AF734659

Anti-social Behaviour

The New Regime

Anesh Pema
District Judge, Leeds Combined Court

Justin Crossley
Barrister, Zenith Chambers, Leeds

JORDAN
PUBLISHING

Published by
Jordan Publishing Limited
21 St Thomas Street
Bristol BS1 6JS

Whilst the publishers and the author have taken every care in preparing the material included in this work, any statements made as to the legal or other implications of particular transactions are made in good faith purely for general guidance and cannot be regarded as a substitute for professional advice. Consequently, no liability can be accepted for loss or expense incurred as a result of relying in particular circumstances on statements made in this work.

© Jordan Publishing Ltd 2015

All rights reserved. No part of this publication may be reproduced, stored in a retrieval system, or transmitted in any way or by any means, including photocopying or recording, without the written permission of the copyright holder, application for which should be addressed to the publisher.

Crown Copyright material is reproduced with kind permission of the Controller of Her Majesty's Stationery Office.

'National Policing Guidelines on the Prosecution for Breaches of Community Protection Notices and Public Spaces Protection Order' produced by the Association of Chief Police Officers is reproduced with permission.

British Library Cataloguing-in-Publication Data

A catalogue record for this book is available from the British Library.

ISBN 978 1 84661 947 2

Typeset by Letterpart Limited, Caterham on the Hill, Surrey CR3 5XL

Printed in Great Britain by Hobbs the Printers Limited, Totton, Hampshire SO40 3WX

City University
Library Information Services
Law Gray's Inn Place
WITHDRAWN

9i 3d1
345.410243 PEM

Anti-social Behaviour

The New Regime

Library Services

City, University of London

Law Library

165 Goswell Road, London, EC1V 7HD

T: 020 7040 8191

W: https://libraryservices.city.ac.uk/

WITHDRAWN

LONG LOAN

Return or renew this item by the date on your library account to avoid overdue charges

Preface

This book aims to be a single volume guide to the new anti-social behaviour legislation. It is intended for use by all those involved in tackling anti-social behaviour and those who act on behalf of persons accused of behaving in such a manner.

We have attempted to explain the new procedures and remedies in a way that should mean the process of applying for, or defending, such applications is as straightforward as the new Act allows. We have included discussion of the preceding legislation concerning anti-social behaviour where relevant, together with case-law decided under the old provision where we believe it will assist in interpreting the new provisions.

The authors would like to thank Rachel McKevitt, Solicitor with the City of York Council for her considerable assistance, enthusiasm and advice, all of which has helped to shape this book.

They are also grateful to Tom Tyson, Head of Zenith Chambers Housing Group for his help and his keen critical eye.

Justin would wish to give particular thanks to Ghazal, Noushin, Ariana and Dariush for their patience and love. He promises that we will now go swimming.

Anesh would also like to thank his ever patient wife, Louise and their daughters Ella and Sophia for their understanding whilst this book has been brought together.

Finally we would both like to thank Tony Hawitt and Kate Hather of Jordan Publishing for their patience and guidance in assembling this book and to apologise to them for last minute wholesale changes that the most recent statutory provisions have required to the book.

We have endeavoured to state the law as at 15 April 2015. All errors are the authors' own.

Anesh Pema
Justin Crossley
Leeds, March 2015

CONTENTS

TABLE OF CASES

References are to paragraph numbers.

TABLE OF STATUTES

References are to paragraph numbers.

TABLE OF STATUTORY INSTRUMENTS

References are to paragraph numbers.

TABLE OF EUROPEAN MATERIAL

References are to paragraph numbers

CHAPTER 1

INTRODUCTION

BACKGROUND TO THE NEW LEGISLATION

1.01 In May 2012 the Home Office published a White Paper entitled 'Putting victims first: more effective responses to anti-social behaviour'. That paper was the preamble for what is now the Anti-social Behaviour, Crime and Policing Act 2014 ('the 2014 Act'). The 2014 Act received Royal Assent on 13 March 2014. On the release of the White Paper the Home Secretary, Theresa May, stated that the Home Office would:

> 'Introduce faster and more effective powers to stop the dangerous and yobbish behaviour of those who make victims lives a misery. We will replace 19 complex existing powers with simply new ones. The powers will include a new court order available on conviction that will stop the behaviour of the most destructive individuals and will address the underlying causes of that behaviour – addressing one of the main failings of the ASBO. There will be new civil injunction that agencies can use immediately to protect victims in communities; simpler powers to close premises that are a magnet for trouble; and a more effective police power to stop anti-social behaviour in public places. We will also speed up the eviction of anti-social tenants to stop "nightmare neighbours" who ruin the lives of those around them ...'

1.02 In most respects the 2014 Act remains loyal to these intentions. Whether it will be effective in tackling the behaviour described by the Home Secretary remains to be seen.

1.03 A central aim of the new legislation, in respect of anti-social behaviour, is to make the process for addressing such behaviour more victim centred. The legislation also intends to simplify the approach to preventing anti-social behaviour by seeking to consolidate remedies within a single act. Previously the provisions for addressing antisocial behaviour were to be found in a number of different acts ranging from the Housing Act 1996 to certain provisions within the Highways Act 1980.

1.04 The Act also seeks to strengthen the powers of landlords when encountering anti-social behaviour from tenants and/or visitors. This includes a new mandatory ground for possession following anti-social behaviour and amending and adding to the existing discretionary grounds.

THE 2014 ACT: AN OVERVIEW

1.05 In respect of anti-social behaviour the Act introduces six new tools for agencies wishing to tackle the same:

(i) New anti-social behaviour injunctions known as civil injunctions (see Chapter 2).

(ii) Criminal behaviour orders (see Chapter 3).

(iii) Dispersal powers (see Chapter 7).

(iv) Community protection notice and orders (see Chapter 8).

(v) Public space protection orders (see Chapter 9).

(vi) Closure of premises orders (see Chapter 10).

1.06 The Act also introduces local involvement and accountability, thereby seeking to further the victim-centric approach, by introducing the following two measures:

(i) Response to complaints (see Chapter 11).

(ii) Community remedies (see Chapter 12).

1.07 For landlords there are changes to the basis upon which they can recover possession of properties let to those perpetrating or allowing anti-social behaviour to be perpetrated at their property.

IMPLEMENTATION OF THE 2014 ACT

1.08 The provisions of the 2014 Act have been implemented in stages. In England and Wales the bulk of the provisions came into force on 10 October 2014. Certain parts of the Act came in to force on the 13 May 2014. However the main provision concerning the new anti-social behaviour injunctions are to come into force on 24 March 2015.

1.09 In July 2014 the Home Office released statutory guidance to accompany the Act entitled 'Anti-social Behaviour, Crime and Policing Act 2014: Reform of anti-social behaviour powers – Statutory guidance for frontline professionals'. The diagrams on the following pages provide an overview of the new Act, setting out the new powers and how these relate to the previous orders and remedies.

OVERVIEW OF NEW POWERS UNDER THE 2014 ACT

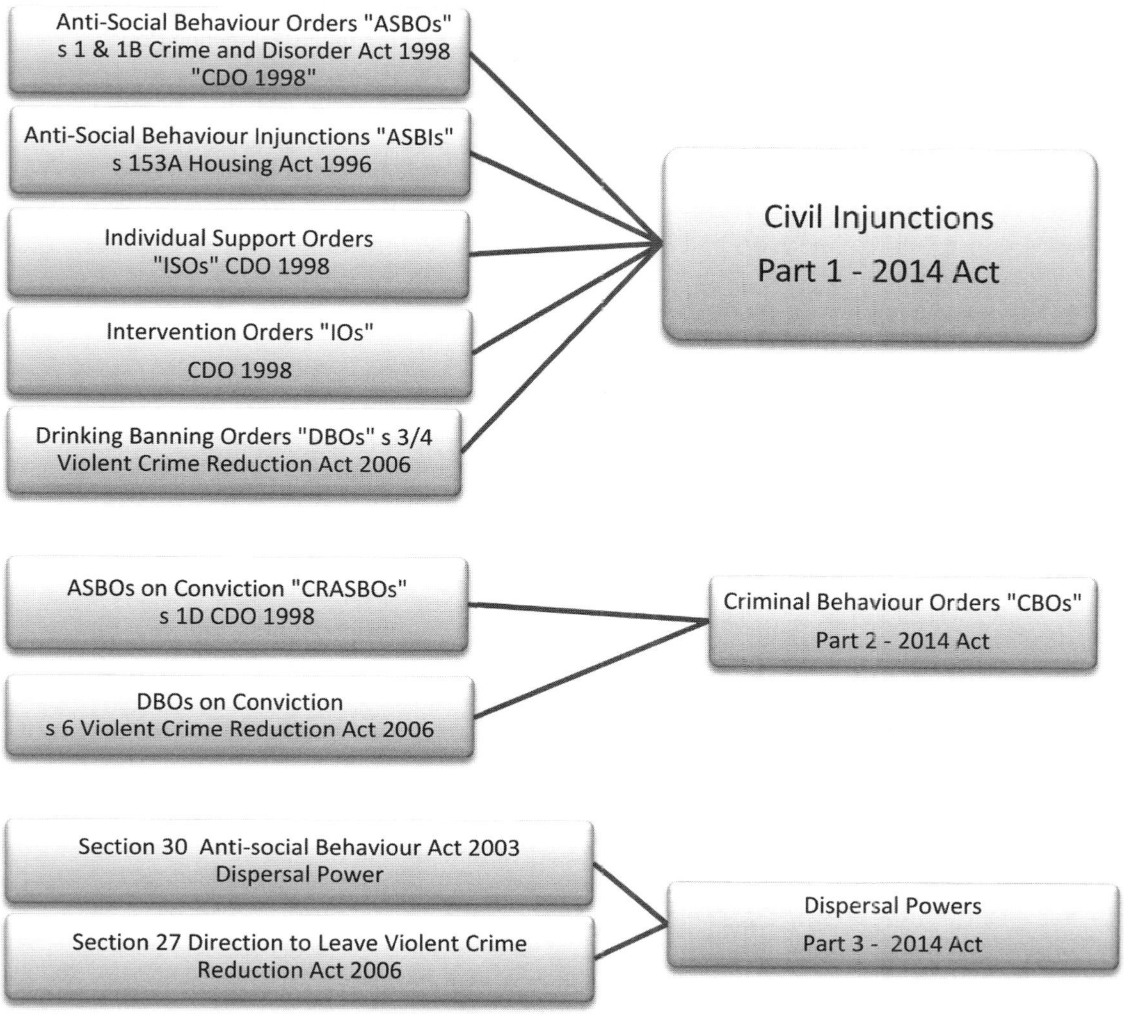

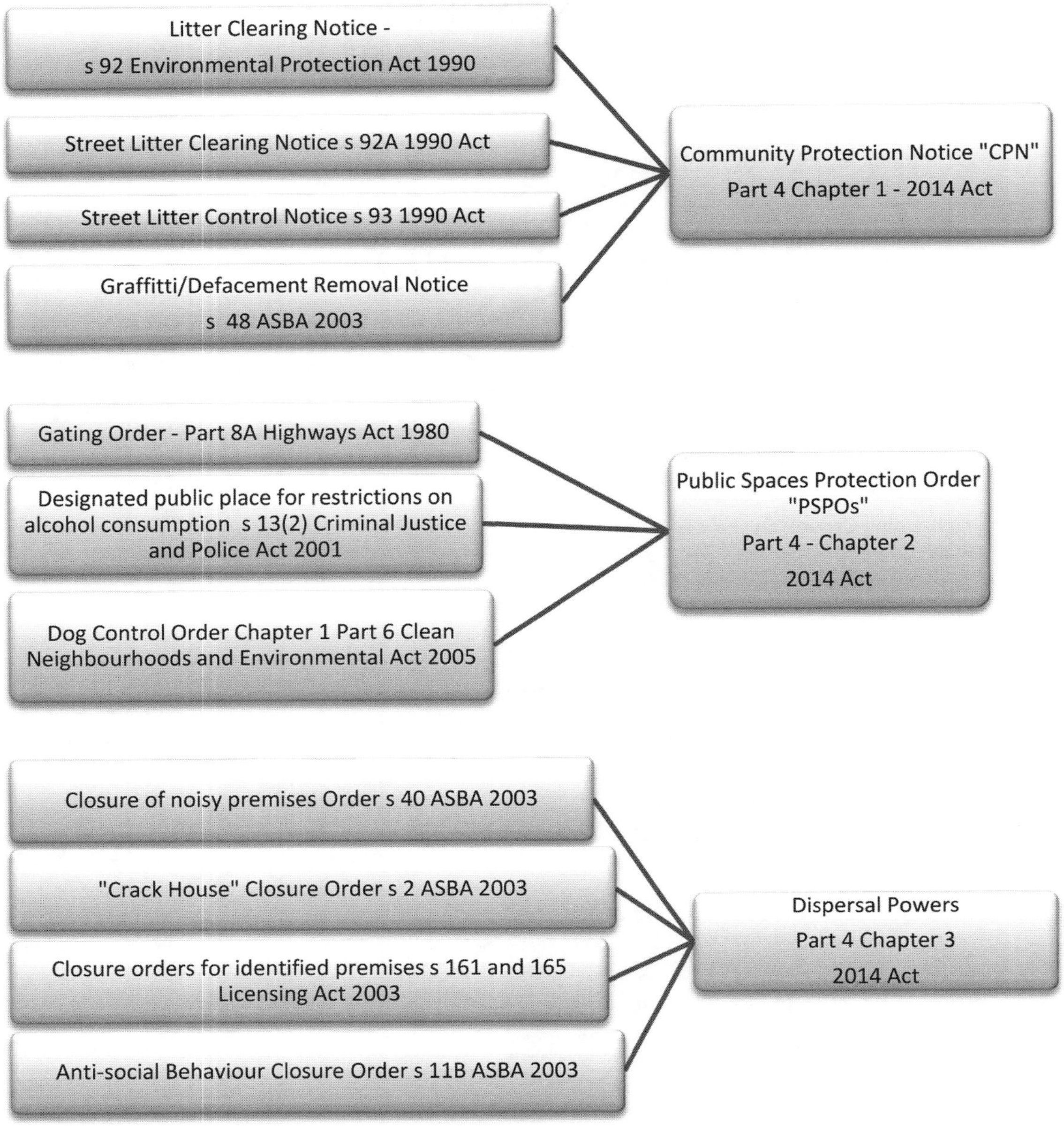
Litter Clearing Notice -
s 92 Environmental Protection Act 1990
Street Litter Clearing Notice s 92A 1990 Act
Street Litter Control Notice s 93 1990 Act
Graffitti/Defacement Removal Notice
s 48 ASBA 2003
Community Protection Notice "CPN"
Part 4 Chapter 1 - 2014 Act
Gating Order - Part 8A Highways Act 1980
Designated public place for restrictions on alcohol consumption s 13(2) Criminal Justice and Police Act 2001
Dog Control Order Chapter 1 Part 6 Clean Neighbourhoods and Environmental Act 2005
Public Spaces Protection Order "PSPOs"
Part 4 - Chapter 2
2014 Act
Closure of noisy premises Order s 40 ASBA 2003
"Crack House" Closure Order s 2 ASBA 2003
Closure orders for identified premises s 161 and 165 Licensing Act 2003
Anti-social Behaviour Closure Order s 11B ASBA 2003
Dispersal Powers
Part 4 Chapter 3
2014 Act

CHAPTER 2

CIVIL INJUNCTIONS

INTRODUCTION

2.01 Applications for civil injunctions, previously referred to in documentation as IPNAs (injunctions to prevent nuisance and annoyance) are made pursuant to Part 1 of the 2014 Act. They replace Housing Act Injunctions under s 153A of the Housing Act 1996 as amended (better known ASBIs) and Anti-social Behaviour Orders (better known as ASBOs). The 2014 Act is in many ways an amalgam of the two principal types of civil orders, incorporating a number of the tests and requirements from the earlier Acts. Part 1 came into force on 23 March 2015.[1]

2.02 They are intended to be easier to apply for and wider ranging than the previous incarnations, together with the new power to impose positive requirements and obligations upon the defendant. Whilst ASBIs and ASBOs have been repealed the power to seek an injunction under s 222 of the Local Government Act 1972 is unaffected.

WHO CAN BE SUBJECT OF AN APPLICATION?

2.03 Whilst injunctions under the Housing Act 1996 were theoretically available against persons under 18 the need for a litigation friend and limitations on any punishment for breach meant that very few injunctions were obtained against such defendants. The usual application for a court order in respect of a child was for an ASBO whether post conviction or for a civil order in the Magistrates' Court. The 2014 Act permits a civil injunction order to be made against any person who is 10 years or over although an application against a child will be heard in the Youth Court not the County Court and requires the applicant to have consulted with the local Youth Offending Team. An application for a civil injunction against an adult can be heard in the Youth Court but only if an application is made to the Youth Court and the court believes it is in the interests of justice for the applications to be heard together.[2] An injunction against a child is also limited in duration to 12 months and any breach will also be dealt with by the Youth Court.

WHO CAN APPLY?

2.04 An application can only be made by one of the bodies specified in s 5 of the 2014 Act. These include local authorities, housing providers, Chief Officers of Police, Chief

---

1 Anti-social Behaviour, Crime and Policing Act 2014 (Commencement No 8, Saving and Transitional Provisions) Order, SI 2015/373, art 4.

2 Anti-social Behaviour, Crime and Policing Act 2014, s 18(2) and the Magistrates' Courts (Injunctions: Anti-social Behaviour) Rules 2015, r 15.

Constable of the British Transport Police, Transport for London, The Environment Agency and the Secretary of State exercising security management functions. The latter is further defined as meaning functions within s 195(3) of the National Health Service Act 2006,[3] in essence the Secretary of State's power to take action for the purpose of 'protecting and improving the security' of NHS staff and users. This plainly allows applications to prevent offending behaviour within hospitals or towards NHS staff generally. It does not however seem to allow the Secretary of State to apply for an injunction to prevent a person from abuse of the 999 call system as was not uncommonly sought in ASBO proceedings. The proviso that the power to apply has to be in order to protect or improve security of NHS staff or contractors means that it would be necessary to show that there was something beyond the inappropriate use of the 999 service, eg abuse which went to threaten the security of the staff who attended the call.

2.05 Housing Providers are widely defined in the Act and include all manner of social landlords (s 20). Housing Providers are limited to making applications for injunctions which relate to behaviour which directly or indirectly relates to or affects its housing management functions (s 5(3)). The housing management functions of a housing provider are said to include, and therefore by implication are not limited to, functions conferred by an enactment and powers and duties of the housing provider as a holder of an estate or interest in housing accommodation, (s 5(4)). This phrase and that of 'housing related conduct' referred to in the definition of anti-social behaviour in s 2(1)(c) is taken from the Housing Act 1996 as amended and has been interpreted widely.

2.06 In *Swindon BC v Redpath*,[4] where an ex tenant of the council waged a campaign of anti-social behaviour against a current tenant the House of Lords held it was clear that the concept of 'housing management functions' was a broad one, having regard to s 21 of the Housing Act 1985, s 111 of the Local Government Act 1972 and s 2 Local Government Act 2000. Parliament had intended the jurisdiction of what was to be covered by 'housing related conduct' to be a broad one, which was shown by the fact that it had consistently extended the scope of what is now s 153A since 1996. It was 'clearly part of a relevant landlord's housing functions to preserve the peace in the neighbourhood of its residential properties by seeking ASBIs to restrain anti-social behaviour' and a person need not live, work or own property in the area to be subject to the Act.

WHAT IS THE TEST FOR A CIVIL INJUNCTION?

2.07 The 2014 Act follows the unhappy precedent set by the 2006 amendment to the Housing Act 1996 by having a statutory test which is split over several sections of the Act with cross-references. The Guidance is also arguably inconsistent with the 2014 Act and therefore has to be considered with caution in relation to interpretation of to the law as the words of the statute, if different, must clearly prevail.

2.08 In contrast to the Guidance (see below) the Act simply states[5] that the court may grant an injunction if two conditions are met, namely that on a balance of probabilities:

---

3 NHS Protect for England and NHS Protect (Wales) as currently named.
4 [2009] EWCA Civ 943, [2010] All ER 100.
5 Anti-social Behaviour, Crime and Policing Act 2014, s 1(1).

(i) the defendant has engaged in or threatens to engage in anti-social behaviour (s 1(2)); and

(ii) it is just and convenient to grant the injunction to prevent the defendant from engaging in anti-social behaviour (s 1(3)).

2.09 This is therefore a two-stage test which has to be applied to any application. Section 2(1) of the Act states that for the purposes of Part 1 anti-social behaviour means any of three alternative definitions:

> '(a) conduct that has caused, or is likely to cause, harassment, alarm or distress to any person,
>
> (b) conduct capable of causing nuisance or annoyance to a person in relation to that person's occupation of residential premises, or
>
> (c) conduct capable of causing housing-related nuisance or annoyance to any person.'

2.10 Section 2(2) then provides a condition that s 2(1)(b) only applies if the injunction is applied for by a housing provider, local authority or Chief Officer of Police. Sections 2(3) and 2(4) go on to further define 'housing-related' in s 2(1)(c) to mean directly or indirectly related to the housing management functions of a housing provider or local authority and these include functions conferred by or under an enactment and powers and duties of the housing provide or local authority as the holder of an estate or interest in housing accommodation.

2.11 The Guidance states that there are two different tests for an injunction pursuant to Part 1 of the 2014 Act. It states that it is necessary to determine whether the application is for an order in a housing related or non-housing related context. If the latter then the test is said to be whether the conduct has caused, or is likely to cause, harassment, alarm or distress to any person. If, however, the behaviour is housing related then the test is conduct which is capable of causing nuisance or annoyance to a person in relation to that person's occupation of residential premises.

2.12 The Guidance is therefore not strictly accurate in saying that there are different tests dependent on whether the behaviour complained about is housing or non-housing-related. While it may usually, if not always, be the case that conduct which causes nuisance or annoyance would also cause harassment, alarm or distress it is not usually true. Section 2(1) provides for (a), (b) and (c) to be alternatives, and there is nothing in the statute to prevent the applicant (unless it is a housing provider which is restricted by s 5(3) – see **2.05**) from relying on anti-social behaviour which is shown to be within s 2(1)(a) rather than s 2(1)(b) although in practical terms the test in the former is more difficult to establish than the latter.

2.14 The better way to interpret the statute it seems to the authors is that if the 'victim' of the behaviour is a resident of premises and the behaviour affects their enjoyment of the premises then the three relevant authorised authorities need only establish that it meets the lesser test. Similarly if the conduct affects any of the very widely interpreted, housing management functions of the landlord their application need only be established to the perceived lower hurdle of conduct which is capable of causing nuisance or annoyance. Anyone else, or in relation to any conduct not falling into either of these two, must prove that the conduct caused, or was likely to cause harassment, alarm or distress. It could be argued that this split test is discriminatory in that if the defendant was a resident of the area he has a different lower test imposed than someone who is not. In practical terms it would be wise for applicants to set out what steps have been taken to address the problems caused by the defendant prior to the application and/or the effects which the conduct has had upon the public.

CAUSED OR IS LIKELY TO CAUSE HARASSMENT, ALARM OR DISTRESS

2.15 This definition is taken from the first limb of the test for ASBOs although it does not require the person to have been affected to be of a different household to the perpetrator, presumably to remove the problem posed by anti-social behaviour caused by domestic violence. It must be assumed that the case-law which came from the consideration of the test in the context of ASBOs will have continuing validity for applications under the 2014 Act.

2.16 The phrase bears some relation to s 5 of the Public Order Act 1986. However, an important difference should be noted. There is no need for the anti-social behaviour to have actually caused any person harassment, alarm or distress. Nor is there any need for the conduct to have happened within sight or hearing of a person who might suffer harassment, alarm or distress. The only stipulation is that the conduct was likely to cause harassment, alarm or distress. There is no need to prove that the defendant intended his or her conduct to cause harassment, alarm or distress – only that it did or was likely to do so. The presence of someone who was caused or was likely to have been caused harassment, alarm or distress is however seemingly necessary. There is little doubt that the definition has been widely drawn to ensure that orders are available to meet as many scenarios as possible.

2.17 As there is no need for evidence from the persons who were caused harassment, alarm or distress, orders can still be obtained using the evidence of professionals as witnesses. In such cases, the behaviour will be proved by hearsay evidence or by live evidence from professionals, such as police or housing officers. The use and admissability of hearsay evidence is considered in more detail in Chapter 4.

2.18 If it is to be asserted that the defendant's actions actually caused harassment, alarm or distress to a person, then that must be proved by evidence. This would ordinarily be done by way of direct evidence from the person or persons who were affected or by hearsay evidence from a professional witness who can give evidence has as to how the complainant was affected.

2.19 If, however, the allegation against the defendant is that his or her conduct was likely to cause harassment, alarm or distress, then, clearly, a direct witness of the effect cannot be called. Rather, the court will hear evidence of the conduct of the defendant and then be asked to conclude that this conduct was likely to cause harassment, alarm or distress. The question then arises – what must the applicant show to the court to establish such likelihood?

2.20 The issue was examined in detail in the case of *The Chief Constable of Lancashire v Potter*[6] in the context of an ASBO case. The administrative court was asked to consider

---

6 [2003] EWHC 2272 (Admin).

an appeal by way of case stated against the decision of the deputy district judge, who had refused to make an ASBO against Potter. The Chief Constable had brought the application against Potter, alleging that she had acted as a prostitute in an area of Preston. He called evidence which was almost exclusively hearsay evidence from two police officers that there was a problem with prostitution in the area, of which residents and visitors had complained. Potter had convictions for prostitution outside the 6-month period and had been seen regularly in the area, and, on occasion, had been seen to step forward and look into moving motor cars to attract attention. Potter did not appear and so the evidence was not challenged. The district judge, however, noted that there was no evidence that she had actually caused harassment, alarm or distress, or any direct evidence from local residents (the evidence was hearsay evidence from anonymous sources). Having applied his mind to the weight to be applied to hearsay evidence, he decided that he could not be sure that anyone had actually been caused harassment, alarm or distress and that he did not feel it fair, in the absence of real examples, to find that simply being a prostitute was likely to cause harassment, alarm or distress.

2.21 The Chief Constable appealed. Lord Justice Auld considered various permutations, including that which has been used in the family law jurisdiction for findings of facts in child abuse cases, but discounted them and came to the conclusion that:

> '[32] Accordingly, as to the meaning of "likely" in this context, my view is that a higher threshold of likelihood is called for than, for example, that of "a real possibility" arising in the context of the safety of children under the Children Act 1989. It is true that the making of an anti-social behaviour order is not a criminal sentence, and serves only to prohibit in specified ways further anti-social behaviour of the sort giving rise to it. However, breach of such an order is a serious matter and can lead to a substantial term of imprisonment or fine. I would give "likely" the meaning in this context of "more probable than not". That meaning, it seems to me, is much the same as that of the Divisional Court in *Parkin v Norman* [1983] QB 92, [1982] 2 All ER 583, [1982] 3 WLR 523, which concerned a charge of insulting behaviour "likely" to occasion a breach of the peace. McCullough J, giving the judgment of the Court consisting of Donaldson LJ and himself, emphasised that the test was whether the conduct in question was "likely", not "liable", to have that effect.'

2.22 Lord Justice Auld went on to emphasise the need for the court not to confuse incidents which actually caused and those likely to cause harassment, alarm or distress:

> 'The case demonstrates the importance for a court when dealing with the issue of likelihood in this context of avoiding at least two pitfalls critical to its final decision. The first is not to confuse the second and third constituents of the s 1(1)(a) condition so as to require proof to the criminal standard that a defendant's conduct has actually caused someone harassment, alarm or distress when considering the alternative, whether it is likely to have caused that result. It is in that respect, it seems to me that the Deputy District Judge, in the passages from his paras 6(Q) and (R) of the statement of case that I have set out and emphasised in para 19 above, fell into error. The thrust of those passages is that he rejected the likelihood alternative because the evidence was wanting as to any instances of actual harassment, alarm or distress …'

2.23 In *R v Israilov*[7] the court of appeal found that burglary of an unoccupied dwelling house did not cause harassment or alarm but that it did cause distress. It is, however, strange that they did not consider whether it was likely to do those things. In *R (on the*

---

[7] [2005] EWCA Crim 441, [2005] All ER (D) 279 (Feb).

application of Mills) v Birmingham Magistrates' Court[8] the defendant had been seen by a plain clothes police officer taking three pairs of gloves without paying. The officer followed her outside the shop and arrested her. She was co-operative and in no way abusive. The Divisional Court held that whilst some thefts might cause harassment, alarm or distress this did not mean that all would. In this case there was no evidence of anti-social behaviour by the claimant, the theft was unbeknown to the shop employees and therefore the actions were not likely to have caused them any harassment.

2.24 The definition was however given a more narrow interpretation by Mr Justice Bean in *R (Gosport Borough Council) v Fareham Magistrates.*[9] Here the council had sought an ASBO against a defendant who owned a jet ski and had on three occasions ridden in what was described as a 'grossly excessive speed', circling buoys and riding in the wake of a ferry. The district judge refused to make an ASBO and the matter was brought before the Divisional Court by way of Judicial Review as he also refused to state a case.

2.25 Mr Justice Bean noted that the court had filed a witness statement in which it had said that whilst it had found that the defendant was riding dangerously there was no evidence to prove that there was in fact a swimmer in the area whilst he was riding in that fashion. He went on to hold that the incidents showed that defendant had acted in an '... irresponsible manner in speeding in the harbour and that this would have caused harassment, alarm or distress to any swimmers had there been any there.'

2.26 The judge however went on to find that whilst the 'or was likely to cause' must add something to the word 'caused' in s 1(1)(a) this was not sufficient in this case:

> 'In order to show that the behaviour "caused" harassment, alarm or distress it would probably be necessary to have evidence from one of the harassed, alarmed or distressed victims; whereas the alternative formulation "or was likely to cause" enables police witnesses to demonstrate that there were potential victims present who it was likely were caused harassment, alarm or distress.'

2.27 As the Council was not able to prove that there had been anyone in the water at the time of the incidents the Divisional Court rejected the Council's application. This is a narrow construction of the definition which is not, it is submitted, borne out by the wide construction applied by House of Lords in *McCann* or the Divisional Court in *Potter*, nor is it really in accordance with the plain words of the statute. The statute only requires proof that the defendant's conduct caused or was likely to have caused harassment, alarm or distress; not that anyone was there to witness it. Strangely, the judge went on to give an example which emphasises why we would submit his construction is an unnecessarily narrow one:

> 'if a man is swaggering around in a public place brandishing a knife, but he is the only person in the area, his behaviour is observed on CCTV and police arrive in a police car and arrest him, I doubt very much whether that behaviour would be sufficient to found an ASBO. It would be quite different if the CCTV showed one or more members of the public in the vicinity.'

---

8 [2005] EWHC 2732 (Admin).

9 [2006] EWHC 3047 (Admin).

2.28 It is the authors' belief that such conduct would be likely to cause alarm or distress and therefore the test would be satisfied even in the absence of witnesses who actually were caused such.

NUISANCE OR ANNOYANCE

2.29 This alternative definition of anti-social behaviour plainly arises from s 153A of the Housing Act 1996 as amended, is extremely wide and is easier to satisfy than the test of harassment, alarm or distress. 'Annoyance' is even wider and therefore generally easier to establish than nuisance. Conduct such as graffiti, loud noise/music and general disturbances at a property have been held to be capable of causing both nuisance and annoyance.

STANDARD OF PROOF

2.30 Another significant difference between ASBOs and injunctions under Part 1 is the standard of proof. In an application for an ASBO the applicant had to prove the allegations of anti-social behaviour beyond reasonable doubt. The test for civil injunctions is only that on a balance of probabilities, s 1(2). The burden of establishing the test must still however lie with the applicant.

TIME-LIMITS

2.31 Hidden away in s 21 of the 2014 Act, a section headed 'Saving and Transitional provision', is s 21(7) which provides that the court may take into account conduct occurring up to 6 months before the commencement day (ie, 23 March 2015) when considering an application for an injunction. For no obvious reason the court can rely on matters up to 1 year in an application for a Criminal Behaviour Order. This will have to be considered by any applicant for an order. In applications before the County Court this will be an issue for a period until a time gap has appeared from the commencement date. In the meantime however where an applicant wants to rely on conduct which took place more than 6 months before the commencement date the question is whether the applicant can rely on it? At first glance it could be said that the court will adopt a similar approach to that taken in relation to the '6 month rule' in ASBOs, ie to allow conduct to be relied on to prove the need, or in the case of the 2014 Act, that it is just to make the injunction. However, on consideration of the actual statutory wording, it seems to us that this wider use cannot be extended to applications under the 2014 Act. The wording expressly provides that in deciding whether to grant an injunction under Part 1 the court may take account of conduct occurring up to 6 months before the commencement day. The limitation to 6 months prior to commencement of proceedings in ASBO proceedings in the Magistrates' Court is due to s 127 of the Magistrates' Court Act 1980 which requires presentation of a complaint or information within 6 months of the matters complained of.

DEFENCES

2.32 No specific defence to civil injunction proceedings is provided for in the 2014 Act. The defendant must therefore seek to defend the action on the basis of challenging the two stage test in the Act. In the vast majority of cases, if the claimant is able to establish that there has been anti-social behaviour within the meaning of the Act it will be difficult for the defendant to defeat the application on the basis that it is not just or convenient to make the order. The best arguments for the defendant in that scenario will be if there are only a few isolated incidents of anti-social behaviour which are not serious or perhaps that the last incident was so long ago that an order should not be made.

MENTAL HEALTH

2.33 In *Wookey v Wookey*[10] a non-molestation order with power of arrest had been sought and ordered against a 70-year-old husband who suffered from dementia and had become jealous of his 72-year-old wife. First, it is useful to note what the court in *Wookey*[11] called 'well-established general propositions' about injunctions:

- the court will not act in vain by granting an injunction which is idle and ineffectual and therefore an injunction should not be granted to impose an obligation to do something which is impossible or cannot be enforced;
- the injunction must serve a useful purpose for the person seeking relief and there must be a real possibility that the order, if made, will be enforceable against the defendant;
- the court expects and assumes that its orders will be obeyed and the court will not normally refuse an injunction because of the defendant's likely disobedience to the order.

2.34 In *Wookey* it was held that where the defendant (against whom the injunction was sought) was incapable of understanding what he was doing or that it was wrong then an injunction should not be granted. This was because the defendant would not be capable of complying with it; the injunction would not have a deterrent effect nor operate on the mind so as to regulate conduct; any breach by the defendant would not be subject to effective enforcement proceedings since the defendant would have a clear defence to any application for committal to prison for contempt of court.

2.35 In *P v P (Contempt of Court: Mental Capacity)*[12] an injunction with power of arrest was made which prohibited the husband from returning to the matrimonial home. The husband suffered from Usher's Syndrome, and was described as deaf and dumb. It was alleged that there had been 29 breaches of the injunction. The judge found that although the husband did not understand the legal system he did know that he should not go to the matrimonial home and knew that he would be liable to go to prison if he did so. The judge extended the injunction for 6 months with a power of arrest. The husband appealed. The Court of Appeal dismissed his appeal. The husband did not need to understand the nature and extent of the jurisdiction of the court to deal with the

---

10 [1991] 3 All ER 365.
11 At p 370f.
12 [1999] 2 FLR 897.

disobedience of its order. A potential contemnor needs only to understand that an order has been made, that it forbids certain acts and that if such an act were to be carried out then the potential contemnor would be punished. The case sets out the relevant matters for the defendant to understand. Evidence should therefore be sought as to the defendant's understanding; that an injunction order has been or will be made; as to whether the defendant understands each and all of the prohibitions; of the consequences of breach of such an order. If necessary, expert assistance to explain the order can be utilised and indeed would provide powerful rebuttal to any arguments about lack of understanding on breach. The expert will therefore need to be briefly informed about the court's powers on breach so that the issue of punishment can be investigated with the defendant.

2.36 In *R (on the application of Cooke) v Director of Public Prosecutions*[13] the defendant was a habitual beggar. He was convicted under s 5 of the Protection from Harassment Act 1997 and after a post conviction order was made on the finding that he was an aggressive beggar, had been aggressive to police officers and had self-harmed. The defendant admitted the conduct but submitted that an ASBO was not necessary as it would not protect persons from further ASB since his mental state was such that he would be unable to comply with the order and secondly that it would be unjust to make one. The defendant argued that the only effect would be to 'criminalise the defendant's mental health problems'.

2.37 The defendant called a psychiatric nurse who gave evidence that the defendant had been diagnosed as having an emotionally unstable personal disorder, evidence of PTSD with a possible diagnosis of Asperger's Syndrome. The nurse gave evidence that the defendant's behaviour could be construed as deliberately antagonistic but this was consequential to his mental health problems. He recommended mental health treatment and that his behaviour could not be prevented without it. He was not capable of complying with an ASBO and would repeatedly breach an order.

2.38 The magistrates held that the defendant did know right from wrong and had demonstrated that he was capable of choice. He had chosen not to engage with mental health services. The magistrates made an order for 3 years. In the case stated they found that he had understanding when he was well but could be irrational when unwell. The magistrates recognised that the defendant needed treatment, but this had to be weighed against protection of the public. They considered that the order would not prevent him obtaining treatment nor that he would inevitably breach the order. They did not accept the evidence of the psychiatric nurse was correct as to the absence of risk to the public. The administrative court was asked to consider whether an ASBO should be made against a person whose ASB was caused by, or consequently of, a mental health disorder.

2.39 The defendant argued that if it was impossible for a person to obey an order there was no point in making it and therefore it was not necessary. Alternatively it was unjust and a wrongful exercise of the discretion to make an ASBO. Lord Justice Dyson held:

> '... if the justices had concluded that the appellant's mental state was such that he was truly incapable of complying with the conditions of any ASBO that they were minded to make, they would have been wrong in law to make the order. If by reason of mental incapacity an

---

[13] [2008] EWHC 2703 (Admin).

offender is incapable of complying with an order, then an order is incapable of protecting the public and cannot therefore be said to be necessary to protect the public.'

2.40 This was qualified by the judge later when he stated:

'The justices should not refuse to make an ASBO on such grounds unless the defendant does not have the mental capacity to understand the meaning of the order, or to comply with it. Such an incapacity being a medical matter, evidence should normally be given by a psychiatrist and not by a psychologist or a psychiatric nurse.

A defendant who suffers from a personality disorder may on that account be liable to disobey an ASBO. In my judgment, however, that is not a sufficient reason for holding that an order, which is otherwise necessary to protect the public from a defendant's anti-social behaviour, is not necessary for that purpose, or that the court should not exercise its discretion to make an order.'

2.41 The court held that on the evidence before the Magistrates' Court the defendant did have the mental capacity to understand the order. In answer to the questions the court held that it would be wrong to make an ASBO if the defendant did not have the mental capacity to understand or comply with the order however the fact that he would be likely to breach the order because he suffered from a personality disorder was not of itself a good reason for not making the order. The above reasoning was approved in the case of *Fairweather v Commissioner of Police for the Metropolis*.[14]

2.42 However a different result was found in *Pender v Director of Public Prosecutions*;[15] an ASBO on conviction was made which prohibited the defendant from begging in a particular way within a certain location. The defendant appealed to the Crown Court on the basis that he had no capacity to understand the prohibition or to comply with it. It is a relatively recent case and shows how the points raised above are perennial ones in this area of work. Medical evidence was given, and perhaps crucially was not challenged, which stated that the defendant suffered from learning difficulties, schizophrenia and a severe addiction to nicotine. Medical evidence concluded that the begging behaviour arose directly as a result of the nicotine addiction. Further, it was concluded that the defendant lacked capacity to understand the ASBO prohibition and the consequences of any breach. Finally, the defendant was incapable of complying with the prohibition on begging because he was compelled to seek nicotine by the only means available to him, in effect, begging. The medical evidence here was not challenged and that determined the case.

THE INJUNCTION TERMS

2.43 If the court elects to grant an injunction it may make one for the purpose of preventing the defendant from engaging in anti-social behaviour which prohibits or requires anything described in the injunction (s 1(4)). This is a major change which the 2014 Act brings into effect. There was no power to order a defendant to perform any positive act within applications under the 1996 Act and whilst some limited power existed in ancillary orders to ASBOs, namely intervention orders ('IOs') and individual support orders ('ISOs') they were confined to attendance on particular and very limited

---

14 [2008] EWHC 3073 (Admin).

15 [2013] EWHC 2598 (Admin), [2013] All ER (D) 173 (Jan).

programmes (only drugs in relation to IOs). As will be seen later in this chapter, the 2014 Act has retained a number of the features which were present in those orders.

2.44 A term of an injunction made under the 2014 Act must, as far as practicable, avoid interference with times that the respondent worked or attended school/education or conflict with other court order requirements (presumably matters such as probation, community service orders).

2.45 The Guidance is silent as to what terms may be imposed in an injunction. It may be deliberate as the intention is to have no limits on what might be set as a prohibition term, however, it seems to the authors that inevitably the courts will have to have regard to both what is reasonable and proportionate to impose. Whilst the case-law on appropriate terms in an order was almost entirely centered around ASBO terms and not ASBIs, it would seem reasonable to conclude that the basic principles in those cases remain valid. The court's decision in *R v Boness*[16] and subsequent authorities led to some guidelines for terms for ASBOs which should properly be considered by any applicant when considering the terms which are to be sought in an application under Part 1. The case-law made it clear that simple, plain language should be employed. Two terms rather than one overly complicated one are preferable. If necessary, professional help can be sought to formulate the terms of an order to ensure that the defendant can understand them. In a case brought by Bradford Metropolitan Borough Council, a psychologist specialising in Asperger's Syndrome assisted in drafting the agreed terms of the order for a defendant with that condition and provided an additional pictorial representation to supplement the defendant's understanding of the court order. This was, however, an extreme example and, in the vast majority of cases, plain, simple, ordinary language will be sufficient. A basic checklist could be considered to include terms which:

- cover the range of anti-social acts committed by the defendant;
- be for the purpose of preventing the defendant from committing acts of anti-social behaviour;
- be reasonable and proportionate;
- be realistic and practical;
- be clear, concise and easy to understand;
- be specific when referring to matters of time, if, for example, prohibiting the offender from being outside or in particular areas at certain times;
- be specific when referring to exclusion from an area, include street names and clear boundaries such as the side of the street included in the order (a map with identifiable street names should also be provided);
- be in terms which make it easy to determine and prosecute a breach;
- contain a prohibition on inciting/encouraging similar conduct.

2.46 The terms of the order must be negative and prohibitory in nature unless a positive requirement is to be imposed with the need for supervisor. This was re-stated in *Lonergan (Ashley) v (1) Lewes Crown Court (2) Brighton & Hove City Council & Secretary of State for the Home Department (Interested Party)*[17] in relation to an ASBO where Lord Justice Maurice Kay stated that the statute required the order to be 'substantially

---

[16] [2005] EWCA Crim 2395.

[17] [2005] EWHC 457 (Admin), [2005] 2 All ER 362.

and not just formally prohibitory'. However, the court found nothing objectionable in a term which stated that the defendant was forbidden from 'being in any place other than ... [three addresses] ... or moving between those addresses, between the hours of 11.30 pm and 6.00 am'. Lord Justice Maurice held that he was satisfied that a restraint upon leaving or travelling between specified premises between particular times met that test. As a matter of logical construction this is rather difficult to accept as essentially it requires a person to be in one of three places which would seem mandatory and, if not, certainly if only one place is specified that would seem so. It is however likely that this remains good authority for the terms to be imposed under a Part 1 Injunction and therefore no supervisor would be required.

2.47 A great deal of the case-law which followed the introduction of ASBOs concerned whether terms could be imposed, breach of which would also be a criminal offence. It remains to be seen whether the same arguments will rage in relation to injunctions made under Part 1. However, as breach is a civil contempt and not a criminal offence and there is no longer a requirement that the term be 'necessary' to prevent further offending it may not be such an issue, although it would remain an issue for an order under Part 2 (see Chapter 3). It seems to the authors, however, that whilst it is common place to have a term in injunctions, both in non-molestation proceedings and ASBIs, that prevent the defendant threatening or assaulting the applicant, the previous case-law cannot be ignored. It is therefore the authors' view that whilst wherever possible the terms should not simply be criminal offences and attempts are made to formulate terms which prohibit the actions before the crime, for instance the carrying of spray cans or paint to prevent graffiti being written as advocated in *Boness*. Sometimes, however, this is not feasible and where the conduct is persistent, causes harassment, alarm or distress (or nuisance or annoyance), and its purpose is to prevent the defendant from repeat conduct rather than to seek a greater penalty, the terms can properly include matters which are criminal offences in their own right.

Specific terms and considerations

2.48 It is suggested that, when seeking to draft orders, the general prohibition from anti-social behaviour and the prohibition from approaching or harassing named lay witnesses who provided statements for the application are included as a matter of course. Thereafter, the prohibitions sought should reflect the incidents which have been alleged and proved. This could mean simple prohibitions against abusive or threatening language, but may also prevent the defendant from entering an area where the incidents have occurred. A common prohibition is to prevent a defendant from returning to an estate from which he has been evicted or a young person to a school from which he has been permanently excluded.

Exclusion zones

2.49 Exclusion zones are now regularly imposed. Commonly, they exclude a defendant from a defined zone, giving relief to specific communities. They are easy to police, as it is not necessary to prove that the defendant was acting in an anti-social manner. Such schemes were pioneered in Liverpool, where minors were banned from named streets. The use of exclusion zones is often an important part of the process to curb anti-social behaviour. By denying the defendant access to the places where he or she has displayed anti-social behaviour in the past, the relevant persons in that area are being afforded a measure of direct protection. In the multiple 'Little London' ASBOs, made in Leeds Magistrates' Court, an exclusion zone was made against all the defendants and often provided the defendants with a single route in and out of the area from their homes. The Divisional Court and the Court of Appeal did not comment adversely on these exclusions and the final orders that were made almost always included that exclusion zone.

2.50 If an exclusion zone is to be sought, then certain practical matters should be attended to by the applicant authority. First, the court should be provided with a clear, coloured map of the area from which the applicant seeks to exclude the defendant. If possible, the authority should indicate the size of the area and mark where the incidents of anti-social behaviour are alleged to have occurred. The map should also indicate the defendant's home (if within the area) and other key locations, eg witnesses' homes (assuming that the addresses were known to the defendant). The maps to be used with the order should, however, not be marked, save with the exclusion area being clearly marked by a coloured outline. The map should be marked with the defendant's name and its purpose, ie 'map to show exclusion area for "X"'. The term prohibiting entry to the exclusion zone should provide the defendant (where appropriate) with exceptions when attending pre-arranged medical appointments, schools, solicitors and when accompanied by probation or YOT workers.

Non-association

2.51 There is a difference between a term which requires a defendant not to associate generally in groups of x or more and a term which prevents him associating (generally in public places) with named individuals who also display anti-social behaviour when with the defendant. General terms of non-association with groups of set numbers are rather difficult to impose without raising issues of proportionality. A term which just prevents the defendant being in a group with more than a set number of people means that they cannot go to sporting events, queue up in a supermarket or go to church. It is unlikely that sufficient exceptions can be made that do not make the term unworkable, however there are some local authorities who have had success with them. In *Boness*[18] a term preventing the defendant from 'congregating in groups of people in a manner causing or likely to cause any person to fear for their safety or congregating in groups of six or more in an outdoor public place' was said to be justified as regards the first part of the term but the second part of the term was not.

2.52 The use of terms preventing a defendant associating with specified individuals has rapidly increased in recent years and, indeed, where actions against youths are concerned, it is now commonplace to have such a term included in the application. The obvious purpose is to keep defendants away from others with whom they are liable to commit anti-social behaviour. The equally clear balance to be applied is that it prevents a person from having free choice over his or her associates or friends. One way to limit the restriction posed by this term is to limit the non-association requirement to public places, ie the defendant may associate with whom they like, provided it is not in public (or a place to which the public have access). This allows a measure of conformity with the ECHR in that there is no general right of freedom to associate with others protected by

[18] *R v Boness (Dean) and 10 others* [2005] EWCA Crim 2395, [2005] All ER (D) 153, 169 JP 621, (2005) *The Times*, October 24.

the Convention – only where the association is for political or demonstration ends – see *Anderson v United Kingdom.*[19] If a non-association clause is sought, then it is important to ensure that only those persons against whom there is evidence of anti-social behaviour when together with the defendant are included in the list of names. Often, this is not adhered to and there is little, if any, evidence to link the defendant to any of the persons named.

2.53 In *Hills v Chief Constable of Essex*[20] the court was asked to consider whether it was lawful to make a term in an ASBO preventing the defendant from associating with a person against whom there was no reciprocal order or term. The defendant had argued that the term went much further than that necessary to protect the public and could result in a breach through no fault of the defendant, eg if the other party came up to him in the street and insisted on walking with him. In this case the other party had been present when a number of the incidents had occurred and had been the subject of an interim order. Due to improvement in her behaviour no final order was argued for.

2.54 Mr Justice Keith noted that the report from the working group led by Thomas LJ had considered a non-association clause was a reasonable one. Further that in the situation put forward by the defendant he would have a reasonable excuse for being in her company.

2.55 In *N v DPP*[21] the Crown Court imposed a term in an ASBO which prevented the defendant from 'congregating in groups of three or more in a public place other than when with adults over 21 years'. The Divisional Court noted the guidance on this term in *Boness* above and that the term would put the defendant in breach when at a sporting event. They concluded that it was insufficient protection for the defendant to be able to assert 'reasonable excuse' and amended the term to effectively mirror that in *Boness.*

Curfew

2.56 Curfews and prohibitions on drinking in public places can all be used as terms. The use of curfews was challenged in *Lonergan*[22] (see **2.46**). Having decided that the curfew term was prohibitory and not mandatory the court considered whether the term was a penalty and therefore improper. The court concluded that the proper consideration of whether a term was a penalty was to consider the purpose of its imposition. Whilst, when imposed as a sentence in criminal proceedings it was intended to punish as a prohibition in an ASBO its purpose was preventative and protective. Therefore the court concluded that there was nothing legally objectionable to the inclusion of a curfew provision as it was necessary for the protection of relevant persons. The court did go on to say, however:

> 'Having said that I do think that it behoves magistrates' courts to consider carefully the need for and duration of a curfew provision when making an ASBO. Just because the ASBO must run for a minimum of two years it does not follow that each and every prohibition within a particular order must endure for the life of the order. A curfew for two years in the life of a teenager is a very considerable restriction of freedom. It may be necessary but in many cases

---

19 [1998] EHRR 218.
20 [2010] ECHR 19859/04.
21 [2007] EWHC 833 (Admin).
22 [2005] EWHC 457 (Admin), [2005] 2 All ER 362, [2005] 1 WLR 2570.

I consider it likely that either the period of curfew could properly be set at less than the full life of the order or that, in the light of behavioural progress, an application to vary the curfew under section 1(8) might well succeed.'

Clothing

2.57 In *R (on the application of B) v Greenwich Magistrates' Court v The Commissioner of Police of the Metropolis*[23] the district judge made an ASBO term that the defendant was prohibited from:

> '... wearing any article of clothing with an attached hood in any public place in the London Borough of Greenwich, whether the hood is up or down.'

2.58 The district judge in his reasons noted that the defendant was part of a gang which gathered together in the street, railway stations, bus stops and other locations where members intimidated members of the public through language and gestures wearing hooded tops to help conceal their identity. He concluded that he was 'satisfied that a prohibition would reduce the swagger, menace and fear of anti-social behaviour'. The defendant appealed by way of judicial review contending that the condition was unreasonable in that its purpose and effect was not to reduce anti-social behaviour but to prohibit or restrict a particular appearance or style of clothing the claimant would wish to wear. Further that the claimant's freedom of expression under art 10 was infringed.

2.59 Mr Justice Mitting with Lord Justice Latham held that the imposition was to reduce swagger, menace and fear and could do so by either prohibiting the wearing of what appeared to be part of a gang uniform and secondly by diminishing the confidence of those who wear the uniform that they may escape the identification by wearing and raising the hood. It was clear on the district judge's findings that the claimant wore the hooded tops deliberately for both of those purposes. The prohibition satisfied the tests of clarity, necessity and proportionality identified in *Boness*. Further that the judge had rightly considered that merely prohibiting the raising of the hood would be an ineffective prohibition.

POSITIVE REQUIREMENT TERMS

2.60 If the term imposes a positive requirement on a defendant then the order must specify the person (may be an individual or an organisation) who is responsible for supervising compliance with the requirement. That person or organisation must have provided the court with evidence about the suitability and enforceability of the requirement before the term can be imposed by the court. This mirrors the approach in the Crime and Disorder Act 1998 with respect of IOs and ISOs. In making this additional requirement the Act makes it difficult to impose what might be termed a simple positive requirement, eg clean up the graffiti or the garden of the house.

2.61 The 2014 Act rather inelegantly goes on to state that the person or organisation has a duty under the Act to make 'any necessary arrangements in connection with the requirements for which the person or organisation has responsibility' (s 3(4)), and to

---

[23] [2008] EWHC 2882 (Admin).

promote compliance by the defendant. The relevant person has a duty to inform the applicant and the Chief Officer of Police if they consider that the defendant has failed to comply or had complied fully with the requirements imposed.

2.62 Section 3(6) imposes a standing duty on a defendant who has such a requirement imposed on him to keep in touch with the specified supervisor as directed by them and to notify them of any change of address. Failure to do so is a breach of the main injunction (s 3(6)).

2.63 There is nothing more in the Act as to what activities can be imposed or how. The Guidance provides little greater assistance. It states that agencies will have the discretion to tailor the positive requirements in each case which could include alcohol awareness classes, dog training classes, provided by animal welfare charities or attendance at mediation sessions with neighbours or victims.

2.64 Unlike Individual Support Orders ('ISOs') there is no requirement for the defendant to attend court when a positive obligation is imposed or for them to have to pay for the course. There is however nothing in either the Act or the Guidance as to how these positive obligations are to be financed. Many of the agencies that provide therapeutic work require the participant to be willing or at least committed to treatment, which is often expensive to provide. It is difficult to see such organisations being willing to volunteer space on oversubscribed courses. It would seem unlikely that even if agencies did agree to the course being used that they would agree to have the duty imposed on them that the Act requires. This would mean that someone from the applicant would have to assume such responsibility. It remains to be seen what local authorities (it seems unlikely that the Police or housing providers would have the resources to run courses) will be willing to allocate in terms of finances for such positive obligations. What is clear is that there is no additional government funding available for any activities, and therefore it may be that unless courses are identified which will accept the defendant at no cost, the scope for making positive requirement terms will be limited.

2.65 An injunction can be for any fixed period or even until further order save that if the injunction is imposed on a person who is under 18 years of age, it may not be for more than 12 months' duration (s 1(6)). The court can also make terms which have different periods of effect (s 1(7)).

EXCLUSION FROM HOME

2.66 A civil injunction under the 2014 Act can exclude a person from the place they normally live if all of the three requirements are satisfied (s 13).

2.67 Firstly, the defendant is aged 18 years of age or over. The Guidance states that the court may exclude a person over 18 from any premises or an area specified in the injunction; however there appears to be nothing in the statute to suggest that the court cannot exclude a person under 18 years of age from premises which are not his home or an area in general without satisfying the three-stage test. Indeed, it would be bizarre if the 2014 Act were to prevent the court from preventing a defendant under 18 from, for example, going to a place where he was causing anti-social behaviour but did not live there. In the absence of any section within the statute imposing such astonishing limitation on the Youth Court's powers, it can only be that the Guidance is poorly worded.

2.68 The second requirement for a court when imposing an order excluding a defendant from his or her home is that the application is sought by Police, local authority or if the property is owned or managed by them, a housing provider. The latter may only apply if they are entitled to dispose of the fee simple, whether in possession or in reversion, or if they are entitled to rents and profits under a lease which was granted for not less than 3 years.

2.69 The third and final requirement is that the court considers that the anti-social behaviour found proved included the use, or threatened use of violence against other persons or that there was a significant risk of harm to other persons. The latter is defined further by s 20 in a very wide way as 'serious ill-treatment or abuse whether physical or not', which therefore covers both emotional and psychological abuse.

2.70 The Guidance states that if an application is made by a local authority or the Police against an owner occupier or someone in private rented accommodation the landlord should be consulted if circumstances permit. The above statutory requirements do not on their face pose many difficulties for applicants in seeking such an order however the draconian nature of such an order is reflected in the Guidance, if not the statute itself. The Guidance specifically states that they did not expect the power to exclude from the home to be used often and extols the court to pay special attention to Art 8 of the European Convention on Human Rights and concludes that applications should only be made 'in extreme cases'. The authors would suggest that the Guidance is entirely justified in expressing this view and it would be a rare case indeed where such an order was imposed.

POWER OF ARREST

2.71 A power of arrest can be attached to any term of an injunction which imposes a prohibition or requirement (s 4(1)), however that does not include a requirement which requires participation in particular activities (s 4(1)). The Guidance says that a power of arrest cannot be attached to any positive requirement; however this leaves open a potential conflict between the Act and the Guidance in that a requirement to do a positive act does not have to be a requirement to participate in a particular activity. The Act specifically states it can be attached to either prohibition or requirement. It is only those requirements which require participation in particular activities which are excluded. Therefore, as it would have been a simple drafting step to have made a power of arrest limited to terms imposing prohibitions, it must mean that a power of arrest is available for 'positive' orders notwithstanding the Guidance's assertion that positive requirements are excluded in total. An example that occurs is a curfew order which could be drafted both positively or negatively, or perhaps a requirement to surrender a passport or dispose of a dangerous item.

2.72 If an injunction is made by the Youth Court containing terms which have a power of arrest attached to any of those terms, each of those provisions must be set out in a separate paragraph of the injunction and a copy of the relevant provisions must be delivered by the applicant to any police station for the area where the conduct occurred.[24] The relevant provisions for which the power of arrest has been attached must not however be delivered until the injunction has been served on the respondent[25] and where an order is made varying or discharging the injunction or any provision the applicant must immediately inform any police station which was given the original order and deliver a copy of the new order to the police station as well.

ISSUE AND PROCEDURE

County Court – adults

2.73 The provisions in the Civil Procedure Rules ('CPR') which related to gang-related violence have been deemed to be appropriate to apply wholesale to the new injunction regime. The provisions relating to applications under Part 1 of the 2014 Act therefore commence at CPR 65.42. The Rules state that any application under Part 1 is subject to the Part 8 procedure, CPR 65.43(1), as modified by the rule and the Practice Direction. A District Judge has power to hear any breach by reason of CPR 65[26] and 81 which govern civil contempt proceedings.

2.74 The application must be made by a claim form N16A (CPR 65.43(2)(a) and PD 65, para 1.1(1)). The application may be made at any County Court centre but will then be sent to the centre closest to where the defendant resides or the conduct complained of occurred PD 65, para 1.1(2). The claim form must be accompanied by a supporting witness statement at the time of filing, CPR 65.43(2)(c).

2.75 The claim form must address those matters required by CPR 8.2, namely the question the court wants the court to decide or the remedy the claimant is seeking and the legal basis for that remedy, the enactment under which the claim is being brought and the representative capacity of the parties if appropriate. The claim form must also state the terms of the injunction which is being applied for.

2.76 Any application which is made on notice must however be served, together with the evidence relied upon, by the claimant on the defendant personally (CPR 65.43(5)). Further whilst pursuant to CPR 8.3 the defendant has 14 days to file an acknowledgment of service the application can be listed before that time has expired. If so the claimant must have served the defendant 2 clear days before the hearing and the defendant is entitled to be heard even if he has not filed such acknowledgment (CPR 65.43(6)). This is a cumbersome mechanism as for most injunction cases waiting 2 weeks before a case could even be listed after the acknowledgement of service is unlikely to be appropriate. It will remain to be seen how the courts approach listing however it is suggested that claimants will be seeking listing hearings for at least interim injunctions at a much earlier juncture. It would therefore be wise to set out the request for the same in the initial application so that the court is aware from the start. Most courts also have user group meetings in which the local practice can be established.

---

24 Magistrates' Courts (Injunctions: Anti-Social Behaviour) Rules 2015, r 5(2).

25 Ibid, r 5(3).

26 See CPR 65.47(5).

Applications against a person aged under 18

2.77 An application for a Part 1 injunction against a person aged under 18 must be made in the Youth Court.[27] The procedure is governed by the Magistrates' Courts (Injunctions: Anti-Social Behaviour) Rules 2015 (SI 2015/423) which came into force on 3 March 2015.

Form and content of application

2.78 As stated in the explanatory note to the 2015 Rules and as agreed by most HMCTS areas (although not all and local practice should be checked) the court will not proscribe the form of the application and notice that applicants may use, as long as any documents are prepared in accordance with the 2015 Rules. The Rules require any application to be made by way of complaint in writing[28] and must as a minimum:[29]

(a) state the name, address and date of birth of the respondent;

(b) state the name and address of a parent or guardian of the respondent (except where the respondent is aged 18 or over, permission having been given by the court in relation to that respondent under r 15);

(c) be supported by evidence of the matters of which the court must be satisfied for the first and second conditions under s 1 to be met;

(d) state the terms of the Part 1 injunction applied for; and

(e) in the case of an application made on notice, include a statement that the requirement for consultation in s 14(1) has been complied with.

2.79 An application which is made without notice must additionally state the reasons why it is necessary for the application to be made without notice having been given.[30]

2.80 An application which is made on notice must be served on the respondent personally[31] and on the parent or guardian personally or by posting it to or leaving it at their address.[32]

SPECIAL MEASURES FOR WITNESSES

2.81 The Act[33] expressly applies Chapter 1 of Part 2 of the Youth Justice and Criminal Evidence Act 1999 which create a variety of special measures for vulnerable witnesses into proceedings under Part 1. This is dealt with in more detail in Chapter 4.

---

27 Anti-social Behaviour, Crime and Policing Act 2014, s 1(8).

28 Magistrates' Courts (Injunctions: Anti-Social Behaviour) Rules 2015, r 2.

29 Ibid, r 3(1).

30 Ibid, r 3(2).

31 Ibid, r 3(3)(a).

32 Ibid, r 3(3)(b). It should be noted that the statutory instrument as originally made contains an error referring to para 2(b) of the Rules whereas it should be para 3(1)(b).

33 Anti-social Behaviour, Crime and Policing Act 2014, s 16.

WITHOUT NOTICE

2.82 A civil injunction can be applied for without notice to the defendant in the first instance. A court may grant an interim injunction, dismiss the application entirely or adjourn the application to be heard later (s 6). The application can be made at any County Court hearing centre and can be heard either there or be transferred to the court nearest the defendant's home or the conduct complained of or at another hearing centre at the court considers appropriate (CPR 65.43(4)). The reason for these options must be to allow the greatest flexibility for hearing what by their very nature must be urgent applications. There is of course the out-of-hours procedure for very urgent applications which cannot wait until the next court date. The rules require the witness statement served in support of the application to state the reasons why notice has not been given (CPR 65.43(4)(a)). An appeal against the refusal to make a without notice order is now to be heard without notice to the defendant.

Minors – Youth Court

2.83 There is an equivalent provision (r 3.2) within the Magistrates' Courts (Injunctions: Anti-Social Behaviour) Rules 2015 for applications made for an order against a minor in the Youth Court to state why it is necessary for the application to be made without notice. Whereas in the County Court an interim order made without notice can in certain circumstances be enforced even if formal service has not occurred but the defendant can be shown to have proper notice of the terms and effect of the order, an interim injunction made by the Youth Court without notice must be served personally on the defendant as soon as practicable and will not have effect until it has been served.[34]

2.84 With respect to all without notice applications the decision of the Court of Appeal in *Moat Housing v Harris & Hartless*[35] should be borne firmly in mind. That is to say that any without notice order is a potentially significant interference of the rights of the defendant and should be an exceptional case. Further that there is a significant difference between making a interim order which merely prevents someone from doing something anti-social which they should not be doing anyway pending a full on notice hearing and an order which requires someone to leave their home. The latter would only be justified in the most extreme of cases and with evidence of violence and risk of harm if the order was not to be made.

INTERIM INJUNCTIONS

2.85 The court, whether County Court or Youth Court, also has the power when adjourning an application for an injunction to make an interim order. This applies whether the hearing is on notice or without. The court can make an injunction which lasts until the final hearing of the application or further order (s 7(2)), if considered just to do so. A without notice interim injunction may not include a term requiring participation in

---

[34] Magistrates' Courts (Injunctions: Anti-Social Behaviour) Rules 2015, r 4(b).

[35] [2005] 3 WLR 691.

particular activities. It is hard to see how a court could impose any interim injunction requiring any positive action on the part of a defendant without a trial of the disputed facts.

VARIATION OR DISCHARGE OF INJUNCTIONS

2.86 An application to vary or discharge may be made by either the applicant or the defendant.[36] Such application is made to the court which made the injunction or to the County Court if made against a minor who has since achieved majority. Any application to vary or discharge an order made by the County Court must be made in accordance with Part 23: see CPR 65.45(1). An application made to vary or discharge an order made by the Youth Court however must comply with r 6[37] which requires the party making the application to specify the reason why the application should be granted and if the application is made to vary the injunction, the variation which is sought and if made by a relevant authority, state that the consultation requirements of s 14(3) of the 2014 Act have been complied with.[38]

2.87 When considering the application the court has the power to make additional terms, extend the period of a term or the whole injunction and to impose a power of arrest. Any variation to add a new requirement will however need to comply with s 3 of the 2014 Act as to supervision and evidence of suitability and enforcement. There is seemingly no bar to making an initial application to vary or discharge an injunction at any time, even immediately after imposition. If however the application is dismissed, the applying party will not be allowed to make a further application without the consent of the court or agreement of the other party. The Act is silent as to where the burden of proof lies on any application. The general principle would be that the person applying would bear at least an evidential burden however not always the legal burden. An issue which could arise would where a defendant applies to discharge an injunction after a period of time has elapsed. If he asserts that he has not acted in an anti-social manner since the injunction was made but the relevant authority does not agree, on whom does the burden lie? It is the authors' view that as a negative cannot be proved it would be for the relevant authority to discharge the burden of proof as to any alleged ongoing behaviour. However it must be the case that the burden of proof as to whether the injunction itself should be discharged or varied lies still on the applicant.

BREACH

2.88 Unlike breach of an ASBO, breach of an injunction imposed under the 2014 Act will be a civil contempt of court, in the same way as breach of an ASBI. Schedule 2 of the 2014 Act states if breach of an order made by the Youth Court is proved beyond reasonable doubt it is punishable by the making of a supervision order or detention order.[39] This statutory provision is necessary given the historical difficulties in proceedings against minors for breach of injunctions in the County Court.

---

36 Anti-social Behaviour, Crime and Policing Act 2014, s 8.

37 Magistrates' Courts (Injunctions: Anti-Social Behaviour) Rules 2015.

38 Ibid, r 6(2).

39 Anti-social Behaviour, Crime and Policing Act 2014, Sch 2, para 1(1).

2.89 If no power of arrest exists in relation to the relevant term then the applicant may apply to the court for an arrest warrant. The application is to a High Court judge if the injunction is made by the High Court and otherwise for an adult to a County Court judge and to a justice of the peace for a minor (s 10). The application in the County Court must be made in accordance with CPR 23 and in respect of an order made by the Youth Court the application must be substantiated on oath.[40] The application can and probably will always will be made without notice (CPR 65.46(1)). In the County Court the applicant must file an affidavit, not a statement, setting out the grounds for the application, or must give oral evidence at the hearing (CPR 65.46(2)). If oral evidence is given the applicant has to produce a written record of that evidence which must be served on the defendant at the time of arrest (CPR 65.46(3)). It is submitted that very few courts would be satisfied with oral evidence and then a written record which would have to be checked by the court before it could be served. Indeed, it seems to us that there would be very few circumstances in which it would be appropriate to rely on oral evidence to establish breach which would then in any event have to be committed to writing anyway. It is right however to note that the Practice Direction as opposed to Part 65 of the CPR or the Act states that any application for arrest warrant shall not be issued unless the application is substantiated on oath (PD 65, para 2.1). The Practice Direction is the only place where the test to be applied by the court is to be found. Practice Direction 65, para 2.1(2) provides that the judge must have reasonable grounds for believing that the defendant has failed to comply with the injunction. The Magistrates' Courts (Injunctions: Anti-Social Behaviour) Rules 2015 do not provide any test to be applied by the court however it would seem to the authors that using the test in the Practice Direction is unlikely to be wrong in principle.

Power of arrest

2.90 If there is a power of arrest then the test is that there are reasonable grounds for believing that the defendant has breached a provision of the injunction (s 10(3)). The Police will arrest the defendant and must inform the applicant on so doing (s 10(7)). The Police will have taken statements in the usual criminal format which will be provided to the defendant and the court.

2.91 A person who is in breach of injunction shall, if there is a power of arrest attached to the relevant term, be arrested and brought before a court within 24 hours of arrest.[41] Sundays, Good Friday and Christmas Day are however not taken into account for considering this period. For adults this means a judge of the County Court even if the injunction was imposed by a Youth Court[42] when a minor or when granted was being heard with other defendants who were minors.[43] Those defendants who are under 18 years of age must be brought before a Youth Court. If a person 18 years of age or over at arrest, but is subject to an order made by the Youth Court then it is the responsibility of the applicant for the injunction to provide the judge with the information necessary to determine whether to deal with the matter or adjourn it pursuant to CPR 65.47.

---

40 Magistrates' Courts (Injunctions: Anti-Social Behaviour) Rules 2015, r 7.
41 Anti-social Behaviour, Crime and Policing Act 2014, s 9(3).
42 Ibid, s 9(3)(b)(ii).
43 Ibid, s 18(2).

2.92 With regard to defendants who are aged under 18 years of age who are arrested and brought before the court, it may either deal with the matter or adjourn the proceedings.[44] If the proceedings are adjourned and the person is released then the matter must be dealt with by the Youth Court within 28 days and they must be given not less than 2 days' notice of the hearing.[45] The power of the court to make an order imposing supervision or detention order is not however effected by a failure to deal with the case in that period.[46] If the arrested person appears after arrest by a constable then the justice of the peace is required by s 9(6) of the 2014 Act to remand the person to appear before the Youth Court which granted the injunction.

2.93 REMAND

2.94 If a person is arrested after issue of a warrant or by a constable exercising a power of arrest the County Court has the discretionary power to remand a person in custody or on bail although a person aged less than 18 years of age can only be remanded in custody for the preparation of medical reports (see below).[47] A person who is remanded on bail can be so by the court taking from the person a recognizance, with or without sureties, which may be conditioned for their appearance before the court at the end of the period of remand or at every time and place to which during the course of the proceedings the hearing may be adjourned to. Any such conditioned recognizance will be considered a remand whenever a time is fixed for the next appearance for the respondent.[48] The court can choose to remand the person to custody until the recognizances which the court has set the amount of have been taken, after which they will be remanded to bail.[49] When remanding a person on bail the court may require the respondent to comply, before release or later, with any requirements which appear to the court to be necessary to secure that the person does not interfere with witnesses or otherwise obstruct the course of justice.[50] Clearly this gives the court power to make any conditions to bail it wishes including not to enter an area or approach witnesses.

2.95 The maximum period of remand (save in relation to medical examination, see below) is 8 clear days unless it is a remand on bail and both parties consent to a longer period.[51] If the period of remand into custody is not exceeding 3 days the court can remand the person into the custody of a constable.[52] This sidesteps the issue which often arises on a Friday/Saturday arrest when there are often problems housing the detained respondent in a normal jail. If the court is satisfied that a person who has been remanded is unable by reason of illness or accident to appear or be brought before the court at the appointed time, the court may further remand the person in their absence.[53] If the person was on bail then the person's recognizance can be enlarged (and of any sureties). This

---

44 Magistrates' Courts (Injunctions: Anti-Social Behaviour) Rules 2015, r 8(2).
45 Ibid, r 8(3).
46 Ibid, r 8(4).
47 Anti-social Behaviour, Crime and Policing Act 2014, ss 10(8) and 9(5) respectively and Sch 1, para 2.
48 Ibid, Sch 2, para 3.
49 Ibid, Sch 1, para 2(3).
50 Ibid, Sch 1, para 9.
51 Ibid, Sch 1, para 4(1).
52 Ibid, Sch 1, para 4(2).
53 Ibid, Sch 1, para 7(1).

enlargement is to be treated as a further remand.[54] The 8 clear day maximum period of remand without consent does not apply if these powers under paragraph 7 are exercised by the court.[55]

Remand for medical examination and report

2.96 Where the court has reason to think that a medical report will be needed and remands the person to enable a medical examination to take place and a report made, the person may be remanded in custody for no more than 3 weeks (aged 18 and over) and if no bail, no more than 4 weeks.[56] If the court is satisfied on either written or oral evidence of a registered medical practitioner that there is reason to suspect the person is suffering from mental disorder and that it would be impracticable for a report on the person's mental condition to be made if they were remanded on bail the court may remand the person to a hospital or registered establishment specified by the court for that report to be done.[57] Section 35(4)–(10) of the Mental Health Act 1983 applies[58] for the purposes of Sch 1, para 6(1) of the 2014 Act so that for instance if the judge invokes such power he or she should indicate that pursuant to s 35(8) of the 1983 Act a person remanded to hospital may obtain, at his own expense, an independent report from a registered medical practitioner and use it to apply to the court for his remand to be terminated pursuant to s 35(7).

2.97 Otherwise in the County Court there appears to be a general discretion as to whether to impose bail or not. The Bail Act does not apply. Indeed the Act and CPR appear to have an inherent conflict in that the Act specifically addresses remand on bail or in custody[59] where as the CPR states that the judge before whom a person is brought after arrest may (a) deal with the matter or (b) adjourn the proceedings (CPR 65.47(2)). There is no mention of bail at all in the CPR although the Practice Direction states that an application for bail may be made orally or in an application notice. The latter plainly deals with a situation where a person has been remanded in custody by a judge after arrest. If such an application is made then it must give details of where the defendant is being held, where he would go to if granted bail, the amount of recognizance which the person would agree to be bound to and the grounds of the application. If bail was refused before then the application must give full details of the change of circumstances. The CPR does however go on to say that if the case is adjourned and the person is released, the matter must be dealt with within 28 days and the defendant must be given not less than 2 days' notice of the hearing.

PROCEDURE FOR COMMITTAL PROCEEDINGS IN THE COUNTY COURT

2.98 Committal proceedings are governed by CPR 81 and the practice direction which accompanies it. Every committal order is sent to the official solicitor who may review the

[54] Ibid, Sch 1, para 7(4).
[55] Ibid, Sch 1, para 7(5).
[56] Ibid, Sch 1, para 5.
[57] Ibid, Sch 1, para 6(1).
[58] Ibid, Sch 1, para 6(3).
[59] Ibid, Sch 1, para 2(1).

case and appeal or apply on their own initiative. By reason of s 13 of the Administration of Justice Act 1960 and CPR 52.3(1) an appeal against a committal order lies to the Court of Appeal and is of right, ie no permission is needed.

2.99 At any hearing of the committal application the applicant may only rely on evidence already served and in relation to allegations of breach already set out.[60] The respondent is entitled to give oral evidence at the hearing whether or not they have served a statement of their evidence[61] and with the permission of the court may call a witness to give oral evidence whether or not the witness has made an affidavit or given a witness statement.[62]

2.100 In general terms the respondent should have details of the alleged acts of contempt and should be allowed not less than 14 days' notice of any committal hearing to obtain legal representation and prepare his case.[63] Where there are concurrent criminal proceedings it is not appropriate to adjourn or stay the committal proceedings unless there is a real risk of prejudice which might lead to injustice.[64] The court may of its own initiative strike out a committal application[65] but also waive any procedural defect in the commencement or conduct of the application it is satisfied that no injunctive has been caused to the respondent by the defect.[66] A committal application may not be discontinued without the permission of the court.[67]

2.101 The court has the power to hear and make a committal order in the respondent's absence[68] and may on its own initiative fix a date and time when the respondent is to be brought before the court.[69]

SENTENCING OF ADULTS

2.102 Whilst the case-law relates to breach of s 153A injunctions, as the principles remain the same it is the authors' view that they will remain good law as the sentencing powers are identical. Therefore it would seem that credit will not be given for time spent in custody on remand and the court should have regard to that fact when sentencing.[70] The provisions of the Criminal Justice Act 2003[71] will have effect such that a defendant will serve half of the period for which they are sentenced.

2.103 There has been a number of cases through the year in which the Court of Appeal has considered the appropriate sentence for breach of an ASBI injunction. For instance in *Birmingham City Council v Flatt*[72] Lord Justice Tuckey approved the dicta in *Hale v*

---

[60] CPR 81.28(1).
[61] CPR 81.28(2)(a).
[62] CPR 81.28(2)(b).
[63] PD 81, paras 15.2 and 15.5–15.6 and see *Turnbull v Middlesbrough BC* [2003] EWCA Civ 1327.
[64] *Barnet London Borough Council v Hurst* [2002] EWCA Civ 1009, [2003] 1 WLR 722.
[65] PD 81, para 16.1.
[66] PD 81, para 16.2.
[67] PD 81, para 16.3.
[68] CPR 39.3.
[69] CPR 81.28(6).
[70] *Delaney v Delaney* [1996] QB 387.
[71] Section 258.
[72] [2008] EWCA Civ 739, [2009] HLR 5.

Tanner[73] that it was not the case that imprisonment was the automatic consequence of breach of an order and that it is common practice to take some other course on the first occasion when someone has to be dealt with for contempt of court for breaching an injunction. That said if imprisonment is appropriate, the length of committal should be decided without reference to whether or not there is to be a suspension of the committal to prison. Lord Justice Carnwath agreed and added that there are no guiding principles as to when such a sentence should be suspended. So far as contempt of court is concerned, the court has an absolute discretion as to whether to do so or not. In the instant case had the defendant admitted the breaches and shown some remorse it may well have done so.

2.104 In *Barnet LBC v Hurst*[74] the Court of Appeal held that a sentence of 9 months was too long where the breaches were restricted to being loud and noisy and disturbing neighbours' sleep. A sentence of 3 months was substituted. However in *Longhurst Homes Ltd v Killen*[75] Lord Justice Hughes in upholding a sentence of 9 months imprisonment where there had been no actual violence but repeated, unpleasant and intimidating behaviour over a number of months stated:

> '[14] It is trite to say that there is no tariff for sentences for contempt of court. The reason is simply that every case must inevitably depend upon its own facts. In this case, as it seems to me, the judge was entitled to come to two principal conclusions. The first was that an immediate sentence of imprisonment was called for. It was called for in the face of breaches of the order which were, firstly deliberate and secondly repeated. In reaching that conclusion the judge would have had regard to the twin purposes of imprisonment for breach of an injunction. Those, as it is well known, are first to punish, and to punish principally for disobedience to the order rather than directly for the acts committed, and second to protect the beneficiaries of the order by securing future compliance. As Mr McNamara realistically accepts, in discharging the first of those duties any court has necessarily to look at the gravity of the breach, and the measure of the gravity of the breach is frequently supplied by the nature of the act constituting the breach.'

2.105 Whilst there are a number of authorities which uphold the making of immediate substantial terms of imprisonment for the first breach, the court often imposes a suspended committal order and on further breach adopts an incremental increase to sentences. Whilst appeal to the Court of Appeal is as of right, the appellate court is slow to interfere even if it considers it would not have made the same sentence. Thus sentences of 6 months for a first breach[76] and 12 months[77] where the breaches had involved attempted violence, racist language and threats to kill and there had been previous breaches, have been upheld. The Court of Appeal has however made it clear that the maximum sentence of 2 years should be reserved for the worst cases.[78]

2.106 In more recent cases before the Court of Appeal[79] the court has expressly stated that Sentencing Guidelines Council guidelines for breaches of anti-social behaviour orders issued in December 2008 (see Appendix 6) are 'equally relevant when an anti-social

---

73 *Hale v Tanner* [2000] 2 FLR 879.
74 [2002] EWCA Civ 1009, [2003] 1 WLR 722, [2003] HLR 19.
75 [2008] EWCA Civ 402.
76 *Leicester City Council v Lewis* (2001) 33 HLR 37.
77 *Nottingham City Council v Cutts* (2001) 33 HLR 7.
78 *Turnbull v Middlesbrough BC* [2003] EWCA Civ 1327, (2003) 100(39) LSG 37, (2003) *The Times*, September 15.
79 *Amicus Horizon v Thorley* [2012] EWCA Civ 817, [2012] HLR 43 and *Doey v The Mayor and Burgess of the London Borough of Islington* [2012] EWCA Civ 1825.

behaviour order has been made by a civil court'.[80] The guidelines set out (at section 9, page 9), a table which categorises anti-social conduct in three boxes. The first is where serious harassment alarm or distress has been caused or where it was intended, the second for lesser degrees of the same and the third is where there is no harassment. The Court of Appeal has endorsed the use of these guidelines and boxes with the consequential aggravating and mitigating factors set out in the Guidelines to reach an appropriate sentence. It is however the authors' opinion that one factor seems not to have been drawn to the court of appeal's attention in either of the cases which is that the length of sentences suggested by the Guidelines must in part be dictated by the maximum sentence. A breach of an ASBO carried a maximum sentence of 5 years' imprisonment whereas breach of an injunction carries a maximum of 2 years. It is therefore the authors' opinion that regard must be had to this difference when considering the length of any sentence of imprisonment, ie the starting points should be less than stated in the Guidelines. For a detailed consideration of the factors within the Guidelines, see Chapter 3.

PURGING CONTEMPT

2.107 A person who has been committed to prison for contempt of court may apply to the court to be released from prison.[81] The application has to be in writing and attested to by the governor of the prison or another officer at least of rank of principal officer, show that the person has purged or wishes to purge the contempt and must be served on the original applicant not less than 1 day before the hearing.[82] The judge hearing the application has complete discretion as to whether to grant the application.

BREACH OF INJUNCTIONS – POWERS OF COURT IN RESPECT OF MINORS

2.108 Paragraph 1 of Sch 2 of the 2014 Act provides that if a Youth Court is satisfied beyond reasonable doubt that a person aged under 18 is breach of a provision of an injunction made under Part 1, the court may make either a supervision order or a detention order.[83] Of importance is that this remains a discretionary power. Even if breach of the injunction is established the court does not have to make an order.

2.109 The court can only consider making such an order on the application of the person who applied for the order in the first place and they must prior to making an application consult the Youth Offending Team specified under s 3(1) for a specified activity or if none was specified, the Youth Offending Team where the respondent appears to live.[84] There is also a mirror and equally pointless requirement to s 14 that the applicant must also inform any other body or individual they think appropriate. As before it is hard to see how this has any value in that it is a subjective requirement and therefore no value at all

[80] *Amicus Horizon v Thorley* (above) per Toulson LJ at para 5.
[81] CPR 81.34(1).
[82] CPR 81.34(2).
[83] Anti-social Behaviour, Crime and Policing Act 2014, Sch 2, para 1.
[84] Ibid, Sch 2, para 1(3).

as a check or balance. Paragraph 1(4) of Sch 2 does however make it mandatory for the court to consider any representations from the Youth Offending Team in considering whether and how to exercise its powers.[85]

SUPERVISION ORDERS

2.110 A supervision order is one which imposes on the defendant one or more of the following requirements:[86]

(a) supervision;

(b) activity; and

(c) curfew.

2.111 A court must obtain and consider information about the defendant's family circumstances and the likely effect of a supervision order on those circumstances.[87] If it is intended to impose more than one of the above requirements the court is obliged to consider the requirements compatibility with each other.[88] In imposing any requirement the court must ensure, as far as practicable, that the requirements imposed by a supervision order avoid any interference with the normal attendance at school, education or work and any conflict with other court orders.[89] A supervision order may not exceed 6 months in duration and must specify the maximum period of any requirement under it. The order must also specify the Youth Offending Team in whose area it appears to the court the defendant lives or, if there is more than one area, the area which the court decides is relevant.[90]

SUPERVISION REQUIREMENT

2.112 A supervision requirement is one which requires the defendant to attend appointments at whatever times and places set by the allocated responsible officer or another person nominated by them.[91]

ACTIVITY REQUIREMENT

2.113 Activity requirements are defined in some detail at para 4 of Sch 2 of the Act and are requirements which can require the defendant to participate in specified activities or attend at a place specified and then comply with instructions given by the person in charge or participate in residential exercises. The total number of days which can be specified overall must not be less than 12 or more than 24 days.[92] A residential exercise may not be for more than 7 days and the defendant must reside where specified and

---

[85] Ibid, Sch 2, para 1(4).
[86] Ibid, Sch 2, para 2(1).
[87] Ibid, Sch 2, para 2(2).
[88] Ibid, Sch 2, para 2(3).
[89] Ibid, Sch 2, para 2(4).
[90] Ibid, Sch 2, para 2(7).
[91] Ibid, Sch 2, para 3.
[92] Ibid, Sch 2, para 4(2).

participate in activities as specified in the instructions. The court may however not make such an order unless the parent or guardian of the minor agrees.[93] This is rather an unusual requirement as presumably the vast majority, if not all, curfews will relate to the defendant's usual residence. An application to vary or amend the order can be made by either party and can amend the place or the periods.[94]

2.114 An activity order can be varied in terms of the times, places, activities or number of days (subject to the minimum and maximums above) but only if the court has consulted the Youth Offending Team and it is satisfied that it is feasible to secure compliance with the requirement as varied and that the activities exist.

CURFEW

2.115 A curfew requirement in a supervision order can require a defendant to be in a specified place for specified periods and can have different places or periods for different days but may not amount to a period of less than 2 hours or more than 8 hours in any day.[95] The wording of the Act means that a general curfew order, ie not to be out of a building after a set hour is not available. The court must specify the place that the defendant shall be. Prior to making an order the court must obtain and consider information about the place proposed to be specified including information about the attitude of the person likely to be affected by the enforced presence there of the defaulter.[96]

2.116 If a curfew requirement is made in a supervision order, the requirement can include a requirement of electronic monitoring of compliance with the curfew.[97] The period of monitoring can be specified in the order or left to the responsible officer. The court cannot make a requirement for electronic monitoring unless the Youth Offending Team confirm that arrangements are in place to provide it and the order must include a provision making a person responsible for the monitoring. If monitoring requires the cooperation of another person than the defendant to make it practicable to secure that monitoring takes place, consent of that person is needed.[98]

2.117 A responsible officer nominated by the court in respect of a supervision order has a duty to make arrangements for the requirements and to promote the defendant's compliance with them.[99] A defendant who has a supervision order imposed on them is obliged to keep in touch with the responsible officer as directed and notify them of any change of address. These obligations have the force of a requirement of the order.[100]

---

93 Ibid, Sch 2, para 10(a) – but NB that if the local authority has parental responsibility for the child who is within their care or provided accommodation by the authority in exercise of social services functions, it is the local authority whose consent is required, para 4(14).
94 Anti-social Behaviour, Crime and Policing Act 2014, Sch 2, para 5(5).
95 Ibid, Sch 2, para 5(1)–(3).
96 Ibid, Sch 2, para 5(4).
97 Ibid, Sch 2, para 6(1).
98 Ibid, Sch 2, para 6(3).
99 Ibid, Sch 2, para 7(2).
100 Ibid, Sch 2, para 7(4).

NON-COMPLIANCE WITH A SUPERVISION ORDER

2.118 If the responsible officer considers that the defendant has failed to comply with a requirement of the order they must inform the original applicant who may apply to the Youth Court for an order but must consult with the Youth Offending Team and anyone it thinks appropriate before doing so.[101]

2.119 At the hearing before the Youth Court, if the breach is established beyond reasonable doubt and that the defendant has no reasonable excuse for failure to comply, the court make revoke the supervision order and make a new one or revoke the order and make a detention order. The court may not do so, however, if the defendant has become 18 years of age and must consider the representations of the Youth Offending Team before exercising its powers.[102]

2.120 Either party may apply to a Youth Court to revoke a supervision order or amend it by removing a requirement from it. The original applicant is required to consult with the Youth Offending Team before making the application whereas the defendant is not. The test is set out in para 10 to Sch 2 and is that it appears to the court to be in the interests of justice to do so, having regard to circumstances which have arisen since the supervision order was made. This means that there has to be a change in circumstances for this application to be made. If the application is dismissed then the applicant party may make no further application to revoke or remove a requirement without the consent of the court or the agreement of the other party.[103]

DETENTION ORDERS FOR YOUNG PERSONS

2.121 A detention order detains the defendant in youth detention accommodation (secure training centre or young offender institution or secure accommodation) as determined by the Secretary of State.[104] The detention order may not exceed 3 months[105] and may not be made against a person aged 13 years of age or less[106] nor can a court impose one unless it is satisfied that in view of the severity or extent of the breach, no other power available to the court is appropriate.[107]

2.122 If a detention order is made either party may apply to revoke the order. The court may revoke the order if is appears to the court to be in the interests of justice to do so, having regard to the circumstances which have arisen since the detention order was made. If the application is dismissed the applicant party cannot make another application without the consent of the court or the agreement of the other party.[108] Prior to any application being made the person applying to revoke the detention order must have

---

[101] Ibid, Sch 2, para 12(1)–(3).
[102] Ibid, Sch 2, para 12(6).
[103] Ibid, Sch 2, para 10(4).
[104] Ibid, Sch 2, para 14(1).
[105] Ibid, Sch 2, para 14(2).
[106] Ibid, Sch 2, para 1(5).
[107] Ibid, Sch 2, para 1(6).
[108] Ibid, Sch 2, para 15(4).

consulted with the Youth Offending Team, either as specified in the injunction or under the supervision order if the detention order was made for breach of a supervision requirement.[109]

APPEALS

2.123 One of the problems with ASBOs was that appeals against orders were made to the Crown Court which meant that Crown Court judges with little or no experience of civil evidence were being asked to consider such appeals. Unfortunately the 2014 Act has continued this position in respect of applications against minors. An appeal against a decision of the Youth Court is to the Crown Court (s 15(1)). It is presumed that the appeal is one of right although not expressly provided for in the 2014 Act.

2.124 Appeals against an order of the County Court will, in seems to the authors, follow the same principles of appeals against ASBIs, and be governed by CPR 52 and PD 52. While the Guidance suggests that appeals for an adult can be made to the High Court this would seem to be incorrect. Part 65 makes it clear that proceedings must be made pursuant to Part 8 which, according to PD 52 Table 1, an appeal from a District Judge (whether interim or final order) is to a Circuit Judge. An appeal from a Circuit Judge is to a High Court Judge.

TRANSITIONAL PROVISIONS

2.125 Where an application is made prior to the commencement date of 23 March 2015 for an order under the previous statutory provisions (save for an application for an individual support order) the old provisions will continue to have force (s 21(2)). Orders which have already been made will continue to be governed by the original statutory provisions including applications to vary or enforce save that no existing order (or term of an order) can be extended in length after the commencement date (s 21(4)). The wording of that sub-section seems to mean that even if an application to extend was made before the commencement date it cannot be extended after that date.

2.126 As a long stop s 21(5) states that by 23 March 2020 any orders which are still in force under the repealed statutory provisions shall be deemed an injunction under s 1 with any 'necessary modifications'.

[109] Ibid, Sch 2, para 15(5), (6).

CHAPTER 3

CRIMINAL BEHAVIOUR ORDERS

3.01 Criminal Behaviour Orders are made under Part 2 of the 2014 Act. They replace ASBOs on conviction ('CRASBOs') and are available if the defendant is convicted of an offence.[1] It should be noted that the type of offence is not prescribed; any offence will suffice, even if unconnected with the anti-social behaviour which forms the basis for the application. This mirrors the CRASBO provisions in the 1998 Act. However the orders differ from CRASBOs in a number of ways. First, they are only available on the application of the prosecution[2] and not any other authority or body, unless they are bringing the prosecution. It would seem likely, and indeed appears to be supported by the Home Office Guidance, that other relevant bodies may request that the prosecution seek an order and provide them with the evidence to do so. Secondly, it would seem that the court can not make an order of its own initiative. Thirdly, a criminal behaviour order under Part 2 can impose positive requirements on a defendant unlike a CRASBO.

WHEN CAN AN ORDER BE MADE?

3.02 If convicted of an offence for which the court imposes a sentence or conditional discharge[3] (meaning that an order cannot be made if the defendant is discharged absolutely) the court may make an order if both of the following conditions are satisfied:[4]

(a) It is proved beyond reasonable doubt that the defendant has engaged in behaviour which caused or was likely to cause harassment, alarm or distress to any person.[5]

(b) The court considers that making the order will help in preventing the offender from engaging in such behaviour.[6]

3.03 The first limb of the test is that which was required to obtain an ASBO and is considered in detail at **2.15**. It should be borne in mind that by reason of s 33(5) of the 2014 Act only conduct which occurs up to 1 year prior to the commencement date (20 October 2014) can be taken into account. This is of course greater than the 6 months which is the limit imposed by s 127 of the Magistrates' Court Act 1980.

3.04 The Guidance states that there does not need to be a link between the criminal behaviour which led to the conviction and the anti-social behaviour which is alleged as the grounds for making the order. It seems to the authors that it is highly unlikely that a criminal court will be content for a completely new case to be presented and argued which has no relationship to the criminal charges, whatever the guidance states. It seems

---

1 Anti-social Behaviour, Crime and Policing Act 2014, s 22(1).
2 Ibid s 22(7).
3 Ibid s 22(6).
4 Ibid s 22(2).
5 Ibid s 22(3).
6 Ibid s 22(4).

to the authors that if there is little or no connection then the appropriate course is to issue proceedings in the County Court. There is a significant risk that if this is not done and the criminal judge refuses to entertain the application any new subsequent application to the County Court may be rather 'stale'. There is of course the additional obvious danger that the defendant is acquitted in the criminal proceedings which removes any jurisdiction of the court to consider any application.

3.05 There is another reason why applications for criminal behaviour orders are not as attractive to an applicant as those for civil injunctions, especially those which are not based on behaviour which is not the subject of criminal proceedings. This is because the two-stage test for criminal behaviour orders has one very significant difference to that for the civil injunction order, namely the burden of proof. To obtain a criminal behaviour order the prosecution has to prove that the defendant has committed acts of anti-social behaviour to a criminal standard. The 2014 Act specifically states that the burden of proof for civil injunction orders is the lower of the two standards, namely the balance of probabilities.[7] The standard of proof for criminal behaviour orders mirrors that in ASBOs and the reason for the different standard of proof must be due to the consequence of breach. In the case-law following the 1998 Act[8] the courts held that where the imposition of an order could result in breach proceedings which would be a criminal offence, the standard of proof should be beyond reasonable doubt not the balance of probabilities. The authors are of the view that unless the application for an order is related to the criminal charges, such that it is effectively the criminal charge, then seeking a criminal behaviour order rather then a civil injunction order would seem tactically flawed, unless the other evidence is overwhelming and could not realistically be challenged.

3.06 The second limb of the test carries no statement as to the burden or standard of proof. The use of the word 'considers' suggests that as was the position with the second limb of the test for an ASBO, there is no standard of proof, only an exercise of discretion and evaluation by the court. It is, however, again noteworthy that there is a material difference in the test to be applied between criminal behaviour orders and civil injunction orders. The latter can be imposed if the court considers it to be just and convenient for the purpose of preventing the defendant from engaging in anti-social behaviour whereas a criminal behaviour order can only be imposed if it would help prevent them from engaging in the same. There is also a change in emphasis from the wording of the ASBO legislation in that where previously the second limb of the test was whether the order was necessary to protect persons from further anti-social behaviour, it is now whether it would help prevent the defendant from further behaviour. It may be that in fact this is a conscious change to reflect the unhappy conflicting case-law which began with *R v Boness*[9] as to whether a CRASBO could properly be made when the terms simply reflected a criminal offence and therefore were arguably not necessary to prevent reoccurrence. By focusing on the need to help prevent the defendant from committing further anti-social behaviour this is avoided.

---

7 Ibid, s 1(2).

8 *R (on the application of McCann and others) v Crown Court at Manchester; Clingham v Kensington and Chelsea Royal Borough Council* [2002] UKHL 39, [2002] 3 WLR 1313.

9 [2005] EWCA Crim 2395.

CONSULTATION

3.07 Where the defendant is less than 18 years of age, the prosecution must ascertain the views of the local Youth Offending Team[10] where the defendant lives or appears to live before making the application. The Home Office Guidance states that the views of the Youth Offending Team must be included within the file of evidence forwarded to the prosecution. The Guidance however says that in practice the body asking the prosecution to apply should be conducting the consultation and that those views should be obtained before requesting the CPS to apply.

3.08 Whilst the statute requires the prosecution to ascertain those views, it is noteworthy that there is no longer a requirement to prove such a consultation by way of certificate, nor indeed does there seem to be any necessity to inform the court what the Youth Offending Team said. In practice an applicant would usually make it clear that the views had been sought and that the application was supported.

PROCEDURE FOR APPLYING

3.09 The court can only consider an application for a criminal behaviour order if the original criminal proceedings have not been concluded. The application for the CBO has to follow sentencing for the criminal offence but the court can adjourn the application to be heard on another day. The statute does not address timing specifically save that it states that a criminal behaviour order can only be made if it is in addition to the sentence. The Home Office Guidance states a court cannot consider an application for an order at a hearing unless the court adjourned consideration of the same from the sentencing hearing. It is not clear when the application has to be raised for it not to be considered as being an application after sentencing. It could be argued that unless it was raised by the court prior to the handing down of sentence the application could not be in addition to the sentence. It is doubtful whether the court will adopt such a strict interpretation; however it will be advisable for the prosecution to make the intention to apply for a criminal behaviour order clear before sentencing is conducted.

CRIMINAL PROCEDURE RULES – PART 50

3.10 The procedure for applications before the Youth Court is governed by Part 50 of the Criminal Procedure Rules which was amended to come into force as of 6 October 2014. By virtue of r 50.2 a court must not make a CBO unless the defendant has had the opportunity to consider what order is sought and why, the evidence in support and to make representations at a hearing.[11] There is an exception for interim orders. However the rules unnecessarily repeat the legislation to state that an interim order is not effective unless the defendant is present when it is made or served personally within 7 days of making.[12]

---

10 Anti-social Behaviour, Crime and Policing Act 2014, s 22(8).

11 It is the opportunity to make the representations not whether they attend or make them, see r 50.2(1)(b).

12 CrimPR, r 50.2(2).

3.11 In order for a prosecutor to seek a post conviction order they must serve a notice of intention to apply for such an order on the court officer and the defendant.[13] In fact the Rule additionally requires service on 'any person on whom the order would be likely to have a significant adverse effect' which opens argument to whether members of a family might be so affected.[14] The notice must be in the prescribed form in the Practice Direction and be served as soon as practicable and without waiting for the verdict.[15]

THE CONTENTS OF THE NOTICE

3.12 The notice of intention to seek an order must include:[16]

(a) a summary of the relevant facts;

(b) an identification of the evidence on which the prosecutor relies on in support;

(c) written statements which had not been already served; and

(d) specify the order sought.

To this we would add that a schedule of the alleged acts of anti-social behaviour must be included. Prior to the inception of the above rule, the Court of Appeal, in relation to ASBO appeals, had been repeating the need for every court to make detailed findings of fact on each alleged act or behaviour. It seems strange that this was ignored in the drafting of the rule. It is suggested that as the defendant is entitled to know the case against him and must state whether they agree or disagree to each of the allegations, a schedule setting them out is a pre-requisite for any application.

DEFENDANT'S RESPONSE

3.13 After the defendant has been served with any notice they must serve written notice of any evidence on which he wishes to rely.[17] Again this must be done without waiting for any verdict and must include any written statement which had not already been served.[18]

3.14 It would seem that a defendant facing a post conviction order application is under more onerous duties of disclosure than one facing a free standing application. The defendant is obliged to serve a statement in accordance with the Rules. Further the evidence has to be filed before the outcome of the criminal case. In practice it is most unlikely that any defendant or their legal representatives will focus energy on this element of the case which may require substantial investment of time to obtain evidence. This is particularly so as the work would be 'wasted' if the defendant was acquitted. The more practical situation will be that a defendant will file their supplemental evidence after conviction before the adjourned hearing to consider the post conviction order.

---

[13] CrimPR 2014, r 50.3(2)(a) and (b) respectively.
[14] CrimPR 2014, r 50.3(2)(c).
[15] CrimPR 2014, r 50.3(2).
[16] CrimPR 2014, r 50.3(3).
[17] CrimPR 2014, r 50.3(4).
[18] CrimPR 2014, r 50.3(4).

SPECIAL MEASURES FOR WITNESSES

3.15 If the prosecutor wishes to use the rules relating to special measures to assist a witness then they may do so in an application for a CBO[19] but must apply when serving the notice (see further Chapter 4). Again it appears to the Authors that the timing is strange in that the prosecutor would be alerting the defendant to the identity of witnesses who may be afraid to give evidence in open court and require screens or other protection at a stage when they may or may not actually be allowed to give evidence, ie if the defendant was acquitted.

3.16 If the application is adjourned the court can choose to adjourn the hearing again, issue a warrant for the defendant's arrest or hear the application in his absence.[20] The court may not however issue a warrant unless it is satisfied that the defendant had adequate notice of the time and place of the adjourned hearing.[21] It cannot proceed in his absence unless it is satisfied of the above and also that he had been told that the court may proceed in his absence. It would seem appropriate therefore for the court's notice of hearing to include such warnings as a matter of course.

Hearing

3.17 In considering an application for a criminal behaviour order the court may consider evidence provided by both prosecution and defendant. Plainly principles of natural justice should mean that that the defendant is given the opportunity to challenge the evidence and present evidence in response. The 2014 Act makes it clear that the prosecution may adduce evidence which would not have been admissible in the actual criminal proceedings.[22] This is presumably to allow the use of hearsay evidence and indeed the Guidance refers expressly to evidence from witnesses who may have been reluctant to give evidence in person and their giving of statements or evidence through police officers. This brings into sharp focus all those matters which were in issue when applications for ASBOs were made. Whilst it seems to us that it is theoretically possible to establish the first limb of the test on the basis of hearsay evidence, it is unlikely given the standard of proof that such evidence in isolation will suffice. Hearsay evidence is likely to be far more useful in proving to the court that the imposition of the order will help prevent the behaviour. Evidence and in particular hearsay evidence and the procedural requirements to adduce the same in a CBO application is considered in more detail in Chapter 4.

3.18 There is specific provision in the 2014 Act for the use of the powers in Chapter 1 of Part 2 of the Youth Justice and Criminal Evidence Act 1999 to provide for special measures in the case of vulnerable and intimidated witnesses[23] including the Rules of Court made for the purposes of that Act.[24] Those special measures are dealt with in detail in Chapter 4.

---

19 CrimPR 2014, r 50.7.
20 Anti-social Behaviour, Crime and Policing Act 2014, s 23(4).
21 Ibid, s 23(5).
22 Ibid, s 23(2).
23 Ibid, s 31.
24 Ibid, s 31(3).

Orders

3.19 As with a civil injunction order, a criminal behaviour order must so far as practicable avoid interference with times that the defendant works or attends school/education or conflict with the requirements of other court requirements[25] (presumably probation, community service orders etc). For a detailed consideration of the appropriate terms of an order see Chapter 2.

3.20 If the term imposes a positive requirement on a defendant then the order must specify the person (may be an individual or an organisation) who is responsible for supervising compliance with the requirement.[26] That person or organisation must have provided the court with evidence about the suitability and enforceability of the requirement *before* the term can be imposed by the court.[27] If there is more than one term, the court must consider their compatibility with each other.[28]

3.21 The 2014 Act rather inelegantly goes on to state that the person or organisation has a duty under the Act to make 'any necessary arrangements in connection with the requirements for which the person or organisation has responsibility'[29] and to promote compliance by the defendant.[30] The relevant person has a duty to inform the applicant and the Chief Officer of Police if they consider that the defendant has failed to comply or had complied fully with the requirements imposed.[31]

3.22 The Act also imposes a mandatory duty on a defendant who has such a requirement imposed on him to keep in touch with the specified supervisor as directed by them[32] and to notify them of any change of address.[33] Failure to comply with either amounts to a breach of the injunction.[34]

3.23 There is nothing more in the Act as to what activities can be imposed or how. The Guidance provides little greater assistance. It states that agencies will have the discretion to tailor the positive requirements in each case, which could include alcohol awareness classes, dog training classes provided by animal welfare charities, or attendance at mediation sessions with neighbours or victims.

3.24 There is no requirement for the defendant to attend court when a positive requirement is imposed and they are not liable for the cost. There is however nothing in either the Act or Guidance as to how such positive obligations are to be financed. Many of the agencies that provide therapeutic work require the participant to be willing or at least committed to treatment, which is often expensive to provide. It is difficult to see such organisations being willing to volunteer space on oversubscribed courses. It would seem unlikely that even if agencies did agree to the course being used that they would agree to have the duty imposed on them that the Act requires. This would mean that

25 Ibid, s 22(9).
26 Ibid, s 24(1).
27 Ibid, s 24(2).
28 Ibid, s 24(5).
29 Ibid, s 24(4)(a).
30 Ibid, s 24(4)(b).
31 Ibid, s 24(4)(c).
32 Ibid, s 24(6)(a).
33 Ibid, s 24(6)(b).
34 Ibid, s 24(6).

someone from the applicant would have to assume such responsibility. It remains to be seen what resources will be available or finances for such positive obligations to be imposed. The Youth Offending Team's input is likely to be crucial.

Duration

3.25 A criminal behaviour order made in respect of an adult must be for a period of not less than 2 years and can be of indefinite duration (s 25(5)). An order can have different periods of duration for different terms within the same order (s 25(6)).

3.26 If the defendant is less than 18 then the order must be no less than 1 year and no more than 3 years (s 25(4)). This is of course different to civil injunction orders which can be imposed for a maximum of 1 year against a minor. It seems odd that a longer order can be imposed in circumstances where the application for an order was based on evidence wholly unrelated to the criminal offence, which may have been very minor indeed. For instance the same evidence presented for a civil injunction order application may result in a maximum of 1 year, but the same evidence if used in an application after, say, a conviction for careless driving or even a television licence offence, could result in a 3-year order breach of which carries a criminal sanction.

3.27 A criminal behaviour order commences on the day made unless there is already an order which is in force, in which case the new order can be dated to commence on expiry of the previous order (s 25(2)). It does not appear therefore that an order can be made so to have effect on the release of a person from custody, no doubt because of the uncertainty as to when that may be.

Review of orders

3.28 As a criminal behaviour order can be made for more than 1 year against a minor the 2014 Act requires a review to be conducted. The review shall be done every 12 months commencing from the date the order takes effect[35] or if during the 12 months a variation has occurred, 12 months from the date of the last variation.[36] Similarly a further review has to occur 12 months after any earlier review or 12 months if another variation occurs.[37] A review is not required if the defendant will be over 18 at the time of such review.[38]

3.29 A review must include consideration of the extent to which the defendant has complied, the adequacy of the support available to the defendant to help him comply and generally any matters as to whether the order should be varied or discharged. It seems likely that guidance as to the conducting of the review will be forthcoming as the statute expressly refers to the need for the reviewer to take account of such issued guidance.[39] There is however no guidance that has presently been issued specifically for any review.

---

35 Ibid, s 28(2)(a)(i).
36 Ibid, s 28(2)(a)(ii).
37 Ibid, s 28(2)(b).
38 Ibid, s 28(1).
39 Ibid, s 28(4).

3.30 The review itself must be conducted by the Chief of Police of the area in which the defendant lives or appears to be living[40] but must be done in co-operation with the local council[41] who have a duty to participate. The Chief Officer of Police can invite participation from any other person or body[42] and it would seem to us that the Youth Offending Team and any relevant educational establishment should be invited to participate as a matter of course.

3.31 One point to note is that the statute refers only to the Chief Officer of Police and not his nominate. It will be important for chief police officers (who are not going to attend) to ensure that the power to attend is properly delegated.

INTERIM ORDERS

3.32 Interim criminal behaviour orders can be made if a court adjourns the consideration of the application for a full order (s 26(1)). The order may be made until final hearing of the application or until further order (s 26(2)) if the court considers it just. It is hard to see how it could be just for an interim order to be made until further order rather than one until the final hearing. Rather oddly the 2014 Act disapplies the need for consultation with the Youth Offending Team before making an interim order.

BREACH

3.33 As noted above breach of a criminal behaviour order is a criminal offence[43] unlike breach of a civil injunction order. The defendant may be sentenced to a fine and/or imprisonment of up to 6 months on summary conviction and up to 5 years on indictment.[44] The court may not impose a conditional discharge as a penalty on conviction.[45] In any breach proceedings a copy of the original criminal order, certified by the proper officer of the court which made it, is admissible as evidence of the order having been made and its contents.[46]

3.34 Breach of an interim order will carry the same sanctions as breach of a full order.[47] Further it is highly likely that as in *Parker v DPP*,[48] a case relating to breach of interim ASBOs, that breach of a term of an interim order, which is subsequently not made as a condition of the final order, is still a criminal offence and no less serious for not being continued. In *Parker* the term in the interim order was one against association with another youth. Lord Justice Rose (Vice President of the Court of Appeal, Criminal Division) held:

> 'In my judgment, however, it by no means follows that the absence from the final ASBO of a condition inserted at the interim stage itself affects the gravity or otherwise of the breach of

[40] Ibid, s 29(1).
[41] Ibid, s 29(2).
[42] Ibid, s 29(3).
[43] Ibid, s 30(1).
[44] Ibid, s 30(2).
[45] Ibid, s 30(3).
[46] Ibid, s 30(4).
[47] Ibid, s 26(4).
[48] [2005] EWHC 1485 (Admin).

> that condition. The gravity of the breach of the interim condition depends on all the circumstances of the case by reference, for example without purporting to be exhaustive, to the nature of the conduct giving rise to the breach and the flagrancy of the breach having regard, for example, to the relevant time scale – that is to say, a breach which occurs very soon after an order has been made may very well be a good deal more serious than a breach occurring some time later. Equally, the repetition of the same breach may well result in the sentencing court taking a graver view of the quality of the breach for which sentence is to be passed.
>
> … For my part, in spite of Mr Lofthouse's elegant submissions, I am wholly unpersuaded that omission of a condition from the final order of itself is a matter to which the court should properly have regard when sentencing for the breach of a condition in an interim order …'

3.35 As the provisions for sentence upon breach mirror those for breach of an ASBO it must be assumed that the sentencing principles, case-law and Guidelines will apply in exactly the same way including the Judicial College Sentencing Guidelines.

SENTENCING

3.36 On summary conviction, an adult defendant (see **3.47** for youths) can be sentenced to a maximum of 6 months and a fine not exceeding the present statutory maximum of £5,000 and, on indictment, up to 5 years' imprisonment and/or a fine.[49] It should be noted that, whilst the court has the power to impose community penalties, as well as fines or prison terms, it does not have the power to impose a conditional discharge,[50] although, presumably, an absolute discharge remains available. The penalty for breach is the same, whether the breach is of a final or an interim order.

3.37 The Sentencing Guidelines Council has now produced 'definitive' sentencing Guidelines for breach of ASBOs[51] after 5 January 2009 which every court is statutorily obliged to have regard to it when passing sentence.[52] At the time of publication there are no sentencing guidelines for the breach of a CBO however it seems to the authors as the penalties for breach are the same it is highly likely that they will continue to be relevant and will probably be re-issued for CBOs substantially unchanged.

3.38 The Guidelines state that whilst it applies to adults and youths the sentencing framework that applies to offenders aged under 18 is significantly different from that for older offenders and therefore the guidance for young offenders is in the form of principles particularly regarding the circumstances in which a custodial sentence might be justified.

3.39 The Guidance gives the courts the following general statement:

> 'The main aim of sentencing for breach of a court order is to achieve the purpose of the order; in the case of an ASBO that is to protect the public from behaviour that is likely to cause harassment, alarm or distress. Any perception that the courts do not treat seriously a failure to comply with a court order can undermine public confidence and is therefore an important additional consideration.'

---

49 Anti-social Behaviour, Crime and Policing Act 2014, s 30(2).
50 Ibid, s 30(3).
51 See Appendix 6.
52 Criminal Justice Act 2003, s 172.

It continues:

> 'The main aim of sentencing for breach of a court order is to achieve the purpose of the order. Therefore, the sentence for breach of an ASBO should primarily reflect the harassment, alarm or distress involved; the fact that it constituted breach of a court order is a secondary consideration.'

3.40 In determining how serious a breach is, the Guideline states:

> 'The sentence for breach of an ASBO must be commensurate with the seriousness of the offence; that is determined by assessing the culpability of the offender and any harm which the offence caused, was intended to cause or might foreseeably have caused.'

3.41 The Guidelines note that the breach may itself cause harassment, alarm or distress, which can reduce the quality of life in a community. Further that breach of an ASBO contravenes an order of the court, and this can undermine public confidence in the effective administration of justice. The assessment of the seriousness of an individual offence must take into account not only the harm actually caused by an offence but also any harm that was intended or might foreseeably have been caused. If the defendant was unaware of the breach due to a misunderstanding of the terms this could be a mitigating feature.

3.42 At Annex B the Guidelines set out the factors indicating a more serious breach as being as follows:

- Offence committed whilst on bail for other offences.
- Failure to respond to previous sentences.
- Offence was racially or religiously aggravated.
- Offence motivated by, or demonstrating, hostility to the victim based on his or her sexual orientation (or presumed sexual orientation).
- Offence motivated by, or demonstrating, hostility based on the victim's disability (or presumed disability).
- Previous conviction(s), particularly where a pattern of repeat offending is disclosed.
- Planning of an offence.
- An intention to commit more serious harm than actually resulted from the offence.
- Offenders operating in groups or gangs.
- 'Professional' offending.
- Commission of the offence for financial gain (where this is not inherent in the offence itself).
- High level of profit from the offence.
- An attempt to conceal or dispose of evidence.
- Failure to respond to warnings or concerns expressed by others about the offender's behaviour.
- Offence committed whilst on licence.
- Offence motivated by hostility towards a minority group, or a member or members of it.
- Deliberate targeting of vulnerable victim(s).

- Commission of an offence while under the influence of alcohol or drugs.
- Use of a weapon to frighten or injure victim.
- Deliberate and gratuitous violence or damage to property, over and above what is needed to carry out the offence.

3.43 An even higher degree of seriousness would be indicated by any of the following:

- Multiple victims.
- An especially serious physical or psychological effect on the victim, even if unintended.
- A sustained assault or repeated assaults on the same victim.
- Victim is particularly vulnerable.
- Location of the offence (for example, in an isolated place).
- Offence is committed against those working in the public sector or providing a service to the public.
- Presence of others, eg relatives, especially children or partner of the victim.
- Additional degradation of the victim (eg taking photographs of a victim as part of a sexual offence).
- In property offences, high value (including sentimental value) of property to the victim, or substantial consequential loss (eg where the theft of equipment causes serious disruption to a victim's life or business).

3.44 As to factors indicating a less serious breach the Guidelines indicate the following:

- A greater degree of provocation than normally expected.
- Mental illness or disability.
- Youth or age, where it affects the responsibility of the individual defendant.
- The fact that the offender played only a minor role in the offence.

3.45 Further in terms of personal mitigation the Guidelines indentify the following as non-exhaustive relevant matters:

- the offender has a lower level of understanding due to mental health issues or learning difficulties;
- the offender was acting under the influence of an older or more experienced offender; or
- there has been compliance with an Individual Support Order or Intervention Order imposed when the ASBO was made.

Sentencing starting points

3.46 The Guidelines set out in tabular form[53] the starting points for a first time offender after a trial. It should be noted that a first time offender is within the context of a breach of an ASBO not someone without previous convictions but someone who has not breached an ASBO before. The court is required to assess the nature of the failure and

---

[53] See Appendix 6.

harm intended and caused by the defendant before considering the starting point for sentence within three brackets. The Guidelines make it plain that if there are repeated breaches or where there are several aggravating features a sentence beyond the range given would be justified. The court should then consider the defendant's credit for guilty plea, if any, and personal mitigation before determining sentence. There is a duty on the court to state why it passes any sentence which is of a different kind or outside the range in the Guidelines.[54]

Youths

3.47 The Guidelines states that whilst the above criteria and mechanism of determining seriousness apply to youths, in most cases of breach by a young offender convicted after a trial, the appropriate sentence will be a community sentence. The Guidelines also state that the particular stage of intellectual or emotional maturity of the defendant (which may not correspond with actual age) will also influence sentence. A young offender is likely to perceive a particular time period as being longer in comparison with an adult, and this may be of relevance dependent on how much time has elapsed between imposition and breach of the order.

3.48 The Guidelines state that where a 'first time offender' (normal meaning) pleads guilty it must make a referral order[55] unless it makes a custodial sentence, absolute discharge or hospital order. In some less serious cases, such as where the breach has not involved any harassment, alarm or distress, a fine may be appropriate if it will be paid by the offender, or otherwise a reparation order should be made. The custody threshold should be set at a significantly higher level than the threshold applicable to adult offenders and usually will not be crossed unless the breach involved serious harassment, alarm or distress through either the use of violence, threats or intimidation or the targeting of individuals/groups in a manner that led to a fear of violence. In exceptional cases the custody threshold may also be crossed where a youth is being sentenced for more than one offence of breach (committed on separate occasions within a short period) involving a lesser but substantial degree of harassment, alarm or distress. The Guidelines even go on to say that where the custody threshold is crossed, the court should normally impose a community sentence in preference to a detention and training order (DTO), as custody should be used only as a measure of last resort.

3.49 If the court is to impose a custodial sentence on a youth the Guidelines state the starting point for sentencing should be 4 months' detention, with a range of up to 12 months. Where a youth is being sentenced for more than one breach involving serious harassment, alarm or distress, the sentence may go beyond that range. Where a custodial sentence is imposed in the Youth Court, it must be a DTO, which can only be for 4, 6, 8, 10, 12, 18 or 24 months. Where the offender is aged 10 or 11, no custodial sentence is available in the Youth Court. Where the offender is aged between 12 and 14, a custodial sentence may be imposed only if the child is a 'persistent offender'.[56]

---

[54] Criminal Justice Act 2003, s 174(2)(a).

[55] Referral is to a youth offender panel, and the court may (or 'shall' in the case of a child aged under 16) require at least one parent or guardian to attend the panel meetings unless this would be unreasonable.

[56] Powers of Criminal Courts (Sentencing) Act 2000, s 100.

3.50 The court may request reports prior to sentencing in the usual way. However, it may also take them from a relevant applicant body. In this way, the court is told of the reasons why the ASBO was made originally, which will have an effect on the impact of the breach that has been proved. It is important for any applicant body to have close links with the CPS with regard to prosecutions of breaches (if not prosecuting itself), as the overall conduct of the defendant is only likely to be known to the applicant and not to the CPS representatives. One means of providing more information which has been instituted by some local authorities in the provision of a case summary to the CPS for each ASBO made, including both details of the proved schedule and those incidents outside the 6 months used to show necessity. This ensures that the sentencing court is appraised on the full background before reaching a decision. Further, if the breach has highlighted the need for an extension or variation of the original terms, it is worthwhile ensuring that the application for the same is made prior to any sentence hearing, so that both matters can be heard by the same tribunal. It will, in those circumstances, generally be appropriate for the CPS to allow the sentence hearing to be conducted by the solicitor or barrister whom the applicant body has instructed to deal with the variation or extension application.

VARIATION AND DISCHARGE

3.51 A criminal behaviour order can be varied or discharged by the court which made the order on application of either the prosecution or the defendant.[57] If made by the Magistrates' Court the application can be to any such court acting in the same local justice area as that court.[58] If an application is dismissed no further application can be made without the permission of the court or agreement of the other party.[59] The 2014 Act makes it clear that in line with the case-law[60] on ASBOs, an application to vary can include one to add a term or extend the duration.[61] If the new term is a positive term, requiring a defendant to do something, then the prosecution has to meet all the criteria for the imposition of such a term as if it had been imposed from the outset.[62]

PUBLICITY

3.52 In exactly the same way as for ASBOs, the provision at s 49 of the Children and Young Persons Act 1933 does not apply[63] and s 39 of the same Act does.[64] This means that there is no automatic restriction on publicity on the making of a criminal behaviour order against a minor. There remains the power in the court to make such an order under s 39. The Home Office Guidance states that making the public aware of the offender and the terms of the order can be an important part of the process in dealing with anti-social behaviour. It would also provide the information to local people to be able to identify and report breaches. It is said in the Guidance that the decision to publicise will be taken by the Police or local council if no s 39 order is made. As with the issue of publicity in

---

57 Anti-social Behaviour, Crime and Policing Act 2014, s 27(1).
58 Ibid, s 27(6).
59 Ibid, s 27(2) and (3).
60 *Leeds City Council v G* [2007] EWHC 1612 (Admin).
61 Anti-social Behaviour, Crime and Policing Act 2014, s 27(4).
62 Ibid, s 27(5).
63 Ibid, s 23(8)(a).
64 Ibid, s 23(8)(b).

relation to the making of a civil injunction order the Guidance is limited to saying that each case has to be decided on its own facts and that the authorities must balance the interference with the defendant's right to privacy with the need to re-assure the victims and wider public. Again, it seems to us that the authorities would do well to simply follow the previous very detailed Guidance given on publicity in relation to ASBOs.

CHAPTER 4

EVIDENCE

4.01 As with all court proceedings, evidence is the key to a successful outcome. This chapter will cover the general techniques of evidence-gathering, which are particularly important to an application for a Part 1 Civil injunction or Part 2 Criminal Behaviour Order although for obvious reasons it is more likely to have relevance to applications under Part 1.

4.02 A list of available sources of evidence might include:

- witness statements of officers attending incidents or those affected by the behaviour;
- evidence of complaints recorded by the Police, housing providers or other agencies;
- statements from professional witnesses (eg council or truancy officers or health visitors);
- video or CCTV evidence (effective where resolution is high; alternatively, high-quality still images can be used);
- supporting statements or reports from other agencies (eg probation reports);
- previous successful relevant civil proceedings (eg eviction for similar behaviour);
- previous relevant convictions;
- copies of custody records of previous relevant arrests; and
- information from witness diaries.

SOURCES OF EVIDENCE

Housing services

4.03 The files of the housing department should contain comprehensive information in respect of each tenancy, including allegations of nuisance made by or against the defendant. Further, the file should record housing management matters, such as copies of warning letters sent to the defendant and notices before possession proceedings are issued. Interviews with the defendant should also be recorded, detailing the allegations and responses.

4.04 For the applicant, the file can provide useful background information if past nuisance has been recorded. This can establish a pattern of anti-social behaviour and previous, unheeded warnings. For the defence, if there has been a lack of proper housing management, it can be argued that an injunction is not necessary, as the defendant has not been given the opportunity to change his or her behaviour, or it may provide mitigating circumstances.

Social services

4.05 The social services department encompasses a wide variety of services, including work with young people, mental health and, in some authorities, the YOT. Documentation from their files can be used in support of or against an application. For the applicant, it can prove, for example, that, despite work having been done with a child, anti-social behaviour continues. For the defendant, the file may show that parental requests for support from the department have been ignored. Failure to provide such support can lead to awkward internal questions, especially if the local authority is also the statutory parent. In appropriate cases, a defendant's representative may successfully argue that an injunction or order should not be made if he or she can demonstrate that other, more appropriate actions should have been taken.[1]

4.06 A request for the production of social services files is often met with resistance. In relation to a child, if care proceedings have begun, permission of the court is needed before documentation can be used.[2] The case of *Re M (Care Proceedings: Disclosure: Human Rights)*[3] contains useful observations on the application of the rules in practice. In other circumstances, disclosure should, in theory, be relatively straightforward.

Environmental services

4.07 Evidence of previous convictions or successful applications for seizure of equipment can assist in building a case against a defendant. Similarly, in eviction cases, especially those cases concerning noise complaints, such records may reveal useful information for the defence. If a complaint has been investigated, what have those investigations shown? For instance, the records may show that the use of monitoring equipment failed to prove a statutory nuisance. Such evidence might deliver a blow to the credibility of the complaints.

Education/school records

4.08 Documentation from educational sources can potentially help both applicant and defendant. The applicant may be assisted by information which establishes a pattern of misconduct throughout a defendant's schooling. Conversely, the records may reveal a system that has failed the defendant, eg by not exploring the possibility of specialist units, pupil referral or home tutoring, in order to try and address the defendant's conduct. The defendant may be able successfully to contend that such avenues should have been explored before recourse to the courts.

Police

4.09 Documentary evidence from the Police can include previous convictions (see **4.11–4.12**), as well as police information which is not normally disclosed. Pocketbook

---

1 See *R (on the application of AB and SB) v Nottingham City Council* [2001] EWHC Admin 235, [2001] 3 FCR 350.

2 FPR 1991, r 4.23.

3 [2001] 2 FLR 1316.

entries of police officers can stand as evidence and printouts of calls made to the Police can provide corroborative evidence of complaints, but these are of limited use if they do not identify the perpetrator or nuisance in detail. Where individuals, other than the defendant, are referred to in evidence, the defence may claim that it is discriminatory to take action against one individual and not others.

4.10 The Police can also provide analyses of crime patterns. Such information can provide an indication of crime hotspots involving a particular defendant. A detailed plan can be produced to demonstrate the complaints made to the Police and to highlight the areas in which the anti-social behaviour has taken place. These plans are often very useful in showing to the court the extent of a defendant's behaviour.

Previous convictions

4.11 Evidence of previous convictions can be invaluable to applicants because no witnesses are required to prove the incident. As a matter of course, checks should be made for relevant convictions for use in any application. Proof of convictions can be introduced in court in one of two ways – either by exhibiting police records of convictions to a statement from a police officer or by requesting certificates of conviction from the appropriate Magistrates' Court or Crown Court. It is, however, very important for an applicant to file the statements of the complaints in the criminal conviction, or at least a summary of the facts. Otherwise, the bare facts of the conviction may not tell the whole story.

4.12 Consideration should be given to the provisions of the Rehabilitation of Offenders Act 1974. If a conviction has become 'spent' under the provisions of this Act the defendant shall be treated for all purposes in law as a person who has not committed the offence.[4] A conviction is spent if the period appropriate to that form of sentence has expired.[5] Once it has, a person cannot be asked questions which may indicate that that person has committed that offence.[6] It follows that a person may not have to answer questions in cross-examination that would lead to the disclosure of spent convictions. Whilst the defendant may seek to rely on these provisions in relation to his or her own previous convictions, there is an exception under s 7(3). If a court is satisfied, in the light of any considerations which appear to it to be relevant, that justice cannot be done in the case except by admitting or requiring evidence relating to a person's spent convictions, that authority may admit or, as the case may be, require the evidence in question. It seems likely that a very strong argument can be made by the applicant that previous convictions showing anti-social behaviour by the defendant *are* necessary to do justice in an application for either a Civil Injunction Order or CBO.

Lay witnesses

4.13 Witnesses who suffer nuisance can provide documentary evidence in the form of diary sheets or log sheets, or letters of complaint. They can also provide compelling evidence of anti-social behaviour, in the form of witness statements and, better still, live

---

4 Rehabilitation of Offenders Act 1974, s 4(1).

5 Rehabilitation of Offenders Act 1974, s 5(1).

6 Rehabilitation of Offenders Act 1974, s 4(1)(b).

evidence. Lay witnesses are, however, often reluctant to give evidence for a variety of reasons, including fear of reprisals or intimidation after the court process. Support, encouragement and protection by the Police or through injunctions are very important in securing lay witnesses' co-operation and attendance. As discussed in detail below in the provisions of the Youth Justice and Criminal Evidence Act 1999 to assist vulnerable witnesses have been made available in applications under Part 1 and Part 2.

4.14 The points that have been made in relation to the applicant's lay witnesses apply equally to the defence witnesses, although perhaps naturally, much of the focus of court intimidation and process concerns the applicant's witnesses.

Professional witnesses

4.15 Professional witnesses are widely used in proceedings to combat anti-social behaviour. These can range from council officers, police officers, health authority employees or professional surveillance personnel. Professional witnesses may themselves have been harassed, alarmed or distressed by the defendant, and they may provide information about the defendant's past conduct in order to establish the necessity test.

4.16 There is nothing to prevent the defence from approaching council employees (or similar), eg the family social worker, a YOT worker, a teacher, etc, for witness statements to support their case. The response to such a request may differ from authority to authority. A typical reaction is often to refuse the request so as not to compromise the applicant's case. If the defence feels that the person approached would be likely to assist the case but feels compelled to refuse to give a statement, a witness summons can be served, to require that person's attendance. However, there is a risk that, in such circumstances, the witness may not give helpful evidence at trial. This risk can be reduced, but not removed, by interviewing the witness outside the court, prior to calling him or her.

Videos and CCTV

General

4.17 Video or CCTV footage can provide compelling evidence in court. On a practical note, it is important to provide the court with statements from people identifying defendants on the video. This is often best done by using a still taken from the video, so that the court can readily follow the identified person as he or she appears in the video.

4.18 More and more lay witnesses have access to home video cameras. The use of such equipment should be encouraged, as neighbours are able to monitor the area over a far longer period than could be done by professional witnesses. However, the defendant can also use home video footage to undermine the case against him or her. If the allegations centre on the intimidating behaviour of the defendant, and footage shows the local community happily interacting with him or her, that will undermine the case. Also, if the defendant captures footage of the applicant's witnesses engaging in similar exploits to those levelled against the defendant, this can be raised as explaining the defendant's conduct as reasonable or, in relation to the necessity test, that the claimant's witnesses did not require protection from the defendant, but the converse.

Using video footage

4.19 If video footage is to be used, the other party should be notified as soon as is practicable, and given the opportunity to view it, to avoid any unnecessary court adjournments. Whoever is adducing video evidence should provide the other side with a copy, or should arrange for private viewing facilities at their office. If the receiving party insists on viewing the original or it is not possible to obtain copies, it should be released only on the solicitor's undertaking to hold it to order, return it on demand and keep it safely. There are no rules in the Magistrates' Court that deal with the presentation of video evidence in civil proceedings. Applicant authorities and defendants are, therefore, left with the general powers by which the magistrates control their own procedure. In the County Court, the position is governed by CPR 32.1. This states that the court may control evidence as it sees fit. It can regulate the nature and way in which evidence is presented, and can even exclude evidence that is normally admissible. It can require a party to give evidence by videotape. However, under CPR 32.1(6), the court should not let any party hold back evidence to ambush a witness. Video evidence undermining a claimant's case should be disclosed at an early stage. However, following *Rall v Hume*,[7] the fact that video evidence is disclosed late in the day is not always sufficient to justify its exclusion.

4.20 It is important to notify the court as soon as possible, to ensure that the correct equipment is available at court. No assumption should be made about the nature of the technical facilities available at court. Tapes should be wound to the relevant place to save court time. A chronology may assist in identifying individuals or events, unless self-evident.

HEARSAY EVIDENCE

Use of hearsay evidence

4.21 The court system in England and Wales is adversarial and the rules of evidence are dictated by this doctrine. Persons who have directly witnessed the events giving rise to the application normally give evidence of those events. Their evidence is then tested and challenged through cross-examination by the opposing party. The court then adjudicates on where the truth lies.

4.22 Hearsay evidence is the term given to evidence that the court is asked to accept when the person who directly witnessed events is not giving evidence. The evidence, therefore, cannot be tested in the same way as when a live witness is available to be cross-examined. Hearsay falls into two categories: first-hand or multiple hearsay.

---

[7] [2001] 3 All ER 248.

Adducing hearsay evidence before the court

4.23 There are several types of hearsay evidence. These may be summarised as follows:

- a statement identifying the witness, signed and dated by him or her, giving a direct account of events – this is the best form of hearsay, especially if accompanied by a statement that the witness is too afraid to attend court;
- an anonymous statement in which the witness states the reasons for not attending;
- direct evidence from a professional witness, telling the court what an identified (or even anonymous) witness has told him or her and why that witness will not attend court.

Hearsay notices

4.24 These are the means used to put the other side on notice of the intention to adduce hearsay evidence and can be used as a tactic to give greater weight to hearsay evidence. If hearsay evidence is to be used, notice should be given to the other party. In the County Court the Civil Evidence Act 1995 Act and CPR 33.2 apply; however, in the Youth Court the procedure is governed primarily by r 50 of the Criminal Procedural Rules 2014 which expressly refers to such applications. It is likely that the proceedings for a CBO are civil proceedings and therefore the Magistrates' Courts (Hearsay Evidence in Civil Proceedings) Rules 1999 (SI 1999/681) may still apply as the note to r 50 expressly records that the rule broadly corresponds with the 1999 Rules. It is the authors' view that applicants should ensure that the provisions of r 50 are adhered to.

4.25 Any party wishing to rely on hearsay evidence in civil proceedings must serve a hearsay notice which complies with s 2 of the 1968 Act and CPR 33.2. The recipient of such a notice can apply under s 3 (and further CPR 33.4) to have the person called to give direct evidence. In considering such an application the court should have regard to the case of *Boyd v Incommunities Ltd*[8] where the Court of Appeal dismissed an appeal by a tenant who had been made the subject of a possession order where his landlord had relied heavily on hearsay evidence, in the form of anonymised witness statements. The Court of Appeal endorsed the use of such evidence, but stressed the importance of a trial judge expressly referring to the criteria set out in s 4 of the Civil Evidence Act 1985 when considering such evidence.

4.26 It should, however, be noted that, by virtue of s 2(4) of the Civil Evidence Act 1995, failure to comply with notice requirements will not affect the actual admissibility of the hearsay evidence but will adversely affect the weight to be attached to it. In considering weight, the court will have regard to the various points at s 4(2) in particular. These include whether it would have been reasonable and practical to produce the maker of the hearsay evidence, whether the statement was made contemporaneously with the events described, and whether the person involved had any motive to conceal or misrepresent matters.

4.27 Any party who wishes to introduce hearsay evidence must serve a written notice on the court officer and the other party(ies).[9] The notice must:[10]

---

[8] (2013) EWCA Civ 756.

[9] CrimPR 2014, r 50.6(1)(a).

(i) explain that it is a notice of hearsay evidence;

(ii) identify that evidence;

(iii) identify the person who made the statement which is hearsay, or explain why if that person is not identified; and

(iv) explain why that person will not be called to give oral evidence.

4.28 One notice can deal with hearsay in more than one statement and can cover more than one witness.[11] There is no specified time limit in the 2014 Rules for the service of the hearsay notice save that any evidence to be relied on in an application, which presumably includes hearsay evidence, must be served 'as soon as practicable (without waiting for the verdict)'.[12]

4.29 If a party wishes to cross-examine a person who made a statement which another party wants to introduce as hearsay then they must ask for the court's permission[13] by written application with reasons.[14] The application has to be made not more than 7 days after service of the hearsay notice and must be served on the court officer and the other parties.

4.30 The court could determine the application without a hearing;[15] however it cannot dismiss it unless the applicant[16] has been allowed to make oral representations,[17] nor can it allow one unless everyone served has been 7 days in which to make representations about the application including whether there should be a hearing.[18]

4.31 In essence therefore under the 2005 Rules if an application is made by a party to call a 'hearsay witness' there must be an oral hearing unless it is being rejected. Conversely the court can require a witness to be called without hearing oral representations if it so chooses.

4.32 Where a party wishes to challenge the credibility or consistency of a witness who made a statement which the party wants to introduce as hearsay, they must serve a notice on the court office and the other party. Such notice must be not more than 7 days after the hearsay notice was served.

4.33 If such a notice as above is served the party who served the hearsay notice can call that person to give oral evidence instead but must serve a notice on the court and the other party within 7 days of the above notice.[19]

---

[10] CrimPR 2014, r 50.6(1)(b).
[11] CrimPR 2014, r 50.6(2).
[12] CrimPR 2014, r 50.3(4)(a).
[13] CrimPR 2014, r 50.7(1).
[14] CrimPR 2014, r 50.7(2)(a).
[15] CrimPR 2014, r 50.7(3).
[16] The applicant need not attend personally.
[17] CrimPR 2014, r 50.7(4)(a).
[18] CrimPR 2014, r 50.7(4)(b).
[19] CrimPR 2014, r 50.8(2).

4.34 The court retains a general power to shorten or extend a period for compliance with the above rules even if the time has passed.[20] Further the court can waive the requirement to use a prescribed form or allow the notice or application to be presented orally.[21]

SPECIAL MEASURES

4.35 Section 16 of the 2014 Act in relation to Part 1, Civil Injunctions and s 31 with respect to
Criminal Behaviour Orders ('CBOs') expressly permit the special measures from the Youth Justice and Criminal Evidence Act 1999 for witnesses who are vulnerable or intimidated to be introduced, with certain specified exceptions. Unlike the previous s 1L to the 1998 Act the use of the measures is not limited to the Magistrates' Court and now seemingly includes appeal hearings (which are re-hearings from the Youth Court) which the 1998 Act insertion arguably did not.

4.36 Sections 16(1) and 31(1) therefore incorporate all the measures in Chapter 1 of Part 2 of the YJCEA 1999 Act with necessary modification save for those sections excluded by ss 16(2) and 31(2). Further all rules of court, i e the criminal procedure rules, enacted for the purpose of implementing and applying the special measures shall be applied to proceedings under the 2014 Act, s 16(3).

4.37 The relevant parts of Chapter I of Part II of the YJCEA 1999 runs from ss 16–33. Section 16 states that a witness (other than the defendant)[22] is eligible for special measures if they are 16 years of age or less[23] or if they suffer from a mental disorder within the meaning of the Mental Health Act 1983[24] or have significant impairment of intelligence or social functioning[25] or physical disability or disorder[26] *and* the court considered that the quality of their evidence would be likely to be diminished by this.[27] It is hard to understand what condition could be a physical disorder which is not also a disability. 'Quality of evidence' is said to be in terms of its completeness, coherence and accuracy. Coherence relates to the witnesses' ability to give answers to the questions put.[28]

4.38 Section 17 applies where the court considers that the quality of *any* witness' evidence (not the defendant) was likely to be diminished by reason of fear or distress in connection with testifying in the proceedings.[29] In determining whether a witness falls into the above the court must consider in particular:[30]

---

20 CrimPR 2014, r 50.9(a).
21 CrimPR 2014, r 50.9(b).
22 This exclusion has been held to be neither unfair nor in contravention of the European Convention on Human Rights: *R (on the application of D) v Camberwell Youth Court*; *R (on the application of the DPP) v Camberwell Youth Court* [2005] 1 WLR 393 and *R v Waltham Forest Youth Court* [2004] EWHC 715 Admin, [2004] 2 Cr App R 21.
23 YJCEA 1999, s 16(1).
24 YJCEA 1999, s 16(2)(a)(i).
25 YJCEA 1999, s 16(2)(a)(ii).
26 YJCEA 1999, s 16(2)(b).
27 YJCEA 1999, s 16(1)(b).
28 YJCEA 1999, s 16(5).
29 YJCEA 1999, s 17(1).
30 YJCEA 1999, s 17(2)(a)–(d).

(a) the nature of alleged circumstances of the offence to which the proceedings relate;
(b) the age of the witness;
(c) such of the following which to the court appears to be relevant:
  (i) social and cultural background and ethnic origins of the witness;
  (ii) the domestic and employment circumstances of the witness; and
  (iii) any religious beliefs or political opinions of the witness;
(d) any behaviour towards the witness on the part of –
  (i) the accused;
  (ii) members of the family or associates of the accused; or
  (iii) any other person who is likely to be an accused or a witness in the proceedings.

Further the court must take into account any views expressed by the witness themselves.[31]

4.39 Given the requirement in the 2014 Act to read the YJCEA 1999 with 'necessary modifications' it is submitted that references to 'offence' in (a) above must be read as referring to the alleged anti-social behaviour. The remaining criteria are relatively self-explanatory.

Procedure for applications

4.40 With hearings both in the County Court and in the Youth Court the rules of evidence are governed by different statutes and statutory instruments, ie rules of court. There is of course the oddity created by s 16 and the adoption by it of any rules which govern the use of the 1999 Act which means that for both venues the Criminal Procedure Rules (subject to necessary modification) apply.

4.41 The rules for applications for special measures in the Magistrates' Court, and therefore the Youth Court and by the above to proceedings in County Court, in criminal proceedings are governed by Part 29 of the Criminal Procedure Rules 2014 (CrimPR 2014). There are no specific rules for civil cases nor the 2014 Act and therefore it is assumed that the same rules must apply to them by reason of the 'necessary modifications' permitted by s 16 of the 2014 Act. Any application for special measures must therefore be made in writing on the prescribed practice direction form.[32]

4.42 Any application for special measures direction must:[33]

'(a) explain how the witness is eligible for assistance;
(b) explain why special measures would be likely to improve the quality of the witness' evidence;
(c) propose the measure or measures that in the applicant's opinion would be likely to maximise, so far as practicable, the quality of that evidence;
(d) report any views that the witness has expressed about –
  (i) his or her eligibility for assistance,
  (ii) the likelihood that special measures would improve the quality of his or her evidence, and

[31] YJCEA 1999, s 17(3).
[32] CrimPR 2014, rr 29.1(1) and 29.3 and the Practice Direction which specifies the Form.
[33] CrimPR 2014, r 29.10.

(iii) the measure or measures proposed by the applicant;

(e) in a case in which a child witness or a qualifying witness does not want the primary rule to apply, provide any information that the court may need to assess the witness' views;

(f) in a case in which the applicant proposes that the witness should give evidence by live link –
(i) identify someone to accompany the witness while the witness gives evidence,
(ii) name that person, if possible, and
(iii) explain why that person would be an appropriate companion for the witness, including the witness' own views;

(g) in a case in which the applicant proposes the admission of video recorded evidence, identify –
(i) the date and duration of the recording,
(ii) which part the applicant wants the court to admit as evidence, if the applicant does not want the court to admit all of it;

(h) attach any other material on which the applicant relies; and

(i) if the applicant wants a hearing, ask for one, and explain why it is needed.'

4.43 Any application must be sent to the court officer and at the same time a copy must be sent by the applicant to every other party to the proceedings.[34] The time by which the application must be brought is unclear as the time-limits in the CrimPR 2014 apply to criminal proceedings time references, eg entering a plea of not guilty. It is submitted that the appropriate time period is at most 28 days after the defendant at the first instance hearing states that the application is to be opposed.[35] The Rules do however allow an application to be made to extend the time-limit but must be made accompanied by a statement explaining the reason why the application was late and must be served on all parties.[36] The application is determined by a justice who can decide whether to give, vary or discharge a special measures direction at a hearing, in public or in private or without a hearing and in a party's absence if they applied for the order/variation and had had 14 days to make representations.[37]

4.44 If the applicant wants to rely on matters which it contends should not be disclosed to the other side then a means for doing so is set out in CrimPR 2014, r 29.12. In essence the applicant must serve a redacted version on the other side and a clean copy on the court explaining why it has been withheld. The court will hear any application to withhold information in private unless it orders otherwise. It can also order it to be heard in the absence of a party. The hearing should generally follow the sequence of representations from the applicant, then from the other parties with all parties present and then further representations from the applicant in the absence of the other party.[38]

Opposing an application

4.45 The procedure is governed by the CrimPR 2014 in the Youth Court and presumably by application to the County Court. The defendant must make any objections to an

34 CrimPR 2014, r 29.3.
35 Comparison CrimPR 2014, r 29.3(a).
36 CrimPR 2014, r 29.5.
37 CrimPR 2014, r 29.8.
38 CrimPR 2014, r 29.12(4).

application in writing and within 14 days of receipt of the application to both the court and the applicant.[39] The objections must set out whether (and the reasons why) the defendant:[40]

(i) disputes that the witness is eligible for assistance by virtue of ss 16 or 17 of YJCEA 1999;

(ii) disputes that any of the special measures available would be likely to improve the quality of evidence given by the witness or that such measures (or a combination of them) would be likely to maximise the quality of that evidence; or

(iii) the proposed measure or measures might tend to inhibit the effective testing of that evidence.

The defendant must also state whether they wish a hearing and explain why one is needed if requested.[41]

Defendant's evidence direction

4.46 There is power for a defendant to make an application for special measures for themselves. This is set out in CrimPR 2014, rr 29.15 and 29.16. There is a similar process for representations in response and the court can make a ruling either on paper or in the absence of the parties if it considers that a hearing is not needed.

Witness anonymity order

4.47 This is an order which is exceptional but provides that a witness may provide their evidence but without any revelation as to their identity. Rule 29.19 of the CrimPR 2014 applies to such an application and requires the applicant to set out a number of matters[42] including why no measures such as admission of facts that would be proved by the witness, order restricting public access to the trial, reporting restrictions, special measures directions under s 19 of the YJCEA 1999, use of the statement as hearsay evidence under s 116 of the Criminal Justice Act 2003.[43] A person wishing to make representations against the making of such an order must comply with r 29.22 filing the same not less than 14 days after service. The court would hear representations in a similar order to that which the court would if an application to withhold information from a party had been made. If the application is made by a person who is not a public authority, the court officer must inform the DPP of the application having been made.[44]

4.48 Any application to vary or discharge a special measures direction must be made in writing as soon as reasonably practicable after becoming aware of the grounds for doing so and serve the application on the court officer and the other parties.[45] The applicant

---

39 CrimPR 2014, r 29.13.
40 CrimPR 2014, r 29.13(4).
41 CrimPR 2014, r 29.2.
42 CrimPR 2014, r 29.19.
43 This is a criminal only provision if it can be shown the person is in fear.
44 CrimPR 2014, r 29.20.
45 CrimPR 2014, r 29.11(1).

must explain what material circumstances are said to have changed, explain why the direction should be varied or discharged and if they want a hearing ask for one and explain why it should occur.[46]

Special measures directions

4.49 Section 18 states that those measures in ss 23–30 will be available to those falling into s 16 above and those in ss 23–28 are available to those eligible by falling into s 17.

4.50 Where the court determines that a witness is eligible for special measures under either ss 16 or 17 it is obliged to determine:[47]

(a) whether any of the measures (or combination) would be likely to improve the quality of the evidence; and if so

(b) which would be likely to maximise so far as practicable, the quality of their evidence; and

(c) give a direction providing for those measures.

4.51 If, however, the witness is a child then the court must consider measures in s 21 before considering the above[48] and those in s 21 are to be considered as if they *are* measures which would be likely to maximise the quality of the child witnesses' evidence.[49]

4.52 In determining whether measures would be likely to improve the quality of a witness' evidence the court must consider all the circumstances of the case and in particular:

(a) any views expressed by the witness; and

(b) whether the measure or measures might tend to inhibit such evidence being effectively tested by a party.

4.53 Any direction which is made must specify the particulars of the provision made by the direction in respect of each special measure which is to apply to the evidence.[50] Once made the direction lasts until determination by acquittal, conviction or abandoned. The court has the power to discharge or vary a special measure if it is in the interests of justice to do so.[51] Such power can be exercised of the court's own motion or on application by a party if there has been a material change of circumstances.[52] The court must state in open court its reasons for giving or varying, refusing or discharging a special measures application/provision.[53]

---

46 CrimPR 2014, r 29.11(2).
47 YJCEA 1999, s 19(2)(b).
48 YJCEA 1999, s 21(2)(a) and (b).
49 YJCEA 1999, s 21(2)(b).
50 YJCEA 1999, s 19(4).
51 YJCEA 1999, s 20(2).
52 YJCEA 1999, s 20(2)(a).
53 YJCEA 1999, s 20(5).

Special measures for child witnesses

4.54 If a witness is a child then the primary rule is that unless the court is satisfied that the special measures direction would not be likely to maximise the quality of the witness' evidence or is unavailable in that court,[54] the court *must* give a special measures direction for any video-recorded evidence in chief to be admitted[55] pursuant to s 27 *and* it must provide for any evidence which is not given by video recording to be by means of a live link in accordance with s 24.[56]

4.55 A direction made for a child witness ceases to have effect when they reach 17 years of age unless the direction relates to a relevant recording to be admitted and that recording was made when the child was under 17. The party who wants to introduce the evidence of a witness who is eligible must as soon as reasonably practicable notify the court that the witness is eligible for assistance, provide the court with any information which the court may need to assess the witness' views if the witness does not want the measures to apply and serve any video recorded evidence on the court officer and other parties.[57]

Screens

4.56 A screen may be provided for a witness so that the defendant cannot see them.[58] The screens must, however, not prevent the judge, magistrates or legal representative from being able to see the witness.[59] If the defendant has more than one legal representative only one need be able to see the witness.[60] In pre-1999 cases the instances of use of screens was in more serious criminal cases but included one where a young witness had a fear of reprisals albeit in a murder trial.[61] It is suggested that the use of screens in injunction cases will be more easily obtained especially where witnesses make statements and have stated that they are worried about reprisals or that they do not want the defendant staring at them as they give evidence as it scares them. In *R v X*[62] the Court of Appeal approved the erection of a screen in a courtroom to prevent young children seeing, or being seen by, the defendants. Social workers had been permitted to sit alongside the child witnesses when they gave evidence to comfort and console them when necessary. The Court of Appeal said that plainly this was a course of conduct which had to be undertaken with considerable care and the court had to be astute to see that nothing improper passed and no undue encouragement was given to the witness to say anything other than the truth.

4.57 In *KL and LK v DPP*[63] Mr Justice Richards held that the fact that, on an application to a Magistrates' Court for permission for use of a screen, material adverse to the defendant was placed before the court did not necessarily preclude fair-minded

---

54 YJCEA 1999, s 21(4).
55 YJCEA 1999, s 20(3)(a).
56 YJCEA 1999, s 20(3)(b).
57 CrimPR 2014, r 29.9(2).
58 YJCEA 1999, s 23(1).
59 YJCEA 1999, s 23(2).
60 YJCEA 1999, s 23(3).
61 *R v HM Coroner for Newcastle upon Tyne ex parte P A* (1998) 162 JP 387.
62 (1990) 91 Cr App R 36.
63 (2002) 166 JP 369.

consideration of the case. The magistrates were not debarred from continuing the hearing thereafter and where they had asked for the screen to be brought into court before the application the High Court would not go behind their statement that this was done as a precautionary measure and not a sign that they had pre-judged the issue. From this it can be seen that it is advisable for a defendant to seek to have the application determined before the day of the final hearing to avoid any such potential disclosure to the court trying the main application.

Live link

4.58 This is where the witness gives evidence by a live television link from a place not in the courtroom and can see and hear and can be heard and seen only by the judge or legal representative.[64] The defendant is not mentioned, however, presumably the defendant can hear the evidence even if they cannot see or be seen by the witness. Once a direction has been given for evidence to be given in this way then the evidence from that witness can only be given in that way unless the court gives permission.[65] An application can be made due to a material change in the circumstances or of the court's own motion.[66] In *R v Richards*[67] the Court of Appeal held that any limitation on the principle of open justice caused by a special measures order was countered by the more fundamental rule that the principal object of the courts was to secure that justice was done. The court considered it was proper for the judge to order that the public gallery be cleared save for press when an important prosecution witness was likely to refuse to give evidence. Applications are also governed by r 29.23–26 of the CrimPR 2014. In essence the applicant must identify the place from which the witness will give evidence and explain why it would be in the interests of the efficient administration of justice for the witness to give evidence by live link.[68] Representations in response must be served not less than 14 days after the service of the application and explain why the conditions are not met.[69]

Evidence to be given in private

4.59 A direction can be given to exclude certain persons, including the press (although if such a direction is made then one person nominated by the press must be allowed to be present unless no nomination is made)[70] during the evidence of a witness if the court considers that there are reasonable grounds for believing that any person other than the accused has sought or will seek to intimidate the witness in connection with testifying.[71] The defendant or his legal representative can not be excluded.[72]

64 YJCEA 1999, s 24(8).
65 YJCEA 1999, s 24(2).
66 YJCEA 1999, s 24(3).
67 163 JP 246, CA.
68 CrimPR 2014, r 29.24.
69 CrimPR 2014, r 29.26.
70 YJCEA 1999, s 24(3).
71 YJCEA 1999, s 24(5).
72 YJCEA 1999, s 24(2).

Removal of wigs and gowns

4.60 A direction can be given that wigs and gowns can be dispensed with during the evidence from a witness.[73]

Video-recorded evidence-in-chief

4.61 The court may direct that unless the interests of justice dictate otherwise the whole or part of an interview of any witness may be admitted as the witness' evidence-in-chief.[74] If any part is not to be played then the court must consider whether the prejudice to the defendant in that part being admitted is outweighed by the desirability of showing the whole or substantially the whole.[75] Where a recording is admitted the witness must be called by the party tendering it unless a direction is given contrary to that effect and the witness cannot give further evidence-in-chief as to any matter which the court considers has been dealt with adequately in the recording.[76]

Video-recorded cross-examination or re-examination

4.62 Where the cross-examination is video recorded it is almost inevitable that the re-examination will have been as well. A direction can be given for such evidence to be given in the recorded form.[77] This provision is not yet in force at the time of this publication and no date is given for commencement.

Examination of a witness through an intermediary

4.63 This provision was brought into force on 23 February 2004. It would allow a direction to be made that examination of a witness would be put through an interpreter or other court approved person to communicate questions put to the witness and to explain questions which are put to the witness.[78]

Aids to communication

4.64 A direction may be given for the witness to be provided with any device which the court considers appropriate enabling questions or answers to be communicated to or by the witness despite any disability, disorder or other impairment suffered by the witness.[79] Presumably this relates to a deaf person having written questions or other means.

---

[73] YJCEA 1999, s 26.
[74] YJCEA 1999, s 27.
[75] YJCEA 1999, s 27(3).
[76] YJCEA 1999, s 27(5).
[77] YJCEA 1999, s 28.
[78] YJCEA 1999, s 29.
[79] YJCEA 1999, s 30.

Status of evidence

4.65 Evidence which is given in accordance with a special measures direction is to be treated as if given by a witness in direct oral testimony in court.[80] Evidence given by recordings and not on oath are to be treated as if it was so given. The court in estimating the weight, if any, to be attached to evidence given pursuant to special measures directions should have regard to all the circumstances from which an inference could be reasonably drawn as to the accuracy of the statement or otherwise.[81]

Restrictions on reporting directions under Chapter I

4.66 Unless the court gives permission, any special measures directions given by the court under s 19 cannot be reported.[82] Any person, newspaper editor or corporate body doing so commits a criminal offence which can be punished on summary conviction to a fine not exceeding level 5 on the standard scale.[83]

[80] YJCEA 1999, s 31(2).
[81] YJCEA 1999, s 31(4).
[82] YJCEA 1999, s 47.
[83] YJCEA 1999, ss 49 and 51.

CHAPTER 5

PUBLICITY OF INJUNCTIONS

INTRODUCTION

5.01 There appears to be no reason in law why an injunction granted against an adult pursuant to the 2014 Act cannot be publicised subject to any application by the defendant for anonymity. For the reasons which are considered in relation to publicity of an order against a minor it is highly unlikely that this would succeed.

5.02 In line with the previous statutory provisions and case-law regarding publicity of ASBOs against minors, s 17 of the 2014 Act specifically disapplies s 49 of the Children and Young Persons Act 1933 which automatically restricts the reporting of proceedings in which minors are involved. This means that the court would have to make an order under s 39 of the Children and Young Persons Act 1933 if publicity is to be prevented by order of the court. The Guidance to the 2014 Act confirms the prevailing views of Parliament and the courts that 'making the public aware of the perpetrator and the terms of the order can be an important part of the process in dealing with anti-social behaviour'. The Guidance states that the decision to publicise will be left to the Police or local authority (although presumably this must apply to housing providers or other permitted applicants) to be determined on a case by case basis after balancing the defendant's right to privacy against the wider needs of the victim and rights of the public. In so stating, the Guidance must be taken to endorse the approach outlined by the courts in relation to ASBOs and the title of the Guidance ('Working Together Guidance on Publicising Anti-social Behaviour Orders') would seem to support this. It is odd that no new guidance has been issued; however the underlying principles in that Guidance must, in the authors' view, remain valid and therefore both the matters in the Guidance and the case law which caused it to be brought into being must be valid until and unless fresh and directly applicable guidance is issued.

5.03 Publicising the making of an anti-social behaviour injunction and its terms is said to serve two important functions. The first is to maximise the effectiveness of the order in that breaches are much more likely to be reported if the terms are known to the wider community and, secondly, it shows that effective action will be taken against those who commit anti-social behaviour. An order against an adult can be publicised without difficulty and should be disseminated to police stations and other relevant bodies.

MINORS

5.04 Orders made against a juvenile pose considerations of balancing the interests of the child against the public interest. The prohibition against publicity in s 39 of the Children and Young Persons Act 1933 is a discretionary one. It is very important to note that there is no *automatic* restriction on reporting and, unless an order is made, every detail may be published. This does not include details of any criminal offence which has been relied on in the proceedings. However, where there are breach proceedings which result in a conviction in relation to a minor, the usual restrictions on reporting of proceedings[1] does not apply but the court has a similar power to s 39 above to order a restriction on publicity.[2] The clearest authority is the judgment of Elias J, who gave a single judgment in respect of two ASBO cases,[3] which he heard separately, argued on similar points but with very different facts. The judge explored the various cases[4] which had previously dealt with the competing public and child's interests in relation to publicity after criminal conviction and applied them. The main points in his decision were as follows:

- there is a conflict which must be balanced between the public interest in disclosure and the welfare of the young person who may require anonymity;
- the court should consider whether there are good reasons for naming the defendant;
- considerable weight should be given to the age of the offender and the potential damage of being identified as a criminal before adulthood;
- the court must have regard to the welfare of the child or young person;[5]
- the prospect of being named in court with accompanying disgrace is a powerful deterrent and the naming serves as a deterrent;
- the public has a particular interest in knowing who in their midst has been responsible for outrageous behaviour. This is not simply 'naming and shaming', which is, in any event, a relevant legitimate factor;
- disclosure of the identity of an individual may well make an order efficacious, as the community would be aware that an order has been made and report breaches;
- there is strong public interest in open justice;
- the fact that an appeal has been made may be a material consideration;
- whilst the court need not refer to every factor above, it should briefly summarise relevant factors and the competing interests before setting out its determination;
- there is no presumption against making an order but the strong public interest is a weighty factor against upholding any claim for anonymity; and
- in general, it is not appropriate or relevant to have regard to the effect on members of the defendant's family.

5.05 Of particular note is the concern that the judge had about the lack of a fully reasoned decision by the Crown Court in the *St Albans* case. On the facts of that case, he suggested that the extreme youth of the child (an 11-year-old) should have been expressly referred to and, further, the apparent improvement in the period after the order had been made required special consideration. For applicant authorities, this case makes it clear that it will be important to ensure that the court is appraised of the need for full reasons to be given. For defendant's representatives, it would seem that it is unlikely that an order preventing publicity can be obtained unless there are good reasons which outweigh the strong arguments of public interest and efficacy of enforcement. The latter may possibly be addressed by arguing for an order which allows the naming of the child but not disclosure of his or her address, or arguing that disclosure of the terms of the order to the

---

1 Children and Young Persons Act 1933, s 49.
2 Youth Justice and Criminal Evidence Act 1999, s 45.
3 *R (on the application of T) v St Albans Crown Court*; *Chief Constable of Surrey v JHG and DHG* [2002] EWHC Admin 1129, (unreported) 20 May 2002.
4 In particular, *R v Winchester Crown Court, ex parte B* [1999] 1 WLR 788, [2000] 1 Cr App R 11.
5 Children and Young Persons Act 1933, s 44.

wider community can be permitted but reporting in the newspapers should not. In practice, the one exception is if an appeal is to be lodged, in which case it is highly unlikely that the order will be refused. In this case, the applicant should ensure that the wording of the prohibition is such that the order will expire at the appeal hearing or if the appeal is withdrawn. This prevents the defendant from simply appealing and withdrawing the appeal to secure an order preventing publicity.

5.06 The issue of publicity using leaflets and its compliance with the European Convention after the imposition on an ASBO has been considered by the court in *Stanley v London Borough of Brent*.[6] Brent council applied for ASBOs against a number of youths alleged to have conducted anti-social behaviour in their area. Interim orders were granted and before the main applications were heard the council prepared a draft leaflet which they wanted to distribute if the orders were granted. The leaflets contained images of the defendants taken on arrest, their names, ages and details of the orders issued against them. A district judge made orders and referred to convictions of three youths. The media publicised the orders and the local authority posted details on its community website. Leaflets were distributed by local authority and by police community safety officers. The local authority also published a report of the proceedings in its newsletter to its tenants. Three defendants sought judicial review of the decision to publicise. They sought a declaration that the publicity was unlawful and in breach of their rights under Art 8 of the European Convention.

DEFENDANT'S CASE

5.07

(i) Publicity interfered with their human rights under Art 8 (right to family life) and any interference should only be that necessary and proportionate to the legitimate aim being pursued.

(ii) The council and Police had failed to identify the legitimate ends which were sought to be achieved and therefore used unnecessary and disproportionate publicity.

(iii) It was not necessary to provide photographs or personal details of the individuals especially as they used photographs taken on arrest.

(iv) The leaflets were distributed to an area wider than the individual exclusion order area.

(v) A website was publicity to the world in general and not necessary.

(vi) The newsletter did nothing to aid enforcement as whilst it included photographs, names and partial addresses, it did not spell out the terms of the orders.

(vii) The defendants also contended they should have had an opportunity to vet the material before it was publicised.

---

6 [2004] EWHC 2229 (Admin), (2005) EMLR 3, [2005] UKHRR 115, (2005) HLR 8, (2005) ACD 13, (2004) *The Times*, October 22.

RESPONDENT'S ARGUMENTS

5.08

(i) Article 8 rights of the defendants were engaged but also those of the community and especially the victims of anti-social behaviour.

(ii) Further the community had rights under Art 10 (freedom to receive information), Art 11 (freedom of assembly – there was evidence that the public was afraid to go out in the area) and Art 17 (prohibition of the abuse of rights).

(iii) The state could be held to be under a positive obligation to protect the rights of the community so these had to be balanced against the defendants' rights.

(iv) The publicity was reasonable and proportionate and aided enforcement and legitimate aims including reassuring and informing the public.

COURT OF APPEAL RULING

5.09

(i) The ASBOs were not limited to an exclusion zone but included general clauses without geographical constraint so publicity need not be limited to the exclusion area especially as most defendants lived outside the area.

(ii) The need for assistance in enforcement was an important consideration.

(iii) The use of arrest photographs was acceptable as the images were not secretly obtained or stored.

(iv) Publication by leaflet was neither unnecessary nor disproportionate as to be effective the orders needed to be better targeted than the media could provide.

(v) Use of photographs was necessary and proportionate for a specific public purpose. The identification of the defendants was critical both in relation to enforcement and as the impact of the orders on real people needed to demonstrated. Also the defendants could otherwise easily transfer their activities elsewhere where they were not known.

(vi) Cases may arise in which consultation as to publicity was a realistic possibility especially for those who are very young but not in this case.

(vii) A simple desire to name and shame would never be an appropriate justification for publicity, however, where the decision had been carefully taken some deference had to be accorded to those entrusted with that decision. The results of this process of consideration should, however, be carefully recorded.

(viii) If there had been significant criminal behaviour for years there was no reason why the publicity should not say so.

(ix) The council should have expressly considered whether the publicity was necessary and proportionate to the legitimate aims. Aims, however, did overlap and a resident who was informed about the orders to reassure may end up helping to enforce.

(x) The website was informative and specifically invited assistance in enforcement. Only local residents would be likely to access the website.

(xi) The newsletter was plainly intended to provide information and reassurance to all of the local authority's tenants. Many would not have seen the website or leaflet.

5.10 Where therefore it is determined that publicity is to be sought in relation to a minor which mirrors the above situation every authority will have to ensure that there is a designated officer in each case who takes the appropriate decision as to the type, form and extent of publicity. The decision-making process will have to be recorded. There is no reason why this process cannot be commenced from an early stage; however, it can only be concluded when the court has heard the evidence and made its findings of fact. The designated officer will have to record exactly why they have reached their decisions as to the publicity being given in that particular case. Caution should be taken so as to avoid any suggestion that the decisions are formulaic and any discretion is effectively fettered by policy. This Guidance and approach must, it seems to the authors, be appropriate and valid in relation to the publicity of orders obtained under the 2014 Act and any subsequent successful breach proceedings.

CHAPTER 6

PARENTING ORDERS

INTRODUCTION

6.01 A parenting order is an order which requires the parent to comply with requirements in an order for not more than 12 months and to attend for not more than 3 months such counselling or guidance programme as might be specified in directions given by the responsible officer under the order. Whilst the focus of this chapter is on the court's powers to make a parenting order following other proceedings it should be noted that a parenting order can be made following direct referral by the Youth Offending Team pursuant to s 22(2A) of Powers of Criminal Courts (Sentencing) Act 2000 following a failure by a parent to attend panel meetings at which they are required to attend. The court then has the power pursuant to Sch 1, Pt 1A, para 9D to make an order in the same form as is discussed in this chapter. Such referrals are, however, rare. There is Home Office Guidance in respect of both routes but the Guidance pre-dates the 2014 Act, although there appears little save the references to the statutes which have changed, and it is suggested that it remains valid.

WHEN?

6.02 In any court proceedings where a child or young person is:

(i) convicted of a criminal offence;[1]

(ii) made subject of a child safety order or found to have failed to comply with the terms of a child safety order;[2]

(iii) made subject to a criminal behaviour order;[3]

(iv) made subject to a civil injunction order;[4]

(v) made subject to a sex offender order;[5]

(vi) a person is convicted of an offence under ss 444 or 443 of the Education Act 1996 (failure to comply with school attendance order or failure to secure regular attendance at school);[6]

(vii) a parental compensation order is made in relation to the child's behaviour.[7]

---

1 Crime and Disorder Act 1998 (CDA 1998), s 8(1)(c).
2 CDA 1998, s 8(1)(a).
3 Ibid, s 8(1)(b).
4 Ibid, s 8(1)(b).
5 Ibid, s 8(1)(b).
6 Ibid, s 8(1)(d).
7 Ibid, s 8(1)(aa).

CRITERIA

6.03 The court may make a parenting order if the court is satisfied that the relevant condition is satisfied but may not make a parenting order unless it has been notified by the secretary of state that arrangements for implementing parenting orders are in place.[8]

6.04 The condition which the court must consider is whether a parenting order would be desirable in the interests of preventing a repetition of the kind of behaviour which led to the making of the injunction order, compensation order or offence.[9]

6.05 Where a person aged 15 or less is convicted of an offence or is made subject to a criminal behaviour order or civil injunction order and the court is satisfied that the relevant condition is fulfilled, the court must make a parenting order[10] and if it is not so satisfied it must state in open court that it is not and why not.[11] There is however no need to do so if the court made a referral order for the original offence.[12]

PROCEDURE

6.06 If the defendant is aged 15 or less then the court must obtain and consider information about the defendant's family circumstances and the likely effect of the order on those circumstances before making a parenting order.[13]

6.07 Where a court proposes to make both a referral order and a parenting order then the court must obtain and consider a report from a probation officer, social worker or member of the Youth Offending Team as to the requirements to be proposed for the parenting order, why the requirements would be desirable in the interests of preventing the commission of a further offence and if the child is aged under 16 the information required in **6.06** above.[14]

6.08 Prior to making a parenting order a court is required to explain to the parent in ordinary language the effect of the order and any of the requirements proposed, the consequences of breach and the power of the court to review and/or vary the order on application.[15] The MOJ Guidance states that it should be stressed that parenting orders are not a punishment and emphasis should be placed on building parents' existing strengths and skills.[16] It also suggests that the requirement to explain in ordinary language can be met, if necessary, by written communication rather than court attendance where the parents refuse to attend. It suggests that this is done in advance of a hearing with the letter being delivered by the Youth Offending Team. It would seem to the authors that extreme caution would have to be taken in proving compliance. There would need to be a recording, based on evidence, that the parents are able to read, and that the

---

8 Ibid, s 8(3).
9 Ibid, s 8(6).
10 Ibid, s 9(1)(a) and s 9(1B)(a) respectively.
11 Ibid, s 9(1)(b) and s 9(1B)(b) respectively.
12 Ibid, s 9(1A).
13 Ibid, s 9(2).
14 Ibid, s 9(2A).
15 Ibid, s 9(3).
16 MOJ Guidance at 6.13.

explanation is given in clear plain English sent prior to an attendance at court when they are required to attend with a clear warning that if they did not the order could be made in their absence. The proof of service would it is suggested have to be personal service. The Act does not expressly require oral communication but explanation is most likely to be given orally.

WHAT CAN BE ORDERED

6.09 The parenting order requires the parent to comply with requirements within the order for a period not exceeding 12 months and unless a previous order has been made it must include a period of not more than 3 months on a guidance or counselling programme as may be specified in directions given by the responsible officer. The MOJ Guidance refers to the latter programme as 'the core requirement of a parenting order', and highlights the fact that the commencement of this element does not need to be specified in the order as it can take place at any time within the currency of the wider order which imposes the other requirements. The court does however have to specify the length of the program and therefore the wider order will need to be longer than the parenting programme to allow for programme to be delivered, and, if appropriate, an allowance of time to enable parents to catch up with missed sessions. If the only requirement included in the order is attendance at a programme then the court could set the requirement for up to 12 months if it considers it reasonable to do so.[17] The Guidance suggests that Youth Offending Teams should recommend to the court what the length of the requirement should be and explain why. The Youth Offending Team should therefore make sure the court is aware that the order should allow time for activities including:

- assessing parents in advance of the programme;
- any work with individual parents needed to prepare for the programme;
- any waiting time before the programme can start;
- the duration of the programme itself;
- a contingency for missed sessions to be provided.

6.10 The court may order the parent to attend a residential course in respect of a counselling or guidance programme[18] but only if it is satisfied that this would be likely to be more effective than a non-residential course in preventing repetition of the behaviour or criminal offending[19] *and* that any interference with family life which would result from such attendance was proportionate in all the circumstances.[20]

6.11 Any requirements imposed in a parenting order must, as far as is practicable, be such as to avoid any conflict with the parent's religious beliefs and any interference with the defendant's work or educational attendance.[21]

6.12 A responsible officer in relation to parenting orders means a person specified in the order who is a probation officer, social worker in the social services department or

---

17 MOJ Guidance at 7.5.
18 CDA 1998, s 8(7A).
19 Ibid, s 8(7A)(a).
20 Ibid, s 8(7A)(b).
21 Ibid, s 9(4).

member of a Youth Offending Team or person nominated by a person appointed as a direction of children's services under s 18 of the Children Act 2004.[22]

VARIATION OR DISCHARGE

6.13 The court may, if it considers it is appropriate, vary or discharge a parenting order on application by the parent or the responsible officer.[23] This can include removing a provision or adding any requirement which the original court could lawfully have made.[24] If an application to discharge an order is dismissed by the court then no further application can be made by *any* person except with the consent of the court.[25] This is a very strange requirement for two reasons. First, the prohibition applies to both parent and responsible officer regardless of who applied. This seems nonsensical and could mean that if a parent made a hopeless application to discharge one week into an order but then did very well thereafter so that the responsible officer saw no reason for the order in, say, 3 months the court's permission would be needed for the officer's application to dismiss. There is no reason that we can see for such a hurdle. Further, the hurdle itself is unspecified and without indication as to the test; inevitably the application for permission will be the same hearing as the application to discharge. The evidence, if any, and submissions will be exactly the same. In reality this is a meaningless subsection.

BREACH

6.14 Any parent who without reasonable excuse fails to comply with any requirement in the order or specified in directions given by the responsible officer shall be liable on summary conviction to a fine not exceeding level 3 on the standard scale.[26] The MOJ Guidance highlights that:

> 'The order is primarily designed to help parents to address their child's behaviour so the responsible officer should aim to secure and maintain the parent's co-operation and compliance with the requirements of the order to ensure that it is successfully completed, and will need to make a judgement about what is reasonable in all the circumstances of the case. Where parents have not initially complied with the order, enforcement action short of prosecution such as warning by the responsible officer or police caution may in some cases be sufficient to secure compliance.'[27]

6.15 The MOJ Guidance also highlights that breach of a parenting order is like breach of a community order and therefore is based on referral from the appropriate responsible officer. Where information relating to a failure to comply comes to their attention para 8.78 of the National Standards applies, which states:

---

22 Ibid, s 8(8).
23 Ibid, s 9(5)(a).
24 Ibid, s 9(5)(b).
25 Ibid, s 9(6).
26 Ibid, s 9(7).
27 MOJ Guidance at 8.4.

> 'If the parent(s) fail(s) to comply with a requirement, including missing an appointment, the responsible officer must make contact with the parent within one working day by visit, telephone or letter. If there is no acceptable reason for the failure, a formal warning must be issued …'

Any letter should be sent by registered post and a copy placed on file. Any conversation should be recorded on file. As to reasonable excuse the MOJ Guidance states that where non-compliance relates to a specific requirement, the responsible officer will need to consider the extent to which the parents have tried to meet the requirement and how far they are able to control their child's behaviour. Where the parents have made all reasonable efforts to control the child, even if he or she commits a further offence, this will not constitute a breach of a specific requirement.[28]

APPEALS

6.16 If a parenting order is made following proceedings involving a child safety order then any appeal by a parent is to the High Court.[29] In respect of one imposed following a criminal behaviour order or civil injunction it is to the Crown Court.[30] There does not seem to be any right of appeal against one made consequential to a parental compensation order; however, judicial review proceedings would be available or a case stated. Appeals against parenting orders following criminal conviction or offences relating to school attendance are governed in the same way as appeals against the sentence for the criminal offences,[31] ie to the Crown Court as of right from the Magistrates' Court or Court of Appeal from the Crown Court with permission.

6.17 The Crown or High Court may make orders as if they were the original court or may direct that the application be re-heard by the Magistrates' Court in the case of an appeal to the High Court.

---

[28] MOJ Guidance at 8.24.

[29] CDA 1998, s 10(1)(a).

[30] Ibid, s 10(1)(b).

[31] Ibid, s 10(4) and (5) respectively.

CHAPTER 7

DISPERSAL POWERS

INTRODUCTION

7.01 The dispersal powers provided by Part 3 of the 2014 Act are powers which can be used to require a person or persons to leave a particular area for up to 48 hours. They replace those which were available under s 27 of the Violent Crime Reduction Act 2006 and s 30 of the Anti-social Behaviour Act 2003. The powers under these statutory provisions were generally considered to be cumbersome and difficult to manage as the latter required formal consultation and the former had an alcohol related conduct limitation. The Home Office Guidance suggests that the power is a more flexible power given to the Police to use in a range of situations to provide immediate but short term respite to a local community. The Guidance states that where behaviour is repeated the police force should work with the local council to find a more suitable sustainable long term solution. As drafted however the power allows an individual officer to react to a problem on the ground by seeking speedy authorisation to utilise the power to disperse in a trouble zone that they have just identified. This is of course in addition to the more measured and planned use of the power where persistent problems are being caused in a particular area.

AUTHORISATION TO USE THE POWER

7.02 Part 3 of the 2014 Act[1] states that a police officer of at least the rank of inspector may authorise the use of the power within a specified location for a specified period which may not exceed 48 hours.

7.03 The authorisation must be:

(a) made in writing;

(b) signed by the officer giving authority; and

(c) specify the ground on which it is given.[2]

The Guidance states that this written authorisation may be admitted in evidence if the making of the authorisation is in dispute.

7.04 The officer may only give an authorisation if satisfied on reasonable grounds that the use of the powers may be necessary for the purpose of removing or reducing the likelihood of:

(a) member of the public in the locality being harassed, alarmed or distressed; or

---

1 Anti-social Behaviour, Crime and Policing Act 2014, s 34(1).

2 Ibid, s 34(4).

(b) the occurrence in the locations of crime and disorder.[3]

7.05 The Home Office Guidance states that it should not be used to stop reasonable activities such as busking or other types of street entertainment which are not causing anti-social behaviour. It also states it may be appropriate for an officer of more senior rank than inspector to authorise the use of the power where there was no inspector on duty who knows the area. The Guidance states that it was important to ensure the power was used proportionately and in accordance with the Human Rights Act and in particular Arts 10 and 6. It gives the example the locality should be defined as either listing the streets or giving the streets which formed the boundary of an area rather than a more vague description. It seems to the authors that a map attached to the written authorisation would seem to be a much more sensible addition. Whatever is considered it is imperative that the reasons and grounds for giving authorisation should be recorded in some detail. Whilst a case under the old power in the 2003 Act, the court's approval of the recording of reasons by the Police in *R (Parminder Singh) v Chief Constable of the West Midlands Police*[4] is still worthy of consideration by any police officer who is tasked with providing authorisation for the use of the new power.

7.06 The Guidance states that the Police should where practical consult with the local council or community representatives before making the authorisation and if not then may wish to inform them as soon as the power has been authorised to be used.

DIRECTION TO LEAVE

7.07 Once authorisation has been given a constable in uniform[5] or an authorised community support officer[6] may direct a person who is in a public place[7] within the designated area to leave the area (or part of it) and not to return for a period specified if two conditions are met.[8]

7.08 The conditions are firstly that the constable has reasonable grounds to suspect that the behaviour of the person in the locality has contributed or is likely to contribute to a) member of the public in the locality being harassed, alarmed or distressed or b) the occurrence in the location of crime and disorder,[9] and secondly that the constable considers that giving the direction is necessary for the purpose of removing or reducing the likelihood of either of those matters.[10] In deciding whether to make a direction to a person the constable must have particular regard to the rights of freedom of expression and freedom of assembly set out in Arts 10 and 11 of the European Convention on

---

3 Ibid, s 34(2).

4 [2006] EWCA Civ 1118, [2006] 1 WLR 3374.

5 Anti-social Behaviour, Crime and Policing Act 2014, s 35(1).

6 Section 40 amends Sch 4, Police Reform Act 2002 to permit the same.

7 Defined in s 35(10) as a place the public or a section of the public has access, on payment or otherwise, as of right or by virtue of express or implied permission and therefore cover shopping malls, shops, bars, etc; in essence, all but private dwellings.

8 Anti-social Behaviour, Crime and Policing Act 2014, s 35(1)(a) and (b).

9 Ibid, s 35(2).

10 Ibid, s 35(3).

Human Rights.[11] It should be noted however that following *Anderson v UK*[12] there is no absolute right to associate under the convention, the right to assembly is for political or demonstration ends alone.

7.09 The direction not to return may not be for longer than 48 hours but can expire after the period in which the authorisation would end.[13] This means that a direction to leave and not return given at the forty-seventh hour of an authorisation could prevent the person from returning until the ninety-fifth hour from the making of the initial authorisation. Any constable can withdraw or vary a direction but it may not extend the period beyond 48 hours from when it was first made.

7.10 The direction from the constable must be given in writing unless it is not reasonable practicable, specify the area to which relates and may impose requirements as to the time by which the person must leave, manner and route.[14] The constable must also, unless it is not reasonably practicable, tell the person that failing without reasonable excuse to comply with the direction is an offence.[15] If a withdrawal or variation occurs then unless not reasonably practicable it must be given to the person to whom the direction was given and unless not reasonably practicable be given in writing.[16] That a variation could be made without the person being personally told or provided the notice in writing seems hard to comprehend as being enforceable.

7.11 If the constable believes that the person is less than 16 years of age then he may remove them to the person's home or a place of safety.[17] The Guidance stresses that the Police have a duty to safeguard and promote the welfare of children under the Children Act 1989 and all forces have safeguarding arrangements so that children are not returned to unsafe homes or placed in potentially harmful situations. The Guidance also specifically cites the case of *R (on the application of W by his parent and litigation friend PW) v Commissioner of Police of the Metropolis, Richmond-upon-Thames London Borough Council and the Secretary of state for the Home Department*[18] where the court held that a constable could use reasonable force if necessary.

RESTRICTIONS ON DIRECTIONS TO DISPERSE

7.12 A person who appears to the constable to be under the age of 10 cannot be subject of a direction under Part 3.[19] It is noteworthy that unlike the previous legislation the constable does not have to establish for certain whether the person is 10 or over. If they consider that the person appears to them to be over 10 years of age a direction can be made. A direction cannot be made which prevents the person having access to their home[20] nor attending at a time at a place where they are required to do for the purposes of employment or a contract for services to which they are a party, court or tribunal order

[11] Ibid, s 36(5).
[12] [1988] EHRR 218.
[13] Anti-social Behaviour, Crime and Policing Act 2014, s 35(4).
[14] Ibid, s 35(5).
[15] Ibid, s 35(6).
[16] Ibid, s 35(9).
[17] Ibid, s 35(7).
[18] [2006] EWCA Civ 458.
[19] Anti-social Behaviour, Crime and Policing Act 2014, s 36(1).
[20] Ibid, s 36(2).

or where they are expected to attend for education, training or medical treatment.[21] A constable is also not permitted to give a direction to someone who is engaged in a lawful picket or a lawful public procession as mentioned in s 11(1) of the Public Order Act 1986.

SURRENDER OF PROPERTY

7.13 When giving a direction under s 35 a constable may also direct the person to give up any item in their possession or control which the constable reasonably believes has been used or is likely to be used in behaviour that harasses, alarms or distresses members of the public.[22] The Guidance suggests that typical examples of items would be alcohol, fireworks or spray paint. The Guidance also highlights the fact that the constable has no right to take the item if the person refuses to surrender it but commits an offence by failing to do so.

7.14 Again the constable must give this direction in writing unless that is not reasonably practicable[23] and must, unless not reasonably practicable, tell that person that failing to comply with the direction is an offence and given them information in writing about how they may recover the item.[24] Once surrendered the items must not be return to the person before the end of the exclusion period[25] however if at the end of the period the person ask for it to be returned it must be returned unless it is retained under another enactment.[26] If the item has not been requested for return by the person by 28 days from when the direction was given the item may be destroyed or otherwise disposed of.[27] The Guidance suggests that the items will be held at the police station and that a person under 16 can be required to attend with their parent or guardian before being allowed to collect the item. The intention is seemingly so that the parent would become aware of what their child was doing and encourage parental responsibility. It seems unlikely however that a child who thought their parent would be unhappy with their conduct would seek to reclaim a firework, spray can or similar item.

RECORD KEEPING

7.15 For obvious reasons the 2014 Act imposes strict requirements on the constable about record keeping. The constable must make a record of the person to whom the direction was given, when it was given and the terms, including the area and duration of exclusion.[28] Similarly record in writing must be made of any withdrawal or variation[29] or any direction for the surrender of property under s 37.[30]

7.16 The Home Office Guidance states that police forces may wish to publish data on the use of the dispersal power to show transparency and to highlight 'hotspot' areas. Further

---

[21] Ibid, s 36(3).
[22] Ibid, s 37(1).
[23] Ibid, s 37(2).
[24] Ibid, s 37(3).
[25] Ibid, s 37(4).
[26] Ibid, s 37(6).
[27] Ibid, s 37(7).
[28] Ibid, s 38(1).
[29] Ibid, s 38(2).
[30] Ibid, s 38(3).

the Police and Crime Commissioners are said to have an important role in holding the forces to account about the use of the powers. Whilst there is no provision in the statute for an appeal against the giving of a direction under ss 35 or 37, the Home Office Guidance suggests that any person who feels that they have been incorrectly dealt with should speak to the duty inspector at the local police station. It does not however say what rights the person has for a review of the direction or indeed of the officer's conduct. It seems to us that the only remedy would be judicial review which in light of the 48 hour duration of any direction would be most unlikely to be an effective remedy.

BREACH

7.17 A person who fails without reasonable excuse to comply with a direction given under s 35 commits an offence[31] for which he is liable on summary conviction to a period not exceeding 3 months or a fine not exceeding level 4.[32] A person who fails without reasonable excuse to comply with a direction under s 37 to surrender an item commits an offence[33] for which he is liable on summary conviction to a fine not exceeding level 2.[34]

[31] Ibid, s 39(1).
[32] Ibid, s 39(2).
[33] Ibid, s 39(3).
[34] Ibid, s 39(4).

CHAPTER 8

COMMUNITY PROTECTION NOTICES

WHAT IS A COMMUNITY PROTECTION NOTICE?

8.01 The purpose of the community protection notice ('CPN') is said to be to address particular, ongoing problems or nuisances which negatively affect the community's quality of life by targeting those responsible. The 2014 Act repeals the previous measures of controlling environmental nuisances by litter clearing notices, defacements removal notices and street litter control notices bringing them all under the power to issue the notice. It is expressly stated in the explanatory note to the statute that the CPN is not intended to replace the statutory nuisance regime, eg s 79 of the Environmental Protection Act 1990; however there is no bar to using the power even if the conduct amounts to a statutory nuisance.

8.02 A community protection notice is one which either imposes a requirement to stop doing specified things, to do specified things or alternatively a requirement to take reasonable steps to achieve results. An example given in the explanatory note to the Act states that a where a dog repeatedly escaped from its owner's back garden due to a broken fence: the owner could be issued with a notice requiring them to fix it to prevent further escapes, and indeed could impose a requirement that they attend dog training sessions. The Home Office Guidance highlights graffiti, rubbish and noise as three key areas.

WHO CAN ISSUE A CPN

8.03 The Act states that an authorised person may issue a community protection notice. An authorised person is defined as any of:

(a) a [police] constable;

(b) the relevant local authority[1] which for issuing a community protection notice is the local authority where the conduction specified in the notice has taken place;[2] or

(c) a person designated by the relevant local authority for the purposes of the section.[3]

8.04 The last is designed to allow local authorities, where appropriate, to authorise registered providers of social housing to issue notices however the category of persons who can be authorised is limited by s 53(4) to those in a subsequent enabling order from the Secretary of State. The Anti-social Behaviour (Authorised Persons) Order 2015 (SI 2015/749) came into force on 17 March 2015 and gives authorisation to housing providers as defined in s 20 of the 2014 Act. The explanatory note to the draft Order records that as this would be a power which the housing provider would have to opt into

---

1 Anti-social Behaviour, Crime and Policing Act 2014, s 53(1).

2 Ibid, s 53(2).

3 Ibid, s 53(1)(c).

whilst there would be a cost for the provision of training of staff that would be balanced against benefit and also that it could be part of the general training required for the 2014 Act. The rationale of giving the power to designated housing providers is also reiterated in the explanatory note, namely that

> '... as 42.1% of English and 60% of Welsh local authority areas don't have an out of hours noise service whereas a third of the reports of anti-social behaviour made to social landlords were about noise. So, under the notice, the police and landlords would be able to deal better with persistent and complex cases, allowing them to use their staff time more effectively.'

In essence the Government is accepting that many cash strapped local authorities are not able to deal with out of hours problems anymore and this will pass powers to the landlords (and Police) to do it for them. As it would be the local authority which would be authorising the housing provider to exercise this power it would be very important for local authorities to ensure that they had considered carefully what the parameters of use should be. Individual memoranda of understanding were suggested by the Government during the course of the Parliamentary debates and it is the Authors' view that this is essential. The memorandum should in our view include what training is to be given to staff and a requirement to record and report all those notices and warnings given on perhaps a monthly basis so that it can be monitored. Whilst there is no formal power to remove the authorisation it would seem to us that the local authority must retain such power in appropriate situations.

8.05 It should also be noted that as with many of the sections of the 2014 Act the power of a constable is extended to authorised community support officers where authorised by the Chief Constable of Police.[4]

WHEN?

8.06 The drafting of the Act again lacks simplicity. Whilst there is a formal test before a person authorised under the Act can issue a notice, there is a condition precedent which has also to be fulfilled in relation to a warning notice which appears later in the section.

WARNING NOTICE

8.07 A CPN can only be issued if the individual or body has been given a written warning that the notice will be issued if their conduct continues to have detrimental effect on quality of life of those in the locality[5] and that the authorised person is satisfied that they have had sufficient time to address the conduct, have not done so and the conduct continues to have the detrimental effect.[6]

8.08 It is worthy of note that there whilst the individual or body must be given time to address the conduct which resulted in the warning, the decision as to what is sufficient time is left entirely to the subjective view of the authorised person. There is no need for reasonable time to be allowed, simply that the authorised person considers there to have

---

[4] Ibid, s 53(5).
[5] Ibid, s 43(5)(a).
[6] Ibid, s 43(5)(b).

been sufficient time. This is in fact confirmed in the Home Office Guidance which states it '... will be for the issuing office to decide how long is allowed ...'.

8.09 The Home Office Guidance states that it would be good practice for the warning letter to outline the behaviour which has been considered anti-social and the time by which the behaviour must stop or change.

THE TEST

8.10 Having established that a warning notice and sufficient time for compliance have been allowed a person authorised to issue a CPN then has to be satisfied on reasonable grounds[7] that the conduct of the individual (who is over 16 years of or over[8]) or body:

(1) is having a detrimental effect on the quality of life of those in the locality;

(2) is of a persistent or continuing nature; and

(3) is unreasonable.

8.11 It is to be noted that the notice can be issued against an individual, business or organisation. The Home Office Guidance states that where it is issued against a business or organisation it should be issued to the most appropriate person, ie the store manager in a major supermarket or the owner if a local shop. In the event of a breach the issuing officer has to establish that the person served with the notice had the power to address the requirements of the notice.

8.12 There is no further explanation in the Act of what is persistent or continuing. However the Home Office Guidance suggests that this has to be seen in light of the conduct which is being addressed. Leaving rubbish in a garden for instance can be easily shown to be continuing and persistent over a relatively long period of time, weeks and often months, whereas loud music or using an area for skateboarding could be seen as continuing on the same day having been asked to stop.

8.13 If the notice is to be issued against an individual then they must be 16 years of age or older.[9] It is also a requirement[10] under the Act that before issuing a notice the issuer must inform those persons or bodies they think appropriate. This presumably could be the parents of the person, the landlord or the local authority. It is a mandatory requirement however presumably it will not be necessary to do so if the need to issue a CPN is urgent.

---

7 Ibid, s 43(1)(a) and (b).

8 Ibid, s 43(1).

9 Ibid, s 43(1).

10 Ibid, s 43(6).

WHAT CAN BE ORDERED?

8.14 The only requirements that may be imposed are ones which are 'reasonable' in order to either prevent the detrimental effects from continuing or recurring[11] or to reduce that detrimental effect or to reduce the risk of its continuance or recurrence.[12]

ISSUE/SERVICE OF NOTICES

8.15 The Act defines how issue of notices should occur rather than service. The context however makes it clear that they are synonymous. A notice may be issued/served on an individual by any of three options, namely by handing it to the person, leaving it at the person's proper address or sending it by post to the person at that address.[13] Notices to a corporate body can be issued to the secretary or clerk[14] and notices to a partnership should be issued to a partner or person who has control or management of the partnership business.[15]

8.16 The proper address of a person is defined as the person's last known address,[16] the corporate body's registered or principal officer, or in the case of a partnership the principal office of the partnership.[17] If the company is registered outside the UK or for a partnership carries out business outside the UK, the principal office for service is the principal office within the UK.[18] If a person specifies an address within the UK for service other than his proper address, as where he will accept notices under the statute then this must be treated as his proper address.[19]

8.17 Both the explanatory note to the Act and the Home Office Guidance address service/issue of the notice. The note to the Act states that wherever possible the notice should be issued to the person personally. However where that is not possible it could be posted or left at the proper address. The Home Office Guidance states that the notice can be handed directly or posted. It is suggested that personal service is likely to be highly desirable in most cases given that breach is a criminal offence. It would seem to the authors that a valid defence could be raised by any defendant that they simply had not received any notice sent by post. If posted it is suggested that registered delivery is appropriate to counter this potential problem.

8.18 If the notice to be issued relates to the condition of premises or the use to which premises have been put and the authorised person has made reasonable enquiries to find out the name of proper address of the occupier of the premises (or owner if unoccupied) without success then the authorised person may post the community protection notice on the premises and is authorised to enter the premises to the extent which is reasonably

---

11 Ibid, s 43(4)(a).
12 Ibid, s 43(4)(b).
13 Ibid, s 55(1).
14 Ibid, s 55(2).
15 Ibid, s 55(3).
16 Ibid, s 55(4).
17 Ibid, s 55(4).
18 Ibid, s 55(5).
19 Ibid, s 55(6).

necessary for that purpose.[20] In the Public Bill Committee stage in Parliament, the Minister stated that enquiries with the Land Registry or council records would normally be appropriate. The community protection notice is treated as having been issued to the occupier of the premises (or owner if unoccupied) at the time when the notice is posted.[21]

8.19 As with service of the notice, the burden of proof at any breach prosecution will be on the issuing officer. It is therefore going to be of fundamental importance that the authorised officer keeps detailed notes of the enquiries which are made to ascertain the proper name and/or address of the premises. They should also record how the notice is posted on the premises and it is suggested photographic evidence should be kept. The practice amongst some authorities has been to issue CPNs or warning notices with an old school carbon record book similar to those used by the Police. This means that an exact copy is then available to be later scanned into the appropriate computer system and distributed as required.

8.20 The Act states that any conduct which is on or affects premises that a person owns, leases, occupies, controls, operates or maintains is to be treated as if the conduct was that of that person.[22] If the premises a government department it is to be treated as conduct of the Minister in charge of that department.[23] The exception to these provisions is that a person's conduct is not to be attributed to another person if they cannot reasonably be expected to control or affect it.[24]

8.21 In the Public Bill committee it was said that the intention of s 44 was to ensure that the owner or occupier of premises could be held responsible for the actions of those who commit anti-social behaviour on that property. The example which was given was that a shop owner whose employees were not doing enough to clear up its litter would be liable under s 44. If however a farmer whose barn had been used for illegal raves had erected barriers and cooperated with Police they were not liable. If he had done nothing to prevent the raves or did not work with the Police he could be liable.

APPEAL AGAINST NOTICE

8.22 An appeal against a notice can be made to a Magistrates' Court on a number of specific grounds, in essence that the notice requirements were not made out.

8.23 The grounds of an appeal specified in the Act[25] are fourfold. First the conduct specified in the community protection notice:

(a) did not take place;

(b) has not had a detrimental effect on the quality of life of those in the locality;

(c) has not been of a persistent or continuing nature;

(d) is not unreasonable; or

(e) is conduct that the person cannot reasonably be expected to control or affect.

---

[20] Ibid, s 44(1) and (2).
[21] Ibid, s 44(3).
[22] Ibid, s 44(1).
[23] Ibid, s 44(2).
[24] Ibid, s 44(3).
[25] Ibid, s 46(1).

8.24 Secondly, that the requirements in the notice, or periods for compliance are unreasonable. Thirdly, that there was a material defect or error in, or connected with, the notice. The fourth and final ground of appeal is that the notice was issued to the wrong person.

8.25 Any appeal must be made within 21 days beginning with the day on which the person is issued with the notice.[26]

8.26 If an appeal is in progress[27] any requirement imposed by the notice to stop a specified activity remains in effect unless the court orders otherwise however any other requirement in the notice is not effective.[28]

8.27 The explanatory notes to the Act give the example that if the notice imposed a requirement to remove rubbish from a garden it would not be effective. However if the notice also contained a requirement to stop adding to the rubbish that requirement would continue to have effect even whilst the appeal was ongoing. It should therefore be something which should be borne in mind by those issuing notices as by having both requirements in the notice the rubbish problem would at least not get worse pending the appeal. There is also the prospect for an appellant to ask the court to make an interim order for the prohibitory element of a notice to be suspended pending an appeal. There is no mechanism or procedure given for such an application in the Act nor what would be the grounds for such.

REMEDIAL ACTION BY LOCAL AUTHORITY

8.28 If a person issued with a CPN fails to comply with a requirement in the notice the relevant local authority may take one or both of the following actions.[29] Firstly the local authority may have work carried out to ensure that the failure is remedied but only on land which is open to the air.[30] If the premises are not open to the air, then if the relevant authority issues the defaulter with a notice specifying the work it intends to have carried out to ensure that the failure is remedied, and it specifies the estimated cost of the work and invites the defaulter to consent to the work being carried out, then the local authority may carry out the work if the 'necessary consent' is given. The 'relevant local authority' is not limited to local authorities in that if the notice was not issued by a local authority the relevant local authority is one which could have issued the notice if it had chosen to do so.[31]

8.29 By 'necessary consent' the Act means the consent of the defaulter and the owner of the premises on which work is to be carried out if the owner is not the defaulter. The local authority need not obtain the consent of the owner if reasonable efforts have been made

---

26 Ibid, s 46(2).
27 An appeal is in progress until it is finally determined or is withdrawn (s 46(3)).
28 Anti-social Behaviour, Crime and Policing Act 2014, s 46(3).
29 Ibid, s 47(1).
30 Ibid, s 47(2).
31 Ibid, s 47(9).

to contact the owner without success.[32] In reality therefore unless the defaulter is co-operating with the local authority (and if he was then why would a notice have been issued?) this is a pointless section.

8.30 If consent is provided or the work is to be done on land open to the air then any person who is authorised by the local authority to do work under the sections may enter premises in the first case or land open to the air in the second.[33]

8.31 If work is carried out by the local authority then if they issue a notice to the defaulter giving details of the work that was carried out and specifying an amount (nor more than the cost to the authority) of having the work done, the defaulter is liable to the authority for that amount.[34] A defaulter issued with such a notice may appeal to a Magistrates' Court within 21 days of the issue of the notice, but only on the ground that the amount specified in the notice is excessive.[35] The Magistrates' Court must on appeal confirm the amount or may substitute a lower amount.[36]

EXEMPTION FROM LIABILITY

8.32 A local authority which exercises or purports to exercise a power under s 47(2) or the person carrying out the work is not liable to an occupier or owner of land for damages or otherwise arising out of anything done or omitted to be done in the exercise of purported exercise of that power.[37] This exemption is not operative if the act or omission was in bad faith or was due to a failure to exercise due care and attention.[38] The exemption does not prevent an action under s 6(1) of the Human Right Act 1998 on the ground that the act or omission was unlawful.[39]

FAILURE TO COMPLY WITH NOTICE

8.33 A person who is issued with a community protection notice who fails to comply with it commits an offence which is punishable on summary conviction to a fine not exceeding level 4 in the case of an individual or to a fine not exceeding £20,000 in the case of a body.[40] There is a defence to the offence if the person took all reasonable steps to comply with the notice or there is some other reasonable excuse for the failure to comply with it.[41]

8.34 If a person is convicted of an offence under s 48 the court may make 'whatever order the court thinks appropriate' to ensuring that what the notice requires to be done is done.[42] This is an astonishingly wide and imprecise power. Section 49(2) gives some

---

[32] Ibid, s 47(4).
[33] Ibid, s 47(5).
[34] Ibid, s 47(6).
[35] Ibid, s 47(7).
[36] Ibid, s 47(8).
[37] Ibid, s 54(1) and (2).
[38] Ibid, s 54(3).
[39] Ibid, s 54(4).
[40] Ibid, s 48(1) and (2).
[41] Ibid, s 48(3).
[42] Ibid, s 49(1).

guidance in that it provides that a court may in particular make an order which requires the defendant to carry out specified work or allow specified work to be carried out by or on behalf of a specified local authority.[43] The latter does not however authorise anyone who is to carry out work to enter the defendant's home without consent.[44] Home is defined as house, flat, vehicle or other accommodation where the defendant usually lives or is living at the time when the work is or would be carried out.[45] Whilst the defendant can withhold consent they are capable of being in breach of the court's order if they fail to give that consent.[46]

8.35 If work is carried out under an order made by the court under s 49(2)(b) and the local authority issues a notice to the defaulter which gives details of the work that was carried out and specifying an amount that it is no more than the cost to the authority of having the work carried out, the defaulter is liable to the authority for that amount.[47] The defaulter who is issued with this notice may appeal to a Magistrates' Court within 21 days from the date of issue of the notice but again limited to the ground that the amount specified is excessive.[48] The Magistrates' Court has the power to confirm the amount or reduce it but not increase it.[49]

FORFEITURE

8.36 In addition to the power of the court to make an order under s 49(2)(b), if a person is convicted of an offence under s 48, the court may order the forfeiture of any item which was used in the commission of that offence.[50] The order may require the person to hand the item over to a constable or a person employed by, or designated by a local authority, as soon as reasonably practicable.[51] The court may order the item to be destroyed or disposed of in whatever way the order specifies.[52] If the item is kept by or handed over to a constable, the police force of which the constable is a member must ensure that arrangements are made for its destruction or disposal, either in accordance with the order or if no arrangements are specified in the order, in whatever way seems appropriate to the police force.[53] A mirror term applies to a local authority to whom an item is kept by or handed into.[54]

SEIZURE OF AN ITEM USED IN COMMISSION OF AN OFFENCE

8.37 If a justice of the peace is satisfied on information on oath that there are reasonable grounds for suspecting that an offence under s 48 has been committed and that there is an

[43] Ibid, s 49(2).
[44] Ibid, s 49(4).
[45] Ibid, s 49(5).
[46] Ibid, s 49(4).
[47] Ibid, s 49(6).
[48] Ibid, s 49(7).
[49] Ibid, s 49(8).
[50] Ibid, s 50(1).
[51] Ibid, s 50(2).
[52] Ibid, s 50(3).
[53] Ibid, s 50(4).
[54] Ibid, s 50(5).

item used in the commission of the offence on premises specified in the information, the justice may issue a warrant authorising any constable or designated person to enter the premises within 14 days from the date of issue of the warrant to seize the item.[55] A constable or designated person is authorised to use reasonable force, if necessary, in executing the warrant.[56] A constable or designated person who has seized an item under a warrant under this section may retain the item until any relevant criminal proceedings have been finally determined, if such proceedings are started before the end of 28 days following the day on which the item was seized.[57] If not then the item must be returned to the person from whom it has been seized.[58]

8.38 It will be noted that the statute as drafted states that whilst a CPN or Fixed Penalty notice can be issued by a constable, relevant local authority or designated person. The warrant from the justice to enter and seize an item is limited to a constable or designated person and not the relevant local authority. As discussed at the start of this chapter (see 8.04) there is presently no order from the Secretary of State which would enable anyone to be designated by the local authority. Even, if and when, such an order is given it would seem strange that only a housing provider or constable can be authorised to seize an item by the justices and the relevant local authority cannot. It is assumed that this another piece of poor drafting which will be amended in due course as there can be no logical reason to exclude the relevant local authority from the section.

FIXED PENALTY NOTICES

8.39 An authorised person may issue a fixed penalty notice to anyone who that person has reason to believe has committed an offence under s 48.[59] The fixed penalty notice must give reasonably detailed particulars of the circumstances alleged to constitute the offence, the period during which proceedings will not be taken for the offence, specify the amount of the fixed penalty (which must be specified by a local authority, may not be more than £100[60]) to be paid, state the name and address of the person to whom the fixed penalty may be paid and specify permissible methods of payment.[61] The notice may specify two amounts and specify that if the lower of the amounts is paid in less than 14 days, this is the amount of the fixed penalty.[62] Where a person is issued with a notice, no proceedings may be taken for the offence for 14 days following the date of the notice and a person may not be convicted of the offence if the person pays the fixed penalty before the end of that period.[63] Payment can be made in any event by pre-paying and posting a letter to the designated person together with cash or otherwise.[64] The letter and payment is deemed made when the letter would have been delivered in the ordinary course of post.[65] In any proceedings a certificate that purports to be signed by or on behalf of the

---

55 Ibid, s 51(1).
56 Ibid, s 51(2).
57 Ibid, s 51(4).
58 Ibid, s 51(4)(b).
59 Ibid, s 52(1).
60 Ibid, s 52(7).
61 Ibid, s 51(6).
62 Ibid, s 52(8).
63 Ibid, s 52(5).
64 Ibid, s 52(9).
65 Ibid, s 52(10).

chief finance officer of the local authority concerned and states that payment of a fixed penalty was, or was not, received by the date specified in the certificate, is evidence of the facts stated.[66]

PROSECUTION OF BREACH OF CPN AND ISSUING OF FPNS

8.40 It is to be noted that the National Policing Guidance on the Prosecution for breaches of CPNS and FPNs was issued in December 2014 (see Appendix 7) and states that whilst the authority who issues the CPN or FPN is responsible for prosecution of any breach by s 52(2) the sums payable under the same must be paid to the local authority.

---

[66] Ibid, s 52(11).

CHAPTER 9

PUBLIC SPACES PROTECTION ORDERS

INTRODUCTION

9.01 Public Spaces Protection Orders (PSPOs) are introduced by way of ss 59 to 75 of the Act. PSPOs are intended to control and restrict anti-social behaviour or potential anti-social behaviour in public spaces. They are intended to simplify the law in that a PSPO replaces three existing kinds of order with the same or similar purposes. A PSPO replaces Designated Public Place Orders (DPPOs) which were introduced by the Police in Criminal Justice Act 2001 and provided a discretionary power to require a person to stop drinking and confiscate alcohol in a public place; Gating Orders, introduced by a way of an amendment to the Highways Act 1980 and which allowed a local authority to restrict public access to a public right of way and Dog Control Orders, which were introduced by the Clean Neighbourhoods and Environment Act 2004, which amongst other powers, could ban dogs from certain public places. PSPOs are intended to be more effective in that they can impose positive as well as negative conditions.

WHO CAN MAKE A PSPO

9.02 Only a local authority can issue PSPOs. It is intended that district councils will take the lead in England with county councils undertaking the role, only where there is no district council. In London, borough councils will be able to make an order as will the Common Council of the City of London, and the Council of the Isles of Scilly. In Wales responsibility will fall to county councils or county borough councils. The power is not available to parish councils or town councils in England. It is important to bear in mind that the granting of a PSPO is presently an executive function of a local authority, as distinct from a non-executive function. This will mean the decision to make an order will need to go before the local authority's cabinet or executive board.

9.03 Before applying for a PSPO the local authority must undertake 'the necessary consultation': see s 72(3). Necessary consultation means consulting with the following:

- the Chief Officer of Police, and the local policing body, for the police area that includes the restricted areas;
- whatever community representatives the local authority thinks it appropriate to consult;
- the owner or occupier of land area.

9.04 There is no definition or example of a community representative. The Guidance suggests that this could relate to groups such as residents associations or those involved in specific activities and cites the example of buskers.

9.05 Before the PSPO is made the local authority must undertake 'the necessary publicity': see s 72(3). In terms of the necessary publicity this means publishing the text of the order. The Guidance states that the Draft Order has to be published in accordance with regulations published by the Secretary of State.[1]

THE GROUNDS UPON WHICH TO MAKE AN ORDER

9.06 In order for a local authority to make a PSPO it must be satisfied on reasonable grounds that two conditions are met.

9.07 The first condition is that:

(a) activities carried on in a public space within the authorities area have had a detrimental effect on the quality of life in the locality, or

(b) it is likely that activities will be carried on in a public place within the area and that they will have such an effect.

9.08 The second condition is that the effect or likely effect of the activities:

(a) is of a persistent or continuing nature,

(b) is, or is likely to be, such as to make the activities unreasonable, and

(c) justifies the restrictions imposed by the notice.

9.09 The first aspect of the 'test', namely establishing that the activity has or is likely to have a 'detrimental effect on the quality of life', would appear to be extremely broad. It is a much lower threshold than that imposed by earlier Acts used to restrict behaviour, which required significant public harm or public nuisance. The use of the phrase 'quality of life' inevitably introduces a highly subjective element. What may impact on one person's 'quality of life' may not necessarily impact on someone else's. An obvious example of this is the singing of a busker or some other form of street entertainment. The Guidance does not provide any specific examples of such behaviour which would justify the making of an order. The furthest the Guidance goes is to say that an order can 'prohibit certain activities, such as the drinking of alcohol, as well as placing requirements on individuals carrying out certain activities, for instance making sure that people walking their dogs keep them on a lead'. Some local authorities are seeking to use this broad 'test' to prevent activities such as skatebording and the use of 'legal highs'.

9.10 The second condition, that the activity is or is likely to be 'unreasonable', introduces a similarly subjective element.

9.11 The Act and the Guidance attempt to introduce notional safeguards. The Act expressly requires a local authority to have particular regard to the rights of freedom of expression and freedom of assembly, as set out in Arts 10 and 11 of the Convention of Human Rights (see s 72 of the Act). This should mean that PSPOs are not used to restrict legitimate public protest.

9.12 The Guidance suggests that when considering restrictions on excluding dogs from designated areas local councils will need to consider whether there are suitable

---

1 Anti-social Behaviour, Crime and Policing Act 2014 (Publication of Public Spaces Protection Orders) Regulations 2014, SI 2014/2591.

alternatives for dogs to be exercised without restrictions. This should mean that local authorities consider carefully whether there are alternative sites for dogs to be walked before imposing such an order.

CONTENTS OF PSPO

9.13 The order must identify the public place to which the prohibitions or requirement is to apply. This is referred to as 'the restricted area'.

9.14 The order must also identify the activity which is deemed to have the detrimental effect referred to at s 59(2) of the Act. If the order relates to the consumption of alcohol (see **9.17**) it must explain its effect. The order must also specify the period for which the order has effect.

9.15 The order can contain both prohibitions and requirements. Either or both can be contained within the order provided that they are 'reasonable to impose'. They must be reasonable to impose in the sense of preventing the detrimental effect from continuing, occurring or re-occurring or to reduce that detrimental effect or to reduce the risk of its continuance, occurrence or recurrence. The prohibitions and/or requirements may apply to all persons or specified categories of persons. They can apply at all times or at specified times and in all circumstances or in specified circumstances.

9.16 Beyond containing the above there is no specific form for a PSPO. The Guidance states that such an order 'can be drafted from scratch based on the individual issues being faced in a particular public space'. A single PSPO can include multiple restrictions and requirements in one order, eg it can prevent the consumption of alcohol at the same time as ensuring that those that walk their dog in an area ensure it is on a lead. A single order can relate to a whole town or city but then specify the specific areas which are the subject of the prohibitions and/or requirements. This can be done by way of annexing a map which identifies the specific areas subject to the order. This would allow, for example, a single order addressing dog fouling in a number of different specified areas in a city, thereby avoiding the need for, say, twenty separate orders. This in turn has the benefit that when a review is to be carried out it can be done on one order, rather than twenty.

PROHIBITION ON CONSUMING ALCOHOL

9.17 A PSPO can be used to restrict the consumption of alcohol in public space. It replaces the former Designated Public Place Order which was used to the same effect.

9.18 A PSPO cannot be used to restrict alcohol use when the premises, including their curtilage, which means beer gardens etc, are licensed to supply alcohol by a local authority. There are existing powers to address anti-social behaviour at such premises under the Licensing Act 2003. Under a PSPO prohibiting alcohol consumption a constable or authorised person may require a person not to consume, in breach of the order, alcohol or anything which the constable or authorised person reasonably believes to be alcohol. Further the constable or authorised person may require the person believed to be in breach to surrender anything in their possession which is, or which the constable or authorised person reasonably believes to be, alcohol or a container for alcohol. If a person fails to do this they commit an offence.

9.19 An 'authorised person' means a person authorised for the purposes of this section by the local authority that made the PSPO, eg a park warden or an enforcement officer or a Community Support Officer. The 'authorised person' must inform those subject to the requirement that a failure to comply with the request is an offence. However if the authorised person fails, upon request to show their authorisation, the request made by the authorised person is not valid.

9.20 A person breaches such an order if they fail without reasonable excuse to comply with the requirement imposed on them by the order. In such circumstances they would be liable on summary conviction to a fine not exceeding level 2 on a standard basis. This was considered in the original Explanatory Notes to the Act which stated that this was intended to allow those enforcing the prohibition to exercise their own judgment in that if no nuisance or anti-social behaviour arose from the consumption of alcohol within the area it would not be necessary to enforce the same. The example cited was that of a family having a bottle of wine with a picnic. Whilst discretion is clearly to be encouraged it does raise at least a potential for allegations of injustice in that those sat drinking cider in a park may be targeted in a way that a family drinking wine with a picnic in the same park may not.

RESTRICTIONS ON PUBLIC RIGHTS OF WAY

9.21 A local authority previously had a power to close access to certain public rights of way where there was anti-social behaviour or the risk of anti-social behaviour by virtue of a Gating Order. These are now to be replaced by PSPOs.

9.22 Section 65 of the Act lists a number of categories of highway over which a public right of way may not be restricted. These include, but are not limited to a trunk road, roads classified as principal roads. The definition of these types of roads in contained within the Highways Act 1980.

9.23 Before making an order restricting public right of way over a highway the local authority must notify those potentially affected by the order. They must also inform them how they can see a copy of the proposed order and if they wish to make representations specify the period within which they should do the same.

9.24 Before making such an order the local authority must also consider the effect of such a restriction on the occupiers of premises adjoining or adjacent to the highway. They must also take into account the likely effect of making the order on other persons in the locality. If the highway to be restricted constitutes a through route the Act requires the local authority to consider the availability of reasonably convenient alternative route. What is not contained within the act is whether if there is no reasonable convenient alternative route does this prevent the making of such an order. Common sense would suggest so. However the Act only requires the local authority to consider the availability of a reasonably convenient alternative route, not to actual identify one.

9.25 A PSPO may not restrict the public right of way over a highway for the occupiers of premises adjoining or adjacent to the highway. Similarly an order may not restrict the public right of way over a highway that is the only or principal means of access to a dwelling. In respect of a highway that is the principal means of access to premises which are used for business or recreational purposes the order cannot restrict the public right way of way during periods when the premises are normally used for those purposes.

9.26 There is no detail within the Act as to how a restriction can be imposed, save for stating that a local authority may install barriers.

DURATION OF A PSPO

9.27 A PSPO should be for a maximum duration of 3 years. It can be for a shorter period. There appears to be no statutory minimum contained within the Act. The Act does provide for an extension for a period of not more than 3 years. Therefore it would appear that an order can be extended on an indefinite number of occasions, providing there are grounds to do so. This reflects the reality of some gating orders that have been in place for many years.

VARIATION AND DISCHARGE OF ORDERS

9.28 Once a PSPO is in force a local authority can apply to vary it by increasing or reducing the restricted area and or by altering or removing a prohibition/requirement included in the order. The Act also provides for a local authority to add a new prohibition or requirement during the currency of the order.

9.29 If wanting to vary the order in the way suggested above this can only be done if the local authority can demonstrate that the requirements in s 59(2)–(3) (being conditions 1 and 2 to the making of the order) are met as regard activities in that area.

9.30 When an order is varied, the order as varied must be publicised in accordance with the regulations made by the Secretary of State.[2] Where an order is discharged, a notice identifying the order and stating the date when it ceases to have effect must be publicised in accordance of the same secretary of state regulations.

CHALLENGING THE VALIDITY OF A PSPO

9.31 The only venue to challenge the making of a PSPO is in the High Court. Such a challenge may be brought by an 'interested person'. The challenge can be to the validity of the order itself or a variation of the order. An interested person means an individual who lives in the restricted area or regularly works in or visits that area.

9.32 There are only two grounds upon which an application to challenge may be brought. They are:

- that the local authority do not have power to make the order or variation, or to include particular prohibitions or requirements imposed by the order (or by the order as varied);

---

2 Anti-social Behaviour, Crime and Policing Act 2014 (Publication of Public Spaces Protection Orders) Regulations 2014, SI 2014/2591.

- that a requirement under Chapter 2 and Part 4 of the Act was not complied with in relation to the order or variation

9.33 Such an application to challenge must be made within a period of 6 weeks, beginning with the date on which the order or variation is made.

9.34 If the High Court is satisfied that one of the grounds referred to above is made out all the interests of the Applicant have been substantially prejudice by a failure to comply with a requirement under Chapter 2 of Part 4 of the 2014 Act the court may quash or vary the order or any of the prohibitions requirements imposed by the order.

9.35 Restricting any challenge to the making of the PSPO to the High Court means that any challenge is akin to a Judicial Review. The cost for the same can be substantial. Similarly the short period within which such a challenge can be brought is clearly intended to discourage the same.

ENFORCEMENT OF PSPO

9.36 It is an offence for a person without reasonable excuse to:

- do anything the person is prohibited from doing by a PSPO (other than consume alcohol – see **9.18**); or
- to fail to comply with a requirement to which the person in subject under a PSPO.

9.37 A person guilty of an offence is liable on summary conviction to a fine not exceeding level 3 on the standard scale.

9.38 As stated above it is not an offence to drink alcohol in a controlled drinking zone. However, it is an offence to fail to comply with the request to cease drinking or surrender alcohol in a controlled drinking zone. Committing this offence the person is liable on summary conviction to a fine not exceeding level 2 on the standard scale.

9.39 A constable or authorised person may issue a fixed penalty notice (FPN) to a person that they believe has committed an offence by breaching of PSPO. The Guidance states that in making the decision to issue a fixed penalty notice, the officer should consider that if issued, payment of the fixed penalty notice would discharge any liability to conviction for the offence. However, where the fixed penalty notice is not paid within the requisite time scale court proceedings can be initiated.

9.40 A FPN is issued by virtue of s 68 of the 2014 Act. A FPN is a notice offering the person to whom it is issued the opportunity to discharge any liability to be convicted of the offence by making a payment to a local authority named in the notice. The FPN itself must contain certain specified information, including 'reasonably detailed particulars of the circumstances alleged to constitute the offence'. A FPN can be for a sum that is not more than £100. It can also specify a lesser sum, if the sum is paid within 14 days. It is for the local authority to fix the sums specified in the notice.

CHAPTER 10

CLOSURE OF PREMISES

INTRODUCTION

10.01 An application for a Closure Notice is made pursuant to ss 76–82 of the 2014 Act. They are intended to replace the previous orders that allowed premises to be closed, including those often referred to as 'Crack House Closures' and 'Brothel Closures', which were introduced by the Policing and Crime Act 2009 and also Closure Orders under s 161 of the Licensing Act 2003. The 2014 Act provides a means of closing a premises which have been or are likely to result in nuisance or there has been or likely to be disorder in the area. The Act is intended to allow for such orders to be obtained with more speed and in a more flexible way, with the aim of bringing much quicker relief and protection for potential victims of anti-social behaviour linked to a specific premises.

10.02 The Act distinguishes between the Closure Notice and a Closure Order. The Closure Notice is an order granted by a local authority or the Police, without the involvement of the court. It closes premises for 24 hours or 48 hours depending on the level of authority of the person issuing the notice. There is also provision to extend a notice originally issued for 24 hours for it to last a further 24 hours (totalling 48 hours) by specified officers of the local authority or police force. The Closure Order application is dealt with in the Magistrates' Court and if granted, can close a premises for 3 months (with a power to close for a further 3 months, resulting in a total closure of no more than 6 months).

CLOSURE NOTICES

Who can apply?

10.03 A police officer of at least the rank of inspector, or a local authority, may issue a Closure Notice which closes the property down for a maximum period of 24 hours.[1]

10.04 A police officer of at least the rank of superintendent, or the Chief Executive Officer of the local authority can issue a Closure Notice which closes a property down for a maximum period of 48 hours.[2]

10.05 A police officer of at least the rank of superintendent, or the Chief Executive Officer of the local authority can issue an extension the Closure Notice for a further 24 hours (up to a maximum of 48 hours). It is the authors' view that the Police or the local authority will have planned in advance how long they need the notice to last, and therefore an extension should be the exception rather than the rule.

---

1 Anti-social Behaviour, Crime and Policing Act 2014, ss 76(1) and 77(1).
2 Ibid, s 77(2).

When can a Closure Notice be issued?

10.06 The Police or a local authority may issue a Closure Notice (s 76(1)) if they are satisfied on reasonable grounds that:

'(a) that the use of particular premises has resulted, or (if the Notice is not issued) is likely soon to result, in nuisance to members of the public; or

(b) there has been (if the Notice is not issued) or is likely soon to be, disorder near those premises associated with the use of those premises, and that the Notice is necessary to prevent the nuisance or disorder from continuing, recurring or occurring.'

10.07 The use of the words 'disorder near those premises' has regard to the fact that the disorder that is to be prevented may not occur within the actual premises. The Act foresees a situation, for example, where a public house has to be closed on a match day, in an effort to prevent disorder not just at that public house but within its immediate vicinity.

Duration of the Closure Notice

10.08 The maximum period that may be specified in a Closure Notice is 24 hours unless either the Notice is issued by Chief Officers (see **10.04**) of the Police or local authority, which provides for a maximum period of 48 hours, or an Extension Notice is issued. An Extension Notice is limited to a further 24 hours. The Notice must be issued by a police officer of at least the rank of superintendent or in the case of a local authority by the Chief Executive Officer or a person designated by the Chief Executive Officer for the purpose of the Act. The Chief Executive Officer is defined within the Act as the head of the paid service of the authority designated under s 4 of the Local Government and Housing Act 1989.

10.09 Whilst the Act provides for an Extension Notice and also a 48-hour Closure Notice, there is no stated criterion for the seeking/granting of these notices. One assumes therefore that the criteria for granting the Extension Notice and a 48-hour Closure Notice, remains those for the issuing of the original Closure Notice, as set at s 76(1).

The power of a Closure Notice

10.10 A Closure Notice may prohibit access to premises by all those persons except those specified or all those of a specified description.[3] The starting point is that the Closure Notice cannot prohibit access to anyone habitually living on the premises or the owner.[4] Persons may be prohibited from gaining access to a property at all times or at specific times.[5] For example closing a public house would not prevent the landlord or other employees who could show that they habitually lived on the premises accessing it during the period that the Notice is in force. The definition of premises can be found in s 92(1):

> '"premises" includes any land or other place (whether enclosed or not); any outbuildings that are, or are used as, part of premises.'

---

3 Ibid, s 76(3)(a).
4 Ibid, s 76(4).
5 Ibid, s 76(3)(b).

Content and service of Closure Notice

10.11 A Closure Notice must contain seven specified matters as set out in s 76(5) of the Act. Of the seven matters listed some are more obvious, such as the identity of the premises and the effect of the Notice. However, the Closure Notice must also make clear that an application will be made under s 80 for a Closure Order[6] (see **10.17**). Thereafter the Notice should also specify when and where the application is to be heard and the effect of a Closure Notice.[7] It must also give information regarding the names of, and the means of contacting, persons and organisations in the area that provide advice about housing and legal matters.[8] The requirements are mandatory. One assumes that failure to meet any one of the specified requirements will result in the Order being unlawful. Accordingly, it is the authors' view that it would be a potential defence to a breach of such an order if the notice requirements had not been fulfilled. There is no provision for a court to waive the notice provisions.

10.12 One of the mandatory requirements is to give notice as to when and where the application will be heard. This clearly presupposes the matter is to proceed to court. One assumes therefore that this should deter an applicant issuing a notice and failing to notify the court, on the basis that they did not intend to attend court 24 or 48 hours later, as the risk of the anti-social behaviour would have ceased. Such an approach is arguably likely to constitute an abuse of process.

10.13 The 2014 Act provides that a Closure Notice may be issued only if reasonable efforts have been made to inform the people who live on the premises (whether habitually or not) and any person who has control of or responsibility for the premises or who has an interest in them, that the Notice is going to be issued.[9] The Act does not provide for what constitutes 'reasonable efforts'. One assumes it is simply a matter of common sense. In adopting a cautious approach applicants would be well advised to ensure wherever possible the persons affected or likely to be affected are informed in writing.

10.14 The Closure Notice must be served by either a constable, if issued by the Police, or a representative of the authority that issued the Notice if issued by a local authority.[10] The 2014 Act recognises that service may pose difficulties and therefore states that the person responsible for service 'must if possible' undertake one or all of the five means of service set out in s 79(2). Further, if it is believed at the time of serving the Notice that there are other persons occupying other parts of the building or structure in which the premises is situated whose access may be impeded if a Closure Notice is made, efforts should be made to serve the Notice on them.[11] A constable or local authority representative may enter premises, using reasonable force if necessary, for the purpose of complying with service.[12] Good practice may include taking copies of the Notice to serve on any person found to be in the premises not previously informed.

---

6 Ibid, s 76(5)(d).
7 Ibid, s 76(5)(e) and (f).
8 Ibid, s 76(5)(g).
9 Ibid, s 76(7).
10 Ibid, s 79(1).
11 Ibid, s 76(3).
12 Ibid, s 79(4).

10.15 Before issuing a Closure Notice the Police or local authority is required to ensure that any individual the officer or authority thinks appropriate has been consulted.[13] The Guidance states that this should include the victim, but could also include other members of the public that may be affected positively or negatively by the closure: community representatives, other organisations and bodies, the Police or local council (where not the issuing organisation) or others that regularly use the premises. One potential issue that may arise is when the serving of a Notice occurs at the same time as the Police executing a search warrant at the premises for drugs. In such circumstance the applicant may be limited as to the information they can provide.

10.16 The Guidance makes clear that the method of consultation will depend on the situation and urgency. For example, in a situation where it comes to the attention of the Police at very short notice that there is the potential for disorder, consultation is likely to be limited.

CLOSURE ORDERS

Who can apply?

10.17 Whenever a Closure Notice is issued an application must be made to the Magistrates' Court for a Closure Order.[14] However the Act provides for a relevant officer to issue a Cancellation Notice if there is no longer a need for an order.[15]

10.18 An application for a Closure Order must be made by a constable, if the Closure Notice was issued by a police officer or by the local authority officer that issued the Closure Notice if the Notice was issued by a local authority.[16] Clearly this envisages the Police or the local authority maintaining their own application, rather than the original application for a Closure Notice being made by one party and then for the Closure Order to be undertaken by another.

10.19 The application for a Closure Order must be heard by the Magistrates' Court not later than 48 hours after service of the Closure Notice.[17] Even if the Notice is to last for 24 hours only the hearing must take place within that time. Clearly the Act envisages an extremely swift process whereby if the closure of premises is to continue it is to be the subject of the court's scrutiny within a very short period. On first reading the test for granting a Closure Order appears to be the same as that for a Closure Notice. However, the test, wider in terms of the behaviour considered, is more restrictive when considering the nature of that behaviour. The court may make a Closure Order if it is satisfied:

(a) that a person is engaged, or (if the order is not made) is likely to engage, in disorderly, offensive or criminal behaviour on the premises;[18] or

(b) that the use of the premises has resulted, or (if the order is not made) is likely to result, in serious nuisance to members of the public;[19] or

---

13 Ibid, s 76(7).
14 Ibid, s 80(1).
15 Ibid, s 78(1).
16 Ibid, s 80(2).
17 Ibid, s 80(3).
18 Ibid, s 80(5)(a).
19 Ibid, s 80(5)(b).

(c) that there has been, or (if the order is not made) is likely to be, disorder near those premises associated with the use of those premises and the order is necessary to prevent the behaviour, nuisance or disorder from continuing, recurring or occurring.[20]

10.20 As can be seen from the above, the granting of a Closure Order, as distinct from a Closure Notice, requires there to have been or there be the risk of 'serious nuisance' to the public. What constitutes 'serious nuisance' as opposed to nuisance will be a matter for the court to determine. However the old Premises Closure legislation (Anti-social Behaviour Act 2003) may assist, in which the test to be considered was one of 'significant and persistent or persistent serious nuisance'.

10.21 A Closure Order prohibits access to the premises for a period specified in the order. That period may not exceed 3 months.[21] The prohibition provisions for the Closure Order mirror that of a Closure Notice. Similarly, the Closure Order may be made in respect of the whole or any part of the premises and may include provision regarding access to a part of the building or structure of which the premises form part.[22] On making an order the court is required to notify the relevant licensing authority if the order relates to premises in respect of which a premises licence is in force.[23] Richmond upon Thames Police have used these new powers in innovative ways to protect individuals. A vulnerable male was being preyed upon by various persons who paid unwanted visits to the man's property. The Police, with the permission of the vulnerable man, served a Notice and obtained an order to close down the property, but allowing access to the vulnerable man, close family and his support staff for the duration of the order. By taking out a Closure Order, it avoided the need for several injunctions being sought, preventing a stream of different people coming and going, and thereby avoided the difficulty of dealing with different persons and their identification.

TEMPORARY ORDERS

10.22 When the magistrates are faced with an application for a Closure Order it is open to them to adopt the alternative course of granting a Temporary Order (s 81). The wording of s 81 implies that a Temporary Order is a distinct entity, but in reality, all this section appears to do is give provision for further Notices to be granted. If the court declines to make a Closure Order, it may order that the Closure Notice continues in force for a specified period of not more than 48 hours. The test for this is the same as the granting of the Closure Notice, therefore this does not include the requirement that there has been or there is a risk of 'serious nuisance'.

10.23 The court also has the power to adjourn the hearing of an application for a period of not more than 14 days so as to allow the occupier of the premises, the person with control or responsibility for the premises or any other person with an interest in the premises to show why a Closure Order should not be made.[24] If a case is adjourned for up to the 14-day period, the court can order that that the original Closure Notice

[20] Ibid, s 80(5)(c).
[21] Ibid, s 80(6).
[22] Ibid, s 80(8).
[23] Ibid, s 80(9).
[24] Ibid, s 81(3).

continues during the period of adjournment.[25] That however contradicts s 81(2) that provides for the Closure Notice to continue in force for a specified period of not more than 48 hours. This would appear to mean that s 81(2) allows the court to make a determination to not grant an order, but they can decide to allow the Notice to remain in force for up to 48 hours.

EXTENSION AND DISCHARGE OF CLOSURE ORDERS

10.24 Section 82 of the 2014 Act provides for an extension (or further extension) to Closure Notices. The Act does not appear to see a limit to the number of applications for an extension. When considering an application for an extension the court is to consider the same test as that set out for the making of the original order. The Act however provides for the court to be satisfied that the 'appropriate consultee' has been consulted regarding the intention to make the application.[26] The appropriate consultee is a local authority, if the application has been made by the Police, and vice versa if the application has been made by a local authority.[27]

10.25 A further difference between the application for an extension of a Closure Order and the making of the original order, is that on application for an extension a Justice of the Peace may issue a summons on whom the Closure Notice was served or any other person who appears to the them to have an interest in the premises, but on whom the Closure Notice was not served, requiring that person to appear before the magistrates to respond to the application.[28]

10.26 When extending a Closure Order the magistrates may do so for a period not exceeding 3 months.[29] The order may not be extended so that it lasts for more than 6 months.[30] At any time before the expiry of a Closure Order, an application may be made to a Justice of the Peace, by complaint, for the order to be discharged.[31] Such an application is not restricted to the Police or the authority that applied for the Order but may be made by a person on whom the Closure Notice was served or any other person who has an interest in the premises, on whom the Notice was not served.[32] When such an application is made by a person affected, the Justices *may* issue a summons requiring either appropriate constable or that local authority (depending on who made the application) to appear before the Magistrates' Court to respond to the application.[33] It is of note that this is not a mandatory requirement in the event that a person affected by the Closure Order makes such an application. However, one would have thought it highly unlikely that a representative from either of the two applicant bodies would not attend when an application was made to discharge the order.

10.27 The Magistrates' Court may not make an order discharging the Closure Order unless they are satisfied that the Closure Order is no longer necessary to prevent the

25 Ibid, s 81(4).
26 Ibid, s 82(3).
27 Ibid, s 82(4).
28 Ibid, s 82(5).
29 Ibid, s 82(7).
30 Ibid, s 82(8).
31 Ibid, s 83(1).
32 Ibid, s 83(2).
33 Ibid, s 83(3).

occurrence, recurrence or continuance of those matters set out at s 80(5) of the Act.[34] An obvious situation in which a local authority would wish to discharge an order would be where they had regained possession of a property and wished to re-let it.

APPEALS

10.28 A Closure Notice *cannot* be appealed. A Closure Order *can* be appealed.

10.29 Either a constable[35] or a local authority[36] may appeal against the decision not to make a Closure Order, the decision not to extend such an order or a decision not to order the continuance in force of a Closure Notice. Interestingly, the Act does not provide for either the Police or a local authority to appeal against a successful application to discharge a Closure Order.

10.30 An appeal against the decision to make or extend a Closure Order or not to make an Order etc. to the Crown Court must be brought within 21 days of the decision to which it relates.[37] On an appeal the Court can make any Order it 'thinks appropriate'.[38]

PENALTY ON BREACH

10.31 An offence is committed when a person, without reasonable excuse, remains on or enters premises in contravention of a Closure Notice or a Closure Order.[39]

10.32 Breaching a Closure Notice or Temporary Order carries a penalty of either imprisonment for a period of up to 3 months or an unlimited fine or both.[40] Breaching a Closing Order is a criminal offence carrying a penalty of either imprisonment for up to 6 months or an unlimited fine or both.[41]

10.33 It is a criminal offence to obstruct a police officer or local council employee who is serving a relevant Notice, or entering or securing premises which are subject to a Closure Notice.[42] Such an offence carries a penalty of either imprisonment for up to 3 months or an unlimited fine, or both.[43]

REIMBURSEMENT OF COSTS AND COMPENSATION

10.34 A local policing body or a local authority that incurs expenditure for the purpose of clearing, securing or maintaining premises in respect of which a Closure Order is in force

---

[34] Ibid, s 83(7).
[35] Ibid, s 84(2).
[36] Ibid, s 84(3).
[37] Ibid, s 84(5).
[38] Ibid, s 84(6).
[39] Ibid, s 86(1) and (2).
[40] Ibid, s 86(4).
[41] Ibid, s 86(5).
[42] Ibid, s 86(3).
[43] Ibid, s 86(4).

can be reimbursed from the owner or occupier of the premises for the expenditure incurred.[44] Such an application must be made within 3 months from the day on which the Closure Order ceased to have effect.[45]

10.35 A person who has incurred financial loss as a consequence of a Closure Notice or a Closure Order may apply to the Magistrates' Court (or the Crown Court if the order was made on an appeal) for compensation arising out of the making of the order.[46] On such an application the Court may order payment of compensation out of central funds if all of the following criteria are satisfied:

(a) that the applicant is not associated with the use of the premises, or the behaviour on the premises, on the basis of which the Closure Notice was issued or the Closure Order made;[47]

(b) if the applicant is the owner of the premises, the applicant took reasonable steps to prevent that use or behaviour;[48]

(c) that the applicant has incurred financial loss in a consequence of the notice or order;[49] and

(d) having regard to all the circumstances it is appropriate to order payment of compensation in respect of that loss.[50]

EXCLUSION OF CIVIL LIABILITY

10.36 The Act expressly prevents a claim in damages, whether by way of judicial review or in negligence arising from anything done by either the Police or a local authority 'in the exercise or purported exercise of a power' under this chapter.[51] However the Act does not prevent a claim in damages succeeding if it can be shown that the local authority or Police acted in bad faith, or that it acted unlawfully for the purposes of s 6(1) of the Human Rights Act 1998.[52]

---

44 Ibid, s 86(1).
45 Ibid, s 86(3).
46 Ibid, s 90(1).
47 Ibid, s 90(5)(a).
48 Ibid, s 90(5)(b).
49 Ibid, s 90(5)(c).
50 Ibid, s 90(5)(d).
51 Ibid, s 89.
52 Ibid, s 89(3) and (4) respectively.

CHAPTER 11

COMMUNITY TRIGGER

INTRODUCTION

11.01 One of the few novel parts of the Anti-social Behaviour, Crime and Policing Act 2014 is the provision of the Community Trigger. The Community Trigger is a key tool to implement a principal aim of the Act to put victims first.

11.02 The Community Trigger is intended to give victims and communities the right to demand that persistent anti-social behaviour within their area is dealt with. The words 'community trigger' are not found in the Act itself. Rather they arise from a consideration of the Home Office Guidance, 'Reform of Anti-social Behaviour Powers – Statutory Guidance for Frontline Professionals' in particular as it relates to the section entitled 'Response to complaints of anti-social behaviour'. The legislation refers to the Community Trigger process as an Anti-Social Behaviour Review.

11.03 The Community Trigger has been trialled within four areas. The trials were commenced on the 1 June 2012 in Manchester, Brighton and Hove, West Lindsay and Boston (Lincolnshire). The trial areas designed the procedure that they believed met the needs of their local community. The effectiveness of trials is reported in the Home Office document 'Empowering Communities, Protecting Victims: Summary Report on the Community Trigger Trials' (9 May 2013).

PURPOSE

11.04 The Community Trigger is intended to allow the victims of anti-social behaviour to demand action from those agencies charged with tackling it. It is intended to require such agencies to come together to take a collective approach to address offensive behaviour.

11.05 It is intended to allow victims to compel the relevant agencies to act when they believe anti-social behaviour persists and there has been an inadequate response or when they perceive themselves being ignored by the relevant agencies.

11.06 The Community Trigger can be used by a person of any age and there is a requirement for agencies to make it as accessible as possible to all victims. Individuals, businesses and community groups can all use the Community Trigger. A complaint can be made by an individual on another person's behalf. It is anticipated that groups such as Neighbourhood Watch, Residents' Associations, Community Groups etc, be amongst the type of group who will use the Community Trigger.

'RELEVANT BODIES' AND 'RESPONSIBLE AUTHORITIES'

11.07 'Relevant bodies' are those organisations which have a statutory duty to have a Community Trigger procedure and to undertake case reviews when a person asks for one and the threshold is met (see below). The relevant bodies are:

- district councils;
- Unitary authorities or London borough councils;
- Police forces (Chief Officer of Police, but he/she can delegate the power down);
- Clinical commissioning groups in England, local health boards in Wales; and
- Social Housing providers who are co-opted into the group.

11.08 The Act envisages providers of social housing to be at the forefront of responding to Community Triggers. However, the Act itself does not determine which housing providers are expected to be co-opted into the procedure. The inference is that the larger housing providers will be co-opted. Clearly in certain large urban areas there will be a number of housing providers in that particular area. Agreement will need to be reached by the respective housing providers as to who is co-opted into the group.

11.09 The local Police and Crime Commissioner ('PCC') must be consulted when the Community Trigger procedure is established, and must be consulted whenever the procedure is reviewed. It is the nature of the Community Trigger in that it is to be designed to match certain areas. Notionally, one PCC will need to be consulted with regard to a number of different Community Trigger procedures. There is an option of a county-wide agreed Community Trigger. An example of this is York and North Yorkshire who have introduced an arrangement whereby there is one procedure for the whole of the North Yorkshire Police force area. The procedure needs to be published by the relevant body in each local government area. Publication can be achieved by simply placing the procedure on a website.

THRESHOLD

11.10 The threshold for the Community Trigger is at the discretion of the relevant bodies that are to respond to it. It is set locally. However, the Act provides for a maximum number of complaints for which the threshold must be no higher. The purpose behind the discretion is to allow local areas to set a threshold which best suits the needs of their community and their best working practices. This will mean having regard to the following matters set out at s 104(5) of the Act:

> '(a) the persistence of the Anti-Social Behaviour about which the original complaint was made;
>
> (b) the harm caused, or the potential harm to be caused, by that behaviour;
>
> (c) the adequacy of the response to that behaviour.'

11.11 If a person has made a complaint about anti-social behaviour in a particular Local Government area the relevant bodies in that area must carry out an ASB case review if:

(a) that person, only if the person makes application for such a review (thereby activating the Community Trigger); and

(b) the relevant bodies decide that the threshold for a review is met.

11.12 Whilst each relevant body sets out its own threshold the most common threshold, or alternatively the minimum, is likely to be when there have been three complaints of anti-social behaviour in the preceding 6-month period and action has not been taken.

11.13 The variation in the threshold for the Community Trigger is reflected in the pilot schemes referred to above. Brighton and Hove City Council provided a threshold for the Trigger as follows:

> '(a) anyone can use a Community Trigger if their concern is about Anti-Social Behaviour or a hate incident/crime and meets the criteria below:
>
> either:
>
> - you have reported the issue or concern at least once before and
> - no action has been taken and
> - more than one week has passed since you reported the issue or concern **OR**
> - the issue or concern affects more than one household or business premises.'

11.14 This is to be contrasted with the Leeds ASB Community Trigger Pilot which included the following:

> 'Criteria for a Community Trigger:
>
> You reported three separate incidents relating to the same problem in the past six months to the Council, police or your landlord, and no action has been taken.
>
> OR
>
> You reported one incident or hate crime motivated by hate (due to race, religion, disability, sexual orientation or transgender identity) in the last six months and no action has been taken.
>
> OR
>
> At least five people have made reports about the same problem in the past six months to the Council, police or your landlord and no action has been taken.'

QUALIFYING COMPLAINTS

11.15 Section 104(11) and (12) define what is meant by a 'qualifying complaint'. A complaint about anti-social behaviour is a qualifying complaint if:

(a) the complaint is made within the period of 1 month (or, if a different period is specified in the review procedures, that period, beginning with the date on which the behaviour is alleged to have occurred; and

(b) the application for the ASB case review is made within the period of 6 months (or if a different period is specified in the review procedures, that period, beginning with the date on which the complaint is made.

11.16 The purpose of the above is to make the matter as current as possible and to prevent someone from reporting historical incidents of anti-social behaviour in order to use the

Community Trigger. The legislation provides for agencies to set different levels provided they comply with the minimum as set out above.

11.17 As to what constitutes anti-social behaviour the definition remains as wide as previously contained within legislation, being behaviour causing harassment, alarm or distress to a member, or members, of the public. It is to be noted that this definition of anti-social behaviour is different from that for an injunction under Part 1 of the Act, which provides the lower test of nuisance or annoyance. The rational for this is set out within the Guidance, which suggests that the victims of housing-related anti-social behaviour will be unable to separate themselves from the anti-social behaviour, meaning the level of harm is likely to be greater and therefore likely to cause harassment, alarm or distress. It is envisaged that on occasions what is complained of may well be a criminal act(s), it is the authors' view that this should still be a qualifying complaint as alarm or distress may still have been suffered.

ONCE THE COMMUNITY TRIGGER IS ACTIVATED

11.18 Once the Community Trigger is activated a case review is required. The relevant bodies should have an agreed procedure for carrying out the review. The review should look at what action has previously been taken in response to the victim's report of anti-social behaviour. The relevant bodies are required to share information about the case, consider whether any new relevant information needs to be obtained, review previous actions taken and propose a response. Schedule 4 states that local providers of social housing **must** be consulted when a review is carried out. In addition, the local providers of social housing **must** cooperate with the relevant bodies in the area in any matters specified by that body concerning the review. There is also a provision within Sch 4 regarding any other person. They may be required to disclose information which will assist a relevant body to carry out a review. If that 'other person' is a person who exercises public functions and if that person is in possession of the information requested, which is held in connection with the exercise of their public functions, then again they **must** comply with the request.

11.19 The relevant body which carries out an ASB case review may make recommendations to a person who exercises public functions (including recommendations to a relevant body) in respect of any matters arising from the review, and the relevant body must have regard to the recommendations in exercising public functions (s 104(7)). An example of a relevant body could be a recommendation made to a housing department or housing provider to consider certain remedies. The relevant body must also inform the applicant of the outcome of the review and any recommendations which had been made in accordance with s 107(7) above. Schedule 4 of the Act sets out a requirement for consultation between various bodies when making and revising anti-social case review procedures. It clearly envisages a collaborative approach between local authorities, the Police and social housing providers.

CONCLUSION

11.20 The Community Trigger is at the heart of what is intended to be a more victim-centric piece of legislation. However, for it to succeed, those victims of anti-social behaviour (and particularly the more vulnerable) will need to know of its existence and effect. The pilot schemes did not suggest great public awareness. One local authority reported that only 49 people of the 338 completing the anti-social behaviour survey had heard of the Community Trigger.

11.21 Local authorities and police forces are making efforts to raise awareness, with many websites providing online forms for registering a complaint. The effectiveness or otherwise of the scheme should become more apparent in time, as the Act requires the relevant bodies to publish information every 12 months covering not just the number of applications, but also the number of times the threshold for a review was not met and the number of times it was met and the number of reviews that resulted in recommendations being made. This will place an onus on the relevant body to ensure there are strong local links and an obvious single point of contact in each local area. Good record keeping will be required and a clear understanding locally as to how often, when and who will be responsible for publishing such information.

CHAPTER 12

COMMUNITY REMEDIES

INTRODUCTION

12.01 The Community Remedy is a further example of the aim of the 2014 Act to put victims of anti-social behaviour at the forefront when addressing the problem of such behaviour. Part 6 of the act is entitled 'Local Involvement and Accountability'. Under this heading are 'Community Remedies'. The Act starts with the requirement for a Community Remedy document before going on to consider how out of court disposals can, in certain circumstances, be the remedy of choice where anti-social behaviour has occurred and stressing the need for victim involvement in selecting the action to be taken.

THE COMMUNITY REMEDY DOCUMENT

12.02 Section 101 of the 2014 Act introduces the requirement for each local policing body to prepare a Community Remedy document for its area. The Community Remedy document is a list of actions which it might be appropriate for perpetrator of anti-social behaviour to be required to undertake if it is determined that they have engaged in anti-social behaviour and are to be dealt with for that behaviour or offence without court proceedings.

12.03 The Community Remedy document and any revisions are to be prepared by the local policing body following consultation with members of the public and community representatives. The Police and Crime Commissioner (PCC) has a statutory duty to consult the local authority and Chief Officer of Police for the area and any community representatives the local policing body thinks it appropriate to consult, and to enter into whatever other public consultation the local policing body thinks appropriate.

12.04 The Guidance states that public consultation could be undertaken as part of another consultation, for example, when consulting on the Police and Crime Plan. The Community Remedy document may be revised at any time and there is encouragement to so do. Consultation may be undertaken in whatever form the PCC considers appropriate, for example, online consultation, addressing their community groups and local victim groups or via a local newspaper. In preparing or revising the Community Remedy document a local policing body must have regard to the following:

(a) the need to promote public confidence in the out-of-court disposal process;

(b) any guidance issued by the Secretary of State about how local policing bodies are to discharge their functions in this section;

(c) carrying out the necessary consultation to take account of all views expressed by those consulted.

12.05 Once the Community Remedy document, or revised document, has been agreed with the Chief Officer of Police, the local policing body must publish it in whatever way it thinks appropriate.

12.06 The legislation does not specify what action should be included in the Community Remedy document. This reflects the approach that it is a matter of discretion for the individual local policing body, reflecting the needs of that area and the concerns of local people. The actions included must be deemed appropriate and proportionate to the types of offences for which community resolutions are used, and seek to have a positive impact on the particular perpetrators.

12.07 The Guidance states that the actions selected as appropriate and proportionate must have a:

- punitive element: reflecting the effects on the victim in the wider community; or
- reparative element: achieving appropriate restitution/reparation to the victims; or
- rehabilitative element: helping to address to the causes of the perpetrators' behaviour; or
- combination of the above.

12.08 Section 101(4)(a) states that in preparing or revising the Community Remedy document, the local policing body must have regard to the need to promote public confidence in the out of court disposal process. It is clear therefore that public support for such disposals is an important factor.

12.09 As to what is to be included in the Community Remedy document, the Guidance offers some actions which may be included such as mediation and a written or verbal apology, etc.

12.10 For a more specific example, West Yorkshire Police and Crime Commission has produced a document in which they list the agreed set of actions to include:

- apologising to the victim, face to face or through a letter explanation or apology;
- the offender signing an acceptable behaviour contract where they agree not to behave anti-socially in future, and understand if they do they will face more formal consequences;
- paying compensation to the victim, eg for any damage caused where appropriate;
- reparation to the victim, eg repairing or cleaning up any damage and mess caused (subject to public liability, health and safety and skills checks); and
- acceptable behaviour contract – voluntary agreement where a carer of a young offender agrees to help them stay away from crime.

WHEN WILL A COMMUNITY REMEDY APPLY?

12.11 Section 102 of the Act sets out when a Community Remedy (or an out of court disposal as herein after referred to) can be used. The Guidance states that they are to be used 'typically ... when dealing with low level criminal damage, low value theft, minor assaults (without injury) and anti-social behaviour'. The Community Remedy can apply when a person (such as a police officer) has evidence that an individual:

(a) A (the perpetrator) has engaged in anti-social behaviour or committed an offence;
(b) A admits to P (the Police) that he or she has done so;
(c) P thinks that the evidence is enough for taking proceedings against A for an injunction under s 1, or taking other court proceedings, but decides that it will be appropriate for A to carry out action of some sort instead; and
(d) if the evidence is that A has committed an offence, P does not think it would be more appropriate for A to be given a caution or a fixed penalty notice.

12.12 Central to the notion of a victim-centric approach, the Act requires P to make reasonable efforts to obtain the views of any victim of the anti-social behaviour, and in particular the victims' views as to whether A should carry out any of the actions listed in the Community Remedy document, before deciding what action to require A to carry out. If the victim expresses a view that A should carry out a particular action listed in the Community Remedy document, P must invite A to carry out this action unless it seems to be P that it would be inappropriate to do so.

12.13 Where there are multiple victims to any offence or anti-social behaviours the officer must make reasonable efforts to take the views of all victims into account. If the victims have differing views as to what action, if any, should be undertaken by the perpetrator then the officer should consider these but the final decision would be left to him/her. The requirement to consult victims amends earlier Acts intended to address anti-social behaviour or low level crime. The 2014 Act introduces a new duty into existing legislation to consult victims when a conditional caution or a youth conditional caution was imposed.[1]

12.14 Whilst Community Remedies have been broadly well-received, it is of note that they have been subject to criticism by some organisations such as the Magistrates' Association. The Magistrates' Association has stated their belief that the courts are the proper place for anti-social behaviour to be dealt with so as to ensure transparency and a consistency of sentencing and sanction monitoring. They raise the suggestion that in allowing separate areas to determine their own response to anti-social behaviour; this could cause inconsistencies of practice and ultimately injustice. There is also a criticism of a system which invites individual victims to choose an appropriate sanction. This could lead to an offender who offends against a sensitive victim being treated differently to one who offends against a more robust victim.

---

1 Section 23ZA to Criminal Justice Act 2003 and s 66BA to the Crime and Disorder Act 1998 introduced by s 103(1) and (2) of the 2014 Act.

CHAPTER 13

NEW GROUNDS FOR POSSESSION OF A RESIDENTIAL PROPERTY

INTRODUCTION

13.01 Part 5 of the 2014 Act introduces additional grounds for a landlord to recover possession of a property where anti-social behaviour is alleged. The most significant amendment to the existing legislation is a new mandatory or absolute ground for possession for certain cases of anti-social behaviour or criminality. The Act also makes amendments to the discretionary grounds for possession, which previously existed under the Housing Act 1985 and the Housing Act 1988. The Home Office Guidance explains the amendments on the basis that 'the existing process for evicting anti-social tenants is often very lengthy and expensive for landlords and the courts, and most importantly, prolongs the suffering of victims, witnesses and the community'.

NEW ABSOLUTE GROUNDS FOR POSSESSION

13.02 Sections 94–97 of the Act introduce new absolute grounds of possession for both secure and assured tenancies. In relation to a secure tenancy the Act makes amendments to s 84 of the Housing Act 1985 by introducing s 84A. With regard to an assured tenancy the Act makes amendments to Part 1 of Sch 2 to the Housing Act 1988 by introducing a Ground 7A. The ground is open to both social and private landlords. However the Guidance anticipates private landlords continuing to use s 21 of the Housing Act 1988 to obtain possession, when a 'no fault ground can be used at the end of the fixed term of tenancy'. The Guidance envisages these grounds will be reserved for the most serious cases and not used as a matter of routine.

ABSOLUTE GROUNDS

13.03 In order to secure an absolute ground for possession the landlord will need to have fulfilled certain notice requirements and, where relevant, review procedures followed (see below) and meet at least one of the following five conditions:

- Condition 1: the tenant, a member of the tenants household, or a person visiting the property has been convicted of a serious offence; or
- Condition 2: the tenant, a member of the tenants household or a person visiting had been found by a court to have breached an injunction to prevent nuisance and annoyance obtained under s 1 of the Act; or
- Condition 3: the tenant, a member of the tenants household or a person visiting the property has been convicted of breach of a criminal behaviour order obtained under s 30 of the Act; or

- Condition 4: the tenants property has been closed for more than 48 hours by way of a Closure Order pursuant to s 80 of the Act; or
- Condition 5: the tenant, a member of the tenant's household or a person visiting the property has been convicted of a breach of an abatement notice served pursuant to the Environmental Protection Act 1990. (The nuisance concerned being noise emitted from the dwelling, rather than some other environmental issue.)

SERIOUS OFFENCE

13.04 'Serious offence' is defined by way of s 84A(9) of the Housing Act 1985 as meaning an offence which was committed on or after the day which this sub-section of the Act came in to force (20 October 2014) and is specified or falls within a description specified in Sch 2A of the Housing Act 1985. The list of offences within the schedule includes a wide range of offences from the most serious (such as murder, kidnap, etc) to lesser offences (such as assault with intent to resist arrest and having an article with a blade or point in a public place).

LOCALITY

13.05 Conditions 1–3 listed above may also require an element of locality. However Conditions 1, 2 and 3 can be committed elsewhere if the breach involves a person who lives or has a right to live in the locality or if it involves the landlord or the landlord's employees or a person performing a housing management function on behalf of the landlord. It is of note that Conditions 4 and 5 specifically relate to the property let in any event. The conditions are not satisfied if an appeal is pending or an appeal has overturned a conviction, finding or order.

13.06 In respect of Condition 1, namely the serious offence, this does not need to be committed wholly in the locality of the dwelling house. The Act provides for it to have been committed 'wholly or partly'. As with the existing Housing Acts the word locality is not defined. It is deemed not to require to a specific definition as it is a matter of common sense as to when an offence took place within the 'locality'. It is a question of fact and degree, based on the evidence – see *Manchester City Council v Lawler*.[1]

NOTICE REQUIREMENTS

13.07 In order to secure possession under the new absolute ground the landlord will need to serve a notice of the proceedings on the tenant. The requirement of such a notice is mandatory. Unlike the service of a Notice under the discretionary grounds the Act does not provide for the court to dispense with the service of a Notice if it is just and equitable to so do. The failure to serve a notice will be fatal to an application on the mandatory grounds.

13.08 The notice requirements in relation to a secure tenancy arise through the introduction of s 83ZA of the Housing Act 1985 and an amendment to s 8 of the

---

1 (1999) 31 HLR 119, CA.

Housing Act 1988 in relation to an assured tenancy. There is no prescribed form of notice for a secure tenancy, but it must contain the information listed in para **13.10** below. A new prescribed form of notice is to be used for an assured tenancy from the 6 April 2015 as contained within the Assured Tenancies and Agricultural Occupancies (Forms) (England) Regulations 2015[2] (Form 3) (see Appendix 3).

13.09 If relying on Conditions 1, 2, 3 or 5 the notice must be served on the tenant within 12 months of the relevant conviction or finding of the court being relied on (or if there is an appeal against the finding or conviction, within 12 months of the appeal being finally determined, abandoned or withdrawn). If the application relies on a closure order the notice must be served within 3 months following the making of such an order (or if there is an appeal against the making of the closure order, within 3 months of it being finally determined, abandoned or withdrawn).

13.10 The notice itself is valid for 12 months. The notice must include the following information:

- that it is the landlord's intention to request the court makes an order under s 84A (secure tenant) or Ground 7A (if an assured tenant) for possession of the dwelling house. In short, the notice must specify they are relying on a mandatory ground;
- the reasons for the landlord's decision to apply for the order;
- which of the five conditions of the absolute grounds the landlord proposes to rely upon;
- which conviction, court finding or closure order the landlord proposes to rely on;
- inform the tenant of their right to request a review of the landlords decision and the timescale within such a request must be made;
- where and how a tenant may seek advice on the notice; and
- the date after which possession proceedings may be begun;

if the landlord wishes to seek possession on one or more of the existing discretionary, in addition to a mandatory ground, the landlord must also specify and give details of the discretionary ground(s) in the notice.

STATUTORY REVIEW

13.11 Mirroring the proceedings to bring to an end a starter or introductory tenancy, a tenant who is notified that possession will be sought on one of the mandatory anti-social grounds has a right to request a review of that decision. In a secure tenancy the right to request a review is provided by s 85ZA of the Housing Act 1985, which states that a tenant 'may request' a review of the landlords decision to seek possession under the mandatory ground if the interest of the landlord belongs to (a) a local housing authority; or (b) a housing action trust. The Absolute Ground for Possession for Anti-social Behaviour (Review Procedure) England Regulations 2014[3] govern how such reviews are to be conducted (see Appendix 3). These regulations are similar to those concerning a review of a decision to bring to an end an introductory tenancy.

---

[2] SI 2015/620.

[3] SI 2014/2554.

13.12 There is no corresponding requirement in respect of assured tenancies. However the Guidance states 'we would expect housing associations to offer a similar non-statutory review procedure'. The decision not to require housing association to carry out statutory review is unfortunate. The fact that many such landlords do carry out reviews when seeking to end a starter or a demoted tenancy does not mean they will necessarily adopt such a policy on this mandatory ground. The review is arguably one of the areas which will be challenged by those seeking to defend such proceedings on the basis of a public law challenge (see **13.14**). Electing not to have review procedure may, notionally at least, avoid such a challenge. However from a landlord's perspective if they carry out similar reviews when seeking to end other non-secure tenancies, electing not to carry out a review may in itself be open to challenge.

13.13 The Act specifies a specific time-frame in respect of a review:

- a request for a review must be made in writing within 7 days of the notice to seek possession being served on the tenant;
- a review must be carried out before the end of the notice period;
- the landlord must communicate the outcome of the review to the tenant in writing;
- if the decision is to confirm the original decision to seek possession, the landlord must also notify the tenant of the reasons for the decision;
- if the review upholds the original decision the landlord will then proceed by applying to the court for a possession order.

There is no prescribed form for requesting a review, but the application must contain certain information as set out by reg 2 of the SI 2014/2554 referred to at **13.11** above. The regulations grant the tenant a right to an oral hearing.

DEFENCES TO CLAIMS

13.14 The Act expressly provides for a tenant seeking to defend a claim for possession on such grounds to raise the defence that an order would be contrary to their rights under the European Convention on Human Rights. This is sometimes referred to as a proportionality defence or argument.

13.15 Mirroring the absence of a requirement for a review in respect of an assured tenancy the Act does not amend the Housing Act 1988 so as to recognise the right to raise such a defence. However given that some social landlords in granting an assured tenancy will be carrying out a public function[4] it seems to the authors that they will be likely to face a challenge on proportionality or human rights grounds in just the same way as a local authority landlord.

13.16 It is not within the scope of this book to consider in detail the basis for a human rights/proportionality defence. The relevant line of authorities supporting a public authority tenant's right to rely on a proportionality defence starts with the decision of

---

4 See *R (on the application of Weaver) v London and Quadrant Housing Trust* [2010] 1 WLR 363.

Manchester City Council v Pinnock.[5] There is a useful summary of the relevant principles to be applied when considering such defence in *Thurrock Borough Council v West*.[6]

13.17 Although not expressly stated within the Act the authors envisage that in addition to a tenant raising a proportionality defence they may also defend a claim based on the mandatory ground by way of a public law challenge, heard within the County Court. Such challenges are brought on a relatively regular basis against the termination of other non-secure tenancies: *see Barber v Croydon Borough Council*.[7] Landlords will need to ensure that they comply strictly with the procedural requirements of the new mandatory grounds. Of equal importance they must undertake any requested review properly and above all fairly. Failure to do so will inevitably result in the landlord having to undertake additional work, which would otherwise have been unnecessary and leave them exposed to a meritorious challenge in the County Court.

13.18 The stated purpose of the mandatory ground was to speed up the process of securing eviction where there was serious or persistent anti-social behaviour. It was believed that removing the test of reasonableness (which exists when considering any of the discretionary grounds) would make obtaining such an order more straight forward and speedy. However it is the authors' view that if claims for possession based on mandatory ground face proportionality and/or public law challenges the desired aim will not necessarily be met. Whatever the ground for possession which the landlord relies, the tenant will still have the opportunity to raise a defence. Although it is envisaged that such arguments should be dealt with on a summary basis at a preliminary hearing, bringing/defending such a claim will still entail a reasonably substantial amount of work including disclosure, comprehensive pleadings, preparation of witness statements, allocation to track, case management, skeleton arguments, etc.

13.19 There is also the potential for much more work and delay arising from applications for injunctions under the Act being fully defended in a way that ASBIs under the old powers were not. Under the previous legislation applications for an ASBI were often compromised at court by the defendant giving an undertaking. Landlords may now be extremely reluctant to accept an undertaking as they may see the obtaining of an order as the first step to securing possession of the defendant's property.

POST POSSESSION ORDER

13.20 Unlike when the court grants an order for possession on a discretionary ground, if the court makes an order on one of the mandatory grounds it may not adjourn or suspend the order. Possession should be granted no later than 14 days after the making of the order, unless the tenant can demonstrate exceptional hardship, in which case possession may be postponed for up to 6 weeks.[8]

13.21 Where an order is granted the Act makes provision for a landlord to withhold consent to the assignment of a secure tenancy by way of exchange. Ordinarily such consent would be withheld when the notice seeking possession is served.

---

5 [2012] UKSC 45, [2011] 1 All ER 285.
6 [2012] EWCA CIV 1435, [2013] 1 P&CR 175 at [22]–[26].
7 [2010] EWCA Civ 51, (2010) *The Times*, 24 March.
8 Section 89 of the Housing Act 1980.

AMENDMENTS/ADDITIONS TO THE EXISTING DISCRETIONARY GROUNDS

13.22 Section 98 of the Act, which has been in force since 13 May 2014, amends the existing discretionary grounds in both the Housing Act 1985 and the Housing Act 1988, by introducing a ground based on conduct which has caused a nuisance to a landlord. The ground provides that the court may grant possession where:

> 'The Tenant or a person residing in or visiting the dwelling house:
>
> (aa) has been guilty of conduct causing or likely to cause a nuisance or annoyance to the landlord of the dwelling house, or a person employed (whether or not by the landlord) in connection with the exercise of the landlords housing managements functions, and that is directly or indirectly related to or affects those functions.'

13.23 The discretionary ground above removes the locality requirement which is present within the existing grounds under both of the Housing Acts. This will allow a landlord to seek to evict a tenant when their anti-social behaviour is against his or her landlord or is against the landlord's employee and is outside the locality of the tenant's property.

13.24 The existing Housing Acts are amended further in that the Act now introduces a discretionary ground for possession if the tenant or an adult residing in the dwelling house has been convicted of an offence connected with a riot. This introduction arose following the riots which occurred in London, Manchester and other cities in 2011. This new ground is introduced as Ground 2ZA to Sch 2 of the Housing Act 1985 and Ground 14ZA of Sch 2 of the Housing Act 1988.

13.25 The Grounds read as follows:

> 'The tenant or an adult residing in the dwelling house has been convicted of an indictable offence which took place during, and at the scene of a riot, in the United Kingdom.'

'Riot' has the same definition as that contained within s 1 of the Public Order Act 1986 namely:

> '(1) Where 12 or more persons who are present together use or threaten unlawful violence for a common purpose and the conduct of them (taken together) is such as what cause a person a reasonable firmness present at the scene to fear for his personal safety, each of the persons using unlawful violence for the common purposes guilty or riot.
>
> (2) It is immaterial whether or not the 12 or more use or threaten unlawful violence simultaneously.
>
> (3) The common purpose may be inferred from conduct.
>
> (4) No personal of reasonable firmness need actually be, or be likely to be, present at the scene.
>
> (5) Riot may be committed in private as well as in public places.

(6) A person guilty of riot is liable on conviction or indictment to imprisonment for a term not exceeding 10 years or a fine or both.'

This new ground applies only to dwellings in England.

APPENDIX 1

PRECEDENTS

1. Criminal Behaviour Order

PRECEDENT 1.1 CBO – DRAFT APPLICATION AND HEARSAY NOTICE

NOTICE OF

INTENTION TO APPLY FOR A CRIMINAL BEHAVIOUR ORDER

IF THE DEFENDANT IS CONVICTED

AND

PROPOSED APPLICATION

(Anti-Social Behaviour Crime and Policing Act 2014, s 22;

Criminal Procedure Rules 2014, Rule 50.3)

R v [Defendant Name]

In the Magistrates' Court

1. THIS NOTICE is to tell you

Defendant's name:

Date of birth:

Address:

that if you are convicted of one or more offences with which you have been charged, the prosecutor intends to apply to the court for a Criminal Behaviour Order to be made against you.

2. THE TERM OF THE ORDER the prosecutor wants the court to make is:

The defendant must not:

3. NOTICE TO THE DEFENDANT SERVED with this document:

If you are convicted, you will have an opportunity to explain to the court why you think the proposed order should not be made. (Written notice of any evidence you rely on needs to be served on the court officer and the prosecutor. Criminal Procedure Rules 2014, r 50.3(4).)

4. Name and address of prosecutor:

5. Offence(s) with which the defendant is charged :

[INSERT CHARGE HERE]

6. Attachments in support of the proposed application:

The prosecutor attaches the following material upon which the application will be based.

1. Description of behaviour is set out below:

   •

   •

2. Evidence relied upon (additional to statements and exhibits served in in support of the charges at 5. above)

   (i) ...

   (ii) ...

   (iii) ...

3. Notice of any Hearsay Evidence relied upon

(CRIMINAL PROCEDURE RULES 2014, RULE 50.6)

NOTICE OF INTENTION TO RELY ON HEARSAY EVIDENCE

1 The Applicant intends to rely on hearsay evidence in its application for a criminal behaviour order against the defendant.

2 [Insert reasons here].

The Crown seeks to rely on the said evidence. This evidence is produced under the authority of *Clingham v Kensington & Chelsea London Borough Council: R v Manchester Crown Court, ex parte McCann & Others* (2002) UKHL 39.

4 Other documents served with this notice

Signed (Prosecutor) ....

Date ....

PRECEDENT 1.2 – SCHEDULE OF INCIDENTS

Criminal Behaviour Order Application (CBO) Details of Previous Behaviour to prove harassment, alarm and/or distress				
Defendant:				
Date of Incident	Nature of Incident	Place of Incident	Incident Number/Incident Details	Result

2. Community Protection Notice

PRECEDENT 2.1 – COMMUNITY PROTECTION NOTICE

[Name of Local Authority or Police Force]

Anti-social Behaviour, Crime and Policing Act 2014
Part 4, Chapter 1 – Community Protection Notice

<table>
<tr><td colspan="4">I am satisfied on reasonable grounds that the conduct of:</td></tr>
<tr><td>Name:</td><td></td><td>Date of Birth:</td><td></td></tr>
<tr><td>Address:</td><td colspan="3"></td></tr>
<tr><td>Business Name:</td><td></td><td>Organisation:</td><td></td></tr>
<tr><td>Business Address:</td><td colspan="3"></td></tr>
<tr><td colspan="4">Is having a detrimental effect, of a persistent or continuing nature, on the quality of life of those in the locality, and the conduct is unreasonable.
The nature of the conduct is as follows:</td></tr>
<tr><td colspan="4">You were issued a written warning on [insert date/time of warning] by [name of officer] to ensure the offending conduct had stopped by [put date/time told to stop], but you have failed to do so.</td></tr>
<tr><td colspan="4">In order to address the offending conduct you must abide by the following conditions:</td></tr>
<tr><td>1.</td><td colspan="3"></td></tr>
<tr><td>2.</td><td colspan="3"></td></tr>
<tr><td>3.</td><td colspan="3"></td></tr>
<tr><td>4.</td><td colspan="3"></td></tr>
<tr><td>5.</td><td colspan="3"></td></tr>
<tr><td colspan="4">You have until [insert date/time] to ensure the conditions are completed otherwise you will be in breach of this Community Protection Notice.
If you fail to comply with the requirements of this Community Protection Notice you will commit an offence for which you will be liable on summary conviction:
(a) To a fine not exceeding level 4 on the standard scale, in the case of an individual;
(b) To a fine not exceeding £20,000, in the case of a body.
If you fail to comply with the terms of the Community Protection Notice, the relevant local authority may have work carried out to ensure that the failure is remedied, but only on land that is open to the air.
As regards premises other than land open to the air, if the relevant local authority issues you with a notice specifying work it intends to have carried out to ensure that the failure is remedied, specifying the estimated cost of the work, and, inviting you to consent to the work being carried out, the authority may have the work carried out if the necessary consent is given.
If the work is carried out as above, and the relevant local authority issued a notice to you giving details of the work that was carried out and specifying an amount that is no more than the cost to the authority of having the work carried out, then you are liable to the authority for that amount (subject to the outcome of any appeal).</td></tr>
</table>

Appeal

A person issued with a Community Protection Notice may appeal to a Magistrates' Court against the Notice on any of the following grounds:

1. That the conduct specified in the Community Protection Notice:
   (a) Did not take place,
   (b) Has not had a detrimental effect on the quality of life of those in the locality,
   (c) Has not been of a persistent or continuing nature,
   (d) Is not unreasonable, or
   (e) Is conduct that the person cannot reasonably be expected to control or affect.
2. That any of the requirements in the notice, or any of the periods within which or times by which they are to be complied with, are unreasonable.
3. That there is a material defect or error in, or in connection with, the Notice.
4. That the Notice was issued to the wrong person.

An appeal must be made within the period of 21 days beginning with the day on which the person is issued with the Notice.

Remedial Orders – a court before which a person is convicted of failing to comply with a Community Protection Notice may make whatever order the court thinks appropriate for ensuring that what the Notice requires to be done is done and for which you may be liable to any costs.

A court before which a person is convicted of failing to comply with a Community protection Notice may order the forfeiture of any item that was used in the commission of the offence.

If a justice of the peace is satisfied on information on oath that there are reasonable grounds for suspecting that an offence under Section 48 has been committed (failure to comply with the Notice), and that there is an item used in the commission of the offence on premises specified in the information, the justice may issue a warrant authorising any constable or designated person to enter the premises within 14 days from the date of issue of the warrant to seize the item.

Officer Issuing		**Person Issued Community Protection Notice**	
Name:		Name:	
Signed:		Signed:	
Date:		Date:	

3. Public Spaces Protection Order

PRECEDENT 3.1 – PSPO (GATING)

[Name of Local Authority]

Anti-social Behaviour, Crime and Policing Act 2014, Section 59

[Name of Local Authority]

[Name of are concerned] Public Spaces Protection Order [year of order]

This Order is made by [Name of Local Authority] ("The Council") under the Anti-Social Behaviour, Crime and Policing Act 2014, Section 59 ("the Act").

1 This Order relates to the land described in Paragraph 1 of the Schedule below and defined by [xxxxxxx] on the plan attached to this Order ("the restricted area"), being a public place in the Council's area to which the Act applies:

2 The Council is satisfied that the 2 conditions below have been met, in that:

a activities carried on in the restricted area as described below, have had a detrimental effect on the quality of life of those in the locality, or it is likely that these activities will be carried on in the public place and that they will have such an effect. The said activities being [name activities].

b that the effect, or likely effect of the activities described above, is, or is likely to be, of a persistent or continuing nature, is, or is likely to be, such as to make the activities unreasonable, and justifies the restrictions imposed by the Order.

BY THIS ORDER

3 The effect of the Order is as follows:

a To restrict the public right of way over the highway within the restricted area described in Paragraph 1 of the Schedule below, the restriction being in place at all times.

b This restriction shall not apply to the occupiers of premises adjoining or adjacent to the restricted area so indicated.

c The alternative to the restricted highway is as indicated in Paragraph 2 of the Schedule below;

d There is authorised the installation of a gate at the ends of the restricted highway identified in Paragraph 1 of the Schedule, whose maintenance is the responsibility of the [name and address of person responsible].

4 The Order will remain in force for a period of [number of years] years from the date of this Order, unless extended by further Orders under the Council's statutory powers.

5 A person guilty of an offence under conditions (3)(a) above, under section 67 of the Act is liable on summary conviction to a fine not exceeding level 3 on the standard scale or fixed penalty notice of a maximum £100.

THE SCHEDULE

1 [Identify area here].

2 The alternative route is [identify any alternative route here].

THE COMMON SEAL of the	[	]
[name of local authority] was	[	]
this day of 201X	[	]
hereto affixed in the presence of:-	[	]

[Title of person signing]

PRECEDENT 3.2 – PSPO

[NAME OF LOCAL AUTHORITY]

ANTI-SOCIAL BEHAVIOUR, CRIME AND POLICING ACT 2014, SECTION 59

[Name of Local authority]

[Name of Area Concerned] Public Spaces Protection Order [year of order]

This Order is made by [Name of Local Authority] ("The Council") under the Anti-Social Behaviour, Crime and Policing Act 2014 Section 59 ("the Act").

1. This Order relates to the public highway described in Paragraph 1 of the Schedule below and defined by [XXXXXXX} on the plan attached to this Order ("the restricted area"), being a public place in the Council's area to which the Act applies:

2. The Council is satisfied that the 2 conditions below have been met, in that:

(a) activities carried on in the restricted area as described below, have had a detrimental effect on the quality of life of those in the locality, or it is likely that these activities will be carried on in the public place and that they will have such an effect. The said activities being [Name activities here].

(b) that the effect, or likely effect of the activities described above, is, or is likely to be, of a persistent or continuing nature, is, or is likely to be, such as to make the activities unreasonable, and justifies the restrictions imposed by the Order.

BY THIS ORDER

3. The effect of the Order is to impose the following prohibitions and/or requirements [delete as appropriate] at [all times/during the following times]:

(a) In the restricted area any person who continues to carry out the following activities from which they are prohibited commits an offence:

(i) [XXXXXXXX].

(ii) [XXXXXXXX].

(b) In the restricted area any person who fails to comply with the following activities they are required to undertake commits an offence:

(i) XXXXXXXX].

(ii) [XXXXXXXX].

4. The Order will remain in force for a period of [XXXXX] years from the date of this Order, unless extended by further Orders under the Council's statutory powers.

5. A person guilty of an offence under conditions (a) or (b) above, under Section 67 of the Act is liable on summary conviction to a fine not exceeding level 3 on the standard scale or fixed penalty notice of a maximum £100.

6. In this area any person who continues drinking intoxicating liquor in the Order area when asked to desist by a Police Officer, Police Community Support Officer or authorised person from the Council under Section 63 or fails to surrender any intoxicating liquor in his possession when asked to do so by a Police Officer, Police Community Support Officer or

authorised person from the Council under Section 63 commits an offence and is liable on summary conviction to a fine not exceeding level 2 on the standard scale or fixed penalty notice of a maximum of £100.

THE SCHEDULE

17. [Identify area here].

THE COMMON SEAL of the	[	]
[name of local authority] was	[	]
this day of 201X	[	]
hereto affixed in the presence of:-	[	]

[Title of person signing]

4. Closure Notice

PRECEDENT 4.1 – CLOSURE NOTICE (LA APPLICATION) – FOR COUNTYWIDE USE

[Insert Organisation Logo Here]

Anti-social Behaviour, Crime and Policing Act 2014, Part 4, Chapter 3

Closure Notice

Re:

("the Premises")

Having reasonable grounds to believe that the use of the Premises has resulted or, (if the notice is not issued) is likely soon to result in nuisance to members of the public, or, that there has been, or, (if the notice is not issued) is likely soon to be disorder near those premises associated with the use of those premises, and

That the notice is necessary to prevent the nuisance or disorder from continuing, recurring or occurring.

I, [INSERT NAME OF PERSON], [INSERT JOB TITLE], [INSERT NAME OF ORGANISATION]l, hereby authorise the issue of this **Closure Notice** under Section 76 of the Anti-Social Behaviour, Crime & Policing Act 2014 in respect of the Premises specified above.

Signature: ....

Date: ....

TAKE NOTICE that

Access to the Premises specified above by any person other than a person who habitually lives on the Premises or the owner of the Premises is hereby PROHIBITED.

An application for an order will be made under Section 80 of the Anti-Social Behaviour, Crime & Policing Act 2014 for the closure of the Premises specified above, to [INSERT NAME OF COURT] Magistrates' Court on at am/pm when evidence for the issue of a Closure Order will be considered.

(On this date, should the court adjourn the hearing for the application of the Closure Order, the details of the court, date and time of the hearing shall be shown at the bottom of this notice).

An order under Section 80 of the Anti-Social Behaviour, Crime & Policing Act 2014 would have the effect of prohibiting access to the premises to all persons for such period (not exceeding three months) as the court may decide and would make it an offence for any person to remain on or enter the Premises.

Failure to comply with this notice amounts to an offence under Section 86 of the Anti-Social Behaviour, Crime & Policing Act 2014 punishable by a maximum of 3 months imprisonment, or a fine, or both.

Advice relating to this notice and housing and legal matters generally can be obtained from any firm of solicitors or from the Citizens' Advice Bureau (Tel: 0844 826 9705).

The hearing for the Closure Order has been adjourned to [INSERT NAME OF COURT] Magistrates' Court on at am/pm by Order of the Court.

PRECEDENT 4.2 – CLOSURE ORDER APPLICATION (LA APPLICATION) – FOR COUNTYWIDE USE

APPLICATION FOR CLOSURE ORDER
(ANTI-SOCIAL BEHAVIOUR, CRIME & POLICING ACT 2014, PART 4, CHAPTER 3)
IN THE [NAME OF COURT] MAGISTRATES' COURT

Date:	
Address:	
Lawful Occupier(s) (insert name if applicable) – date of birth:	
Application made by:	[NAME, JOB TITLE & ORGANISATION DETAILS]
Relevant authorities consulted:	[LOCAL AUTHORITY NAME,

In relation to the address (**FULL ADDRESS**) it is alleged that:

(a) A person has engaged, or (if the order is not made) is likely to engage, in disorderly, offensive or criminal behaviour on the premises,

Or,

(b) The use of the premises has resulted, or (if the order is not made) is likely to result, in serious nuisance to members of the public,

Or,

(c) There has been, or (if the order is not made) is likely to be, disorder near those premises associated with the use of those premises,

And,

(d) The order is necessary to prevent the behaviour, nuisance or disorder from continuing, recurring or occurring.

With a Closure Notice having been served on the address on (**DATE & TIME**) application is now made for a Closure Order..
Application is made for a Closure Order for a period of three months.
On the application of: [NAME, JOB TITLE & NAME OF ORGANISATION]
Address: [ADDRESS OF APPLICANT].
Who states that the information given above is correct.
Taken before me ....
Justice of the Peace
[Justices' Clerk]

PRECEDENT 4.3 – CLOSURE ORDER EXTENSION APPLICATION (LA APPLICATION) – FOR COUNTYWIDE USE

APPLICATION FOR AN EXTENSION TO A CLOSURE ORDER (ANTI-SOCIAL BEHAVIOUR ACT 2003, PART 1A, s.11E)

IN THE [NAME OF COURT] MAGISTRATES' COURT

Date:
Address:

Sole Lawful Occupier(s) (insert name if applicable) – date of birth:

Application made by: [APPLICANT NAME, JOB TITLE & ORGANISATION INSERTED HERE]

Relevant authorities consulted: [NAME OF LOCAL AUTHORITY INSERTED HERE],

In relation to the address (**FULL ADDRESS**) it was found at [NAME OF COURT] Magistrates' Court on [**DATE ORDER MADE**] that:

(a) A person has engaged, or (if the order is not made) is likely to engage, in disorderly, offensive or criminal behaviour on the premises,

or

(b) The use of the premises has resulted, or (if the order is not made) is likely to result, in serious nuisance to members of the public,

or

(c) There has been, or (if the order is not made) is likely to be, disorder near those premises associated with the use of those premises,

and

(d) The order is necessary to prevent the behaviour, nuisance or disorder from continuing, recurring or occurring.

A Closure Order was granted for a period of [**INSERT NO. OF MONTHS**] to [**INSERT DATE TO**].

With a Closure Order granted on [**INSERT DATE OF ORDER**] having been served on the address, application is now being made for a Closure Order Extension, as it is believed to be necessary to prevent the occurrence, recurrence or continuance of disorderly, offensive or criminal behaviour on the premises, or, serious nuisance to members of the public resulting from the use of the premises, or, disorder near the premises associated with the use of the premises.

Application is thus made for a Closure Order Extension for a further period of [**INSERT NO. OF MONTHS**].

On the application of: [NAME, JOB TITLE & ORGANISATION NAME OF APPLICANT INSERTED HERE]

Address: [ADDRESS OF APPLICANT]

Who states that the information given above is correct.

Taken before me ....

Justice of the Peace

[Justices' Clerk]

5. Absolute Ground for Possession

PRECEDENT 5.1 – NOTICE – ABSOLUTE GROUND FOR POSSESSION

	Details of Service Served on (person) .... By (Officer) .... at (place). .... at am/pm on (date) .... in following manner ....

NOTICE OF SEEKING POSSESSION

Housing Act 1985, section 83ZA

As amended by Section 147 of the Housing Act 1996 and Section 95 Anti-Social Behaviour, Crime & Policing Act 2014

This Notice is the first step towards requiring you to give up possession of your dwelling. You should read it very carefully.

1. To: [INSERT FULL NAME OF TENANT(S)]

- If you need help or advice about this Notice, and what you should do about it, take it immediately to a Citizens' Advice Bureau, a Housing Aid Centre, or a Law Centre, or to a Solicitor. You may be able to receive Legal Aid but this will depend on your personal circumstances.

2. [Name of Local Authority] intends to apply to the Court for an order requiring you to give up possession of:

[INSERT ADDRESS OF PROPERTY INCLUDING POSTCODE]

- If you are a secure tenant under the Housing Act 1985, you can only be required to leave your dwelling if you landlord obtains an order for possession from the Court. The order must be based on one of the Conditions which are set out in Section 84A of the Housing Act 1985 (see paragraphs **3 and 4** below).
- If you are willing to give up possession without a Court order, you should notify the person who signed this Notice as soon as possible and say when you would leave.

3. Possession will be sought in accordance with Section 84A of the Housing Act 1985, which reads:-

"84A Absolute ground for possession for anti-social behaviour

(1) If the court is satisfied that any of the following conditions is met, it must make an order for the possession of a dwelling-house let under a secure tenancy.
This is subject to subsection (2) (and to any available defence based on the tenant's Convention rights, within the meaning of the Human rights Act 1998).

(2) Subsection (1) applies only where the landlord has complied with any obligations it has under section 85ZA (review of decision to seek possession).

(3) Condition 1 is that-
 (a) The tenant, or a person residing in or visiting the dwelling-house, has been convicted of a serious offence, and
 (b) The serious offence-
  (i) Was committed (wholly or partly) in, or in the locality of, the dwelling-house,
  (ii) Was committed elsewhere against a person with a right (of whatever description) to reside in, or occupy housing accommodation in the locality of, the dwelling-house, or
  (iii) Was committed elsewhere against the landlord of the dwelling-house, or a person employed (whether or not by the landlord) in connection with the exercise of the landlord's housing management functions, and directly or indirectly related to or affected those functions.

(4) Condition 2 is that a court has found in relevant proceedings that the tenant, or a person residing in or visiting the dwelling-house, has breached a provision of an injunction under section 1 of the Anti-social Behaviour, Crime and Policing Act 2014, other than a provision requiring a person to participate in a particular activity, and-

(a) The breach occurred in, or in the locality of, the dwelling-house, or

(b) The breach occurred elsewhere and the provision breached was a provision intended to prevent-

(i) Conduct that is capable of causing nuisance or annoyance to a person with a right (of whatever description) to reside in, or occupy housing accommodation in the locality of, the dwelling-house, or

(ii) Conduct that is capable of causing nuisance or annoyance to the landlord of the dwelling-house, or a person employed (whether or not by the landlord) in connection with the exercise of the landlord's housing management functions, and that is directly or indirectly related to or affects those functions.

(5) Condition 3 is that the tenant, or a person residing in or visiting the dwelling-house, has been convicted of an offence under section 30 of the Anti-social Behaviour, Crime and Policing Act 2014 consisting of a breach of a provision of a criminal behaviour order prohibiting a person from doing anything described in the order, and the offence involved-

(a) A breach that occurred in, or in the locality of, the dwelling-house or

(b) A breach that occurred elsewhere of a provision intended to prevent-

(i) Behaviour that causes or is likely to cause harassment, alarm or distress to a person with a right (of whatever description) to reside in, or occupy housing accommodation in the locality of, the dwelling-house or

(ii) Behaviour that causes or is likely to cause harassment, alarm or distress to the landlord of the dwelling-house, or a person employed (whether or not by the landlord) in connection with the exercise of the landlord's housing management functions, and that is directly or indirectly related to or affects those functions.

(6) Condition 4 is that-

(a) The dwelling-house is or has been subject to a closure order under section 80 of the Anti-social Behaviour, Crime and Policing Act 2014, and

(b) Access to the dwelling-house has been prohibited (under the closure order or under a closure notice issued under section 76 of that Act) for a continuous period of more than 48 hours.

(7) Condition 5 is that-

(a) The tenant, or a person residing in or visiting the dwelling-house, has been convicted of an offence under-

(i) Section 80(4) of the Environmental Protection Act 1990 (breach of abatement notice in relation to statutory nuisance), or

(ii) Section 82(8) of that Act (breach of court order to abate statutory nuisance etc.), and

(b) The nuisance concerned was noise emitted from the dwelling-house which was a statutory nuisance for the pruposes of Part 3 of that Act by virtue of section 79(1)(g) of that Act (noise emitted from premises so as to be prejudicial to health or a nuisance)."

4. Particulars of each Condition are as follows and the reasons for taking this action include but are not limited to:

***************[DELETE CONDITIONS AS APPROPRIATE]************

Condition 1 particulars

You, a person residing with you or visiting you, has been convicted of a serious offence, and the serious offence was committed (wholly or partly) in or in the locality of the dwelling-house, or was committed elsewhere against a person with a right (of whatever description) to reside in, or occupy housing accommodation in the locality of the dwelling-house, or was committed elsewhere against your landlord, or a person employed (whether or not by your landlord) in connection with the exercise of your landlord's housing management functions, and directly or indirectly related to or affected those functions.

In particular it is alleged that:

1. xxxxxxxxx.
2. xxxxxxxxx.
3. xxxxxxxxx.

Condition 2 particulars

A court has found in relevant proceedings that you, or a person residing or visiting you has breached a provision of an injunction under section 1 of the Anti-social Behaviour, Crime and Policing Act 2014, other than a provision requiring a person to participate in a particular activity, and the breach occurred in, or in the locality of the dwelling-house, or, the breach occurred elsewhere and the provision breached was a provision intended to prevent conduct that is capable of causing a nuisance or annoyance to a person with a right (of whatever description) to reside in, or occupy housing accommodation in the locality of the dwelling-house, or conduct that is capable of causing nuisance or annoyance to the landlord of the dwelling-house, or a person employed (whether or not by the landlord) in connection with the exercise of the landlord's housing management functions, and that is directly or indirectly related to of affects those functions.

In particular it is alleged that:

1. xxxxxxxxx.
2. xxxxxxxxx.
3. xxxxxxxxx.

Condition 3 particulars

You, or a person residing in or visiting you, has been convicted of an offence under section 30 of the Anti-social Behaviour, Crime and Policing Act 2014 consisting of a breach of a provision of a criminal behaviour order prohibiting a person from doing anything described in the order, and the offence involved a breach that occurred in, or in the locality of the dwelling-house or a breach that occurred elsewhere of a provision intended to prevent behaviour that causes or is likely to cause harassment, alarm or distress to a person with a right (of whatever description) to reside in, or occupy housing accommodation in the locality of, the dwelling-house or behaviour that causes or is likely to cause harassment, alarm or distress to the landlord of the dwelling-house, or a person employed (whether or not by the landlord) in connection with the exercise of the landlord's housing management functions, and that is directly or indirectly related to or affects those functions.

In particular it is alleged that:

1. xxxxxxxxx.
2. xxxxxxxxx.
3. xxxxxxxxx.

Condition 4 particulars

The dwelling-house is or has been subject to a closure order under section 80 of the Anti-social Behaviour, Crime and Policing Act 2014 and access to the dwelling-house has been prohibited (under the closure order or under a closure notice issued under section 76 of that Act) for a continuous period of more than 48 hours.

In particular it is alleged that:-

1. xxxxxxxxx.
2. xxxxxxxxx.
3. xxxxxxxxx.

Condition 5 particulars

You, or a person residing with or visiting you, has been convicted of an offence under section 80(4) of the Environmental Protection Act 1990 (breach of abatement notice in relation to statutory nuisance), or section 82(8) of that Act (breach of court order to abate statutory nuisance etc.) and the nuisance concerned was noise emitted from the dwelling-house which was a statutory nuisance for the purposes of Part 3 of that Act by virtue of section 79(1)(g) of that Act (noise emitted from premises so as to be prejudicial to health or a nuisance).

In particular it is alleged that:-

1. xxxxxxxxx.
2. xxxxxxxxx.
3. xxxxxxxxx.

5. The date after which proceedings for the possession of the dwelling-house may be begun is [INSERT DATE TENANT TO GIVE UP POSSESSION].

- Court proceedings may be begun at once or at any time during the following twelve months. Once the twelve months are up this Notice will lapse and a new notice must be served before possession can be sought.
- Possession of your dwelling-house cannot be obtained until after this date, which cannot be earlier than the date when your tenancy or licence could have been brought to an end. This means that if you have a weekly or fortnightly tenancy, there should be at least 4 weeks between the date this notice is given and the date possession is ordered.
- A notice seeking possession on section 84A must be served on you within specified time periods which vary depending on which condition is relied upon:
  - Where the landlord proposes to rely on condition 1, 3 or 5: within 12 months of the conviction (or if the conviction is appealed; within 12 months of the conclusion of the appeal);
  - Where the landlord proposes to rely on condition 2: within 12 months of the court's finding that the injunction has been breached (or if the finding is appealed: within 12 months of the conclusion of the appeal);
  - Where the landlord proposes to rely on condition 4: within 3 months of the closure order (or if the order is appealed: within 3 months of the conclusion of the appeal).

6. You have the right to ask the Council to hold a review of the decision to end your tenancy, such a request must be made in writing before the end of the period of 7 days beginning with the day on which the notice under section 83ZA was served. The request must be made by [INSERT TIME WITHIN WHICH REQUEST MUST BE MADE].

A review request form is attached at the end of this notice for your convenience.

Signed .... on behalf of [NAME OF LOCAL AUTHORITY], [ADDRESS OF LOCAL AUTHORITY. Tel: [TELEPHONE NUMBER OF LOCAL AUTHORITY]

Date: 20 .

I...[NAME & JOB TITLE OF SERVING OFFICER] of [NAME OF SERVING ORGANISATION] hereby certify that at ....am/pm on the.........day of 20

I served of

with Notice of Seeking Possession, of which this is a true copy by:

Delivering the said Notice of Seeking Possession to him/her personally:

By leaving the said Notice of Seeking Possession at... (address)

Being the said last known or usual place of abode.

Signature: ....

Date: ....

<u>**Office use only**</u>
Date received:
Signed:

PLEASE RETURN TO [INSERT FULL NAME, JOB TITLE AND ADDRESS OF PERSON TO WHOM REVIEW REQUEST SHOULD BE RETURNED TO]. PLEASE MARK THE ENVELOPE – URGENT REVIEW OF DECISION TO END SECURE TENANCY.

Request for a review of the Council's decision to seek an order for possession of a dwelling-house under section 84A Housing Act 1985.

[NAME OF LOCAL AUTHORITY] must receive this form or written request for a review before the end of 7 days beginning with the day on which the notice under section 83ZA was served.

Name:

Address:

Telephone Number:

Date upon which decision made (date Notice Served):

Tenancy Start Date:

Description of the decision: Council's decision to seek an order for possession of [ADDRESS OF DWELLING-HOUSE], full details of particulars can be found within section 4 of the Notice of Seeking Possession (particulars of conditions relied upon):

[INSERT HERE SECTION 4 WORDING]

Do you agree with the information provided within section 4 of the Notice (particulars of conditions relied upon)?

Yes/No

Please state the grounds upon which you are seeking a review.
(continue on a separate sheet if necessary)

Do you require the review to be conduct by way of oral hearing:

Yes/No

Do you agree to receive communications relating to the review by email? If so, please write below your email address to which communications will be sent.

Yes/No

Email Address:

If you have requested an oral review hearing, you will be sent a letter telling you the date, time and place of review at least 5 days before the hearing. If a review is carried out, you will be notified before the day specified in the notice under section 83ZA as the day after which proceedings for possession of the dwelling-house may be begun, as to the decision on the review and any reasons for the decision.

Signature: ....

Date: ....

APPENDIX 2

STATUTES

Anti-social Behaviour, Crime and Policing Act 2014 (ss 1–105, Sch 2)

Arrangement of Sections

PART 1
INJUNCTIONS

PART 3
DISPERSAL POWERS

PART 4
COMMUNITY PROTECTION

Chapter 1
Community Protection Notices

Chapter 2
Public Spaces Protection Orders

Chapter 3
Closure of Premises Associated with Nuisance or Disorder etc

PART 1

INJUNCTIONS

Injunctions

1 Power to grant injunctions

(1) A court may grant an injunction under this section against a person aged 10 or over ('the respondent') if two conditions are met.

(2) The first condition is that the court is satisfied, on the balance of probabilities, that the respondent has engaged or threatens to engage in anti-social behaviour.

(3) The second condition is that the court considers it just and convenient to grant the injunction for the purpose of preventing the respondent from engaging in anti-social behaviour.

(4) An injunction under this section may for the purpose of preventing the respondent from engaging in anti-social behaviour –

(a) prohibit the respondent from doing anything described in the injunction;
(b) require the respondent to do anything described in the injunction.

(5) Prohibitions and requirements in an injunction under this section must, so far as practicable, be such as to avoid –

(a) any interference with the times, if any, at which the respondent normally works or attends school or any other educational establishment;
(b) any conflict with the requirements of any other court order or injunction to which the respondent may be subject.

(6) An injunction under this section must –

(a) specify the period for which it has effect, or
(b) state that it has effect until further order.

In the case of an injunction granted before the respondent has reached the age of 18, a period must be specified and it must be no more than 12 months.

(7) An injunction under this section may specify periods for which particular prohibitions or requirements have effect.

(8) An application for an injunction under this section must be made to –

(a) a youth court, in the case of a respondent aged under 18;
(b) the High Court or the county court, in any other case.

Paragraph (b) is subject to any rules of court made under section 18(2).

2 Meaning of 'anti-social behaviour'

(1) In this Part 'anti-social behaviour' means –

(a) conduct that has caused, or is likely to cause, harassment, alarm or distress to any person,
(b) conduct capable of causing nuisance or annoyance to a person in relation to that person's occupation of residential premises, or
(c) conduct capable of causing housing-related nuisance or annoyance to any person.

(2) Subsection (1)(b) applies only where the injunction under section 1 is applied for by –

(a) a housing provider,
(b) a local authority, or
(c) a chief officer of police.

(3) In subsection (1)(c) 'housing-related' means directly or indirectly relating to the housing management functions of –

(a) a housing provider, or
(b) a local authority.

(4) For the purposes of subsection (3) the housing management functions of a housing provider or a local authority include –

(a) functions conferred by or under an enactment;
(b) the powers and duties of the housing provider or local authority as the holder of an estate or interest in housing accommodation.

Contents of injunctions

3 Requirements included in injunctions

(1) An injunction under section 1 that includes a requirement must specify the person who is to be responsible for supervising compliance with the requirement.

The person may be an individual or an organisation.

(2) Before including a requirement, the court must receive evidence about its suitability and enforceability from –

(a) the individual to be specified under subsection (1), if an individual is to be specified;
(b) an individual representing the organisation to be specified under subsection (1), if an organisation is to be specified.

(3) Before including two or more requirements, the court must consider their compatibility with each other.

(4) It is the duty of a person specified under subsection (1) –

(a) to make any necessary arrangements in connection with the requirements for which the person has responsibility (the 'relevant requirements');
(b) to promote the respondent's compliance with the relevant requirements;
(c) if the person considers that the respondent –

(i) has complied with all the relevant requirements, or
(ii) has failed to comply with a relevant requirement,

to inform the person who applied for the injunction and the appropriate chief officer of police.

(5) In subsection (4)(c) 'the appropriate chief officer of police' means –

(a) the chief officer of police for the police area in which it appears to the person specified under subsection (1) that the respondent lives, or
(b) if it appears to that person that the respondent lives in more than one police area, whichever of the relevant chief officers of police that person thinks it most appropriate to inform.

(6) A respondent subject to a requirement included in an injunction under section 1 must –

(a) keep in touch with the person specified under subsection (1) in relation to that requirement, in accordance with any instructions given by that person from time to time;
(b) notify the person of any change of address.

These obligations have effect as requirements of the injunction.

4 Power of arrest

(1) A court granting an injunction under section 1 may attach a power of arrest to a prohibition or requirement of the injunction if the court thinks that –

(a) the anti-social behaviour in which the respondent has engaged or threatens to engage consists of or includes the use or threatened use of violence against other persons, or
(b) there is a significant risk of harm to other persons from the respondent.

'Requirement' here does not include one that has the effect of requiring the respondent to participate in particular activities.

(2) If the court attaches a power of arrest, the injunction may specify a period for which the power is to have effect which is shorter than that of the prohibition or requirement to which it relates.

Applications for injunctions

5 Applications for injunctions

(1) An injunction under section 1 may be granted only on the application of –

(a) a local authority,
(b) a housing provider,
(c) the chief officer of police for a police area,
(d) the chief constable of the British Transport Police Force,
(e) Transport for London,
(f) the Environment Agency,
(g) the Natural Resources Body for Wales,
(h) the Secretary of State exercising security management functions, or a Special Health Authority exercising security management functions on the direction of the Secretary of State, or
(i) the Welsh Ministers exercising security management functions, or a person or body exercising security management functions on the direction of the Welsh Ministers or under arrangements made between the Welsh Ministers and that person or body.

(2) In subsection (1) 'security management functions' means –

(a) the Secretary of State's security management functions within the meaning given by section 195(3) of the National Health Service Act 2006;
(b) the functions of the Welsh Ministers corresponding to those functions.

(3) A housing provider may make an application only if the application concerns anti-social behaviour that directly or indirectly relates to or affects its housing management functions.

(4) For the purposes of subsection (3) the housing management functions of a housing provider include –

(a) functions conferred by or under an enactment;
(b) the powers and duties of the housing provider as the holder of an estate or interest in housing accommodation.

(5) The Secretary of State may by order –

(a) amend this section;
(b) amend section 20 in relation to expressions used in this section.

6 Applications without notice

(1) An application for an injunction under section 1 may be made without notice being given to the respondent.

(2) If an application is made without notice the court must either –

(a) adjourn the proceedings and grant an interim injunction (see section 7), or
(b) adjourn the proceedings without granting an interim injunction, or
(c) dismiss the application.

Interim injunctions

7 Interim injunctions

(1) This section applies where the court adjourns the hearing of an application (whether made with notice or without) for an injunction under section 1.

(2) The court may grant an injunction under that section lasting until the final hearing of the application or until further order (an 'interim injunction') if the court thinks it just to do so.

(3) An interim injunction made at a hearing of which the respondent was not given notice may not have the effect of requiring the respondent to participate in particular activities.

(4) Subject to that, the court has the same powers (including powers under section 4) whether or not the injunction is an interim injunction.

Variation and discharge

8 Variation or discharge of injunctions

(1) The court may vary or discharge an injunction under section 1 on the application of –

(a) the person who applied for the injunction, or
(b) the respondent.

(2) In subsection (1) 'the court' means –

(a) the court that granted the injunction, except where paragraph (b) applies;
(b) the county court, where the injunction was granted by a youth court but the respondent is aged 18 or over.

(3) The power to vary an injunction includes power –

(a) to include an additional prohibition or requirement in the injunction, or to extend the period for which a prohibition or requirement has effect;
(b) to attach a power of arrest, or to extend the period for which a power of arrest has effect.

(4) If an application under this section is dismissed, the party by which the dismissed application was made may make no further application under this section without –

(a) the consent of the court, or
(b) the agreement of the other party.

(5) Section 3 applies to additional requirements included under subsection (3)(a) above as it applies to requirements included in a new injunction.

Breach of injunctions

9 Arrest without warrant

(1) Where a power of arrest is attached to a provision of an injunction under section 1, a constable may arrest the respondent without warrant if he or she has reasonable cause to suspect that the respondent is in breach of the provision.

(2) A constable who arrests a person under subsection (1) must inform the person who applied for the injunction.

(3) A person arrested under subsection (1) must, within the period of 24 hours beginning with the time of the arrest, be brought before –

(a) a judge of the High Court or a judge of the county court, if the injunction was granted by the High Court;
(b) a judge of the county court, if –

(i) the injunction was granted by the county court, or
(ii) the injunction was granted by a youth court but the respondent is aged 18 or over;

(c) a justice of the peace, if neither paragraph (a) nor paragraph (b) applies.

(4) In calculating when the period of 24 hours ends, Christmas Day, Good Friday and any Sunday are to be disregarded.

(5) The judge before whom a person is brought under subsection (3)(a) or (b) may remand the person if the matter is not disposed of straight away.

(6) The justice of the peace before whom a person is brought under subsection (3)(c) must remand the person to appear before the youth court that granted the injunction.

10 Issue of arrest warrant

(1) If the person who applied for an injunction under section 1 thinks that the respondent is in breach of any of its provisions, the person may apply for the issue of a warrant for the respondent's arrest.

(2) The application must be made to –

(a) a judge of the High Court, if the injunction was granted by the High Court;
(b) a judge of the county court, if –

  (i) the injunction was granted by the county court, or
  (ii) the injunction was granted by a youth court but the respondent is aged 18 or over;

(c) a justice of the peace, if neither paragraph (a) nor paragraph (b) applies.

(3) A judge or justice may issue a warrant under this section only if the judge or justice has reasonable grounds for believing that the respondent is in breach of a provision of the injunction.

(4) A warrant issued by a judge of the High Court must require the respondent to be brought before that court.

(5) A warrant issued by a judge of the county court must require the respondent to be brought before that court.

(6) A warrant issued by a justice of the peace must require the respondent to be brought before –

(a) the youth court that granted the injunction, if the person is aged under 18;
(b) the county court, if the person is aged 18 or over.

(7) A constable who arrests a person under a warrant issued under this section must inform the person who applied for the injunction.

(8) If the respondent is brought before a court by virtue of a warrant under this section but the matter is not disposed of straight away, the court may remand the respondent.

11 Remands

Schedule 1 (remands under sections 9 and 10) has effect.

12 Powers in respect of under-18s

Schedule 2 (breach of injunctions: powers of court in respect of under-18s) has effect.

Exclusion from home

13 Power to exclude person from home in cases of violence or risk of harm

(1) An injunction under section 1 may have the effect of excluding the respondent from the place where he or she normally lives ('the premises') only if –

(a) the respondent is aged 18 or over,
(b) the injunction is granted on the application of –

  (i) a local authority,
  (ii) the chief officer of police for the police area that the premises are in, or
  (iii) if the premises are owned or managed by a housing provider, that housing provider, and

(c) the court thinks that –

  (i) the anti-social behaviour in which the respondent has engaged or threatens to engage consists of or includes the use or threatened use of violence against other persons, or
  (ii) there is a significant risk of harm to other persons from the respondent.

(2) For the purposes of this section a housing provider owns a place if –

(a) the housing provider is a person (other than a mortgagee not in possession) entitled to dispose of the fee simple of the place, whether in possession or in reversion, or
(b) the housing provider is a person who holds or is entitled to the rents and profits of the place under a lease that (when granted) was for a term of not less then 3 years.

Supplemental

14 Requirements to consult etc

(1) A person applying for an injunction under section 1 must before doing so –

(a) consult the local youth offending team about the application, if the respondent will be aged under 18 when the application is made;
(b) inform any other body or individual the applicant thinks appropriate of the application.

This subsection does not apply to a without-notice application.

(2) Where the court adjourns a without-notice application, before the date of the first on-notice hearing the applicant must –

(a) consult the local youth offending team about the application, if the respondent will be aged under 18 on that date;
(b) inform any other body or individual the applicant thinks appropriate of the application.

(3) A person applying for variation or discharge of an injunction under section 1 granted on that person's application must before doing so –

(a) consult the local youth offending team about the application for variation or discharge, if the respondent will be aged under 18 when that application is made;
(b) inform any other body or individual the applicant thinks appropriate of that application.

(4) In this section –

'local youth offending team' means –

(a) the youth offending team in whose area it appears to the applicant that the respondent lives, or
(b) if it appears to the applicant that the respondent lives in more than one such area, whichever one or more of the relevant youth offending teams the applicant thinks it appropriate to consult;

'on-notice hearing' means a hearing of which notice has been given to the applicant and the respondent in accordance with rules of court;

'without-notice application' means an application made without notice under section 6.

15 Appeals against decisions of youth courts

(1) An appeal lies to the Crown Court against a decision of a youth court made under this Part.

(2) On an appeal under this section the Crown Court may make –

(a) whatever orders are necessary to give effect to its determination of the appeal;
(b) whatever incidental or consequential orders appear to it to be just.

(3) An order of the Crown Court made on an appeal under this section (other than one directing that an application be re-heard by the youth court) is to be treated for the purposes of section 8 as an order of the youth court.

16 Special measures for witnesses

(1) Chapter 1 of Part 2 of the Youth Justice and Criminal Evidence Act 1999 (special measures directions in the case of vulnerable and intimidated witnesses) applies to proceedings under this Part as it applies to criminal proceedings, but with –

(a) the omission of the provisions of that Act mentioned in subsection (2) (which make provision appropriate only in the context of criminal proceedings), and
(b) any other necessary modifications.

(2) The provisions are –

(a) section 17(4) to (7);
(b) section 21(4C)(e);
(c) section 22A;
(d) section 27(10);
(e) section 32.

(3) Rules of court made under or for the purposes of Chapter 1 of Part 2 of that Act apply to proceedings under this Part –

(a) to the extent provided by rules of court, and
(b) subject to any modifications provided by rules of court.

(4) Section 47 of that Act (restrictions on reporting special measures directions etc) applies with any necessary modifications –

(a) to a direction under section 19 of that Act as applied by this section;
(b) to a direction discharging or varying such a direction.

Sections 49 and 51 of that Act (offences) apply accordingly.

17 Children and young persons: disapplication of reporting restrictions

Section 49 of the Children and Young Persons Act 1933 (restrictions on reports of proceedings in which children and young persons are concerned) does not apply to proceedings under this Part.

18 Rules of court

(1) Rules of court may provide that an appeal from a decision of the High Court, the county court or a youth court –

(a) to dismiss an application for an injunction under section 1 made without notice being given to the respondent, or
(b) to refuse to grant an interim injunction when adjourning proceedings following such an application,

may be made without notice being given to the respondent.

(2) Rules of court may provide for a youth court to give permission for an application for an injunction under section 1 against a person aged 18 or over to be made to the youth court if –

(a) an application to the youth court has been made, or is to be made, for an injunction under that section against a person aged under 18, and
(b) the youth court thinks that it would be in the interests of justice for the applications to be heard together.

(3) In relation to a respondent attaining the age of 18 after proceedings under this Part have begun, rules of court may –

(a) provide for the transfer of the proceedings from the youth court to the High Court or the county court;
(b) prescribe circumstances in which the proceedings may or must remain in the youth court.

19 Guidance

(1) The Secretary of State may issue guidance to persons entitled to apply for injunctions under section 1 (see section 5) about the exercise of their functions under this Part.

(2) The Secretary of State may revise any guidance issued under this section.

(3) The Secretary of State must arrange for any guidance issued or revised under this section to be published.

20 Interpretation etc

(1) In this Part –

'anti-social behaviour' has the meaning given by section 2;
'harm' includes serious ill-treatment or abuse, whether physical or not;
'housing accommodation' includes –

(a) flats, lodging-houses and hostels;
(b) any yard, garden, outhouses and appurtenances belonging to the accommodation or usually enjoyed with it;
(c) any common areas used in connection with the accommodation;

'housing provider' means –

(a) a housing trust, within the meaning given by section 2 of the Housing Associations Act 1985, that is a charity;
(b) a housing action trust established under section 62 of the Housing Act 1988;
(c) in relation to England, a non-profit private registered provider of social housing;
(d) in relation to Wales, a Welsh body registered as a social landlord under section 3 of the Housing Act 1996;
(e) any body (other than a local authority or a body within paragraphs (a) to (d)) that is a landlord under a secure tenancy within the meaning given by section 79 of the Housing Act 1985;

'local authority' means –

(a) in relation to England, a district council, a county council, a London borough council, the Common Council of the City of London or the Council of the Isles of Scilly;
(b) in relation to Wales, a county council or a county borough council;

'respondent' has the meaning given by section 1(1).

(2) A person's age is treated for the purposes of this Part as being that which it appears to the court to be after considering any available evidence.

21 Saving and transitional provision

(1) In this section 'existing order' means any of the following injunctions and orders –

- (a) an anti-social behaviour injunction under section 153A of the Housing Act 1996;
- (b) an injunction under section 153B of that Act (injunction against unlawful use of premises);
- (c) an injunction in which anything is included by virtue of section 153D(3) or (4) of that Act (power to include provision banning person from premises or area, or to include power of arrest, in injunction against breach of tenancy agreement);
- (d) an order under section 1 or 1B of the Crime and Disorder Act 1998 (anti-social behaviour orders etc);
- (e) an individual support order under section 1AA of that Act made in connection with an order under section 1 or 1B of that Act;
- (f) an intervention order under section 1G of that Act;
- (g) a drinking banning order under section 3 or 4 of the Violent Crime Reduction Act 2006.

(2) The repeal or amendment by this Act of provisions about any of the existing orders specified in subsection (1)(a) to (d), (f) and (g) does not apply in relation to –

- (a) an application made before the commencement day for an existing order;
- (b) an existing order (whether made before or after that day) applied for before that day;
- (c) anything done in connection with such an application or order.

(3) The repeal or amendment by this Act of provisions about an order specified in subsection (1)(e) does not apply in relation to –

- (a) an individual support order made before the commencement day;
- (b) anything done in connection with such an order.

(4) As from the commencement day there may be no variation of an existing order that extends the period of the order or of any of its provisions.

(5) At the end of the period of 5 years beginning with the commencement day –

- (a) in relation to any of the existing orders specified in subsection (1)(a), (b) and (d) to (g) that is still in force, this Part has effect, with any necessary modifications (and with any modifications specified in an order under section 185(7)), as if the provisions of the order were provisions of an injunction under section 1;
- (b) the provisions of this Part set out in subsection (6) apply to any injunction specified in subsection (1)(c) that is still in force as they apply to an injunction under section 1;
- (c) subsections (2) to (4) cease to have effect.

(6) The provisions referred to in subsection (5)(b) are –

- (a) section 1(7);
- (b) sections 4(2) and 9 (if a power of arrest is attached);
- (c) sections 6 to 8;
- (d) section 10;
- (e) section 11 and Schedule 1;
- (f) section 12 and Schedule 2;
- (g) section 18(1).

(7) In deciding whether to grant an injunction under section 1 a court may take account of conduct occurring up to 6 months before the commencement day.

(8) In this section 'commencement day' means the day on which this Part comes into force.

PART 2
CRIMINAL BEHAVIOUR ORDERS

Criminal behaviour orders

22 Power to make orders

(1) This section applies where a person ('the offender') is convicted of an offence.

(2) The court may make a criminal behaviour order against the offender if two conditions are met.

(3) The first condition is that the court is satisfied, beyond reasonable doubt, that the offender has engaged in behaviour that caused or was likely to cause harassment, alarm or distress to any person.

(4) The second condition is that the court considers that making the order will help in preventing the offender from engaging in such behaviour.

(5) A criminal behaviour order is an order which, for the purpose of preventing the offender from engaging in such behaviour –

(a) prohibits the offender from doing anything described in the order;
(b) requires the offender to do anything described in the order.

(6) The court may make a criminal behaviour order against the offender only if it is made in addition to –

(a) a sentence imposed in respect of the offence, or
(b) an order discharging the offender conditionally.

(7) The court may make a criminal behaviour order against the offender only on the application of the prosecution.

(8) The prosecution must find out the views of the local youth offending team before applying for a criminal behaviour order to be made if the offender will be under the age of 18 when the application is made.

(9) Prohibitions and requirements in a criminal behaviour order must, so far as practicable, be such as to avoid –

(a) any interference with the times, if any, at which the offender normally works or attends school or any other educational establishment;
(b) any conflict with the requirements of any other court order or injunction to which the offender may be subject.

(10) In this section 'local youth offending team' means –

(a) the youth offending team in whose area it appears to the prosecution that the offender lives, or
(b) if it appears to the prosecution that the offender lives in more than one such area, whichever one or more of the relevant youth offending teams the prosecution thinks appropriate.

23 Proceedings on an application for an order

(1) For the purpose of deciding whether to make a criminal behaviour order the court may consider evidence led by the prosecution and evidence led by the offender.

(2) It does not matter whether the evidence would have been admissible in the proceedings in which the offender was convicted.

(3) The court may adjourn any proceedings on an application for a criminal behaviour order even after sentencing the offender.

(4) If the offender does not appear for any adjourned proceedings the court may –

- (a) further adjourn the proceedings,
- (b) issue a warrant for the offender's arrest, or
- (c) hear the proceedings in the offender's absence.

(5) The court may not act under paragraph (b) of subsection (4) unless it is satisfied that the offender has had adequate notice of the time and place of the adjourned proceedings.

(6) The court may not act under paragraph (c) of subsection (4) unless it is satisfied that the offender –

- (a) has had adequate notice of the time and place of the adjourned proceedings, and
- (b) has been informed that if the offender does not appear for those proceedings the court may hear the proceedings in his or her absence.

(7) Subsection (8) applies in relation to proceedings in which a criminal behaviour order is made against an offender who is under the age of 18.

(8) In so far as the proceedings relate to the making of the order –

- (a) section 49 of the Children and Young Persons Act 1933 (restrictions on reports of proceedings in which children and young persons are concerned) does not apply in respect of the offender;
- (b) section 39 of that Act (power to prohibit publication of certain matters) does so apply.

24 Requirements included in orders

(1) A criminal behaviour order that includes a requirement must specify the person who is to be responsible for supervising compliance with the requirement.

The person may be an individual or an organisation.

(2) Before including a requirement, the court must receive evidence about its suitability and enforceability from –

- (a) the individual to be specified under subsection (1), if an individual is to be specified;
- (b) an individual representing the organisation to be specified under subsection (1), if an organisation is to be specified.

(3) Before including two or more requirements, the court must consider their compatibility with each other.

(4) It is the duty of a person specified under subsection (1) –

- (a) to make any necessary arrangements in connection with the requirements for which the person has responsibility (the 'relevant requirements');
- (b) to promote the offender's compliance with the relevant requirements;
- (c) if the person considers that the offender –
  - (i) has complied with all the relevant requirements, or
  - (ii) has failed to comply with a relevant requirement,

  to inform the prosecution and the appropriate chief officer of police.

(5) In subsection (4)(c) 'the appropriate chief officer of police' means –

- (a) the chief officer of police for the police area in which it appears to the person specified under subsection (1) that the offender lives, or
- (b) if it appears to that person that the offender lives in more than one police area, whichever of the relevant chief officers of police that person thinks it most appropriate to inform.

(6) An offender subject to a requirement in a criminal behaviour order must –

(a) keep in touch with the person specified under subsection (1) in relation to that requirement, in accordance with any instructions given by that person from time to time;
(b) notify the person of any change of address.

These obligations have effect as requirements of the order.

25 Duration of order etc

(1) A criminal behaviour order takes effect on the day it is made, subject to subsection (2).

(2) If on the day a criminal behaviour order ('the new order') is made the offender is subject to another criminal behaviour order ('the previous order'), the new order may be made so as to take effect on the day on which the previous order ceases to have effect.

(3) A criminal behaviour order must specify the period ('the order period') for which it has effect.

(4) In the case of a criminal behaviour order made before the offender has reached the age of 18, the order period must be a fixed period of –

(a) not less than 1 year, and
(b) not more than 3 years.

(5) In the case of a criminal behaviour order made after the offender has reached the age of 18, the order period must be –

(a) a fixed period of not less than 2 years, or
(b) an indefinite period (so that the order has effect until further order).

(6) A criminal behaviour order may specify periods for which particular prohibitions or requirements have effect.

Interim orders

26 Interim orders

(1) This section applies where a court adjourns the hearing of an application for a criminal behaviour order.

(2) The court may make a criminal behaviour order that lasts until the final hearing of the application or until further order ('an interim order') if the court thinks it just to do so.

(3) Section 22(6) to (8) and section 25(3) to (5) do not apply in relation to the making of an interim order.

(4) Subject to that, the court has the same powers whether or not the criminal behaviour order is an interim order.

Variation and discharge

27 Variation or discharge of orders

(1) A criminal behaviour order may be varied or discharged by the court which made it on the application of –

(a) the offender, or
(b) the prosecution.

(2) If an application by the offender under this section is dismissed, the offender may make no further application under this section without –

(a) the consent of the court which made the order, or
(b) the agreement of the prosecution.

(3) If an application by the prosecution under this section is dismissed, the prosecution may make no further application under this section without –

(a) the consent of the court which made the order, or
(b) the agreement of the offender.

(4) The power to vary an order includes power to include an additional prohibition or requirement in the order or to extend the period for which a prohibition or requirement has effect.

(5) Section 24 applies to additional requirements included under subsection (4) as it applies to requirements included in a new order.

(6) In the case of a criminal behaviour order made by a magistrates' court, the references in this section to the court which made the order include a reference to any magistrates' court acting in the same local justice area as that court.

Review of orders (under-18s)

28 Review of orders

(1) If –

(a) a person subject to a criminal behaviour order will be under the age of 18 at the end of a review period (see subsection (2)),
(b) the term of the order runs until the end of that period or beyond, and
(c) the order is not discharged before the end of that period,

a review of the operation of the order must be carried out before the end of that period.

(2) The 'review periods' are –

(a) the period of 12 months beginning with –

(i) the day on which the criminal behaviour order takes effect, or
(ii) if during that period the order is varied under section 27, the day on which it is varied (or most recently varied, if the order is varied more than once);

(b) a period of 12 months beginning with –

(i) the day after the end of the previous review period, or
(ii) if during that period of 12 months the order is varied under section 27, the day on which it is varied (or most recently varied, if the order is varied more than once).

(3) A review under this section must include consideration of –

(a) the extent to which the offender has complied with the order;
(b) the adequacy of any support available to the offender to help him or her comply with it;
(c) any matters relevant to the question whether an application should be made for the order to be varied or discharged.

(4) Those carrying out or participating in a review under this section must have regard to any relevant guidance issued by the Secretary of State under section 32 when considering –

(a) how the review should be carried out;
(b) what particular matters the review should deal with;
(c) what action (if any) it would be appropriate to take as a result of the findings of the review.

29 Carrying out and participating in reviews

(1) A review under section 28 is to be carried out by the chief officer of police of the police force maintained for the police area in which the offender lives or appears to be living.

(2) The chief officer, in carrying out a review under section 28, must act in co-operation with the council for the local government area in which the offender lives or appears to be living; and the council must co-operate in the carrying out of the review.

(3) The chief officer may invite the participation in the review of any other person or body.

(4) In this section 'local government area' means –

(a) in relation to England, a district or London borough, the City of London, the Isle of Wight and the Isles of Scilly;
(b) in relation to Wales, a county or a county borough.

For the purposes of this section, the council for the Inner and Middle Temples is the Common Council of the City of London.

Breach of orders

30 Breach of order

(1) A person who without reasonable excuse –

(a) does anything he or she is prohibited from doing by a criminal behaviour order, or
(b) fails to do anything he or she is required to do by a criminal behaviour order,

commits an offence.

(2) A person guilty of an offence under this section is liable –

(a) on summary conviction, to imprisonment for a period not exceeding 6 months or to a fine, or to both;
(b) on conviction on indictment, to imprisonment for a period not exceeding 5 years or to a fine, or to both.

(3) If a person is convicted of an offence under this section, it is not open to the court by or before which the person is convicted to make an order under subsection (1)(b) of section 12 of the Powers of Criminal Courts (Sentencing) Act 2000 (conditional discharge).

(4) In proceedings for an offence under this section, a copy of the original criminal behaviour order, certified by the proper officer of the court which made it, is admissible as evidence of its having been made and of its contents to the same extent that oral evidence of those things is admissible in those proceedings.

(5) In relation to any proceedings for an offence under this section that are brought against a person under the age of 18 –

(a) section 49 of the Children and Young Persons Act 1933 (restrictions on reports of proceedings in which children and young persons are concerned) does not apply in respect of the person;
(b) section 45 of the Youth Justice and Criminal Evidence Act 1999 (power to restrict reporting of criminal proceedings involving persons under 18) does so apply.

(6) If, in relation to any proceedings mentioned in subsection (5), the court does exercise its power to give a direction under section 45 of the Youth Justice and Criminal Evidence Act 1999, it must give its reasons for doing so.

Supplemental

31 Special measures for witnesses

(1) Chapter 1 of Part 2 of the Youth Justice and Criminal Evidence Act 1999 (special measures directions in the case of vulnerable and intimidated witnesses) applies to criminal behaviour order proceedings as it applies to criminal proceedings, but with –

- (a) the omission of the provisions of that Act mentioned in subsection (2) (which make provision appropriate only in the context of criminal proceedings), and
- (b) any other necessary modifications.

(2) The provisions are –

- (a) section 17(4) to (7);
- (b) section 21(4C)(e);
- (c) section 22A;
- (d) section 27(10);
- (e) section 32.

(3) Rules of court made under or for the purposes of Chapter 1 of Part 2 of that Act apply to criminal behaviour order proceedings –

- (a) to the extent provided by rules of court, and
- (b) subject to any modifications provided by rules of court.

(4) Section 47 of that Act (restrictions on reporting special measures directions etc) applies with any necessary modifications –

- (a) to a direction under section 19 of that Act as applied by this section;
- (b) to a direction discharging or varying such a direction.

Sections 49 and 51 of that Act (offences) apply accordingly.

(5) In this section 'criminal behaviour order proceedings' means proceedings in a magistrates' court or the Crown Court so far as relating to the issue whether to make a criminal behaviour order.

32 Guidance

(1) The Secretary of State may issue guidance to –

- (a) chief officers of police, and
- (b) the councils mentioned in section 29(2),

about the exercise of their functions under this Part.

(2) The Secretary of State may revise any guidance issued under this section.

(3) The Secretary of State must arrange for any guidance issued or revised under this section to be published.

33 Saving and transitional provision

(1) The repeal or amendment by this Act of provisions about any of the orders specified in subsection (2) does not –

- (a) prevent an order specified in that subsection from being made in connection with criminal proceedings begun before the commencement day;
- (b) apply in relation to an order specified in that subsection which is made in connection with criminal proceedings begun before that day;

(c) apply in relation to anything done in connection with such an order.

(2) The orders are –

(a) an order under section 1C of the Crime and Disorder Act 1998 (orders on conviction in criminal proceedings);
(b) an individual support order under section 1AA of that Act made in connection with an order under section 1C of that Act;
(c) a drinking banning order under section 6 of the Violent Crime Reduction Act 2006 (orders on conviction in criminal proceedings).

(3) As from the commencement day there may be no variation of an order specified in subsection (2) that extends the period of the order or of any provision of the order.

(4) At the end of the period of 5 years beginning with the commencement day –

(a) this Part has effect in relation to any order specified in subsection (2) that is still in force as if the provisions of the order were provisions of a criminal behaviour order;
(b) subsections (1) to (3) cease to have effect.

This Part, as it applies by virtue of paragraph (a), has effect with any necessary modifications (and with any modifications specified in an order under section 185(7)).

(5) In deciding whether to make a criminal behaviour order a court may take account of conduct occurring up to 1 year before the commencement day.

(6) In this section 'commencement day' means the day on which this Part comes into force.

PART 3

DISPERSAL POWERS

34 Authorisations to use powers under section 35

(1) A police officer of at least the rank of inspector may authorise the use in a specified locality, during a specified period of not more than 48 hours, of the powers given by section 35.

'Specified' means specified in the authorisation.

(2) An officer may give such an authorisation only if satisfied on reasonable grounds that the use of those powers in the locality during that period may be necessary for the purpose of removing or reducing the likelihood of –

(a) members of the public in the locality being harassed, alarmed or distressed, or
(b) the occurrence in the locality of crime or disorder.

(3) In deciding whether to give such an authorisation an officer must have particular regard to the rights of freedom of expression and freedom of assembly set out in articles 10 and 11 of the Convention.

'Convention' has the meaning given by section 21(1) of the Human Rights Act 1998.

(4) An authorisation under this section –

(a) must be in writing,
(b) must be signed by the officer giving it, and
(c) must specify the grounds on which it is given

35 Directions excluding a person from an area

(1) If the conditions in subsections (2) and (3) are met and an authorisation is in force under section 34, a constable in uniform may direct a person who is in a public place in the locality specified in the authorisation –

- (a) to leave the locality (or part of the locality), and
- (b) not to return to the locality (or part of the locality) for the period specified in the direction ('the exclusion period').

(2) The first condition is that the constable has reasonable grounds to suspect that the behaviour of the person in the locality has contributed or is likely to contribute to –

- (a) members of the public in the locality being harassed, alarmed or distressed, or
- (b) the occurrence in the locality of crime or disorder.

(3) The second condition is that the constable considers that giving a direction to the person is necessary for the purpose of removing or reducing the likelihood of the events mentioned in subsection (2)(a) or (b).

(4) The exclusion period may not exceed 48 hours.

The period may expire after (as long as it begins during) the period specified in the authorisation under section 34.

(5) A direction under this section –

- (a) must be given in writing, unless that is not reasonably practicable;
- (b) must specify the area to which it relates;
- (c) may impose requirements as to the time by which the person must leave the area and the manner in which the person must do so (including the route).

(6) The constable must (unless it is not reasonably practicable) tell the person to whom the direction is given that failing without reasonable excuse to comply with the direction is an offence.

(7) If the constable reasonably believes that the person to whom the direction is given is under the age of 16, the constable may remove the person to a place where the person lives or a place of safety.

(8) Any constable may withdraw or vary a direction under this section; but a variation must not extend the duration of a direction beyond 48 hours from when it was first given.

(9) Notice of a withdrawal or variation of a direction –

- (a) must be given to the person to whom the direction was given, unless that is not reasonably practicable, and
- (b) if given, must be given in writing unless that is not reasonably practicable.

(10) In this section 'public place' means a place to which at the material time the public or a section of the public has access, on payment or otherwise, as of right or by virtue of express or implied permission.

(11) In this Part 'exclusion period' has the meaning given by subsection (1)(b).

36 Restrictions

(1) A constable may not give a direction under section 35 to a person who appears to the constable to be under the age of 10.

(2) A constable may not give a direction under section 35 that prevents the person to whom it is given having access to a place where the person lives.

(3) A constable may not give a direction under section 35 that prevents the person to whom it is given attending at a place which the person is –

(a) required to attend for the purposes of the person's employment, or a contract of services to which the person is a party,
(b) required to attend by an obligation imposed by or under an enactment or by the order of a court or tribunal, or
(c) expected to attend for the purposes of education or training or for the purposes of receiving medical treatment,

at a time when the person is required or expected (as the case may be) to attend there.

(4) A constable may not give a direction to a person under section 35 if the person is one of a group of persons who are –

(a) engaged in conduct that is lawful under section 220 of the Trade Union and Labour Relations (Consolidation) Act 1992 (peaceful picketing), or
(b) taking part in a public procession of the kind mentioned in subsection (1) of section 11 of the Public Order Act 1986 in respect of which –
   (i) written notice has been given in accordance with that section, or
   (ii) written notice is not required to be given as provided by subsections (1) and (2) of that section.

(5) In deciding whether to give a direction under section 35 a constable must have particular regard to the rights of freedom of expression and freedom of assembly set out in articles 10 and 11 of the Convention.

'Convention' has the meaning given by section 21(1) of the Human Rights Act 1998.

37 Surrender of property

(1) A constable who gives a person a direction under section 35 may also direct the person to surrender to the constable any item in the person's possession or control that the constable reasonably believes has been used or is likely to be used in behaviour that harasses, alarms or distresses members of the public.

(2) A direction under this section must be given in writing, unless that is not reasonably practicable.

(3) A constable who gives a person a direction under this section must (unless it is not reasonably practicable) –

(a) tell the person that failing without reasonable excuse to comply with the direction is an offence, and
(b) give the person information in writing about when and how the person may recover the surrendered item.

(4) The surrendered item must not be returned to the person before the end of the exclusion period.

(5) If after the end of that period the person asks for the item to be returned, it must be returned (unless there is power to retain it under another enactment).

(6) But if it appears to a constable that the person is under the age of 16 and is not accompanied by a parent or other responsible adult, the item may be retained until the person is so accompanied.

(7) If the person has not asked for the return of the item before the end of the period of 28 days beginning with the day on which the direction was given, the item may be destroyed or otherwise disposed of.

38 Record-keeping

(1) A constable who gives a direction under section 35 must make a record of –

(a) the individual to whom the direction is given,

(b) the time at which the direction is given, and
(c) the terms of the direction (including in particular the area to which it relates and the exclusion period).

(2) A constable who withdraws or varies a direction under section 35 must make a record of –

(a) the time at which the direction is withdrawn or varied,
(b) whether notice of the withdrawal or variation is given to the person to whom the direction was given and if it is, at what time, and
(c) if the direction is varied, the terms of the variation.

(3) A constable who gives a direction under section 37 must make a record of –

(a) the individual to whom the direction is given,
(b) the time at which the direction is given, and
(c) the item to which the direction relates.

39 Offences

(1) A person given a direction under section 35 who fails without reasonable excuse to comply with it commits an offence.

(2) A person guilty of an offence under subsection (1) is liable on summary conviction –

(a) to imprisonment for a period not exceeding 3 months, or
(b) to a fine not exceeding level 4 on the standard scale,

(3) A person given a direction under section 37 who fails without reasonable excuse to comply with it commits an offence.

(4) A person guilty of an offence under subsection (3) is liable on summary conviction to a fine not exceeding level 2 on the standard scale.

40 Powers of community support officers

(1) Schedule 4 to the Police Reform Act 2002 (powers of community support officers) is amended as follows.

(2) In paragraph 2(6), for paragraph (aa) there is substituted –

'(aa) an offence under section 39 of the Anti-social Behaviour, Crime and Policing Act 2014;'.

(3) For paragraph 4A of Schedule 4 there is substituted –

'4A

Where a designation applies this paragraph to a person, that person has within the relevant police area the powers conferred on a constable by section 35 of the Anti-social Behaviour, Crime and Policing Act 2014.

4AB

(1) Where a designation applies this paragraph to a person, that person has within the relevant police area the powers conferred on a constable by section 37 of the Anti-social Behaviour, Crime and Policing Act 2014.

(2) A designation may not apply this paragraph to a person unless a designation also applies paragraph 4A to that person.'

41 Guidance

(1) The Secretary of State may issue guidance to chief officers of police about the exercise, by officers under their direction or control, of those officers' functions under this Part.

(2) The Secretary of State may revise any guidance issued under this section.

(3) The Secretary of State must arrange for any guidance issued or revised under this section to be published.

42 Saving and transitional provision

(1) The repeal by this Act of Part 4 of the Anti-social Behaviour Act 2003, and the repeal or amendment by this Act of provisions related to that Part, do not apply in relation to –

(a) an authorisation given under section 30(2) of that Act before the commencement day, or
(b) anything done in connection with such an authorisation.

(2) The repeal by this Act of section 27 of the Violent Crime Reduction Act 2006, and the repeal or amendment by this Act of provisions related to that section, do not apply in relation to –

(a) a direction given under that section before the commencement day, or
(b) anything done in connection with such a direction.

(3) In this section 'commencement day' means the day on which this Part comes into force.

PART 4
COMMUNITY PROTECTION

Chapter 1
Community Protection Notices

Community protection notices

43 Power to issue notices

(1) An authorised person may issue a community protection notice to an individual aged 16 or over, or a body, if satisfied on reasonable grounds that –

(a) the conduct of the individual or body is having a detrimental effect, of a persistent or continuing nature, on the quality of life of those in the locality, and
(b) the conduct is unreasonable.

(2) In subsection (1) 'authorised person' means a person on whom section 53 (or an enactment amended by that section) confers power to issue community protection notices.

(3) A community protection notice is a notice that imposes any of the following requirements on the individual or body issued with it –

(a) a requirement to stop doing specified things;
(b) a requirement to do specified things;
(c) a requirement to take reasonable steps to achieve specified results.

(4) The only requirements that may be imposed are ones that are reasonable to impose in order –

(a) to prevent the detrimental effect referred to in subsection (1) from continuing or recurring, or
(b) to reduce that detrimental effect or to reduce the risk of its continuance or recurrence.

(5) A person (A) may issue a community protection notice to an individual or body (B) only if –

(a) B has been given a written warning that the notice will be issued unless B's conduct ceases to have the detrimental effect referred to in subsection (1), and
(b) A is satisfied that, despite B having had enough time to deal with the matter, B's conduct is still having that effect.

(6) A person issuing a community protection notice must before doing so inform any body or individual the person thinks appropriate.

(7) A community protection notice must –

(a) identify the conduct referred to in subsection (1);
(b) explain the effect of sections 46 to 51.

(8) A community protection notice may specify periods within which, or times by which, requirements within subsection (3)(b) or (c) are to be complied with.

44 Occupiers of premises etc

(1) Conduct on, or affecting, premises (other than premises within subsection (2)) that a particular person –

(a) owns,
(b) leases,
(c) occupies,
(d) controls,
(e) operates, or
(f) maintains,

is treated for the purposes of section 43 as conduct of that person.

(2) Conduct on, or affecting, premises occupied for the purposes of a government department is treated for the purposes of section 43 as conduct of the Minister in charge of that department.

(3) This section does not treat an individual's conduct as that of another person if that person cannot reasonably be expected to control or affect it.

45 Occupier or owner unascertainable

(1) This section applies where –

(a) an authorised person has power to issue a community protection notice,
(b) the detrimental effect referred to in section 43(1) arises from the condition of premises or the use to which premises have been put, and
(c) the authorised person has made reasonable enquiries to find out the name or proper address of the occupier of the premises (or, if the premises are unoccupied, the owner) but without success.

(2) The authorised person may –

(a) post the community protection notice on the premises;
(b) enter the premises, or other premises, to the extent reasonably necessary for that purpose.

(3) The community protection notice is treated as having been issued to the occupier of the premises (or, if the premises are unoccupied, the owner) at the time the notice is posted.

(4) In this section 'authorised person' has the same meaning as in section 43(1).

46 Appeals against notices

(1) A person issued with a community protection notice may appeal to a magistrates' court against the notice on any of the following grounds.

1. That the conduct specified in the community protection notice –

   (a) did not take place,
   (b) has not had a detrimental effect on the quality of life of those in the locality,
   (c) has not been of a persistent or continuing nature,
   (d) is not unreasonable, or
   (e) is conduct that the person cannot reasonably be expected to control or affect.

2. That any of the requirements in the notice, or any of the periods within which or times by which they are to be complied with, are unreasonable.
3. That there is a material defect or error in, or in connection with, the notice.
4. That the notice was issued to the wrong person.

(2) An appeal must be made within the period of 21 days beginning with the day on which the person is issued with the notice.

(3) While an appeal against a community protection notice is in progress –

(a) a requirement imposed by the notice to stop doing specified things remains in effect, unless the court orders otherwise, but
(b) any other requirement imposed by the notice is of no effect.

For this purpose an appeal is 'in progress' until it is finally determined or is withdrawn.

(4) A magistrates' court hearing an appeal against a community protection notice must –

(a) quash the notice,
(b) modify the notice (for example by extending a period specified in it), or
(c) dismiss the appeal.

Failure to comply with notice

47 Remedial action by local authority

(1) Where a person issued with a community protection notice ('the defaulter') fails to comply with a requirement of the notice, the relevant local authority may take action under subsection (2) or subsection (3) (or both).

(2) The relevant local authority may have work carried out to ensure that the failure is remedied, but only on land that is open to the air.

(3) As regards premises other than land open to the air, if the relevant local authority issues the defaulter with a notice –

(a) specifying work it intends to have carried out to ensure that the failure is remedied,
(b) specifying the estimated cost of the work, and
(c) inviting the defaulter to consent to the work being carried out,

the authority may have the work carried out if the necessary consent is given.

(4) In subsection (3) 'the necessary consent' means the consent of –

(a) the defaulter, and
(b) the owner of the premises on which the work is to be carried out (if that is not the defaulter).

Paragraph (b) does not apply where the relevant authority has made reasonable efforts to contact the owner of the premises but without success.

(5) A person authorised by a local authority to carry out work under this section may enter any premises to the extent reasonably necessary for that purpose, except that a person who is only authorised to carry out work under subsection (2) may only enter land that is open to the air.

(6) If work is carried out under subsection (2) or (3) and the relevant local authority issues a notice to the defaulter –

(a) giving details of the work that was carried out, and
(b) specifying an amount that is no more than the cost to the authority of having the work carried out,

the defaulter is liable to the authority for that amount (subject to the outcome of any appeal under subsection (7)).

(7) A person issued with a notice under subsection (6) may appeal to a magistrates' court, within the period of 21 days beginning with the day on which the notice was issued, on the ground that the amount specified under subsection (6)(b) is excessive.

(8) A magistrates' court hearing an appeal under subsection (7) must –

(a) confirm the amount, or
(b) substitute a lower amount.

(9) In this section 'the relevant local authority' means –

(a) the local authority that issued the community protection notice;
(b) if the community protection notice was not issued by a local authority, the local authority (or, as the case may be, one of the local authorities) that could have issued it.

48 Offence of failing to comply with notice

(1) A person issued with a community protection notice who fails to comply with it commits an offence.

(2) A person guilty of an offence under this section is liable on summary conviction –

(a) to a fine not exceeding level 4 on the standard scale, in the case of an individual;
(b) to a fine not exceeding £20,000, in the case of a body.

(3) A person does not commit an offence under this section if –

(a) the person took all reasonable steps to comply with the notice, or
(b) there is some other reasonable excuse for the failure to comply with it.

49 Remedial orders

(1) A court before which a person is convicted of an offence under section 48 in respect of a community protection notice may make whatever order the court thinks appropriate for ensuring that what the notice requires to be done is done.

(2) An order under this section may in particular require the defendant –

(a) to carry out specified work, or
(b) to allow specified work to be carried out by or on behalf of a specified local authority.

(3) To be specified under subsection (2)(b) a local authority must be –

(a) the local authority that issued the community protection notice;
(b) if the community protection notice was not issued by a local authority, the local authority (or, as the case may be, one of the local authorities) that could have issued it.

(4) A requirement imposed under subsection (2)(b) does not authorise the person carrying out the work to enter the defendant's home without the defendant's consent.

But this does not prevent a defendant who fails to give that consent from being in breach of the court's order.

(5) In subsection (4) 'the defendant's home' means the house, flat, vehicle or other accommodation where the defendant –

(a) usually lives, or
(b) is living at the time when the work is or would be carried out.

(6) If work is carried out under subsection (2)(b) and the local authority specified under that subsection issues a notice to the defaulter –

(a) giving details of the work that was carried out, and
(b) specifying an amount that is no more than the cost to the authority of having the work carried out,

the defaulter is liable to the authority for that amount (subject to the outcome of any appeal under subsection (7)).

(7) A person issued with a notice under subsection (6) may appeal to a magistrates' court, within the period of 21 days beginning with the day on which the notice was issued, on the ground that the amount specified under subsection (6)(b) is excessive.

(8) A magistrates' court hearing an appeal under subsection (7) must –

(a) confirm the amount, or
(b) substitute a lower amount.

50 Forfeiture of item used in commission of offence

(1) A court before which a person is convicted of an offence under section 48 may order the forfeiture of any item that was used in the commission of the offence.

(2) An order under this section may require a person in possession of the item to hand it over as soon as reasonably practicable –

(a) to a constable, or
(b) to a person employed by a local authority or designated by a local authority under section 53(1)(c).

(3) An order under this section may require the item –

(a) to be destroyed, or
(b) to be disposed of in whatever way the order specifies.

(4) Where an item ordered to be forfeited under this section is kept by or handed over to a constable, the police force of which the constable is a member must ensure that arrangements are made for its destruction or disposal, either –

(a) in accordance with the order, or
(b) if no arrangements are specified in the order, in whatever way seems appropriate to the police force.

(5) Where an item ordered to be forfeited under this section is kept by or handed over to a person within subsection (2)(b), the local authority by whom the person is employed or was designated must ensure that arrangements are made for its destruction or disposal, either –

(a) in accordance with the order, or
(b) if no arrangements are specified in the order, in whatever way seems appropriate to the local authority.

51 Seizure of item used in commission of offence

(1) If a justice of the peace is satisfied on information on oath that there are reasonable grounds for suspecting –

- (a) that an offence under section 48 has been committed, and
- (b) that there is an item used in the commission of the offence on premises specified in the information,

the justice may issue a warrant authorising any constable or designated person to enter the premises within 14 days from the date of issue of the warrant to seize the item.

(2) In this section 'designated person' means a person designated by a local authority under section 53(1)(c).

(3) A constable or designated person may use reasonable force, if necessary, in executing a warrant under this section.

(4) A constable or designated person who has seized an item under a warrant under this section –

- (a) may retain the item until any relevant criminal proceedings have been finally determined, if such proceedings are started before the end of the period of 28 days following the day on which the item was seized;
- (b) otherwise, must before the end of that period return the item to the person from whom it was seized.

(5) In subsection (4) 'relevant criminal proceedings' means proceedings for an offence under section 48 in the commission of which the item is alleged to have been used.

52 Fixed penalty notices

(1) An authorised person may issue a fixed penalty notice to anyone who that person has reason to believe has committed an offence under section 48.

(2) In subsection (1) 'authorised person' means a person on whom section 53 (or an enactment amended by that section) confers power to issue fixed penalty notices under this section.

(3) A fixed penalty notice is a notice offering the person to whom it is issued the opportunity of discharging any liability to conviction for the offence by payment of a fixed penalty to a local authority specified in the notice.

(4) The local authority specified under subsection (3) must be –

- (a) the local authority that issued the community protection notice to which the fixed penalty notice relates;
- (b) if the community protection notice was not issued by a local authority, the local authority (or, as the case may be, one of the local authorities) that could have issued it.

(5) Where a person is issued with a notice under this section in respect of an offence –

- (a) no proceedings may be taken for the offence before the end of the period of 14 days following the date of the notice;
- (b) the person may not be convicted of the offence if the person pays the fixed penalty before the end of that period.

(6) A fixed penalty notice must –

- (a) give reasonably detailed particulars of the circumstances alleged to constitute the offence;
- (b) state the period during which (because of subsection (5)(a)) proceedings will not be taken for the offence;
- (c) specify the amount of the fixed penalty;
- (d) state the name and address of the person to whom the fixed penalty may be paid;
- (e) specify permissible methods of payment.

(7) An amount specified under subsection (6)(c) must not be more than £100.

(8) A fixed penalty notice may specify two amounts under subsection (6)(c) and specify that, if the lower of those amounts is paid within a specified period (of less than 14 days), that is the amount of the fixed penalty.

(9) Whatever other method may be specified under subsection (6)(e), payment of a fixed penalty may be made by pre-paying and posting to the person whose name is stated under subsection (6)(d), at the stated address, a letter containing the amount of the penalty (in cash or otherwise).

(10) Where a letter is sent as mentioned in subsection (9), payment is regarded as having been made at the time at which that letter would be delivered in the ordinary course of post.

(11) In any proceedings, a certificate that –

- (a) purports to be signed by or on behalf of the chief finance officer of the local authority concerned, and
- (b) states that payment of a fixed penalty was, or was not, received by the dated specified in the certificate,

is evidence of the facts stated.

(12) In this section 'chief finance officer', in relation to a local authority, means the person with responsibility for the authority's financial affairs.

Who may issue notices

53 Authorised persons

(1) A community protection notice or a fixed penalty notice may be issued by –

- (a) a constable;
- (b) the relevant local authority (see subsections (2) and (3));
- (c) a person designated by the relevant local authority for the purposes of this section.

(2) For a community protection notice, 'the relevant local authority' means the local authority (or, as the case may be, any of the local authorities) within whose area the conduct specified in the notice has, according to the notice, been taking place.

(3) For a fixed penalty notice, 'the relevant local authority' means the local authority (or, as the case may be, any of the local authorities) within whose area the offence in question is alleged to have taken place.

(4) Only a person of a description specified in an order made by the Secretary of State for the purposes of subsection (1)(c) may be designated under that subsection.

(5) In Part 1 of Schedule 4 to the Police Reform Act 2002 (powers exercisable by community support officers), after paragraph 1ZA there is inserted –

> **'1ZB Power to issue community protection notices**
>
> A person shall have the power of a constable to issue a community protection notice under section 43 of the Anti-social Behaviour, Crime and Policing Act 2014 if –
>
> (a) a designation applies this paragraph to that person, and
> (b) the conduct specified in the notice has (according to the notice) been taking place within the relevant police area.'

(6) In paragraph 1 of that Schedule (power of community support officers to issue fixed penalty notices), after paragraph (ab) of sub-paragraph (2) there is inserted –

'(ac) the power of a constable to issue a fixed penalty notice under section 52 of the Anti-social Behaviour, Crime and Policing Act 2014 (fixed penalty notice in respect of failure to comply with community protection notice);'.

Supplemental

54 Exemption from liability

(1) A local authority exercising or purporting to exercise a power under section 47(2) is not liable to an occupier or owner of land for damages or otherwise (whether at common law or otherwise) arising out of anything done or omitted to be done in the exercise or purported exercise of that power.

(2) A person carrying out work under section 47(2), or a person by or on whose behalf work is carried out under section 49(2)(b), is not liable to an occupier or owner of land for damages or otherwise (whether at common law or otherwise) arising out of anything done or omitted to be done in carrying out that work.

(3) Subsections (1) and (2) do not apply –

- (a) to an act or omission shown to have been in bad faith, or
- (b) to liability arising out of a failure to exercise due care and attention.

(4) Subsections (1) and (2) do not apply so as to prevent an award of damages made in respect of an act or omission on the ground that the act or omission was unlawful by virtue of section 6(1) of the Human Rights Act 1998.

(5) This section does not affect any other exemption from liability (whether at common law or otherwise).

55 Issuing of notices

(1) A notice under this Chapter may be issued to a person by –

- (a) handing it to the person,
- (b) leaving it at the person's proper address, or
- (c) sending it by post to the person at that address.

(2) A notice under this Chapter to a body corporate may be issued to the secretary or clerk of that body.

(3) A notice under this Chapter to a partnership may be issued to a partner or a person who has the control or management of the partnership business.

(4) For the purposes of this section and of section 7 of the Interpretation Act 1978 (service of documents by post) in its application to this section, the proper address of a person is the person's last known address, except that –

- (a) in the case of a body corporate or its secretary or clerk, it is the address of the body's registered or principal office;
- (b) in the case of a partnership or person having the control or the management of the partnership business, it is the principal office of the partnership.

(5) For the purposes of subsection (4) the principal office of a company registered outside the United Kingdom, or of a partnership carrying on business outside the United Kingdom, is its principal office within the United Kingdom.

(6) If a person has specified an address in the United Kingdom, other than the person's proper address within the meaning of subsection (4), as the one at which the person or someone on the person's behalf will accept notices of the same description as a notice under this Chapter, that address is also treated for the purposes of this section and section 7 of the Interpretation Act 1978 as the person's proper address.

56 Guidance

(1) The Secretary of State may issue –

(a) guidance to chief officers of police about the exercise, by officers under their direction or control, of those officers' functions under this Chapter;

(b) guidance to local authorities about the exercise of their functions under this Chapter and those of persons designated under section 53(1)(c).

(2) The Secretary of State may revise any guidance issued under this section.

(3) The Secretary of State must arrange for any guidance issued or revised under this section to be published.

57 Interpretation of Chapter 1

In this Chapter –

'conduct' includes a failure to act;
'local authority' means –

(a) in relation to England, a district council, a county council for an area for which there is no district council, a London borough council, the Common Council of the City of London or the Council of the Isles of Scilly;

(b) in relation to Wales, a county council or a county borough council;

'owner', in relation to premises, means –

(a) a person (other than a mortgagee not in possession) entitled to dispose of the fee simple of the premises, whether in possession or in reversion;

(b) a person who holds or is entitled to the rents and profits of the premises under a lease that (when granted) was for a term of not less then 3 years;

'premises' includes any land.

58 Saving and transitional provision

(1) The repeal or amendment by this Act of provisions about any of the notices specified in subsection (2) does not apply in relation to –

(a) a notice specified in that subsection served before the commencement day;

(b) anything done in connection with such a notice.

(2) The notices are –

(a) a litter abatement notice under section 92 of the Environmental Protection Act 1990;

(b) a litter clearing notice under section 92A of that Act;

(c) a street litter control notice under section 93 of that Act;

(d) a defacement removal notice under section 48 of the Anti-social Behaviour Act 2003.

(3) A community protection notice that contains no requirement that could not have been contained in one of the notices specified in subsection (2) may be issued in respect of conduct before the commencement day.

(4) Subsection (3) applies only during the period of 3 months beginning with the commencement day.

(5) In this section 'commencement day' means the day on which this Chapter comes into force.

Chapter 2

Public Spaces Protection Orders

Public spaces protection orders

59 Power to make orders

(1) A local authority may make a public spaces protection order if satisfied on reasonable grounds that two conditions are met.

(2) The first condition is that –

- (a) activities carried on in a public place within the authority's area have had a detrimental effect on the quality of life of those in the locality, or
- (b) it is likely that activities will be carried on in a public place within that area and that they will have such an effect.

(3) The second condition is that the effect, or likely effect, of the activities –

- (a) is, or is likely to be, of a persistent or continuing nature,
- (b) is, or is likely to be, such as to make the activities unreasonable, and
- (c) justifies the restrictions imposed by the notice.

(4) A public spaces protection order is an order that identifies the public place referred to in subsection (2) ('the restricted area') and –

- (a) prohibits specified things being done in the restricted area,
- (b) requires specified things to be done by persons carrying on specified activities in that area, or
- (c) does both of those things.

(5) The only prohibitions or requirements that may be imposed are ones that are reasonable to impose in order –

- (a) to prevent the detrimental effect referred to in subsection (2) from continuing, occurring or recurring, or
- (b) to reduce that detrimental effect or to reduce the risk of its continuance, occurrence or recurrence.

(6) A prohibition or requirement may be framed –

- (a) so as to apply to all persons, or only to persons in specified categories, or to all persons except those in specified categories;
- (b) so as to apply at all times, or only at specified times, or at all times except those specified;
- (c) so as to apply in all circumstances, or only in specified circumstances, or in all circumstances except those specified.

(7) A public spaces protection order must –

- (a) identify the activities referred to in subsection (2);
- (b) explain the effect of section 63 (where it applies) and section 67;
- (c) specify the period for which the order has effect.

(8) A public spaces protection order must be published in accordance with regulations made by the Secretary of State.

60 Duration of orders

(1) A public spaces protection order may not have effect for a period of more than 3 years, unless extended under this section.

(2) Before the time when a public spaces protection order is due to expire, the local authority that made the order may extend the period for which it has effect if satisfied on reasonable grounds that doing so is necessary to prevent –

(a) occurrence or recurrence after that time of the activities identified in the order, or
(b) an increase in the frequency or seriousness of those activities after that time.

(3) An extension under this section –

(a) may not be for a period of more than 3 years.
(b) must be published in accordance with regulations made by the Secretary of State.

(4) A public spaces protection order may be extended under this section more than once.

61 Variation and discharge of orders

(1) Where a public spaces protection order is in force, the local authority that made the order may vary it –

(a) by increasing or reducing the restricted area;
(b) by altering or removing a prohibition or requirement included in the order, or adding a new one.

(2) A local authority may make a variation under subsection (1)(a) that results in the order applying to an area to which it did not previously apply only if the conditions in section 59(2) and (3) are met as regards activities in that area.

(3) A local authority may make a variation under subsection (1)(b) that makes a prohibition or requirement more extensive, or adds a new one, only if the prohibitions and requirements imposed by the order as varied are ones that section 59(5) allows to be imposed.

(4) A public spaces protection order may be discharged by the local authority that made it.

(5) Where an order is varied, the order as varied must be published in accordance with regulations made by the Secretary of State.

(6) Where an order is discharged, a notice identifying the order and stating the date when it ceases to have effect must be published in accordance with regulations made by the Secretary of State.

Prohibition on consuming alcohol

62 Premises etc to which alcohol prohibition does not apply

(1) A prohibition in a public spaces protection order on consuming alcohol does not apply to –

(a) premises (other than council-operated licensed premises) authorised by a premises licence to be used for the supply of alcohol;
(b) premises authorised by a club premises certificate to be used by the club for the supply of alcohol;
(c) a place within the curtilage of premises within paragraph (a) or (b);
(d) premises which by virtue of Part 5 of the Licensing Act 2003 may at the relevant time be used for the supply of alcohol or which, by virtue of that Part, could have been so used within the 30 minutes before that time;
(e) a place where facilities or activities relating to the sale or consumption of alcohol are at the relevant time permitted by virtue of a permission granted under section 115E of the Highways Act 1980 (highway-related uses).

(2) A prohibition in a public spaces protection order on consuming alcohol does not apply to council-operated licensed premises –

(a) when the premises are being used for the supply of alcohol, or

(b) within 30 minutes after the end of a period during which the premises have been used for the supply of alcohol.

(3) In this section –

'club premises certificate' has the meaning given by section 60 of the Licensing Act 2003;
'premises licence' has the meaning given by section 11 of that Act;
'supply of alcohol' has the meaning given by section 14 of that Act.

(4) For the purposes of this section, premises are 'council-operated licensed premises' if they are authorised by a premises licence to be used for the supply of alcohol and –

(a) the licence is held by a local authority in whose area the premises (or part of the premises) are situated, or
(b) the licence is held by another person but the premises are occupied by a local authority or are managed by or on behalf of a local authority.

63 Consumption of alcohol in breach of prohibition in order

(1) This section applies where a constable or an authorised person reasonably believes that a person (P) –

(a) is or has been consuming alcohol in breach of a prohibition in a public spaces protection order, or
(b) intends to consume alcohol in circumstances in which doing so would be a breach of such a prohibition.

In this section 'authorised person' means a person authorised for the purposes of this section by the local authority that made the public spaces protection order (or authorised by virtue of section 69(1)).

(2) The constable or authorised person may require P –

(a) not to consume, in breach of the order, alcohol or anything which the constable or authorised person reasonably believes to be alcohol;
(b) to surrender anything in P's possession which is, or which the constable or authorised person reasonably believes to be, alcohol or a container for alcohol.

(3) A constable or an authorised person who imposes a requirement under subsection (2) must tell P that failing without reasonable excuse to comply with the requirement is an offence.

(4) A requirement imposed by an authorised person under subsection (2) is not valid if the person –

(a) is asked by P to show evidence of his or her authorisation, and
(b) fails to do so.

(5) A constable or an authorised person may dispose of anything surrendered under subsection (2)(b) in whatever way he or she thinks appropriate.

(6) A person who fails without reasonable excuse to comply with a requirement imposed on him or her under subsection (2) commits an offence and is liable on summary conviction to a fine not exceeding level 2 on the standard scale.

Restrictions on public rights of way

64 Orders restricting public right of way over highway

(1) A local authority may not make a public spaces protection order that restricts the public right of way over a highway without considering –

(a) the likely effect of making the order on the occupiers of premises adjoining or adjacent to the highway;
(b) the likely effect of making the order on other persons in the locality;

(c) in a case where the highway constitutes a through route, the availability of a reasonably convenient alternative route.

(2) Before making such an order a local authority must –

(a) notify potentially affected persons of the proposed order,
(b) inform those persons how they can see a copy of the proposed order,
(c) notify those persons of the period within which they may make representations about the proposed order, and
(d) consider any representations made.

In this subsection 'potentially affected persons' means occupiers of premises adjacent to or adjoining the highway, and any other persons in the locality who are likely to be affected by the proposed order.

(3) Before a local authority makes a public spaces protection order restricting the public right of way over a highway that is also within the area of another local authority, it must consult that other authority if it thinks it appropriate to do so.

(4) A public spaces protection order may not restrict the public right of way over a highway for the occupiers of premises adjoining or adjacent to the highway.

(5) A public spaces protection order may not restrict the public right of way over a highway that is the only or principal means of access to a dwelling.

(6) In relation to a highway that is the only or principal means of access to premises used for business or recreational purposes, a public spaces protection order may not restrict the public right of way over the highway during periods when the premises are normally used for those purposes.

(7) A public spaces protection order that restricts the public right of way over a highway may authorise the installation, operation and maintenance of a barrier or barriers for enforcing the restriction.

(8) A local authority may install, operate and maintain barriers authorised under subsection (7).

(9) A highway over which the public right of way is restricted by a public spaces protection order does not cease to be regarded as a highway by reason of the restriction (or by reason of any barrier authorised under subsection (7)).

(10) In this section –

'dwelling' means a building or part of a building occupied, or intended to be occupied, as a separate dwelling;
'highway' has the meaning given by section 328 of the Highways Act 1980.

65 Categories of highway over which public right of way may not be restricted

(1) A public spaces protection order may not restrict the public right of way over a highway that is –

(a) a special road;
(b) a trunk road;
(c) a classified or principal road;
(d) a strategic road;
(e) a highway in England of a description prescribed by regulations made by the Secretary of State;
(f) a highway in Wales of a description prescribed by regulations made by the Welsh Ministers.

(2) In this section –

'classified road', 'special road' and 'trunk road' have the meaning given by section 329(1) of the Highways Act 1980;
'highway' has the meaning given by section 328 of that Act;
'principal road' has the meaning given by section 12 of that Act (and see section 13 of that Act);

'strategic road' has the meaning given by section 60(4) of the Traffic Management Act 2004.

Validity of orders

66 Challenging the validity of orders

(1) An interested person may apply to the High Court to question the validity of –

(a) a public spaces protection order, or
(b) a variation of a public spaces protection order.

'Interested person' means an individual who lives in the restricted area or who regularly works in or visits that area.

(2) The grounds on which an application under this section may be made are –

(a) that the local authority did not have power to make the order or variation, or to include particular prohibitions or requirements imposed by the order (or by the order as varied);
(b) that a requirement under this Chapter was not complied with in relation to the order or variation.

(3) An application under this section must be made within the period of 6 weeks beginning with the date on which the order or variation is made.

(4) On an application under this section the High Court may by order suspend the operation of the order or variation, or any of the prohibitions or requirements imposed by the order (or by the order as varied), until the final determination of the proceedings.

(5) If on an application under this section the High Court is satisfied that –

(a) the local authority did not have power to make the order or variation, or to include particular prohibitions or requirements imposed by the order (or by the order as varied), or
(b) the interests of the applicant have been substantially prejudiced by a failure to comply with a requirement under this Chapter,

the Court may quash the order or variation, or any of the prohibitions or requirements imposed by the order (or by the order as varied).

(6) A public spaces protection order, or any of the prohibitions or requirements imposed by the order (or by the order as varied), may be suspended under subsection (4) or quashed under subsection (5) –

(a) generally, or
(b) so far as necessary for the protection of the interests of the applicant.

(7) An interested person may not challenge the validity of a public spaces protection order, or of a variation of a public spaces protection order, in any legal proceedings (either before or after it is made) except –

(a) under this section, or
(b) under subsection (3) of section 67 (where the interested person is charged with an offence under that section).

Failure to comply with orders

67 Offence of failing to comply with order

(1) It is an offence for a person without reasonable excuse –

(a) to do anything that the person is prohibited from doing by a public spaces protection order, or
(b) to fail to comply with a requirement to which the person is subject under a public spaces protection order.

(2) A person guilty of an offence under this section is liable on summary conviction to a fine not exceeding level 3 on the standard scale.

(3) A person does not commit an offence under this section by failing to comply with a prohibition or requirement that the local authority did not have power to include in the public spaces protection order.

(4) Consuming alcohol in breach of a public spaces protection order is not an offence under this section (but see section 63).

68 Fixed penalty notices

(1) A constable or an authorised person may issue a fixed penalty notice to anyone he or she has reason to believe has committed an offence under section 63 or 67 in relation to a public spaces protection order.

(2) A fixed penalty notice is a notice offering the person to whom it is issued the opportunity of discharging any liability to conviction for the offence by payment of a fixed penalty to a local authority specified in the notice.

(3) The local authority specified under subsection (2) must be the one that made the public spaces protection order.

(4) Where a person is issued with a notice under this section in respect of an offence –

- (a) no proceedings may be taken for the offence before the end of the period of 14 days following the date of the notice;
- (b) the person may not be convicted of the offence if the person pays the fixed penalty before the end of that period.

(5) A fixed penalty notice must –

- (a) give reasonably detailed particulars of the circumstances alleged to constitute the offence;
- (b) state the period during which (because of subsection (4)(a)) proceedings will not be taken for the offence;
- (c) specify the amount of the fixed penalty;
- (d) state the name and address of the person to whom the fixed penalty may be paid;
- (e) specify permissible methods of payment.

(6) An amount specified under subsection (5)(c) must not be more than £100.

(7) A fixed penalty notice may specify two amounts under subsection (5)(c) and specify that, if the lower of those amounts is paid within a specified period (of less than 14 days), that is the amount of the fixed penalty.

(8) Whatever other method may be specified under subsection (5)(e), payment of a fixed penalty may be made by pre-paying and posting to the person whose name is stated under subsection (5)(d), at the stated address, a letter containing the amount of the penalty (in cash or otherwise).

(9) Where a letter is sent as mentioned in subsection (8), payment is regarded as having been made at the time at which that letter would be delivered in the ordinary course of post.

(10) In any proceedings, a certificate that –

- (a) purports to be signed by or on behalf of the chief finance officer of the local authority concerned, and
- (b) states that payment of a fixed penalty was, or was not, received by the dated specified in the certificate,

is evidence of the facts stated.

(11) In this section –

'authorised person' means a person authorised for the purposes of this section by the local authority that made the order (or authorised by virtue of section 69(2));
'chief finance officer,' in relation to a local authority, means the person with responsibility for the authority's financial affairs.

Supplemental

69 Powers of community support officers

(1) In Part 1 of Schedule 4 to the Police Reform Act 2002 (powers exercisable by community support officers), for paragraph 5 there is substituted –

'5 Alcohol consumption in restricted areas

Where a designation applies this paragraph to any person, that person shall, within the relevant police area, have the powers of a constable under section 63 of the Anti-social Behaviour, Crime and Policing Act 2014 (consumption of alcohol in breach of prohibition in public spaces protection order) –

(a) to impose a requirement under subsection (2) of that section; and
(b) to dispose under subsection (5) of that section of anything surrendered to the person;

and that section shall have effect in relation to the exercise of those powers by that person as if the references to a constable were references to that person.'

(2) In paragraph 1 of that Schedule (power of community support officers to issue fixed penalty notices), after paragraph (e) of sub-paragraph (2) there is inserted –

'(f) the power of a constable to issue a fixed penalty notice under section 68 of the Anti-social Behaviour, Crime and Policing Act 2014 (fixed penalty notice in respect of failure to comply with public spaces protection order).'

70 Byelaws

A byelaw that prohibits, by the creation of an offence, an activity regulated by a public spaces protection order is of no effect in relation to the restricted area during the currency of the order.

71 Bodies other than local authorities with statutory functions in relation to land

(1) The Secretary of State may by order –

(a) designate a person or body (other than a local authority) that has power to make byelaws in relation to particular land, and
(b) specify land in England to which the power relates.

(2) This Chapter has effect as if –

(a) a person or body designated under subsection (1) (a 'designated person') were a local authority, and
(b) land specified under that subsection were within its area.

But references in the rest of this section to a local authority are to a local authority that is not a designated person.

(3) The only prohibitions or requirements that may be imposed in a public spaces protection order made by a designated person are ones that it has power to impose (or would, but for section 70, have power to impose) by making a byelaw in respect of the restricted area.

(4) A public spaces protection order made by a designated person may not include provision regulating, in relation to a particular public space, an activity that is already regulated in relation to that space by a public spaces protection order made by a local authority.

(5) Where a public spaces protection order made by a local authority regulates, in relation to a particular public space, an activity that a public spaces protection order made by a designated person already regulates, the order made by the designated person ceases to have that effect.

(6) If a person or body that may be designated under subsection (1)(a) gives a notice in writing under this subsection, in respect of land in relation to which it has power to make byelaws, to a local authority in whose area the land is situated –

- (a) no part of the land may form, or fall within, the restricted area of any public spaces protection order made by the local authority;
- (b) if any part of the land –
    - (i) forms the restricted area of a public spaces protection order already made by the local authority, or
    - (ii) falls within such an area,

the order has ceases to have effect (where sub-paragraph (i) applies), or has effect as if the restricted area did not include the land in question (where sub-paragraph (ii) applies).

72 Convention rights, consultation, publicity and notification

(1) A local authority, in deciding –

- (a) whether to make a public spaces protection order (under section 59) and if so what it should include,
- (b) whether to extend the period for which a public spaces protection order has effect (under section 60) and if so for how long,
- (c) whether to vary a public spaces protection order (under section 61) and if so how, or
- (d) whether to discharge a public spaces protection order (under section 61),

must have particular regard to the rights of freedom of expression and freedom of assembly set out in articles 10 and 11 of the Convention.

(2) In subsection (1) 'Convention' has the meaning given by section 21(1) of the Human Rights Act 1998.

(3) A local authority must carry out the necessary consultation and the necessary publicity, and the necessary notification (if any), before –

- (a) making a public spaces protection order,
- (b) extending the period for which a public spaces protection order has effect, or
- (c) varying or discharging a public spaces protection order.

(4) In subsection (3) –

'the necessary consultation' means consulting with –

- (a) the chief officer of police, and the local policing body, for the police area that includes the restricted area;
- (b) whatever community representatives the local authority thinks it appropriate to consult;
- (c) the owner or occupier of land within the restricted area;

the necessary publicity' means –

- (a) in the case of a proposed order or variation, publishing the text of it;
- (b) in the case of a proposed extension or discharge, publicising the proposal;

'the necessary notification' means notifying the following authorities of the proposed order, extension, variation or discharge –

- (a) the parish council or community council (if any) for the area that includes the restricted area;
- (b) in the case of a public spaces protection order made or to be made by a district council in England, the county council (if any) for the area that includes the restricted area.

(5) The requirement to consult with the owner or occupier of land within the restricted area –

(a) does not apply to land that is owned and occupied by the local authority;
(b) applies only if, or to the extent that, it is reasonably practicable to consult the owner or occupier of the land.

(6) In the case of a person or body designated under section 71, the necessary consultation also includes consultation with the local authority which (ignoring subsection (2) of that section) is the authority for the area that includes the restricted area.

(7) In relation to a variation of a public spaces protection order that would increase the restricted area, the restricted area for the purposes of this section is the increased area.

73 Guidance

(1) The Secretary of State may issue –

(a) guidance to local authorities about the exercise of their functions under this Chapter and those of persons authorised by local authorities under section 63 or 68;
(b) guidance to chief officers of police about the exercise, by officers under their direction or control, of those officers' functions under this Part.

(2) The Secretary of State may revise any guidance issued under this section.

(3) The Secretary of State must arrange for any guidance issued or revised under this section to be published.

74 Interpretation of Chapter 2

(1) In this Chapter –

'alcohol' has the meaning given by section 191 of the Licensing Act 2003;
'community representative', in relation to a public spaces protection order that a local authority proposes to make or has made, means any individual or body appearing to the authority to represent the views of people who live in, work in or visit the restricted area;
'local authority' means –

(a) in relation to England, a district council, a county council for an area for which there is no district council, a London borough council, the Common Council of the City of London (in its capacity as a local authority) or the Council of the Isles of Scilly;
(b) in relation to Wales, a county council or a county borough council;

'public place' means any place to which the public or any section of the public has access, on payment or otherwise, as of right or by virtue of express or implied permission;
'restricted area' has the meaning given by section 59(4).

(2) For the purposes of this Chapter, a public spaces protection order 'regulates' an activity if the activity is –

(a) prohibited by virtue of section 59(4)(a), or
(b) subjected to requirements by virtue of section 59(4)(b),

whether or not for all persons and at all times.

75 Saving and transitional provision

(1) The repeal or amendment by this Act of provisions about any of the orders specified in subsection (2) does not apply in relation to –

(a) an order specified in that subsection made before the commencement day;
(b) anything done in connection with such an order.

(2) The orders are –

(a) a gating order under Part 8A of the Highways Act 1980;
(b) an order under section 13(2) of the Criminal Justice and Police Act 2001 (power of local authority to designate public place for restrictions on alcohol consumption);
(c) a dog control order under Chapter 1 of Part 6 of the Clean Neighbourhoods and Enironment Act 2005.

(3) At the end of the period of 3 years beginning with the commencement day –

(a) this Chapter has effect in relation to any order specified in subsection (2) that is still in force as if the provisions of the order were provisions of a public spaces protection order;
(b) subsection (1) ceases to have effect.

This Part, as it applies by virtue of paragraph (a), has effect with any necessary modifications (and with any modifications specified in an order under section 185(7)).

(4) In this section 'commencement day' means the day on which this Chapter comes into force.

Chapter 3

Closure of Premises Associated with Nuisance or Disorder etc

Closure notices

76 Power to issue closure notices

(1) A police officer of at least the rank of inspector, or the local authority, may issue a closure notice if satisfied on reasonable grounds –

(a) that the use of particular premises has resulted, or (if the notice is not issued) is likely soon to result, in nuisance to members of the public, or
(b) that there has been, or (if the notice is not issued) is likely soon to be, disorder near those premises associated with the use of those premises,

and that the notice is necessary to prevent the nuisance or disorder from continuing, recurring or occurring.

(2) A closure notice is a notice prohibiting access to the premises for a period specified in the notice.

For the maximum period, see section 77.

(3) A closure notice may prohibit access –

(a) by all persons except those specified, or by all persons except those of a specified description;
(b) at all times, or at all times except those specified;
(c) in all circumstances, or in all circumstances except those specified.

(4) A closure notice may not prohibit access by –

(a) people who habitually live on the premises, or
(b) the owner of the premises,

and accordingly they must be specified under subsection (3)(a).

(5) A closure notice must –

(a) identify the premises;
(b) explain the effect of the notice;
(c) state that failure to comply with the notice is an offence;
(d) state that an application will be made under section 80 for a closure order;

(e) specify when and where the application will be heard;
(f) explain the effect of a closure order;
(g) give information about the names of, and means of contacting, persons and organisations in the area that provide advice about housing and legal matters.

(6) A closure notice may be issued only if reasonable efforts have been made to inform –

(a) people who live on the premises (whether habitually or not), and
(b) any person who has control of or responsibility for the premises or who has an interest in them,

that the notice is going to be issued.

(7) Before issuing a closure notice the police officer or local authority must ensure that any body or individual the officer or authority thinks appropriate has been consulted.

(8) The Secretary of State may by regulations specify premises or descriptions of premises in relation to which a closure notice may not be issued.

77 Duration of closure notices

(1) The maximum period that may be specified in a closure notice is 24 hours unless subsection (2) applies.

(2) The maximum period is 48 hours –

(a) if, in the case of a notice issued by a police officer, the officer is of at least the rank of superintendent, or
(b) if, in the case of a notice issued by a local authority, the notice is signed by the chief executive officer of the authority or a person designated by him or her for the purposes of this subsection.

(3) In calculating when the period of 48 hours ends, Christmas Day is to be disregarded.

(4) The period specified in a closure notice to which subsection (2) does not apply may be extended by up to 24 hours –

(a) if, in the case of a notice issued by a police officer, an extension notice is issued by an officer of at least the rank of superintendent, or
(b) if, in the case of a notice issued by a local authority, the authority issues an extension notice signed by the chief executive officer of the authority or a person designated by the chief executive officer for the purposes of this subsection.

(5) An extension notice is a notice which –

(a) identifies the closure notice to which it relates, and
(b) specifies the period of the extension.

(6) In this section 'chief executive officer', in relation to a local authority, means the head of the paid service of the authority designated under section 4 of the Local Government and Housing Act 1989.

78 Cancellation or variation of closure notices

(1) This section applies where a closure notice is in force and the relevant officer or authority is no longer satisfied as mentioned in section 76(1), either –

(a) as regards the premises as a whole, or
(b) as regards a particular part of the premises.

(2) In a case within subsection (1)(a) the relevant officer or authority must issue a cancellation notice.

A cancellation notice is a notice cancelling the closure notice.

(3) In a case within subsection (1)(b) the relevant officer or authority must issue a variation notice.

A variation notice is a notice varying the closure notice so that it does not apply to the part of the premises referred to in subsection (1)(b).

(4) A cancellation notice or a variation notice that relates to a closure notice which was –

(a) issued by a local authority, and
(b) signed as mentioned in section 77(2)(b),

must be signed by the person who signed the closure notice (or, if that person is not available, by another person who could have signed as mentioned in section 77(2)(b)).

(5) A cancellation notice or a variation notice that relates to a closure notice which was –

(a) issued by a local authority, and
(b) extended under section 77(4)(b),

must be signed by the person who signed the extension notice (or, if that person is not available, by another person who could have signed the extension notice).

(6) In this section 'the relevant officer or authority' means –

(a) in the case of a closure notice issued by a police officer and not extended under section 77(4)(a), that officer (or, if that officer is not available, another officer of the same or higher rank);
(b) in the case of a closure notice issued by a police officer and extended under section 77(4)(a), the officer who issued the extension notice (or, if that officer is not available, another officer of the same or higher rank);
(c) in the case of a closure notice issued by a local authority, that authority.

79 Service of notices

(1) A closure notice, an extension notice, a cancellation notice or a variation notice must be served by –

(a) a constable, in the case of a notice issued by a police officer;
(b) a representative of the authority that issued the notice, in the case of a notice issued by a local authority.

(2) The constable or local authority representative must if possible –

(a) fix a copy of the notice to at least one prominent place on the premises,
(b) fix a copy of the notice to each normal means of access to the premises,
(c) fix a copy of the notice to any outbuildings that appear to the constable or representative to be used with or as part of the premises,
(d) give a copy of the notice to at least one person who appears to the constable or representative to have control of or responsibility for the premises, and
(e) give a copy of the notice to the people who live on the premises and to any person who does not live there but was informed (under section 76(6)) that the notice was going to be issued.

(3) If the constable or local authority representative reasonably believes, at the time of serving the notice, that there are persons occupying another part of the building or other structure in which the premises are situated whose access to that part will be impeded if a closure order is made under section 80, the constable or representative must also if possible serve the notice on those persons.

(4) The constable or local authority representative may enter any premises, using reasonable force if necessary, for the purposes of complying with subsection (2)(a).

(5) In this section 'representative' in relation to a local authority, means –

(a) an employee of the authority, or
(b) a person, or employee or a person, acting on behalf of the authority.

Closure orders

80 Power of court to make closure orders

(1) Whenever a closure notice is issued an application must be made to a magistrates' court for a closure order (unless the notice has been cancelled under section 78).

(2) An application for a closure order must be made –

(a) by a constable, if the closure notice was issued by a police officer;
(b) by the authority that issued the closure notice, if the notice was issued by a local authority.

(3) The application must be heard by the magistrates' court not later than 48 hours after service of the closure notice.

(4) In calculating when the period of 48 hours ends, Christmas Day is to be disregarded.

(5) The court may make a closure order if it is satisfied –

(a) that a person has engaged, or (if the order is not made) is likely to engage, in disorderly, offensive or criminal behaviour on the premises, or
(b) that the use of the premises has resulted, or (if the order is not made) is likely to result, in serious nuisance to members of the public, or
(c) that there has been, or (if the order is not made) is likely to be, disorder near those premises associated with the use of those premises,

and that the order is necessary to prevent the behaviour, nuisance or disorder from continuing, recurring or occurring.

(6) A closure order is an order prohibiting access to the premises for a period specified in the order.

The period may not exceed 3 months.

(7) A closure order may prohibit access –

(a) by all persons, or by all persons except those specified, or by all persons except those of a specified description;
(b) at all times, or at all times except those specified;
(c) in all circumstances, or in all circumstances except those specified.

(8) A closure order –

(a) may be made in respect of the whole or any part of the premises;
(b) may include provision about access to a part of the building or structure of which the premises form part.

(9) The court must notify the relevant licensing authority if it makes a closure order in relation to premises in respect of which a premises licence is in force.

81 Temporary orders

(1) This section applies where an application has been made to a magistrates' court under section 80 for a closure order.

(2) If the court does not make a closure order it may nevertheless order that the closure notice continues in force for a specified further period of not more than 48 hours, if satisfied –

(a) that the use of particular premises has resulted, or (if the notice is not continued) is likely soon to result, in nuisance to members of the public, or

(b) that there has been, or (if the notice is not continued) is likely soon to be, disorder near those premises associated with the use of those premises,

and that the continuation of the notice is necessary to prevent the nuisance or disorder from continuing, recurring or occurring.

(3) The court may adjourn the hearing of the application for a period of not more than 14 days to enable –

(a) the occupier of the premises,
(b) the person with control of or responsibility for the premises, or
(c) any other person with an interest in the premises,

to show why a closure order should not be made.

(4) If the court adjourns the hearing under subsection (3) it may order that the closure notice continues in force until the end of the period of the adjournment.

82 Extension of closure orders

(1) At any time before the expiry of a closure order, an application may be made to a justice of the peace, by complaint, for an extension (or further extension) of the period for which the order is in force.

(2) Those entitled to make an application under this section are –

(a) where the closure order was made on the application of a constable, a police officer of at least the rank of inspector;
(b) where the closure order was made on the application of a local authority, that authority.

(3) A police officer or local authority may make an application under this section only if satisfied on reasonable grounds that it is necessary for the period of the order to be extended to prevent the occurrence, recurrence or continuance of –

(a) disorderly, offensive or criminal behaviour on the premises,
(b) serious nuisance to members of the public resulting from the use of the premises, or
(c) disorder near the premises associated with the use of the premises,

and also satisfied that the appropriate consultee has been consulted about the intention to make the application.

(4) In subsection (3) 'the appropriate consultee' means –

(a) the local authority, in the case of an application by a police officer;
(b) the chief officer of police for the area in which the premises are situated, in the case of an application by a local authority.

(5) Where an application is made under this section, the justice of the peace may issue a summons directed to –

(a) any person on whom the closure notice was served under section 79, or
(b) any other person who appears to the justice to have an interest in the premises but on whom the closure notice was not served,

requiring the person to appear before the magistrates' court to respond to the application.

(6) If a summons is issued under subsection (5), a notice stating the date, time and place of the hearing of the application must be served on the persons to whom the summons is directed.

(7) If the magistrates' court is satisfied as mentioned in subsection (3)(a), (b) or (c), it may make an order extending (or further extending) the period of the closure order by a period not exceeding 3 months.

(8) The period of a closure order may not be extended so that the order lasts for more than 6 months.

83 Discharge of closure orders

(1) At any time before the expiry of a closure order, an application may be made to a justice of the peace, by complaint, for the order to be discharged.

(2) Those entitled to make an application under this section are –

(a) a constable, where the closure order was made on the application of a constable;
(b) the authority that applied for the closure order, where the order was made on the application of a local authority;
(c) a person on whom the closure notice was served under section 79;
(d) anyone else who has an interest in the premises but on whom the closure notice was not served.

(3) Where a person other than a constable makes an application under this section for the discharge of an order that was made on the application of a constable, the justice may issue a summons directed to a constable considered appropriate by the justice requiring him or her to appear before the magistrates' court to respond to the application.

(4) If a summons is issued under subsection (3), a notice stating the date, time and place of the hearing of the application must be served on –

(a) the constable to whom the summons is directed;
(b) the persons mentioned in subsection (2)(c) and (d) (other than the complainant).

(5) Where –

(a) the order in question was made on the application of a local authority, and
(b) a person other than that authority makes an application under this section for the discharge of the order,

the justice may issue a summons directed to that authority requiring it to appear before the magistrates' court to respond to the application.

(6) If a summons is issued under subsection (5), a notice stating the date, time and place of the hearing of the application must be served on –

(a) the authority mentioned in that subsection;
(b) the persons mentioned in subsection (2)(c) and (d) (other than the complainant).

(7) The magistrates' court may not make an order discharging the closure order unless satisfied that the closure order is no longer necessary to prevent the occurrence, recurrence or continuance of –

(a) disorderly, offensive or criminal behaviour on the premises,
(b) serious nuisance to members of the public resulting from the use of the premises, or
(c) disorder near the premises associated with the use of the premises.

Appeals

84 Appeals

(1) An appeal against a decision to make or extend a closure order may be made by –

(a) a person on whom the closure notice was served under section 79;
(b) anyone else who has an interest in the premises but on whom the closure notice was not served.

(2) A constable may appeal against –

(a) a decision not to make a closure order applied for by a constable;

(b) a decision not to extend a closure order made on the application of a constable;
(c) a decision (under section 81) not to order the continuation in force of a closure notice issued by a constable.

(3) A local authority may appeal against –

(a) a decision not to make a closure order applied for by that authority;
(b) a decision not to extend a closure order made on the application of that authority;
(c) a decision (under section 81) not to order the continuation in force of a closure notice issued by that authority.

(4) An appeal under this section is to the Crown Court.

(5) An appeal under this section must be made within the period of 21 days beginning with the date of the decision to which it relates.

(6) On an appeal under this section the Crown Court may make whatever order it thinks appropriate.

(7) The Crown Court must notify the relevant licensing authority if it makes a closure order in relation to premises in respect of which a premises licence is in force.

Enforcement

85 Enforcement of closure orders

(1) An authorised person may –

(a) enter premises in respect of which a closure order is in force;
(b) do anything necessary to secure the premises against entry.

(2) In this section 'authorised person' –

(a) in relation to a closure order made on the application of a constable, means a constable or a person authorised by the chief officer of police for the area in which the premises are situated;
(b) in relation to a closure order made on the application of a local authority, means a person authorised by that authority.

(3) A person acting under subsection (1) may use reasonable force.

(4) A person seeking to enter premises under subsection (1) must, if required to do so by or on behalf of the owner, occupier or other person in charge of the premises, produce evidence of his or her identity and authority before entering the premises.

(5) An authorised person may also enter premises in respect of which a closure order is in force to carry out essential maintenance or repairs to the premises.

86 Offences

(1) A person who without reasonable excuse remains on or enters premises in contravention of a closure notice (including a notice continued in force under section 81) commits an offence.

(2) A person who without reasonable excuse remains on or enters premises in contravention of a closure order commits an offence.

(3) A person who without reasonable excuse obstructs a person acting under section 79 or 85(1) commits an offence.

(4) A person guilty of an offence under subsection (1) or (3) is liable on summary conviction –

(a) to imprisonment for a period not exceeding 3 months, or
(b) to a fine,

or to both.

(5) A person guilty of an offence under subsection (2) is liable on summary conviction –

(a) to imprisonment for a period not exceeding 51 weeks, or
(b) to a fine,

or to both.

(6) In relation to an offence committed before the commencement of section 281(5) of the Criminal Justice Act 2003, the reference in subsection (5)(a) to 51 weeks is to be read as a reference to 6 months.

Supplemental

87 Access to other premises

(1) Where –

(a) access to premises is prohibited or restricted by, or as a result of, an order under section 80, 81, 82 or 84,
(b) those premises are part of a building or structure, and
(c) there is another part of that building or structure that is not subject to the prohibition or restriction,

an occupier or owner of that other part may apply to the appropriate court for an order under this section.

(2) The appropriate court is –

(a) the magistrates' court, in the case of an order under section 80, 81 or 82;
(b) the Crown Court, in the case of an order under section 84.

(3) Notice of an application under this section must be given to –

(a) whatever constable the court thinks appropriate;
(b) the local authority;
(c) a person on whom the closure notice was served under section 79;
(d) anyone else who has an interest in the premises but on whom the closure notice was not served.

(4) On an application under this section the court may make whatever order it thinks appropriate in relation to access to any part of the building or structure mentioned in subsection (1).

It does not matter whether provision has been made under section 80(8)(b).

88 Reimbursement of costs

(1) A local policing body or a local authority that incurs expenditure for the purpose of clearing, securing or maintaining premises in respect of which a closure order is in force may apply to the court that made the order for an order under this section.

(2) On an application under this section the court may make whatever order it thinks appropriate for the reimbursement (in full or in part) by the owner or occupier of the premises of the expenditure mentioned in subsection (1).

(3) An application for an order under this section may not be heard unless it is made before the end of the period of 3 months starting with the day on which the closure order ceases to have effect.

(4) An order under this section may be made only against a person who has been served with the application for the order.

(5) An application under this section must also be served on –

(a) the local policing body for the area in which the premises are situated, if the application is made by a local authority;
(b) the local authority, if the application is made by a local policing body.

89 Exemption from liability

(1) A police officer, or the chief officer of police under whose direction or control he or she acts, is not liable for damages in proceedings for –

(a) judicial review, or
(b) the tort of negligence or misfeasance in public office,

arising out of anything done or omitted to be done by the police officer in the exercise or purported exercise of a power under this Chapter.

(2) A local authority is not liable for damages in proceedings for –

(a) judicial review, or
(b) the tort of negligence or misfeasance in public office,

arising out of anything done or omitted to be done by the authority in the exercise or purported exercise of a power under this Chapter.

(3) Subsections (1) and (2) do not apply to an act or omission shown to have been in bad faith.

(4) Subsections (1) and (2) do not apply so as to prevent an award of damages made in respect of an act or omission on the ground that the act or omission was unlawful by virtue of section 6(1) of the Human Rights Act 1998.

(5) This section does not affect any other exemption from liability (whether at common law or otherwise).

90 Compensation

(1) A person who claims to have incurred financial loss in consequence of a closure notice or a closure order may apply to the appropriate court for compensation.

(2) The appropriate court is –

(a) the magistrates' court that considered the application for a closure order (except where paragraph (b) applies);
(b) the Crown Court, in the case of a closure order that was made or extended by an order of that Court on an appeal under section 84.

(3) An application under this section may not be heard unless it is made before the end of the period of 3 months starting with whichever of the following is applicable –

(a) the day on which the closure notice was cancelled under section 78;
(b) the day on which a closure order was refused;
(c) the day on which the closure order ceased to have effect.

(4) For the purposes of subsection (3)(b) the day on which a closure order was refused is –

(a) the day on which the magistrates' court decided not to make a closure order (except where paragraph (b) applies);

(b) the day on which the Crown Court dismissed an appeal against a decision not to make a closure order.

(5) On an application under this section the court may order the payment of compensation out of central funds if it is satisfied –

(a) that the applicant is not associated with the use of the premises, or the behaviour on the premises, on the basis of which the closure notice was issued or the closure order made,
(b) if the applicant is the owner or occupier of the premises, that the applicant took reasonable steps to prevent that use or behaviour,
(c) that the applicant has incurred financial loss in consequence of the notice or order, and
(d) that having regard to all the circumstances it is appropriate to order payment of compensation in respect of that loss.

(6) In this section 'central funds' has the same meaning as in enactments providing for the payment of costs.

91 Guidance

(1) The Secretary of State may issue –

(a) guidance to chief officers of police about the exercise, by officers under their direction or control, of those officers ' functions under this Chapter;
(b) guidance to local authorities about the exercise of their functions under this Chapter and those of their representatives (within the meaning of section 79).

(2) The Secretary of State may revise any guidance issued under this section.

(3) The Secretary of State must arrange for any guidance issued or revised under this section to be published.

92 Interpretation of Chapter 3

(1) In this Chapter –

'cancellation notice' has the meaning given by section 78(2);
'criminal behaviour' means behaviour that constitutes a criminal offence;
'extension notice' has the meaning given by section 77(5);
'local authority' means –

(a) in relation to England, a district council, a county council for an area for which there is no district council, a London borough council, the Common Council of the City of London or the Council of the Isles of Scilly;
(b) in relation to Wales, a county council or a county borough council;

'offensive behaviour' means behaviour by a person that causes or is likely to cause harassment, alarm or distress to one or more other persons not of the same household as that person;
'owner', in relation to premises, means –

(a) a person (other than a mortgagee not in possession) entitled to dispose of the fee simple of the premises, whether in possession or in reversion;
(b) a person who holds or is entitled to the rents and profits of the premises under a lease that (when granted) was for a term of not less then 3 years;

'premises' includes –

(a) any land or other place (whether enclosed or not);
(b) any outbuildings that are, or are used as, part of premises;

'premises licence' has the meaning given by section 11 of the Licensing Act 2003;
'relevant licensing authority' has the meaning given by section 12 of that Act;
'variation notice' has the meaning given by section 78(3).

(2) A reference in this Chapter to 'the local authority', in relation to any premises or a notice or order relating to any premises, is a reference to the local authority (or, as the case may be, any of the local authorities) within whose area the premises are situated.

(3) A reference in this Chapter to 'the premises', in relation to a closure notice or a closure order, is a reference to the premises to which the notice or order relates.

93 Saving and transitional provision

(1) The repeal or amendment by this Act of provisions about any of the notices specified in subsection (2) or orders specified in subsection (3) does not apply in relation to –

(a) any such notice issued or order made before the commencement day;
(b) anything done in connection with any such notice or order.

(2) The notices are –

(a) a notice issued under section 1 of the Anti-social Behaviour Act 2003;
(b) a notice issued under section 11A of that Act.

(3) The orders are –

(a) an order made under section 2 of the Anti-social Behaviour Act 2003;
(b) an order made under section 11B of that Act;
(c) an order made under section 40 of that Act;
(d) an order made under section 161 of the Licensing Act 2003;
(e) an order made under section 165(2)(b), (c) or (d) of that Act.

(4) A person deciding whether to issue a closure notice may take into account things that –

(a) happened before the commencement day, and
(b) would have given rise to the power to issue one of the notices specified in subsection (2) or to make an order specified in subsection (3)(c) or (d).

(5) A court deciding whether to make a closure order may take into account things that –

(a) happened before the commencement day, and
(b) would have given rise to the power to make an order specified in subsection (3)(a), (b) or (e).

(6) Subsections (4) and (5) apply only during the period of 3 months beginning with the commencement day.

(7) In this section 'commencement day' means the day on which this Chapter comes into force.

PART 5

RECOVERY OF POSSESSION OF DWELLING-HOUSES: ANTI-SOCIAL BEHAVIOUR GROUNDS

Absolute ground for possession: secure tenancies

94 New ground for serious offences or breach of prohibitions etc

(1) After section 84 of the Housing Act 1985 (secure tenancies: grounds and orders for possession) there is inserted –

'84A Absolute ground for possession for anti-social behaviour

(1) If the court is satisfied that any of the following conditions is met, it must make an order for the possession of a dwelling-house let under a secure tenancy.

This is subject to subsection (2) (and to any available defence based on the tenant's Convention rights, within the meaning of the Human Rights Act 1998).

(2) Subsection (1) applies only where the landlord has complied with any obligations it has under section 85ZA (review of decision to seek possession).

(3) Condition 1 is that –

(a) the tenant, or a person residing in or visiting the dwelling-house, has been convicted of a serious offence, and
(b) the serious offence –

(i) was committed (wholly or partly) in, or in the locality of, the dwelling-house,
(ii) was committed elsewhere against a person with a right (of whatever description) to reside in, or occupy housing accommodation in the locality of, the dwelling-house, or
(iii) was committed elsewhere against the landlord of the dwelling-house, or a person employed (whether or not by the landlord) in connection with the exercise of the landlord's housing management functions, and directly or indirectly related to or affected those functions.

(4) Condition 2 is that a court has found in relevant proceedings that the tenant, or a person residing in or visiting the dwelling-house, has breached a provision of an injunction under section 1 of the Anti-social Behaviour, Crime and Policing Act 2014, other than a provision requiring a person to participate in a particular activity, and –

(a) the breach occurred in, or in the locality of, the dwelling-house, or
(b) the breach occurred elsewhere and the provision breached was a provision intended to prevent –

(i) conduct that is capable of causing nuisance or annoyance to a person with a right (of whatever description) to reside in, or occupy housing accommodation in the locality of, the dwelling-house, or
(ii) conduct that is capable of causing nuisance or annoyance to the landlord of the dwelling-house, or a person employed (whether or not by the landlord) in connection with the exercise of the landlord's housing management functions, and that is directly or indirectly related to or affects those functions.

(5) Condition 3 is that the tenant, or a person residing in or visiting the dwelling-house, has been convicted of an offence under section 30 of the Anti-social Behaviour, Crime and Policing Act 2014 consisting of a breach of a provision of a criminal behaviour order prohibiting a person from doing anything described in the order, and the offence involved –

(a) a breach that occurred in, or in the locality of, the dwelling-house, or
(b) a breach that occurred elsewhere of a provision intended to prevent –

(i) behaviour that causes or is likely to cause harassment, alarm or distress to a person with a right (of whatever description) to reside in, or occupy housing accommodation in the locality of, the dwelling-house, or
(ii) behaviour that causes or is likely to cause harassment, alarm or distress to the landlord of the dwelling-house, or a person employed (whether or not by the landlord) in connection with the exercise of the landlord's housing management functions, and that is directly or indirectly related to or affects those functions.

(6) Condition 4 is that –

(a) the dwelling-house is or has been subject to a closure order under section 80 of the Anti-social Behaviour, Crime and Policing Act 2014, and
(b) access to the dwelling-house has been prohibited (under the closure order or under a closure notice issued under section 76 of that Act) for a continuous period of more than 48 hours.

(7) Condition 5 is that –

(a) the tenant, or a person residing in or visiting the dwelling-house, has been convicted of an offence under –

(i) section 80(4) of the Environmental Protection Act 1990 (breach of abatement notice in relation to statutory nuisance), or

(ii) section 82(8) of that Act (breach of court order to abate statutory nuisance etc), and

(b) the nuisance concerned was noise emitted from the dwelling-house which was a statutory nuisance for the purposes of Part 3 of that Act by virtue of section 79(1)(g) of that Act (noise emitted from premises so as to be prejudicial to health or a nuisance).

(8) Condition 1, 2, 3, 4 or 5 is not met if –

(a) there is an appeal against the conviction, finding or order concerned which has not been finally determined, abandoned or withdrawn, or
(b) the final determination of the appeal results in the conviction, finding or order being overturned.

(9) In this section –

'relevant proceedings' means proceedings for contempt of court or proceedings under Schedule 2 to the Anti-social Behaviour, Crime and Policing Act 2014;
'serious offence' means an offence which –

(a) was committed on or after the day on which subsection (3) comes into force,
(b) is specified, or falls within a description specified, in Schedule 2A at the time the offence was committed and at the time the court is considering the matter, and
(c) is not an offence that is triable only summarily by virtue of section 22 of the Magistrates' Courts Act 1980 (either-way offences where value involved is small).

(10) The Secretary of State may by order amend Schedule 2A as it applies in relation to dwelling-houses in England by –

(a) adding an indictable offence;
(b) removing an offence.

(11) The Welsh Ministers may by order amend Schedule 2A as it applies in relation to dwelling-houses in Wales by –

(a) adding an indictable offence;
(b) removing an offence.

(12) An order under subsection (10) or (11) –

(a) is to be made by statutory instrument;
(b) may make different provision for different purposes;
(c) may include incidental, supplementary, consequential, transitional or saving provision.

(13) A statutory instrument containing an order under subsection (10) or (11) may not be made unless a draft of the instrument has been laid before and approved by a resolution of –

(a) each House of Parliament (in the case of an order of the Secretary of State), or
(b) the National Assembly for Wales (in the case of an order of the Welsh Ministers).

(2) After Schedule 2 to that Act there is inserted the Schedule set out in Schedule 3 to this Act.

95 Notice requirements for new ground

After section 83 of the Housing Act 1985 (proceedings for possession or termination: notice requirements) there is inserted –

'83ZA Notice requirements in relation to proceedings for possession on absolute ground for anti-social behaviour

(1) This section applies in relation to proceedings for possession of a dwelling-house under section 84A (absolute ground for possession for anti-social behaviour), including proceedings where possession is also sought on one or more of the grounds set out in Schedule 2.

(2) The court must not entertain the proceedings unless the landlord has served on the tenant a notice under this section.

(3) The notice must –

(a) state that the court will be asked to make an order under section 84A for the possession of the dwelling-house,
(b) set out the reasons for the landlord's decision to apply for the order (including the condition or conditions in section 84A on which the landlord proposes to rely), and
(c) inform the tenant of any right that the tenant may have under section 85ZA to request a review of the landlord's decision and of the time within which the request must be made.

(4) In a case where possession is also sought on one or more of the grounds set out in Schedule 2, the notice must also –

(a) specify the ground on which the court will be asked to make the order, and
(b) give particulars of that ground.

(5) A notice which states that the landlord proposes to rely upon condition 1, 3 or 5 in section 84A –

(a) must also state the conviction on which the landlord proposes to rely, and
(b) must be served on the tenant within –

(i) the period of 12 months beginning with the day of the conviction, or
(ii) if there is an appeal against the conviction, the period of 12 months beginning with the day on which the appeal is finally determined or abandoned.

(6) A notice which states that the landlord proposes to rely upon condition 2 in section 84A –

(a) must also state the finding on which the landlord proposes to rely, and
(b) must be served on the tenant within –

(i) the period of 12 months beginning with the day on which the court has made the finding, or
(ii) if there is an appeal against the finding, the period of 12 months beginning with the day on which the appeal is finally determined, abandoned or withdrawn.

(7) A notice which states that the landlord proposes to rely upon condition 4 in section 84A –

(a) must also state the closure order concerned, and
(b) must be served on the tenant within –

(i) the period of 3 months beginning with the day on which the closure order was made, or
(ii) if there is an appeal against the making of the order, the period of 3 months beginning with the day on which the appeal is finally determined, abandoned or withdrawn.

(8) A notice under this section must also inform the tenant that, if the tenant needs help or advice about the notice and what to do about it, the tenant should take it immediately to a Citizens' Advice Bureau, a housing aid centre, a law centre or a solicitor.

(9) The notice –

(a) must also specify the date after which proceedings for the possession of the dwelling-house may be begun, and
(b) ceases to be in force 12 months after the date so specified.

(10) The date specified in accordance with subsection (9)(a) must not be earlier than –

(a) in the case of a periodic tenancy, the date on which the tenancy could, apart from this Part, be brought to an end by notice to quit given by the landlord on the same day as the notice under this section;
(b) in the case of a secure tenancy for a term certain, one month after the date of the service of the notice.

(11) Where a notice under this section is served with respect to a secure tenancy for a term certain, it has effect also with respect to any periodic tenancy arising on the termination of that tenancy by virtue of section 86; and subsection (10)(a) does not apply to the notice.'

96 Review requirements for new ground

After section 85 of the Housing Act 1985 (extended discretion of court in certain proceedings for possession) there is inserted –

'85ZA Review of decision to seek possession on absolute ground for anti-social behaviour

(1) A tenant may request a review of a landlord's decision to seek an order for possession of a dwelling-house under section 84A if the interest of the landlord belongs to –

(a) a local housing authority, or
(b) a housing action trust.

(2) Such a request must be made in writing before the end of the period of 7 days beginning with the day on which the notice under section 83ZA is served.

(3) On a request being duly made to it, the landlord must review its decision.

(4) The landlord must notify the tenant in writing of the decision on the review.

(5) If the decision is to confirm the original decision, the landlord must also notify the tenant of the reasons for the decision.

(6) The review must be carried out, and the tenant notified, before the day specified in the notice under section 83ZA as the day after which proceedings for the possession of the dwelling-house may be begun.

(7) The Secretary of State may by regulations make provision about the procedure to be followed in connection with a review under this section that relates to an order for possession of a dwelling-house in England.

(8) The Welsh Ministers may by regulations make provision about the procedure to be followed in connection with a review under this section that relates to an order for possession of a dwelling-house in Wales.

(9) Regulations under subsections (7) and (8) may, in particular, make provision –

(a) requiring the decision on review to be made by a person of appropriate seniority who was not involved in the original decision, and
(b) as to the circumstances in which the person concerned is entitled to an oral hearing, and whether and by whom the person may be represented at such a hearing.

(10) Regulations under this section –

(a) may contain transitional or saving provision;
(b) are to be made by statutory instrument which –

(i) in the case of regulations made by the Secretary of State, is subject to annulment in pursuance of a resolution of either House of Parliament;
(ii) in the case of regulations made by the Welsh Ministers, is subject to annulment in pursuance of a resolution of the National Assembly for Wales.'

Absolute ground for possession: assured tenancies

97 Corresponding new ground and notice requirements for assured tenancies

(1) In Part 1 of Schedule 2 to the Housing Act 1988 (assured tenancies: grounds on which court must order possession), after ground 7 there is inserted –

'Ground 7A

Any of the following conditions is met.

Condition 1 is that –

(a) the tenant, or a person residing in or visiting the dwelling-house, has been convicted of a serious offence, and
(b) the serious offence –

(i) was committed (wholly or partly) in, or in the locality of, the dwelling-house,

- (ii) was committed elsewhere against a person with a right (of whatever description) to reside in, or occupy housing accommodation in the locality of, the dwelling-house, or
- (iii) was committed elsewhere against the landlord of the dwelling-house, or a person employed (whether or not by the landlord) in connection with the exercise of the landlord's housing management functions, and directly or indirectly related to or affected those functions.

Condition 2 is that a court has found in relevant proceedings that the tenant, or a person residing in or visiting the dwelling-house, has breached a provision of an injunction under section 1 of the Anti-social Behaviour, Crime and Policing Act 2014, other than a provision requiring a person to participate in a particular activity, and –

- (a) the breach occurred in, or in the locality of, the dwelling-house, or
- (b) the breach occurred elsewhere and the provision breached was a provision intended to prevent –
  - (i) conduct that is capable of causing nuisance or annoyance to a person with a right (of whatever description) to reside in, or occupy housing accommodation in the locality of, the dwelling-house, or
  - (ii) conduct that is capable of causing nuisance or annoyance to the landlord of the dwelling-house, or a person employed (whether or not by the landlord) in connection with the exercise of the landlord's housing management functions, and that is directly or indirectly related to or affects those functions.

Condition 3 is that the tenant, or a person residing in or visiting the dwelling-house, has been convicted of an offence under section 30 of the Anti-social Behaviour, Crime and Policing Act 2014 consisting of a breach of a provision of a criminal behaviour order prohibiting a person from doing anything described in the order, and the offence involved –

- (a) a breach that occurred in, or in the locality of, the dwelling-house, or
- (b) a breach that occurred elsewhere of a provision intended to prevent –
  - (i) behaviour that causes or is likely to cause harassment, alarm or distress to a person with a right (of whatever description) to reside in, or occupy housing accommodation in the locality of, the dwelling-house, or
  - (ii) behaviour that causes or is likely to cause harassment, alarm or distress to the landlord of the dwelling-house, or a person employed (whether or not by the landlord) in connection with the exercise of the landlord's housing management functions, and that is directly or indirectly related to or affects those functions.

Condition 4 is that –

- (a) the dwelling-house is or has been subject to a closure order under section 80 of the Anti-social Behaviour, Crime and Policing Act 2014, and
- (b) access to the dwelling-house has been prohibited (under the closure order or under a closure notice issued under section 76 of that Act) for a continuous period of more than 48 hours.

Condition 5 is that –

- (a) the tenant, or a person residing in or visiting the dwelling-house, has been convicted of an offence under –
  - (i) section 80(4) of the Environmental Protection Act 1990 (breach of abatement notice in relation to statutory nuisance), or
  - (ii) section 82(8) of that Act (breach of court order to abate statutory nuisance etc), and
- (b) the nuisance concerned was noise emitted from the dwelling-house which was a statutory nuisance for the purposes of Part 3 of that Act by virtue of section 79(1)(g) of that Act (noise emitted from premises so as to be prejudicial to health or a nuisance).

Condition 1, 2, 3, 4 or 5 is not met if –

- (a) there is an appeal against the conviction, finding or order concerned which has not been finally determined, abandoned or withdrawn, or
- (b) the final determination of the appeal results in the conviction, finding or order being overturned.

In this ground –

'relevant proceedings' means proceedings for contempt of court or proceedings under Schedule 2 to the Anti-social Behaviour, Crime and Policing Act 2014;
'serious offence' means an offence which –

- (a) was committed on or after the day on which this ground comes into force,

(b) is specified, or falls within a description specified, in Schedule 2A to the Housing Act 1985 at the time the offence was committed and at the time the court is considering the matter, and
(c) is not an offence that is triable only summarily by virtue of section 22 of the Magistrates' Courts Act 1980 (either-way offences where value involved is small).'

(2) In section 8 of that Act (notice of proceedings for possession) –

(a) in subsection (3)(b), for 'subsections (4)' there is substituted 'subsections (3A)';
(b) after subsection (3) there is inserted –

'(3A) If a notice under this section specifies in accordance with subsection (3)(a) Ground 7A in Schedule 2 to this Act (whether with or without other grounds), the date specified in the notice as mentioned in subsection (3)(b) is not to be earlier than –

(a) in the case of a periodic tenancy, the earliest date on which, apart from section 5(1), the tenancy could be brought to an end by a notice to quit given by the landlord on the same date as the date of service of the notice under this section;
(b) in the case of a fixed term tenancy, one month after the date on which the notice was served';

(c) in subsection (4), for '(whether with or without other grounds)' there is substituted '(whether without other grounds or with any ground other than Ground 7A)';
(d) in subsection (4A), after 'other than Ground' there is inserted '7A or';
(e) after subsection (4B) there is inserted –

'(4C) A notice under this section that specifies in accordance with subsection (3)(a) Ground 7A in Schedule 2 to this Act (whether with or without other grounds) must be served on the tenant within the time period specified in subsection (4D), (4E) or (4F).

(4D) Where the landlord proposes to rely on condition 1, 3 or 5 in Ground 7A, the notice must be served on the tenant within –

(a) the period of 12 months beginning with the day of the conviction, or
(b) if there is an appeal against the conviction, the period of 12 months beginning with the day on which the appeal is finally determined or abandoned.

(4E) Where the landlord proposes to rely on condition 2 in Ground 7A, the notice must be served on the tenant within –

(a) the period of 12 months beginning with the day on which the court has made the finding, or
(b) if there is an appeal against the finding, the period of 12 months beginning with the day on which the appeal is finally determined, abandoned or withdrawn.

(4F) Where the landlord proposes to rely on condition 4 in Ground 7A, the notice must be served on the tenant within –

(a) the period of 3 months beginning with the day on which the closure order was made, or
(b) if there is an appeal against the making of the order, the period of 3 months beginning with the day on which the appeal is finally determined, abandoned or withdrawn.';

(f) in subsection (5), after 'Ground' there is inserted '7A or'.

Discretionary grounds: secure and assured tenancies

98 Conduct causing nuisance to landlord etc

(1) In Part 1 of Schedule 2 to the Housing Act 1985 (grounds on which court may order possession in relation to secure tenancies if it considers it reasonable), in Ground 2, at the end of paragraph (a) (but before the 'or') there is inserted –

'(aa) has been guilty of conduct causing or likely to cause a nuisance or annoyance to the landlord of the dwelling-house, or a person employed (whether or not by the landlord) in connection with the exercise of the landlord's housing management functions, and that is directly or indirectly related to or affects those functions'.

(2) In Part 2 of Schedule 2 to the Housing Act 1988 (grounds on which court may order possession in relation to assured tenancies if it considers it reasonable), in Ground 14, at the end of paragraph (a) (but before the 'or') there is inserted –

> '(aa) has been guilty of conduct causing or likely to cause a nuisance or annoyance to the landlord of the dwelling-house, or a person employed (whether or not by the landlord) in connection with the exercise of the landlord's housing management functions, and that is directly or indirectly related to or affects those functions'.

99 Offences connected with riot

(1) In Part 1 of Schedule 2 to the Housing Act 1985 (grounds on which court may order possession in relation to secure tenancies if it considers it reasonable), after Ground 2 there is inserted –

> **'Ground 2ZA**
>
> The tenant or an adult residing in the dwelling-house has been convicted of an indictable offence which took place during, and at the scene of, a riot in the United Kingdom.
>
> In this Ground –
>
> 'adult' means a person aged 18 or over;
> 'indictable offence' does not include an offence that is triable only summarily by virtue of section 22 of the Magistrates' Courts Act 1980 (either way offences where value involved is small);
> 'riot' is to be construed in accordance with section 1 of the Public Order Act 1986.
>
> This Ground applies only in relation to dwelling-houses in England.'

(2) In Part 2 of Schedule 2 to the Housing Act 1988 (grounds on which court may order possession in relation to assured tenancies if it considers it reasonable), after Ground 14 there is inserted –

> **'Ground 14ZA**
>
> The tenant or an adult residing in the dwelling-house has been convicted of an indictable offence which took place during, and at the scene of, a riot in the United Kingdom.
>
> In this Ground –
>
> 'adult' means a person aged 18 or over;
> 'indictable offence' does not include an offence that is triable only summarily by virtue of section 22 of the Magistrates' Courts Act 1980 (either way offences where value involved is small);
> 'riot' is to be construed in accordance with section 1 of the Public Order Act 1986.
>
> This Ground applies only in relation to dwelling-houses in England.'

Supplemental

100 Restrictions where new possession proceedings in progress etc

(1) In section 138 of the Housing Act 1985 (right to buy: suspension of duty of landlord to convey freehold or grant lease) –

(a) in subsection (2A)(a), for 'or Ground 2 possession order' there is substituted, 'Ground 2 or 2ZA possession order or section 84A possession order';
(b) in subsection (2B)(a), for 'or an operative Ground 2 possession order' there is substituted, 'an operative Ground 2 or 2ZA possession order or an operative section 84A possession order';
(c) in subsection (2C), for the definition of 'Ground 2 possession order' there is substituted –

'Ground 2 or 2ZA possession order' means an order for possession under Ground 2 or Ground 2ZA in Schedule 2';

(d) for the definition of 'operative Ground 2 possession order' there is substituted –

'operative Ground 2 or 2ZA possession order' means an order made under Ground 2 or Ground 2ZA in Schedule 2 which requires possession of the dwelling-house to be given up on a date specified in the order;'

(e) after that definition there is inserted –

'operative section 84A possession order' means an order under section 84A which requires possession of the dwelling-house to be given up on a date specified in the order;

'section 84A possession order' means an order for possession under section 84A;'.

(2) In Schedule 3 to that Act (grounds for withholding consent to assignment of secure tenancy by way of exchange), after Ground 2 there is inserted –

'Ground 2ZA

Proceedings have been begun for possession of the dwelling-house, of which the tenant or the proposed assignee is the secure tenant, under section 84A (absolute ground for possession for anti-social behaviour), or there has been served on the tenant or the proposed assignee a notice under section 83ZA (notice requirements in relation to proceedings for possession on absolute ground for anti-social behaviour) which is still in force.'

(3) In Schedule 14 to the Localism Act 2011 (grounds on which landlord may refuse to surrender and grant tenancies in pursuance of a request under section 158 of that Act) –

(a) after Ground 4 there is inserted –

'4A Ground 4A

(1) This ground is that either of the following conditions is met.

(2) The first condition is that –

(a) proceedings have begun for possession of a dwelling-house let on an existing tenancy which is a secure tenancy, and

(b) possession is sought under section 84A of the Housing Act 1985 (absolute ground for possession for anti-social behaviour).

(3) The second condition is that –

(a) a notice has been served on a relevant tenant under section 83ZA of that Act (notice requirements in relation to proceedings for possession on absolute ground for anti-social behaviour), and

(b) the notice is still in force.';

(b) after Ground 5 there is inserted –

'5A Ground 5A

(1) This ground is that either of the following conditions is met.

(2) The first condition is that –

(a) proceedings have begun for possession of a dwelling-house let on an existing tenancy which is an assured tenancy, and

(b) possession is sought on ground 7A in Part 1 of Schedule 2 to the Housing Act 1988 (absolute ground for possession for anti-social behaviour).

(3) The second condition is that –

(a) a notice has been served on a relevant tenant under section 8 of that Act (notice of proceedings for possession), and

(b) the notice specifies ground 7A and is still in force.'

PART 6

LOCAL INVOLVEMENT AND ACCOUNTABILITY

Community remedies

101 The community remedy document

(1) Each local policing body must prepare a community remedy document for its area, and may revise it at any time.

(2) A community remedy document is a list of actions any of which might, in the opinion of the local policing body, be appropriate in a particular case to be carried out by a person who –

- (a) has engaged in anti-social behaviour or has committed an offence, and
- (b) is to be dealt with for that behaviour or offence without court proceedings.

(3) For the purposes of subsection (2), an action is appropriate to be carried out by a person only if it has one or more of the following objects –

- (a) assisting in the person's rehabilitation;
- (b) ensuring that the person makes reparation for the behaviour or offence in question;
- (c) punishing the person.

(4) In preparing or revising the community remedy document for its area a local policing body must –

- (a) have regard to the need to promote public confidence in the out-of-court disposal process;
- (b) have regard to any guidance issued by the Secretary of State about how local policing bodies are to discharge their functions under this section;
- (c) carry out the necessary consultation and take account of all views expressed by those consulted.

(5) In subsection (4)(c) 'the necessary consultation' means –

- (a) consultation with the chief officer of police for the area,
- (b) consultation with the local authority for any part of the area,
- (c) consultation with whatever community representatives the local policing body thinks it appropriate to consult, and
- (d) whatever other public consultation the local policing body thinks appropriate.

(6) A local policing body must agree the community remedy document for its area, and any revised document, with the chief officer of police for the area.

(7) Once the community remedy document, or a revised document, has been agreed with the chief officer of police, the local policing body must publish it in whatever way it thinks appropriate.

(8) The Secretary of State must publish any guidance issued under subsection (4)(b).

(9) In this section –

'anti-social behaviour' has the meaning given by section 2 (ignoring subsection (2) of that section);

'community representative', in relation to a police area, means any individual or body appearing to the local policing body to represent the views of people who live in, work in or visit the area;

'local authority' means –

- (a) in relation to England, a district council, a county council for an area for which there is no district council, a London borough council, the Common Council of the City of London or the Council of the Isles of Scilly;
- (b) in relation to Wales, a county council or a county borough council;

'out-of-court disposal process' means the process by which a person is dealt with under section 102 or by means of a conditional caution or youth conditional caution.

102 Anti-social behaviour etc: out-of-court disposals

(1) This section applies where –

(a) a person (P) within subsection (2) has evidence that an individual (A) has engaged in anti-social behaviour or committed an offence,
(b) A admits to P that he or she has done so,
(c) P thinks that the evidence is enough for taking proceedings against A for an injunction under section 1, or taking other court proceedings, but decides that it would be appropriate for A to carry out action of some sort instead, and
(d) if the evidence is that A has committed an offence, P does not think that it would be more appropriate for A to be given a caution or a fixed penalty notice.

(2) The persons within this subsection are –

(a) a constable;
(b) an investigating officer;
(c) a person authorised by a relevant prosecutor for the purposes of section 22 of the Criminal Justice Act 2003 (conditional cautions) or section 66A of the Crime and Disorder Act 1998 (youth conditional cautions).

(3) Before deciding what action to invite A to carry out, P must make reasonable efforts to obtain the views of the victim (if any) of the anti-social behaviour or the offence, and in particular the victim's views as to whether A should carry out any of the actions listed in the community remedy document.

(4) If the victim expresses the view that A should carry out a particular action listed in the community remedy document, P must invite A to carry out that action unless it seems to P that it would be inappropriate to do so.

(5) Where –

(a) there is more than one victim and they express different views, or
(b) for any other reason subsection (4) does not apply,

P must nevertheless take account of any views expressed by the victim (or victims) in deciding what action to invite A to carry out.

(6) In this section –

'action' includes the making of a payment to the victim (but does not include the payment of a fixed penalty);
'anti-social behaviour' has the meaning given by section 2 (ignoring subsection (2) of that section);
'community remedy document' means the community remedy document (as revised from time to time) published under section 101 for the police area in which A's anti-social behaviour or offence took place;
'caution' –

(a) in the case of a person aged 18 or over, includes a conditional caution within the meaning of Part 3 of the Criminal Justice Act 2003;
(b) in the case of a person under that age, means a youth caution or youth conditional caution within the meaning of Chapter 1 of Part 4 of the Crime and Disorder Act 1998;

'investigating officer' and 'relevant prosecutor' have the same meaning as in Part 3 of the Criminal Justice Act 2003 (see section 27 of that Act);
'victim' means the particular person who seems to P to have been affected, or principally affected, by A's anti-social behaviour or offence.

103 Criminal behaviour: conditional cautions

(1) In Part 3 of the Criminal Justice Act 2003 (conditional cautions), after section 23 there is inserted –

'23ZA Duty to consult victims

(1) Before deciding what conditions to attach to a conditional caution, a relevant prosecutor or the authorised person must make reasonable efforts to obtain the views of the victim (if any) of the offence, and in particular the victim's views as to whether the offender should carry out any of the actions listed in the community remedy document.

(2) If the victim expresses the view that the offender should carry out a particular action listed in the community remedy document, the prosecutor or authorised person must attach that as a condition unless it seems to the prosecutor or authorised person that it would be inappropriate to do so.

(3) Where –

(a) there is more than one victim and they express different views, or
(b) for any other reason subsection (2) does not apply,

the prosecutor or authorised person must nevertheless take account of any views expressed by the victim (or victims) in deciding what conditions to attach to the conditional caution.

(4) In this section –

'community remedy document' means the community remedy document (as revised from time to time) published under section 101 of the Anti-social Behaviour, Crime and Policing Act 2014 for the police area in which the offence was committed;
'victim' means the particular person who seems to the relevant prosecutor or authorised person to have been affected, or principally affected, by the offence.'

(2) After section 66B of the Crime and Disorder Act 1998 (requirements for youth conditional cautions) there is inserted –

'66BA Duty to consult victims

(1) Before deciding what conditions to attach to a youth conditional caution, a relevant prosecutor or the authorised person must make reasonable efforts to obtain the views of the victim (if any) of the offence, and in particular the victim's views as to whether the offender should carry out any of the actions listed in the community remedy document.

(2) If the victim expresses the view that the offender should carry out a particular action listed in the community remedy document, the prosecutor or authorised person must attach that as a condition unless it seems to the prosecutor or authorised person that it would be inappropriate to do so.

(3) Where –

(a) there is more than one victim and they express different views, or
(b) for any other reason subsection (2) does not apply,

the prosecutor or authorised person must nevertheless take account of any views expressed by the victim (or victims) in deciding what conditions to attach to the conditional caution.

(4) In this section –

'community remedy document ' means the community remedy document (as revised from time to time) published under section 101 of the Anti-social Behaviour, Crime and Policing Act 2014 for the police area in which the offence was committed;
'victim' means the particular person who seems to the relevant prosecutor or authorised person to have been affected, or principally affected, by the offence.'

Response to complaints about anti-social behaviour

104 Review of response to complaints

(1) In a case where a person has made a complaint about anti-social behaviour in a particular local government area, the relevant bodies in that area must carry out a review of the response to that behaviour (an 'ASB case review)' if –

(a) that person, or any other person, makes an application for such a review, and
(b) the relevant bodies decide that the threshold for a review is met.

(2) The relevant bodies in each local government area must –

(a) make arrangements about the carrying out of ASB case reviews by those bodies ('review procedures'), and
(b) ensure that the current review procedures are published.

(3) The review procedures must include provision about the making of applications for ASB case reviews; and, in particular, must –

(a) specify the point of contact for making applications, and
(b) ensure that applications made to that point of contact are passed on to all the relevant bodies in the local government area.

(4) In a situation where –

(a) an application for an ASB case review is made, and
(b) at least three (or, if a different number is specified in the review procedures, at least that number of) qualifying complaints have been made about the anti-social behaviour to which the application relates,

the relevant bodies must decide that the threshold for a review is met.

(5) In any other situation where an application for an ASB case review is made, the question whether the threshold for a review is met must be decided by the relevant bodies in accordance with the review procedures; and the procedures may, in particular, include provision for this purpose which is framed by reference to any of these matters –

(a) the persistence of the anti-social behaviour about which the original complaint was made;
(b) the harm caused, or the potential for harm to be caused, by that behaviour;
(c) the adequacy of the response to that behaviour.

(6) After the relevant bodies have decided whether or not the threshold for a review is met, they must inform the applicant of their decision.

(7) The relevant bodies who carry out an ASB case review may make recommendations to a person who exercises public functions (including recommendations to a relevant body) in respect of any matters arising from the review; and the person must have regard to the recommendations in exercising public functions.

(8) The relevant bodies who carry out an ASB case review must inform the applicant of –

(a) the outcome of the review, and
(b) any recommendations made in accordance with subsection (7).

(9) As soon as practicable after the end of a reporting period, the relevant bodies in a local government area must publish information about the following matters which relates to that period –

(a) the number of applications for ASB case reviews made to those bodies;
(b) the number of times those bodies decided that the threshold for a review was not met;
(c) the number of ASB case reviews those bodies have carried out;

(d) the number of ASB case reviews carried out by those bodies that have resulted in recommendations being made.

(10) The question whether a complaint made about anti-social behaviour is a 'qualifying complaint' for the purposes of subsection (4) is to be determined in accordance with subsections (11) and (12).

(11) A complaint about anti-social behaviour is a qualifying complaint if –

(a) the complaint is made within the period of one month (or, if a different period is specified in the review procedures, that period) beginning with the date on which the behaviour is alleged to have occurred; and
(b) the application for the ASB case review is made within the period of six months (or, if a different period is specified in the review procedures, that period) beginning with the date on which the complaint is made.

(12) But where a person makes two or more complaints about anti-social behaviour which meet the requirements in subsection (11), the question of which complaint is, or which complaints are, qualifying complaints is to be decided by the relevant bodies in accordance with the review procedures.

The procedures may, in particular, include provision for this purpose which is framed by reference to whether different complaints relate to different aspects of particular anti-social behaviour (including different incidents comprised in particular anti-social behaviour).

(13) Schedule 4 (ASB case reviews: supplementary provision) has effect.

105 ASB case reviews: interpretation

(1) This section applies for the purposes of section 104, this section and Schedule 4.

(2) In relation to England –

'local government area' means an area for which there is –

(a) a relevant district council, or
(b) a unitary authority;

'relevant district council' means the council of a district so far as it is not a unitary authority;
'unitary authority' means –

(a) the council of a county so far as it is the council for an area for which there are no district councils,
(b) the council of any district comprised in an area for which there is no county council,
(c) a London borough council,
(d) the Common Council of the City of London in its capacity as a local authority, or
(e) the Council of the Isles of Scilly;

and, in relation to a local government area in England –

'local provider of social housing' means a private registered provider of social housing that –

(a) grants tenancies of dwelling-houses in that area, or
(b) manages any house or other property in that area;

'relevant bodies' means –

(a) the relevant district council or the unitary authority,
(b) the chief officer of police for the police area which that local government area is within,
(c) each clinical commissioning group established under section 14V of the National Health Service Act 2006 whose area is wholly or partly within that local government area, and
(d) any local providers of social housing who are among the relevant bodies by virtue of the co-option arrangements made in relation to that local government area.

(3) In relation to Wales –

'local government area' means –

(a) a county, or
(b) a county borough;

and, in relation to a local government area in Wales –

'local provider of social housing' means a body registered as a social landlord under section 3 of the Housing Act 1996 that –

(a) grants tenancies of dwelling-houses in that area, or
(b) manages any house or other property in that area;

'relevant bodies' means –

(a) the council for the area,
(b) the chief officer of police for the police area which that local government area is within,
(c) each Local Health Board whose area is wholly or partly within that local government area, and
(d) any local providers of social housing who are among the relevant bodies by virtue of the co-option arrangements made in relation to that local government area.

(4) These expressions have the meanings given –

'anti-social behaviour' means behaviour causing harassment, alarm or distress to members or any member of the public;
'applicant' means a person who makes an application for an ASB case review;
'ASB case review' has the meaning given in section 104(1);
'dwelling-house' has the same meaning as in the Housing Act 1985;
'co-option arrangements' has the meaning given in paragraph 5 of Schedule 4;
'reporting period', in relation to the publication of information by the relevant bodies in a local government area, means a period, not exceeding 12 months, determined by those bodies.

Schedule 2

Breach of Injunctions: Powers of Court in Respect of Under-18s

Section 12

PART 1

INTRODUCTORY

Power to make supervision order or detention order

1 (1) A youth court, if satisfied beyond reasonable doubt that a person aged under 18 is in breach of a provision of an injunction under section 1 to which he or she is subject, may make in respect of the person –

(a) a supervision order (see Part 2 of this Schedule), or
(b) a detention order (see Part 3 of this Schedule).

(2) An order under sub-paragraph (1) may be made only on the application of the person who applied for the injunction.

(3) A person making an application for an order under sub-paragraph (1) must before doing so –

(a) consult any youth offending team specified under section 3(1) or, if a youth offending team is not specified under that subsection, the local youth offending team within the meaning of section 14;
(b) inform any other body or individual the applicant thinks appropriate.

(4) In considering whether and how to exercise its powers under this paragraph, the court must consider any representations made by the youth offending team referred to in sub-paragraph (3)(a).

(5) A detention order may not be made under sub-paragraph (1) in respect of a person aged under 14.

(6) The court may not make a detention order under sub-paragraph (1) unless it is satisfied that, in view of the severity or extent of the breach, no other power available to the court is appropriate.

PART 2

SUPERVISION ORDERS

2 (1) A supervision order is an order imposing on the person in respect of whom it is made ("the defaulter") one or more of the following requirements –

(a) a supervision requirement (see paragraph 3);
(b) an activity requirement (see paragraph 4);
(c) a curfew requirement (see paragraph 5).

(2) Before making a supervision order the court must obtain and consider information about the defaulter's family circumstances and the likely effect of a supervision order on those circumstances.

(3) Before making a supervision order imposing two or more requirements, the court must consider their compatibility with each other.

(4) The court must ensure, as far as practicable, that requirements imposed by a supervision order are such as to avoid –

(a) any interference with the times, if any, at which the defaulter normally works or attends school or any other educational establishment;
(b) any conflict with the requirements of any other court order or injunction to which the defaulter may be subject.

(5) A supervision order must for the purposes of this Schedule specify a maximum period for the operation of any requirement contained in the order.

(6) The period specified under sub-paragraph (5) may not exceed 6 months (not counting the day on which the order is made).

(7) A supervision order must for the purposes of this Schedule specify –

(a) the youth offending team in whose area it appears to the court that the respondent will live during the period specified under sub-paragraph (5), or
(b) if it appears to the court that the defaulter will live in more than one such area, whichever of the relevant youth offending teams the court decides.

Supervision requirements

3 (1) In this Schedule "supervision requirement", in relation to a supervision order, means a requirement that the defaulter attend appointments with –

(a) the responsible officer (see paragraph 7), or
(b) another person decided by the responsible officer,

at whatever times and places the responsible officer instructs.

(2) The appointments must be within the period for the time being specified in the order under paragraph 2(5).

Activity requirements

4 (1) In this Schedule "activity requirement", in relation to a supervision order, means a requirement that the defaulter do any or all of the following within the period for the time being specified in the order under paragraph 2(5) –

(a) participate, on however many days are specified in the order, in activities at a place or places specified in it;
(b) participate in an activity or activities specified in the order on however many days are specified in it;
(c) participate in one or more residential exercises for a continuous period or periods comprising however many days are specified in the order;
(d) in accordance with sub-paragraphs (8) to (10), engage in activities in accordance with instructions of the responsible officer on however many days are specified in the order.

(2) The aggregate number of days specified in a supervision order in relation to an activity requirement must not be less than 12 or more than 24.

(3) A requirement referred to in sub-paragraph (1)(a) operates to require the defaulter, in accordance with instructions given by the responsible officer, on the number of days specified in the order in relation to the requirement –

(a) to present himself or herself at a place specified in the order to a person of a description specified in it;
(b) on each day, to comply with instructions given by, or under the authority of, the person in charge of the place.

(4) A requirement referred to in sub-paragraph (1)(b) operates to require the defaulter, in accordance with instructions given by the responsible officer, on the number of days specified in the order in relation to the requirement –

(a) to participate in an activity specified in the order;
(b) on each day, to comply with instructions given by, or under the authority of, the person in charge of the activity.

(5) Where the order includes a requirement referred to in sub-paragraph (1)(c) to participate in a residential exercise, it must specify either –

(a) a place, or
(b) an activity,

in relation to the exercise.

(6) A requirement under sub-paragraph (1)(c) to participate in a residential exercise in relation to which a place is specified under sub-paragraph (5) operates to require the defaulter, in accordance with instructions given by the responsible officer –

(a) to present himself or herself at the beginning of the period specified in the order in relation to the exercise, at the place specified in it, to a person of a description specified in the instructions;
(b) to live there for that period;
(c) during that period to comply with instructions given by, or under the authority of, the person in charge of the place.

(7) A requirement under sub-paragraph (1)(c) to participate in a residential exercise in relation to which an activity is specified under sub-paragraph (5) operates to require the defaulter, in accordance with instructions given by the responsible officer –

(a) to participate, for the period specified in the order in relation to the exercise, in the activity specified in it;
(b) during that period to comply with instructions given by, or under the authority of, the person in charge of the activity.

(8) Subject to sub-paragraph (9), instructions under sub-paragraph (1)(d) relating to any particular day must require the defaulter to do either of the following –

(a) to present himself or herself to a person of a description specified in the instructions at a place specified in them;
(b) to participate in an activity specified in the instructions.

The instructions operate to require the defaulter, on that day or while participating in that activity, to comply with instructions given by, or under the authority of, the person in charge of the place or activity.

(9) If the supervision order so provides, instructions under sub-paragraph (1)(d) may require the defaulter to participate in a residential exercise for a period comprising not more than seven days, and for that purpose –

(a) to present himself or herself at the beginning of that period to a person of a description specified in the instructions at a place specified in them, and to live there for that period, or
(b) to participate for that period in an activity specified in the instructions.

(10) Instructions of the kind mentioned in sub-paragraph (9) –

(a) may not be given except with the consent of a parent or guardian of the defaulter;
(b) operate to require the defaulter, during the period specified under that sub-paragraph, to comply with instructions given by, or under the authority of, the person in charge of the place or activity specified under paragraph (a) or (b) of that sub-paragraph.

(11) Instructions given by, or under the authority of, a person in charge of a place under sub-paragraph (3)(b), (6)(c), (8) or (10)(b) may require the defaulter to engage in activities otherwise than at that place.

(12) Where a supervision order contains an activity requirement, the court may, on the application of the original applicant or the defaulter, amend the order by substituting for a number of days, place, activity, period or description of persons specified in the order a new number of days, place, activity, period or description (subject, in the case of a number of days, to sub-paragraph (2)).

(13) A court may include an activity requirement in a supervision order or vary an activity requirement under sub-paragraph (12) only if –

(a) it has consulted the youth offending team that is to be, or is, specified in the order,
(b) it is satisfied that it is feasible to secure compliance with the requirement, or the requirement as varied,
(c) it is satisfied that provision for the defaulter to participate in the activities proposed can be made under the arrangements for persons to participate in those activities which exist in the area of the youth offending team that is to be, or is, specified in the order, and
(d) in a case where the requirement, or the requirement as varied, would involve the co-operation of a person other than the defaulter and the responsible officer, that person consents to its inclusion or variation.

(14) In sub-paragraph (10) "guardian" has the same meaning as in the Children and Young Persons Act 1933.

But where a local authority has parental responsibility (within the meaning given by section 3 of the Children Act 1989) for a defaulter who –

(a) is in the authority's care, or
(b) is provided with accommodation by the authority in the exercise of social services functions (within the meaning given by section 1A of the Local Authority Social Services Act 1970),

the reference to "guardian" in sub-paragraph (10) is to be read as a reference to that authority.

Curfew requirements

5 (1) In this Schedule "curfew requirement", in relation to a supervision order, means a requirement that the defaulter remain at a place specified in the order for the periods specified in it.

(2) A supervision order imposing a curfew requirement may specify different places or different periods for different days.

(3) The periods specified under sub-paragraph (1) –

(a) must be within the period for the time being specified in the order under paragraph 2(5);
(b) may not amount to less than 2 or more than 8 hours in any day.

(4) Before specifying a place under sub-paragraph (1), the court making the order must obtain and consider information about the place proposed to be specified (including information as to the attitude of persons likely to be affected by the enforced presence there of the defaulter).

(5) Where a supervision order contains a curfew requirement, the court may, on the application of the original applicant or the defaulter, amend the order by –

(a) substituting new periods for the periods specified in the order under this paragraph (subject to sub-paragraph (3));
(b) substituting a new place for the place specified in the order under this paragraph (subject to sub-paragraph (4)).

Electronic monitoring requirements

6 (1) A supervision order containing a curfew requirement may also contain a requirement (an "electronic monitoring requirement") for securing the electronic monitoring of compliance with the curfew requirement during a period –

(a) specified in the order, or
(b) determined by the responsible officer in accordance with the order.

(2) In the case referred to in sub-paragraph (1)(b), the responsible officer must, before the beginning of the period when the electronic monitoring requirement is to take effect, notify –

(a) the defaulter,
(b) the person responsible for the monitoring, and
(c) any person within sub-paragraph (3)(b),

of the time when that period is to begin.

(3) Where –

(a) it is proposed to include an electronic monitoring requirement in a supervision order, but
(b) there is a person (other than the defaulter) without whose co-operation it will not be practicable to secure that the monitoring takes place,

the requirement may not be included in the order without that person's consent.

(4) A supervision order imposing an electronic monitoring requirement must include provision for making a person responsible for the monitoring.

(5) An electronic monitoring requirement may not be included in a supervision order unless the court making the order –

(a) has been notified by the youth offending team for the time being specified in the order that arrangements for electronic monitoring are available in the area that includes the place the court proposes to specify in the order for the purposes of the curfew requirement, and

(b) is satisfied that the necessary provision can be made under the arrangements currently available.

(6) Where a supervision order contains an electronic monitoring requirement, the court may, on the application of the original applicant or the defaulter, amend the order by substituting a new period for the period specified in the order under this paragraph.

(7) Sub-paragraph (3) applies in relation to the variation of an electronic monitoring requirement under sub-paragraph (6) as it applies in relation to the inclusion of a requirement.

"Responsible officer"

7 (1) For the purposes of this Part of this Schedule, the "responsible officer", in relation to a supervision order, means –

(a) in a case where the order imposes a curfew requirement and an electronic monitoring requirement, but does not impose an activity or supervision requirement, the person who under paragraph 6(4) is responsible for the electronic monitoring;

(b) in any other case, the member of the youth offending team for the time being specified in the order who is for the time being responsible for discharging the functions conferred by this Schedule on the responsible officer.

(2) Where a supervision order has been made, it is the duty of the responsible officer –

(a) to make any arrangements that are necessary in connection with the requirements contained in the order;

(b) to promote the defaulter's compliance with those requirements.

(3) The responsible officer must ensure, so far as practicable, that any instructions given by the officer under a supervision order are such as to avoid the things referred to in paragraph 2(4).

(4) A defaulter in respect of whom a supervision order is made must –

(a) keep in touch with the responsible officer, in accordance with any instructions given by the responsible officer from time to time;

(b) notify the responsible officer of any change of address.

These obligations have effect as requirements of the order.

Amendment of operative period

8 (1) The court may, on the application of the original applicant, amend a supervision order by substituting a new period for the one specified in the order for the time being under paragraph 2(5) (subject to paragraph 2(6)).

(2) A court amending a supervision order under sub-paragraph (1) may make whatever other amendments to the order the court considers appropriate in relation to a requirement imposed by the order.

Amendment on change of area of residence

9 (1) This paragraph applies where, on an application made in relation to a supervision order by the original applicant or the defaulter, the court is satisfied that the defaulter proposes to live, or is living, in the area of a youth offending team other than the team for the time being specified in the order.

(2) If the application is made by the defaulter, the court may amend the order by substituting for the youth offending team specified in the order the youth offending team for the area referred to in sub-paragraph (1) (or, if there is more than one youth offending team for that area, whichever of them the court decides).

(3) If the application is made by the original applicant, the court must amend the order in the way mentioned in sub-paragraph (2) (subject to sub-paragraph (5)).

(4) Where a court amends the supervision order under sub-paragraph (2) or (3) but the order contains a requirement that, in the opinion of the court, cannot reasonably be complied with if the defaulter lives in the area referred to in sub-paragraph (1), the court must also amend the order by –

(a) removing that requirement, or
(b) substituting for that requirement a new requirement that can reasonably be complied with if the defaulter lives in that area.

(5) Sub-paragraph (3) does not require a court to amend the supervision order if in its opinion sub-paragraph (4) would produce an inappropriate result.

(6) The original applicant must consult the youth offending team for the time being specified in the order before making an application under sub-paragraph (1).

Revocation of supervision order

10 (1) The original applicant or the defaulter may apply to a youth court –

(a) to revoke a supervision order;
(b) to amend a supervision order by removing a requirement from it.

(2) If it appears to the court to be in the interests of justice to do so, having regard to circumstances that have arisen since the supervision order was made, the court may grant an application under sub-paragraph (1) and revoke or amend the order accordingly.

(3) The circumstances referred to in sub-paragraph (2) include the conduct of the defaulter.

(4) If an application under this paragraph is dismissed, the party by which the dismissed application was made may make no further application under this paragraph without –

(a) the consent of the court, or
(b) the agreement of the other party.

(5) The original applicant must consult the youth offending team for the time being specified in the supervision order before making an application under sub-paragraph (1).

Compliance with supervision order

11 If the responsible officer considers that the defaulter has complied with all the requirements of the supervision order, the officer must inform the original applicant.

Non-compliance with supervision order

12 (1) If the responsible officer considers that the defaulter has failed to comply with a requirement of the supervision order, the officer must inform the original applicant.

(2) On being informed under sub-paragraph (1) the original applicant may apply to a youth court.

(3) Before making an application under sub-paragraph (2) the original applicant must –

(a) consult the youth offending team for the time being specified in the order;
(b) inform any other body or individual the original applicant thinks appropriate.

(4) If on an application under sub-paragraph (2) the court is satisfied beyond reasonable doubt that the defaulter has without reasonable excuse failed to comply with a requirement of the supervision order, the court may –

(a) revoke the supervision order and make a new one;
(b) revoke the order and make a detention order (see Part 3 of this Schedule).

(5) The powers in sub-paragraph (4) –

(a) may not be exercised after the defaulter reaches the age of 18;
(b) are in addition to any other power of the court in relation to the breach of the supervision order.

(6) The court must consider any representations made by the youth offending team for the time being specified in the order before exercising its powers under this paragraph.

Copies of supervision order etc

13 (1) A court that makes a supervision order must straight away provide a copy of the order to –

(a) the defaulter;
(b) the youth offending team for the time being specified in the order.

(2) Where a supervision order is made, the original applicant must straight away provide a copy of so much of the order as is relevant –

(a) in a case where the order includes an activity requirement specifying a place under paragraph 4(1)(a), to the person in charge of that place;
(b) in a case where the order includes an activity requirement specifying an activity under paragraph 4(1)(b), to the person in charge of that activity;
(c) in a case where the order includes an activity requirement specifying a residential exercise under paragraph 4(1)(c), to the person in charge of the place or activity specified under paragraph 4(5) in relation to that residential exercise;
(d) in a case where the order contains an electronic monitoring requirement, to –
    (i) any person who by virtue of paragraph 6(4) will be responsible for the electronic monitoring, and
    (ii) any person without whose consent that requirement could not have been included in the order.

(3) A court that revokes or amends a supervision order must straight away provide a copy of the revoking order, or of the order as amended, to –

(a) the defaulter;
(b) the youth offending team for the time being specified in the order.

(4) Where –

(a) a copy of a supervision order (or part of a supervision order) has been given to a person under sub-paragraph (2) by virtue of a requirement contained in the order, and
(b) the order is revoked, or amended in respect of that requirement,

the original applicant must straight away give a copy of the revoking order, or of so much of the order as amended as is relevant, to that person.

PART 3
DETENTION ORDERS

Detention orders

14 (1) A detention order is an order that the person in respect of whom it is made ("the defaulter") be detained for a period specified in the order in whatever youth detention accommodation the Secretary of State decides.

(2) The period specified under sub-paragraph (1) may not exceed the period of 3 months (not counting the day on which the order is made).

(3) In sub-paragraph (1) "youth detention accommodation" means –

(a) a secure training centre;
(b) a young offender institution;
(c) secure accommodation, as defined by section 23(12) of the Children and Young Persons Act 1969.

(4) The function of the Secretary of State under sub-paragraph (1) is exercisable concurrently with the Youth Justice Board.

(5) A person detained under a detention order is in legal custody.

Revocation of detention order

15 (1) Where a detention order is made, the original applicant or the defaulter may apply to a youth court to revoke it.

(2) If it appears to the court to be in the interests of justice to do so, having regard to circumstances that have arisen since the detention order was made, the court may grant an application under sub-paragraph (1) and revoke the order accordingly.

(3) The circumstances referred to in sub-paragraph (2) include the conduct of the defaulter.

(4) If an application under this paragraph is dismissed, the party by which the dismissed application was made may make no further application under this paragraph without –

(a) the consent of the court, or
(b) the agreement of the other party.

(5) A person making an application under this paragraph in relation to a detention order made under paragraph 1 must before doing so consult any youth offending team specified in the injunction under section 3(1) or, if none is specified, the local youth offending team within the meaning of section 14.

(6) A person making an application under this paragraph in relation to a detention order made under paragraph 12(4)(b) must before doing so consult the youth offending team for the time being specified in the relevant supervision order.

Youth Justice, Crime and Evidence Act 1999 (ss 16–63)

Arrangement of Sections

PART II

GIVING OF EVIDENCE OR INFORMATION FOR PURPOSES OF CRIMINAL PROCEEDINGS

Chapter I

PART II

GIVING OF EVIDENCE OR INFORMATION FOR PURPOSES OF CRIMINAL PROCEEDINGS

Chapter I

Special Measures Directions in Case of Vulnerable and Intimidated Witnesses

Preliminary

16 Witnesses eligible for assistance on grounds of age or incapacity

(1) For the purposes of this Chapter a witness in criminal proceedings (other than the accused) is eligible for assistance by virtue of this section –

(a) if under the age of 18 at the time of the hearing; or

(b) if the court considers that the quality of evidence given by the witness is likely to be diminished by reason of any circumstances falling within subsection (2).

(2) The circumstances falling within this subsection are –

(a) that the witness –

(i) suffers from mental disorder within the meaning of the Mental Health Act 1983, or
(ii) otherwise has a significant impairment of intelligence and social functioning;

(b) that the witness has a physical disability or is suffering from a physical disorder.

(3) In subsection (1)(a) "the time of the hearing", in relation to a witness, means the time when it falls to the court to make a determination for the purposes of section 19(2) in relation to the witness.

(4) In determining whether a witness falls within subsection (1)(b) the court must consider any views expressed by the witness.

(5) In this Chapter references to the quality of a witness's evidence are to its quality in terms of completeness, coherence and accuracy; and for this purpose "coherence" refers to a witness's ability in giving evidence to give answers which address the questions put to the witness and can be understood both individually and collectively.

17 Witnesses eligible for assistance on grounds of fear or distress about testifying

(1) For the purposes of this Chapter a witness in criminal proceedings (other than the accused) is eligible for assistance by virtue of this subsection if the court is satisfied that the quality of evidence given by the witness is likely to be diminished by reason of fear or distress on the part of the witness in connection with testifying in the proceedings.

(2) In determining whether a witness falls within subsection (1) the court must take into account, in particular –

(a) the nature and alleged circumstances of the offence to which the proceedings relate;
(b) the age of the witness;
(c) such of the following matters as appear to the court to be relevant, namely –

(i) the social and cultural background and ethnic origins of the witness,
(ii) the domestic and employment circumstances of the witness, and
(iii) any religious beliefs or political opinions of the witness;

(d) any behaviour towards the witness on the part of –

(i) the accused,
(ii) members of the family or associates of the accused, or
(iii) any other person who is likely to be an accused or a witness in the proceedings.

(3) In determining that question the court must in addition consider any views expressed by the witness.

(4) here the complainant in respect of a sexual offence or an offence under section 4 of the Asylum and Immigration (Treatment of Claimants, etc) Act 2004 is a witness in proceedings relating to that offence (or to that offence and any other offences), the witness is eligible for assistance in relation to those proceedings by virtue of this subsection unless the witness has informed the court of the witness' wish not to be so eligible by virtue of this subsection.

(5) A witness in proceedings relating to a relevant offence (or to a relevant offence and any other offences) is eligible for assistance in relation to those proceedings by virtue of this subsection unless the witness has informed the court of the witness' wish not to be so eligible by virtue of this subsection.

(6) For the purposes of subsection (5) an offence is a relevant offence if it is an offence described in Schedule 1A.

(7) The Secretary of State may by order amend Schedule 1A.

18 Special measures available to eligible witnesses

(1) For the purposes of this Chapter –

(a) the provision which may be made by a special measures direction by virtue of each of sections 23 to 30 is a special measure available in relation to a witness eligible for assistance by virtue of section 16; and
(b) the provision which may be made by such a direction by virtue of each of sections 23 to 28 is a special measure available in relation to a witness eligible for assistance by virtue of section 17;

but this subsection has effect subject to subsection (2).

(2) Where (apart from this subsection) a special measure would, in accordance with subsection (1)(a) or (b), be available in relation to a witness in any proceedings, it shall not be taken by a court to be available in relation to the witness unless –

(a) the court has been notified by the Secretary of State that relevant arrangements may be made available in the area in which it appears to the court that the proceedings will take place, and
(b) the notice has not been withdrawn.

(3) In subsection (2) "relevant arrangements" means arrangements for implementing the measure in question which cover the witness and the proceedings in question.

(4) The withdrawal of a notice under that subsection relating to a special measure shall not affect the availability of that measure in relation to a witness if a special measures direction providing for that measure to apply to the witness' evidence has been made by the court before the notice is withdrawn.

(5) The Secretary of State may by order make such amendments of this Chapter as he considers appropriate for altering the special measures which, in accordance with subsection (1)(a) or (b), are available in relation to a witness eligible for assistance by virtue of section 16 or (as the case may be) section 17, whether –

(a) by modifying the provisions relating to any measure for the time being available in relation to such a witness,
(b) by the addition –
    (i) (with or without modifications) of any measure which is for the time being available in relation to a witness eligible for assistance by virtue of the other of those sections, or
    (ii) of any new measure, or
(c) by the removal of any measure.

Special measures directions

19 Special measures direction relating to eligible witness

(1) This section applies where in any criminal proceedings –

(a) a party to the proceedings makes an application for the court to give a direction under this section in relation to a witness in the proceedings other than the accused, or
(b) the court of its own motion raises the issue whether such a direction should be given.

(2) Where the court determines that the witness is eligible for assistance by virtue of section 16 or 17, the court must then –

(a) determine whether any of the special measures available in relation to the witness (or any combination of them) would, in its opinion, be likely to improve the quality of evidence given by the witness; and
(b) if so –
    (i) determine which of those measures (or combination of them) would, in its opinion, be likely to maximise so far as practicable the quality of such evidence; and
    (ii) give a direction under this section providing for the measure or measures so determined to apply to evidence given by the witness.

(3) In determining for the purposes of this Chapter whether any special measure or measures would or would not be likely to improve, or to maximise so far as practicable, the quality of evidence given by the witness, the court must consider all the circumstances of the case, including in particular –

(a) any views expressed by the witness; and
(b) whether the measure or measures might tend to inhibit such evidence being effectively tested by a party to the proceedings.

(4) A special measures direction must specify particulars of the provision made by the direction in respect of each special measure which is to apply to the witness' evidence.

(5) In this Chapter "special measures direction" means a direction under this section.

(6) Nothing in this Chapter is to be regarded as affecting any power of a court to make an order or give leave of any description (in the exercise of its inherent jurisdiction or otherwise) –

(a) in relation to a witness who is not an eligible witness, or
(b) in relation to an eligible witness where (as, for example, in a case where a foreign language interpreter is to be provided) the order is made or the leave is given otherwise than by reason of the fact that the witness is an eligible witness.

20 Further provisions about directions: general

(1) Subject to subsection (2) and section 21(8), a special measures direction has binding effect from the time it is made until the proceedings for the purposes of which it is made are either –

(a) determined (by acquittal, conviction or otherwise), or
(b) abandoned,

in relation to the accused or (if there is more than one) in relation to each of the accused.

(2) The court may discharge or vary (or further vary) a special measures direction if it appears to the court to be in the interests of justice to do so, and may do so either –

(a) on an application made by a party to the proceedings, if there has been a material change of circumstances since the relevant time, or
(b) of its own motion.

(3) In subsection (2) "the relevant time" means –

(a) the time when the direction was given, or
(b) if a previous application has been made under that subsection, the time when the application (or last application) was made.

(4) Nothing in section 24(2) and (3), 27(4) to (7) or 28(4) to (6) is to be regarded as affecting the power of the court to vary or discharge a special measures direction under subsection (2).

(5) The court must state in open court its reasons for –

(a) giving or varying,
(b) refusing an application for, or for the variation or discharge of, or
(c) discharging,

a special measures direction and, if it is a magistrates' court, must cause them to be entered in the register of its proceedings.

(6) Criminal Procedure Rules may make provision –

(a) for uncontested applications to be determined by the court without a hearing;
(b) for preventing the renewal of an unsuccessful application for a special measures direction except where there has been a material change of circumstances;

(c) for expert evidence to be given in connection with an application for, or for varying or discharging, such a direction;
(d) for the manner in which confidential or sensitive information is to be treated in connection with such an application and in particular as to its being disclosed to, or withheld from, a party to the proceedings.

21 Special provisions relating to child witnesses

(1) For the purposes of this section –

(a) a witness in criminal proceedings is a "child witness" if he is an eligible witness by reason of section 16(1)(a) (whether or not he is an eligible witness by reason of any other provision of section 16 or 17);
(b) and
(c) a "relevant recording", in relation to a child witness, is a video recording of an interview of the witness made with a view to its admission as evidence in chief of the witness.

(2) Where the court, in making a determination for the purposes of section 19(2), determines that a witness in criminal proceedings is a child witness, the court must –

(a) first have regard to subsections (3) to (4C) below; and
(b) then have regard to section 19(2);

and for the purposes of section 19(2), as it then applies to the witness, any special measures required to be applied in relation to him by virtue of this section shall be treated as if they were measures determined by the court, pursuant to section 19(2)(a) and (b)(i), to be ones that (whether on their own or with any other special measures) would be likely to maximise, so far as practicable, the quality of his evidence.

(3) The primary rule in the case of a child witness is that the court must give a special measures direction in relation to the witness which complies with the following requirements –

(a) it must provide for any relevant recording to be admitted under section 27 (video recorded evidence in chief); and
(b) it must provide for any evidence given by the witness in the proceedings which is not given by means of a video recording (whether in chief or otherwise) to be given by means of a live link in accordance with section 24.

(4) The primary rule is subject to the following limitations –

(a) the requirement contained in subsection (3)(a) or (b) has effect subject to the availability (within the meaning of section 18(2)) of the special measure in question in relation to the witness;
(b) the requirement contained in subsection (3)(a) also has effect subject to section 27(2);
(ba) if the witness informs the court of the witness' wish that the rule should not apply or should apply only in part, the rule does not apply to the extent that the court is satisfied that not complying with the rule would not diminish the quality of the witness' evidence; and
(c) the rule does not apply to the extent that the court is satisfied that compliance with it would not be likely to maximise the quality of the witness' evidence so far as practicable (whether because the application to that evidence of one or more other special measures available in relation to the witness would have that result or for any other reason).

(4A) Where as a consequence of all or part of the primary rule being disapplied under subsection (4)(ba) a witness' evidence or any part of it would fall to be given as testimony in court, the court must give a special measures direction making such provision as is described in section 23 for the evidence or that part of it.

(4B) The requirement in subsection (4A) is subject to the following limitations –

(a) if the witness informs the court of the witness 's wish that the requirement in subsection (4A) should not apply, the requirement does not apply to the extent that the court is satisfied that not complying with it would not diminish the quality of the witness' evidence; and
(b) the requirement does not apply to the extent that the court is satisfied that making such a provision would not be likely to maximise the quality of the witness' evidence so far as practicable (whether

because the application to that evidence of one or more other special measures available in relation to the witness would have that result or for any other reason).

(4C) In making a decision under subsection (4)(ba) or (4B)(a), the court must take into account the following factors (and any others it considers relevant) –

- (a) the age and maturity of the witness;
- (b) the ability of the witness to understand the consequences of giving evidence otherwise than in accordance with the requirements in subsection (3) or (as the case may be) in accordance with the requirement in subsection (4A);
- (c) the relationship (if any) between the witness and the accused;
- (d) the witness' social and cultural background and ethnic origins;
- (e) the nature and alleged circumstances of the offence to which the proceedings relate.

(5) [*repealed*]

(6) [*repealed*]

(7) [*repealed*]

(8) Where a special measures direction is given in relation to a child witness who is an eligible witness by reason only of section 16(1)(a), then –

- (a) subject to subsection (9) below, and
- (b) except where the witness has already begun to give evidence in the proceedings,

the direction shall cease to have effect at the time when the witness attains the age of 18.

(9) Where a special measures direction is given in relation to a child witness who is an eligible witness by reason only of section 16(1)(a) and –

- (a) the direction provides –
  - (i) for any relevant recording to be admitted under section 27 as evidence in chief of the witness, or
  - (ii) for the special measure available under section 28 to apply in relation to the witness, and
- (b) if it provides for that special measure to so apply, the witness is still under the age of 18 when the video recording is made for the purposes of section 28,

then, so far as it provides as mentioned in paragraph (a)(i) or (ii) above, the direction shall continue to have effect in accordance with section 20(1) even though the witness subsequently attains that age.

22 Extension of provisions of section 21 to certain witnesses over 18

(1) For the purposes of this section –

- (a) a witness in criminal proceedings (other than the accused) is a "qualifying witness" if he –
  - (i) is not an eligible witness at the time of the hearing (as defined by section 16(3)), but
  - (ii) was under the age of 18 when a relevant recording was made;
- (b) and
- (c) a "relevant recording", in relation to a witness, is a video recording of an interview of the witness made with a view to its admission as evidence in chief of the witness.

(2) Subsections (2) to (4) and (4C) of section 21, so far as relating to the giving of a direction complying with the requirement contained in section 21(3)(a), apply to a qualifying witness in respect of the relevant recording as they apply to a child witness (within the meaning of that section).

22A Special provisions relating to sexual offences

(1) This section applies where in criminal proceedings relating to a sexual offence (or to a sexual offence and other offences) the complainant in respect of that offence is a witness in the proceedings.

(2) This section does not apply if the place of trial is a magistrates' court.

(3) This section does not apply if the complainant is an eligible witness by reason of section 16(1)(a) (whether or not the complainant is an eligible witness by reason of any other provision of section 16 or 17).

(4) If a party to the proceedings makes an application under section 19(1)(a) for a special measures direction in relation to the complainant, the party may request that the direction provide for any relevant recording to be admitted under section 27 (video recorded evidence in chief).

(5) Subsection (6) applies if –

(a) a party to the proceedings makes a request under subsection (4) with respect to the complainant, and
(b) the court determines for the purposes of section 19(2) that the complainant is eligible for assistance by virtue of section 16(1)(b) or 17.

(6) The court must –

(a) first have regard to subsections (7) to (9); and
(b) then have regard to section 19(2);

and for the purposes of section 19(2), as it then applies to the complainant, any special measure required to be applied in relation to the complainant by virtue of this section is to be treated as if it were a measure determined by the court, pursuant to section 19(2)(a) and (b)(i), to be one that (whether on its own or with any other special measures) would be likely to maximise, so far as practicable, the quality of the complainant's evidence.

(7) The court must give a special measures direction in relation to the complainant that provides for any relevant recording to be admitted under section 27.

(8) The requirement in subsection (7) has effect subject to section 27(2).

(9) The requirement in subsection (7) does not apply to the extent that the court is satisfied that compliance with it would not be likely to maximise the quality of the complainant's evidence so far as practicable (whether because the application to that evidence of one or more other special measures available in relation to the complainant would have that result or for any other reason).

(10) In this section "relevant recording", in relation to a complainant, is a video recording of an interview of the complainant made with a view to its admission as the evidence in chief of the complainant.

Special measures

23 Screening witness from accused

(1) A special measures direction may provide for the witness, while giving testimony or being sworn in court, to be prevented by means of a screen or other arrangement from seeing the accused.

(2) But the screen or other arrangement must not prevent the witness from being able to see, and to be seen by –

(a) the judge or justices (or both) and the jury (if there is one);
(b) legal representatives acting in the proceedings; and
(c) any interpreter or other person appointed (in pursuance of the direction or otherwise) to assist the witness.

(3) Where two or more legal representatives are acting for a party to the proceedings, subsection (2)(b) is to be regarded as satisfied in relation to those representatives if the witness is able at all material times to see and be seen by at least one of them.

24 Evidence by live link

(1) A special measures direction may provide for the witness to give evidence by means of a live link.

(1A) Such a direction may also provide for a specified person to accompany the witness while the witness is giving evidence by live link.

(1B) In determining who may accompany the witness, the court must have regard to the wishes of the witness.

(2) Where a direction provides for the witness to give evidence by means of a live link, the witness may not give evidence in any other way without the permission of the court.

(3) The court may give permission for the purposes of subsection (2) if it appears to the court to be in the interests of justice to do so, and may do so either –

(a) on an application by a party to the proceedings, if there has been a material change of circumstances since the relevant time, or
(b) of its own motion.

(4) In subsection (3) "the relevant time" means –

(a) the time when the direction was given, or
(b) if a previous application has been made under that subsection, the time when the application (or last application) was made.

(5) …

(6) …

(7) …

(8) In this Chapter "live link" means a live television link or other arrangement whereby a witness, while absent from the courtroom or other place where the proceedings are being held, is able to see and hear a person there and to be seen and heard by the persons specified in section 23(2)(a) to (c).

25 Evidence given in private

(1) A special measures direction may provide for the exclusion from the court, during the giving of the witness' evidence, of persons of any description specified in the direction.

(2) The persons who may be so excluded do not include –

(a) the accused,
(b) legal representatives acting in the proceedings, or
(c) any interpreter or other person appointed (in pursuance of the direction or otherwise) to assist the witness.

(3) A special measures direction providing for representatives of news gathering or reporting organisations to be so excluded shall be expressed not to apply to one named person who –

(a) is a representative of such an organisation, and
(b) has been nominated for the purpose by one or more such organisations,

unless it appears to the court that no such nomination has been made.

(4) A special measures direction may only provide for the exclusion of persons under this section where –

(a) the proceedings relate to a sexual offence or an offence under section 4 of the Asylum and Immigration (Treatment of Claimants, etc) Act 2004; or

(b) it appears to the court that there are reasonable grounds for believing that any person other than the accused has sought, or will seek, to intimidate the witness in connection with testifying in the proceedings.

(5) Any proceedings from which persons are excluded under this section (whether or not those persons include representatives of news gathering or reporting organisations) shall nevertheless be taken to be held in public for the purposes of any privilege or exemption from liability available in respect of fair, accurate and contemporaneous reports of legal proceedings held in public.

26 Removal of wigs and gowns

A special measures direction may provide for the wearing of wigs or gowns to be dispensed with during the giving of the witness' evidence.

27 Video recorded evidence in chief

(1) A special measures direction may provide for a video recording of an interview of the witness to be admitted as evidence in chief of the witness.

(2) A special measures direction may, however, not provide for a video recording, or a part of such a recording, to be admitted under this section if the court is of the opinion, having regard to all the circumstances of the case, that in the interests of justice the recording, or that part of it, should not be so admitted.

(3) In considering for the purposes of subsection (2) whether any part of a recording should not be admitted under this section, the court must consider whether any prejudice to the accused which might result from that part being so admitted is outweighed by the desirability of showing the whole, or substantially the whole, of the recorded interview.

(4) Where a special measures direction provides for a recording to be admitted under this section, the court may nevertheless subsequently direct that it is not to be so admitted if –

(a) it appears to the court that –

(i) the witness will not be available for cross-examination (whether conducted in the ordinary way or in accordance with any such direction), and

(ii) the parties to the proceedings have not agreed that there is no need for the witness to be so available; or

(b) any Criminal Procedure Rules requiring disclosure of the circumstances in which the recording was made have not been complied with to the satisfaction of the court.

(5) Where a recording is admitted under this section –

(a) the witness must be called by the party tendering it in evidence, unless –

(i) a special measures direction provides for the witness' evidence on cross-examination to be given in any recording admissible under section 28, or

(ii) the parties to the proceedings have agreed as mentioned in subsection (4)(a)(ii); and

(b) the witness may not without the permission of the court give evidence in chief otherwise than by means of the recording as to any matter which, in the opinion of the court, is dealt with in the witness' recorded testimony.

(6) Where in accordance with subsection (2) a special measures direction provides for part only of a recording to be admitted under this section, references in subsections (4) and (5) to the recording or to the witness' recorded testimony are references to the part of the recording or testimony which is to be so admitted.

(7) The court may give permission for the purposes of subsection (5)(b) if it appears to the court to be in the interests of justice to do so, and may do so either –

(a) on an application by a party to the proceedings, ... or
(b) of its own motion.

(8) ...

(9) The court may, in giving permission for the purposes of subsection (5)(b), direct that the evidence in question is to be given by the witness by means of a live link.

(9A) If the court directs under subsection (9) that evidence is to be given by live link, it may also make such provision in that direction as it could make under section 24(1A) in a special measures direction.

(10) ...

(11) Nothing in this section affects the admissibility of any video recording which would be admissible apart from this section.

28 Video recorded cross-examination or re-examination

(1) Where a special measures direction provides for a video recording to be admitted under section 27 as evidence in chief of the witness, the direction may also provide –

(a) for any cross-examination of the witness, and any re-examination, to be recorded by means of a video recording; and
(b) for such a recording to be admitted, so far as it relates to any such cross-examination or re-examination, as evidence of the witness under cross-examination or on re-examination, as the case may be.

(2) Such a recording must be made in the presence of such persons as Criminal Procedure Rules or the direction may provide and in the absence of the accused, but in circumstances in which –

(a) the judge or justices (or both) and legal representatives acting in the proceedings are able to see and hear the examination of the witness and to communicate with the persons in whose presence the recording is being made, and
(b) the accused is able to see and hear any such examination and to communicate with any legal representative acting for him.

(3) Where two or more legal representatives are acting for a party to the proceedings, subsection (2)(a) and (b) are to be regarded as satisfied in relation to those representatives if at all material times they are satisfied in relation to at least one of them.

(4) Where a special measures direction provides for a recording to be admitted under this section, the court may nevertheless subsequently direct that it is not to be so admitted if any requirement of subsection (2) or Criminal Procedure Rules or the direction has not been complied with to the satisfaction of the court.

(5) Where in pursuance of subsection (1) a recording has been made of any examination of the witness, the witness may not be subsequently cross-examined or re-examined in respect of any evidence given by the witness in the proceedings (whether in any recording admissible under section 27 or this section or otherwise than in such a recording) unless the court gives a further special measures direction making such provision as is mentioned in subsection (1)(a) and (b) in relation to any subsequent cross-examination, and re-examination, of the witness.

(6) The court may only give such a further direction if it appears to the court –

(a) that the proposed cross-examination is sought by a party to the proceedings as a result of that party having become aware, since the time when the original recording was made in pursuance of subsection (1), of a matter which that party could not with reasonable diligence have ascertained by then, or
(b) that for any other reason it is in the interests of justice to give the further direction.

(7) Nothing in this section shall be read as applying in relation to any cross-examination of the witness by the accused in person (in a case where the accused is to be able to conduct any such cross-examination).

29 Examination of witness through intermediary

(1) A special measures direction may provide for any examination of the witness (however and wherever conducted) to be conducted through an interpreter or other person approved by the court for the purposes of this section ("an intermediary").

(2) The function of an intermediary is to communicate –

(a) to the witness, questions put to the witness, and
(b) to any person asking such questions, the answers given by the witness in reply to them,

and to explain such questions or answers so far as necessary to enable them to be understood by the witness or person in question.

(3) Any examination of the witness in pursuance of subsection (1) must take place in the presence of such persons as Criminal Procedure Rules or the direction may provide, but in circumstances in which –

(a) the judge or justices (or both) and legal representatives acting in the proceedings are able to see and hear the examination of the witness and to communicate with the intermediary, and
(b) (except in the case of a video recorded examination) the jury (if there is one) are able to see and hear the examination of the witness.

(4) Where two or more legal representatives are acting for a party to the proceedings, subsection (3)(a) is to be regarded as satisfied in relation to those representatives if at all material times it is satisfied in relation to at least one of them.

(5) A person may not act as an intermediary in a particular case except after making a declaration, in such form as may be prescribed by Criminal Procedure Rules, that he will faithfully perform his function as intermediary.

(6) Subsection (1) does not apply to an interview of the witness which is recorded by means of a video recording with a view to its admission as evidence in chief of the witness; but a special measures direction may provide for such a recording to be admitted under section 27 if the interview was conducted through an intermediary and –

(a) that person complied with subsection (5) before the interview began, and
(b) the court's approval for the purposes of this section is given before the direction is given.

(7) Section 1 of the Perjury Act 1911 (perjury) shall apply in relation to a person acting as an intermediary as it applies in relation to a person lawfully sworn as an interpreter in a judicial proceeding; and for this purpose, where a person acts as an intermediary in any proceeding which is not a judicial proceeding for the purposes of that section, that proceeding shall be taken to be part of the judicial proceeding in which the witness' evidence is given.

30 Aids to communication

A special measures direction may provide for the witness, while giving evidence (whether by testimony in court or otherwise), to be provided with such device as the court considers appropriate with a view to enabling questions or answers to be communicated to or by the witness despite any disability or disorder or other impairment which the witness has or suffers from.

Supplementary

31 Status of evidence given under Chapter I

(1) Subsections (2) to (4) apply to a statement made by a witness in criminal proceedings which, in accordance with a special measures direction, is not made by the witness in direct oral testimony in court but forms part of the witness' evidence in those proceedings.

(2) The statement shall be treated as if made by the witness in direct oral testimony in court; and accordingly –

(a) it is admissible evidence of any fact of which such testimony from the witness would be admissible;
(b) it is not capable of corroborating any other evidence given by the witness.

(3) Subsection (2) applies to a statement admitted under section 27 or 28 which is not made by the witness on oath even though it would have been required to be made on oath if made by the witness in direct oral testimony in court.

(4) In estimating the weight (if any) to be attached to the statement, the court must have regard to all the circumstances from which an inference can reasonably be drawn (as to the accuracy of the statement or otherwise).

(5) Nothing in this Chapter (apart from subsection (3)) affects the operation of any rule of law relating to evidence in criminal proceedings.

(6) Where any statement made by a person on oath in any proceeding which is not a judicial proceeding for the purposes of section 1 of the Perjury Act 1911 (perjury) is received in evidence in pursuance of a special measures direction, that proceeding shall be taken for the purposes of that section to be part of the judicial proceeding in which the statement is so received in evidence.

(7) Where in any proceeding which is not a judicial proceeding for the purposes of that Act –

(a) a person wilfully makes a false statement otherwise than on oath which is subsequently received in evidence in pursuance of a special measures direction, and
(b) the statement is made in such circumstances that had it been given on oath in any such judicial proceeding that person would have been guilty of perjury,

he shall be guilty of an offence and liable to any punishment which might be imposed on conviction of an offence under section 57(2) (giving of false unsworn evidence in criminal proceedings).

(8) In this section "statement" includes any representation of fact, whether made in words or otherwise.

32 Warning to jury

Where on a trial on indictment with a jury evidence has been given in accordance with a special measures direction, the judge must give the jury such warning (if any) as the judge considers necessary to ensure that the fact that the direction was given in relation to the witness does not prejudice the accused.

33 Interpretation etc of Chapter I

(1) In this Chapter –

"eligible witness" means a witness eligible for assistance by virtue of section 16 or 17;
"live link" has the meaning given by section 24(8);
"quality", in relation to the evidence of a witness, shall be construed in accordance with section 16(5);
"special measures direction" means (in accordance with section 19(5)) a direction under section 19.

(2) In this Chapter references to the special measures available in relation to a witness shall be construed in accordance with section 18.

(3) In this Chapter references to a person being able to see or hear, or be seen or heard by, another person are to be read as not applying to the extent that either of them is unable to see or hear by reason of any impairment of eyesight or hearing.

(4) In the case of any proceedings in which there is more than one accused –

(a) any reference to the accused in sections 23 to 28 may be taken by a court, in connection with the giving of a special measures direction, as a reference to all or any of the accused, as the court may determine, and
(b) any such direction may be given on the basis of any such determination.

(5) For the purposes of this Chapter as it applies in relation to a witness who is the complainant in respect of a relevant offence, where the age of the witness is uncertain and there are reasons to believe that the witness is under the age of 18, that witness is presumed to be under the age of 18.

(6) In subsection (5) "relevant offence" means –

(a) a sexual offence;
(b) an offence under section 1 of the Protection of Children Act 1978;
(c) an offence under section 160 of the Criminal Justice Act 1988;
(d) an offence under section 4 of the Asylum and Immigration (Treatment of Claimants, etc) Act 2004.

Use of Live Link and Intermediary for Evidence of Certain Accused Persons

33A Live link directions

(1) This section applies to any proceedings (whether in a magistrates' court or before the Crown Court) against a person for an offence.

(2) The court may, on the application of the accused, give a live link direction if it is satisfied –

(a) that the conditions in subsection (4) or, as the case may be, subsection (5) are met in relation to the accused, and
(b) that it is in the interests of justice for the accused to give evidence through a live link.

(3) A live link direction is a direction that any oral evidence to be given before the court by the accused is to be given through a live link.

(4) Where the accused is aged under 18 when the application is made, the conditions are that –

(a) his ability to participate effectively in the proceedings as a witness giving oral evidence in court is compromised by his level of intellectual ability or social functioning, and
(b) use of a live link would enable him to participate more effectively in the proceedings as a witness (whether by improving the quality of his evidence or otherwise).

(5) Where the accused has attained the age of 18 at that time, the conditions are that –

(a) he suffers from a mental disorder (within the meaning of the Mental Health Act 1983) or otherwise has a significant impairment of intelligence and social function,
(b) he is for that reason unable to participate effectively in the proceedings as a witness giving oral evidence in court, and
(c) use of a live link would enable him to participate more effectively in the proceedings as a witness (whether by improving the quality of his evidence or otherwise).

(6) While a live link direction has effect the accused may not give oral evidence before the court in the proceedings otherwise than through a live link.

(7) The court may discharge a live link direction at any time before or during any hearing to which it applies if it appears to the court to be in the interests of justice to do so (but this does not affect the power to give a further live link direction in relation to the accused).

The court may exercise this power of its own motion or on an application by a party.

(8) The court must state in open court its reasons for –

- (a) giving or discharging a live link direction, or
- (b) refusing an application for or for the discharge of a live link direction,

and, if it is a magistrates' court, it must cause those reasons to be entered in the register of its proceedings.

33B Section 33A: meaning of "live link"

(1) In section 33A "live link" means an arrangement by which the accused, while absent from the place where the proceedings are being held, is able –

- (a) to see and hear a person there, and
- (b) to be seen and heard by the persons mentioned in subsection (2),

and for this purpose any impairment of eyesight or hearing is to be disregarded.

(2) The persons are –

- (a) the judge or justices (or both) and the jury (if there is one),
- (b) where there are two or more accused in the proceedings, each of the other accused,
- (c) legal representatives acting in the proceedings, and
- (d) any interpreter or other person appointed by the court to assist the accused.

33C Saving

Nothing in this Chapter affects –

- (a) any power of a court to make an order, give directions or give leave of any description in relation to any witness (including an accused), or
- (b) the operation of any rule of law relating to evidence in criminal proceedings.

Chapter II

Protection of Witnesses from Cross-Examination by Accused in Person

General prohibitions

34 Complainants in proceedings for sexual offences

No person charged with a sexual offence may in any criminal proceedings cross-examine in person a witness who is the complainant, either –

- (a) in connection with that offence, or
- (b) in connection with any other offence (of whatever nature) with which that person is charged in the proceedings.

35 Child complainants and other child witnesses

(1) No person charged with an offence to which this section applies may in any criminal proceedings cross-examine in person a protected witness, either –

(a) in connection with that offence, or
(b) in connection with any other offence (of whatever nature) with which that person is charged in the proceedings.

(2) For the purposes of subsection (1) a "protected witness" is a witness who –

(a) either is the complainant or is alleged to have been a witness to the commission of the offence to which this section applies, and
(b) either is a child or falls to be cross-examined after giving evidence in chief (whether wholly or in part) –

(i) by means of a video recording made (for the purposes of section 27) at a time when the witness was a child, or
(ii) in any other way at any such time.

(3) The offences to which this section applies are –

(a) any offence under –

(i) ...
(ii) ...
(iii) ...
(iv) ...
(iva) any of sections 33 to 36 of the Sexual Offences Act 1956,
(v) the Protection of Children Act 1978; or
(vi) Part 1 of the Sexual Offences Act 2003 or any relevant superseded enactment;

(b) kidnapping, false imprisonment or an offence under section 1 or 2 of the Child Abduction Act 1984;
(c) any offence under section 1 of the Children and Young Persons Act 1933;
(d) any offence (not within any of the preceding paragraphs) which involves an assault on, or injury or a threat of injury to, any person.

(3A) In subsection (3)(a)(vi) "relevant superseded enactment" means –

(a) any of sections 1 to 32 of the Sexual Offences Act 1956;
(b) the Indecency with Children Act 1960;
(c) the Sexual Offences Act 1967;
(d) section 54 of the Criminal Law Act 1977.

(4) In this section "child" means –

(a) where the offence falls within subsection (3)(a), a person under the age of 18; or
(b) where the offence falls within subsection (3)(b), (c) or (d), a person under the age of 14.

(5) For the purposes of this section "witness" includes a witness who is charged with an offence in the proceedings.

Prohibition imposed by court

36 Direction prohibiting accused from cross-examining particular witness

(1) This section applies where, in a case where neither of sections 34 and 35 operates to prevent an accused in any criminal proceedings from cross-examining a witness in person –

(a) the prosecutor makes an application for the court to give a direction under this section in relation to the witness, or
(b) the court of its own motion raises the issue whether such a direction should be given.

(2) If it appears to the court –

(a) that the quality of evidence given by the witness on cross-examination –

(i) is likely to be diminished if the cross-examination (or further cross-examination) is conducted by the accused in person, and
(ii) would be likely to be improved if a direction were given under this section, and

(b) that it would not be contrary to the interests of justice to give such a direction,

the court may give a direction prohibiting the accused from cross-examining (or further cross-examining) the witness in person.

(3) In determining whether subsection (2)(a) applies in the case of a witness the court must have regard, in particular, to –

(a) any views expressed by the witness as to whether or not the witness is content to be cross-examined by the accused in person;
(b) the nature of the questions likely to be asked, having regard to the issues in the proceedings and the defence case advanced so far (if any);
(c) any behaviour on the part of the accused at any stage of the proceedings, both generally and in relation to the witness;
(d) any relationship (of whatever nature) between the witness and the accused;
(e) whether any person (other than the accused) is or has at any time been charged in the proceedings with a sexual offence or an offence to which section 35 applies, and (if so) whether section 34 or 35 operates or would have operated to prevent that person from cross-examining the witness in person;
(f) any direction under section 19 which the court has given, or proposes to give, in relation to the witness.

(4) For the purposes of this section –

(a) "witness", in relation to an accused, does not include any other person who is charged with an offence in the proceedings; and
(b) any reference to the quality of a witness' evidence shall be construed in accordance with section 16(5).

37 Further provisions about directions under section 36

(1) Subject to subsection (2), a direction has binding effect from the time it is made until the witness to whom it applies is discharged.

In this section "direction" means a direction under section 36.

(2) The court may discharge a direction if it appears to the court to be in the interests of justice to do so, and may do so either –

(a) on an application made by a party to the proceedings, if there has been a material change of circumstances since the relevant time, or
(b) of its own motion.

(3) In subsection (2) "the relevant time" means –

(a) the time when the direction was given, or
(b) if a previous application has been made under that subsection, the time when the application (or last application) was made.

(4) The court must state in open court its reasons for –

(a) giving, or
(b) refusing an application for, or for the discharge of, or
(c) discharging,

a direction and, if it is a magistrates' court, must cause them to be entered in the register of its proceedings.

(5) Criminal Procedure Rules may make provision –

(a) for uncontested applications to be determined by the court without a hearing;
(b) for preventing the renewal of an unsuccessful application for a direction except where there has been a material change of circumstances;
(c) for expert evidence to be given in connection with an application for, or for discharging, a direction;
(d) for the manner in which confidential or sensitive information is to be treated in connection with such an application and in particular as to its being disclosed to, or withheld from, a party to the proceedings.

Cross-examination on behalf of accused

38 Defence representation for purposes of cross-examination

(1) This section applies where an accused is prevented from cross-examining a witness in person by virtue of section 34, 35 or 36.

(2) Where it appears to the court that this section applies, it must –

(a) invite the accused to arrange for a legal representative to act for him for the purpose of cross-examining the witness; and
(b) require the accused to notify the court, by the end of such period as it may specify, whether a legal representative is to act for him for that purpose.

(3) If by the end of the period mentioned in subsection (2)(b) either –

(a) the accused has notified the court that no legal representative is to act for him for the purpose of cross-examining the witness, or
(b) no notification has been received by the court and it appears to the court that no legal representative is to so act,

the court must consider whether it is necessary in the interests of justice for the witness to be cross-examined by a legal representative appointed to represent the interests of the accused.

(4) If the court decides that it is necessary in the interests of justice for the witness to be so cross-examined, the court must appoint a qualified legal representative (chosen by the court) to cross-examine the witness in the interests of the accused.

(5) A person so appointed shall not be responsible to the accused.

(6) Criminal Procedure Rules may make provision –

(a) as to the time when, and the manner in which, subsection (2) is to be complied with;
(b) in connection with the appointment of a legal representative under subsection (4), and in particular for securing that a person so appointed is provided with evidence or other material relating to the proceedings.

(7) Criminal Procedure Rules made in pursuance of subsection (6)(b) may make provision for the application, with such modifications as are specified in the rules, of any of the provisions of –

(a) Part I of the Criminal Procedure and Investigations Act 1996 (disclosure of material in connection with criminal proceedings), or
(b) the Sexual Offences (Protected Material) Act 1997.

(8) For the purposes of this section –

(a) any reference to cross-examination includes (in a case where a direction is given under section 36 after the accused has begun cross-examining the witness) a reference to further cross-examination; and
(b) "qualified legal representative" means a legal representative who has a right of audience (within the meaning of the Courts and Legal Services Act 1990) in relation to the proceedings before the court.

39 Warning to jury

(1) Where on a trial on indictment with a jury an accused is prevented from cross-examining a witness in person by virtue of section 34, 35 or 36, the judge must give the jury such warning (if any) as the judge considers necessary to ensure that the accused is not prejudiced –

(a) by any inferences that might be drawn from the fact that the accused has been prevented from cross-examining the witness in person;
(b) where the witness has been cross-examined by a legal representative appointed under section 38(4), by the fact that the cross-examination was carried out by such a legal representative and not by a person acting as the accused's own legal representative.

(2) Subsection (8)(a) of section 38 applies for the purposes of this section as it applies for the purposes of section 38.

40 Funding of defence representation

(1) In section 19(3) of the Prosecution of Offences Act 1985 (regulations authorising payments out of central funds), after paragraph (d) there shall be inserted –

> '(e) to cover the proper fee or costs of a legal representative appointed under section 38(4) of the Youth Justice and Criminal Evidence Act 1999 (defence representation for purposes of cross-examination) and any expenses properly incurred in providing such a person with evidence or other material in connection with his appointment.'

(2) …

Chapter III

Protection of Complainants in Proceedings for Sexual Offences

41 Restriction on evidence or questions about complainant's sexual history

(1) If at a trial a person is charged with a sexual offence, then, except with the leave of the court –

(a) no evidence may be adduced, and
(b) no question may be asked in cross-examination,

by or on behalf of any accused at the trial, about any sexual behaviour of the complainant.

(2) The court may give leave in relation to any evidence or question only on an application made by or on behalf of an accused, and may not give such leave unless it is satisfied –

(a) that subsection (3) or (5) applies, and
(b) that a refusal of leave might have the result of rendering unsafe a conclusion of the jury or (as the case may be) the court on any relevant issue in the case.

(3) This subsection applies if the evidence or question relates to a relevant issue in the case and either –

(a) that issue is not an issue of consent; or
(b) it is an issue of consent and the sexual behaviour of the complainant to which the evidence or question relates is alleged to have taken place at or about the same time as the event which is the subject matter of the charge against the accused; or
(c) it is an issue of consent and the sexual behaviour of the complainant to which the evidence or question relates is alleged to have been, in any respect, so similar –

   (i) to any sexual behaviour of the complainant which (according to evidence adduced or to be adduced by or on behalf of the accused) took place as part of the event which is the subject matter of the charge against the accused, or

(ii) to any other sexual behaviour of the complainant which (according to such evidence) took place at or about the same time as that event,

that the similarity cannot reasonably be explained as a coincidence.

(4) For the purposes of subsection (3) no evidence or question shall be regarded as relating to a relevant issue in the case if it appears to the court to be reasonable to assume that the purpose (or main purpose) for which it would be adduced or asked is to establish or elicit material for impugning the credibility of the complainant as a witness.

(5) This subsection applies if the evidence or question –

(a) relates to any evidence adduced by the prosecution about any sexual behaviour of the complainant; and
(b) in the opinion of the court, would go no further than is necessary to enable the evidence adduced by the prosecution to be rebutted or explained by or on behalf of the accused.

(6) For the purposes of subsections (3) and (5) the evidence or question must relate to a specific instance (or specific instances) of alleged sexual behaviour on the part of the complainant (and accordingly nothing in those subsections is capable of applying in relation to the evidence or question to the extent that it does not so relate).

(7) Where this section applies in relation to a trial by virtue of the fact that one or more of a number of persons charged in the proceedings is or are charged with a sexual offence –

(a) it shall cease to apply in relation to the trial if the prosecutor decides not to proceed with the case against that person or those persons in respect of that charge; but
(b) it shall not cease to do so in the event of that person or those persons pleading guilty to, or being convicted of, that charge.

(8) Nothing in this section authorises any evidence to be adduced or any question to be asked which cannot be adduced or asked apart from this section.

42 Interpretation and application of section 41

(1) In section 41 –

(a) "relevant issue in the case" means any issue falling to be proved by the prosecution or defence in the trial of the accused;
(b) "issue of consent" means any issue whether the complainant in fact consented to the conduct constituting the offence with which the accused is charged (and accordingly does not include any issue as to the belief of the accused that the complainant so consented);
(c) "sexual behaviour" means any sexual behaviour or other sexual experience, whether or not involving any accused or other person, but excluding (except in section 41(3)(c)(i) and (5)(a)) anything alleged to have taken place as part of the event which is the subject matter of the charge against the accused; and
(d) subject to any order made under subsection (2), "sexual offence" shall be construed in accordance with section 62.

(2) The Secretary of State may by order make such provision as he considers appropriate for adding or removing, for the purposes of section 41, any offence to or from the offences which are sexual offences for the purposes of this Act by virtue of section 62.

(3) Section 41 applies in relation to the following proceedings as it applies to a trial, namely –

(a) …
(b) …
(c) the hearing of an application under paragraph 2(1) of Schedule 3 to the Crime and Disorder Act 1998 (application to dismiss charge by person sent for trial under section 51 or 51A of that Act),

(d) any hearing held, between conviction and sentencing, for the purpose of determining matters relevant to the court's decision as to how the accused is to be dealt with, and
(e) the hearing of an appeal,

and references (in section 41 or this section) to a person charged with an offence accordingly include a person convicted of an offence.

43 Procedure on applications under section 41

(1) An application for leave shall be heard in private and in the absence of the complainant.

In this section "leave" means leave under section 41.

(2) Where such an application has been determined, the court must state in open court (but in the absence of the jury, if there is one) –

(a) its reasons for giving, or refusing, leave, and
(b) if it gives leave, the extent to which evidence may be adduced or questions asked in pursuance of the leave,

and, if it is a magistrates' court, must cause those matters to be entered in the register of its proceedings.

(3) Criminal Procedure Rules may make provision –

(a) requiring applications for leave to specify, in relation to each item of evidence or question to which they relate, particulars of the grounds on which it is asserted that leave should be given by virtue of subsection (3) or (5) of section 41;
(b) enabling the court to request a party to the proceedings to provide the court with information which it considers would assist it in determining an application for leave;
(c) for the manner in which confidential or sensitive information is to be treated in connection with such an application, and in particular as to its being disclosed to, or withheld from, parties to the proceedings.

Chapter IV

Reporting Restrictions

Reports relating to persons under 18

44 Restrictions on reporting alleged offences involving persons under 18

(1) This section applies (subject to subsection (3)) where a criminal investigation has begun in respect of –

(a) an alleged offence against the law of –

(i) England and Wales, or
(ii) Northern Ireland; or

(b) an alleged civil offence (other than an offence falling within paragraph (a)) committed (whether or not in the United Kingdom) by a person subject to service law.

(2) No matter relating to any person involved in the offence shall while he is under the age of 18 be included in any publication if it is likely to lead members of the public to identify him as a person involved in the offence.

(3) The restrictions imposed by subsection (2) cease to apply once there are proceedings in a court (whether a court in England and Wales, a service court or a court in Northern Ireland) in respect of the offence.

(4) For the purposes of subsection (2) any reference to a person involved in the offence is to –

(a) a person by whom the offence is alleged to have been committed; or
(b) if this paragraph applies to the publication in question by virtue of subsection (5) –

(i) a person against or in respect of whom the offence is alleged to have been committed, or
(ii) a person who is alleged to have been a witness to the commission of the offence;

except that paragraph (b)(i) does not include a person in relation to whom section 1 of the Sexual Offences (Amendment) Act 1992 (anonymity of victims of certain sexual offences) applies in connection with the offence.

(5) Subsection (4)(b) applies to a publication if –

(a) where it is a relevant programme, it is transmitted, or
(b) in the case of any other publication, it is published,

on or after such date as may be specified in an order made by the Secretary of State.

(5A) In the application of this section to Northern Ireland, the reference in subsection (5) to the Secretary of State shall be construed as a reference to the Department of Justice in Northern Ireland.

(6) The matters relating to a person in relation to which the restrictions imposed by subsection (2) apply (if their inclusion in any publication is likely to have the result mentioned in that subsection) include in particular –

(a) his name,
(b) his address,
(c) the identity of any school or other educational establishment attended by him,
(d) the identity of any place of work, and
(e) any still or moving picture of him.

(7) Any appropriate criminal court may by order dispense, to any extent specified in the order, with the restrictions imposed by subsection (2) in relation to a person if it is satisfied that it is necessary in the interests of justice to do so.

(8) However, when deciding whether to make such an order dispensing (to any extent) with the restrictions imposed by subsection (2) in relation to a person, the court shall have regard to the welfare of that person.

(9) In subsection (7) "appropriate criminal court" means –

(a) in a case where this section applies by virtue of subsection (1)(a)(i) or (ii), any court in England and Wales or (as the case may be) in Northern Ireland which has any jurisdiction in, or in relation to, any criminal proceedings (but not a service court unless the offence is alleged to have been committed by a person subject to service law);
(b) in a case where this section applies by virtue of subsection (1)(b), any court falling within paragraph (a) or a service court.

(10) The power under subsection (7) of a magistrates' court in England and Wales may be exercised by a single justice.

(11) In the case of a decision of a magistrates' court in England and Wales, or a court of summary jurisdiction in Northern Ireland, to make or refuse to make an order under subsection (7), the following persons, namely –

(a) any person who was a party to the proceedings on the application for the order, and
(b) with the leave of the Crown Court, or in Northern Ireland a county court, any other person,

may, in accordance with Criminal Procedure Rules in England and Wales, or rules of court in Northern Ireland, appeal to the Crown Court, or in Northern Ireland a county court against that decision or appear or be represented at the hearing of such an appeal.

(12) On such an appeal the Crown Court or in Northern Ireland a county court –

(a) may make such order as is necessary to give effect to its determination of the appeal; and
(b) may also make such incidental or consequential orders as appear to it to be just.

(13) In this section –

(a) "civil offence" means an act or omission which, if committed in England and Wales, would be an offence against the law of England and Wales;
(b) any reference to a criminal investigation, in relation to an alleged offence, is to an investigation conducted by police officers, or other persons charged with the duty of investigating offences, with a view to it being ascertained whether a person should be charged with the offence;
(c) any reference to a person subject to service law is to –

    (i) a person subject to service law within the meaning of the Armed Forces Act 2006; or
    (ii) a civilian subject to service discipline within the meaning of that Act.

45 Power to restrict reporting of criminal proceedings involving persons under 18

(1) This section applies (subject to subsection (2)) in relation to –

(a) any criminal proceedings in any court (other than a service court) in England and Wales or Northern Ireland; and
(b) any proceedings (whether in the United Kingdom or elsewhere) in any service court.

(2) This section does not apply in relation to any proceedings to which section 49 of the Children and Young Persons Act 1933 applies.

(3) The court may direct that no matter relating to any person concerned in the proceedings shall while he is under the age of 18 be included in any publication if it is likely to lead members of the public to identify him as a person concerned in the proceedings.

(4) The court or an appellate court may by direction ("an excepting direction") dispense, to any extent specified in the excepting direction, with the restrictions imposed by a direction under subsection (3) if it is satisfied that it is necessary in the interests of justice to do so.

(5) The court or an appellate court may also by direction ("an excepting direction") dispense, to any extent specified in the excepting direction, with the restrictions imposed by a direction under subsection (3) if it is satisfied –

(a) that their effect is to impose a substantial and unreasonable restriction on the reporting of the proceedings, and
(b) that it is in the public interest to remove or relax that restriction;

but no excepting direction shall be given under this subsection by reason only of the fact that the proceedings have been determined in any way or have been abandoned.

(6) When deciding whether to make –

(a) a direction under subsection (3) in relation to a person, or
(b) an excepting direction under subsection (4) or (5) by virtue of which the restrictions imposed by a direction under subsection (3) would be dispensed with (to any extent) in relation to a person,

the court or (as the case may be) the appellate court shall have regard to the welfare of that person.

(7) For the purposes of subsection (3) any reference to a person concerned in the proceedings is to a person –

(a) against or in respect of whom the proceedings are taken, or
(b) who is a witness in the proceedings.

(8) The matters relating to a person in relation to which the restrictions imposed by a direction under subsection (3) apply (if their inclusion in any publication is likely to have the result mentioned in that subsection) include in particular –

(a) his name,
(b) his address,
(c) the identity of any school or other educational establishment attended by him,
(d) the identity of any place of work, and
(e) any still or moving picture of him.

(9) A direction under subsection (3) may be revoked by the court or an appellate court.

(10) An excepting direction –

(a) may be given at the time the direction under subsection (3) is given or subsequently; and
(b) may be varied or revoked by the court or an appellate court.

(11) In this section "appellate court", in relation to any proceedings in a court, means a court dealing with an appeal (including an appeal by way of case stated) arising out of the proceedings or with any further appeal.

45A Power to restrict reporting of criminal proceedings for lifetime of witnesses and victims under 18

(1) This section applies in relation to –

(a) any criminal proceedings in any court (other than a service court) in England and Wales, and
(b) any proceedings (whether in the United Kingdom or elsewhere) in any service court.

(2) The court may make a direction ("a reporting direction") that no matter relating to a person mentioned in subsection (3) shall during that person's lifetime be included in any publication if it is likely to lead members of the public to identify that person as being concerned in the proceedings.

(3) A reporting direction may be made only in respect of a person who is under the age of 18 when the proceedings commence and who is –

(a) a witness, other than an accused, in the proceedings;
(b) a person against whom the offence, which is the subject of the proceedings, is alleged to have been committed.

(4) For the purposes of subsection (2), matters relating to a person in respect of whom the reporting direction is made include –

(a) the person's name,
(b) the person's address,
(c) the identity of any school or other educational establishment attended by the person,
(d) the identity of any place of work of the person, and
(e) any still or moving picture of the person.

(5) The court may make a reporting direction in respect of a person only if it is satisfied that –

(a) the quality of any evidence given by the person, or
(b) the level of co-operation given by the person to any party to the proceedings in connection with that party's preparation of its case,

is likely to be diminished by reason of fear or distress on the part of the person in connection with being identified by members of the public as a person concerned in the proceedings.

(6) In determining whether subsection (5) is satisfied, the court must in particular take into account –

(a) the nature and alleged circumstances of the offence to which the proceedings relate;
(b) the age of the person;
(c) such of the following as appear to the court to be relevant –

(i) the social and cultural background and ethnic origins of the person,

(ii) the domestic, educational and employment circumstances of the person, and
(iii) any religious beliefs or political opinions of the person;

(d) any behaviour towards the person on the part of –

(i) an accused,
(ii) members of the family or associates of an accused, or
(iii) any other person who is likely to be an accused or a witness in the proceedings.

(7) In determining that question the court must in addition consider any views expressed –

(a) by the person in respect of whom the reporting restriction may be made, and
(b) where that person is under the age of 16, by an appropriate person other than an accused.

(8) In determining whether to make a reporting direction in respect of a person, the court must have regard to –

(a) the welfare of that person,
(b) whether it would be in the interests of justice to make the direction, and
(c) the public interest in avoiding the imposition of a substantial and unreasonable restriction on the reporting of the proceedings.

(9) A reporting direction may be revoked by the court or an appellate court.

(10) The court or an appellate court may by direction ("an excepting direction") dispense, to any extent specified in the excepting direction, with the restrictions imposed by a reporting direction.

(11) The court or an appellate court may only make an excepting direction if –

(a) it is satisfied that it is necessary in the interests of justice to do so, or
(b) it is satisfied that –

(i) the effect of the reporting direction is to impose a substantial and unreasonable restriction on the reporting of the proceedings, and
(ii) it is in the public interest to remove or relax that restriction.

(12) No excepting direction shall be given under subsection (11)(b) by reason only of the fact that the proceedings have been determined in any way or have been abandoned.

(13) In determining whether to make an excepting direction in respect of a person, the court or the appellate court must have regard to the welfare of that person.

(14) An excepting direction –

(a) may be given at the time the reporting direction is given or subsequently, and
(b) may be varied or revoked by the court or an appellate court.

(15) For the purposes of this section –

(a) criminal proceedings in a court other than a service court commence when proceedings are instituted for the purposes of Part 1 of the Prosecution of Offences Act 1985, in accordance with section 15(2) of that Act;
(b) proceedings in a service court commence when the charge is brought under section 122of the Armed Forces Act 2006.

(16) In this section –

(a) "appellate court", in relation to any proceedings in a court, means a court dealing with an appeal (including an appeal by way of case stated) arising out of the proceedings or with any further appeal;
(b) "appropriate person" has the same meaning as in section 50;

(c) references to the quality of evidence given by a person are to its quality in terms of completeness, coherence and accuracy (and for this purpose "coherence" refers to a person's ability in giving evidence to give answers which address the questions put to the person and can be understood both individually and collectively);

(d) references to the preparation of the case of a party to any proceedings include, where the party is the prosecution, the carrying out of investigations into any offence at any time charged in the proceedings.

Reports relating to adult witnesses

46 Power to restrict reports about certain adult witnesses in criminal proceedings

(1) This section applies where –

(a) in any criminal proceedings in any court (other than a service court) in England and Wales or Northern Ireland, or

(b) in any proceedings (whether in the United Kingdom or elsewhere) in any service court,

a party to the proceedings makes an application for the court to give a reporting direction in relation to a witness in the proceedings (other than the accused) who has attained the age of 18.

In this section "reporting direction" has the meaning given by subsection (6).

(2) If the court determines –

(a) that the witness is eligible for protection, and

(b) that giving a reporting direction in relation to the witness is likely to improve –

(i) the quality of evidence given by the witness, or

(ii) the level of co-operation given by the witness to any party to the proceedings in connection with that party's preparation of its case,

the court may give a reporting direction in relation to the witness.

(3) For the purposes of this section a witness is eligible for protection if the court is satisfied –

(a) that the quality of evidence given by the witness, or

(b) the level of co-operation given by the witness to any party to the proceedings in connection with that party's preparation of its case,

is likely to be diminished by reason of fear or distress on the part of the witness in connection with being identified by members of the public as a witness in the proceedings.

(4) In determining whether a witness is eligible for protection the court must take into account, in particular –

(a) the nature and alleged circumstances of the offence to which the proceedings relate;

(b) the age of the witness;

(c) such of the following matters as appear to the court to be relevant, namely –

(i) the social and cultural background and ethnic origins of the witness,

(ii) the domestic and employment circumstances of the witness, and

(iii) any religious beliefs or political opinions of the witness;

(d) any behaviour towards the witness on the part of –

(i) the accused,

(ii) members of the family or associates of the accused, or

(iii) any other person who is likely to be an accused or a witness in the proceedings.

(5) In determining that question the court must in addition consider any views expressed by the witness.

(6) For the purposes of this section a reporting direction in relation to a witness is a direction that no matter relating to the witness shall during the witness' lifetime be included in any publication if it is likely to lead members of the public to identify him as being a witness in the proceedings.

(7) The matters relating to a witness in relation to which the restrictions imposed by a reporting direction apply (if their inclusion in any publication is likely to have the result mentioned in subsection (6)) include in particular –

(a) the witness' name,
(b) the witness' address,
(c) the identity of any educational establishment attended by the witness,
(d) the identity of any place of work, and
(e) any still or moving picture of the witness.

(8) In determining whether to give a reporting direction the court shall consider –

(a) whether it would be in the interests of justice to do so, and
(b) the public interest in avoiding the imposition of a substantial and unreasonable restriction on the reporting of the proceedings.

(9) The court or an appellate court may by direction ("an excepting direction") dispense, to any extent specified in the excepting direction, with the restrictions imposed by a reporting direction if –

(a) it is satisfied that it is necessary in the interests of justice to do so, or
(b) it is satisfied –
  (i) that the effect of those restrictions is to impose a substantial and unreasonable restriction on the reporting of the proceedings, and
  (ii) that it is in the public interest to remove or relax that restriction;

but no excepting direction shall be given under paragraph (b) by reason only of the fact that the proceedings have been determined in any way or have been abandoned.

(10) A reporting direction may be revoked by the court or an appellate court.

(11) An excepting direction –

(a) may be given at the time the reporting direction is given or subsequently; and
(b) may be varied or revoked by the court or an appellate court.

(12) In this section –

(a) "appellate court", in relation to any proceedings in a court, means a court dealing with an appeal (including an appeal by way of case stated) arising out of the proceedings or with any further appeal;
(b) references to the quality of a witness' evidence are to its quality in terms of completeness, coherence and accuracy (and for this purpose "coherence" refers to a witness' ability in giving evidence to give answers which address the questions put to the witness and can be understood both individually and collectively);
(c) references to the preparation of the case of a party to any proceedings include, where the party is the prosecution, the carrying out of investigations into any offence at any time charged in the proceedings.

Reports relating to directions under Chapter I or II Chapter 1, 1A or 2

47 Restrictions on reporting directions under Chapter I or II Chapter 1, 1A or 2

(1) Except as provided by this section, no publication shall include a report of a matter falling within subsection (2).

(2) The matters falling within this subsection are –

(a) a direction under section 19, 33A or 36 or an order discharging, or (in the case of a direction under section 19) varying, such a direction;

(aa) a direction under Article 7 or 24 of the Criminal Evidence (Northern Ireland) Order 1999 or an order discharging, or (in the case of a direction under Article 7) varying, such a direction;

(b) proceedings –

(i) on an application for such a direction or order, or

(ii) where the court acts of its own motion to determine whether to give or make any such direction or order.

(3) The court dealing with a matter falling within subsection (2) may order that subsection (1) is not to apply, or is not to apply to a specified extent, to a report of that matter.

(4) Where –

(a) there is only one accused in the relevant proceedings, and

(b) he objects to the making of an order under subsection (3),

the court shall make the order if (and only if) satisfied after hearing the representations of the accused that it is in the interests of justice to do so; and if the order is made it shall not apply to the extent that a report deals with any such objections or representations.

(5) Where –

(a) there are two or more accused in the relevant proceedings, and

(b) one or more of them object to the making of an order under subsection (3),

the court shall make the order if (and only if) satisfied after hearing the representations of each of the accused that it is in the interests of justice to do so; and if the order is made it shall not apply to the extent that a report deals with any such objections or representations.

(6) Subsection (1) does not apply to the inclusion in a publication of a report of matters after the relevant proceedings are either –

(a) determined (by acquittal, conviction or otherwise), or

(b) abandoned,

in relation to the accused or (if there is more than one) in relation to each of the accused.

(7) In this section "the relevant proceedings" means the proceedings to which any such direction as is mentioned in subsection (2) relates or would relate.

(8) Nothing in this section affects any prohibition or restriction by virtue of any other enactment on the inclusion of matter in a publication.

Other restrictions

48 Amendments relating to other reporting restrictions

Schedule 2, which contains amendments relating to reporting restrictions under –

(a) the Children and Young Persons Act 1933,

(b) the Sexual Offences (Amendment) Act 1976,

(c) the Sexual Offences (Northern Ireland) Order 1978,

(d) the Sexual Offences (Amendment) Act 1992, and

(e) the Criminal Justice (Northern Ireland) Order 1994,

shall have effect.

Offences

49 Offences under Chapter IV

(1) This section applies if a publication –

(a) includes any matter in contravention of section 44(2) or of a direction under section 45(3) or 46(2); or

(b) includes a report in contravention of section 47.

(1A) This section also applies –

(a) in England and Wales, Scotland and Northern Ireland, if a publication includes any matter in contravention of a direction under section 45A(2) made by a service court;

(b) in England and Wales, if a publication includes any matter in contravention of a direction under section 45A(2) made by a court other than a service court.

(2) Where the publication is a newspaper or periodical, any proprietor, any editor and any publisher of the newspaper or periodical is guilty of an offence.

(3) Where the publication is a relevant programme –

(a) any body corporate or Scottish partnership engaged in providing the programme service in which the programme is included, and

(b) any person having functions in relation to the programme corresponding to those of an editor of a newspaper,

is guilty of an offence.

(4) In the case of any other publication, any person publishing it is guilty of an offence.

(5) A person guilty of an offence under this section is liable on summary conviction to a fine not exceeding level 5 on the standard scale.

(6) Proceedings for an offence under this section in respect of a publication falling within subsection (1)(b) may not be instituted –

(a) in England and Wales otherwise than by or with the consent of the Attorney General, or

(b) in Northern Ireland otherwise than by or with the consent of the Attorney General for Northern Ireland.

(7) Schedule 2A makes special provision in connection with the operation of this section, so far as it relates to a publication that includes matter in contravention of a direction under section 45A(2), in relation to persons providing information society services.

50 Defences

(1) Where a person is charged with an offence under section 49 it shall be a defence to prove that at the time of the alleged offence he was not aware, and neither suspected nor had reason to suspect, that the publication included the matter or report in question.

(2) Where –

(a) a person is charged with an offence under section 49, and

(b) the offence relates to the inclusion of any matter in a publication in contravention of section 44(2),

it shall be a defence to prove that at the time of the alleged offence he was not aware, and neither suspected nor had reason to suspect, that the criminal investigation in question had begun.

(3) Where –

(a) paragraphs (a) and (b) of subsection (2) apply, and
(b) the contravention of section 44(2) does not relate to either –

(i) the person by whom the offence mentioned in that provision is alleged to have been committed, or
(ii) (where that offence is one in relation to which section 1 of the Sexual Offences (Amendment) Act 1992 applies) a person who is alleged to be a witness to the commission of the offence,

it shall be a defence to show to the satisfaction of the court that the inclusion in the publication of the matter in question was in the public interest on the ground that, to the extent that they operated to prevent that matter from being so included, the effect of the restrictions imposed by section 44(2) was to impose a substantial and unreasonable restriction on the reporting of matters connected with that offence.

(4) Subsection (5) applies where –

(a) paragraphs (a) and (b) of subsection (2) apply, and
(b) the contravention of section 44(2) relates to a person ("the protected person") who is neither –

(i) the person mentioned in subsection (3)(b)(i), nor
(ii) a person within subsection (3)(b)(ii) who is under the age of 16.

(5) In such a case it shall be a defence, subject to subsection (6), to prove that written consent to the inclusion of the matter in question in the publication had been given –

(a) by an appropriate person, if at the time when the consent was given the protected person was under the age of 16, or
(b) by the protected person, if that person was aged 16 or 17 at that time,

and (where the consent was given by an appropriate person) that written notice had been previously given to that person drawing to his attention the need to consider the welfare of the protected person when deciding whether to give consent.

(6) The defence provided by subsection (5) is not available if –

(a) (where the consent was given by an appropriate person) it is proved that written or other notice withdrawing the consent –

(i) was given to the appropriate recipient by any other appropriate person or by the protected person, and
(ii) was so given in sufficient time to enable the inclusion in the publication of the matter in question to be prevented; or

(b) subsection (8) applies.

(6A) Where –

(a) a person is charged with an offence under section 49, and
(b) the offence relates to the inclusion of any matter in a publication in contravention of a direction under section 45A(2),

it shall be a defence, unless subsection (6B) or (8) applies, to prove that the person in relation to whom the direction was given had given written consent to the inclusion of that matter in the publication.

(6B) Written consent is not a defence by virtue of subsection (6A) if the person was under the age of 18 at the time the consent was given.

(7) Where –

(a) a person is charged with an offence under section 49, and
(b) the offence relates to the inclusion of any matter in a publication in contravention of a direction under section 46(2),

it shall be a defence, unless subsection (8) applies, to prove that the person in relation to whom the direction was given had given written consent to the inclusion of that matter in the publication.

(8) Written consent is not a defence if it is proved that any person interfered –

(a) with the peace or comfort of the person giving the consent, or
(b) (where the consent was given by an appropriate person) with the peace or comfort of either that person or the protected person,

with intent to obtain the consent.

(9) In this section –

"an appropriate person" means (subject to subsections (10) to (12)) –

(a) in England and Wales or Northern Ireland, a person who is a parent or guardian of the protected person, or
(b) in Scotland, a person who has parental responsibilities (within the meaning of section 1(3) of the Children (Scotland) Act 1995) in relation to the protected person;

"guardian", in relation to the protected person, means any person who is not a parent of the protected person but who has parental responsibility for the protected person within the meaning of –

(a) (in England and Wales) the Children Act 1989, or
(b) (in Northern Ireland) the Children (Northern Ireland) Order 1995.

(10) Where the protected person is (within the meaning of the Children Act 1989) a child who is looked after by a local authority, "an appropriate person" means a person who is –

(a) a representative of that authority, or
(b) a parent or guardian of the protected person with whom the protected person is allowed to live.

(11) Where the protected person is (within the meaning of the Children (Northern Ireland) Order 1995) a child who is looked after by an authority, "an appropriate person" means a person who is –

(a) an officer of that authority, or
(b) a parent or guardian of the protected person with whom the protected person is allowed to live.

(12) Where the protected person is (within the meaning of section 17(6) of the Children (Scotland) Act 1995) a child who is looked after by a local authority, "an appropriate person" means a person who is –

(a) a representative of that authority, or
(b) a person who has parental responsibilities (within the meaning of section 1(3) of that Act) in relation to the protected person and with whom the protected person is allowed to live.

(13) However, no person by whom the offence mentioned in section 44(2) is alleged to have been committed is, by virtue of subsections (9) to (12), an appropriate person for the purposes of this section.

(14) In this section "the appropriate recipient", in relation to a notice under subsection (6)(a), means –

(a) the person to whom the notice giving consent was given,
(b) (if different) the person by whom the matter in question was published, or
(c) any other person exercising, on behalf of the person mentioned in paragraph (b), any responsibility in relation to the publication of that matter;

and for this purpose "person" includes a body of persons and a partnership.

51 Offences committed by bodies corporate or Scottish partnerships

(1) If an offence under section 49 committed by a body corporate is proved –

(a) to have been committed with the consent or connivance of, or
(b) to be attributable to any neglect on the part of,

an officer, the officer as well as the body corporate is guilty of the offence and liable to be proceeded against and punished accordingly.

(2) In subsection (1) "officer" means a director, manager, secretary or other similar officer of the body, or a person purporting to act in any such capacity.

(3) If the affairs of a body corporate are managed by its members, "director" in subsection (2) means a member of that body.

(4) Where an offence under section 49 is committed by a Scottish partnership and is proved to have been committed with the consent or connivance of a partner, he as well as the partnership shall be guilty of the offence and shall be liable to be proceeded against and punished accordingly.

Supplementary

52 Decisions as to public interest for purposes of Chapter IV

(1) Where for the purposes of any provision of this Chapter it falls to a court to determine whether anything is (or, as the case may be, was) in the public interest, the court must have regard, in particular, to the matters referred to in subsection (2) (so far as relevant).

(2) Those matters are –

- (a) the interest in each of the following –
  - (i) the open reporting of crime,
  - (ii) the open reporting of matters relating to human health or safety, and
  - (iii) the prevention and exposure of miscarriages of justice;
- (b) the welfare of any person in relation to whom the relevant restrictions imposed by or under this Chapter apply or would apply (or, as the case may be, applied); and
- (c) any views expressed –
  - (i) by an appropriate person on behalf of a person within paragraph (b) who is under the age of 16 ("the protected person"), or
  - (ii) by a person within that paragraph who has attained that age.

(3) In subsection (2) "an appropriate person", in relation to the protected person, has the same meaning as it has for the purposes of section 50.

Chapter V

Competence of Witnesses and Capacity to be Sworn

Competence of witnesses

53 Competence of witnesses to give evidence

(1) At every stage in criminal proceedings all persons are (whatever their age) competent to give evidence.

(2) Subsection (1) has effect subject to subsections (3) and (4).

(3) A person is not competent to give evidence in criminal proceedings if it appears to the court that he is not a person who is able to –

- (a) understand questions put to him as a witness, and
- (b) give answers to them which can be understood.

(4) A person charged in criminal proceedings is not competent to give evidence in the proceedings for the prosecution (whether he is the only person, or is one of two or more persons, charged in the proceedings).

(5) In subsection (4) the reference to a person charged in criminal proceedings does not include a person who is not, or is no longer, liable to be convicted of any offence in the proceedings (whether as a result of pleading guilty or for any other reason).

54 Determining competence of witnesses

(1) Any question whether a witness in criminal proceedings is competent to give evidence in the proceedings, whether raised –

(a) by a party to the proceedings, or
(b) by the court of its own motion,

shall be determined by the court in accordance with this section.

(2) It is for the party calling the witness to satisfy the court that, on a balance of probabilities, the witness is competent to give evidence in the proceedings.

(3) In determining the question mentioned in subsection (1) the court shall treat the witness as having the benefit of any directions under section 19 which the court has given, or proposes to give, in relation to the witness.

(4) Any proceedings held for the determination of the question shall take place in the absence of the jury (if there is one).

(5) Expert evidence may be received on the question.

(6) Any questioning of the witness (where the court considers that necessary) shall be conducted by the court in the presence of the parties.

Giving of sworn or unsworn evidence

55 Determining whether witness to be sworn

(1) Any question whether a witness in criminal proceedings may be sworn for the purpose of giving evidence on oath, whether raised –

(a) by a party to the proceedings, or
(b) by the court of its own motion,

shall be determined by the court in accordance with this section.

(2) The witness may not be sworn for that purpose unless –

(a) he has attained the age of 14, and
(b) he has a sufficient appreciation of the solemnity of the occasion and of the particular responsibility to tell the truth which is involved in taking an oath.

(3) The witness shall, if he is able to give intelligible testimony, be presumed to have a sufficient appreciation of those matters if no evidence tending to show the contrary is adduced (by any party).

(4) If any such evidence is adduced, it is for the party seeking to have the witness sworn to satisfy the court that, on a balance of probabilities, the witness has attained the age of 14 and has a sufficient appreciation of the matters mentioned in subsection (2)(b).

(5) Any proceedings held for the determination of the question mentioned in subsection (1) shall take place in the absence of the jury (if there is one).

(6) Expert evidence may be received on the question.

(7) Any questioning of the witness (where the court considers that necessary) shall be conducted by the court in the presence of the parties.

(8) For the purposes of this section a person is able to give intelligible testimony if he is able to –

(a) understand questions put to him as a witness, and
(b) give answers to them which can be understood.

See further, in relation to the application of sub-s (5) above, with modifications, to proceedings before the Court Martial: the Youth Justice and Criminal Evidence Act 1999 (Application to Service Courts) Order 2009, SI 2009/2083, arts 9(3), (4)(f), 10(1)–(3), (7).

56 Reception of unsworn evidence

(1) Subsections (2) and (3) apply to a person (of any age) who –

(a) is competent to give evidence in criminal proceedings, but
(b) (by virtue of section 55(2)) is not permitted to be sworn for the purpose of giving evidence on oath in such proceedings.

(2) The evidence in criminal proceedings of a person to whom this subsection applies shall be given unsworn.

(3) A deposition of unsworn evidence given by a person to whom this subsection applies may be taken for the purposes of criminal proceedings as if that evidence had been given on oath.

(4) A court in criminal proceedings shall accordingly receive in evidence any evidence given unsworn in pursuance of subsection (2) or (3).

(5) Where a person ("the witness") who is competent to give evidence in criminal proceedings gives evidence in such proceedings unsworn, no conviction, verdict or finding in those proceedings shall be taken to be unsafe for the purposes of any of sections 2(1), 13(1) and 16(1) of the Criminal Appeal Act 1968 (grounds for allowing appeals) by reason only that it appears to the Court of Appeal that the witness was a person falling within section 55(2) (and should accordingly have given his evidence on oath).

57 Penalty for giving false unsworn evidence

(1) This section applies where a person gives unsworn evidence in criminal proceedings in pursuance of section 56(2) or (3).

(2) If such a person wilfully gives false evidence in such circumstances that, had the evidence been given on oath, he would have been guilty of perjury, he shall be guilty of an offence and liable on summary conviction to –

(a) imprisonment for a term not exceeding 6 months, or
(b) a fine not exceeding £1,000,

or both.

(3) In relation to a person under the age of 14, subsection (2) shall have effect as if for the words following "on summary conviction" there were substituted "to a fine not exceeding £250".

Chapter VI

Restrictions on use of Evidence

Additional restrictions

58 Inferences from silence not permissible where no prior access to legal advice

(1) Sections 34 and 36 to 38 of the Criminal Justice and Public Order Act 1994 (inferences from accused's silence) shall be amended as follows.

(2) In section 34 (effect of accused's failure to mention facts when questioned or charged), after subsection (2) there shall be inserted –

> "(2A) Where the accused was at an authorised place of detention at the time of the failure, subsections (1) and (2) above do not apply if he had not been allowed an opportunity to consult a solicitor prior to being questioned, charged or informed as mentioned in subsection (1) above."

(3) In section 36 (effect of accused's failure or refusal to account for objects, substances or marks), after subsection (4) there shall be inserted –

> "(4A) Where the accused was at an authorised place of detention at the time of the failure or refusal, subsections (1) and (2) above do not apply if he had not been allowed an opportunity to consult a solicitor prior to the request being made."

(4) In section 37 (effect of accused's failure or refusal to account for presence at a particular place), after subsection (3) there shall be inserted –

> "(3A) Where the accused was at an authorised place of detention at the time of the failure or refusal, subsections (1) and (2) do not apply if he had not been allowed an opportunity to consult a solicitor prior to the request being made."

(5) In section 38 (interpretation), after subsection (2) there shall be inserted –

> "(2A) In each of sections 34(2A), 36(4A) and 37(3A) "authorised place of detention" means –
>
> (a) a police station; or
> (b) any other place prescribed for the purposes of that provision by order made by the Secretary of State;
>
> and the power to make an order under this subsection shall be exercisable by statutory instrument which shall be subject to annulment in pursuance of a resolution of either House of Parliament."

59 Restriction on use of answers etc obtained under compulsion

Schedule 3, which amends enactments providing for the use of answers and statements given under compulsion so as to restrict in criminal proceedings their use in evidence against the persons giving them, shall have effect.

Removal of restriction

60 Removal of restriction on use of evidence from computer records

Section 69 of the Police and Criminal Evidence Act 1984 (evidence from computer records inadmissible unless conditions relating to proper use and operation of computer shown to be satisfied) shall cease to have effect.

Chapter VII

General

61 Application of Part II to service courts

(1) The Secretary of State may by order direct that any provision of –

(a) Chapters I to III and V, or
(b) sections 62, 63 and 65 so far as having effect for the purposes of any of those Chapters,

shall apply, subject to such modifications as he may specify, to any proceedings before a service court.

(2) Chapter IV (and sections 62, 63 and 65 so far as having effect for the purposes of that Chapter) shall have effect for the purposes of proceedings before a service court subject to any modifications which the Secretary of State may by order specify.

(3) The power to make an order under section 39 of the Criminal Justice and Public Order Act 1994 (power to apply sections 34 to 38 to the armed forces) in relation to any provision of sections 34 to 38 of that Act shall be exercisable in relation to any provision of those sections as amended by section 58 above.

62 Meaning of "sexual offence" and other references to offences

(1) In this Part "sexual offence" means any offence under Part 1 of the Sexual Offences Act 2003 or any relevant superseded offence.

(1A) In subsection (1) "relevant superseded offence" means –

(a) rape or burglary with intent to rape;
(b) an offence under any of sections 2 to 12 and 14 to 17 of the Sexual Offences Act 1956 (unlawful intercourse, indecent assault, forcible abduction etc);
(c) an offence under section 128 of the Mental Health Act 1959 (unlawful intercourse with person receiving treatment for mental disorder by member of hospital staff etc);
(d) an offence under section 1 of the Indecency with Children Act 1960 (indecent conduct towards child under 14);
(e) an offence under section 54 of the Criminal Law Act 1977 (incitement of child under 16 to commit incest).

(2) In this Part any reference (including a reference having effect by virtue of this subsection) to an offence of any description ("the substantive offence") is to be taken to include a reference to an offence which consists of attempting or conspiring to commit, or of aiding, abetting, counselling, procuring or inciting the commission of, the substantive offence.

63 General interpretation etc of Part II

(1) In this Part (except where the context otherwise requires) –

"accused", in relation to any criminal proceedings, means any person charged with an offence to which the proceedings relate (whether or not he has been convicted);
"the complainant", in relation to any offence (or alleged offence), means a person against or in relation to whom the offence was (or is alleged to have been) committed;
"court" (except in Chapter IV or V or subsection (2)) means a magistrates' court, the Crown Court or the criminal division of the Court of Appeal;
"legal representative" means a person who, for the purposes of the Legal Services Act 2007, is an authorised person in relation to an activity which constitutes the exercise of a right of audience or the conduct of litigation (within the meaning of that Act);
"picture" includes a likeness however produced;
"the prosecutor" means any person acting as prosecutor, whether an individual or body;

"publication" includes any speech, writing, relevant programme or other communication in whatever form, which is addressed to the public at large or any section of the public (and for this purpose every relevant programme shall be taken to be so addressed), but does not include an indictment or other document prepared for use in particular legal proceedings;

"relevant programme" means a programme included in a programme service, within the meaning of the Broadcasting Act 1990;

"service court" means –

(a) the Court Martial;
(b) the Service Civilian Court; or
(c) the Court Martial Appeal Court;

"video recording" means any recording, on any medium, from which a moving image may by any means be produced, and includes the accompanying sound-track;

"witness", in relation to any criminal proceedings, means any person called, or proposed to be called, to give evidence in the proceedings.

(2) Nothing in this Part shall affect any power of a court to exclude evidence at its discretion (whether by preventing questions being put or otherwise) which is exercisable apart from this Part.

Crime and Disorder Act 1998 (ss 8–10)

Arrangement of Sections

Youth crime and disorder

8 Parenting orders

(1) This section applies where, in any court proceedings –

(a) a child safety order is made in respect of a child or the court determines on an application under section 12(6) below that a child has failed to comply with any requirement included in such an order;
(aa) a parental compensation order is made in relation to a child's behaviour;
(b) an injunction is granted under section 1 of the Anti-social Behaviour, Crime and Policing Act 2014, an order is made under section 22 of that Act or a sexual harm prevention order is made in respect of a child or young person;
(c) a child or young person is convicted of an offence; or
(d) a person is convicted of an offence under section 443 (failure to comply with school attendance order) or section 444 (failure to secure regular attendance at school of registered pupil) of the Education Act 1996.

(2) Subject to subsection (3) and section 9(1) below, if in the proceedings the court is satisfied that the relevant condition is fulfilled, it may make a parenting order in respect of a person who is a parent or guardian of the child or young person or, as the case may be, the person convicted of the offence under section 443 or 444 ("the parent").

(3) A court shall not make a parenting order unless it has been notified by the Secretary of State that arrangements for implementing such orders are available in the area in which it appears to the court that the parent resides or will reside and the notice has not been withdrawn.

(4) A parenting order is an order which requires the parent –

(a) to comply, for a period not exceeding twelve months, with such requirements as are specified in the order, and
(b) subject to subsection (5) below, to attend, for a concurrent period not exceeding three months, such counselling or guidance programme as may be specified in directions given by the responsible officer.

(5) A parenting order may, but need not, include such a requirement as is mentioned in subsection (4)(b) above in any case where a parenting order under this section or any other enactment has been made in respect of the parent on a previous occasion.

(6) The relevant condition is that the parenting order would be desirable in the interests of preventing –

(a) in a case falling within paragraph (a), (aa) or (b) of subsection (1) above, any repetition of the kind of behaviour which led to parental compensation order, sexual harm prevention order being made the order being made or the injunction granted;
(b) in a case falling within paragraph (c) of that subsection, the commission of any further offence by the child or young person;
(c) in a case falling within paragraph (d) of that subsection, the commission of any further offence under section 443 or 444 of the Education Act 1996.

(7) The requirements that may be specified under subsection (4)(a) above are those which the court considers desirable in the interests of preventing any such repetition or, as the case may be, the commission of any such further offence.

(7A) A counselling or guidance programme which a parent is required to attend by virtue of subsection (4)(b) above may be or include a residential course but only if the court is satisfied –

(a) that the attendance of the parent at a residential course is likely to be more effective than his attendance at a non-residential course in preventing any such repetition or, as the case may be, the commission of any such further offence, and
(b) that any interference with family life which is likely to result from the attendance of the parent at a residential course is proportionate in all the circumstances.

(8) In this section and section 9 below "responsible officer", in relation to a parenting order, means one of the following who is specified in the order, namely –

(a) an officer of a local probation board or an officer of a provider of probation services;
(b) a social worker of a local authority; and
(bb) a person nominated by a person appointed as director of children 's services under section 18 of the Children Act 2004 or by a person appointed as chief education officer under section 532 of the Education Act 1996;
(c) a member of a youth offending team.

(9) In this section "sexual harm prevention order" means an order under section 103A of the Sexual Offences Act 2003 (sexual harm prevention orders).

9 Parenting orders: supplemental

(1) Where a person under the age of 16 is convicted of an offence, the court by or before which he is so convicted –

(a) if it is satisfied that the relevant condition is fulfilled, shall make a parenting order; and
(b) if it is not so satisfied, shall state in open court that it is not and why it is not.

(1A) The requirements of subsection (1) do not apply where the court makes a referral order in respect of the offence.

(1B) If an injunction under section 1 of the Anti-social Behaviour, Crime and Policing Act 2014 is granted or an order is made under section 22 of that Act is made in respect of a person under the age of 16 the court which makes the order –

(a) must make a parenting order if it is satisfied that the relevant condition is fulfilled;
(b) if it is not so satisfied, must state in open court that it is not and why it is not.

(2) Before making a parenting order –

(a) in a case falling within paragraph (a) of subsection (1) of section 8 above;
(b) in a case falling within paragraph (b) or (c) of that subsection, where the person concerned is under the age of 16; *or*
(c) in a case falling within paragraph (d) of that subsection, where the person to whom the offence related is under that age.
(d) [repealed].

a court shall obtain and consider information about the person's family circumstances and the likely effect of the order on those circumstances.

(2A) In a case where a court proposes to make both a referral order in respect of a child or young person convicted of an offence and a parenting order, before making the parenting order the court shall obtain and consider a report by an appropriate officer –

(a) indicating the requirements proposed by that officer to be included in the parenting order;
(b) indicating the reasons why he considers those requirements would be desirable in the interests of preventing the commission of any further offence by the child or young person; and
(c) if the child or young person is aged under 16, containing the information required by subsection (2) above.

(2AA) [repealed].

(2B) In subsection (2A) above "an appropriate officer" means –

(a) an officer of a local probation board or an officer of a provider of probation services;
(b) a social worker of a local authority; or
(c) a member of a youth offending team.

(3) Before making a parenting order, a court shall explain to the parent in ordinary language –

(a) the effect of the order and of the requirements proposed to be included in it;
(b) the consequences which may follow (under subsection (7) below) if he fails to comply with any of those requirements; and
(c) that the court has power (under subsection (5) below) to review the order on the application either of the parent or of the responsible officer.

(4) Requirements specified in, and directions given under, a parenting order shall, as far as practicable, be such as to avoid –

(a) any conflict with the parent's religious beliefs; and
(b) any interference with the times, if any, at which he normally works or attends an educational establishment.

(5) If while a parenting order is in force it appears to the court which made it, on the application of the responsible officer or the parent, that it is appropriate to make an order under this subsection, the court may make an order discharging the parenting order or varying it –

(a) by cancelling any provision included in it; or
(b) by inserting in it (either in addition to or in substitution for any of its provisions) any provision that could have been included in the order if the court had then had power to make it and were exercising the power.

(6) Where an application under subsection (5) above for the discharge of a parenting order is dismissed, no further application for its discharge shall be made under that subsection by any person except with the consent of the court which made the order.

(7) If while a parenting order is in force the parent without reasonable excuse fails to comply with any requirement included in the order, or specified in directions given by the responsible officer, he shall be liable on summary conviction to a fine not exceeding level 3 on the standard scale.

(7A) In this section "referral order" means an order under section 16(2) or (3) of the Powers of Criminal Courts (Sentencing) Act 2000 (referral of offender to youth offender panel).

10 Appeals against parenting orders

(1) An appeal shall lie –

- (a) to the county court against the making of a parenting order by virtue of paragraph (a) of subsection (1) of section 8 above; and
- (b) to the Crown Court against the making of a parenting order by virtue of paragraph (b) of that subsection.

(2) On an appeal under subsection (1) above the county court or the Crown Court –

- (a) may make such orders as may be necessary to give effect to its determination of the appeal; and
- (b) may also make such incidental or consequential orders as appear to it to be just.

(3) Any order of the county court or the Crown Court made on an appeal under subsection (1) above (other than one directing that an application be re-heard by a magistrates' court) shall, for the purposes of subsections (5) to (7) of section 9 above, be treated as if it were an order of the court from which the appeal was brought and not an order of the county court or the Crown Court.

(4) A person in respect of whom a parenting order is made by virtue of section 8(1)(c) above shall have the same right of appeal against the making of the order as if –

- (a) the offence that led to the making of the order were an offence committed by him; and
- (b) the order were a sentence passed on him for the offence.

(5) A person in respect of whom a parenting order is made by virtue of section 8(1)(d) above shall have the same right of appeal against the making of the order as if the order were a sentence passed on him for the offence that led to the making of the order.

(6) The Lord Chancellor may, with the concurrence of the Lord Chief Justice, by order make provision as to the circumstances in which appeals under subsection (1)(a) above may be made against decisions taken by courts on questions arising in connection with the transfer, or proposed transfer, of proceedings by virtue of any order under paragraph 2 of Schedule 11 (jurisdiction) to the Children Act 1989 ("the 1989 Act").

(7) Except to the extent provided for in any order made under subsection (6) above, no appeal may be made against any decision of a kind mentioned in that subsection.

(8) The Lord Chief Justice may nominate a judicial office holder (as defined in section 109(4) of the Constitutional Reform Act 2005) to exercise his functions under this section.

Civil Evidence Act 1995 (ss 1–16)

Arrangement of Sections

Admissibility of hearsay evidence

1 Admissibility of hearsay evidence

(1) In civil proceedings evidence shall not be excluded on the ground that it is hearsay.

(2) In this Act –

(a) 'hearsay' means a statement made otherwise than by a person while giving oral evidence in the proceedings which is tendered as evidence of the matters stated; and
(b) references to hearsay include hearsay of whatever degree.

(3) Nothing in this Act affects the Admissibility of evidence admissible apart from this section.

(4) The provisions of sections 2 to 6 (safeguards and supplementary provisions relating to hearsay evidence) do not apply in relation to hearsay evidence admissible apart from this section, notwithstanding that it may also be admissible by virtue of this section.

Safeguards in relation to hearsay evidence

2 Notice of proposal to adduce hearsay evidence

(1) A party proposing to adduce hearsay evidence in civil proceedings shall, subject to the following provisions of this section, give to the other party or parties to the proceedings –

(a) such notice (if any) of that fact, and
(b) on request, such particulars of or relating to the evidence,

as is reasonable and practicable in the circumstances for the purpose of enabling him or them to deal with any matters arising from its being hearsay.

(2) Provision may be made by rules of court –

(a) specifying classes of proceedings or evidence in relation to which subsection (1) does not apply, and
(b) as to the manner in which (including the time within which) the duties imposed by that subsection are to be complied with in the cases where it does apply.

(3) Subsection (1) may also be excluded by agreement of the parties; and compliance with the duty to give notice may in any case be waived by the person to whom notice is required to be given.

(4) A failure to comply with subsection (1), or with rules under subsection (2)(b), does not affect the Admissibility of the evidence but may be taken into account by the court –

(a) in considering the exercise of its powers with respect to the course of proceedings and costs, and
(b) as a matter adversely affecting the weight to be given to the evidence in accordance with section 4.

3 Power to call witness for cross-examination on hearsay statement

Rules of court may provide that where a party to civil proceedings adduces hearsay evidence of a statement made by a person and does not call that person as a witness, any other party to the proceedings may, with the leave of the court, call that person as a witness and cross-examine him on the statement as if he had been called by the first-mentioned party and as if the hearsay statement were his evidence in chief.

4 Considerations relevant to weighing of hearsay evidence

(1) In estimating the weight (if any) to be given to hearsay evidence in civil proceedings the court shall have regard to any circumstances from which any inference can reasonably be drawn as to the reliability or otherwise of the evidence.

(2) Regard may be had, in particular, to the following –

(a) whether it would have been reasonable and practicable for the party by whom the evidence was adduced to have produced the maker of the original statement as a witness;
(b) whether the original statement was made contemporaneously with the occurrence or existence of the matters stated;
(c) whether the evidence involves multiple hearsay;
(d) whether any person involved had any motive to conceal or misrepresent matters;
(e) whether the original statement was an edited account, or was made in collaboration with another or for a particular purpose;
(f) whether the circumstances in which the evidence is adduced as hearsay are such as to suggest an attempt to prevent proper evaluation of its weight.

Supplementary provisions as to hearsay evidence

5 Competence and credibility

(1) Hearsay evidence shall not be admitted in civil proceedings if or to the extent that it is shown to consist of, or to be proved by means of, a statement made by a person who at the time he made the statement was not competent as a witness.

For this purpose 'not competent as a witness' means suffering from such mental or physical infirmity, or lack of understanding, as would render a person incompetent as a witness in civil proceedings; but a child shall be treated as competent as a witness if he satisfies the requirements of section 96(2)(a) and (b) of the Children Act 1989 (conditions for reception of unsworn evidence of child).

(2) Where in civil proceedings hearsay evidence is adduced and the maker of the original statement, or of any statement relied upon to prove another statement, is not called as a witness –

(a) evidence which if he had been so called would be admissible for the purpose of attacking or supporting his credibility as a witness is admissible for that purpose in the proceedings; and
(b) evidence tending to prove that, whether before or after he made the statement, he made any other statement inconsistent with it is admissible for the purpose of showing that he had contradicted himself.

Provided that evidence may not be given of any matter of which, if he had been called as a witness and had denied that matter in cross-examination, evidence could not have been adduced by the cross-examining party.

6 Previous statements of witnesses

(1) Subject as follows, the provisions of this Act as to hearsay evidence in civil proceedings apply equally (but with any necessary modifications) in relation to a previous statement made by a person called as a witness in the proceedings.

(2) A party who has called or intends to call a person as a witness in civil proceedings may not in those proceedings adduce evidence of a previous statement made by that person, except –

(a) with the leave of the court, or
(b) for the purpose of rebutting a suggestion that his evidence has been fabricated.

This shall not be construed as preventing a witness statement (that is, a written statement of oral evidence which a party to the proceedings intends to lead) from being adopted by a witness in giving evidence or treated as his evidence.

(3) Where in the case of civil proceedings sections 3, 4 or 5 of the Criminal Procedure Act 1865 applies, which make provision as to –

(a) how far a witness may be discredited by the party producing him,
(b) the proof of contradictory statements made by a witness, and
(c) cross-examination as to previous statements in writing,

this Act does not authorise the adducing of evidence of a previous inconsistent or contradictory statement otherwise than in accordance with those sections.

This is without prejudice to any provision made by rules of court under section 3 above (power to call witness for cross-examination on hearsay statement).

(4) Nothing in this Act affects any of the rules of law as to the circumstances in which, where a person called as a witness in civil proceedings is cross-examined on a document used by him to refresh his memory, that document may be made evidence in the proceedings.

(5) Nothing in this section shall be construed as preventing a statement of any description referred to above from being admissible by virtue of section 1 as evidence of the matters stated.

7 Evidence formerly admissible at common law

(1) The common law rule effectively preserved by section 9(1) and (2)(a) of the Civil Evidence Act 1968 (Admissibility of admissions adverse to a party) is superseded by the provisions of this Act.

(2) The common law rules effectively preserved by section 9(1) and (2)(b) to (d) of the Civil Evidence Act 1968, that is, any rule of law whereby in civil proceedings –

- (a) published works dealing with matters of a public nature (for example, histories, scientific works, dictionaries and maps) are admissible as evidence of facts of a public nature stated in them,
- (b) public documents (for example, public registers, and returns made under public authority with respect to matters of public interest) are admissible as evidence of facts stated in them, or
- (c) records (for example, the records of certain courts, treaties, Crown grants, pardons and commissions) are admissible as evidence of facts stated in them,

shall continue to have effect.

(3) The common law rules effectively preserved by section 9(3) and (4) of the Civil Evidence Act 1968, that is, any rule of law whereby in civil proceedings –

- (a) evidence of a person's reputation is admissible for the purpose of proving his good or bad character, or
- (b) evidence of reputation or family tradition is admissible –
  - (i) for the purpose of proving or disproving pedigree or the existence of a marriage, or
  - (ii) for the purpose of proving or disproving the existence of any public or general right or of identifying any person or thing,

shall continue to have effect in so far as they authorise the court to treat such evidence as proving or disproving that matter.

Where any such rule applies, reputation or family tradition shall be treated for the purposes of this Act as a fact and not as a statement or multiplicity of statements about the matter in question.

(4) The words in which a rule of law mentioned in this section is described are intended only to identify the rule and shall not be construed as altering it in any way.

Other matters

8 Proof of statements contained in documents

(1) Where a statement contained in a document is admissible as evidence in civil proceedings, it may be proved –

- (a) by the production of that document, or
- (b) whether or not that document is still in existence, by the production of a copy of that document or of the material part of it,

authenticated in such manner as the court may approve.

(2) It is immaterial for this purpose how many removes there are between a copy and the original.

9 Proof of records of business or public authority

(1) A document which is shown to form part of the records of a business or public authority may be received in evidence in civil proceedings without further proof.

(2) A document shall be taken to form part of the records of a business or public authority if there is produced to the court a certificate to that effect signed by an officer of the business or authority to which the records belong.

For this purpose –

(a) a document purporting to be a certificate signed by an officer of a business or public authority shall be deemed to have been duly given by such an officer and signed by him; and
(b) a certificate shall be treated as signed by a person if it purports to bear a facsimile of his signature.

(3) The absence of an entry in the records of a business or public authority may be proved in civil proceedings by affidavit of an officer of the business or authority to which the records belong.

(4) In this section –

'records' means records in whatever form;
'business' includes any activity regularly carried on over a period of time, whether for profit or not, by any body (whether corporate or not) or by an individual;
'officer' includes any person occupying a responsible position in relation to the relevant activities of the business or public authority or in relation to its records; and
'public authority' includes any public or statutory undertaking, any government department and any person holding office under Her Majesty.

(5) The court may, having regard to the circumstances of the case, direct that all or any of the above provisions of this section do not apply in relation to a particular document or record, or description of documents or records.

10 Admissibility of proof of Ogden Tables

(1) The actuarial tables (together with explanatory notes) for use in personal injury and fatal accident cases issued from time to time by the Government Actuary's Department are admissible in evidence for the purpose of assessing, in an action for personal injury, the sum to be awarded as general damages for future pecuniary loss.

(2) They may be proved by the production of a copy published by Her Majesty's Stationery Office.

(3) For the purposes of this section –

(a) 'personal injury' includes any disease and any impairment of a person's physical or mental condition; and
(b) 'action for personal injury' includes an action brought by virtue of the Law Reform (Miscellaneous Provisions) Act 1934 or the Fatal Accidents Act 1976.

General

11 Meaning of 'civil proceedings'

In this Act 'civil proceedings' means civil proceedings, before any tribunal, in relation to which the strict rules of evidence apply, whether as a matter of law or by agreement of the parties.

References to 'the court' and 'rules of court' shall be construed accordingly.

12 Provisions as to rules of court

(1) Any power to make rules of court regulating the practice or procedure of the court in relation to civil proceedings includes power to make such provision as may be necessary or expedient for carrying into effect the provisions of this Act.

(2) Any rules of court made for the purposes of this Act as it applies in relation to proceedings in the High Court apply, except in so far as their operation is excluded by agreement, to arbitration proceedings to which this Act applies, subject to such modifications as may be appropriate.

Any question arising as to what modifications are appropriate shall be determined, in default of agreement, by the arbitrator or umpire, as the case may be.

13 Interpretation

In this Act –

'civil proceedings' has the meaning given by section 11 and 'court' and 'rules of court' shall be construed in accordance with that section;
'document' means anything in which information of any description is recorded, and 'copy', in relation to a document, means anything onto which information recorded in the document has been copied, by whatever means and whether directly or indirectly;
'hearsay' shall be construed in accordance with section 1(2);
'oral evidence' includes evidence which, by reason of a defect of speech or hearing, a person called as a witness gives in writing or by signs;
'the original statement', in relation to hearsay evidence, means the underlying statement (if any) by –

(a) in the case of evidence of fact, a person having personal knowledge of that fact, or
(b) in the case of evidence of opinion, the person whose opinion it is; and

'statement' means any representation of fact or opinion, however made.

14 Savings

(1) Nothing in this Act affects the exclusion of evidence on grounds other than that it is hearsay.

This applies whether the evidence falls to be excluded in pursuance of any enactment or rule of law, for failure to comply with rules of court or an order of the court, or otherwise.

(2) Nothing in this Act affects the proof of documents by means other than those specified in section 8 or 9.

(3) Nothing in this Act affects the operation of the following enactments –

(a) section 2 of the Documentary Evidence Act 1868 (mode of proving certain official documents);
(b) section 2 of the Documentary Evidence Act 1882 (documents printed under the superintendence of Stationery Office);
(c) section 1 of the Evidence (Colonial Statutes) Act 1907 (proof of statutes of certain legislatures);
(d) section 1 of the Evidence (Foreign, Dominion and Colonial Documents) Act 1933 (proof and effect of registers and official certificates of certain countries);
(e) section 5 of the Oaths and Evidence (Overseas Authorities and Countries) Act 1963 (provision in respect of public registers of other countries).

15 Consequential amendments and repeals

(1) The enactments specified in Schedule 1 are amended in accordance with that Schedule, the amendments being consequential on the provisions of this Act.

(2) The enactments specified in Schedule 2 are repealed to the extent specified.

16 Short title, commencement and extent

(1) This Act may be cited as the Civil Evidence Act 1995.

(2) The provisions of this Act come into force on such day as the Lord Chancellor may appoint by order made by statutory instrument, and different days may be appointed for different provisions and for different purposes.

(3) Subject to subsection (3A), the provisions of this Act shall not apply in relation to proceedings begun before commencement.

(3A) Transitional provisions for the application of the provisions of this Act to proceedings begun before commencement may be made by rules of court or practice directions.

(4) This Act extends to England and Wales.

(5) Section 10 (admissibility and proof of Ogden Tables) also extends to Northern Ireland.

As it extends to Northern Ireland, the following shall be substituted for subsection (3)(b) –

> '(b) "action for personal injury" includes an action brought by virtue of the Law Reform (Miscellaneous Provisions) (Northern Ireland) Act 1937 or the Fatal Accidents (Northern Ireland) Order 1977.'

(6) The provisions of Schedules 1 and 2 (consequential amendments and repeals) have the same extent as the enactments respectively amended or repealed.

Housing Act 1988 (ss 8, 21, Sch 2)

8 Notice of proceedings for possession

(1) The court shall not entertain proceedings for possession of a dwelling-house let on an assured tenancy unless –

- (a) the landlord or, in the case of joint landlords, at least one of them has served on the tenant a notice in accordance with this section and the proceedings are begun within the time limits stated in the notice in accordance with subsections (3) to (4B) below, or
- (b) the court considers it just and equitable to dispense with the requirement of such a notice.

(2) The court shall not make an order for possession on any of the grounds in Schedule 2 to this Act unless that ground and particulars of it are specified in the notice under this section; but the grounds specified in such a notice may be altered or added to with the leave of the court.

(3) A notice under this section is one in the prescribed form informing the tenant that –

- (a) the landlord intends to begin proceedings for possession of the dwelling-house on one or more of the grounds specified in the notice; and
- (b) those proceedings will not begin earlier than a date specified in the notice in accordance with subsections (3A) to (4B) below; and
- (c) those proceedings will not begin later than twelve months from the date of service of the notice.

(3A) If a notice under this section specifies in accordance with subsection (3)(a) Ground 7A in Schedule 2 to this Act (whether with or without other grounds), the date specified in the notice as mentioned in subsection (3)(b) is not to be earlier than –

- (a) in the case of a periodic tenancy, the earliest date on which, apart from section 5(1), the tenancy could be brought to an end by a notice to quit given by the landlord on the same date as the date of service of the notice under this section;

(b) in the case of a fixed term tenancy, one month after the date on which the notice was served.

(4) If a notice under this section specifies in accordance with subsection (3)(a) above Ground 14 in Schedule 2 to this Act (whether without other grounds or with any ground other than Ground 7A or 14), the date specified in the notice as mentioned in subsection (3)(b)above shall not be earlier than the date of the service of the notice.

(4A) If a notice under this section specifies in accordance with subsection (3)(a) above, any of Grounds 1, 2, 5 to 7, 9 and 16 in Schedule 2 to this Act (whether without other grounds or with any ground other than Ground 14), the date specified in the notice as mentioned in subsection (3)(b) above shall not be earlier than –

(a) two months from the date of service of the notice; and
(b) if the tenancy is a periodic tenancy, the earliest date on which, apart from section 5(1) above, the tenancy could be brought to an end by a notice to quit given by the landlord on the same date as the date of service of the notice under this section.

(4B) In any other case, the date specified in the notice as mentioned in subsection (3)(b) above shall not be earlier than the expiry of the period of two weeks from the date of the service of the notice.

(4C) A notice under this section that specifies in accordance with subsection (3)(a) Ground 7A in Schedule 2 to this Act (whether with or without other grounds) must be served on the tenant within the time period specified in subsection (4D), (4E) or (4F).

(4D) Where the landlord proposes to rely on condition 1, 3 or 5 in Ground 7A, the notice must be served on the tenant within –

(a) the period of 12 months beginning with the day of the conviction, or
(b) if there is an appeal against the conviction, the period of 12 months beginning with the day on which the appeal is finally determined or abandoned.

(4E) Where the landlord proposes to rely on condition 2 in Ground 7A, the notice must be served on the tenant within –

(a) the period of 12 months beginning with the day on which the court has made the finding, or
(b) if there is an appeal against the finding, the period of 12 months beginning with the day on which the appeal is finally determined, abandoned or withdrawn.

(4F) Where the landlord proposes to rely on condition 4 in Ground 7A, the notice must be served on the tenant within –

(a) the period of 3 months beginning with the day on which the closure order was made, or
(b) if there is an appeal against the making of the order, the period of 3 months beginning with the day on which the appeal is finally determined, abandoned or withdrawn.

(5) The court may not exercise the power conferred by subsection (1)(b) above if the landlord seeks to recover possession on Ground 7A or 8 in Schedule 2 to this Act.

(6) Where a notice under this section –

(a) is served at a time when the dwelling-house is let on a fixed term tenancy, or
(b) is served after a fixed term tenancy has come to an end but relates (in whole or in part) to events occurring during that tenancy,

the notice shall have effect notwithstanding that the tenant becomes or has become tenant under a statutory periodic tenancy arising on the coming to an end of the fixed term tenancy.

21 Recovery of possession on expiry or termination of assured shorthold tenancy

(1) Without prejudice to any right of the landlord under an assured shorthold tenancy to recover possession of the dwelling-house let on the tenancy in accordance with Chapter I above, on or after the coming to an end of an assured shorthold tenancy which was a fixed term tenancy, a court shall make an order for possession of the dwelling-house if it is satisfied –

(a) that the assured shorthold tenancy has come to an end and no further assured tenancy (whether shorthold or not) is for the time being in existence, other than an assured shorthold periodic tenancy (whether statutory or not); and
(b) the landlord or, in the case of joint landlords, at least one of them has given to the tenant not less than two months' notice in writing stating that he requires possession of the dwelling-house.

(1A) Subsection (1B) applies to an assured shorthold tenancy of a dwellinghouse in England if –

(a) it is a fixed term tenancy for a term certain of not less than two years, and
(b) the landlord is a private registered provider of social housing.

(1B) The court may not make an order for possession of the dwelling-house let on the tenancy unless the landlord has given to the tenant not less than six months' notice in writing –

(a) stating that the landlord does not propose to grant another tenancy on the expiry of the fixed term tenancy, and
(b) informing the tenant of how to obtain help or advice about the notice and, in particular, of any obligation of the landlord to provide help or advice.

(2) A notice under paragraph (b) of subsection (1) above may be given before or on the day on which the tenancy comes to an end; and that subsection shall have effect notwithstanding that on the coming to an end of the fixed term tenancy a statutory periodic tenancy arises.

(3) Where a court makes an order for possession of a dwelling-house by virtue of subsection (1) above, any statutory periodic tenancy which has arisen on the coming to an end of the assured shorthold tenancy shall end (without further notice and regardless of the period) in accordance with section 5(1A).

(4) Without prejudice to any such right as is referred to in subsection (1) above, a court shall make an order for possession of a dwelling-house let on an assured shorthold tenancy which is a periodic tenancy if the court is satisfied –

(a) that the landlord or, in the case of joint landlords, at least one of them has given to the tenant a notice in writing stating that, after a date specified in the notice, being the last day of a period of the tenancy and not earlier than two months after the date the notice was given, possession of the dwelling-house is required by virtue of this section; and
(b) that the date specified in the notice under paragraph (a) above is not earlier than the earliest day on which, apart from section 5(1) above, the tenancy could be brought to an end by a notice to quit given by the landlord on the same date as the notice under paragraph (a) above.

(4A) Where a court makes an order for possession of a dwelling-house by virtue of subsection (4) above, the assured shorthold tenancy shall end in accordance with section 5(1A)

(5) Where an order for possession under subsection (1) or (4) above is made in relation to a dwelling-house let on a tenancy to which section 19A above applies, the order may not be made so as to take effect earlier than –

(a) in the case of a tenancy which is not a replacement tenancy, six months after the beginning of the tenancy, and
(b) in the case of a replacement tenancy, six months after the beginning of the original tenancy.

(5A) Subsection (5) above does not apply to an assured shorthold tenancy to which section 20B (demoted assured shorthold tenancies) applies.

(6) In subsection (5)(b) above, the reference to the original tenancy is –

(a) where the replacement tenancy came into being on the coming to an end of a tenancy which was not a replacement tenancy, to the immediately preceding tenancy, and
(b) where there have been successive replacement tenancies, to the tenancy immediately preceding the first in the succession of replacement tenancies.

(7) For the purposes of this section, a replacement tenancy is a tenancy –

(a) which comes into being on the coming to an end of an assured short-hold tenancy, and
(b) under which, on its coming into being –

(i) the landlord and tenant are the same as under the earlier tenancy as at its coming to an end, and
(ii) the premises let are the same or substantially the same as those let under the earlier tenancy as at that time.

SCHEDULE 2

GROUNDS FOR POSSESSION OF DWELLING-HOUSES LET ON ASSURED TENANCIES

PART I

GROUNDS ON WHICH COURT MUST ORDER POSSESSION

Ground 1

Not later than the beginning of the tenancy the landlord gave notice in writing to the tenant that possession might be recovered on this ground or the court is of the opinion that it is just and equitable to dispense with the requirement of notice and (in either case) –

(a) at some time before the beginning of the tenancy, the landlord who is seeking possession or, in the case of joint landlords seeking possession, at least one of them occupied the dwelling-house as his only or principal home; or
(b) the landlord who is seeking possession or, in the case of joint landlords seeking possession, at least one of them requires the dwelling-house as his, his spouse's or his civil partner's only or principal home and neither the landlord (or, in the case of joint landlords, any one of them) nor any other person who, as landlord, derived title under the landlord who gave the notice mentioned above acquired the reversion on the tenancy for money or money's worth.

Ground 2

The dwelling-house is subject to a mortgage granted before the beginning of the tenancy and –

(a) the mortgagee is entitled to exercise a power of sale conferred on him by the mortgage or by section 101of the Law of Property Act 1925; and
(b) the mortgagee requires possession of the dwelling-house for the purpose of disposing of it with vacant possession in exercise of that power; and
(c) either notice was given as mentioned in Ground 1 above or the court is satisfied that it is just and equitable to dispense with the requirement of notice;

and for the purposes of this ground 'mortgage' includes a charge and 'mortgagee' shall be construed accordingly.

Ground 3

The tenancy is a fixed term tenancy for a term not exceeding eight months and –

(a) not later than the beginning of the tenancy the landlord gave notice in writing to the tenant that possession might be recovered on this ground; and

(b) at some time within the period of twelve months ending with the beginning of the tenancy, the dwelling-house was occupied under a right to occupy it for a holiday.

Ground 4

The tenancy is a fixed term tenancy for a term not exceeding twelve months and –

(a) not later than the beginning of the tenancy the landlord gave notice in writing to the tenant that possession might be recovered on this ground, and
(b) at some time within the period of twelve months ending with the beginning of the tenancy, the dwelling-house was let on a tenancy falling within paragraph 8 of Schedule l to this Act.

Ground 5

The dwelling-house is held for the purpose of being available for occupation by a minister of religion as a residence from which to perform the duties of his office and –

(a) not later than the beginning of the tenancy the landlord gave notice in writing to the tenant that possession might be recovered on this ground; and
(b) the court is satisfied that the dwelling-house is required for occupation by a minister of religion as such a residence.

Ground 6

The landlord who is seeking possession or, if that landlord is a non-profit registered provider of social housing, registered social landlord or charitable housing trust, or (where the dwelling-house is social housing within the meaning of Part 2 of the Housing and Regeneration Act 2008) a profit-making registered provider of social housing, a superior landlord intends to demolish or reconstruct the whole or a substantial part of the dwelling-house or to carry out substantial works on the dwelling-house or any part thereof or any building of which it forms part and the following conditions are fulfilled –

(a) the intended work cannot reasonably be carried out without the tenant giving up possession of the dwelling-house because –

   (i) the tenant is not willing to agree to such a variation of the terms of the tenancy as would give such access and other facilities as would permit the intended work to be carried out, or
   (ii) the nature of the intended work is such that no such variation is practicable, or
   (iii) the tenant is not willing to accept an assured tenancy of such part only of the dwelling-house (in this sub-paragraph referred to as 'the reduced part') as would leave in the possession of his landlord so much of the dwelling-house as would be reasonable to enable the intended work to be carried out and, where appropriate, as would give such access and other facilities over the reduced part as would permit the intended work to be carried out, or
   (iv) the nature of the intended work is such that such a tenancy is not practicable; and

(b) either the landlord seeking possession acquired his interest in the dwelling-house before the grant of the tenancy or that interest was in existence at the time of that grant and neither that landlord (or, in the case of joint landlords, any of them) nor any other person who, alone or jointly with others, has acquired that interest since that time acquired it for money or money's worth; and
(c) the assured tenancy on which the dwelling-house is let did not come into being by virtue of any provision of Schedule 1 to the Rent Act 1977, as amended by Part I of Schedule 4 to this Act or, as the case may be, section 4 of the Rent (Agriculture) Act 1976, as amended by Part II of that Schedule.

For the purposes of this ground, if, immediately before the grant of the tenancy, the tenant to whom it was granted or, if it was granted to joint tenants, any of them was the tenant or one of the joint tenants of the dwelling-house concerned under an earlier assured tenancy or, as the case may be, under a tenancy to which Schedule 10 to the Local Government and Housing Act 1989 applied, any reference in paragraph (b) above to the grant of the tenancy is a reference to the grant of that earlier assured tenancy or, as the case may be, to the grant of the tenancy to which the said Schedule 10 applied.

For the purposes of this ground 'registered social landlord' has the same meaning as in the Housing Act 1985 (see section 5(4) and (5) of that Act) and 'charitable housing trust' means a housing trust within the meaning of the Housing Associations Act 1985, which is a charity.

Ground 7

The tenancy or a fixed term tenancy of a dwelling-house in England is a periodic tenancy (including a statutory periodic tenancy) which has devolved under the will or intestacy of the former tenant and the proceedings for the recovery of possession are begun not later than twelve months after the death of the former tenant or, if the court so directs, after the date on which, in the opinion of the court, the landlord or, in the case of joint landlords, any one of them became aware of the former tenant's death.

For the purposes of this ground, the acceptance by the landlord of rent from a new tenant after the death of the former tenant shall not be regarded as creating a new tenancy, unless the landlord agrees in writing to a change (as compared with the tenancy before the death) in the amount of the rent, the period of length of term of the tenancy, the premises which are let or any other term of the tenancy.

This ground does not apply to a fixed term tenancy that is a lease of a dwelling-house 8–

(a) granted on payment of a premium calculated by reference to a percentage of the value of the dwelling house or of the cost of providing it, or
(b) under which the lessee (or the lessee's personal representatives) will or may be entitled to a sum calculated by reference, directly or indirectly, to the value of the dwelling-house.

Ground 7A

Any of the following conditions is met.

Condition 1 is that –

(a) the tenant, or a person residing in or visiting the dwelling-house, has been convicted of a serious offence, and
(b) the serious offence –
    (i) was committed (wholly or partly) in, or in the locality of, the dwelling-house,
    (ii) was committed elsewhere against a person with a right (of whatever description) to reside in, or occupy housing accommodation in the locality of, the dwelling-house, or
    (iii) was committed elsewhere against the landlord of the dwelling-house, or a person employed (whether or not by the landlord) in connection with the exercise of the landlord's housing management functions, and directly or indirectly related to or affected those functions.

Condition 2 is that a court has found in relevant proceedings that the tenant, or a person residing in or visiting the dwelling-house, has breached a provision of an injunction under section 1 of the Anti-Social Behaviour, Crime and Policing Act 2014, other than a provision requiring a person to participate in a particular activity, and –

(a) the breach occurred in, or in the locality of, the dwelling-house, or
(b) the breach occurred elsewhere and the provision breached was a provision intended to prevent –
    (i) conduct that is capable of causing nuisance or annoyance to a person with a right (of whatever description) to reside in, or occupy housing accommodation in the locality of, the dwelling-house, or
    (ii) conduct that is capable of causing nuisance or annoyance to the landlord of the dwelling-house, or a person employed (whether or not by the landlord) in connection with the exercise of the landlord's housing management functions, and that is directly or indirectly related to or affects those functions.

Condition 3 is that the tenant, or a person residing in or visiting the dwelling-house, has been convicted of an offence under section 30 of the Anti-social Behaviour, Crime and Policing Act 2014 consisting of a breach of a provision of a criminal behaviour order prohibiting a person from doing anything described in the order, and the offence involved –

(a) a breach that occurred in, or in the locality of, the dwelling house, or
(b) a breach that occurred elsewhere of a provision intended to prevent –

 (i) behaviour that causes or is likely to cause harassment, alarm or distress to a person with a right (of whatever description) to reside in, or occupy housing accommodation in the locality of, the dwelling-house, or
 (ii) behaviour that causes or is likely to cause harassment, alarm or distress to the landlord of the dwelling house, or a person employed (whether or not by the landlord) in connection with the exercise of the landlord's housing management functions, and that is directly or indirectly related to or affects those functions.

Condition 4 is that –

(a) the dwelling-house is or has been subject to a closure order under section 80 of the Anti-social Behaviour, Crime and Policing Act 2014, and
(b) access to the dwelling-house has been prohibited (under the closure order or under a closure notice issued under section 76 of that Act) for a continuous period of more than 48 hours.

Condition 5 is that –

(a) the tenant, or a person residing in or visiting the dwelling house, has been convicted of an offence under

 (i) section 80(4) of the Environmental Protection Act 1990 (breach of abatement notice in relation to statutory nuisance), or
 (ii) section 82(8) of that Act (breach of court order to abate statutory nuisance etc.), and

(b) the nuisance concerned was noise emitted from the dwelling-house which was a statutory nuisance for the purposes of

Part 3 of that Act by virtue of section 79(1)(g) of that Act (noise emitted from premises so as to be prejudicial to health or a nuisance).

Condition 1, 2, 3, 4 or 5 is not met if –

(a) there is an appeal against the conviction, finding or order concerned which has not been finally determined, abandoned or withdrawn, or (b) the final determination of the appeal results in the conviction, finding or order being overturned.

In this ground –

'relevant proceedings' means proceedings for contempt of court or proceedings under Schedule 2 to the Anti-social Behaviour, Crime and Policing Act 2014;
'serious offence' means an offence which –

(a) was committed on or after the day on which this ground comes into force,
(b) is specified, or falls within a description specified, in Schedule 2A to the Housing Act 1985 at the time the offence was committed and at the time the court is considering the matter, and
(c) is not an offence that is triable only summarily by virtue of section 22 of the Magistrates' Courts Act 1980 (either-way offences where value involved is small).

Ground 8

Both at the date of the service of the notice under section 8 of this Act relating to the proceedings for possession and at the date of the hearing –

(a) if rent is payable weekly or fortnightly, at least eight weeks rent is unpaid;
(b) if rent is payable monthly, at least two months rent is unpaid;

(c) if rent is payable quarterly, at least one quarter's rent is more than three months in arrears; and
(d) if rent is payable yearly, at least three months' rent is more than three months in arrears; and for the purpose of this ground 'rent' means rent lawfully due from the tenant.

PART II

GROUNDS ON WHICH COURT MAY ORDER POSSESSION

Ground 9

Suitable alternative accommodation is available for the tenant or will be available for him when the order for possession takes effect.

Ground 10

Some rent lawfully due from the tenant –

(a) is unpaid on the date on which the proceedings for possession are begun; and
(b) except where subsection (1)(b) of section 8 of this Act applies, was in arrears at the date of the service of the notice under that section relating to those proceedings.

Ground 11

Whether or not any rent is in arrears on the date on which proceedings for possession are begun, the tenant has persistently delayed paying rent which has become lawfully due.

Ground 12

Any obligation of the tenancy (other than one related to the payment of rent) has been broken or not performed.

Ground 13

The condition of the dwelling-house or any of the common parts has deteriorated owing to acts of waste by, or the neglect or default of, the tenant or any other person residing in the dwelling-house and, in the case of an act of waste by, or the neglect or default of, a person lodging with the tenant or a sub-tenant of his, the tenant has not taken such steps as he ought reasonably to have taken for the removal of the lodger or sub-tenant.

For the purposes of this ground, 'common parts' means any part of a building comprising the dwelling-house and any other premises which the tenant is entitled under the terms of the tenancy to use in common with the occupiers of other dwelling-houses in which the landlord has an estate or interest.

Ground 14

The tenant or a person residing in or visiting the dwelling-house –

(a) has been guilty of conduct causing or likely to cause a nuisance or annoyance to a person residing, visiting or otherwise engaging in a lawful activity in the locality,
(aa) has been guilty of conduct causing or likely to cause a nuisance or annoyance to the landlord of the dwelling-house, or a person employed (whether or not by the landlord) in connection with the exercise of the landlord's housing management functions, and that is directly or indirectly related to or affects those functions,
(b) has been convicted of –

(i) using the dwelling-house or allowing it to be used for immoral or illegal purposes, or

(ii) an indictable offence committed in, or in the locality of, the dwelling-house.

Ground 14ZA

The tenant or an adult residing in the dwelling-house has been convicted of an indictable offence which took place during, and at the scene of, a riot in the United Kingdom.

In this Ground –

'adult' means a person aged 18 or over;
'indictable offence' does not include an offence that is triable only summarily by virtue of section 22 of the Magistrates' Courts Act 1980 (either way offences where value involved is small);
'riot' is to be construed in accordance with section 1 of the Public Order Act 1986.

This Ground applies only in relation to dwelling-houses in England.

Ground 14A

The dwelling-house was occupied (whether alone or with others) by a married couple, a couple who are civil partners of each other, a couple living together as husband and wife or a couple living together as if they were civil partners and –

(a) one or both of the partners is a tenant of the dwelling-house,
(b) the landlord who is seeking possession is a non-profit registered provider of social housing, a registered social landlord or a charitable housing trust or, where the dwelling-house is social housing within the meaning of Part 2 of the Housing and Regeneration Act 2008, a profit-making registered provider of social housing,
(c) one partner has left the dwelling-house because of violence or threats of violence by the other towards –
    (i) that partner, or
    (ii) a member of the family of that partner who was residing with that partner immediately before the partner left, and.
(d) the court is satisfied that the partner who has left is unlikely to return.

For the purposes of this ground 'registered social landlord' and 'member of the family' have the same meaning as in Part I of the Housing Act 1996 and 'charitable housing trust' means a housing trust, within the meaning of the Housing Associations Act 1985, which is a charity within the meaning of the Charities Act 1993.

Ground 15

The condition of any furniture provided for use under the tenancy has, in the opinion of the court, deteriorated owing to ill-treatment by the tenant or any other person residing in the dwelling-house and, in the case of ill-treatment by a person lodging with the tenant or by a sub-tenant of his, the tenant has not taken such steps as he ought reasonably to have taken for the removal of the lodger or sub-tenant.

Ground 16

The dwelling-house was let to the tenant in consequence of his employment by the landlord seeking possession or a previous landlord under the tenancy and the tenant has ceased to be in that employment.

For the purposes of this ground, at a time when the landlord is or was the Secretary of State, employment by a health service body, as defined in section 60(7) of the National Health Service and Community Care Act 1990, or by a Local Health Board, shall be regarded as employment by the Secretary of State.

Ground 17

The tenant is the person, or one of the persons, to whom the tenancy was granted and the landlord was induced to grant the tenancy by a false statement made knowingly or recklessly by –

(a) the tenant or,
(b) a person acting at the tenant's instigation.

Housing Act 1985 (ss 83ZA, 83, 84, 84A, 85, 85ZA, Sch 2, Sch 2A)

83ZA Notice requirements in relation to proceedings for possession on absolute ground for anti-social behaviour

(1) This section applies in relation to proceedings for possession of a dwelling-house under section 84A (absolute ground for possession for anti-social behaviour), including proceedings where possession is also sought on one or more of the grounds set out in Schedule 2.

(2) The court must not entertain the proceedings unless the landlord has served on the tenant a notice under this section.

(3) The notice must –

(a) state that the court will be asked to make an order under section 84A for the possession of the dwelling-house,
(b) set out the reasons for the landlord's decision to apply for the order (including the condition or conditions in section 84A on which the landlord proposes to rely), and
(c) inform the tenant of any right that the tenant may have under section 85ZA to request a review of the landlord's decision and of the time within which the request must be made.

(4) In a case where possession is also sought on one or more of the grounds set out in Schedule 2, the notice must also –

(a) specify the ground on which the court will be asked to make the order, and
(b) give particulars of that ground.

(5) A notice which states that the landlord proposes to rely upon condition 1, 3 or 5 in section 84A –

(a) must also state the conviction on which the landlord proposes to rely, and
(b) must be served on the tenant within –
    (i) the period of 12 months beginning with the day of the conviction, or
    (ii) if there is an appeal against the conviction, the period of 12 months beginning with the day on which the appeal is finally determined or abandoned.

(6) A notice which states that the landlord proposes to rely upon condition 2 in section 84A –

(a) must also state the finding on which the landlord proposes to rely, and
(b) must be served on the tenant within –
    (i) the period of 12 months beginning with the day on which the court has made the finding, or
    (ii) if there is an appeal against the finding, the period of 12 months beginning with the day on which the appeal is finally determined, abandoned or withdrawn.

(7) A notice which states that the landlord proposes to rely upon condition 4 in section 84A –

(a) must also state the closure order concerned, and
(b) must be served on the tenant within –

(i) the period of 3 months beginning with the day on which the closure order was made, or
(ii) if there is an appeal against the making of the order, the period of 3 months beginning with the day on which the closure order was made, or
(ii) if there is an appeal against the making of the order, the period of 3 months beginning with the day on which the appeal is finally determined, abandoned or withdrawn.

(8) A notice under this section must also inform the tenant that, if the tenant needs help or advice about the notice and what to do about it, the tenant should take it immediately to a Citizens' Advice Bureau, a housing aid centre, a law centre or a solicitor.

(9) The notice –

(a) must also specify the date after which proceedings for the possession of the dwelling-house may be begun, and
(b) ceases to be in force 12 months after the date so specified.

(10) The date specified in accordance with subsection (9)(a) must not be earlier than –

(a) in the case of a periodic tenancy, the date on which the tenancy could, apart from this Part, be brought to an end by notice to quit given by the landlord on the same day as the notice under this section;
(b) in the case of a secure tenancy for a term certain, one month after the date of the service of the notice.

(11) Where a notice under this section is served with respect to a secure tenancy for a term certain, it has effect also with respect to any periodic tenancy arising on the termination of that tenancy by virtue of section 86; and subsection (10)(a) does not apply to the notice.

83A Additional requirements in relation to certain proceedings for possession

(1) Where a notice under section 83 has been served on a tenant containing the information mentioned in subsection (3)(a) of that section, the court shall not entertain proceedings for the possession of the dwelling-house unless they are begun at a time when the notice is still in force.

(2) Where –

(a) a notice under section 83 has been served on a tenant, and
(b) a date after which proceedings may be begun has been specified in the notice in accordance with subsection (4)(a) of that section,

the court shall not entertain proceedings for the possession of the dwelling-house unless they are begun after the date so specified and at a time when the notice is still in force.

(3) Where –

(a) the ground or one of the grounds specified in a notice under section 83 is Ground 2A in Schedule 2 (domestic violence), and
(b) the partner who has left the dwelling-house as mentioned in that ground is not a tenant of the dwelling-house,

the court shall not entertain proceedings for the possession of the dwelling-house unless it is satisfied that the landlord has served a copy of the notice on the partner who has left or has taken all reasonable steps to serve a copy of the notice on that partner.

This subsection has effect subject to subsection (5).

(4) Where –

(a) Ground 2A in Schedule 2 is added to a notice under section 83 with the leave of the court after proceedings for possession are begun, and

(b) the partner who has left the dwelling-house as mentioned in that ground is not a party to the proceedings,

the court shall not continue to entertain the proceedings unless it is satisfied that the landlord has served a notice under subsection (6) on the partner who has left or has taken all reasonable steps to serve such a notice on that partner.

This subsection has effect subject to subsection (5).

(5) Where subsection (3) or (4) applies and Ground 2 in Schedule 2 (nuisance or other anti-social behaviour) is also specified in the notice under section 83, the court may dispense with the requirements as to service in relation to the partner who has left the dwelling-house if it considers it just and equitable to do so.

(6) A notice under this subsection shall –

(a) state that proceedings for the possession of the dwelling-house have begun,
(b) specify the ground or grounds on which possession is being sought, and
(c) give particulars of the ground or grounds.

84 Grounds and orders for possession

(1) The court shall not make an order for the possession of a dwelling-house let under a secure tenancy except on one or more of the grounds set out in Schedule 2 or in accordance with section 107D (recovery of possession on expiry of flexible tenancy).

(2) The court shall not make an order for possession –

(a) on the grounds set out in Part I of that Schedule (grounds 1 to 8), unless it considers it reasonable to make the order,
(b) on the grounds set out in Part II of that Schedule (grounds 9 to 11), unless it is satisfied that suitable accommodation will be available for the tenant when the order takes effect,
(c) on the grounds set out in Part III of that Schedule (grounds 12 to 16), unless it both considers it reasonable to make the order and is satisfied that suitable accommodation will be available for the tenant when the order takes effect;

and Part IV of that Schedule has effect for determining whether suitable accommodation will be available for a tenant.

(3) Where a notice under section 83 has been served on the tenant, the court shall not make such an order on any of those grounds above unless the ground is specified in the notice; but the grounds so specified may be altered or added to with the leave of the court.

(4) Where a date is specified in a notice under section 83 in accordance with subsection (3) of that section, the court shall not make an order which requires the tenant to give up possession of the dwelling-house in question before the date so specified.

84A Absolute ground for possession for anti-social behaviour

(1) If the court is satisfied that any of the following conditions is met, it must make an order for the possession of a dwelling-house let under a secure tenancy.

This is subject to subsection (2) (and to any available defence based on the tenant's Convention rights, within the meaning of the Human Rights Act 1998).

(2) Subsection (1) applies only where the landlord has complied with any obligations it has under section 85ZA (review of decision to seek possession).

(3) Condition 1 is that

(a) the tenant, or a person residing in or visiting the dwelling-house, has been convicted of a serious offence, and
(b) the serious offence –

(i) was committed (wholly or partly) in, or in the locality of, the dwelling-house,
(ii) was committed elsewhere against a person with a right (of whatever description) to reside in, or occupy housing accommodation in the locality of, the dwelling-house, or
(iii) was committed elsewhere against the landlord of the dwelling-house, or a person employed (whether or not by the landlord) in connection with the exercise of the landlord's housing management functions, and directly or indirectly related to or affected those functions.

(4) Condition 2 is that a court has found in relevant proceedings that the tenant, or a person residing in or visiting the dwelling-house, has breached a provision of an injunction under section 1 of the Anti-social Behaviour, Crime and Policing Act 2014, other than a provision requiring a person to participate in a particular activity, and –

(a) the breach occurred in, or in the locality of, the dwelling-house, or
(b) the breach occurred elsewhere and the provision breached was a provision intended to prevent –

(i) conduct that is capable of causing nuisance or annoyance to a person with a right (of whatever description) to reside in, or occupy housing accommodation in the locality of, the dwelling-house, or
(ii) conduct that is capable of causing nuisance or annoyance to the landlord of the dwelling-house, or a person employed (whether or not by the landlord) in connection with the exercise of the landlord's housing management functions, and that is directly or indirectly related to or affects those functions.

(5) Condition 3 is that the tenant, or a person residing in or visiting the dwelling-house, has been convicted of an offence under section 30 of the Anti-social Behaviour, Crime and Policing Act 2014 consisting of a breach of a provision of a criminal behaviour order prohibiting a person from doing anything described in the order, and the offence involved –

(a) a breach that occurred in, or in the locality of, the dwellinghouse, or
(b) a breach that occurred elsewhere of a provision intended to prevent –

(i) behaviour that causes or is likely to cause harassment, alarm or distress to a person with a right (of whatever description) to reside in, or occupy housing accommodation in the locality of, the dwelling-house, or
(ii) behaviour that causes or is likely to cause harassment, alarm or distress to the landlord of the dwelling-house, or a person employed (whether or not by the landlord) in connection with the exercise of the landlord's housing management functions, and that is directly or indirectly related to or affects those functions.

(6) Condition 4 is that –

(a) the dwelling-house is or has been subject to a closure order under section 80 of the Anti-social Behaviour, Crime and Policing Act 2014, and
(b) access to the dwelling-house has been prohibited (under the closure order or under a closure notice issued under section 76 of that Act) for a continuous period of more than 48 hours.

(7) Condition 5 is that –

(a) the tenant, or a person residing in or visiting the dwelling-house, has been convicted of an offence under –

(i) section 80(4) of the Environmental Protection Act 1990 (breach of abatement notice in relation to statutory nuisance), or
(ii) section 82(8) of that Act (breach of court order to abate statutory nuisance etc.), and

(b) the nuisance concerned was noise emitted from the dwelling-house which was a statutory nuisance for the purposes of Part 3 of that Act by virtue of section 79(1)(g) of that Act (noise emitted from premises so as to be prejudicial to health or a nuisance).

(8) Condition 1, 2, 3, 4 or 5 is not met if –

(a) there is an appeal against the conviction, finding or order concerned which has not been finally determined, abandoned or withdrawn, or
(b) the final determination of the appeal results in the conviction, finding or order being overturned.

(9) In this section –

'relevant proceedings' means proceedings for contempt of court or proceedings under Schedule 2 to the Anti-social Behaviour, Crime and Policing Act 2014;
'serious offence' means an offence which –

(a) was committed on or after the day on which subsection (3) comes into force,
(b) is specified, or falls within a description specified, in Schedule 2A at the time the offence was committed and at the time the court is considering the matter, and
(c) is not an offence that is triable only summarily by virtue of section 22 of the Magistrates' Courts Act 1980 (eitherway offences where value involved is small).

(10) The Secretary of State may by order amend Schedule 2A as it applies in relation to dwelling-houses in England by –

(a) adding an indictable offence;
(b) removing an offence.

(11) The Welsh Ministers may by order amend Schedule 2A as it applies in relation to dwelling-houses in Wales by –

(a) adding an indictable offence;
(b) removing an offence.

(12) An order under subsection (10) or (11) –

(a) is to be made by statutory instrument;
(b) may make different provision for different purposes;
(c) may include incidental, supplementary, consequential, transitional or saving provision.

(13) A statutory instrument containing an order under subsection (10) or (11) may not be made unless a draft of the instrument has been laid before and approved by a resolution of –

(a) each House of Parliament (in the case of an order of the Secretary of State), or
(b) the National Assembly for Wales (in the case of an order of the Welsh Ministers).

85 Extended discretion of court in certain proceedings for possession

(1) Where proceedings are brought for possession of a dwelling-house let under a secure tenancy on any of the grounds set out in Part I or Part III of Schedule 2 (grounds 1 to 8 and 12 to 16: cases in which the court must be satisfied that it is reasonable to make a possession order), the court may adjourn the proceedings for such period or periods as it thinks fit.

(2) On the making of an order for possession of such a dwelling-house on any of those grounds, or at any time before the execution of the order, the court may –

(a) stay or suspend the execution of the order, or
(b) postpone the date of possession,

for such period or periods as the court thinks fit.

(3) On such an adjournment, stay, suspension or postponement the court –

(a) shall impose conditions with respect to the payment by the tenant of arrears of rent (if any) and rent unless it considers that to do so would cause exceptional hardship to the tenant or would otherwise be unreasonable, and
(b) may impose such other conditions as it thinks fit.

(4) If the conditions are complied with, the court may, if it thinks fit, discharge or rescind the order for possession.

(5), (5A) …

85ZA Review of decision to seek possession on absolute ground for antisocial behaviour

(1) A tenant may request a review of a landlord's decision to seek an order for possession of a dwelling-house under section 84A if the interest of the landlord belongs to –

(a) a local housing authority, or
(b) a housing action trust.

(2) Such a request must be made in writing before the end of the period of 7 days beginning with the day on which the notice under section 83ZA is served.

(3) On a request being duly made to it, the landlord must review its decision.

(4) The landlord must notify the tenant in writing of the decision on the review.

(5) If the decision is to confirm the original decision, the landlord must also notify the tenant of the reasons for the decision.

(6) The review must be carried out, and the tenant notified, before the day specified in the notice under section 83ZA as the day after which proceedings for the possession of the dwelling-house may be begun.

(7) The Secretary of State may by regulations make provision about the procedure to be followed in connection with a review under this section that relates to an order for possession of a dwelling-house in England.

(8) The Welsh Ministers may by regulations make provision about the procedure to be followed in connection with a review under this section that relates to an order for possession of a dwelling-house in Wales.

(9) Regulations under subsections (7) and (8) may, in particular, make provision –

(a) requiring the decision on review to be made by a person of appropriate seniority who was not involved in the original decision, and
(b) as to the circumstances in which the person concerned is entitled to an oral hearing, and whether and by whom the person may be represented at such a hearing.

(10) Regulations under this section –

(a) may contain transitional or saving provision;
(b) are to be made by statutory instrument which –
    (i) in the case of regulations made by the Secretary of State, is subject to annulment in pursuance of a resolution of either House of Parliament;
    (ii) in the case of regulations made by the Welsh Ministers, is subject to annulment in pursuance of a resolution of the National Assembly for Wales.

SCHEDULE 2

GROUNDS FOR POSSESSION OF DWELLING-HOUSES LET UNDER SECURE TENANCIES

PART I

GROUNDS ON WHICH COURT MAY ORDER POSSESSION IF IT CONSIDERS IT REASONABLE

Ground 1

Rent lawfully due from the tenant has not been paid or an obligation of the tenancy has been broken or not performed.

Ground 2

The tenant or a person residing in or visiting the dwelling-house –

(a) has been guilty of conduct causing or likely to cause a nuisance or annoyance to a person residing, visiting or otherwise engaging in a lawful activity in the locality, or
(aa) has been guilty of conduct causing or likely to cause a nuisance or annoyance to the landlord of the dwelling-house, or a person employed (whether or not by the landlord) in connection with the exercise of the landlord's housing management functions, and that is directly or indirectly related to or affects those functions,
(b) has been convicted of –

  (i) using the dwelling-house or allowing it to be used for immoral or illegal purposes, or
  (ii) an indictable offence committed in, or in the locality of, the dwelling-house.

Ground 2ZA

The tenant or an adult residing in the dwelling-house has been convicted of an indictable offence which took place during, and at the scene of, a riot in the United Kingdom.

In this Ground –

'adult' means a person aged 18 or over;
'indictable offence' does not include an offence that is triable only summarily by virtue of section 22 of the Magistrates' Courts Act 1980 (either way offences where value involved is small);
'riot' is to be construed in accordance with section 1 of the Public Order Act 1986.

This Ground applies only in relation to dwelling-houses in England.

Ground 2A

The dwelling-house was occupied (whether alone or with others) by a married couple, a couple who are civil partners of each other, a couple living together as husband and wife or a couple living together as if they were civil partners and –

(a) one or both of the partners is a tenant of the dwelling-house,
(b) one partner has left because of violence or threats of violence by the other towards –

  (i) that partner, or
  (ii) a member of the family of that partner who was residing with that partner immediately before the partner left, and

(c) the court is satisfied that the partner who has left is unlikely to return.

Ground 3

The condition of the dwelling-house or of any of the common parts has deteriorated owing to acts of waste by, or the neglect or default of, the tenant or a person residing in the dwelling-house and, in the case of an act of waste by, or the neglect or default of, a person lodging with the tenant or a sub-tenant of his, the tenant has not taken such steps as he ought reasonably to have taken for the removal of the lodger or sub-tenant.

Ground 4

The condition of furniture provided by the landlord for use under the tenancy, or for use in the common parts, has deteriorated owing to ill-treatment by the tenant or a person residing in the dwelling-house and, in the case of ill-treatment by a person lodging with the tenant or a sub-tenant of his, the tenant has not taken such steps as he ought reasonably to have taken for the removal of the lodger or sub-tenant.

Ground 5

The tenant is the person, or one of the persons, to whom the tenancy was granted and the landlord was induced to grant the tenancy by a false statement made knowingly or recklessly by –

(a) the tenant, or
(b) a person acting at the tenant's instigation.

Ground 6

The tenancy was assigned to the tenant, or to a predecessor in title of his who is a member of his family and is residing in the dwelling-house, by an assignment made by virtue of section 92 (assignments by way of exchange) and a premium was paid either in connection with that assignment or the assignment which the tenant or predecessor himself made by virtue of that section.

In this paragraph 'premium' means any fine or other like sum and any other pecuniary consideration in addition to rent.

Ground 7

The dwelling-house forms part of, or is within the curtilage of, a building which, or so much of it as is held by the landlord, is held mainly for purposes other than housing purposes and consists mainly of accommodation other than housing accommodation, and –

(a) the dwelling-house was let to the tenant or a predecessor in title of his in consequence of the tenant or predecessor being in the employment of the landlord, or of –

a local authority,
a development corporation,
a housing action trust,
a Mayoral development corporation.
an urban development corporation, or
the governors of an aided school, and

(b) the tenant or a person residing in the dwelling-house has been guilty of conduct such that, having regard to the purpose for which the building is used, it would not be right for him to continue in occupation of the dwelling-house.

Ground 8

The dwelling-house was made available for occupation by the tenant (or a predecessor in title of his) while works were carried out on the dwelling-house which he previously occupied as his only or principal home and –

(a) the tenant (or predecessor) was a secure tenant of the other dwelling-house at the time when he ceased to occupy it as his home,
(b) the tenant (or predecessor) accepted the tenancy of the dwelling-house of which possession is sought on the understanding that he would give up occupation when, on completion of the works, the other dwelling-house was again available for occupation by him under a secure tenancy, and
(c) the works have been completed and the other dwelling-house is so available.

SCHEDULE 2A

Section 84A (9)

ABSOLUTE GROUND FOR POSSESSION FOR ANTI-SOCIAL BEHAVIOUR: SERIOUS OFFENCES

Violent offences

1 Murder.

2 Manslaughter.

3 Kidnapping.

4 False imprisonment.

5 An offence under any of the following sections of the Offences against the Person Act 1861 –

(a) section 4 (soliciting murder),
(b) section 16 (threats to kill),
(c) section 18 (wounding with intent to cause grievous bodily harm),
(d) section 20 (malicious wounding),
(e) section 21 (attempting to choke, suffocate or strangle in order to commit or assist in committing an indictable offence),
(f) section 22 (using chloroform etc. to commit or assist in the committing of any indictable offence),
(g) section 23 (maliciously administering poison etc. so as to endanger life or inflict grievous bodily harm),
(h) section 24 (maliciously administering poison etc. with intent to injure, aggrieve or annoy any other person),
(i) section 27 (abandoning or exposing children whereby life is endangered or health permanently injured),
(j) section 28 (causing bodily injury by explosives),
(k) section 29 (using explosives etc. with intent to do grievous bodily harm),
(l) section 30 (placing explosives with intent to do bodily injury),
(m) section 31 (setting spring guns etc. with intent to do grievous bodily harm),
(n) section 38 (assault with intent to resist arrest),
(o) section 47 (assault occasioning actual bodily harm).

6 An offence under any of the following sections of the Explosive Substances Act 1883 –

(a) section 2 (causing explosion likely to endanger life or property),
(b) section 3 (attempt to cause explosion, or making or keeping explosive with intent to endanger life or property),
(c) section 4 (making or possession of explosive under suspicious circumstances).

7 An offence under section 1 of the Infant Life (Preservation) Act 1929 (child destruction).

8 An offence under section 1 of the Children and Young Persons Act 1933 (cruelty to children).

9 An offence under section 1 of the Infanticide Act 1938 (infanticide).

10 An offence under any of the following sections of the Public Order Act 1986 –

(a) section 1 (riot),
(b) section 2 (violent disorder),
(c) section 3 (affray).

11 An offence under either of the following sections of the Protection from Harassment Act 1997 –

(a) section 4 (putting people in fear of violence),
(b) section 4A (stalking involving fear of violence or serious alarm or distress).

12 An offence under any of the following provisions of the Crime and Disorder Act 1998 –

(a) section 29 (racially or religiously aggravated assaults),
(b) section 31(1)(a) or (b) (racially or religiously aggravated offences under section 4 or 4A of the Public Order Act 1986),
(c) section 32 (racially or religiously aggravated harassment etc.).

13 An offence under either of the following sections of the Female Genital Mutilation Act 2003 –

(a) section 1 (female genital mutilation),
(b) section 2 (assisting a girl to mutilate her own genitalia).

14 An offence under section 5 of the Domestic Violence, Crime and Victims Act 2004 (causing or allowing the death of a child or vulnerable adult).

15 Sexual offences

An offence under section 33A of the Sexual Offences Act 1956 (keeping a brothel used for prostitution).

16

An offence under section 1 of the Protection of Children Act 1978 (indecent photographs of children).

17

An offence under section 160 of the Criminal Justice Act 1988 (possession of indecent photograph of a child).

18

An indictable offence under Part 1 of the Sexual Offences Act 2003 (sexual offences).

19 Offensive weapons

An offence under either of the following sections of the Prevention of Crime Act 1953 –

(a) section 1 (prohibition of the carrying of offensive weapons without lawful authority or reasonable excuse),
(b) section 1A (threatening with offensive weapon in public).

20 An offence under any of the following provisions of the Firearms Act 1968 –

(a) section 16 (possession of firearm with intent to endanger life),
(b) section 16A (possession of firearm with intent to cause fear of violence),
(c) section 17(1) (use of firearm to resist arrest),
(d) section 17(2) (possession of firearm at time of committing or being arrested for offence specified in Schedule 1 to the Act of 1968),
(e) section 18 (carrying a firearm with criminal intent),
(f) section 19 (carrying a firearm in a public place),
(g) section 20 (trespassing with firearm),
(h) section 21 (possession of firearms by persons previously convicted of crime).

21 An offence under either of the following sections of the Criminal Justice Act 1988 –

(a) section 139 (having article with blade or point in public place),
(b) section 139AA (threatening with article with blade or point or offensive weapon).

22 Offences against property

An offence under any of the following sections of the Theft Act 1968 –

(a) section 8 (robbery or assault with intent to rob),
(b) section 9 (burglary),
(c) section 10 (aggravated burglary).

23 An offence under section 1 of the Criminal Damage Act 1971 (destroying or damaging property).

24 An offence under section 30 of the Crime and Disorder Act 1998 (racially or religiously aggravated criminal damage).

25 Road traffic offences

An offence under section 35 of the Offences against the Person Act 1861 (injuring persons by furious driving).

26 An offence under section 12A of the Theft Act 1968 (aggravated vehicle-taking involving an accident which caused the death of any person).

27 An offence under any of the following sections of the Road Traffic Act 1988 –

(a) section 1 (causing death by dangerous driving),
(b) section 1A (causing serious injury by dangerous driving),
(c) section 3A (causing death by careless driving when under influence of drink or drugs).

28 Drug-related offences

An offence under any of the following provisions of the Misuse of Drugs Act 1971 –

(a) section 4 (restriction of production and supply of controlled drugs),
(b) section 5(3) (possession of controlled drugs with intent to supply),
(c) section 8(a) or (b) (occupiers etc. of premises to be punishable for permitting unlawful production or supply etc. of controlled drugs there).

29 An offence under section 6 of that Act (restrictions of cultivation of cannabis plant) where the cultivation is for profit and the whole or a substantial part of the dwelling-house concerned is used for the cultivation.

30 Inchoate offences

(1) An offence of attempting or conspiring the commission of an offence specified or described in this Schedule.

(2) An offence under Part 2 of the Serious Crime Act 2007 (encouraging or assisting) where the offence (or one of the offences) which the person in question intends or believes would be committed is an offence specified or described in this Schedule.

(3) An offence of aiding, abetting, counselling or procuring the commission of an offence specified or described in this Schedule.

31 Scope of offences

Where this Schedule refers to offences which are offences under the law of England and Wales and another country or territory, the reference is to be read as limited to the offences so far as they are offences under the law of England and Wales.

Children and Young Persons Act 1933 (ss 39, 49)

39 Power to prohibit publication of certain matter in newspapers

(1) In relation to any proceedings, other than criminal proceedings, in any court the court may direct that the following may not be included in a publication –

(a) no newspaper report of the proceedings shall reveal the name, address, or school, or include any particulars calculated to lead to the identification, of any child or young person concerned in the proceedings, either as being the person by or against or in respect of whom the proceedings are taken, or as being a witness therein;

(aa) any particulars calculated to lead to the identification of a child or young person so concerned in the proceedings;

(b) no picture shall be published in any newspaper as being or including a picture that is or includes a picture of any child or young person so concerned in the proceedings as aforesaid;

except in so far (if at all) as may be permitted by the direction of the court.

(2) Any person who publishes any matter includes matter in a publication in contravention of any such direction shall on summary conviction be liable in respect of each offence to a fine not exceeding level 5 on the standard scale.

(3) In this section –

"publication" includes any speech, writing, relevant programme or other communication in whatever form, which is addressed to the public at large or any section of the public (and for this purpose every relevant programme shall be taken to be so addressed), but does not include a document prepared for use in particular legal proceedings;

"relevant programme" means a programme included in a programme service within the meaning of the Broadcasting Act 1990.

****

49 Restrictions on reports of proceedings in which children or young persons are concerned

(1) No matter relating to any child or young person concerned in proceedings to which this section applies shall while he is under the age of 18 be included in any publication if it is likely to lead members of the public to identify him as someone concerned in the proceedings.

(2) The proceedings to which this section applies are –

- (a) proceedings in a youth court;
- (b) proceedings on appeal from a youth court (including proceedings by way of case stated);
- (c) proceedings in a magistrates' court under Schedule 2 to the Criminal Justice and Immigration Act 2008 (proceedings for breach, revocation or amendment of youth rehabilitation orders);
- (d) proceedings on appeal from a magistrates' court arising out of any proceedings mentioned in paragraph (c) (including proceedings by way of case stated).

(3) In this section "publication" includes any speech, writing, relevant programme or other communication in whatever form, which is addressed to the public at large or any section of the public (and for this purpose every relevant programme shall be taken to be so addressed), but does not include an indictment or other document prepared for use in particular legal proceedings.

(3A) The matters relating to a person in relation to which the restrictions imposed by subsection (1) above apply (if their inclusion in any publication is likely to have the result mentioned in that subsection) include in particular –

- (a) his name,
- (b) his address,
- (c) the identity of any school or other educational establishment attended by him,
- (d) the identity of any place of work, and
- (e) any still or moving picture of him.

(4) For the purposes of this section a child or young person is "concerned" in any proceedings if he is –

- (a) a person against or in respect of whom the proceedings are taken, or
- (b) a person called, or proposed to be called, to give evidence in the proceedings.

(4A) If a court is satisfied that it is in the public interest to do so, it may, in relation to a child or young person who has been convicted of an offence, by order dispense to any specified extent with the restrictions imposed by subsection (1) above in relation to any proceedings before it to which this section applies by virtue of subsection (2)(a) or (b) above, being proceedings relating to –

- (a) the prosecution or conviction of the offender for the offence;
- (b) the manner in which he, or his parent or guardian, should be dealt with in respect of the offence;
- (c) the enforcement, amendment, variation, revocation or discharge of any order made in respect of the offence;
- (d) where an attendance centre order is made in respect of the offence, the enforcement of any rules made under section 222(1)(d) or (e) of the Criminal Justice Act 2003; or
- (e) where a detention and training order is made, the enforcement of any requirements imposed under section 103(6)(b) of the Powers of Criminal Courts (Sentencing) Act 2000.

(4B) A court shall not exercise its power under subsection (4A) above without –

- (a) affording the parties to the proceedings an opportunity to make representations; and
- (b) taking into account any representations which are duly made.

(5) Subject to subsection (7) below, a court may, in relation to proceedings before it to which this section applies, by order dispense to any specified extent with the requirements of this section in relation to a child or young person who is concerned in the proceedings if it is satisfied –

- (a) that it is appropriate to do so for the purpose of avoiding injustice to the child or young person; or
- (b) that, as respects a child or young person to whom this paragraph applies who is unlawfully at large, it is necessary to dispense with those requirements for the purpose of apprehending him and bringing him before a court or returning him to the place in which he was in custody.

(6) Paragraph (b) of subsection (5) above applies to any child or young person who is charged with or has been convicted of –

- (a) a violent offence,
- (b) a sexual offence, or
- (c) an offence punishable in the case of a person aged 18 or over with imprisonment for fourteen years or more.

(7) The court shall not exercise its power under subsection (5)(b) above –

- (a) except in pursuance of an application by or on behalf of the Director of Public Prosecutions; and
- (b) unless notice of the application has been given by the Director of Public Prosecutions to any legal representative of the child or young person.

(8) The court's power under subsection (4A) or (5) above may be exercised by a single justice.

(9) If a publication includes any matter in contravention of subsection (1) above, the following persons shall be guilty of an offence and liable on summary conviction to a fine not exceeding level 5 on the standard scale –

- (a) where the publication is a newspaper or periodical, any proprietor, any editor and any publisher of the newspaper or periodical;
- (b) where the publication is a relevant programme –
  - (i) any body corporate or Scottish partnership engaged in providing the programme service in which the programme is included; and
  - (ii) any person having functions in relation to the programme corresponding to those of an editor of a newspaper;
- (c) in the case of any other publication, any person publishing it.

(9A) Where a person is charged with an offence under subsection (9) above it shall be a defence to prove that at the time of the alleged offence he was not aware, and neither suspected nor had reason to suspect, that the publication included the matter in question.

(9B) If an offence under subsection (9) above committed by a body corporate is proved –

- (a) to have been committed with the consent or connivance of, or
- (b) to be attributable to any neglect on the part of,

an officer, the officer as well as the body corporate is guilty of the offence and liable to be proceeded against and punished accordingly.

(9C) In subsection (9B) above "officer" means a director, manager, secretary or other similar officer of the body, or a person purporting to act in any such capacity.

(9D) If the affairs of a body corporate are managed by its members, "director" in subsection (9C) above means a member of that body.

(9E) Where an offence under subsection (9) above is committed by a Scottish partnership and is proved to have been committed with the consent or connivance of a partner, he as well as the partnership shall be guilty of the offence and shall be liable to be proceeded against and punished accordingly.

(10) In any proceedings under Schedule 2 to the Criminal Justice and Immigration Act 2008 (proceedings for breach, revocation or amendment of youth rehabilitation orders) before a magistrates' court other than a youth court or on appeal from such a court it shall be the duty of the magistrates' court or the appellate court to announce in the course of the proceedings that this section applies to the proceedings; and if the court fails to do so this section shall not apply to the proceedings.

(11) In this section –

"picture" includes a likeness however produced;

"relevant programme" means a programme included in a programme service, within the meaning of the Broadcasting Act 1990;
"sexual offence" means an offence listed in Part 2 of Schedule 15 to the Criminal Justice Act 2003;
"specified" means specified in an order under this section;
"violent offence" means an offence listed in Part 1 of Schedule 15 to the Criminal Justice Act 2003;

and a person who, having been granted bail, is liable to arrest (whether with or without a warrant) shall be treated as unlawfully at large.

(12) This section extends to England and Wales, Scotland and Northern Ireland, but no reference in this section to any court includes a court in Scotland.

****

APPENDIX 3

STATUTORY INSTRUMENTS

The Magistrates' Courts (Injunctions: Anti-Social Behaviour) Rules 2015

SI 2015/423

Made	*25th February 2015*
Laid before Parliament	*3rd March 2015*
Coming into force in accordance with Rule 1(2)	

The Lord Chief Justice, with the concurrence of the Lord Chancellor, makes the following Rules in exercise of the powers conferred by section 144 of the Magistrates' Courts Act 1980 and section 18(2) and (3) of the Anti-Social Behaviour, Crime and Policing Act 2014.

1 Citation, commencement and interpretation

(1) These Rules may be cited as the Magistrates' Courts (Injunctions: Anti-Social Behaviour) Rules 2015.

(2) These Rules come into force on the day on which, and immediately after, section 1 of the 2014 Act comes into force.

(3) In these Rules –

- (a) "the 2014 Act" means the Anti-Social Behaviour, Crime and Policing Act 2014;
- (b) a reference to a section or Schedule by number alone means the section or Schedule so numbered in the 2014 Act;
- (c) "applicant" means the person applying or who applied for the injunction, and "respondent" means the person against whom the injunction is or was applied for;
- (d) "defaulter" has the meaning given in paragraph 2 of Schedule 2 to the 2014 Act;
- (e) "original applicant" has the meaning given in paragraph 1(2) of Schedule 2 to the 2014 Act;
- (f) "Part 1 injunction" means an injunction under Part 1 of the 2014 Act.

2 Applications to be by complaint

An application to which these rules apply must be made by way of complaint in writing.

3 Applications for injunctions

(1) An application to a youth court for a Part 1 injunction must –

- (a) state the name, address and date of birth of the respondent;
- (b) state the name and address of a parent or guardian of the respondent (except where the respondent is aged 18 or over, permission having been given by the court in relation to that respondent under rule 15);
- (c) be supported by evidence of the matters of which the court must be satisfied for the first and second conditions under section 1 to be met;
- (d) state the terms of the Part 1 injunction applied for; and
- (e) in the case of an application made on notice, include a statement that the requirement for consultation in section 14(1) has been complied with.

(2) If an application without notice is made by virtue of section 6, the application must also state the reasons why it is necessary for the application to be made without notice having been given.

(3) In the case of an application made on notice, a copy of the application must be served by the applicant on –

(a) the respondent personally; and
(b) the parent or guardian mentioned in paragraph (2)(b) personally, or by posting it to or leaving it at that parent or guardian's address.

4 Interim Part 1 injunctions

An interim Part 1 injunction which is made on an application made without notice –

(a) must be served on the respondent personally as soon as practicable; and

(b) will not take effect until it has been so served.

5 Part 1 injunction containing provisions to which a power of arrest is attached

(1) In this rule, "relevant provision" means a provision of a Part 1 injunction to which a power of arrest is attached.

(2) Where a Part 1 injunction contains one or more relevant provisions –

(a) each relevant provision must be set out in a separate paragraph of the injunction; and
(b) subject to paragraph (3), the applicant must deliver a copy of the relevant provisions to any police station for the area where the conduct occurred.

(3) Where the Part 1 injunction has been granted without notice under section 41, the applicant must not deliver a copy of the relevant provisions to any police station under paragraph (2)(b) before the injunction containing the relevant provisions has been served on the respondent.

(4) Where an order is made varying or discharging any relevant provision, the applicant must –

(a) immediately inform any police station to which a copy of the relevant provisions was delivered under paragraph (2)(b); and
(b) deliver a copy of the order to any police station so informed.

6 Application to vary or discharge a Part 1 injunction

(1) An application under section 8(1) to vary or discharge a Part 1 injunction must be made to the court which granted the injunction.

(2) Such an application must –

(a) specify –

    (i) the reason why the person applying for variation or discharge believes the court should vary or discharge the injunction; and
    (ii) if the application is to vary the injunction, the variation which is sought; and

(b) where the application is made by the person on whose application the injunction was granted, include a statement that the consultation requirement under section 14(3) has been complied with.

7 Application for warrant of arrest

(1) An application for a warrant of arrest under section 10(1) must be substantiated on oath. (2) Such an application may be made without notice.

8 Proceedings following arrest under the 2014 Act

(1) This rule applies where a person under the age of 18 is arrested pursuant to –

(a) a power of arrest attached to a provision of a Part 1 injunction; or
(b) a warrant of arrest.

(2) A youth court before which a person is brought following such arrest may –

(a) deal with the matter; or
(b) adjourn the proceedings.

(3) If proceedings are adjourned and the arrested person is released –

(a) the matter must be dealt with (either by the same or another youth court) within 28 days of the date on which the arrested person appears in court; and
(b) the arrested person must be given not less than 2 days' notice of the hearing.

(4) An application under paragraph 1(2) of Schedule 2 may be made even if the arrested person is not dealt with within the period in paragraph (3)(a) of this rule.

9 Recognizance

Where, in accordance with paragraph 2(3)(b) of Schedule 1, the court fixes the amount of any recognizance with a view to it being taken subsequently, the recognizance may be taken by –

(a) a District Judge (Magistrates' Court);
(b) a justice of the peace;
(c) a justices' clerk; or
(d) a police officer of the rank of inspector or above, or in charge of a police station, with the same consequences as if it had been entered into before the court.

10 Application for supervision order or detention order

An application under paragraph 1(2) of Schedule 2 must –

(a) be supported by evidence of the breach of any provisions of the injunction which is alleged; and
(b) include a statement that the consultation required by paragraph 1(3) of Schedule 2 has been undertaken.

11 Non-compliance with supervision order

An application under paragraph 12(2) of Schedule 2 must –

(a) be supported by evidence of the failure to comply with provisions of the supervision order which is alleged; and
(b) include a statement that the consultation required by paragraph 12(3) of Schedule 2 has been undertaken.

12 Application to amend or revoke a supervision order

(1) An application under paragraph 8(1) of Schedule 2 must state the new period which it is proposed to have substituted for that specified in the supervision order.

(2) An application under paragraph 9(1) of Schedule 2 must include –

(a) confirmation of the area in which the defaulter intends to reside or is now residing; and
(b) if the application is made by the original applicant, a statement that the consultation required by paragraph 9(6) of Schedule 2 has been undertaken.

(3) An application under paragraph 10(1) of Schedule 2 must include –

(a) the reasons why it is in the interests of justice for the order to be revoked or (as the case may be) amended by removing any requirement from it; and
(b) if the application is made by the original applicant, a statement that the consultation required by paragraph 10(5) of Schedule 2 has been undertaken.

13 Application to revoke a detention order

An application under paragraph 15(1) of Schedule 2 must include –

(a) the reasons why it is in the interests of justice for the order to be revoked; and
(b) if the application is made by the injunction applicant, a statement that the consultation required by paragraph 15(5) or (6) (as applicable) of Schedule 2 has been undertaken.

14 Applications for which court's consent is required

(1) Where the consent of the court is required by section 8(4), or paragraph 10(4) or 15(4) of Schedule 2, for the making of a further application, the application for consent must include –

(a) confirmation of the date on which, and the court by which, the previous application was dismissed; and
(b) a statement of the reasons why consent should be given.

(2) Such consent –

(a) may be given by a court comprising a single justice; but
(b) may not be refused without the applicant having been given an opportunity to make oral representations.

15 Application for permission for an application for a Part 1 injunction against a person aged 18 or over

(1) A youth court may, on application, give permission for an application for a Part 1 injunction against a person aged 18 or over to be made to the youth court if the conditions in section 18(2)(a) and (b) are fulfilled.

(2) The application for permission must include –

(a) in relation to the condition in section 18(2)(a), details of the application which has been made, or is to be made, for a Part 1 injunction against a person aged under 18; and
(b) in relation to the condition in section 18(2)(b), a statement of the reasons why it is in the interests of justice for the applications to be heard together.

16 Respondent attaining age of 18 after commencement of proceedings

(1) Where a respondent attains the age of 18 after the commencement of proceedings under Part 1 of the 2014 Act, the proceedings must remain in a youth court, subject to paragraphs (2) and (3).

(2) The court in which the proceedings were continuing when the respondent attained the age of

18 may, at the request of the applicant or the respondent or of its own motion –

(a) make a direction under paragraph (3); or
(b) direct that the proceedings be transferred to a youth court for the local justice area in which the respondent currently resides, in order for that court to consider whether to make a direction under paragraph (3).

(3) The court may direct that the proceedings be transferred to the High Court or county court, having had regard in particular to –

(a) the stage which the proceedings have reached;
(b) the circumstances of the applicant and the respondent; and
(c) the need to ensure fairness between the applicant and the respondent.

(4) The court may not make a direction under paragraph (3) without a hearing, on notice to both the applicant and the respondent.

(5) The applicant and the respondent must submit to the court –

(a) in writing; and
(b) no less than 7 days before the date specified for the hearing, or such other time as the court directs,

any reasons why the proceedings should either remain in a youth court or be transferred to the High Court or county court, having regard in particular the matters mentioned in paragraph (3).

Assured Tenancies and Agricultural Occupancies (Forms) (England) Regulations 2015

SI 2015/620

Made	*9th March 2015*
Coming into force	*6th April 2015*

The Secretary of State, in exercise of powers conferred by sections 6(2) and (3), 8(3), 13(2) and (4), 22(1) and 45(1) and (5) of, and paragraphs 7(2) and 9(2)(a) of Schedule 2A to, the Housing Act 1988 makes the following Regulations:

1 Citation and commencement

These Regulations may be cited as the Assured Tenancies and Agricultural Occupancies (Forms) (England) Regulations 2015 and come into force on 6th April 2015.

2 Interpretation

In these Regulations any reference to a section or Schedule is a reference to a section of, or Schedule to, the Housing Act 1988 and any reference to a numbered form is a reference to the form bearing that number in the Schedule to these Regulations, or to a form substantially to the same effect.

3 Prescribed forms

The forms prescribed for the purposes of Part I (rented accommodation) of the Housing Act 1988 are –

(a) for a notice under section 6(2) proposing terms of a statutory periodic tenancy different from the implied terms, Form No 1;

(b) for an application under section 6(3) referring a notice under section 6(2) to a tribunal, Form No 2;

(c) for a notice under section 8 informing a tenant or licensee that the landlord intends to begin proceedings for possession of a dwelling-house let on an assured tenancy or an assured agricultural occupancy, Form No 3;

(d) for a notice under section 13(2) proposing a new rent for an assured tenancy of premises situated in England, Form No 4;

(e) for a notice under section 13(2) proposing a new rent or licence fee for an assured agricultural occupancy of premises situated in England, Form No 5;

(f) for an application under section 13(4) referring to a tribunal a notice under section 13(2) relating to an assured tenancy or an assured agricultural occupancy, Form No 6;

(g) for an application under section 22(1) to a tribunal for a determination of rent under an assured shorthold tenancy, Form No 7;

(h) for a notice under paragraph 7 of Schedule 2A, by the tenant to the landlord proposing that an assured tenancy be replaced by an assured shorthold tenancy, Form No 8;

(i) for a notice under paragraph 9 of Schedule 2A, by the landlord to the prospective tenant, proposing an assured shorthold tenancy where the tenancy meets the conditions for an assured agricultural occupancy, Form No 9.

4 Revocations and savings

(1) The Assured Tenancies and Agricultural Occupancies (Forms) Regulations 1997 are revoked in relation to England.

(2) The Assured Tenancies and Agricultural Occupancies (Forms) (Amendment) (England) Regulations 2003 are revoked.

(3) Nothing in paragraphs (1) and (2) affects the validity of a notice served before the coming into force of these Regulations if, at the date of service of the notice, the notice was in the form then prescribed by the Assured Tenancies and Agricultural Occupancies (Forms) Regulations 1997 or a form substantially to the same effect.

SCHEDULE

Forms Prescribed for the Purposes of Part I of the Housing Act 1988

Regulation 3

FORM No. 3

Housing Act 1988 section 8, as amended by section 151 of the Housing Act 1996 and section 97 of the Anti-social Behaviour, Crime and Policing Act 2014

FORM 3

Notice seeking possession of a property let on an Assured Tenancy or an Assured Agricultural Occupancy

Housing Act 1988 section 8 as amended by section 151 of the Housing Act 1996 and section 97 of the Anti-social Behaviour, Crime and Policing Act 2014

- Please write clearly in black ink.
- Please cross out text marked with an asterisk (*) that does not apply.
- This form should be used where possession of accommodation let under an assured tenancy, an assured agricultural occupancy or an assured shorthold tenancy is sought on one of the grounds in Schedule 2 to the Housing Act 1988.
- Do not use this form if possession is sought on the "shorthold" ground under section 21 of the Housing Act 1988 from an assured shorthold tenant where the fixed term has come to an end or, for assured shorthold tenancies with no fixed term which started on or after 28th February 1997, after six months has elapsed. There is no prescribed form for these cases, but you must give notice in writing.

1 To: ....

*Name(s) of tenant(s)/licensee(s)**

2 Your landlord/licensor* intends to apply to the court for an order requiring you to give up possession of: ....
....
....
....

Address of premises

3 Your landlord/licensor* intends to seek possession on ground(s) .... in Schedule 2 to the Housing Act 1988 (as amended), which read(s): ....
....
....
....

Give the full text (as set out in the Housing Act 1988 (as amended) of each ground which is being relied on. Continue on a separate sheet if necessary.

4 Give a full explanation of why each ground is being relied on: ....
....
....
....

Continue on a separate sheet if necessary.

Notes on the grounds for possession

- If the court is satisfied that any of grounds 1 to 8 is established, it must make an order (but see below in respect of fixed term tenancies).
- Before the court will grant an order on any of grounds 9 to 17, it must be satisfied that it is reasonable to require you to leave. This means that, if one of these grounds is set out in section 3, you will be able to suggest to the court that it is not reasonable that you should have to leave, even if you accept that the ground applies.
- The court will not make an order under grounds 1, 3 to 7, 9 or 16, to take effect during the fixed term of the tenancy (if there is one) and it will only make an order during the fixed term on grounds 2, 8, 10 to 15 or 17 if the terms of the tenancy make provision for it to be brought to an end on any of these grounds.
- Where the court makes an order for possession solely on ground 6 or 9, the landlord must pay your reasonable removal expenses.

5 The court proceedings will not begin until after: ....

Give the earliest date on which court proceedings can be brought

Notes on the earliest date on which court proceedings can be brought

- Where the landlord is seeking possession on grounds 1, 2, 5 to 7, 9 or 16 (without ground 7A or 14), court proceedings cannot begin earlier than 2 months from the date this notice is served on you and not before the date on which the tenancy (had it not been assured) could have been brought to an end by a notice to quit served at the same time as this notice. This applies even if one of grounds 3, 4, 8, 10 to 13, 14ZA, 14A, 15 or 17 is also specified.
- Where the landlord is seeking possession on grounds 3, 4, 8, 10 to 13, 14ZA, 14A, 15 or 17 (without ground 7A or 14), court proceedings cannot begin earlier than 2 weeks from the date this notice is served. If one of 1, 2, 5 to 7, 9 or 16 grounds is also specified court proceedings cannot begin earlier than two months from the date this notice is served.
- Where the landlord is seeking possession on ground 7A (with or without other grounds), court proceedings cannot begin earlier than 1 month from the date this notice is served on you and not before the date on which the tenancy (had it not been assured) could have been brought to an end by a notice to quit served at the same time as this notice. A notice seeking possession on ground 7A must be served on you within specified time periods which vary depending on which condition is relied upon:
  - Where the landlord proposes to rely on condition 1, 3 or 5: within 12 months of the conviction (or if the conviction is appealed: within 12 months of the conclusion of the appeal);
  - Where the landlord proposes to rely on condition 2: within 12 months of the court's finding that the injunction has been breached (or if the finding is appealed: within 12 months of the conclusion of the appeal);
  - Where the landlord proposes to rely on condition 4: within 3 months of the closure order (or if the order is appealed: within 3 months of the conclusion of the appeal).
- Where the landlord is seeking possession on ground 14 (with or without other grounds other than ground 7A), court proceedings cannot begin before the date this notice is served.
- Where the landlord is seeking possession on ground 14A, court proceedings cannot begin unless the landlord has served, or has taken all reasonable steps to serve, a copy of this notice on the partner who has left the property.
- After the date shown in section 5, court proceedings may be begun at once but not later than 12 months from the date on which this notice is served. After this time the notice will lapse and a new notice must be served before possession can be sought.

6 Name and address of landlord/licensor*.

To be signed and dated by the landlord or licensor or the landlord's or licensor's agent (someone acting for him). If there are joint landlords each landlord or the agent must sign unless one signs on behalf of the rest with their agreement.

Signed .... *Date* ....

Please specify whether: landlord/licensor/joint landlords/landlord's agent

Name(s) (Block Capitals)..

Address ....

Telephone: Daytime .... *Evening* ....

What to do if this notice is served on you

- This notice is the first step requiring you to give up possession of your home. You should read it very carefully.
- Your landlord cannot make you leave your home without an order for possession issued by a court. By issuing this notice your landlord is informing you that he intends to seek such an order. If you are willing to give up possession without a court order, you should tell the person who signed this notice as soon as possible and say when you are prepared to leave.
- Whichever grounds are set out in section 3 of this form, the court may allow any of the other grounds to be added at a later date. If this is done, you will be told about it so you can discuss the additional grounds at the court hearing as well as the grounds set out in section 3.
- If you need advice about this notice, and what you should do about it, take it immediately to a citizens' advice bureau, a housing advice centre, a law centre or a solicitor.

The Absolute Ground for Possession for Anti-social Behaviour (Review Procedure) (England) Regulations 2014

SI 2014/2554

Made	*22nd September 2014*
Laid before Parliament	*25th September 2014*
Coming into force	*20th October 2014*

The Secretary of State, in exercise of the power conferred by section 85ZA(7) of the Housing Act 1985, makes the following Regulations:

1 Citation, commencement, application and interpretation

(1) These Regulations may be cited as the Absolute Ground for Possession for Anti-social Behaviour (Review Procedure) (England) Regulations 2014 and come into force on 20th October 2014.

(2) These Regulations apply in relation to dwelling-houses in England only. (3) In these Regulations –

"the Act" means the Housing Act 1985;
"applicant" means a tenant who has requested a review;
"business day" means any day other than a Saturday, Sunday, Christmas Day, Good Friday, or a day which is a bank holiday in England under the Banking and Financial Dealings Act 1971;
"landlord" means a person to whom a request for a review is made;
"original decision" means a landlord's decision to seek an order for possession of a dwelling- house under section 84A of the Act (absolute ground for possession for anti-social behaviour);
"review" means a review under section 85ZA(1) of the Act (review of decision to seek possession on absolute ground for anti-social behaviour).

2 Application

An application for a review must include –

(a) the applicant's name and address;
(b) a description of the original decision in respect of which the review is sought including the date on which the decision was made;
(c) a statement of the grounds on which the review is sought;
(d) a statement to the effect that the applicant does, or does not, require the review to be conducted by way of an oral hearing;
(e) a statement to the effect that the applicant does, or does not, agree to receive communications relating to the review by email, and if the former, the email address to which such communications should be sent.

3 Right to a hearing

(1) Where an application includes a statement to the effect that the applicant requires the review to be conducted by way of an oral hearing, the review must be conducted in accordance with regulations 6 to 10.

(2) In any other case, the review must be conducted in accordance with regulation 5.

4 Communication

(1) Where an application includes a statement to the effect that the applicant agrees to receive communications relating to the review by email, any notice, document or other communication sent in connection with the review by the landlord to the email address referred to in regulation 2(e) is to be taken as having been received by the applicant on the day on which it was sent to that address.

(2) In any other case, a notice, document or other communication sent in connection with the review by the landlord is to be taken as having been received by the applicant on –

(a) the day it is given to the applicant in person;
(b) the second business day after it is sent by first class post to the address referred to in regulation 2(a); or
(c) the day it is delivered by hand to the address referred to in regulation 2(a).

5 Review without a hearing

(1) Where regulation 3(2) applies, the landlord must send a written notice to the applicant stating that the applicant may make written representations in support of the application before a time specified in the notice.

(2) The time specified pursuant to paragraph (1) must not be earlier than five days after the day on which the notice referred to in that paragraph is received by the applicant.

(3) In making a decision on the review the person conducting the review must take into account any representations received in accordance with this regulation.

(4) The review must be conducted by a person appointed for that purpose by the landlord, who may be an officer or employee of the landlord.

(5) A person appointed under paragraph (4) who is an officer or employee of the landlord must be a person of greater seniority than the person who made the original decision.

(6) The person referred to in paragraph (4) must not be a person who was involved in the making of the original decision.

6 Review by way of a hearing

(1) Where regulation 3(1) applies, the landlord must send a written notice to the applicant stating the date, time and place of the oral hearing.

(2) The date referred to in paragraph (1) must not be earlier than five days after the day on which the notice referred to in that paragraph is received by the applicant.

(3) If at any time before the date on which the hearing is due to take place the applicant so requests, the landlord may postpone the hearing to a later date.

7 Procedure at hearing

(1) The hearing must be conducted by a person appointed for that purpose by the landlord, who may be an officer or employee of the landlord.

(2) A person appointed under paragraph (1) who is an officer or employee of the landlord must be a person of greater seniority than the person who made the original decision.

(3) The person referred to in paragraph (1) must not be a person who was involved in the making of the original decision.

(4) The hearing must be conducted with the minimum amount of formality and in accordance with any directions given by the person conducting it.

(5) At the hearing the applicant may –

(a) make oral or written representations relevant to the decision to be made on the review;
(b) be accompanied or represented by another person appointed by the applicant for that purpose (whether that person is professionally qualified or not);
(c) call persons to give evidence on any matter relevant to the decision to be made on the review; and
(d) put questions to any person who gives evidence at the hearing.

(6) The person who made the original decision may attend the hearing and may do any of the things the applicant may do pursuant to paragraph (5).

(7) A person appointed as a representative pursuant to paragraph (5)(b) has the same rights as the applicant (or, as the case may be, the person who made the original decision) for the purposes of the conduct of the hearing.

8 Absence of applicant at hearing

If the applicant fails to attend the hearing, the person conducting it may, having regard to all the circumstances (including any explanation offered for the absence) proceed with the hearing or give such directions with a view to the further conduct of the review as that person may think appropriate.

9 Adjournment of hearing

(1) The hearing may be adjourned by the person conducting it (on the application of the applicant or otherwise).

(2) Where the hearing is adjourned for more than one day, the person conducting it must specify a date on which the hearing is to be resumed by sending a notice in writing to that effect to the applicant and any other person whose attendance is required at the resumed hearing.

10 Decision on review

Where regulation 3(1) applies, the decision on the review must be made by the person who conducted the hearing.

Anti-social Behaviour, Crime and Policing Act 2014 (Publication of Public Spaces Protection Orders) Regulations 2014

SI 2014/2591

Made	*24th September 2014*
Laid before Parliament	*26th September 2014*
Coming into force	*20th October 2014*

The Secretary of State, in exercise of the powers conferred by sections 59(8), 60(3)(b), 61(5) and (6) of the Anti-social Behaviour, Crime and Policing Act 2014, makes the following Regulations.

1 Citation and commencement

These Regulations may be cited as the Anti-social Behaviour, Crime and Policing Act 2014 (Publication of Public Spaces Protection Orders) Regulations 2014 and come into force on 20th October 2014.

2 Publication of a public spaces protection order which has been made, extended or varied

In relation to a public spaces protection order that a local authority has made, extended or varied, that local authority must –

(a) publish the order as made, extended or varied (as the case may be) on its website; and

(b) cause to be erected on or adjacent to the public place to which the order relates such notice (or notices) as it considers sufficient to draw the attention of any member of the public using that place to –

(i) the fact that the order has been made, extended or varied (as the case may be); and

(ii) the effect of that order being made, extended or varied (as the case may be).

3 Publication of a notice of discharge of a public spaces protection order

(1) In relation to a public spaces protection order that a local authority has discharged, that local authority must –

(a) publish a notice on its website identifying the order which has been discharged and the date on which it ceases to have effect; and

(b) cause to be erected on or adjacent to the public place to which the order relates, a notice (or notices) –

(i) identifying the order which has been discharged; and

(ii) the date on which it ceases to have effect.

(2) The notice (or notices) mentioned in paragraph (1)(b) must be positioned in a manner that the local authority considers sufficient to draw it to the attention of any member of the public using that place.

APPENDIX 4

PROCEDURAL RULES

Civil Procedure Rules 1998 (CPR 33.1–33.5, 65.37–65.49; PD 65, SS. I, II, VII; CPR 81.1–10, 81.28–31; PD 81, S. 8)

PART 33

MISCELLANEOUS RULES ABOUT EVIDENCE

33.1 Introductory

In this Part –

(a) 'hearsay' means a statement made, otherwise than by a person while giving oral evidence in proceedings, which is tendered as evidence of the matters stated; and
(b) references to hearsay include hearsay of whatever degree.

33.2 Notice of intention to rely on hearsay evidence

(1) Where a party intends to rely on hearsay evidence at trial and either –

(a) that evidence is to be given by a witness giving oral evidence; or
(b) that evidence is contained in a witness statement of a person who is not being called to give oral evidence;

that party complies with section 2(1)(a) of the Civil Evidence Act 1995[1] serving a witness statement on the other parties in accordance with the court's order.

(2) Where paragraph (1)(b) applies, the party intending to rely on the hearsay evidence must, when he serves the witness statement –

(a) inform the other parties that the witness is not being called to give oral evidence; and
(b) give the reason why the witness will not be called.

(3) In all other cases where a party intends to rely on hearsay evidence at trial, that party complies with section 2(1)(a) of the Civil Evidence Act 1995 by serving a notice on the other parties which –

(a) identifies the hearsay evidence;
(b) states that the party serving the notice proposes to rely on the hearsay evidence at trial; and
(c) gives the reason why the witness will not be called.

(4) The party proposing to rely on the hearsay evidence must –

(a) serve the notice no later than the latest date for serving witness statements; and
(b) if the hearsay evidence is to be in a document, supply a copy to any party who requests him to do so.

33.3 Circumstances in which notice of intention to rely on hearsay evidence is not required

Section 2(1) of the Civil Evidence Act 1995 (duty to give notice of intention to rely on hearsay evidence) does not apply –

(a) to evidence at hearings other than trials;
(aa) to an affadavit or witness statement which is to be used at trial but which does not contain hearsay evidence;
(b) to a statement which a party to a probate action wishes to put in evidence and which is alleged to have been made by the person whose estate is the subject of the proceedings; or
(c) where the requirement is excluded by a practice direction.

33.4 Power to call witness for cross-examination on hearsay evidence

(1) Where a party –

(a) proposes to rely on hearsay evidence; and
(b) does not propose to call the person who made the original statement to give oral evidence,

the court may, on the application of any other party, permit that party to call the maker of the statement to be cross-examined on the contents of the statement.

(2) An application for permission to cross-examine under this rule must be made not more than 14 days after the day on which a notice of intention to rely on the hearsay evidence was served on the applicant.

33.5 Credibility

(1) Where a party –

(a) proposes to rely on hearsay evidence; but
(b) does not propose to call the person who made the original statement to give oral evidence; and
(c) another party wishes to call evidence to attack the credibility of the person who made the statement,

the party who so wishes must give notice of his intention to the party who proposes to give the hearsay statement in evidence.

(2) A party must give notice under paragraph (1) not more than 14 days after the day on which a hearsay notice relating to the hearsay evidence was served on him.

****

PART 65

PROCEEDINGS RELATING TO ANTI-SOCIAL BEHAVIOUR AND HARASSMENT

****

VII Parenting Orders Under the Anti-social Behaviour Act 2003

65.37 Scope of this Section and interpretation

(1) This Section of this Part applies in relation to applications for parenting orders under sections 26A and 26B of the Anti-social Behaviour Act 2003 by a relevant authority.

(2) In this Section –

(a) 'the 2003 Act' means the Anti-social Behaviour Act 2003; and

(b) 'relevant authority' has the same meaning as in section 26C of the 2003 Act.

65.38 Applications for parenting orders

(1) Subject to paragraph (2) –

(a) where the relevant authority is the claimant in the proceedings, an application for an order under section 26A or 26B of the 2003 Act must be made in the claim form; and
(b) where the relevant authority is a defendant in the proceedings, an application for such an order must be made by application notice which must be filed with the defence.

(2) Where the relevant authority becomes aware of the circumstances that led it to apply for an order after its claim is issued or its defence filed, the application must be made by application notice as soon as possible thereafter.

(3) Where the application is made by application notice, it must normally be made on notice to the person against whom the order is sought.

65.39 Applications by the relevant authority to be joined to proceedings

(1) Where the relevant authority is not a party to the proceedings –

(a) an application under section 26C(2) of the 2003 Act to be made a party must be made in accordance with Section I of Part 19; and
(b) the application to be made a party and the application for an order under section 26A or 26B of the 2003 Act must be made in the same application notice.

(2) The applications –

(a) must be made as soon as possible after the relevant authority becomes aware of the proceedings; and
(b) must normally be made on notice to the person against whom the order is sought.

65.40 Applications by the relevant authority to join a parent to proceedings

(1) An application under section 26C(3) of the 2003 Act by a relevant authority which is a party to the proceedings to join a parent to those proceedings must be made –

(a) in the same application notice as the application for an order under section 26A or 26B of the 2003 Act; and
(b) as soon as possible after the relevant authority considers that the grounds for the application are met.

(2) Rule 19.2 does not apply in relation to an application made by a relevant authority under section 26C(3) of the 2003 Act to join a parent to the proceedings.

(3) The application notice must contain –

(a) the relevant authority's reasons for claiming the anti-social behaviour of the child or young person is material in relation to the proceedings; and
(b) details of the behaviour alleged.

(4) The application must normally be made on notice to the person against whom the order is sought.

65.41 Evidence

An application under section 26A, 26B or 26C of the 2003 Act must be accompanied by written evidence.

VIII Injunctions under the Policing and Crime Act 2009 and under Part 1 of the Anti-social Behaviour, Crime and Policing Act 2014

65.42 Scope of this Section and interpretation

(1) This Section applies to applications for an injunction and other related proceedings under Part 4 of the Policing and Crime Act 2009 (Injunctions: gang-related violence) and under Part 1 of the Anti-Social Behaviour, Crime and Policing Act 2014 (Injunctions).

(2) In this Section –

(a) "the 2009 Act" means the Policing and Crime Act 2009(b)"; and
(b) "the 2014 Act" means the Anti-Social Behaviour, Crime and Policing Act 2014.

65.43 Applications for an injunction

(1) An application for an injunction under Part 4 of the 2009 Act or Part 1 of the 2014 Act is subject to the Part 8 procedure as modified by this rule and Practice Direction 65.

(2) The application –

(a) must be made by a claim form in accordance with Practice Direction 65;
(b) may be made at any County Court hearing centre; and
(c) must be supported by a witness statement which must be filed with the claim form.

(2A) If the application –

(a) is on notice; and
(b) is made at a County Court hearing centre which does not serve the address where –

 (i) the defendant resides or carries on business' or
 (ii) the claimant resides or carries on business,

the application will be issued by the County Court hearing centre where the application is made and sent to the hearing centre serving the address (b)(i) or (ii), as appropriate.

(Practice Direction 65 makes further provision in respect of applications which are not made at the County Court hearing centre which serves the address where the defendant resides or the conduct complained of occurred.)

(3) The claim form must state –

(a) the matters required by rule 8.2; and
(b) the terms of the injunction applied for.

(4) An application under this rule may be made without notice and where such an application without notice is made –

(a1) the application may –

 (i) be made at any County Court hearing centre;
 (ii) be heard at the hearing centre where the application is made; and
 (iii) at any stage of the proceedings, be transferred by the court to –
  (aa) the hearing centre which serves the address where the defendant resides or where the conduct complained of occurred; or
  (bb) another hearing centre as the court considers appropriate;

(a) the witness statement in support of the application must state the reasons why notice has not been given; and
(b) the following rules do not apply –

 (i) 8.3;

(ii) 8.4;
(iii) 8.5(2) to (6);
(iv) 8.6(1);
(v) 8.7; and
(vi) 8.8.

(5) In every application made on notice, the application notice must be served, together with a copy of the witness statement, by the claimant on the defendant personally.

(6) An application made on notice may be listed for hearing before the expiry of the time for the defendant to file an acknowledgment of service under rule 8.3, and in such a case –

(a) the claimant must serve the application notice and witness statement on the defendant not less than 2 days before the hearing; and
(b) the defendant may take part in the hearing whether or not the defendant has filed an acknowledgment of service.

65.44 Injunction containing provisions to which a power of arrest is attached

(1) In this rule 'relevant provision' means a provision of an injunction to which a power of arrest is attached.

(Section 36(6) and (7) and section 40(3) and 41(4) of the 2009 Act and section 4(1) (a) and (b) of the 2014 Act confer powers to attach a power of arrest to an injunction.)

(2) Where an injunction contains one or more relevant provisions –

(a) each relevant provision must he set out in a separate paragraph of the injunction; and
(b) subject to paragraph (3), the claimant must deliver a copy of the relevant provisions to any police station for the area where the conduct occurred.

(3) Where the injunction has been granted without notice, the claimant must not deliver a copy of the relevant provisions to any police station for the area where the conduct occurred before the defendant has been served with the injunction containing the relevant provisions.

(4) Where an order is made varying or discharging any relevant provision, the claimant must –

(a) immediately inform the police station to which a copy of the relevant provisions was delivered under paragraph (2)(b); and
(b) deliver a copy of the order to any police station so informed.

65.45 Application to vary or discharge an injunction

(1) An application to vary or discharge an injunction under section 42(1)(b) of the 2009 Act or section 8(1)(a) and (b) of the 2014 Act must be made in accordance with Part 23.

(2) An application by the claimant to vary or discharge the injunction under section 42(1)(b) of the 2009 Act may be made without notice.

(3) If an application under this rule is made without giving notice, the application notice must state the reasons why notice has not been given.

65.46 Application for warrant of arrest under section 44(2) of the 2009 Act or section 10 of the 2014 Act

(1) An application for a warrant of arrest under section 44(2) of the 2009 Act or section 10 of the 2014 Act must be made in accordance with Part 23 and may be made without notice.

(2) An applicant for a warrant of arrest under section 44(2) of the 2009 Act or section 10 of the 2014 Act must –

(a) file an affidavit setting out grounds for the application with the application notice; or
(b) give oral evidence of the grounds for the application at the hearing.

(3) Where in accordance with sub-paragraph (2)(b), oral evidence is given, the applicant must produce a written record of that evidence which must be served on the person arrested at the time of the arrest.

65.47 Proceedings following arrest under the 2009 Act

(1) This rule applies where a person is arrested pursuant to –

(a) a power of arrest attached to a provision of an injunction; or
(b) a warrant of arrest.

(2) The judge before whom a person is brought following his arrest may –

(a) deal with the matter; or
(b) adjourn the proceedings.

(3) If proceedings under section 33 or 44 of the 2009 Act or section 9 or 10 of the 2014 Act are adjourned and the arrested person is released –

(a) the matter must be dealt with (whether by the same or another judge) within 28 days of the date on which the arrested person appears in court; and
(b) the arrested person must be given not less than 2 days' notice of the hearing.

(4) An application notice seeking the committal for contempt of court of the arrested person may be issued even if the arrested person is not dealt with within the period in sub-paragraph (3)(a).

(5) Sections 2 and 8 of Part 81 apply where an application is made in a County Court to commit a person for breach of an injunction as if references in those Sections to the judge include references to a District Judge.

(For applications for the discharge of a person committed to prison for contempt of court see rules 81.31 and 81.32.)

65.48 Recognizance

(1) Where, in accordance with paragraph 2(2)b) of Schedule 5 to the 2009 Act or paragraph 2(3)(b) of Schedule 1 to the 2014 Act, the court fixes the amount of any recognizance with a view to it being taken subsequently, the recognizance may be taken by –

(a) a judge;
(b) a justice of the peace;
(c) a justices' clerk;
(d) a police officer of the rank of inspector or above, or in charge of a police station; or
(e) where the arrested person is in custody. the governor or keeper of a prison,

with the same consequences as if it had been entered into before the court.

(2) The person having custody of an applicant for bail must release that person if satisfied that the required recognizances have been taken.

65.49 Applications for a power of arrest to be attached to any provision of an injunction

(1) An application under section 34 or 39 of the 2009 Act or section 5 or 6 of the 2014 Act which includes an application for a power of arrest to be attached to any provision of an injunction must be made in the proceedings seeking the injunction by –

(a) the claim form; or
(b) an application under Part 23.

(2) Every application must be supported by written evidence.

(3) Every application made on notice must be served personally, together with a copy of the written evidence, by the applicant on the person against whom the injunction is sought not less than 2 days before the hearing.

(Attention is drawn to rule 25.3(3) – applications without notice.)

Practice Direction 65 –

Anti-Social Behaviour and Harassment

This Practice Direction supplements CPR Part 65 (PD65)

SECTION I – HOUSING ACT 1996, POLICING AND CRIME ACT 2009 AND ANTI-SOCIAL BEHAVIOUR, CRIME AND POLICING ACT 2014 INJUNCTIONS

Issuing the claim

1.1

(1) An application for an injunction under Chapter III of Part V of the 1996 Act and Part 4 of the 2009 Act or Part 1 of the 2014 Act must be made by form N16A and for the purposes of applying Practice Direction 8A to applications under Section I or Section VIII of Part 65, form N16A shall be treated as the Part 8 claim form.

(2) An application on notice under rules 65.3 or 65.43 will be issued by the County Court hearing centre where the claim is made but will then be sent to the County Court hearing centre which serves the address where the defendant resides or the conduct complained of occurred. An applicant should consider the potential delay which may result if an application is not made at the appropriate County Court hearing centre in the first instance.

Proceedings transferred from youth court, or breach of injunction made by youth court

1A.1 Where proceedings under Part 4 of the 2009 Act or Part 1 of the 2014 Act which were commenced in a youth court have been transferred to the High Court or County Court after the respondent attained the age of 18, anything done in the youth court in or in relation to those proceedings will have effect, for the purposes of continuing the proceedings in the High Court or County Court, as if it had been done in the High Court or County Court as the case may be.

1A.2 Proceedings transferred to the County Court will be sent to the County Court hearing centre which serves the address where the respondent resides.

1A.3 Where a person aged 18 or over is brought before a judge following arrest for a breach of an injunction granted by a youth court (whether pursuant to a power of arrest attached to the injunction or to a warrant issued for that person's arrest under section 44 of the 2009 Act or section 10 of the 2014 Act), it is the responsibility of the injunction applicant (within the meaning of paragraph 1(9) of Schedule 5A to the 2009 Act) or original applicant (within the meaning of paragraph 1(2) of Schedule 2 to the 2014 Act) to provide the judge with the information necessary to determine whether to deal with the matter or adjourn the proceedings under rule 65.47.

Hearings – Part 4 of the 2009 Act

1.2 Unless the court otherwise orders, an application on notice for an injunction under Part 4 of the 2009 Act under rule 65.43 or any other hearing in relation to such an injunction requiring the respondent's attendance must be heard at one of the following County Court hearing centres –

(a) Birmingham
(b) Bradford
(c) Brighton
(d) Bristol
(e) Cardiff
(f) Chelmsford
(g) Croydon
(h) Hammersmith (formerly known as West London)
(i) Leicester
(j) Liverpool
(k) Luton
(l) Manchester
(m) Newcastle
(n) Norwich
(o) Nottingham
(p) Oxford
(q) Peterborough
(r) Portsmouth
(s) Preston
(t) Sheffield

(Attention is drawn to the statutory guidance on listing for hearings. These hearings will take place in courts which have been identified as having suitable facilities if special measures are needed for potential witnesses or security.)

Warrant of arrest on an application under section 155(3) of the 1996 Act, section 44(2) of the 2009 Act and section 10 of the 2014 Act

2.1 In accordance with section 155(4) of the 1996 Act , section 44(3) of the 2009 Act and section 10(3) of the 2014 Act, a warrant of arrest on an application under section 155(3) of the 1996 Act , section 44(2) of the 2009 Act or section 10 of the 2014 Act shall not be issued unless –

(1) the application is substantiated on oath; and
(2) in any proceedings under the 1996 Act or the 2014 Act the judge has reasonable grounds for believing that the defendant has failed to comply with the injunction.

Application for bail

3.1 An application for bail by a person arrested under –

(1) a power of arrest attached to an injunction under Chapter III of Part V of the 1996 Act , Part 4 of the 2009 Act or Part 1 of the 2014 Act or
(2) a warrant of arrest issued on an application under section 155(3) of the 1996 Act, Part 4 of the 2009 Act or Part 1 of the 2014 Act,

may be made either orally or in an application notice.

3.2 An application notice seeking bail must contain –

(1) the full name of the person making the application;
(2) the address of the place where the person making the application is detained at the time when the application is made;
(3) the address where the person making the application would reside if that person were to be granted bail;
(4) the amount of the recognizance in which that person would agree to be bound; and
(5) the grounds on which the application is made and, where previous application has been refused, full details of any change in circumstances which has occurred since that refusal.

3.3 A copy of the application notice must be served on the person who obtained the injunction.

Remand for medical examination and report

4.1 Section 156(4) of the 1996 Act, section 45(5) of the 2009 Act and paragraph 6 of Schedule 1 to the 2014 Act provides that the judge has power to make an order under section 35 of the Mental Health Act 1983 in certain circumstances. If he does so attention is drawn to section 35(8) of that Act, which provides that a person remanded to hospital under that section may obtain at his own expense an independent report on his mental condition from a registered medical practitioner chosen by him and apply to the court on the basis of it for his remand to be terminated under section 35(7).

SECTION II – APPLICATIONS BY LOCAL AUTHORITIES FOR POWER OF ARREST TO BE ATTACHED TO AN INJUNCTION

Application for Bail under the 2006 Act

4A.1 The following paragraphs of Section I of this practice direction apply in relation to an application for bail by a person arrested under a power of arrest attached to an injunction under section 27 of the 2006 Act –

(1) paragraph 3.1(1), as if a reference to Chapter III of Part V of the Housing Act 1996 was a reference to section 27 of the 2006 Act;
(2) paragraph 3.2; and
(3) paragraph 3.3.

Remand for Medical Examination and Report

4A.2 Paragraph 4.1 of Section I of this practice direction applies in relation to section 27 of the 2006 Act, as if a reference in paragraph 4.1 to section 156(4) of the Housing Act 1996 was a reference to section 27(11) of the 2006 Act.

****

SECTION VII – PARENTING ORDERS UNDER THE ANTI-SOCIAL BEHAVIOUR ACT 2003

Applications for Parenting Orders

16.1 Where the applicant is a registered social landlord or a private registered provider of social housing, the application must be supported by evidence that the relevant local authority has been consulted in accordance with section 26B(8) of the 2003 Act.

16.2 An order under section 26A or 26B of the 2003 Act must be served personally on the defendant.

16.3 An application by a relevant authority under section 26C(3) of the 2003 Act to join a person to the proceedings may only be made against a person aged 18 or over.

PART 81

APPLICATIONS AND PROCEEDINGS IN RELATION TO CONTEMPT OF COURT

Section 1 – Scope and interpretation

81.1 Scope

(1) This Part sets out the procedure in respect of –

(a) contempt of court; and
(b) the penal, contempt and disciplinary provisions of the County Courts Act 1984.

(2) So far as applicable, and with the necessary modifications, this Part applies in relation to an order requiring a person –

(a) guilty of contempt of court; or
(b) punishable by virtue of any enactment as if that person had been guilty of contempt of the High Court, to pay a fine or to give security for good behaviour, as it applies in relation to an order of committal.

(3) Unless otherwise stated, this Part applies to procedure in the Court of Appeal, the High Court and the County Court.

81.2 Saving for other powers

(1) This Part is concerned only with procedure and does not itself confer upon the court the power to make an order for –

(a) committal;
(b) sequestration; or
(c) the imposition of a fine in respect of contempt of court.

(2) Nothing in this Part affects the power of the court to make an order requiring a person –

(a) guilty of contempt of court; or
(b) punishable by virtue of any enactment as if that person had been guilty of contempt of the High Court, to pay a fine or to give security for good behaviour.

(3) Nothing in this Part affects any statutory or inherent power of the court to make a committal order of its own initiative against a person guilty of contempt of court.

81.3 Interpretation

In this Part –

"applicant" means a person making –

(i) an application for permission to make a committal application;
(ii) a committal application; or
(iii) an application for a writ of sequestration;

"committal application" means any application for an order committing a person to prison;
"respondent" means a person –

(i) against whom a committal application is made or is intended to be made; or
(ii) against whose property it is sought to issue a writ of sequestration; and

"undertaking" means an undertaking to the court.

Section 2 – Committal for breach of a judgment, order or undertaking to do or abstain from doing an act

81.4 Enforcement of judgment, order or undertaking to do or abstain from doing an act

(1) If a person –

(a) required by a judgment or order to do an act does not do it within the time fixed by the judgment or order; or
(b) disobeys a judgment or order not to do an act,

then, subject to the Debtors Acts 1869 and 1878 and to the provisions of these Rules, the judgment or order may be enforced by an order for committal.

(2) If the time fixed by the judgment or order for doing an act has been varied by a subsequent order or agreement of the parties under rule 2.11, then references in paragraph (1)(a) to the time fixed are references to the time fixed by that subsequent order or agreement.

(3) If the person referred to in paragraph (1) is a company or other corporation, the committal order may be made against any director or other officer of that company or corporation.

(4) So far as applicable, and with the necessary modifications, this Section applies to undertakings given by a party as it applies to judgments or orders.

(Rules 81.17(3) and (4) make provision for cases in which both this Section and Section 6 (Committal for making a false statement of truth or disclosure statement) may be relevant.)

(5) If a judgment or order requires a person to deliver goods or pay their value –

- (a) the judgment or order may not be enforced by a committal order under paragraph (1);
- (b) the person entitled to enforce the judgment or order may apply to the court for an order requiring that the goods be delivered within a specified time; and (c) where the court grants such an order, that order may be enforced under paragraph (1).

81.5 Requirement for service of a copy of the judgment or order and time for service

(1) Unless the court dispenses with service under rule 81.8, a judgment or order may not be enforced under rule 81.4 unless a copy of it has been served on the person required to do or not do the act in question, and in the case of a judgment or order requiring a person to do an act –

- (a) the copy has been served before the end of the time fixed for doing the act, together with a copy of any order fixing that time;
- (b) where the time for doing the act has been varied by a subsequent order or agreement under rule 2.11, a copy of that subsequent order or agreement has also been served; and
- (c) where the judgment or order was made under rule 81.4(5), or was made pursuant to an earlier judgment or order requiring the act to be done, a copy of the earlier judgment or order has also been served.

(2) Where the person referred to in paragraph (1) is a company or other corporation, a copy of the judgment or order must also be served on the respondent before the end of the time fixed for doing the act.

(3) Copies of the judgment or order and any orders or agreements fixing or varying the time for doing an act must be served in accordance with rule 81.6 or 81.7, or in accordance with an order for alternative service made under rule 81.8(2)(b).

81.6 Method of service – copies of judgments or orders

Subject to rules 81.7 and 81.8, copies of judgments or orders and any orders or agreements fixing or varying the time for doing an act must be served personally.

81.7 Method of service – copies of undertakings

(1) Subject to paragraph (2) and rule 81.8, a copy of any document recording an undertaking will be delivered by the court to the person who gave the undertaking –

- (a) by handing to that person a copy of the document before that person leaves the court building;
- (b) by posting a copy to that person at the residence or place of business of that person where this is known; or
- (c) by posting a copy to that person's solicitor.

(2) If delivery cannot be effected in accordance with paragraph (1), the court officer will deliver a copy of the document to the party for whose benefit the undertaking was given and that party must serve it personally on the person who gave the undertaking as soon as practicable.

(3) Where the person referred to in paragraph (1) is a company or other corporation, a copy of the judgment or order must also be served on the respondent.

81.8 Dispensation with personal service

(1) In the case of a judgment or order requiring a person not to do an act, the court may dispense with service of a copy of the judgment or order in accordance with rules 81.5 to 81.7 if it is satisfied that the person has had notice of it –

(a) by being present when the judgment or order was given or made; or
(b) by being notified of its terms by telephone, email or otherwise.

(2) In the case of any judgment or order the court may –

(a) dispense with service under rules 81.5 to 81.7 if the court thinks it just to do so; or
(b) make an order in respect of service by an alternative method or at an alternative place.

81.9 Requirement for a penal notice on judgments and orders

(1) Subject to paragraph (2), a judgment or order to do or not do an act may not be enforced under rule 81.4 unless there is prominently displayed, on the front of the copy of the judgment or order served in accordance with this Section, a warning to the person required to do or not do the act in question that disobedience to the order would be a contempt of court punishable by imprisonment, a fine or sequestration of assets.

(2) The following may be enforced under rule 81.4 notwithstanding that they do not contain the warning described in paragraph (1) –

(a) an undertaking to do or not do an act which is contained in a judgment or order; and
(b) an incoming protection measure.

(3) In this rule, "incoming protection measure" has the meaning given to it in rule 74.34(1).

(Paragraphs 2.1 to 2.4 of the Practice Direction supplementing this Part and form N117 contain provisions about penal notices and warnings in relation to undertakings.)

81.10 How to make the committal application

(1) A committal application is made by an application notice under Part 23 in the proceedings in which the judgment or order was made or the undertaking was given.

(2) Where the committal application is made against a person who is not an existing party to the proceedings, it is made against that person by an application notice under Part 23.

(3) The application notice must –

(a) set out in full the grounds on which the committal application is made and must identify, separately and numerically, each alleged act of contempt including, if known, the date of each of the alleged acts; and
(b) be supported by one or more affidavits containing all the evidence relied upon.

(4) Subject to paragraph (5), the application notice and the evidence in support must be served personally on the respondent.

(5) The court may –

(a) dispense with service under paragraph (4) if it considers it just to do so; or
(b) make an order in respect of service by an alternative method or at an alternative place.

****

Section 8 – General rules about committal applications, orders for committal and writs of sequestration

81.28 The hearing

(1) Unless the court hearing the committal application or application for sequestration otherwise permits, the applicant may not rely on –

(a) any grounds other than –

(i) those set out in the claim form or application notice; or
(ii) in relation to a committal application under Section 3 or 4, the statement of grounds required by rule 81.14(1)(a) (where not included in the claim form) or 81.15(4)(a); or

(b) any evidence unless it has been served in accordance with the relevant Section of this Part or the Practice Direction supplementing this Part.

(2) At the hearing, the respondent is entitled –

(a) to give oral evidence, whether or not the respondent has filed or served written evidence, and, if doing so, may be cross-examined; and
(b) with the permission of the court, to call a witness to give oral evidence whether or not the witness has made an affidavit or witness statement.

(3) The court may require or permit any party or other person (other than the respondent) to give oral evidence at the hearing.

(4) The court may give directions requiring the attendance for cross-examination of a witness who has given written evidence.

(5) If the court hearing an application in private decides to make a committal order against the respondent, it will in public state –

(a) the name of the respondent;
(b) in general terms, the nature of the contempt of court in respect of which the committal order is being made; and
(c) the length of the period of the committal order.

(Rule 39.2 contains provisions about hearings in private.)

(6) Where a committal order is made in the absence of the respondent, the court may on its own initiative fix a date and time when the respondent is to be brought before the court.

81.29 Power to suspend execution of a committal order

(1) The court making the committal order may also order that its execution will be suspended for such period or on such terms or conditions as it may specify.

(2) Unless the court otherwise directs, the applicant must serve on the respondent a copy of any order made under paragraph (1).

81.30 Warrant of committal

(1) If a committal order is made, the order will be for the issue of a warrant of committal.

(2) Unless the court orders otherwise –

- (a) a copy of the committal order must be served on the respondent either before or at the time of the execution of the warrant of committal; or
- (b) where the warrant of committal has been signed by the judge, the committal order may be served on the respondent at any time within 36 hours after the execution of the warrant.

(3) Without further order of the court, a warrant of committal must not be enforced more than 2 years after the date on which the warrant is issued.

81.31 Discharge of a person in custody

(1) A person committed to prison for contempt of court may apply to the court to be discharged.

(2) The application must –

- (a) be in writing and attested by the governor of the prison (or any other officer of the prison not below the rank of principal officer);
- (b) show that the person committed to prison for contempt has purged, or wishes to purge, the contempt; and
- (c) be served on the person (if any) at whose instance the warrant of committal was issued at least one day before the application is made.

(3) Paragraph (2) does not apply to –

- (a) a warrant of committal to which CCR Order 27 rule 8, or CCR Order 28 rule 4 or 14 relates; or
- (b) an application made by the Official Solicitor acting with official authority for the discharge of a person in custody.

(4) If the committal order is made in a County Court and –

- (a) does not direct that any application for discharge must be made to a judge; or
- (b) was made by a District Judge under section 118 of the County Courts Act 1984, the application for discharge may be made to a District Judge.

(5) If the committal order is made in the High Court, the application for discharge may be made to a single judge of the Division in which the committal order was made.

****

Practice Direction 81 –

Applications and proceedings in realtion to contempt of court

****

Section 8 of Part 81 – General rules about committal applications, orders for committal and writs of sequestration

General rules

8.1 Subject to paragraph 8.2, this Section of the Practice Direction applies in relation to all matters covered by Part 81.

8.2 Where there is a conflict between the provisions in this Section of the Practice Direction and specific provisions elsewhere in this Practice Direction or in Part 81, the specific provisions prevail.

Human rights

9 In all cases the Convention rights of those involved should particularly be borne in mind. It should be noted that the standard of proof, having regard to the possibility that a person may be sent to prison, is that the allegation be proved beyond reasonable doubt.

(Section 1 of the Human Rights Act 1998 defines 'the Convention rights'.)

Court to which applications should be made and levels of judiciary

10.1 A committal application or an application for permission to make a committal application –

(1) may be made in the County Court if the alleged contempt is a contempt which the County Court has power to punish; and
(2) must otherwise be made in the High Court.

10.2 Except where under an enactment a Master or District Judge has power to make a committal order, a committal order can only be made–

(1) in High Court proceedings, by a High Court Judge or a person authorised to act as such; or
(2) in County Court proceedings, by a judge of the County Court other than a District Judge of that court, unless they are exercising the jurisdiction of a Circuit Judge with the permission of the Designated Civil Judge.

10.3 Paragraph 10.4 applies in relation to proceedings in any court (the first court) where the judge or judges exercising the jurisdiction of the first court are deemed to constitute a court of the High Court by virtue of an enactment.

10.4 The reference in paragraph 10.2(1) to a High Court Judge will be construed as a reference to a judge of the first court.

General rules about applications: applications which cannot be made without permission

11 If the committal application is one which cannot be made without permission –

(1) the permission may only be granted by a judge who would have power to hear the committal application if permission were granted;
(2) the date on which and the name of the judge by whom the requisite permission was granted must be stated on the claim form or application notice by which the committal application is commenced;
(3) the claim form or application notice may not be issued or filed until the requisite permission has been granted; and
(4) Rules 23.9 and 23.10 do not apply.

General rules about applications: applications by claim form

12 If the application for permission to make a committal application or the committal application is commenced by the issue of a claim form –

(1) Part 8 will apply –

    (a) subject to the provisions of Part 81 and this Practice Direction, in particular sub-paragraphs (2) to (4);
    (b) as though references to'claimant' were references to the applicant; and
    (c) as though references to'defendant' were references to the respondent;

(2) an amendment to the claim form may be made with the permission of the court but not otherwise;
(3) rule 8.4 does not apply; and

(4) the claim form must contain a prominent notice stating the possible consequences of the court making a committal order and of the respondent not attending the hearing. A form of notice which may be used is annexed to this Practice Direction at Annex 3.

General rules about applications: applications by application notice

13.1 Where the application is made by application notice, the application notice must state that the application is made in the proceedings in question, and its title and reference number must correspond with the title and reference number of those proceedings.

13.2 If the application for permission to make a committal application or the committal application is commenced by the filing of an application notice –

(1) Part 23 will apply subject to the provisions of Part 81 and this Practice Direction, in particular sub-paragraphs (2) to (4);
(2) an amendment to the application notice may be made with the permission of the court but not otherwise;
(3) the court may not dispose of the application without a hearing; and
(4) the application notice must contain a prominent notice stating the possible consequences of the court making a committal order and of the respondent not attending the hearing. A form of notice which may be used is annexed to this Practice Direction at Annex 3.

Evidence and information

14.1 Written evidence in support of or in opposition to a committal application must be given by affidavit.

14.2 Written evidence served in support of or in opposition to a committal application must, unless the court otherwise directs, be filed.

14.3 The following rules do not apply to committal applications –

(1) rule 35.7 (Court's power to direct that evidence is to be given by a single joint expert);
(2) rule 35.8 (Instructions to single joint expert); and
(3) rule 35.9 (Power of court to direct a party to provide information).

14.4 An order under rule 18.1 (Obtaining further information) may not be made against a respondent to a committal application.

The hearing – Rule 81.28

15.1 When issuing or filing the claim form or application notice for a committal application, the applicant must obtain from the court a date for the hearing of the committal application.

15.2 Unless the court otherwise directs, the hearing date of a committal application must not be less than 14 days after service of the claim form or application notice on the respondent. The hearing date must be specified in the claim form or application notice or in a Notice of Hearing attached to and served with the claim form or application notice.

15.3 Paragraphs 15.1 and 15.2 apply to certifications of conduct and applications under section 336 of the Charities Act 2011 ('section 336 application') referred to in Section 4 of Part 81 as if references to the claim form or application notice were references to the certification or section 336 application.

(The definition of'applicant' in rule 81.3 includes a person who makes a committal application by way of certification or section 336 application.)

15.4 The court may on the hearing date –

(1) give case management directions with a view to a hearing of the committal application on a future date; or

(2) if the committal application is ready to be heard, proceed to hear it.

15.5 In dealing with any committal application, the court will have regard to the need for the respondent to have details of the alleged acts of contempt and the opportunity to respond to the committal application.

15.6 The court will also have regard to the need for the respondent to be –

(1) allowed a reasonable time for responding to the committal application including, if necessary, preparing a defence;
(2) made aware of the possible availability of criminal legal aid and how to contact the Legal Aid Agency;
(3) given the opportunity, if unrepresented, to obtain legal advice; and
(4) if unable to understand English, allowed to make arrangements, seeking the assistance of the court if necessary, for an interpreter to attend the hearing.

Striking out, procedural defects and discontinuance

16.1 On application by the respondent or on its own initiative, the court may strike out a committal application if it appears to the court –

(1) that the application and the evidence served in support of it disclose no reasonable ground for alleging that the respondent is guilty of a contempt of court;
(2) that the application is an abuse of the court's process or, if made in existing proceedings, is otherwise likely to obstruct the just disposal of those proceedings; or
(3) that there has been a failure to comply with a rule, practice direction or court order.

16.2 The court may waive any procedural defect in the commencement or conduct of a committal application if satisfied that no injustice has been caused to the respondent by the defect.

16.3 A committal application may not be discontinued without the permission of the court.

Criminal Procedure Rules 2014 (Pts 29, 50; CrimPD Div V and Application Form)

PART 29

MEASURES TO ASSIST A WITNESS OR DEFENDANT TO GIVE EVIDENCE

Section 1

Understanding and Applying this Part

29.1 When this Part applies

This Part applies –

(a) where the court can give a direction (a 'special measures direction'), under section 19 of the Youth Justice and Criminal Evidence Act 1999, on an application or on its own initiative, for any of the following measures –

  (i) preventing a witness from seeing the defendant (section 23 of the 1999 Act),
  (ii) allowing a witness to give evidence by live link (section 24 of the 1999 Act),
  (iii) hearing a witness' evidence in private (section 25 of the 1999 Act),
  (iv) dispensing with the wearing of wigs and gowns (section 26 of the 1999 Act),
  (v) admitting video recorded evidence (sections 27 and 28 of the 1999 Act),

(vi) questioning a witness through an intermediary (section 29 of the 1999 Act),
(vii) using a device to help a witness communicate (section 30 of the 1999 Act);

(b) where the court can vary or discharge such a direction, under section 20 of the 1999 Act;
(c) where the court can give, vary or discharge a direction (a 'defendant's evidence direction') for a defendant to give evidence –

(i) by live link, under section 33A of the 1999 Act, or
(ii) through an intermediary, under sections 33BA and 33BB of the 1999 Act;

(d) where the court can –

(i) make a witness anonymity order, under section 86 of the Coroners and Justice Act 2009, or
(ii) vary or discharge such an order, under section 91, 92 or 93 of the 2009 Act;

(e) where the court can give or discharge a direction (a 'live link direction'), on an application or on its own initiative, for a witness to give evidence by live link under –

(i) section 32 of the Criminal Justice Act 1988, or
(ii) sections 51 and 52 of the Criminal Justice Act 2003;

(f) where the court can exercise any other power it has to give, vary or discharge a direction for a measure to help a witness give evidence.

29.2 Meaning of 'witness'

In this Part, 'witness' means anyone (other than a defendant) for whose benefit an application, direction or order is made.

Note: At the end of this Part is a summary of the circumstances in which a witness or defendant may be eligible for the assistance of one of the measures to which this Part applies.

Section 2

General Rules

29.3 Making an application for a direction or order

A party who wants the court to exercise its power to give or make a direction or order must –

(a) apply in writing as soon as reasonably practicable, and in any event not more than –

(i) 28 days after the defendant pleads not guilty, in a magistrates' court, or
(ii) 14 days after the defendant pleads not guilty, in the Crown Court; and

(b) serve the application on –

(i) the court officer, and
(ii) each other party.

Note: See also rule 29.10 (content of application for a special measures direction), rule 29.15 (content of application for a defendant's evidence direction), rule 29.19 (content and conduct of application for a witness anonymity order) and rule 29.24 (content of application for a live link direction).

The Practice Direction sets out forms for use in connection with –

(a) an application under rule 29.10 for a special measures direction;

(b) an application under rule 29.24 for a live link direction (otherwise than as a special measures direction).

29.4 Decisions and reasons

(1) A party who wants to introduce the evidence of a witness who is the subject of an application, direction or order must –

(a) inform the witness of the court's decision as soon as reasonably practicable; and
(b) explain to the witness the arrangements that as a result will be made for him or her to give evidence.

(2) The court must announce, at a hearing in public before the witness gives evidence, the reasons for a decision –

(a) to give, make, vary or discharge a direction or order; or
(b) to refuse to do so.

29.5 Court's power to vary requirements under this Part

(1) The court may –

(a) shorten or extend (even after it has expired) a time limit under this Part; and
(b) allow an application or representations to be made in a different form to one set out in the Practice Direction, or to be made orally.

(2) A person who wants an extension of time must –

(a) apply when serving the application or representations for which it is needed; and
(b) explain the delay.

29.6 Custody of documents

Unless the court otherwise directs, the court officer may –

(a) keep a written application or representations; or
(b) arrange for the whole or any part to be kept by some other appropriate person, subject to any conditions that the court may impose.

29.7 Declaration by intermediary

(1) This rule applies where –

(a) a video recorded interview with a witness is conducted through an intermediary;
(b) the court directs the examination of a witness or defendant through an intermediary.

(2) An intermediary must make a declaration –

(a) before such an interview begins;
(b) before the examination begins (even if such an interview with the witness was conducted through the same intermediary).

(3) The declaration must be in these terms –

'I solemnly, sincerely and truly declare [*or* I swear by Almighty God] that I will well and faithfully communicate questions and answers and make true explanation of all matters and things as shall be required of me according to the best of my skill and understanding.'

Section 3

Special Measures Directions

29.8 Exercise of court's powers

The court may decide whether to give, vary or discharge a special measures direction –

(a) at a hearing, in public or in private, or without a hearing;
(b) in a party's absence, if that party –

  (i) applied for the direction, variation or discharge, or
  (ii) has had at least 14 days in which to make representations.

Note: The rules in Section 2 (general rules) also apply.

29.9 Special measures direction for a young witness

(1) This rule applies where, under section 21 or section 22 of the Youth Justice and Criminal Evidence Act 1999, the primary rule requires the court to give a direction for a special measure to assist a child witness or a qualifying witness –

(a) on an application, if one is made; or
(b) on the court's own initiative, in any other case.

(2) A party who wants to introduce the evidence of such a witness must as soon as reasonably practicable –

(a) notify the court that the witness is eligible for assistance;
(b) provide the court with any information that the court may need to assess the witness' views, if the witness does not want the primary rule to apply; and
(c) serve any video recorded evidence on –

(i) the court officer, and
(ii) each other party.

Note: Under sections 21 and 22 of the Youth Justice and Criminal Evidence Act 1999, a 'child witness' is one who is under 18, and a 'qualifying witness' is one who was a child witness when interviewed.

Under those sections, the 'primary rule' requires the court to give a direction –

(a) for the evidence of a child witness or of a qualifying witness to be admitted –

(i) by means of a video recording of an interview with the witness, in the place of examination-in-chief, and

(ii) after that, by live link; or

(b) if one or both of those measures is not taken, for the witness while giving evidence to be screened from seeing the defendant.

The primary rule always applies unless –

(a) the witness does not want it to apply, and the court is satisfied that to omit a measure usually required by that rule would not diminish the quality of the witness' evidence; or

(b) the court is satisfied that to direct one of the measures usually required by that rule would not be likely to maximise, so far as practicable, the quality of the witness' evidence.

29.10 Content of application for a special measures direction

An applicant for a special measures direction must –

(a) explain how the witness is eligible for assistance;
(b) explain why special measures would be likely to improve the quality of the witness' evidence;
(c) propose the measure or measures that in the applicant's opinion would be likely to maximise, so far as practicable, the quality of that evidence;
(d) report any views that the witness has expressed about –

(i) his or her eligibility for assistance,
(ii) the likelihood that special measures would improve the quality of his or her evidence, and
(iii) the measure or measures proposed by the applicant;

(e) in a case in which a child witness or a qualifying witness does not want the primary rule to apply, provide any information that the court may need to assess the witness' views;
(f) in a case in which the applicant proposes that the witness should give evidence by live link –

(i) identify someone to accompany the witness while the witness gives evidence,
(ii) name that person, if possible, and
(iii) explain why that person would be an appropriate companion for the witness, including the witness' own views;

(g) in a case in which the applicant proposes the admission of video recorded evidence, identify –

(i) the date and duration of the recording,
(ii) which part the applicant wants the court to admit as evidence, if the applicant does not want the court to admit all of it;

(h) attach any other material on which the applicant relies; and
(i) if the applicant wants a hearing, ask for one, and explain why it is needed.

Note: The Practice Direction sets out a form of application for use in connection with this rule.

29.11 Application to vary or discharge a special measures direction

(1) A party who wants the court to vary or discharge a special measures direction must –

- (a) apply in writing, as soon as reasonably practicable after becoming aware of the grounds for doing so; and
- (b) serve the application on –
  - (i) the court officer, and
  - (ii) each other party.

(2) The applicant must –

- (a) explain what material circumstances have changed since the direction was given (or last varied, if applicable);
- (b) explain why the direction should be varied or discharged; and
- (c) ask for a hearing, if the applicant wants one, and explain why it is needed.

Note: Under section 20 of the Youth Justice and Criminal Evidence Act 1999, the court can vary or discharge a special measures direction –

- (a) on application, if there has been a material change of circumstances; or
- (b) on the court's own initiative.

29.12 Application containing information withheld from another party

(1) This rule applies where –

- (a) an applicant serves an application for a special measures direction, or for its variation or discharge; and
- (b) the application includes information that the applicant thinks ought not be revealed to another party.

(2) The applicant must –

- (a) omit that information from the part of the application that is served on that other party;
- (b) mark the other part to show that, unless the court otherwise directs, it is only for the court; and
- (c) in that other part, explain why the applicant has withheld that information from that other party.

(3) Any hearing of an application to which this rule applies –

- (a) must be in private, unless the court otherwise directs; and
- (b) if the court so directs, may be, wholly or in part, in the absence of a party from whom information has been withheld.

(4) At any hearing of an application to which this rule applies –

- (a) the general rule is that the court must consider, in the following sequence –
  - (i) representations first by the applicant and then by each other party, in all the parties' presence, and then
  - (ii) further representations by the applicant, in the absence of a party from whom information has been withheld; but
- (b) the court may direct other arrangements for the hearing.

Note: See section 20 of the Youth Justice and Criminal Evidence Act 1999.

29.13 Representations in response

(1) This rule applies where a party wants to make representations about –

- (a) an application for a special measures direction;

(b) an application for the variation or discharge of such a direction; or
(c) a direction, variation or discharge that the court proposes on its own initiative.

(2) Such a party must –

(a) serve the representations on –

(i) the court officer, and
(ii) each other party;

(b) do so not more than 14 days after, as applicable –

(i) service of the application, or
(ii) notice of the direction, variation or discharge that the court proposes; and

(c) ask for a hearing, if that party wants one, and explain why it is needed.

(3) Where representations include information that the person making them thinks ought not be revealed to another party, that person must –

(a) omit that information from the representations served on that other party;
(b) mark the information to show that, unless the court otherwise directs, it is only for the court; and
(c) with that information include an explanation of why it has been withheld from that other party.

(4) Representations against a special measures direction must explain, as appropriate –

(a) why the witness is not eligible for assistance;
(b) if the witness is eligible for assistance, why –

(i) no special measure would be likely to improve the quality of the witness' evidence,
(ii) the proposed measure or measures would not be likely to maximise, so far as practicable, the quality of the witness' evidence, or
(iii) the proposed measure or measures might tend to inhibit the effective testing of that evidence;

(c) in a case in which the admission of video recorded evidence is proposed, why it would not be in the interests of justice for the recording, or part of it, to be admitted as evidence.

(5) Representations against the variation or discharge of a special measures direction must explain why it should not be varied or discharged.

Note: Under sections 21 and 22 of the Youth Justice and Criminal Evidence Act 1999, where the witness is a child witness or a qualifying witness the special measures that the court usually must direct must be treated as likely to maximise, so far as practicable, the quality of the witness' evidence, irrespective of representations to the contrary.

Section 4

Defendant's Evidence Directions

29.14 Exercise of court's powers

The court may decide whether to give, vary or discharge a defendant's evidence direction –

(a) at a hearing, in public or in private, or without a hearing;
(b) in a party's absence, if that party –

(i) applied for the direction, variation or discharge, or
(ii) has had at least 14 days in which to make representations.

Note: The rules in Section 2 (general rules) also apply.

29.15 Content of application for a defendant's evidence direction

An applicant for a defendant's evidence direction must –

(a) explain how the proposed direction meets the conditions prescribed by the Youth Justice and Criminal Evidence Act 1999;
(b) in a case in which the applicant proposes that the defendant give evidence by live link –

(i) identify a person to accompany the defendant while the defendant gives evidence, and
(ii) explain why that person is appropriate;

(c) ask for a hearing, if the applicant wants one, and explain why it is needed.

Note: See sections 33A and 33BA of the Youth Justice and Criminal Evidence Act 1999.

29.16 Application to vary or discharge a defendant's evidence direction

(1) A party who wants the court to vary or discharge a defendant's evidence direction must –

(a) apply in writing, as soon as reasonably practicable after becoming aware of the grounds for doing so; and
(b) serve the application on –

(i) the court officer, and
(ii) each other party.

(2) The applicant must –

(a) on an application to discharge a live link direction, explain why it is in the interests of justice to do so;
(b) on an application to discharge a direction for an intermediary, explain why it is no longer necessary in order to ensure that the defendant receives a fair trial;
(c) on an application to vary a direction for an intermediary, explain why it is necessary for the direction to be varied in order to ensure that the defendant receives a fair trial; and
(d) ask for a hearing, if the applicant wants one, and explain why it is needed.

29.17 Representations in response

(1) This rule applies where a party wants to make representations about –

(a) an application for a defendant's evidence direction;
(b) an application for the variation or discharge of such a direction; or
(c) a direction, variation or discharge that the court proposes on its own initiative.

(2) Such a party must –

(a) serve the representations on –

(i) the court officer, and
(ii) each other party;

(b) do so not more than 14 days after, as applicable –

(i) service of the application, or
(ii) notice of the direction, variation or discharge that the court proposes; and

(c) ask for a hearing, if that party wants one, and explain why it is needed.

(3) Representations against a direction, variation or discharge must explain why the conditions prescribed by the Youth Justice and Criminal Evidence Act 1999 are not met.

Section 5

Witness Anonymity Orders

29.18 Exercise of court's powers

(1) The court may decide whether to make, vary or discharge a witness anonymity order –

(a) at a hearing (which must be in private, unless the court otherwise directs), or without a hearing (unless any party asks for one);
(b) in the absence of a defendant.

(2) The court must not exercise its power to make, vary or discharge a witness anonymity order, or to refuse to do so –

(a) before or during the trial, unless each party has had an opportunity to make representations;
(b) on an appeal by the defendant to which applies Part 63 (appeal to the Crown Court) or Part 68 (appeal to the Court of Appeal about conviction or sentence), unless in each party's case –

(i) that party has had an opportunity to make representations, or
(ii) the appeal court is satisfied that it is not reasonably practicable to communicate with that party;

(c) after the trial and any such appeal are over, unless in the case of each party and the witness –

(i) each has had an opportunity to make representations, or
(ii) the court is satisfied that it is not reasonably practicable to communicate with that party or witness.

Note: The rules in Section 2 (general rules) also apply.

29.19 Content and conduct of application for a witness anonymity order

(1) An applicant for a witness anonymity order must –

(a) include in the application nothing that might reveal the witness' identity;
(b) describe the measures proposed by the applicant;
(c) explain how the proposed order meets the conditions prescribed by section 88 of the Coroners and Justice Act 2009;
(d) explain why no measures other than those proposed will suffice, such as –

(i) an admission of the facts that would be proved by the witness,
(ii) an order restricting public access to the trial,
(iii) reporting restrictions, in particular under section 46 of the Youth Justice and Criminal Evidence Act 1999 or under section 39 of the Children and Young Persons Act 1933,
(iv) a direction for a special measure under section 19 of the Youth Justice and Criminal Evidence Act 1999,
(v) introduction of the witness' written statement as hearsay evidence, under section 116 of the Criminal Justice Act 2003, or
(vi) arrangements for the protection of the witness;

(e) attach to the application –

(i) a witness statement setting out the proposed evidence, edited in such a way as not to reveal the witness' identity,
(ii) where the prosecutor is the applicant, any further prosecution evidence to be served, and any further prosecution material to be disclosed under the Criminal Procedure and Investigations Act 1996, similarly edited, and
(iii) any defence statement that has been served, or as much information as may be available to the applicant that gives particulars of the defence; and

(f) ask for a hearing, if the applicant wants one.

(2) At any hearing of the application, the applicant must –

(a) identify the witness to the court, unless at the prosecutor's request the court otherwise directs; and
(b) present to the court, unless it otherwise directs –
   (i) the unedited witness statement from which the edited version has been prepared,
   (ii) where the prosecutor is the applicant, the unedited version of any further prosecution evidence or material from which an edited version has been prepared, and
   (iii) such further material as the applicant relies on to establish that the proposed order meets the conditions prescribed by section 88 of the 2009 Act.

(3) At any such hearing –

(a) the general rule is that the court must consider, in the following sequence –
   (i) representations first by the applicant and then by each other party, in all the parties' presence, and then
   (ii) information withheld from a defendant, and further representations by the applicant, in the absence of any (or any other) defendant; but
(b) the court may direct other arrangements for the hearing.

(4) Before the witness gives evidence, the applicant must identify the witness to the court –

(a) if not already done;
(b) without revealing the witness' identity to any other party or person; and
(c) unless at the prosecutor's request the court otherwise directs.

29.20 Duty of court officer to notify the Director of Public Prosecutions

The court officer must notify the Director of Public Prosecutions of an application, unless the prosecutor is, or acts on behalf of, a public authority.

29.21 Application to vary or discharge a witness anonymity order

(1) A party who wants the court to vary or discharge a witness anonymity order, or a witness who wants the court to do so when the case is over, must –

(a) apply in writing, as soon as reasonably practicable after becoming aware of the grounds for doing so; and
(b) serve the application on –
   (i) the court officer, and
   (ii) each other party.

(2) The applicant must –

(a) explain what material circumstances have changed since the order was made (or last varied, if applicable);
(b) explain why the order should be varied or discharged, taking account of the conditions for making an order; and
(c) ask for a hearing, if the applicant wants one.

(3) Where an application includes information that the applicant thinks might reveal the witness' identity, the applicant must –

(a) omit that information from the application that is served on a defendant;
(b) mark the information to show that it is only for the court and the prosecutor (if the prosecutor is not the applicant); and
(c) with that information include an explanation of why it has been withheld.

(4) Where a party applies to vary or discharge a witness anonymity order after the trial and any appeal are over, the party who introduced the witness' evidence must serve the application on the witness.

Note: Under sections 91, 92 and 93 of the Coroners and Justice Act 2009, the court can vary or discharge a witness anonymity order –

(a) on an application, if there has been a material change of circumstances since it was made or previously varied; or

(b) on the court's own initiative, unless the trial and any appeal are over.

29.22 Representations in response

(1) This rule applies where a party or, where the case is over, a witness, wants to make representations about –

(a) an application for a witness anonymity order;
(b) an application for the variation or discharge of such an order; or
(c) a variation or discharge that the court proposes on its own initiative.

(2) Such a party or witness must –

(a) serve the representations on –

(i) the court officer, and
(ii) each other party;

(b) do so not more than 14 days after, as applicable –

(i) service of the application, or
(ii) notice of the variation or discharge that the court proposes; and

(c) ask for a hearing, if that party or witness wants one.

(3) Where representations include information that the person making them thinks might reveal the witness' identity, that person must –

(a) omit that information from the representations served on a defendant;
(b) mark the information to show that it is only for the court (and for the prosecutor, if relevant); and
(c) with that information include an explanation of why it has been withheld.

(4) Representations against a witness anonymity order must explain why the conditions for making the order are not met.

(5) Representations against the variation or discharge of such an order must explain why it would not be appropriate to vary or discharge it, taking account of the conditions for making an order.

(6) A prosecutor's representations in response to an application by a defendant must include all information available to the prosecutor that is relevant to the conditions and considerations specified by sections 88 and 89 of the Coroners and Justice Act 2009.

Section 6

Live Link Directions

29.23 Exercise of court's powers

The court may decide whether to give or discharge a live link direction –

(a) at a hearing, in public or in private, or without a hearing;
(b) in a party's absence, if that party –

(i) applied for the direction or discharge, or
(ii) has had at least 14 days in which to make representations.

Note: The rules in Section 2 (general rules) also apply. The rules in this Section do not apply to an application for a special measures direction allowing a witness to give evidence by live link: as to which, see the rules in Section 3 (special measures directions).

29.24 Content of application for a live link direction

An applicant for a live link direction must –

(a) unless the court otherwise directs, identify the place from which the witness will give evidence;
(b) if that place is in the United Kingdom, explain why it would be in the interests of the efficient or effective administration of justice for the witness to give evidence by live link;
(c) if the applicant wants the witness to be accompanied by another person while giving evidence –

  (i) name that person, if possible, and
  (ii) explain why it is appropriate for the witness to be accompanied;

(d) ask for a hearing, if the applicant wants one, and explain why it is needed.

Note: See section 32 of the Criminal Justice Act 1988 and section 51 of the Criminal Justice Act 2003.

The Practice Direction sets out a form of application for use in connection with this rule.

29.25 Application to discharge a live link direction

(1) A party who wants the court to discharge a live link direction must –

(a) apply in writing, as soon as reasonably practicable after becoming aware of the grounds for doing so; and
(b) serve the application on –

  (i) the court officer, and
  (ii) each other party.

(2) The applicant must –

(a) explain what material circumstances have changed since the direction was given;
(b) explain why it is in the interests of justice to discharge the direction; and
(c) ask for a hearing, if the applicant wants one, and explain why it is needed.

Note: See section 32(4) of the Criminal Justice Act 1988 and section 52(3) of the Criminal Justice Act 2003.

29.26 Representations in response

(1) This rule applies where a party wants to make representations about –

(a) an application for a live link direction;
(b) an application for the discharge of such a direction; or
(c) a direction or discharge that the court proposes on its own initiative.

(2) Such a party must –

(a) serve the representations on –

  (i) the court officer, and
  (ii) each other party;

(b) do so not more than 14 days after, as applicable –

  (i) service of the application, or
  (ii) notice of the direction or discharge that the court proposes; and

(c) ask for a hearing, if that party wants one, and explain why it is needed.

(3) Representations against a direction or discharge must explain, as applicable, why the conditions prescribed by the Criminal Justice Act 1988 or the Criminal Justice Act 2003 are not met.

SUMMARY OF ELIGIBILITY FOR MEASURES TO WHICH THIS PART APPLIES

Special measures direction

Under section 16 of the Youth Justice and Criminal Evidence Act 1999, a witness is eligible for the assistance of a special measures direction given under section 19 of that Act if –

- *(a)* *the witness is under 18; or*
- *(b)* *the witness has –*
  - *(i)* *a mental disorder, or a significant impairment of intelligence and social functioning, or*
  - *(ii)* *a physical disability or disorder*

  and the court considers that the completeness, coherence and accuracy (the 'quality') of evidence given by the witness is likely to be diminished by reason of those circumstances.

Under section 17 of the 1999 Act, a witness is eligible for such assistance if –

- *(a)* *the court is satisfied that the quality of evidence given by the witness is likely to be diminished because of his or her fear or distress in connection with giving evidence, taking account particularly of –*
  - *(i)* *the circumstances of the offence,*
  - *(ii)* *the witness' age, social and cultural background, ethnic origins, domestic and employment circumstances, religious beliefs or political opinions,*
  - *(iii)* *any behaviour towards the witness on the part of the defendant, the defendant's family or associates, or any other potential defendant or witness, and*
  - *(iv)* *the witness' own views;*
- *(b)* *the witness is the complainant in respect of a sexual offence, and has not declined such assistance; or*
- *(c)* *the offence is one of a list of offences involving weapons, and the witness has not declined such assistance.*

Section 28 of the 1999 Act (video recorded cross-examination or re-examination) is not yet in force. With that exception, all the special measures listed in rule 29.1 potentially are available where the witness is eligible for assistance under section 16 of the Act. Those numbered (i) to (v) are available where the witness is eligible for assistance under section 17.

As a general rule, but with exceptions, the court must give a special measures direction –

- *(a)* *under section 21 or 22 of the 1999 Act, where the witness –*
  - *(i)* *is under 18, or*
  - *(ii)* *was under that age when interviewed*

  whether or not an application for a direction is made;
- *(b)* *under section 22A of the 1999 Act, where an application is made in the Crown Court for the evidence of a witness who is the complainant of a sexual offence to be admitted by means of a video recording of an interview with the witness in the place of examination-in-chief.*

Defendant's evidence direction

Under section 33A of the 1999 Act, the court can allow a defendant to give evidence by live link, or (when the Coroners and Justice Act 2009 comes into force) under section 33BA can allow a defendant to give evidence through an intermediary, if –

- *(a)* *the defendant –*
  - *(i)* *is under 18, and the defendant's ability to participate effectively as a witness giving oral evidence is compromised by his or her level of intellectual ability or social functioning; or*
  - *(ii)* *suffers from a mental disorder or some other significant impairment of intelligence and social functioning and cannot participate effectively as a witness giving oral evidence for that reason;*

(b) *the use of a live link –*

(i) *would enable the defendant to participate more effectively, and*
(ii) *is in the interests of justice;*

(c) *the examination of the defendant through an intermediary is necessary to ensure that the defendant receives a fair trial.*

Witness anonymity order

Under section 86 of the Coroners and Justice Act 2009, a witness anonymity order is an order that specifies measures to be taken to ensure that the identity of a witness is not disclosed, such as withholding the witness' name from materials disclosed to a party to the proceedings, the use of a pseudonym, the screening of the witness from view, the modulation of the witness' voice, and the prohibition of questions that might reveal his or her identity. Before making such an order, the court must –

(a) *be satisfied that three conditions prescribed by the Act are met (section 88 of the 2009 Act); and*
(b) *have regard to considerations specified by the Act (section 89 of the 2009 Act).*

Live link direction

Under section 32 of the Criminal Justice Act 1988, the court can allow a witness who is outside the United Kingdom to give evidence by live link –

(a) *in proceedings in a youth court, or on appeal from such proceedings; or*
(b) *at a trial in the Crown Court, or on appeal from such a trial.*

Under section 51 of the Criminal Justice Act 2003, on an application or on its own initiative, the court can allow a witness who is in the United Kingdom, but outside the building in which the proceedings are held, to give evidence by live link. The court must be satisfied that that is in the interests of the efficient or effective administration of justice.

If a witness is eligible for the assistance of a special measures direction (as to which, see the note above), the court can allow the witness to give evidence by live link under sections 19 and 24 of the 1999 Act. Section 3 of this Part contains relevant rules.

Criminal Practice Directions Division V

****

Part 29 Measures to assist a witness or defendant to give evidence

CPD V Evidence 29A: Measures to assist a witness or defendant to give evidence

29A.1 For special measures applications, the procedures at Part 29 should be followed. However, assisting a vulnerable witness to give evidence is not merely a matter of ordering the appropriate measure. Further directions about vulnerable people in the courts, ground rules hearings and intermediaries are given in the Practice Direction accompanying Part 3.

29A.2 Special measures need not be considered or ordered in isolation. The needs of the individual witness should be ascertained, and a combination of special measures may be appropriate. For example, if a witness who is to give evidence by live link wishes, screens can be used to shield the live link screen from the defendant and the public, as would occur if screens were being used for a witness giving evidence in the court room.

CPD V Evidence 29B: Witnesses giving evidence by live link

29B.1 A special measures direction for the witness to give evidence by live link may also provide for a specified person to accompany the witness (Rule 29.10(f)). In determining who this should be, the court must have regard to the wishes of the witness. The presence of a supporter is designed to provide emotional support to the witness, helping reduce the witness's anxiety and stress and contributing to the ability to give best evidence. It is preferable for the direction to be made well before the trial begins and to ensure that the designated person is available on the day of the witness's testimony so as to provide certainty for the witness.

29B.2 An increased degree of flexibility is appropriate as to who can act as supporter. This can be anyone known to and trusted by the witness who is not a party to the proceedings and has no detailed knowledge of the evidence in the case. The supporter may be a member of the Witness Service but need not be an usher or court official. Someone else may be appropriate.

29B.3 The usher should continue to be available both to assist the witness and the witness supporter, and to ensure that the court's requirements are properly complied with in the live link room.

29B.4 In order to be able to express an informed view about special measures, the witness is entitled to practise speaking using the live link (and to see screens in place). Simply being shown the room and equipment is inadequate for this purpose.

29B.5 If, with the agreement of the court, the witness has chosen not to give evidence by live link but to do so in the court room, it may still be appropriate for a witness supporter to be selected in the same way, and for the supporter to sit alongside the witness while the witness is giving evidence.

CPD V Evidence 29C: Visually recorded interviews: memory refreshing and watching at a different time from the jury

29C.1 Witnesses are entitled to refresh their memory from their statement or visually recorded interview. The court should enquire at the PCMH or other case management hearing about arrangements for memory refreshing. The witness's first viewing of the visually recorded interview can be distressing or distracting. It should not be seen for the first time immediately before giving evidence. Depending upon the age and vulnerability of the witness several competing issues have to be considered and it may be that the assistance of the intermediary is needed to establish exactly how memory refreshing should be managed.

29C.2 If the interview is ruled inadmissible, the court must decide what constitutes an acceptable alternative method of memory refreshing.

29C.3 Decisions about how, when and where refreshing should take place should be court-led and made on a case-by-case basis in respect of each witness. General principles to be addressed include:

i. the venue for viewing. The delicate balance between combining the court familiarisation visit and watching the DVD, and having them on two separate occasions, needs to be considered in respect of each witness as combining the two may lead to 'information overload'. Refreshing need not necessarily take place within the court building but may be done, for example, at the police ABE suite.

ii. requiring that any viewing is monitored by a person (usually the officer in the case) who will report to the court about anything said by the witness.

iii. whether it is necessary for the witness to see the DVD more than once for the purpose of refreshing. The court will need to ask the advice of the intermediary, if any, with respect to this. iv. arrangements, if the witness will not watch the DVD at the same time as the trial bench or judge and jury, for the witness to watch it before attending to be cross examined, (depending upon their ability to retain information this may be the day before).

29C.4 There is no legal requirement that the witness should watch the interview at the same time as the trial bench or jury. Increasingly, this is arranged to occur at a different time, with the advantages that breaks can be taken as needed without disrupting the trial, and cross-examination starts while the witness is fresh. An intermediary may be present to facilitate communication but should not act as the independent person designated to take a note and report to the court if anything is said. Where the viewing takes place at a different time from that of the jury, the witness is sworn just before cross-examination, asked if he or she has watched the interview and if its contents are 'true' (or other words tailored to the witness's understanding).

CPD V Evidence 29D: Witness anonymity orders

29D.1 This direction supplements Part 29 of the Rules, which governs the procedure to be followed on an application for a witness anonymity order. The court's power to make such an order is conferred by the Coroners and Justice Act 2009 (in this section, 'the Act'); section 87 of the Act provides specific relevant powers and obligations.

29D.2 As the Court of Appeal stated in *R v Mayers and Others* [2008] EWCA Crim 2989, [2009] 1 W.L.R. 1915, [2009] 1 Cr. App. R. 30 and emphasised again in *R v Donovan and Kafunda* [2012] EWCA Crim 2749, unreported, 'a witness anonymity order is to be regarded as a special measure of the last practicable resort': Lord Chief Justice, Lord Judge. In making such an application, the prosecution's obligations of disclosure 'go much further than the ordinary duties of disclosure' (*R v Mayers*); reference should be made to the Judicial Protocol on Disclosure, see the Practice Direction accompanying Part 22.

Case management

29D.3 Where such an application is proposed, with the parties' active assistance the court should set a realistic timetable, in accordance with the duties imposed by Rules 3.2 and 3.3. Where possible, the trial judge should determine the application, and any hearing should be attended by the parties' trial advocates. Service of evidence and disclosure of prosecution material pending an application.

29D.4 Where the prosecutor proposes an application for a witness anonymity order, it is not necessary for that application to have been determined before the proposed evidence is served. In most cases, an early indication of what that evidence will be if an order is made will be consistent with a party's duties under Rules 1.2 and 3.3. The prosecutor should serve with the other prosecution evidence a witness statement setting out the proposed evidence, redacted in such a way as to prevent disclosure of the witness' identity, as permitted by section 87(4) of the Act. Likewise the prosecutor should serve with other prosecution material disclosed under the Criminal Procedure and Investigations Act 1996 any such material appertaining to the witness, similarly redacted.

The application

29D.5 An application for a witness anonymity order should be made as early as possible and within the period for which Rule 29.3 provides. The application, and any hearing of it, must comply with the requirements of that rule and with those of Rule 29.19. In accordance with Rules 1.2 and 3.3, the applicant must provide the court with all available information relevant to the considerations to which the Act requires a court to have regard.

Response to the application

29D.6 A party upon whom an application for a witness anonymity order is served must serve a response in accordance with Rule 29.22. That period may be extended or shortened in the court's discretion: Rule 29.5.

29D.7 To avoid the risk of injustice, a respondent, whether the Prosecution or a defendant, must actively assist the court. If not already done, a respondent defendant should serve a defence statement under section 5 or 6 of the Criminal Procedure and Investigations Act 1996, so that the court is fully informed of what is in issue. When a defendant makes an application for a witness anonymity order the prosecutor should consider the continuing duty to disclose material under section 7A of the Criminal Procedure and Investigations Act 1996; therefore a prosecutor's response should include confirmation that that duty has been considered. Great care should be taken to ensure that nothing disclosed contains anything that might reveal the witness' identity. A respondent prosecutor should provide the court with all available information relevant to the considerations to which the Act requires a court to have regard, whether or not that information falls to be disclosed under the 1996 Act.

Determination of the application

29D.8 All parties must have an opportunity to make oral representations to the court on an application for a witness anonymity order: section 87(6) of the Act. However, a hearing may not be needed if none is sought: Rule 29.18(1)(a). Where, for example, the witness is an investigator who is recognisable by the defendant but known only by an assumed name, and there is no likelihood that the witness' credibility will be in issue, then the court may indicate a provisional decision and invite representations within a defined period, usually 14 days, including representations about whether there should be a hearing. In such a case, where the parties do not object the court may make an order without a hearing. Or where the court provisionally considers an application to be misconceived, an applicant may choose to withdraw it without requiring a hearing. Where the court directs a hearing of the application then it should allow adequate time for service of the representations in response.

29D.9 The hearing of an application for a witness anonymity order usually should be in private: Rule 29.18(1)(a). The court has power to hear a party in the absence of a defendant and that defendant's representatives: section 87(7) of the Act and Rule 29.18(1)(b). In the Crown Court, a recording of the proceedings will be made, in accordance with Rule 5.5. The Crown Court officer must treat such a recording in the same way as the recording of an application for a public interest ruling. It must be kept in secure conditions, and the arrangements made by the Crown Court officer for any transcription must impose restrictions that correspond with those under rule 5.5(2).

29D.10 Where confidential supporting information is presented to the court before the last stage of the hearing, the court may prefer not to read that information until that last stage.

29D.11 The court may adjourn the hearing at any stage, and should do so if its duty under rule 3.2 so requires.

29D.12 On a prosecutor's application, the court is likely to be assisted by the attendance of a senior investigator or other person of comparable authority who is familiar with the case.

29D.13 During the last stage of the hearing it is essential that the court test thoroughly the information supplied in confidence in order to satisfy itself that the conditions prescribed by the Act are met. At that stage, if the court concludes that this is the only way in which it can satisfy itself as to a relevant condition or consideration, exceptionally it may invite the applicant to present the proposed witness to be questioned by the court. Any such questioning should be carried out at such a time, and the witness brought to the court in such a way, as to prevent disclosure of his or her identity.

29D.14 The court may ask the Attorney General to appoint special counsel to assist. However, it must be kept in mind that, 'Such an appointment will always be exceptional, never automatic; a course of last and never first resort. It should not be ordered unless and until the trial judge is satisfied that no other course will adequately meet the overriding requirement of fairness to the defendant': *R v H* [2004] UKHL 3, [2004] 2 A.C. 134 (at paragraph 22), [2004] 2 Cr. App. R. 10. Whether to accede to such a request is a matter for the Attorney General, and adequate time should be allowed for the consideration of such a request.

29D.15 The Court of Appeal in *R v Mayers* 'emphasise[d] that all three conditions, A, B and C, must be met before the jurisdiction to make a witness anonymity order arises. Each is mandatory. Each is distinct.' The Court also noted that if there is more than one anonymous witness in a case any link, and the nature of any link, between the witnesses should be investigated: 'questions of possible improper collusion between them, or cross-contamination of one another, should be addressed.'

29D.16 Following a hearing the court should announce its decision on an application for a witness anonymity order in the parties' presence and in public: rule 29.4(2). The court should give such reasons as it is possible to give without revealing the witness' identity. In the Crown Court, the court will be conscious that reasons given in public may be reported and reach the jury. Consequently, the court should ensure that nothing in its decision or its reasons could undermine any warning it may give jurors under section 90(2) of the Act. A record of the reasons must be kept. In the Crown Court, the announcement of those reasons will be recorded.

Order

29D.17 Where the court makes a witness anonymity order, it is essential that the measures to be taken are clearly specified in a written record of that order approved by the court and issued on its behalf. An order made in a magistrates' court must be recorded in the court register, in accordance with rule 5.4.

29D.18 Self-evidently, the written record of the order must not disclose the identity of the witness to whom it applies. However, it is essential that there be maintained some means of establishing a clear correlation between witness and order, and especially where in the same proceedings witness anonymity orders are made in respect of more than one witness, specifying different measures in respect of each. Careful preservation of the application for the order, including the confidential part, ordinarily will suffice for this purpose.

Discharge or variation of the order

29D.19 Section 91 of the Act allows the court to discharge or vary a witness anonymity order: on application, if there has been a material change of circumstances since the order was made or since any previous variation of it; or on its own initiative. Rule 29.21 allows the parties to apply for the variation of a pre-trial direction where circumstances have changed.

29D.20 The court should keep under review the question of whether the conditions for making an order are met. In addition, consistently with the parties' duties under rules 1.2 and 3.3, it is incumbent on each, and in particular on the applicant for the order, to keep the need for it under review.

29D.21 Where the court considers the discharge or variation of an order, the procedure that it adopts should be appropriate to the circumstances. As a general rule, that procedure should approximate to the procedure for determining an application for an order. The court may need to hear further representations by the applicant for the order in the absence of a respondent defendant and that defendant's representatives.

Retention of confidential material

29D.22 If retained by the court, confidential material must be stored in secure conditions by the court officer. Alternatively, subject to such directions as the court may give, such material may be committed to the safe keeping of the applicant or any other appropriate person in exercise of the powers conferred by rule 29.6. If the material is released to any such person, the court should ensure that it will be available to the court at trial.

APPLICATION FOR A SPECIAL MEASURES DIRECTION

(Criminal Procedure Rules, rule 29.3 and 29.10)

Case details

Name of defendant:

Court:

Case reference number:

Charge(s):

How to use this form. This form includes notes to help you complete it. They explain when a witness may be eligible for the assistance of special measures.

1. Complete the box above and give the details required in the boxes below. You must complete Parts A and B in all cases, and Parts C to G as appropriate. If you use an electronic version of this form, the boxes will expand. If you use a paper version and need more space, you may attach extra sheets.

2. Sign and date the completed form.

3. Send a copy of the completed form to:

(a) the court, and

(b) each other party to the case.[1]

Notes:

1. You must send this form so as to reach the recipients within the time prescribed by Criminal Procedure Rule 29.3. The court may extend that time limit, **but if you are late you must explain why.**

2. A party who wants to make representations about this application must serve those representations under Criminal Procedure Rule 29.13 **not more than 14 days after service of this application.**

PART A: information about this application

A1. Do you want a hearing of this application ?

No ☐ **Yes** ☐ If yes, explain why.

A2. Is this application late ?

No ☐ **Yes** ☐ If yes, explain why.

A3. Have you applied for a special measures direction for this witness in this case before ?

No ☐ **Yes** ☐ If yes, give details and explain what has changed since then.

[1] In some circumstances, an applicant may omit information from the copy of this application that is served on another party: see Criminal Procedure Rule 29.12.

PART B: information about the witness

B1. Witness' details

Name of witness:

Date of birth:

B2. Explain how the witness is eligible for assistance.[2] Tick the category. If the witness is eligible because of **disability**, or **fear or distress**, give details and explain why the quality of the witness' evidence is likely to be diminished because of that.

- Youth ☐
- Disability ☐
- Fear or distress ☐
- Sexual offence ☐
- Weapons offence ☐

B3. Explain why special measures would be likely to improve the quality of the witness' evidence.

B4. Which measure(s) would be likely to maximise so far as practicable the quality of the witness' evidence ? Tick what you propose.

Screening witness from defendant	☐	
Evidence by live link	☐	complete Part C
Evidence in private	☐	complete Part D
Removal of wigs and gowns	☐	
Video recorded interview as evidence in chief	☐	complete Part E
Intermediary	☐	complete Part F
Aids to communication	☐	complete Part G

B5. What has been done to help the witness express an informed opinion about special measures ? Care must be taken to explain to the witness (a) what is meant by special measures, (b) what measure(s) may be available, and (c) what they would involve for the witness.[3]

[2] See the notes for guidance at the end of this form.

[3] If the witness does not want a special measure, he or she should be asked to explain why. The witness should also be told that if he or she changes his or her mind as the trial approaches, a further application to the court can be made.

B6. What views has the witness expressed about:

(a) his or her eligibility ?

(b) whether special measures would be likely to improve the quality of his or her evidence ?

(c) the measure(s) that you propose ?

The views, concerns and requests expressed by the witness, or on his or her behalf, must be set out in detail.

PART C: evidence by live link[4]

C1. Do you want the witness to give evidence:

using the court's own live link ? ☐ or

from somewhere else ? ☐

Tick which you propose. If you want the witness to give evidence by live link from somewhere else, answer question C2.

C2. Explain why you want the witness to give evidence from somewhere else. Give the address from which you propose the witness should give evidence, unless you want the court to direct that the address need not be revealed.

C3. Who do you propose should accompany the witness while he or she gives evidence ? Give that person's name, if known, and relationship to the witness (if any).

C4. Why would that person be an appropriate companion for the witness ? Include the witness' own views.

[4] See the notes for guidance at the end of this form.

PART D: evidence in private[5]

Explain on what grounds you want the witness to give evidence in private.

PART E: video recorded interview as evidence in chief[6]

E1. When was the interview ? .... (date)

E2. Was the interview conducted through an intermediary ?[7]

No ☐ **Yes** ☐ If yes, complete Part F as well.

E3. Was any aid to communication used in conducting the interview ?

No ☐ **Yes** ☐ If yes, give details.

E4. How long is the full version of the recording ? .... (hours / minutes)

E5. Has an edited version been prepared for use in evidence ?

No ☐ **Yes** ☐

E6. When did you serve[8]**:**

(a) the full version ? .... (date)

(b) the edited version (if any) ? .... (date)

E7. Do you want the court's permission for the witness to give evidence in chief otherwise than by means of the recording ?

No ☐ **Yes** ☐ If yes, explain why.

---

[5] See the notes for guidance at the end of this form.

[6] See the notes for guidance at the end of this form. In some cases, the court must give a direction for this measure. By completing this part the applicant indicates that the witness will be available to be cross-examined at trial.

[7] The court can give retrospective approval for the use of an intermediary in a video recorded interview. See Part F and the notes for guidance at the end of this form.

[8] A defendant need not serve a recording of defence evidence on the prosecution until the close of the prosecution case at trial.

PART F: intermediary[9]

F1. Describe the witness' communication needs, and the proposed arrangements for questioning the witness. Attach any relevant report, including an intermediary's assessment if available. 'Ground rules' for questioning must be discussed between the court, the advocates and the intermediary before the witness gives evidence, to establish (a) how questions should be put to help the witness understand them, and (b) how the proposed intermediary will alert the court if the witness has not understood, or needs a break.

F2. Is the proposed intermediary registered with the Ministry of Justice Intermediaries Registration Board ?

No ☐ **Yes** ☐

F3. Give the proposed intermediary's (a) name and (b) (if relevant) occupation, skills and professional qualifications.

F4. Is the intermediary known, or related, to the witness ?

No ☐ **Yes** ☐ If yes, give details.

F5. Has the intermediary been used in any other part of the investigation or pre-trial preparation ?

No ☐ **Yes** ☐ If yes, give details.

F6. Where a video recorded interview was conducted through an intermediary:

(a) was that intermediary the person named above ? Yes ☐ **No** ☐

If no, attach an additional Part F in respect of that intermediary, giving the details required by questions F2, F3, F4 and F5.

(b) did that intermediary make a declaration ?[10] **Yes** ☐**No** ☐

[9] See the notes for guidance at the end of this form.

[10] The declaration required by Criminal Procedure Rule 29.7.

PART G: aids to communication

G1. What device is proposed as a communication aid ?

G2. Might the use of this device affect the conduct of the trial ?

No ☐ **Yes** ☐ If yes, give details.

PART H: supporting material

Have you included with this application any other material ?

No ☐ **Yes** ☐ If yes, list it here.

Signed: .... **[prosecutor]**
[defendant / defendant's solicitor]

Date: ....

PART 50

CIVIL BEHAVIOUR ORDERS AFTER VERDICT OR FINDING

When this Part applies

50.1. (1) This Part applies in magistrates' courts and in the Crown Court where the court could decide to make, vary or revoke a civil order –

(a) under a power that the court can exercise after reaching a verdict or making a finding, and
(b) that requires someone to do, or not do, something.

(2) A reference to a 'behaviour order' in this Part is a reference to any such order.

(3) A reference to 'hearsay evidence' in this Part is a reference to evidence consisting of hearsay within the meaning of section 1(2) of the Civil Evidence Act 1995(a).

Note. In the circumstances set out in the Acts listed, the court can make a behaviour order:

(a) on conviction, under –

(i) section 14A of the Football Spectators Act 1989 (football banning orders),
(ii) section 5 of the Protection from Harassment Act 1997 (restraining orders),
(iii) sections 1C and 1D of the Crime and Disorder Act 1998 (anti-social behaviour orders and interim anti-social behaviour orders),
(iv) sections 8 and 9 of the Crime and Disorder Act 1998 (parenting orders),
(v) section 103A of the Sexual Offences Act 2003 (sexual harm prevention orders),
(vi) section 104 of the Sexual Offences Act 2003 (sexual offences prevention orders),
(vii) section 19 of the Serious Crime Act 2007 (serious crime prevention orders),
(viii) section 6 of the Violent Crime Reduction Act 2006 (drinking banning orders),
(ix) section 22 of the Anti-social Behaviour, Crime and Policing Act 2014 (criminal behaviour orders);

(b) on acquittal, under section 5A of the Protection from Harassment Act 1997

(restraining orders on acquittal); and

(c) on the making of a finding of (i) not guilty by reason of insanity, or (ii) disability, under section 104 of the Sexual Offences Act 2003 (sexual offences prevention orders).

Section 1(2) of the Civil Evidence Act 1995 defines hearsay as meaning "a statement made otherwise than by a person while giving oral evidence in the proceedings which is tendered as evidence of the matters stated". Section 13 of that Act defines a statement as meaning "any representation of fact or opinion, however made".

Behaviour orders: general rules

50.2. (1) The court must not make a behaviour order unless the person to whom it is directed has had an opportunity –

(a) to consider –

(i) what order is proposed and why, and
(ii) the evidence in support; and

(b) to make representations at a hearing (whether or not that person in fact attends).

(2) That restriction does not apply to making an interim behaviour order, but such an order has no effect unless the person to whom it is directed –

(a) is present when it is made; or
(b) is handed a document recording the order not more than 7 days after it is made.

(3) Where the court decides not to make, where it could –

(a) a football banning order;

(b) a parenting order, after a person under 16 is convicted of an offence; or
(c) a drinking banning order,

the court must announce, at a hearing in public, the reasons for its decision.

Note: The Acts listed in the note to rule 50.1 impose requirements specific to each different type of behaviour order. Not all allow the court to make an interim behaviour order.

See section 14A(3) of the Football Spectators Act 1989(**g**); sections 8A(4) and 9(1) of the Crime and Disorder Act 1998(**h**); and section 6(4) of the Violent Crime Reduction Act 2006(**a**).

Application for behaviour order and notice of terms of proposed order: special rules

50.3. (1) This rule applies where –

(a) a prosecutor wants the court to make –

(i) an anti-social behaviour order,
(ii) a serious crime prevention order, or
(iii) a criminal behaviour order; or

(b) a prosecutor proposes, on the prosecutor's initiative or at the court's request –

(i) a sexual offences prevention order, or
(ii) a sexual harm prevention order if the defendant is convicted.

(2) Where paragraph (1)(a) applies, the prosecutor must serve a notice of intention to apply for such an order on –

(a) the court officer;
(b) the defendant against whom the prosecutor wants the court to make the order; and
(c) any person on whom the order would be likely to have a significant adverse effect, as soon as practicable (without waiting for the verdict).

(3) A notice under paragraph (2) must –

(a) summarise the relevant facts;
(b) identify the evidence on which the prosecutor relies in support;
(c) attach any written statement that the prosecutor has not already served; and
(d) specify the order that the prosecutor wants the court to make. (4) A defendant served with a notice under paragraph (2) must –
(a) serve written notice of any evidence on which the defendant relies on –

(i) the court officer, and
(ii) the prosecutor,

as soon as practicable (without waiting for the verdict); and
(b) in the notice, identify that evidence and attach any written statement that has not already been served.

(5) Where paragraph (1)(b) applies, the prosecutor must –

(a) serve a draft order on the court officer and on the defendant not less than 2 business days before the hearing at which the order may be made;
(b) in a case in which a sexual offences prevention order is proposed, in the draft order specify those prohibitions which the prosecutor proposes as necessary for the purpose of protecting the public or any particular members of the public from serious sexual harm from the defendant;
(c) in a case in which a sexual harm prevention order is proposed, in the draft order specify those prohibitions which the prosecutor proposes as necessary for the purpose of –

(i) protecting the public or any particular members of the public from sexual harm from the defendant, or
(ii) protecting children or vulnerable adults generally, or any particular children or vulnerable adults, from sexual harm from the defendant outside the United Kingdom.

(6) This rule does not apply to an application for an interim anti-social behaviour order.

(7) Where the prosecutor wants the court to make an anti-social behaviour order or a criminal behaviour order, the rules about special measures directions in Part 29 (Measures to assist a witness or defendant to give evidence) apply, but –

(a) the prosecutor must apply when serving a notice under paragraph (2); and
(b) the time limits in rule 29.3(a) do not apply.

Note: The Practice Direction sets out a form of notice for use in connection with this rule.

Under section 8 of the Serious Crime Act 2007 a serious crime prevention order may be made only on an application by the Director of Public Prosecutions or the Director of the Serious Fraud Office. See also paragraphs 2, 7 and 13 of Schedule 2 to the 2007 Act.

Section 107 of the Sexual Offences Act 2003(**a**) describes the content and effect of a sexual offences prevention order.

Under section 1I of the Crime and Disorder Act 1998(**b**), on an application for an anti-social behaviour order the court may give a special measures direction under the Youth Justice and Criminal Evidence Act 1999. Under section 31 of the Anti-social Behaviour, Crime and Policing Act 2014(**c**) the court may give such a direction on an application for a criminal behaviour order.

If a party relies on hearsay evidence, see also rules 50.6, 50.7, and 50.8.

Evidence to assist the court: special rules

50.4. (1) This rule applies where the court can make on its own initiative –

(a) a football banning order;
(b) a restraining order;
(c) an anti-social behaviour order; or
(d) a drinking banning order.

(2) A party who wants the court to take account of evidence not already introduced must –

(a) serve notice in writing on –

(i) the court officer, and
(ii) every other party,

as soon as practicable (without waiting for the verdict); and
(b) in the notice, identify that evidence; and
(c) attach any written statement containing such evidence.

Note: If a party relies on hearsay evidence, see also rules 50.6, 50.7, and 50.8.

Application to vary or revoke behaviour order

50.5. (1) The court may vary or revoke a behaviour order if –

(a) the legislation under which it is made allows the court to do so; and
(b) one of the following applies –

(i) the prosecutor,
(ii) the person to whom the order is directed, (iii) any other person mentioned in the order,
(iv) the relevant authority or responsible officer,
(v) the relevant Chief Officer of Police, or
(vi) the Director of Public Prosecutions.

(2) A person applying under this rule must –

(a) apply in writing as soon as practicable after becoming aware of the grounds for doing so, explaining –

(i) what material circumstances have changed since the order was made, and
(ii) why the order should be varied or revoked as a result; and

(b) serve the application on –

(i) the court officer,

(ii) as appropriate, the prosecutor or defendant, and
(iii) any other person listed in paragraph (1)(b), if the court so directs.

(3) A party who wants the court to take account of any particular evidence before making its decision must, as soon as practicable –

(a) serve notice in writing on –

(i) the court officer,
(ii) as appropriate, the prosecutor or defendant, and
(iii) any other person listed in paragraph (1)(b) on whom the court directed the application to be served; and

(b) in that notice identify the evidence and attach any written statement that has not already been served.

(4) The court may decide an application under this rule with or without a hearing.

(5) But the court must not –

(a) dismiss an application under this rule unless the applicant has had an opportunity to make representations at a hearing (whether or not the applicant in fact attends); or
(b) allow an application under this rule unless everyone required to be served, by this rule or by the court, has had at least 14 days in which to make representations, including representations about whether there should be a hearing.

(6) The court officer must –

(a) serve the application on any person, if the court so directs; and
(b) give notice of any hearing to –

(i) the applicant, and
(ii) any person required to be served, by this rule or by the court.

Note: The legislation that gives the court power to make a behaviour order may limit the circumstances in which it may be varied or revoked and may require a hearing.

If a party relies on hearsay evidence, see also rules 50.6, 50.7 and 50.8.

Notice of hearsay evidence

50.6. (1) A party who wants to introduce hearsay evidence must –

(a) serve a notice in writing on –

(i) the court officer, and
(ii) every other party directly affected; and

(b) in that notice –

(i) explain that it is a notice of hearsay evidence, (ii) identify that evidence,
(iii) identify the person who made the statement which is hearsay, or explain why if that person is not identified, and
(iv) explain why that person will not be called to give oral evidence.

(2) A party may serve one notice under this rule in respect of more than one notice and more than one witness.

Note: For the time within which to serve a notice of hearsay evidence, see rule 50.3(2) to (4), rule

50.4(2) and rule 50.5(3). See also the requirement in section 2 of the Civil Evidence Act 1995 for reasonable and practicable notice of a proposal to introduce hearsay evidence.

Rules 50.6, 50.7 and 50.8 broadly correspond with rules 3, 4 and 5 of the Magistrates' Courts (Hearsay Evidence in Civil Proceedings) Rules 1999(**a**), which apply in civil proceedings in magistrates' courts. Rule 3 of the 1999 Rules however includes a time limit, which may be varied by the court, or a justices' clerk, of 21 days before the date fixed for the hearing, for service of a hearsay notice.

Cross-examination of maker of hearsay statement

50.7. (1) This rule applies where a party wants the court's permission to cross-examine a person who made a statement which another party wants to introduce as hearsay.

(2) The party who wants to cross-examine that person must –

(a) apply in writing, with reasons, not more than 7 days after service of the notice of hearsay evidence; and

(b) serve the application on –

(i) the court officer,

(ii) the party who served the hearsay evidence notice, and

(iii) every party on whom the hearsay evidence notice was served.

(3) The court may decide an application under this rule with or without a hearing.

(4) But the court must not –

(a) dismiss an application under this rule unless the applicant has had an opportunity to make representations at a hearing (whether or not the applicant in fact attends); or

(b) allow an application under this rule unless everyone served with the application has had at least 7 days in which to make representations, including representations about whether there should be a hearing.

Note: See also section 3 of the Civil Evidence Act 1995.

Credibility and consistency of maker of hearsay statement

50.8. (1) This rule applies where a party wants to challenge the credibility or consistency of a person who made a statement which another party wants to introduce as hearsay.

(2) The party who wants to challenge the credibility or consistency of that person must – (a) serve a written notice of intention to do so on –

(i) the court officer, and

(ii) the party who served the notice of hearsay evidence

not more than 7 days after service of that hearsay evidence notice; and

(b) in the notice, identify any statement or other material on which that party relies. (3) The party who served the hearsay notice –

(a) may call that person to give oral evidence instead; and

(b) if so, must serve a notice of intention to do so on –

(i) the court officer, and

(ii) every party on whom the hearsay notice was served

not more than 7 days after service of the notice under paragraph (2).

Note: Section 5(2) of the Civil Evidence Act 1995 describes the procedure for challenging the credibility of the maker of a statement of which hearsay evidence is introduced. See also section 6 of that Act. The 1995 Act does not allow the introduction of evidence of a previous inconsistent statement otherwise than in accordance with sections 5, 6 and 7 of the Criminal Procedure Act 1865(**a**).

Court's power to vary requirements under this Part

50.9. The court may –

(a) shorten a time limit or extend it (even after it has expired);

(b) allow a notice or application to be given in a different form, or presented orally.

APPENDIX 5

ANTI-SOCIAL BEHAVIOUR AND CRIME AND POLICING ACT 2014: REFORM OF ANTI-SOCIAL BEHAVIOUR POWERS

STATUTORY GUIDANCE FOR FRONTLINE PROFESSIONALS (JULY 2014)

Home Office

Anti-social Behaviour, Crime and Policing Act 2014: Reform of anti-social behaviour powers

Statutory guidance for frontline professionals

July 2014

Contents

Introduction

Anti-social behaviour is a broad term used to describe the day-to-day incidents of crime, nuisance and disorder that make many people's lives a misery – from litter and vandalism, to public drunkenness or aggressive dogs, to noisy or abusive neighbours. Such a wide range of behaviours means that responsibility for dealing with anti-social behaviour is shared between a number of agencies, particularly the police, councils and social landlords.

Victims can feel helpless, bounced from one agency to another and then back again. In many cases, the behaviour is targeted against the most vulnerable in our society and even what is perceived as 'low level' anti-social behaviour, when targeted and persistent, can have devastating effects on a victim's life.

Our reforms are designed to put victims at the heart of the response to anti-social behaviour, and give professionals the flexibility they need to deal with any given situation.

This is statutory guidance issued under sections 19, 32, 41, 56, 73 and 91 of the Anti-social Behaviour, Crime and Policing Act 2014 and replaces the draft guidance issued in October 2013.

This guidance is written primarily for the police officers, council staff and social landlords who will use the new powers. Part 1 looks at the new measures being introduced to give victims a greater say in the way their reports of anti-social behaviour are dealt with. Part 2 then outlines the new powers. We have worked closely with frontline professionals, victims and others in the development of the legislation, and we will continue to work to ensure that this guidance helps professionals make best use of the new powers to protect the public.

In addition to this guidance, the Government has produced specific advice on how the new anti-social behaviour powers can be used to deal with irresponsible dog ownership. That document has been produced in conjunction with the Welsh Assembly Government and is available at **https://www.gov.uk/government/publications/tackling-irresponsible-dog-ownership-draft-practitioners-manual**

Part 1: Putting victims first

This Government has set out a new approach to crime, policing and community safety, based on a fundamental shift from bureaucratic to democratic accountability through directly elected Police and Crime Commissioners, increased transparency, and increasing professional discretion. This new approach includes overhauling the whole system of dealing with anti-social behaviour to ensure agencies are putting the needs of victims first.

This marks a decisive shift from the target-driven, top-down, directive approach of the past. It makes no sense for officials in Whitehall to decide local anti-social behaviour priorities, say how agencies should respond to specific issues, or set crude targets that can result in perverse working practices and outcomes.

Over the past few years, the police, councils and others have started to adopt a range of effective mechanisms that improve the response they provide to victims. From Multi-Agency Risk Assessment Conferences to taking on board the lessons identified in the anti-social behaviour call handling trials, victims have now become the focus of the response in many areas. This has resulted in an end-to-end risk assessment process, ensuring that vulnerable victims are better supported in cases of anti-social behaviour.

In terms of the behaviour itself, what is seen as 'anti-social' will vary from victim to victim, and community to community. This is one reason why we changed the way in which incidents of anti-social behaviour are reported, no longer focusing on the behaviour, but on the impact it has on the victim.

The right response will depend on a range of factors, but most importantly, on the needs of the victim and the impact the behaviour is having on their lives. Solutions need to be jointly developed by local agencies, each bringing their own experience and expertise to work together with communities and victims. Frontline professionals must be free to use their judgment rather than following a prescribed 'one size fits all' approach.

Giving victims a say

The Anti-social Behaviour, Crime and Policing Act 2014 includes two new measures which are designed to give victims and communities a say in the way anti-social behaviour is dealt with:

- The **Community Trigger**, gives victims the ability to demand action, starting with a review of their case, where the locally defined threshold is met.
- The **Community Remedy**, gives victims a say in the out-of-court punishment of perpetrators for low-level crime and anti-social behaviour.

These measures are covered in more detail in this section of the guidance.

1.1 Community Trigger

Purpose	Gives victims and communities the right to request a review of their case and bring agencies together to take a joined up, problem-solving approach to find a solution.
Relevant bodies and responsible authorities	• Councils; • Police; • Clinical Commissioning Groups in England and Local Health Boards in Wales; • Registered providers of social housing who are co-opted into this group.
Threshold	To be defined by the local agencies but not more than: • three complaints in the previous six month period. May also take account of: • the persistence of the anti-social behaviour; • the harm or potential harm caused by the anti-social behaviour; • the adequacy of response to the anti-social behaviour.
Details	• When a request to use the Community Trigger is received, agencies must decide whether the threshold has been met and communicate this to the victim; • If the threshold is met, a case review will be undertaken by the partner agencies. Agencies will share information related to the case, review what action has previously been taken and decide whether additional actions are possible. The local Community Trigger procedure should clearly state the timescales in which the review will be undertaken; • The review encourages a problem-solving approach aimed at dealing with some of the most persistent, complex cases of anti-social behaviour; • The victim is informed of the outcome of the review. Where further actions are necessary an action plan will be discussed with the victim, including timescales.
Who can use the Community Trigger?	• A victim of anti-social behaviour or another person acting on behalf of the victim such as a carer or family member, Member of Parliament or councillor. • The victim can be an individual, a business or a community group.

Community Trigger

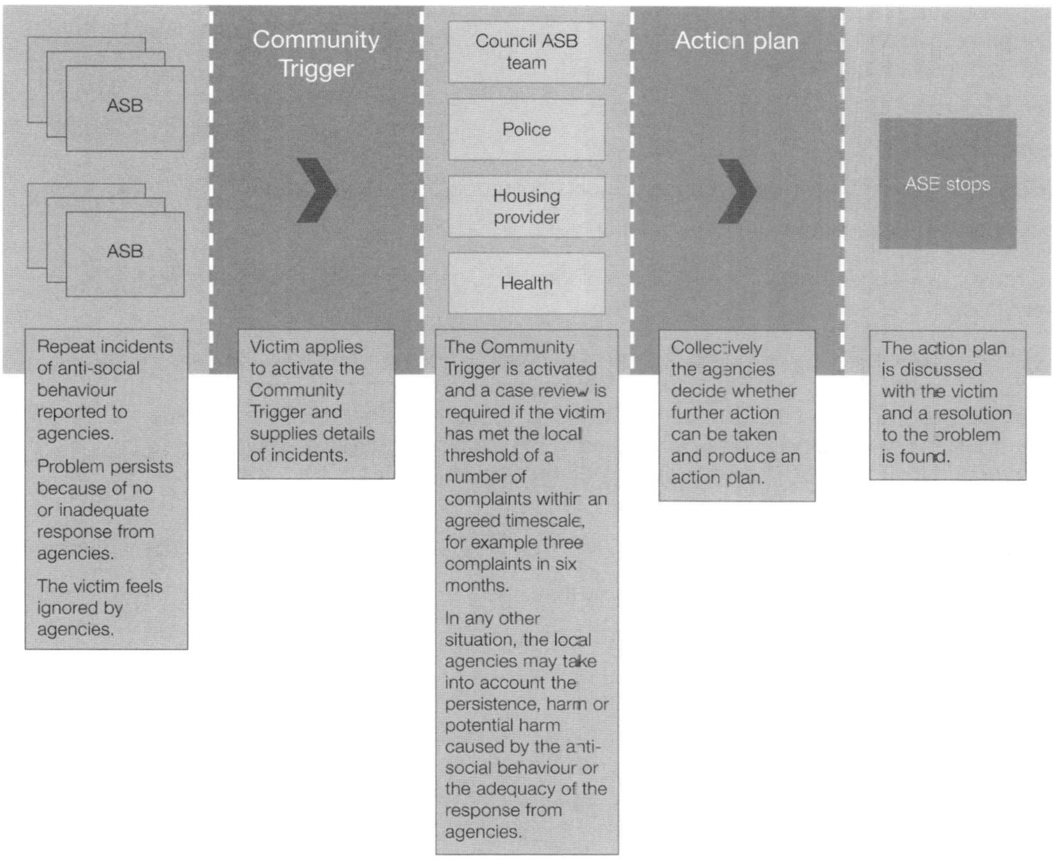

Purpose

Victims will be able to use the Community Trigger to demand action, starting with a review of their case. Agencies including councils, the police, local health teams and registered providers of social housing will have a duty to undertake a case review when someone requests one and the case meets a locally defined threshold.

The Community Trigger can also be used by any person on behalf of a victim, for example a family member, friend, carer, councillor, Member of Parliament or other professional person. This is intended to ensure that all victims are able to use the Community Trigger. However, the victim's consent should be sought by the person using the Community Trigger on their behalf.

The Community Trigger can be used by a person of any age, and agencies should make it as accessible as possible to all victims.

Putting victims first: The Community Trigger will help to reassure victims that agencies take their reports of anti-social behaviour seriously, but it cannot in itself increase reporting from vulnerable victims. Agencies should consider how to maximise awareness of the Community Trigger, in particular among vulnerable people and professionals who work with vulnerable people.

Relevant bodies and responsible authorities

'Relevant bodies' are those organisations which have a statutory duty to have a Community Trigger procedure and to undertake case reviews when a person asks for one (and the threshold is met). The relevant bodies are:

- district councils, unitary authorities or London borough councils;
- police forces;
- clinical commissioning groups in England, local health boards in Wales; and
- social housing providers who are co-opted into the group.

There must be arrangements for the inclusion of local providers of social housing among the relevant bodies in an area.

The Act does not determine which housing providers should be co-opted into the procedures. It may be more effective to co-opt the larger housing providers so that they can be involved in developing and reviewing the Community Trigger procedures on behalf of the sector. Smaller housing providers need only be involved in the Community Trigger when a case involves one of their tenants. For the purposes of the Community Trigger, a 'local provider of social housing' includes:

In England:

- A private registered provider of social housing that:
  - grants tenancies of dwelling-houses in that area; or
  - manages any house or other property in that area.

In Wales:

- A body registered as a social landlord under section 3 of the Housing Act 1996 that:
  - grants tenancies of dwelling-houses in that area; or
  - manages any house or other property in that area.

Box A: How to co-opt a social landlord

Where there are a number of housing providers in an area, they could be represented by one housing provider on behalf of the sector. There may be an established working group or organisation which can provide this role, for example, in Birmingham there is an established partnership organisation.

Birmingham Social Housing Partnership is the representative organisation for housing providers in Birmingham, representing in excess of 35 housing providers. The purpose of the organisation is to ensure that registered housing providers are engaged in community safety in the city. An important part of the work is to lead the development of an action plan for providers to contribute to reducing crime, disorder and anti-social behaviour. The group supports partner agencies in their operational responses to community safety issues, anti-social behaviour, hate crime, domestic abuse and gang violence.

Role of the Police and Crime Commissioner (PCC): The local PCC must be consulted on the Community Trigger procedure when it is set up, and must also be consulted whenever the procedure is reviewed. Depending on how the local council areas are arranged for the purposes of the Community Trigger, there may be a number of different procedures in one police force area. Arrangements may be made for the PCC to be directly involved in the Community Trigger, for example by:

- auditing case reviews;
- providing a route for victims to query the decision on whether the threshold was met or the way a Community Trigger review was carried out; or
- monitoring use of the Community Trigger to identify any learning and best practice.

Threshold

The relevant bodies should work together to agree an appropriate Community Trigger threshold, taking into consideration the nature of anti-social behaviour experienced by victims in their area and working practices of the agencies involved. **The threshold must be no higher than three complaints of anti-social behaviour in a six months period. Where a person makes an application for a case review and the number of qualifying complaints has been made, the threshold for a review is met.**

In any other situation, in setting the threshold, reference may be had to any of the following matters:

- the persistence of the anti-social behaviour;
- the harm or potential harm caused by the anti-social behaviour;
- the adequacy of the response from agencies.

The relevant bodies may wish to consult the local community about what they would consider to be an appropriate threshold in their area.

The harm, or the potential for harm to be caused to the victim, is an important consideration in determining whether the threshold is met because those who are vulnerable are likely to be less resilient to anti-social behaviour. People can be vulnerable for a number of reasons, and vulnerability or resilience can vary over time depending on personal circumstances and the nature of the anti-social behaviour. The relevant bodies should use their risk assessment procedure as part of the decision on whether the threshold is met. Risk assessment matrices cannot provide a definitive assessment of someone's needs, but will assist agencies in judging an appropriate response. It may be beneficial for the relevant bodies to adopt a common risk assessment matrix, or to have one agreed matrix for the Community Trigger.

Behaviour which falls below the level of harassment, alarm or distress, may not meet the threshold, but when assessed on the grounds of potential harm to the victim, the impact of the behaviour may be such that the threshold will be met.

One of the aims of the Community Trigger is to encourage those who are most vulnerable, or may not otherwise engage with agencies, to report incidents of anti-social behaviour.

When the victim is considered vulnerable, the relevant bodies should consider what additional practical and emotional support is offered to the victim.

Qualifying complaints: The legislation sets out what will be considered a 'qualifying complaint' for using the Community Trigger. The purpose of this is to prevent someone reporting historical incidents of anti-social behaviour in order to use the Community Trigger. The legislation sets out the following standards but agencies can set different levels if appropriate for their area as long as it does not lower the standard as set out:

- the anti-social behaviour was reported within one month of the alleged behaviour taking place; and
- the application to use the Community Trigger is made within six months of the report of anti-social behaviour.

For the purpose of the Community Trigger, anti-social behaviour is defined as behaviour causing harassment, alarm or distress to a member, or members, of the public. However, when deciding whether the threshold is met, agencies should consider the cumulative effect of the incidents and consider the harm or potential harm caused to the victim, rather than rigidly deciding whether each incident reached the level of harassment, alarm or distress.

Even though housing-related anti-social behaviour has a lower test of nuisance or annoyance for an injunction under Part 1 of the Act, because of the victim's inability to separate themselves from the anti-social behaviour the harm experienced is highly likely, depending upon the circumstances, to result in harassment, alarm or distress for the purposes of the Community Trigger.

The Community Trigger is specifically designed to deal with anti-social behaviour. However anti-social behaviour can often be motivated by hate and the relevant bodies may wish to include reports of these incidents in their Community Trigger.

Box B: Hate crime

A hate crime is any criminal offence which is perceived by the victim or any other person to be motivated by hostility or prejudice based on a personal characteristic. Incidents can range from harassment, abusive language, criminal damage/damage to property, to threats and physical violence. Incidents of hate crime may manifest themselves in low level forms of anti-social behaviour, which on the surface may appear minor but the impact on the victim and their families may be devastating and life changing. Hate crime can also have a negative impact on cohesion and integration in communities if incidents are not dealt with quickly and effectively.

There are a number of laws in place to deal with those who commit hate crimes, including public order offences and racially and religiously aggravated offences and the courts also have powers to enhance a perpetrator's sentence for any offence that is motivated by hatred or hostility towards the victim.

In March 2012, the Government published 'Challenge it, Report it, Stop it: The Government's Plan to Tackle Hate Crime' (https://www.gov.uk/government/uploads/system/uploads/attachment_data/file/97849/action-plan.pdf). The plan brings together the work of a number of departments and agencies under three important objectives: to prevent hate crime happening in the first place; to increase reporting and access to support, and to improve the operational response to hate crime. Whilst the Government plays a vital role in setting a national direction, the response to hate crime should be led at the local level. An effective multi-agency response to hate crime will involve professionals, the voluntary sector and communities working together to develop effective responses to tackle incidents early before they can escalate.

Details

The Community Trigger was piloted in Manchester, Brighton and Hove, West Lindsey and Boston, and Richmond upon Thames. The Home Office report 'Empowering Communities, Protecting Victims: summary report on the community trigger trials', published in May 2013 (**https://www.gov.uk/government/uploads/system/uploads/attachment_data/file/207468/community-trigger-trials-report-v4.pdf**), highlights the lessons identified by the pilot areas and will help assist the relevant bodies which are setting up their Community Trigger procedures.

Information sharing: The effective operation of the legislation requires the relevant bodies to share relevant information for the purpose of carrying out the case review. This may include details of previous complaints made by the victim, information about the effect the problem has had on others in the area, and details of what action has previously been taken. Relevant bodies should therefore have agreements in place for information sharing, risk assessments and a common understanding of the aims of the Community Trigger.

The relevant bodies may request any person to disclose information for the purpose of a Community Trigger review. If the request is made to a person who exercises public functions and they possess the information they must disclose it. The only exception to that is where to share the information would be either:

- in contravention of any of the provisions of the Data Protection Act 1998; or
- prohibited by Part 1 of the Regulation of Investigatory Powers Act 2000.

Other than these two exceptions, disclosing information for the Community Trigger does not breach any obligation of confidence or any other restriction on the disclosure of information.

Housing providers undertake several functions, including some that are public in nature and some that are not. If a request is made in relation to their functions that are considered to be public in nature, the information sharing duty applies. This is the case for housing providers who are co-opted into the group of relevant bodies as well as those who are not.

Box C: Sharing information

The Homes and Communities Agency's Regulatory Framework, Neighbourhood and Community Standard, requires registered housing providers:

- to co-operate with relevant partners to help improve social, environmental and economic wellbeing in areas where they own properties; and
- to work in partnership with other agencies to prevent and tackle anti-social behaviour in the neighbourhoods where they own homes.

Publishing the Community Trigger procedure and contact details: The relevant bodies must publish the Community Trigger procedure, including the point of contact for making an application to use the Community Trigger. The relevant bodies can decide an appropriate method and format for publishing this depending on the needs of the community, for example, it may be necessary to translate the information into different languages.

The relevant bodies must publish a 'point of contact' for victims (or anyone acting on their behalf) who have decided to use the Community Trigger. This may include a phone number, email address, postal address, and a form which can be completed online.

Putting victims first: Using the Community Trigger must be straightforward for the victim. It is good practice to have a number of methods to contact an agency, and consideration should be given to the fact that some victims may feel more comfortable contacting one agency than another. The Community Trigger can be used by any person and agencies should consider how to make it as accessible as possible to young people, those who are vulnerable, have learning difficulties or do not speak English.

The Community Trigger procedure: The relevant bodies must work together to devise and agree the procedure for the Community Trigger. The procedure must include provision for a person to request a review of the way an application for a Community Trigger was dealt with, and also the way their Community Trigger review was carried out.

Box D: Basic procedure for a Community Trigger

Each area should agree a procedure that suits the needs of victims and communities locally. However, the basic outline of that procedure is likely to include the following steps:

- A victim of anti-social behaviour (or someone acting on their behalf) makes an application to use the Community Trigger.
- The relevant bodies decide whether the threshold is met.
- If it has been, then the relevant bodies share information about the case, consider whether any new relevant information needs to be obtained, review previous actions taken and propose a response. The victim is informed of the outcome or agencies will work with the victim to devise and implement an action plan.
- If necessary, escalation and review.

The case review: The relevant bodies should have an agreed procedure for carrying out the Community Trigger review. The review will look at what action has previously been taken in response to the victim's reports of anti-social behaviour.

When setting up the procedure the relevant bodies should consider how the Community Trigger can be built into existing processes. Many areas have a regular multi-agency meeting to discuss cases of anti-social behaviour, such as an Anti-social Behaviour Risk Assessment Conference or a Multi-Agency Risk Assessment Conference. These may be the best-placed forums to undertake the case review. Alternatively, the relevant bodies may decide that it is more appropriate to have a separate forum to discuss cases. It will be up to local relevant bodies to decide what works best in their area. If the perpetrator is under the age of 18 the youth offending team should be invited to attend the review.

The Community Trigger will not prompt a review of decisions previously made by the Crown Prosecution Service (CPS). If a victim is not satisfied with a decision made by the CPS they should refer to the CPS complaints process, and the Victims' Right to Review Scheme. The Victims' Right to Review Scheme makes it easier for victims to seek a review of a CPS decision not to bring charges against a suspect or to terminate proceedings, in relation to decisions made after 5 June 2013.

Making recommendations: The relevant bodies who undertake a case review may make recommendations to other agencies. The legislation places a duty on a person who carries out public functions to have regard to those recommendations. This means that they are not obliged to carry out the recommendations, but that they should acknowledge them and may be challenged if they choose not to carry them out without good reason.

The recommendations are likely to take the form of an action plan to resolve the anti-social behaviour. Whenever possible, the relevant bodies should involve the victim in devising the action plan to help ensure it meets the needs of the victim. The relevant bodies will not be able to recommend the CPS to take action. The CPS operates independently under the superintendence of the Attorney General, and must make decisions in accordance with the Code for Crown Prosecutors.

Responding to the victim: The Act places a duty on the relevant bodies to respond to the victim at particular points in the process. These include:

- the decision as to whether or not the threshold is met;
- the outcome of the review; and
- any recommendations made as an outcome of the review.

The relevant bodies should agree as part of the procedure whether one agency will communicate with all victims, or whether an appropriate agency will lead in a specific case. People who use the Community Trigger may feel that they have been let down by agencies in the past so it is important that victims receive timely and consistent communication regarding their case.

Publishing data: The legislation states that relevant bodies must publish information covering:

- the number of applications for Community Triggers received;
- the number of times the threshold for review was not met;
- the number of anti-social behaviour case reviews carried out; and
- the number of anti-social behaviour case reviews that resulted in recommendations being made.

This data can represent the whole area; it does not need to be broken down by relevant body. One relevant body can publish the information on behalf of all the relevant bodies in the area. The data must be published at least annually. The relevant bodies may wish to publish data more frequently, or to publish additional details. For example, the relevant bodies may publish information about which area the triggers came from, or which the relevant bodies they related to, if this information is useful to communities and victims. Published information must not include details which could identify the victim.

Who can use the Community Trigger?

Individuals, businesses and community groups can all use the Community Trigger. Relevant bodies may decide to have a different threshold for the community to use it collectively to encourage them to work together to share and find solutions to problems. Forums such as Neighbourhood Watch, Home Watch, residents' associations, community groups, Safer Neighbourhood meetings and Neighbourhood Policing community meetings are among the ways in which communities can share experiences and problems.

1.2 Community Remedy

Purpose	The Community Remedy gives victims a say in the out-of-court punishment of perpetrators for low-level crime and anti-social behaviour.
The Community Remedy document	The Act places a duty on the Police and Crime Commissioner to consult with members of the public and community representatives on what punitive, reparative or rehabilitative actions they would consider appropriate to be on the Community Remedy document.
Applicants / who can use the Community Remedy	• Police officer; • An investigating officer (which can include Police Community Support Officers for certain offences, if designated the power by their chief constable); • A person authorised by a relevant prosecutor for conditional cautions or youth conditional cautions.
Community resolutions	When dealing with anti-social behaviour or low-level offences through a community resolution the police officer may use the Community Remedy document as a means to engage the victim in having a say in the punishment of the perpetrator.
Test	• The officer must have evidence that the person has engaged in anti-social behaviour or committed an offence; • The person must admit to the behaviour or the offence (and agree to participate); • The officer must think that the evidence is enough for court proceedings including for a civil injunction, or impose a caution, but considers that a community resolution would be more appropriate.
Conditional cautions	The Community Remedy document should be considered when it is proposed that a perpetrator be given a conditional caution or youth conditional caution as a means of consulting the victim about the possible conditions to be attached to the caution.
Failure to comply	If the perpetrator fails to comply with a conditional caution or youth conditional caution they can face court action for the offence.
Important changes/ differences	The Community Remedy document is a list of actions which may be chosen by the victim for the perpetrator to undertake in consequence of their behaviour or offending.

Community Remedy

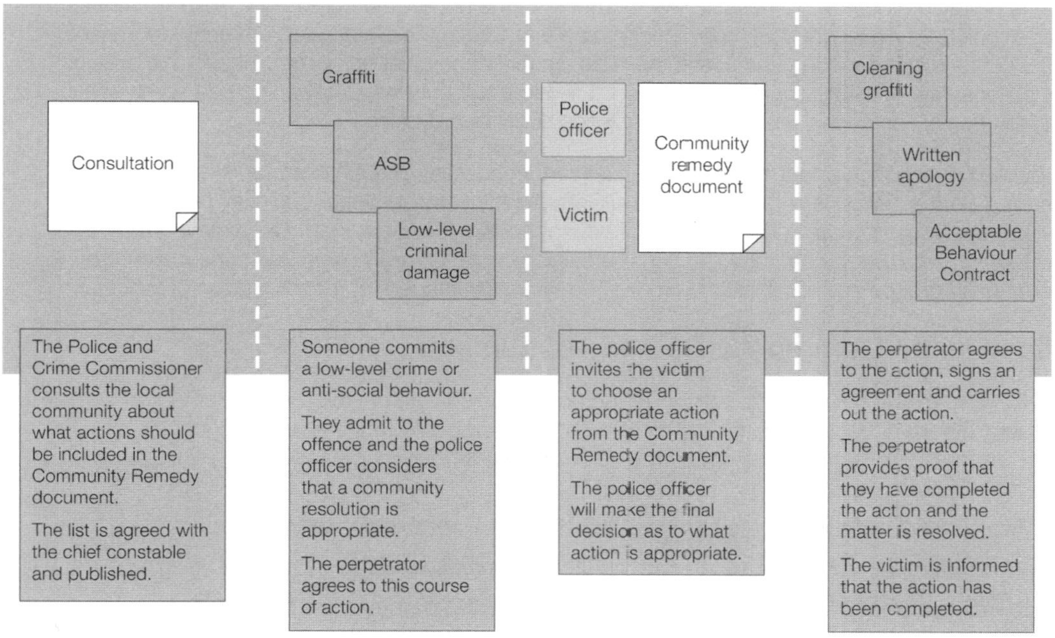

Purpose

This section explains how the Community Remedy document should be developed and how it should be used when a community resolution, conditional caution or youth conditional caution is the chosen disposal.

The Community Remedy document will be used as part of the existing process for delivering community resolutions. It will give victims of low-level crime and anti-social behaviour a say in the punishment of perpetrators out of court. The Community Remedy may also be used when a conditional caution or youth conditional caution is given, as a means of consulting the victim about the possible conditions to be attached to the caution.

The community remedy is for anti-social behaviour and low-level criminal offences.

The Community Remedy document

The Community Remedy document is a list of actions that the victim will be invited to choose from when a community resolution is to be used. The list of actions may vary from one police force area to another, based on what is available in the area and what the Police and Crime Commissioner (PCC) and chief constable agree are appropriate. The Community Remedy document must be published.

Consultation

There is a duty on the PCC to consult with members of the public and community representatives on what actions they would consider appropriate to be included in the Community Remedy document. The PCC has a statutory duty to consult the local authority and chief officer of police for the area on what actions they consider should be included. The local authority youth offending and community safety teams will know what resources and facilities are available locally.

The public consultation could be undertaken as part of another consultation, for example, when consulting on the Police and Crime Plan. The Community Remedy document may be revised at any time and it may be desirable to do this if new options are to be added. Consultation may be undertaken in whatever format the PCC considers appropriate (for example, online consultation, talking to community groups and local victims groups, via local newspapers or a combination of formats).

Actions in the Community Remedy document

The PCC and the chief constable will agree the actions listed on the Community Remedy document. These actions must be appropriate and proportionate to the types of offences for which community resolutions are used, and seek to have a positive impact on the perpetrator. Each of the actions must have a:

- punitive element: reflecting the effects on the victim and the wider community; or
- reparative element: achieving appropriate restitution/reparation to the victim; or
- rehabilitative element: helping to address the causes of the perpetrator's behaviour; or
- combination of these.

The actions available must help improve public confidence in the use of out-of-court disposals and must be compatible with the perpetrator's human rights.

Box E: What could be included?

The legislation does not specify what actions should be included in the Community Remedy document. This will vary from one police force to another depending on the views of local people and the availability of actions or activities. Actions in the Community Remedy document may include:

- mediation (for example, to resolve a neighbour dispute);
- a written or verbal apology;
- the perpetrator signing an Acceptable Behaviour Contract – where they agree not to behave anti-socially in the future – or face more formal consequences;
- take part in a restorative justice activity such as a neighbourhood justice panel;
- paying an appropriate amount for damage to be repaired or stolen property to be replaced;
- participation in structured activities that are either educational or rehabilitative, funded by the PCC as part of their efforts to reduce crime; or
- reparation to the community (for example, by doing local unpaid work for a short period).

Community Resolutions

Typically, community resolutions are used when dealing with low-level criminal damage, low value theft, minor assaults (without injury) and anti-social behaviour.

Community resolutions can be used by a police officer or an investigating officer. Police community support officers (PCSOs) can carry out community resolutions for offences which their chief constable has designated them powers to deal with. Community resolutions may also be delivered by PCSOs on the authority of a police officer of the appropriate rank.

Section 38 of the Police Reform Act 2002 defines an investigating officer as a person employed by a police force or Office of the Police and Crime Commissioner, or who is under the direction and control of the chief officer, and has been designated as an investigating officer.

Before deciding on a community resolution the police officer must:

- have evidence that the person has engaged in anti-social behaviour;
- have an admission of guilt from the person engaged in the behaviour (and they agree to participate and are capable of understanding the situation and process);
- believe that the evidence is sufficient for taking proceedings for a civil injunction, or other court proceedings, caution, or fixed penalty notice, but considers that a community resolution would be more appropriate.

Further information can be found in the ACPO Guidelines on the use of Community Resolutions (CR) Incorporating Restorative Justice (RJ) 2012 (http://www.acpo.police.uk/documents/criminaljustice/2012/201208CJBAComResandRJ.pdf).

Using the community remedy document with community resolutions

When a community resolution is to be used, the officer must make reasonable efforts to obtain the views of the victim as to whether the perpetrator should carry out any of the actions listed in the Community Remedy document. If the officer considers that the action chosen by the victim is appropriate, the perpetrator should be asked to carry out that action. The police officer or investigating officer in question will have ultimate responsibility for ensuring that the action offered to the perpetrator is appropriate and proportionate to the offence.

If there are multiple victims of the offence, the officer must make reasonable efforts to take the views of all the victims into account. If the victims have different views then the officer should consider these but will make the final decision as to which action it is appropriate for the perpetrator to undertake.

Community resolutions are entirely voluntary. The officer should ensure the victim understands the purpose of community resolutions and that the victim knows that they can choose not to be involved. This will help to ensure the victim has realistic expectations of what can be achieved. For example, the resolution may not be legally enforceable if the perpetrator fails to complete the agreed action.

It is not necessary for the victim to meet the perpetrator in order to choose the action in the Community Remedy document. The officer may consider undertaking a risk assessment, particularly if the victim is known to the perpetrator, or if the resolution involves the victim meeting the perpetrator.

Putting victims first: The Community Remedy is intended to give victims more say in the punishment of perpetrators out of court. However, the victim's involvement is voluntary and the victim must not be made to feel they should take part in a process they are not comfortable with, that they think may put them at risk, or that they do not believe will be of benefit to them.

When using the Community Remedy the officer should consider the most appropriate way to involve the victim. If the victim is under 18 or vulnerable, they may require a family member or carer to assist them understand the purpose of community resolutions and choose an action from the Community Remedy document.

If the victim is not contactable, or it cannot be ascertained who the victim is, for example, if the offence is graffiti in a public place, the officer will choose an appropriate action for the perpetrator to undertake.

Conditional caution and youth conditional caution

When a conditional caution or a youth conditional caution is to be used, the officer or authorised person must make reasonable efforts to obtain the views of the victim as to whether the perpetrator should carry out any of the actions listed in the Community Remedy document. If the officer issuing the conditional caution considers that the action chosen by the victim is appropriate, the action can form part of the conditions of the caution. The police officer or investigating officer in question (or prosecutor in some cases) will have ultimate responsibility for ensuring that the sanction offered to the perpetrator is appropriate and proportionate to the offence.

If there are multiple victims of the offence, the officer must make reasonable efforts to take the views of all the victims into account. If the victims have different views then the officer should consider these but will make the final decision as to which action it is appropriate for the perpetrator to undertake.

Conditional cautions are available for all offences except domestic violence and hate crimes, which are excluded from the conditional caution scheme. For full details of the considerations to apply when deciding whether to use a conditional caution, see the Ministry of Justice's Statutory Code of Practice for Adult Conditional Cautions.

https://www.gov.uk/government/publications/code-of-practice-for-adult-conditional-cautions

A youth conditional caution is available for any offence, except for domestic violence or hate crime, which scores four on the ACPO Gravity Matrix. Full details can be found in the Ministry of Justice's Statutory Code of Practice for Youth Conditional Cautions.

https://www.gov.uk/government/publications/code-of-practice-for-youth-conditional-cautions--2

Part 2: More effective powers

Dealing with anti-social behaviour is rarely simple. The new powers are designed to be flexible, allowing professionals to adapt them to protect victims in a wide range of situations. However, the new powers will work best when complemented by more effective ways of working – in particular, working in partnership, sharing information and using early and informal interventions.

Working together and sharing information

The new powers will allow the police, councils, social landlords and others to deal with problems quickly. However, local agencies should still work together where appropriate to ensure the best results for victims. Each agency brings with it a range of expertise and experience that when brought together can assist in resolving issues more effectively.

As part of this joined-up approach, an effective information-sharing protocol is essential. There is already a duty on some bodies (such as the police and councils) to work together and in areas where this works well, with information flowing between partners quickly, victims can see a real difference in the response to their reports of anti-social behaviour. The Community Trigger outlined in Part 1 of this guidance includes a specific duty on some bodies to share information when the trigger is activated, however, partners should not wait until a victim feels they are being ignored before coming together to prepare a response.

Case management

Effective case management should underpin all activity to deal with anti-social behaviour, starting from when a complaint is received until the matter is resolved. The welfare, safety and well-being of victims whose complaints form the basis of any action must be the main consideration at every stage of the process. This will ensure that agencies provide a fair and consistent service to the public, taking timely appropriate action to tackle anti-social behaviour.

Assessing the risk to victims

It is good practice for agencies to assess the risk of harm to the victim, and their potential vulnerability, when they receive a complaint about anti-social behaviour. This should mark the start of the case-management process. It is important to identify the effect the anti-social behaviour is having on the victim, particularly if repeated incidents of anti-social behaviour are having a cumulative effect on their well-being. A continuous and organised risk assessment will help identify cases that are causing, or could result in serious harm to the victim, either as a one-off incident or as part of a targeted and persistent campaign of anti-social behaviour against the victim.

2.1 Early and informal interventions

Early intervention, especially through informal approaches, can be successful in stopping the anti-social behaviour committed by the majority of perpetrators. For example, a 2013 HouseMark survey showed that over 80% of anti-social behaviour cases dealt with by social landlords were successfully resolved through some form of early or informal intervention.

Early and informal interventions can establish clear standards of behaviour and reinforce the message that anti-social behaviour will not be tolerated. In many cases, awareness of the impact of their behaviour on victims, and the threat of more formal enforcement tools, can be a sufficient incentive for an individual to change their behaviour. It should be for frontline professionals to decide when and how to use these approaches, but the Government encourages use of informal methods where it is deemed to be appropriate.

Informal interventions should be considered first in most cases, particularly when dealing with young people, as they can stop bad behaviour before it escalates. This should be determined by professionals on a case by case basis. However, some of the most common forms of informal intervention are included below for reference. Alternatively, in cases where informal intervention is not the appropriate first step, perhaps because the victim is at risk of harm, professionals should consider progressing directly to formal sanctions.

Warnings

Verbal warnings: In deciding to use a verbal warning, the officer should still consider the evidence. For instance, the officer should have reason to believe that the anti-social behaviour has occurred, or is likely to occur, and that the individual's behaviour could be considered to be unreasonable. In issuing a verbal warning, the police, council or housing officer should make clear to the individual what behaviour is causing the issue and what effect this is having on the victim or community and the consequences of non-compliance are explained clearly.

Written warnings: As with a verbal warning, a written warning should contain specifics about what behaviour has occurred and why this is not acceptable, including the impact on any victims or local community. Local agencies should alert each other that the warning has been given so that it can be effectively monitored.

Each agency needs to ensure that it keeps a record of any verbal or written warning given so that it may be used as evidence in court proceedings if required.

Local agencies may wish to consider what level of detail they go into at this stage regarding the consequences of further anti-social behaviour and more serious sanctions – for instance, an Acceptable Behaviour Contract, court proceedings for a civil injunction or even criminal proceedings if the behaviour escalates.

Community resolution

'Community resolution' is the nationally recognised term for the resolution of a less serious offence or anti-social behaviour, through informal agreement between the parties involved as opposed to progression through the criminal justice process. A community resolution may be used with both youth and adult perpetrators. It enables the police to deal more proportionately with lower level crime and anti-social behaviour in a timely and transparent manner that takes into account the needs of the victim, perpetrator and wider community, outside the formal criminal justice system.

Community resolutions are primarily aimed at first time perpetrators where genuine remorse has been expressed, and where an out-of-court disposal is more appropriate than taking more formal action. Community resolutions can help to reduce reoffending by encouraging perpetrators to face up to the impact of their behaviour and to take responsibility for making good the harm caused.

Further information can be found in the ACPO Guidelines on the use of Community Resolutions (CR) Incorporating Restorative Justice (RJ) 2012.

The new Community Remedy document outlined in Part 1.2 must be used when dealing with anti-social behaviour or lower-level offences out of court through community resolutions.

Mediation

In many cases of anti-social behaviour, mediation can be an effective tool, solving the issue by bringing all parties to the table. This can be very effective in neighbour disputes, family conflicts, lifestyle differences such as noise nuisance complaints and similar situations where it can sometimes be difficult to identify the victim and the perpetrator.

Mediation does not work if it is forced on those involved. All parties must be willing to come to the table and discuss their issues and agencies should consider whether mediation is appropriate, who should attend and set clear ground rules for participation.

It is not for the mediator to establish a solution to the issue as, in most cases, they will have already tried this with each party unsuccessfully. For mediation to deliver long-term solutions, those in dispute should agree a solution. The mediator should facilitate this conversation and ensure all parties adhere to the ground rules. They can also draw up an agreement if required for all parties to sign to formalise what has been agreed.

Acceptable Behaviour Contracts

Acceptable behaviour contracts (ABCs), sometimes called acceptable behaviour agreements, can be an effective way of dealing with anti-social individuals, especially where there are a number of problem behaviours. They can also be very effective at dealing with young people early, to nip problem behaviours in the bud before they escalate.

ABCs are a written agreement between a perpetrator of anti-social behaviour and the agency or agencies acting locally to prevent that behaviour. The terms of an ABC can be discussed with the perpetrator before they are drafted and signed to encourage compliance. However, there is no formal sanction associated with refusing to sign an ABC, so if an individual does not wish to sign, they cannot be forced to do so. However, refusal to sign an ABC may persuade a court that only a civil injunction or a criminal behaviour order will prevent the anti-social behaviour.

While there are no formal sanctions associated with breaching the conditions of an ABC, agencies should consider further steps if the individual does not change their behaviour. Potential further action should be made clear in the ABC so that the perpetrator is aware of the consequences of failing to comply. In the case of graffiti, for example, this could be the issue of a community protection notice or an application for a civil injunction.

In cases where court proceedings are subsequently deemed necessary, the work undertaken as part of drafting an ABC can form part of the evidence pack. For instance, any discussion with victims and communities to assess the impact of the behaviour could form the basis of a community impact statement for the court.

Parenting contracts

Where informal interventions are used against under 18s, the parents or guardians of the young person should be contacted in advance of the decision to take action. In many cases, the parents or guardians can play an important role in ensuring the individual changes their behaviour. While there are formal routes such as parenting orders, at this stage it may be appropriate to include a role for the parent in an ABC. In addition, if the behaviour of the parent is part of the issue (either because they are a bad influence on the child or fail to provide suitable supervision) agencies could consider a parenting contract. These are similar to an ABC but are signed by the parent or guardian. They could also be considered where the child in question is under 10 and so other interventions are not appropriate for the perpetrator themselves.

With a potentially troubled family, agencies should consider discussing the matter with other bodies with an interest – for instance the local youth offending team, social services and school to assess the scale of the problem. Family intervention programmes and the local Troubled Families Unit should also be contacted where appropriate to discuss potential interventions.

Support and counselling

In many cases, there are underlying causes of the anti-social behaviour. The new powers allow professionals to actively deal with these through the use of positive requirements. However, there is no need to wait until formal court action before offering help.

Substance misuse or alcohol dependency can drive anti-social behaviour and low-level crime, and support can have a positive impact. Catching someone before they fall into a criminal way of life by supporting them to escape addiction can save thousands of pounds in enforcement action over a person's lifetime.

The Troubled Families Programme has already identified many of the issues faced by young people (https://www.gov.uk/government/policies/helping-troubled-families-turn-their-lives-around). The young person being dealt with may already be known by the Troubled Families Unit, but if not, it may be useful to discuss the issues with local experts to see whether there is a wider support programme that can be put in place.

Conclusion

These are only a selection of the informal approaches that have been successful across England and Wales in recent years. In many cases, informal early intervention is successful in changing behaviours and protecting communities. Local enforcement agencies should develop a framework of early and informal interventions that reflects the needs of victims and communities. Early and informal interventions may be included in a plan to deal with anti-social behaviour locally, but should not replace formal interventions where they are the most effective means of dealing with anti-social behaviour.

2.2 Civil injunction

Purpose	To stop or prevent individuals engaging in anti-social behaviour quickly, nipping problems in the bud before they escalate.
Applicants	• Local councils; • Social landlords; • Police (including British Transport Police); • Transport for London; • Environment Agency and Natural Resources Wales; and • NHS Protect and NHS Protect (Wales)
Test	• On the balance of probabilities; • Behaviour likely to cause harassment, alarm or distress (non-housing related anti-social behaviour); or • Conduct capable of causing nuisance or annoyance (housing-related anti-social behaviour); and • Just and convenient to grant the injunction to prevent anti-social behaviour.
Details	• Issued by the county court and High Court for over 18s and the youth court for under 18s. • Injunction will include prohibitions and can also include positive requirements to get the perpetrator to address the underlying causes of their anti-social behaviour. • Agencies must consult youth offending teams in applications against under 18s.
Penalty on breach	• Breach of the injunction is not a criminal offence, but breach must be proved to the criminal standard, that is, beyond reasonable doubt. • Over 18s: civil contempt of court with unlimited fine or up to two years in prison. • Under 18s: supervision order or, as a very last resort, a civil detention order of up to three months for 14-17 year olds.
Appeals	• Over 18s to the High Court; and • Under 18s to the Crown Court.
Important changes/ differences	• Available to a wider range of agencies than Anti-Social Behaviour Injunctions. • Obtainable on a civil standard of proof unlike Anti-Social Behaviour Orders (ASBOs). • No need to prove "necessity" unlike ASBOs. • Breach is not a criminal offence. • Scope for positive requirements to focus on long-term solutions.

Civil injunction

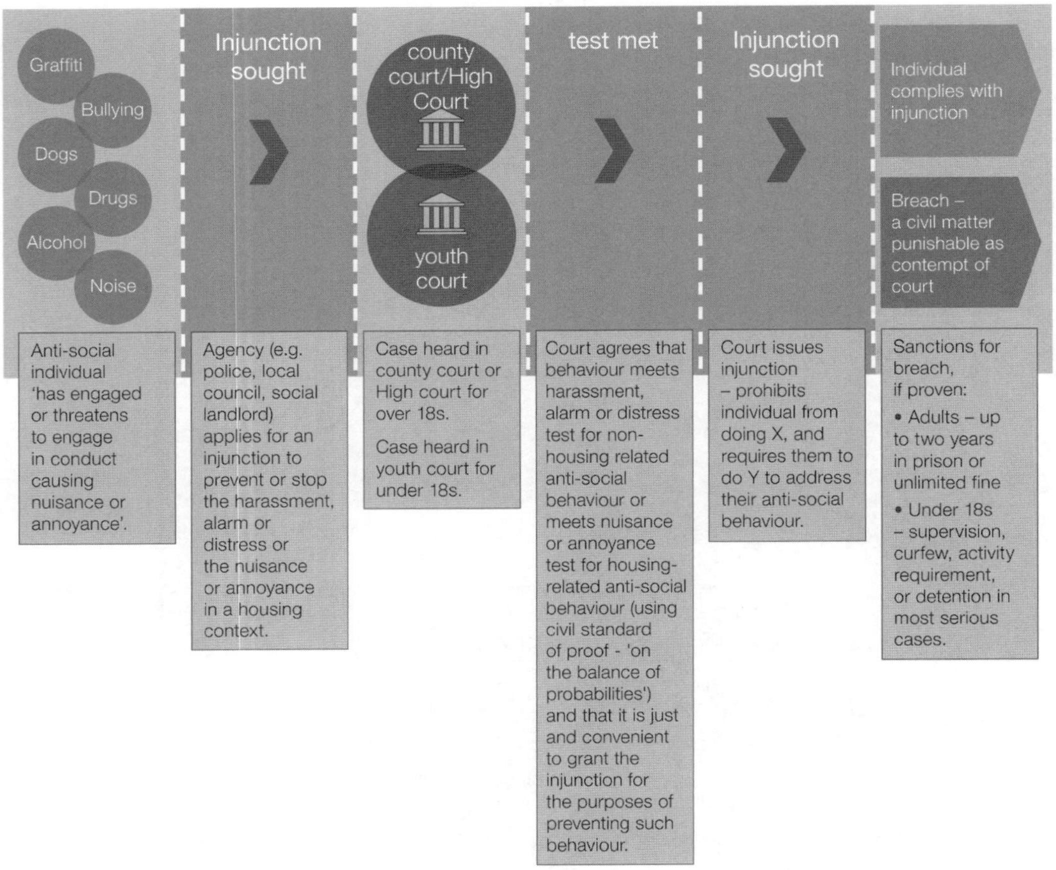

Purpose

The injunction under Part 1 of the Anti-social Behaviour, Crime and Policing Act 2014 is a civil power which can be applied for to deal with anti-social individuals. The injunction can offer fast and effective protection for victims and communities and set a clear standard of behaviour for perpetrators, stopping the person's behaviour from escalating.

Although the injunction is a civil power, it is still a formal sanction and many professionals will want to consider informal approaches before resorting to court action, especially in the case of under 18s. However, where informal approaches have not worked or professionals decide that a formal response is needed more quickly, they should be free to do so.

Applicants

A number of agencies can apply for the injunction to ensure that the body best placed to lead on a specific case can do so. These are:

- A local council;
- A housing provider;

- The chief officer of police for the local area;
- The chief constable of the British Transport Police;
- Transport for London;
- The Environment Agency and Natural Resources Wales;
- NHS Protect and NHS Protect (Wales).

Putting victims first: Anti-social behaviour should be tackled with agencies working together, rather than in isolation. Agencies may consider establishing local consultation protocols and arrangements for applying for injunctions.

Test

There are two tests for an injunction under Part 1 of the 2014 Act.

Non-housing related

For anti-social behaviour in a non-housing related context the test is conduct that has caused, or is likely to cause, harassment, alarm or distress to any person. This will apply, for example, where the anti-social behaviour has occurred in a public place, such as a town or city centre, shopping mall, or local park, and where the behaviour does not affect the housing management functions of a social landlord or people in their homes.

Housing-related

For anti-social behaviour in a housing context the nuisance or annoyance test will apply, that is, where the conduct is capable of causing nuisance or annoyance to a person in relation to that person's occupation of residential premises or the conduct is capable of causing housing-related nuisance or annoyance to any person. Only social landlords, local councils or the police will be able to apply for an injunction under these provisions in the legislation. In the case of social landlords only, "housing-related" means directly or indirectly relating to their housing management function.

The injunction can be applied for by the police, local councils and social landlords against perpetrators in social housing, the private-rented sector and owner-occupiers. This means that it can be used against perpetrators who are not even tenants of the social landlord who is applying for the order.

The injunction can also be used in situations where the perpetrator has allowed another person to engage in anti-social behaviour, as opposed to actively engaging in such behaviour themselves. For example, in a case where another person, such as a visitor or lodger, is or has been behaving anti-socially, the injunction could be used against the problem visitor, lodger or owner if applicable. An agency seeking to apply for the injunction must produce evidence (to the civil standard of proof, that is, 'on the balance of probabilities') and satisfy the court that it is both 'just and convenient' to grant the order.

Putting victims first: In deciding whether the individual's conduct has caused or is likely to cause harassment, alarm or distress or is capable of causing nuisance or annoyance, agencies should communicate with all potential victims and witnesses to understand the wider harm to individuals and the community. Not only will this ensure that victims and communities feel that their problem is being taken seriously, but it will also aid the evidence-gathering process for application to the court.

Details

Who can the injunction be issued against? A court may grant the injunction against anyone who is 10 years of age or over. Applications against individuals who are 18 years of age or over must be made in the county court or High Court, whilst applications against individuals who are under 18 years of age must be made in the youth court.

Intergenerational or 'mixed aged' cases: Mostly, hearings for injunction applications will be heard in the youth court for under 18s and the county court for over 18s. However, there are some cases of anti-social behaviour where the individuals involved include both over 18s and under 18s. In such cases, the applicant can apply to the youth court to have such cases heard together as joint hearings. The youth court must find that it is in the interests of justice to hear the 'mixed aged' case and, if it does so, the case can only be heard in that court – the joint hearing cannot be heard in the county court. However, subsequent hearings (breach etc.) involving individuals over 18 will take place in the county court.

Dealing with young people: Applicants must consult the local youth offending team (YOT) if the application is against someone under the age of 18 and inform any other body or individual the applicant thinks appropriate, for example, a youth charity that is already working with the young person. Although the consultation requirement does not mean that the YOT can veto the application, it is important that applicants fully consider and take into account representations from the YOT as part of developing good partnership working in cases involving young people. YOTs play a central role in preventing and reducing anti-social behaviour by young people, working with them to try and help them stay away from crime. For more information on YOTs and how to find your local team you should visit https://www.gov.uk/youth-offending-team.

YOTs will be important in getting the young person to adhere to the conditions in the injunction and that they are understood. The conditions will be overseen by a responsible officer in the YOT or children's and family services. YOTs will also work with applicants as part of a multi-agency approach to ensure that positive requirements in the injunction are tailored to the needs of the young person.

When can injunctions be used? The injunction can be used to deal with a wide range of behaviours, many of which can cause serious harm to victims and communities in both housing-related and non-housing related situations. This can include vandalism, public drunkenness, aggressive begging, irresponsible dog ownership, noisy or abusive behaviour towards neighbours, or bullying. Agencies must make proportionate and reasonable judgements before applying for the injunction. Injunctions should not be used to stop reasonable, trivial or benign behaviours that have not caused, or are not likely to cause, anti-social behaviour to victims or communities. Failure to make such reasonable and proportionate judgements will increase the likelihood that an application will not be successful.

What to include: The injunction will include relevant prohibitions to get individuals to stop behaving anti-socially. It can also include positive requirements to get the individual to deal with the underlying cause of their behaviour. Agencies will have the discretion to tailor the positive requirements in each case to address the respondent's individual circumstances, behaviour and needs. Positive requirements could include the following:

- The respondent attending alcohol awareness classes for alcohol-related problems;
- Irresponsible dog owners attending dog training classes provided by animal welfare charities; or
- The respondent attending mediation sessions with neighbours or victims.

The prohibitions or requirements in the injunction must be reasonable and must not, so far as practicable:

- interfere with the times, if any, at which the respondent normally works or attends school or any other educational establishment; or
- conflict with the requirements of any other court order or injunction to which the respondent may be subject.

In addition to these factors, applicants should consider the impact on any caring responsibilities the perpetrator may have and, in the event that they have a disability, whether he or she is capable of complying with the proposed prohibitions or requirements.

A draft of the proposed terms of the injunction should include all proposed prohibitions and requirements, their duration and any powers of arrest attached. Applicants will need to be prepared for the court to examine each prohibition and requirement, and will need to be able to prove how each will help stop or prevent the respondent from engaging in or threatening to engage in anti-social behaviour in the future.

Putting victims first: Keeping victims and communities updated on enforcement action at key points can help them deal with the impact the behaviour is having. Victims may feel that their complaint has been ignored if they don't see immediate changes to the behaviour. However, simply informing them of what is happening can make a huge difference.

Duration of injunctions: Prohibitions or requirements in the injunction can be for a fixed or indefinite period for adult perpetrators. In the case of under 18s the prohibitions or requirements must have a specified time limit, and the maximum term is 12 months.

Exclusion from the home: The court may exclude a perpetrator over the age of 18 from any premises or an area specified within the terms of the injunction. This can include their home, where the court thinks that the anti-social behaviour includes the use, or threatened use, of violence against other persons, or there is a significant risk of harm. The word harm is defined in section 20 of the legislation as including "serious ill-treatment or abuse, whether physical or not" – which means that it could include emotional or psychological harm, such as harassment or racial abuse.

Social landlords will only be able to apply to the court to exclude their own tenants and visitors to properties managed by them, whilst councils and the police will be the lead agencies in applying to exclude private tenants or owner-occupiers from their homes. In cases where the police or the local council is the lead agency in an application to exclude a social tenant, they should consult the landlord. If the exclusion is applied against someone in privately rented accommodation or in residential leasehold housing, the police force or council should, where circumstances permit, inform and consult the landlord (generally referred to in the leasehold as the freeholder) beforehand.

We do not expect the power of exclusion to be used often and the court will pay special attention to proportionality in light of the Article 8 (Right to respect for private and family life, European Convention on Human Rights) implications. As such, applications should only be made for exclusion in extreme cases that meet the higher threshold set out above.

Publicising the injunction issued to a young person: Making the public aware of the perpetrator and the terms of the order can be an important part of the process in dealing with anti-social behaviour. It can provide reassurance to communities that action is being taken when they report anti-social behaviour. It will also provide the information local people need to identify and report breaches. The decision to publicise the injunction will be taken by the police or council unless the court has made a section 39 order (Children and Young Persons Act 1933) prohibiting publication. When deciding whether to publicise the injunction, public authorities (including the courts) must consider that it is necessary and proportionate to interfere with the young person's right to privacy, and the likely impact on a young person's behaviour. This will need to be balanced against the need to provide re-assurance to the victims and the wider community as well as providing them with information so that they can report any breaches. Each case should be decided carefully on its own facts.

'Without notice' applications: Injunctions can be applied for 'without notice' being given to the perpetrator in exceptional cases to stop serious harm to victims. They should not be made routinely or in place of inadequate preparation for normal 'with notice' applications. The notification and consultation requirements that apply to 'with notice' applications do not apply to 'without notice' applications.

Interim injunctions: The court will grant an interim injunction if a 'without notice' application is successful. The court may also grant an interim injunction where a standard application is adjourned. The interim injunction can only include prohibitions, not positive requirements. When applying for an interim injunction, the applicant should ensure that the application presents the victim's case and also why the interim injunction is necessary.

Variation and discharge of injunctions: The court has the power to vary or discharge the injunction upon application by either the perpetrator or the applicant. If the applicant wishes to discharge or vary the injunction, they should notify the people and organisations they consulted as part of the initial application process. Applicants may consider applying to vary the injunction in response to changes in the respondent's behaviour. The powers of the court to vary the injunction include:

- to remove a prohibition or requirement in the injunction;
- to include a prohibition or requirement in the injunction;
- to reduce the period for which a prohibition or requirement has effect;
- to extend the period for which a prohibition or requirement has effect; or
- to attach a power of arrest, or extend the period for which a power of arrest has effect.

If the court dismisses an application to vary the injunction, the relevant party is not allowed to make a further application without the consent of the court or the agreement of the other party.

Power of arrest: The court can attach a power of arrest to any prohibition or requirement in the injunction, except a positive requirement, that is, a requirement that the respondent participates in a particular activity. The court can only attach a power of arrest if:

- the anti-social behaviour in which the respondent has engaged, or threatens to engage, consists of or includes the use, or threatened use, of violence against other persons; or
- there is a significant risk of harm to other persons from the respondent.

If the applicant believes a power of arrest is appropriate, they should present this by way of written evidence. Such evidence may indicate that the respondent poses a high level of risk to the victim or the community should any of the conditions in the injunction be breached, for example, a history of violent behaviour. Where a power of arrest is attached to a condition of the injunction, a police officer can arrest the respondent without warrant if he or she has reasonable cause to believe that a breach has occurred. The police must present the respondent to court within 24 hours of their arrest (except on Sunday, Christmas Day and Good Friday).

If the applicant thinks that the respondent has breached a term of the injunction to which a power of arrest has not been attached, they may apply to the court for an arrest warrant. The application must be made to a judge in the county court in the case of an adult and a justice of the peace in the case of respondents who are below the age of 18. The court may then issue a warrant for the respondent's arrest and to be brought before the court but only if it has reasonable grounds for believing the respondent has breached a provision in the injunction. The police must inform the applicant when the respondent is arrested.

Hearsay evidence: Hearsay and professional witness evidence allow for the identities of those who are unable to give evidence due to fear or intimidation, to be protected. This is especially important as cases can involve anti-social behaviour in residential areas where local people and those targeted by the behaviour may feel unable to come forward for fear of reprisals. Hearsay evidence could be provided by a police officer, healthcare official, or any other professional who has interviewed the witness directly.

Penalty on breach

The breach of the injunction is not a criminal offence. However, due to the potential severity of the penalties which the court can impose on respondents, the criminal standard of proof – 'beyond reasonable doubt' – is applied in breach proceedings.

For adults, breach is dealt with by a civil contempt of court, which is punishable by up to two years in prison and/or an unlimited fine. The imprisonment is for contempt of court, not for the conduct. For under 18s, breach proceedings are dealt with in the youth court and could result in a supervision order with a supervision, curfew or activity requirement. In the most serious cases, (that is, 'where the court determines that because of the severity or extent of the breach no other power available to it is appropriate') the court may impose a detention order on a young person for breaching the terms of the injunction – including breach of a positive requirement. For under 18s, only those between 14 and 17 years of age can be detained for breaching the injunction and they cannot be detained for longer than three months.

Remands: The court has the power to remand a perpetrator in custody or on bail after they have been arrested for suspected breach of the injunction (with or without warrant). An under 18 can only be remanded in custody on medical grounds, that is, after obtaining evidence from a registered medical practitioner the court is satisfied that the young person is suffering from a mental disorder and it would be impracticable to get a medical report for the young person if they were granted bail. The court has discretion as to whether to remand a person on bail or in custody.

Appeals

Appeals may be lodged by both the applicant and perpetrator following the grant, refusal, variation or discharge of the injunction. A decision by the county court (in the case of proceedings in respect of an adult) may be appealed to the High Court. Appeals against decisions of the youth court in under 18 cases are heard in the Crown Court.

2.3 Criminal behaviour order

Purpose	Issued by any criminal court against a person who has been convicted of an offence to tackle the most persistently anti-social individuals who are also engaged in criminal activity.
Applicants	The prosecution, in most cases the Crown Prosecution Service (CPS), either at its own initiative or following a request from the police or council.
Test	• If the court is satisfied beyond reasonable doubt that the offender has engaged in behaviour that has caused or is likely to cause harassment, alarm or distress to any person; and • The court considers that making the order will help prevent the offender from engaging in such behaviour.
Details	• Issued by any criminal court for any criminal offence. • The anti-social behaviour does not need to be part of the criminal offence. • Order will include prohibitions to stop the anti-social behaviour but it can also include positive requirements to get the offender to address the underlying causes of the offender's behaviour. • Agencies must find out the view of the youth offending team (YOT) for applications for under 18s.
Penalty on breach	• Breach of the order is a criminal offence and must be proved to a criminal standard of proof, that is, beyond reasonable doubt. • For over 18s on summary conviction: up to six months imprisonment or a fine or both. • For over 18s on conviction on indictment: up to five years imprisonment or a fine or both. • For under 18s: the sentencing powers in the youth court apply.
Appeals	• Appeals against orders made in the magistrates' court (which includes the youth court) lie to the Crown Court. • Appeals against orders made in the Crown Court lie to the Court of Appeal.
Important changes/ differences	• Consultation requirement with YOTs for under 18s. • No need to prove "necessity" unlike Anti-Social Behaviour Orders. • Scope for positive requirements to focus on long-term solutions.

Criminal behaviour order

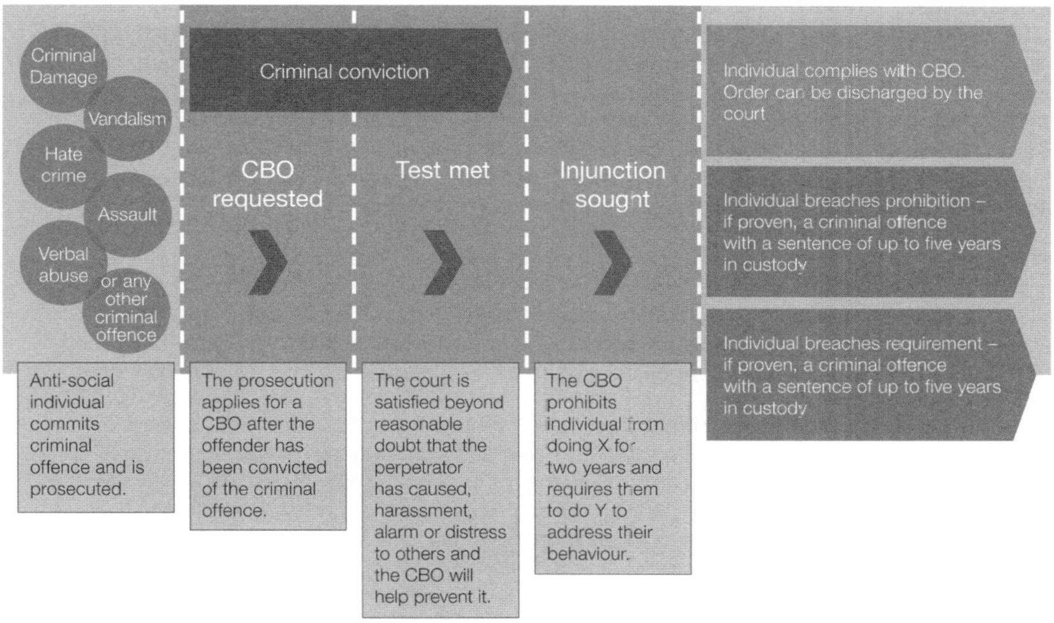

Purpose

The Criminal Behaviour Order (CBO) is available on conviction for any criminal offence in any criminal court. The order is aimed at tackling the most serious and persistent offenders where their behaviour has brought them before a criminal court.

Applicants

The prosecution, usually the Crown Prosecution Service (CPS), but in some cases it could be a local council, may apply for the CBO after the offender has been convicted of a criminal offence. The prosecution can apply for a CBO at its own initiative or following a request from a council or the police. The CBO hearing will occur after, or at the same time as, the sentencing for the criminal conviction.

Good relationships will be important between local agencies and the CPS to ensure the CBO application can be properly reviewed and notice of it served as soon as practicable, without waiting for the verdict in the criminal case. The court cannot consider an application for a CBO at a hearing after the offender has been sentenced, unless the court has adjourned proceedings from the sentence date for the application to be considered. Agencies should consider setting up local information exchanges to make sure that the CBO is considered every time an anti-social behaviour offender is brought to a criminal court.

The test

For a CBO to be made:

- the court must be satisfied, beyond reasonable doubt, that the offender has engaged in behaviour that caused, or was likely to cause, harassment, alarm or distress to any person; and
- that the court considers making the order will help in preventing the offender from engaging in such behaviour.

Details

When can a CBO be used? The CBO can deal with a wide range of anti-social behaviours following the individual's conviction for a criminal offence, for example, threatening violence against others in the community, persistently being drunk and aggressive in public or criminal damage. Agencies must make proportionate and reasonable judgements before applying for a CBO and conditions of an order **should not** be designed to stop reasonable, trivial or benign behaviours that have not caused, or are not likely to cause, anti-social behaviour to victims or communities. An application for a CBO does not require a link between the criminal behaviour which led to the conviction and the anti-social behaviour for it to be issued by the court.

Consultation: The only formal consultation requirement applies where an offender is under 18 years of age. In those cases, the prosecution must find out the views of the local youth offending team (YOT) before applying for the CBO. The views of the YOT must be included in the file of evidence forwarded to the prosecution. In practice, the consultation with the YOT must be carried out by the organisation preparing the application for the CBO, namely the council or police force.

The legislation has deliberately kept formal consultation requirements to a minimum, to enable agencies to act quickly where needed to protect victims and communities. However, in most cases it is likely there would be a number of agencies the police or local council would wish to consult with. This could include local organisations that have come into contact with the individual, such as schools and colleges of further education, providers of probation services, social services, mental health services, housing providers or others.

These views should be considered before the decision is made to ask the CPS to consider applying for a CBO. This will ensure that an order is the proper course of action in each case and that the terms of the order are appropriate.

Evidence not heard in the criminal case can still be admissible at the CBO hearing, for example, evidence of other anti-social behaviour by the offender and information about why an order is appropriate in the terms asked for. Witnesses who might be reluctant to give evidence in person may have their evidence accepted as a written statement, or given by someone such as a police officer as hearsay evidence, but this will depend on the circumstances of the individual case.

Special measures are available in proceedings for CBOs in the case of witnesses who are under 18 and vulnerable and intimidated adult witnesses (sections 16 and 17, Youth Justice and Criminal Evidence Act 1999). The court has to satisfy itself that the special measure, or combination of special measures, is likely to maximise the quality of the witness's evidence before granting an application for special measures.

Interim orders: In cases where an offender is convicted of an offence but the court is adjourned for sentencing, or the CBO hearing is adjourned after sentence, an interim order can be granted, if the court thinks that it is just to do so. The prosecution can apply for the interim order.

Duration of a CBO: The terms of the CBO must include the duration of the order. For adults this is a minimum of two years up to an indefinite period. For under 18s the order must be between one and three years.

Prohibitions and requirements: The CBO must clearly describe the details of what the offender is not allowed to do (prohibitions) as well as what they must do (requirements). Orders can include prohibitions or requirements or both. It is up to the court to decide which are needed to help prevent further anti-social behaviour and which measures are most appropriate and available, to tackle the underlying cause of the behaviour. So far as practicable, these must not interfere with an offender's education or work commitments or conflict with any other court order or injunction the offender is subject to. In addition to these factors, practitioners should, in proposing prohibitions or requirements to the court, also consider the impact on any caring responsibilities the respondent may have and, in the event that the respondent has any disability, whether he or she is capable of complying with the proposed prohibitions or requirements.

Local agencies will be familiar with the prohibitions element of the order. However, as with the civil injunction, requirements could also be included if the court believes that it will help stop further anti-social behaviour by the offender. Requirements should aim to tackle the underlying cause of the anti-social behaviour and be tailored to the specific needs of each offender. They could include:

- attendance at an anger management course where an offender finds it difficult to respond without violence;
- youth mentoring;
- a substance misuse awareness session where an offender's anti-social behaviour occurs when they have been drinking or using drugs; or
- a job readiness course to help an offender get employment and move them away from the circumstances that cause them to commit anti-social behaviour.

The court must receive evidence about the suitability and enforceability of any requirement from the person or organisation who will be responsible for supervising compliance with the requirement.

Putting victims first: The potential impact on the victim(s) will be at the heart of the considerations of the terms of the order. Stopping the anti-social behaviour is for the benefit of the victim and the CBO is not a punitive measure. Always stop to think how the terms of the order will impact on the victim(s): What would they think? Would they be satisfied? It is also good practice to take the time to explain the terms of the order to the victim(s) so that they are aware of the outcome of the court case.

Publicising a CBO issued to a young person: Making the public aware of the offender and the terms of the order can be an important part of the process in dealing with anti-social behaviour. It can provide reassurance to communities that action is being taken when they report anti-social behaviour. It will also provide the information local people need to identify and report breaches. The decision to publicise a CBO will be taken by the police or council unless the court has made a section 39 order (Children and Young Persons Act 1933) prohibiting publication. When deciding whether to publicise a CBO, public authorities (including the courts) must consider that it is necessary and proportionate to interfere with the young person's right to privacy, and the likely impact on a young person's behaviour. This will need to be balanced against the need to provide re-assurance to the victims and the wider community as well as providing them with information so that they can report any breaches. Each case should be decided carefully on its own facts.

Applications to vary or discharge the order: A CBO may be varied or discharged by the court which made the original order. Either the offender or the prosecution can make an application but if this is dismissed by the court neither party can make a subsequent application without the consent of either the court or the other party.

The power to vary the order includes extending the term of the order or including additional prohibitions or requirements in the order. This flexibility allows for those monitoring the progress of offenders to alter the conditions of the order to suit any developing new circumstances.

Annual reviews for under 18s: Where the order is made against someone under 18 years of age, there is a requirement to conduct annual reviews. The review must include consideration of:

- the extent to which the offender has complied with their order;
- the adequacy of any support available to help them to comply with the order; and
- anything else relevant to the question of whether an application should be made to vary or discharge the order.

Under the legislation, the police have overall responsibility for carrying out such a review, with a requirement to act in co-operation with the council. The police may invite any other person or body to participate in the review. This could include youth offending teams, educational establishments or other organisations who have been working with the young person. As a result of the review an application to vary or discharge the CBO may be made to the court.

Penalty on breach

It is a criminal offence if an offender fails to comply, without reasonable excuse, with either the requirements or prohibitions in the CBO. Failure to comply with a prohibition or requirement should be notified to the police. The court has the power to impose serious penalties on conviction, including:

- on summary conviction in the magistrates' court: a maximum of six months in prison or a fine or both.
- on conviction on indictment in the Crown Court: a maximum of five years in prison or a fine or both.

Hearings for those under 18 will take place in the youth court where the maximum sentence is a two year detention and training order.

2.4 Dispersal power

Purpose	Requires a person committing or likely to commit anti-social behaviour, crime or disorder to leave an area for up to 48 hours.
Used by	• Police officers in uniform; and • Police Community Support Officers (if designated the power by their chief constable).
Test	• Contributing or likely to contribute to members of the public in the locality being harassed, alarmed or distressed (or the occurrence of crime and disorder); and • Direction necessary to remove or reduce the likelihood of the anti-social behaviour, crime or disorder.
Details	• Must specify the area to which it relates and can determine the time and the route to leave by. • Can confiscate any item that could be used to commit anti-social behaviour, crime or disorder. • Use in a specified locality must be authorised by a police inspector and can last for up to 48 hours. • A direction can be given to anyone who is, or appears to be, over the age of 10. • A person who is under 16 and given a direction can be taken home or to a place of safety.
Penalty on breach	• Breach is a criminal offence. • Failure to comply with a direction to leave: up to a level 4 fine and/or up to three months in prison although under 18s cannot be imprisoned. • Failure to hand over items: up to a level 2 fine.
Appeals	A person who is given a direction and feels they have been incorrectly dealt with should speak to the duty inspector at the local police station. Details should be given to the person on the written notice.
Important changes/ differences	• It is a more flexible power; it can be used to provide immediate respite to a community from anti-social behaviour, crime or disorder. • An area does not need to be designated as a dispersal zone in advance. • Although there is no requirement to consult the local council, the authorising officer may consider doing so in some circumstances before authorising use of the dispersal. • Police Community Support Officers may use all elements of the dispersal power (if designated the power by their chief constable).

Dispersal power

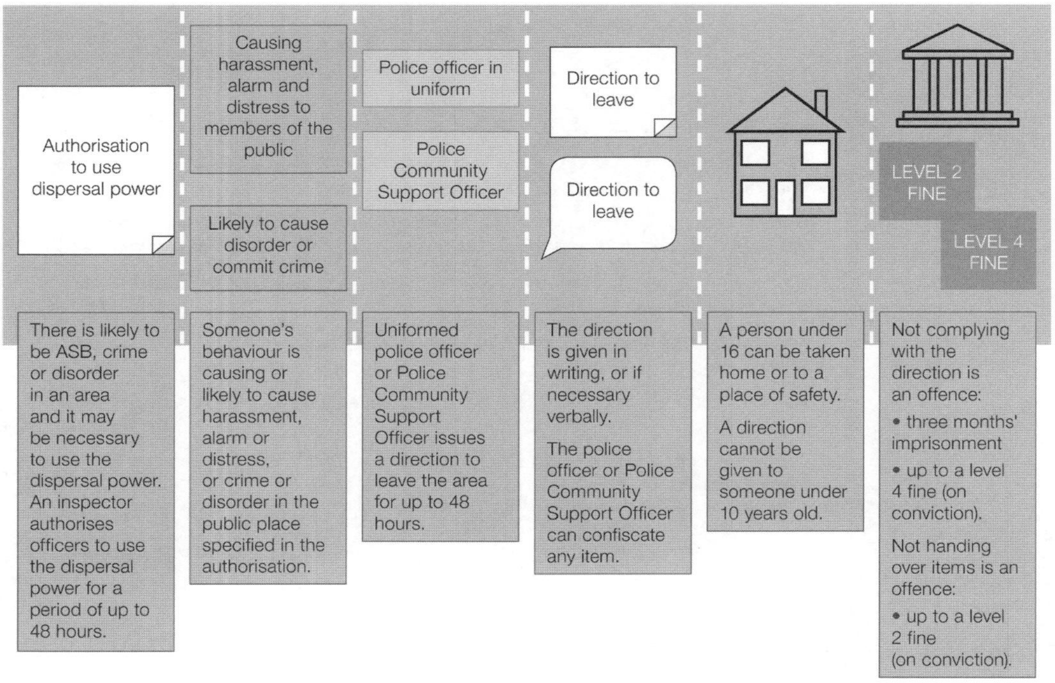

Purpose

The dispersal power is a flexible power which the police can use in a range of situations to disperse anti-social individuals and provide immediate short-term respite to a local community. The power is preventative as it allows an officer to deal instantly with someone's behaviour and nip the problem in the bud before it escalates. In areas where there are regular problems, the police force should work with the local council to find sustainable long-term solutions. In all instances, the impact on the local community should be considered before using the dispersal power.

Who can use it?

The dispersal power can be used by police officers in uniform. Police Community Support Officers (PCSOs) can also use this power if designated by their chief constable. Use of the dispersal power must be authorised by an officer of at least the rank of inspector before use. This will ensure that the dispersal power is not used to stop reasonable activities such as busking or other types of street entertainment which are not causing anti-social behaviour. It may be appropriate for an officer of a more senior rank than inspector to authorise the use of the dispersal power where, for example, there is not an inspector on duty who knows the specific circumstances of the area. The authorising officer can sanction use of the power in a specified locality for a period of up to 48 hours or make a decision on a case by case basis.

The inspector (or above) must record the authorisation in writing, specifying the grounds on which it is given and sign the authorisation. The decision should be based on objective grounds; this may include local knowledge of the area and intelligence that there are likely to be problems at a specific time. The authorising police officer should ensure that the wider impacts on, for example, community relations, are considered properly before use. The written authorisation may be admitted in evidence if the making of the authorisation is in dispute.

It is important that this power is used proportionately and reasonably in a manner compatible with the Human Rights Act 1998. As such, when pre-authorising or authorising an area, the locality should be defined as a specific geographic location, for example by listing the streets to which it applies or the streets which form the boundary of the area rather than stating 'in and around the area of'. The authorisation should not cover an area larger than necessary.

The dispersal power can only be used in the specific location authorised by the inspector. If the anti-social behaviour is occurring outside the authorised area, the inspector (or above) will have to increase the area or the officer cannot issue the dispersal.

The authorising police officer may wish, where practical, to consult with the local council or community representatives before making the authorisation. This may help to understand the implications of using the power within a particular community or whether the community will benefit from the authorisation or use of the dispersal power. Working with the local authority can also assist the police in gaining community consensus and support when it is necessary to use the dispersal power or assist community relations where there are concerns about the use of the dispersal power in a particular area. When it has not been practical to consult the local authority, the authorising officer may wish to notify the local authority if authorisation of the dispersal power has been given or the dispersal power has been used.

In authorising the dispersal power the inspector (or above) must have regard to Articles 10 and 11 of the European Convention on Human Rights that provide for the right for lawful freedom of expression and freedom of assembly.

The test

Two conditions need to be met for a direction to be given:

- The officer must have reasonable grounds to suspect that the behaviour of the person has contributed, or is likely to contribute, to:
  - members of the public in the locality being harassed, alarmed or distressed; or
  - crime and disorder occurring in the locality.
- The officer considers that giving a direction to the person is necessary for the purpose of removing or reducing the likelihood of anti-social behaviour, crime or disorder.

The test includes behaviour that is **likely** to cause harassment, alarm or distress, allowing the dispersal to be used as a preventative measure. The dispersal power is for use in public places; this includes places to which the public has access by virtue of express or implied permission, for example a shopping centre.

Details

Written notice: The direction must be given in writing, unless that is not reasonably practicable. The written notice will specify the locality to which the direction relates and for how long the person must leave the area. The officer can also impose requirements as to the time by which the person must leave the locality and the route they must take. The officer must also tell the person that failure to comply, without reasonable excuse, is an offence unless it is not reasonably practicable to do so.

The information should be provided as clearly as possible and the officer should ensure the person has understood it. If the direction is given verbally a written record of it must also be kept in order to enforce it in the event that it is breached, and for the police force to be able to monitor use of the power. The written notice may also be admitted in evidence in breach proceedings.

Many forces have already established good practice in relation to the use of dispersal powers. For instance, in some forces, officers carry a pre-printed notepad to provide details of the direction, the consequences of a failure to comply, where to collect any confiscated items, and a map to clarify the area a person is excluded from.

Dispersing young people: A police officer (or PCSO where designated) can give a direction to anyone who is, or appears to be, over the age of 10. If the officer reasonably believes the person given the direction to be under the age of 16, the officer can take them home or to another place of safety. Under the provisions of the Children Act 2004 the police have a duty to 'safeguard and promote the welfare of children'. Police forces have safeguarding arrangements in place to ensure that children are not returned to unsafe homes or placed in potentially harmful situations.

Case law in relation to Part 4 of the Anti-social Behaviour Act 2003 states that to 'remove' a person under 16 to their place of residence carries with it a power to use reasonable force if necessary to do so. See R (on the application of W by his parent and litigation friend PW) (Claimant) v (1) Commissioner of Police for the Metropolis, (2) Richmond-upon-Thames London Borough Council (Defendants) and the Secretary of State for the Home Department (Interested Party) [2006].

Putting victims first: If the dispersal power is used in response to a complaint from a member of the public, the officer should update them about what has been done in response to their complaint. Keeping victims updated on enforcement action can provide reassurance to the community and result in fewer follow up calls on the issue.

Restrictions: A direction cannot be given to someone engaged in peaceful picketing that is lawful under section 220 of the Trade Union and Labour Relations (Consolidation) Act 1992 or if they are taking part in a public procession as defined in section 11 of the Public Order Act 1986. In addition, the direction cannot restrict someone from having access to the place where they live or from attending a place where they:

- work, or are contracted to work for that period of time;
- are required to attend by a court or tribunal;
- are expected for education or training, or to receive medical treatment during the period of time that the direction applies.

Providing information to the public: Where use of the dispersal power has been authorised in advance, the police force may wish to consider providing information to those who may be affected.

Surrender of property: The police officer or PCSO can require the person given the direction to hand over items causing or likely to cause anti-social behaviour. This could be any item but typical examples are alcohol, fireworks or spray paint.

The officer does not have the power to seize the item; therefore the person's consent is required to take the item. However, it is an offence for the person not to hand over the item if asked to do so.

Surrendered items will be held at the police station and can be collected after the period of the direction has expired. If the item is not collected within 28 days it can be destroyed or disposed of. If the individual is under the age of 16 they can be required to be accompanied by a parent or other responsible adult to collect the item; this will mean that the adult can be made aware of the young person's behaviour and will help encourage parental responsibility.

Recording information and publishing data: The officer giving the direction must record:

- the individual to whom the direction is given;
- the time at which the direction is given; and
- the terms of the direction (including the area to which it relates and the exclusion period).

If a direction is varied or withdrawn the officer must record the time this was done and the terms of the variation.

Police forces may wish to publish data on the use of the dispersal power to be transparent about their use of it. Police and Crime Commissioners will have an important role in holding forces to account to ensure that officers are using the power proportionately. Publication of data locally will help highlight any 'hotspot' areas that may need a longer-term solution, such as diversionary activities for young people or security measures in pubs and clubs to prevent alcohol-related anti-social behaviour in town centres.

Penalty on breach

Failure to comply with the direction is a summary only criminal offence which will be dealt with in the magistrates' court or youth court for people under the age of 18. On conviction it carries a maximum penalty of a level 4 fine and/or three months imprisonment, although those people under the age of 18 cannot be imprisoned. Failure to surrender items is also a criminal offence with a maximum penalty of a level 2 fine.

Appeals

A person who is given a direction and feels they have been incorrectly dealt with should speak to the duty inspector at the local police station. Details should be given to the person on the written notice.

A more effective power

The new dispersal power is a more flexible tool available to uniformed police officers and designated PCSOs to deal with individuals engaging in anti-social behaviour, crime and disorder not only when they have occurred or are occurring, but when they are likely to occur and in any locality. This extends the capability of the police to prevent incidents of anti-social behaviour, crime and disorder before they take place. The new dispersal power replaces those available under section 27 of the Violent Crime Reduction Act 2006 and section 30 of the Anti-social Behaviour Act 2003.

Important features of the new power are that:

- PCSOs will be able to use the power to enable them to take swift action to prevent anti-social behaviour or to stop its escalation;
- There is no longer a requirement for the pre-designation of a "dispersal zone' in which the power can be used therefore it can be used in any locality immediately;
- The power is also available to disperse individuals without a requirement that two or more people be engaged in the offending behaviour;
- The new power can be used across the spectrum of anti-social behaviour, crime and disorder; not just in dealing with anti-social behaviour and disorder associated with the night-time economy and problem licensed premises;

- There is an additional power to confiscate items associated with the behaviour of the person being directed to disperse, for example alcohol, offensive material, noisy equipment or eggs and other missiles used for Halloween "tricks";
- The period of a person's exclusion from a specified area has been extended to a maximum of 48 hours;
- There is no longer a requirement for the police officer or PCSO to definitively establish the person's age as the new power is available if the person appears to be aged 10 or over;
- Authorisation from a senior officer is a safeguard to ensure that the power is used fairly and proportionately and only in circumstances in which it is necessary. In many cases, the pre-authorisation will fit into current operational processes. For example, many current section 27 directions are given during Friday and Saturday nights while policing the night time economy. In this situation, pre-authorisation could be given during the pre-brief before officers begin;
- The requirement to keep a written record of when the power is used enables effective enforcement of any breach and will be evidentially important for prosecution of breaches.

2.5 Community protection notice

Purpose	To stop a person aged 16 or over, business or organisation committing anti-social behaviour which spoils the community's quality of life.
Who can issue a CPN	• Council officers; • Police officers; • Police community support officers (PCSOs) if designated; and • Social landlords (if designated by the council).
Test	Behaviour has to: • have a detrimental effect on the quality of life of those in the locality; • be of a persistent or continuing nature; and • be unreasonable.
Details	• Written warning issued informing the perpetrator of problem behaviour, requesting them to stop, and the consequences of continuing. • Community protection notice (CPN) issued including requirement to stop things, do things or take reasonable steps to avoid further anti-social behaviour. • Can allow council to carry out works in default on behalf of a perpetrator.
Penalty on breach	• Breach is a criminal offence. • A fixed penalty notice can be issued of up to £100 if appropriate. • A fine of up to level 4 (for individuals), or £20,000 for businesses.
Appeals	• Terms of a CPN can be appealed by the perpetrator within 21 days of issue. • The cost of works undertaken on behalf of the perpetrator by the council can be challenged by the perpetrator if they think they are disproportionate.
Important changes/ differences	• The CPN can deal with a wider range of behaviours for instance, it can deal with noise nuisance and litter on private land open to the air. • The CPN can be used against a wider range of perpetrators. • The CPN can include requirements to ensure that problems are rectified and that steps are taken to prevent the anti-social behaviour occurring again.

Community protection notice

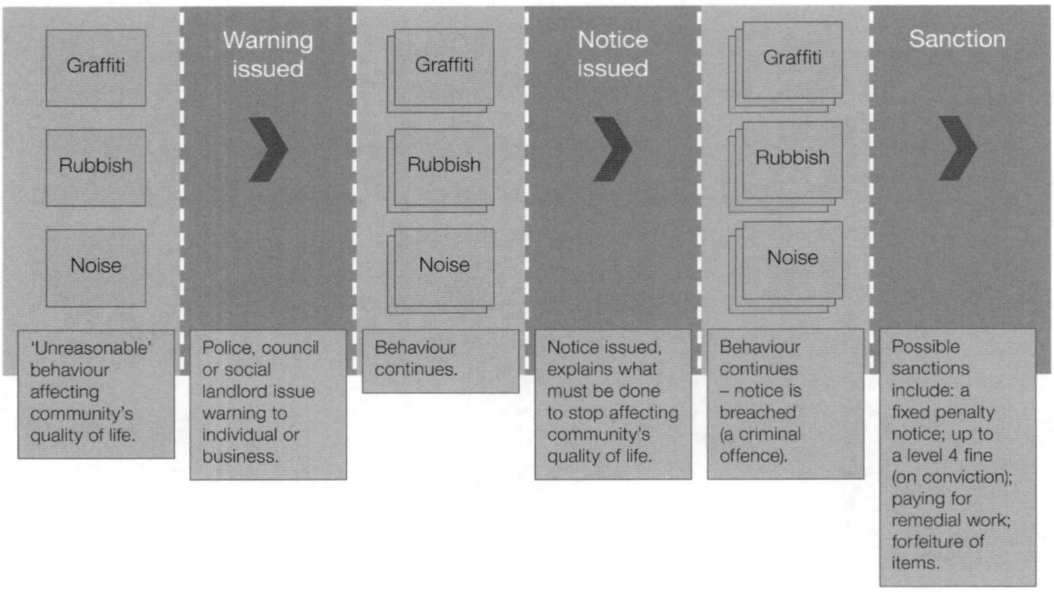

Purpose

The community protection notice (CPN) is intended to deal with particular, ongoing problems or nuisances which negatively affect the community's quality of life by targeting those responsible.

Who can issue a CPN

In many areas, councils already take the lead in dealing with these kinds of issues and they will continue to be able to issue the new notice. However, the move towards neighbourhood policing and community safety teams in recent years has seen the police take a more active role in dealing with these issues, working with councils, and so police officers and police community support officers will also be able to issue CPNs.

In addition, there is a formal role for social landlords. Social landlords in England and Wales manage over four million dwellings and deal with hundreds of thousands of complaints of anti-social behaviour every year. Where it is appropriate, local councils can designate social landlords in their area to issue CPNs.

Test

The test is designed to be broad and focus on the impact anti-social behaviour is having on victims and communities. A CPN can be issued by one of the bodies above if they are satisfied on reasonable grounds that the conduct of the individual, business or organisation:

- is having a detrimental effect on the quality of life of those in the locality;
- is persistent or continuing in nature; and
- is unreasonable.

Putting victims first: In deciding whether the behaviour is having a detrimental effect on the quality of life of those in the locality, issuing officers should consider speaking to potential victims to understand the wider harm to individuals and the community. Not only will this ensure that victims feel that their problem is being taken seriously, but also add to the case against the alleged perpetrator. It will also ensure that officers do not use the notice to stop reasonable activities such as busking or other types of street entertainment which are not causing anti-social behaviour.

Decisions on whether behaviour is persistent should be taken on a case by case basis by issuing officers. Where an individual is storing rubbish in their garden for many months, proving persistence may be simple, but there may be cases where behaviour is continuing over a very short time period. An example could be where an individual is playing loud music in a park. If the officer had asked the individual to stop the music and they had refused, this could be considered continuing in nature and a CPN could be used.

The issuing officer must also make a judgement on whether the behaviour is unreasonable. For instance, a baby crying in the middle of the night may well be having a detrimental effect on those living next door and is likely to be persistent in nature. However, it would not be reasonable to issue the parents with a CPN as there is not a great deal they can do to control or affect the behaviour.

There is significant merit in involving the local council, which will have many years of experience in tackling environmental issues, when deciding whether or not to serve a CPN.

Details

Who can a CPN be issued to? A CPN can be issued against any person aged 16 or over or a body, including a business. Where a body is issued with a CPN, it should be issued to the most appropriate person. In the case of a small business, it could be the shop owner whereas in the case of a major supermarket it could be the store manager. The issuing officer will have to be able to prove that the person issued with the CPN can be reasonably expected to control or affect the behaviour. The CPN can be handed directly to the person in question or it could be posted to them. In circumstances where the owner or occupier cannot be determined, the issuing officer can post the CPN on the premises and it is considered as having been served at that point. In that scenario, the issuing officer would need to demonstrate that reasonable enquiries had been undertaken to ascertain the identity of the owner or occupier, for instance, checking with the Land Registry.

Box F: Considering statutory nuisance

Issuing a community protection notice (CPN) does not discharge the council from its duty to issue an Abatement Notice where the behaviour constitutes a statutory nuisance for the purposes of Part 3 of the Environmental Protection Act 1990. A statutory nuisance is one of the matters listed in section 79(1) of that Act that, given all the surrounding circumstances, is judged to be 'prejudicial to health or a nuisance'. For England and Wales, statutory nuisances are listed as:

- the state of the premises;
- smoke emitted from premises;
- fumes or gases emitted from (domestic) premises;
- any dust, steam, smell or other effluvia arising on industrial, trade or business premises;
- any accumulation or deposit;
- any animal kept in such a place or manner;
- any insects emanating from relevant industrial, trade or business premises;
- artificial light emitted from premises;
- noise emitted from premises;
- noise emitted from or caused by a vehicle, machinery or equipment in a street;
- any other matter declared by any enactment to be a statutory nuisance.

Many of these terms have special meanings, either under the 1990 Act or following decisions of the courts. In particular, 'nuisance' means something different to 'bothersome' or an 'annoyance'. The assessment of nuisance is an objective test, taking into account a range of factors and is based on what is reasonable for the 'average' person. 'Prejudicial to health' means 'injurious or likely to cause injury to health' under section 79(7) of the 1990 Act. While a CPN can be issued for behaviour that may constitute a statutory nuisance, the interaction between the two powers should be considered. It remains a principle of law that a specific power should be used in preference to a general one.

As CPNs can only be issued for behaviours that are persistent or continuing and unreasonable, in most cases, social landlords or the police will have sufficient time to contact the relevant council team in advance of issuing a CPN if they believe the behaviour could be a statutory nuisance. If it could be a statutory nuisance, the issuing authority may wish to consider whether issuing a CPN is necessary given the powers afforded to council under the 1990 Act. If they do decide to issue a CPN in parallel, they should work with the relevant council team to ensure any restrictions or requirements complement those that may be included in any future Abatement Notice.

The written warning: In many cases, the behaviour in question will have been ongoing for some time. Informal interventions may well have been exhausted by the time the applicant decides to go down the formal route of issuing a CPN. However, before a CPN can be issued, a written warning must be issued to the person committing anti-social behaviour.

The written warning must make clear to the individual that if they do not stop the anti-social behaviour, they could be issued with a CPN. However, local agencies may wish to include other information in the written warning, for instance:

- outlining the behaviour that is considered anti-social as this will ensure there is little doubt over what needs to be done to avoid the CPN being issued;

- outlining the time by which the behaviour is expected to have changed in order to give the alleged perpetrator a clear understanding of when the CPN might be served;
- setting out the potential consequences of being issued with a CPN – namely the potential sanctions on breach which could act as an incentive for the individual to change their behaviour before a formal CPN is issued.

How this written warning is discharged is up to each agency. In cases where a problem has been continuing for a period of time, the written warning may be included in other correspondence. However, in cases where issue of a written warning is required more quickly, it could be a standard form of words, adaptable to any situation – for instance, a pre-agreed form of words that can be used by the officer on the spot.

Enough time should be left between the issue of a written warning and the issue of a CPN to allow the individual or body to deal with the matter. It will be for the issuing officer to decide how long is allowed on a case by case basis. For instance, in an example where a garden is to be cleared of waste, several days or weeks may be required to enable the individual to make arrangements. However, where an individual is playing loud music in a park, as outlined above, the officer could require the behaviour to stop immediately.

Putting victims first: Keeping victims and communities updated on enforcement action at important points can help them to deal with the impact of the behaviour. Victims may feel that their complaint has been ignored if they don't see immediate changes to the behaviour. However, simply informing them of what is happening can make a huge difference and result in fewer follow up calls on the issue. If a CPN has been issued, the officer may wish to speak to those affected by the anti-social behaviour again to inform them of what steps have been taken, potential timescales and possible implications for the perpetrator.

Partnership working: In many cases, the issuing agency will have already had contact with other partners in dealing with a persistent issue. For instance, in a case dealing with a build-up of litter, the council may have spoken to the local neighbourhood policing team or social landlord. However, in situations that develop more quickly, the relevant officer will have to decide whether there are other individuals or bodies that should be informed. In particular, for matters that could amount to a statutory nuisance (see Box F) it will often be advisable to seek the expert view of council environmental health officers before issuing a CPN.

What to include in a CPN? A CPN can be drafted from scratch if necessary so that it is appropriate to the situation and can include any or all of the following:

- A requirement to stop doing specified things;
- A requirement to do specified things;
- A requirement to take reasonable steps to achieve specified results.

This means that not only can the relevant officer stop someone being anti-social, but they can also put steps in place to ensure the behaviour does not recur.

In deciding what should be included as a requirement in a CPN, issuing officers should consider what is reasonable to include in a notice of this type and any timescales they wish to add. CPNs are designed to deal with short or medium-term issues. While restrictions and requirements may be similar to those in a civil injunction (see part 2.2), more serious conditions, such as attendance at a drug rehabilitation course, would clearly be more appropriate to a court issued order.

Putting victims first: When the issuing officer has decided what to include as a requirement in the community protection notice they should consider the desired outcome for the community. Victims don't just want the behaviour to stop; they also want it not to occur again. Consideration should be given to whether there are requirements that could ensure the anti-social behaviour does not recur.

Penalty on breach

Failure to comply with a CPN is an offence. Where an individual, business or organisation fails to comply with the terms of a CPN, a number of options are available for the issuing authority and these are outlined in more detail below.

Putting victims first: When deciding which sanction to choose on non-compliance with a CPN, the issuing authority should consider the potential wishes of the victim. While issuing a fixed penalty notice may be considered appropriate, if it does nothing to alleviate the impact on the community or leaves victims feeling ignored, this may not be the best course of action and may lead to further complaints and the requirement for more action.

Fixed penalty notices: Depending on the behaviour in question, the issuing officer could decide that a fixed penalty notice (FPN) would be the most appropriate sanction. The FPN can be issued by a police officer, PCSO, council officer or, if designated, a social landlord. In making the decision to issue a FPN, the officer should be mindful that if issued, payment of the FPN would discharge any liability to conviction for the offence.

A FPN should not be more than £100 and can specify two amounts, for instance, a lower payment if settled early, say within 14 days. In order to allow the individual time to pay the FPN, no other associated proceedings can be taken until at least 14 days after the issue. The exact wording or design of a FPN can be determined locally to fit with local standards and protocols but must:

- give reasonably detailed particulars of the circumstances alleged to constitute the offence;
- state the period during which proceedings will not be taken for the offence;
- specify the amount or amounts payable;
- state the name and address of the person to whom the FPN should be paid; and
- specify permissible methods of payment (for example, cash, cheque, bank transfer).

Remedial action: If an individual or body fails to comply with a CPN issued by the council, the council may decide to take remedial action to address the issue. Where the CPN has been issued by the police or a social landlord, but they believe remedial action is an appropriate sanction, they should approach the council to discuss the best way to move forward. For instance, the social landlord could undertake the work on behalf of the council.

If it is decided that remedial action is the best way forward, the council (or the other agency in discussion with the council) should establish what works are required to put the situation right. For instance, in a situation where the complaint relates to a significant build up of rubbish in someone's front garden, remedial action could take the form of clearing the garden on the perpetrator's behalf.

Putting victims first: Punishment of the perpetrator may not be top of the victim's priority list; they may just want to see the situation fixed. If remedial action is chosen as the most appropriate action, it may help those affected by the behaviour to know when they can expect remedial works to be undertaken.

Where this work is to be undertaken on land 'open to the air', the council or their agent (for instance, a rubbish disposal contractor) can undertake these works without the consent of the owner or occupier. Where works are required indoors the permission of the owner or occupier is required. When it has been decided what works are required, the council has to specify to the perpetrator what work it intends to carry out and the estimated cost. Once the work has been completed, the council should give the perpetrator details of the work completed and the final amount payable. In determining a 'reasonable' charge, local authorities should ensure the costs are no more than is necessary to restore the land to the standard specified in the notice. Such costs may include officer time, use of cleaning equipment (unless of a specialised nature), and administration costs relating to the clearance itself.

Remedial orders: On conviction for an offence of failing to comply with a CPN, the prosecuting authority may ask the court to impose a remedial order and/or a forfeiture order. This could be for a number of reasons, for instance:

- The matter may be deemed so serious that a court order is warranted;
- Works may be required to an area that requires the owner's or occupier's consent and this is not forthcoming; or
- The issuing authority may believe that forfeiture or seizure of one or more items is required as a result of the behaviour (for instance, sound making equipment).

A remedial order may require the defendant:

- to carry out specified work (this could set out the original CPN requirements); or
- to allow work to be carried out by, or on behalf of, a specified local authority.

Where works are required indoors, the defendant's permission is still required. But this does not prevent a defendant who fails to give that consent from being in breach of the court's order.

Forfeiture orders: Following conviction for an offence under section 45, the court may also order the forfeiture of any item that was used in the commission of the offence. This could be spray paints, sound making equipment or a poorly socialised dog where the court feels the individual is not able to manage the animal appropriately (re-homed in the case of a dog). Where items are forfeited, they can be destroyed or disposed of appropriately.

Seizure: In some circumstances, the court may issue a warrant authorising the seizure of items that have been used in the commission of the offence of failing to comply with a CPN. In these circumstances, an enforcement officer may use reasonable force, if necessary, to seize the item or items.

Failure to comply with any of the requirements in the court order constitutes contempt of court and could lead to a custodial sentence. If an individual is convicted of an offence under section 48, they may receive up to a level 4 fine (up to £20,000 in the case of a business or organisation).

Appeals

Anyone issued with a CPN has the opportunity to appeal it. Appeals are heard in a magistrates' court and the CPN should provide details of the process and how an individual can appeal. As the legislation makes clear, an appeal can be made on the following grounds:

The test was not met if:

- **the behaviour did not take place.** In most cases, officers will have collected evidence to place beyond any reasonable doubt that the behaviour occurred. However, in cases where the officer has relied on witness statements alone, they should consider the potential for this appeal route and build their case accordingly.
- **the behaviour has not had a detrimental effect on the quality of life of those in the locality.** Again, the importance of witness statements and any other evidence that the behaviour in question is having a negative impact on those nearby should be collected to ensure this defence is covered.
- **the behaviour was not persistent or continuing.** In some cases, judging persistence will be straightforward. However, in cases where a decision to issue a CPN is taken more quickly, officers should use their professional judgement to decide whether this test is met and may need to justify this on appeal.
- **the behaviour is not unreasonable.** In many cases, individuals, businesses or organisations that are presented with evidence of the detrimental impact of their behaviour will take steps to address it. Where they do not, they may argue that what they are doing is reasonable. In deciding whether behaviour is unreasonable, officers should consider the impact the behaviour is having on the victim, whether steps could be taken to alleviate this impact and whether the behaviour is necessary at all.
- **the individual cannot reasonably be expected to control or affect the behaviour.** In issuing the CPN, the officer must make a judgement as to whether the individual or business or organisation can reasonably be expected to do something to change the behaviour. The officer should be prepared to justify this decision in court if required.

Other reasons:

- **Any of the requirements are unreasonable.** Requirements in a CPN should either prevent the anti-social behaviour from continuing or recurring, or reduce the detrimental effect or reduce the risk of its continuance or recurrence. As such, it should be related to the behaviour in question.
- **There is a material defect or error with the CPN.** This ground for appeal could be used if there was a failure to comply with a requirement in the Act, such as a failure to provide a written warning before issuing a CPN.
- **The CPN was issued to the wrong person.** This could be grounds for appeal if the CPN was posted to the wrong address or the wrong person was identified in a business or organisation.

The person issued with the CPN must appeal within 21 days of issue. Where an appeal is made, any requirement included under section 43(3)(b) or (c), namely a requirement to do specified things or take reasonable steps to achieve specified results, is suspended until the outcome of the appeal. However, requirements stopping the individual or body from doing specified things under section 43(3)(a) continue to have effect. In addition, where remedial action is taken by a council under section 47 or 49 the individual has the opportunity to appeal on the grounds that the cost of the work being undertaken on their behalf is disproportionate.

2.6 Public spaces protection order

Purpose	Designed to stop individuals or groups committing anti-social behaviour in a public space
Who can make a PSPO	• Councils issue a public spaces protection order (PSPO) after consultation with the police, Police and Crime Commissioner and other relevant bodies.
Test	Behaviour being restricted has to: • be having, or be likely to have, a detrimental effect on the quality of life of those in the locality; • be persistent or continuing nature; and • be unreasonable.
Details	• Restrictions and requirements set by the council. • These can be blanket restrictions or requirements or can be targeted against certain behaviours by certain groups at certain times. • Can restrict access to public spaces (including certain types of highway) where that route is being used to commit anti-social behaviour. • Can be enforced by a police officer, police community support officers and council officers.
Penalty on breach	• Breach is a criminal offence. • Enforcement officers can issue a fixed penalty notice of up to £100 if appropriate. • A fine of up to level 3 on prosecution.
Appeals	• Anyone who lives in, or regularly works in or visits the area can appeal a PSPO in the High Court within six weeks of issue. • Further appeal is available each time the PSPO is varied by the council.
Important changes/ differences	• More than one restriction can be added to the same PSPO, meaning that a single PSPO can deal with a wider range of behaviours than the orders it replaces.

Public spaces protection order

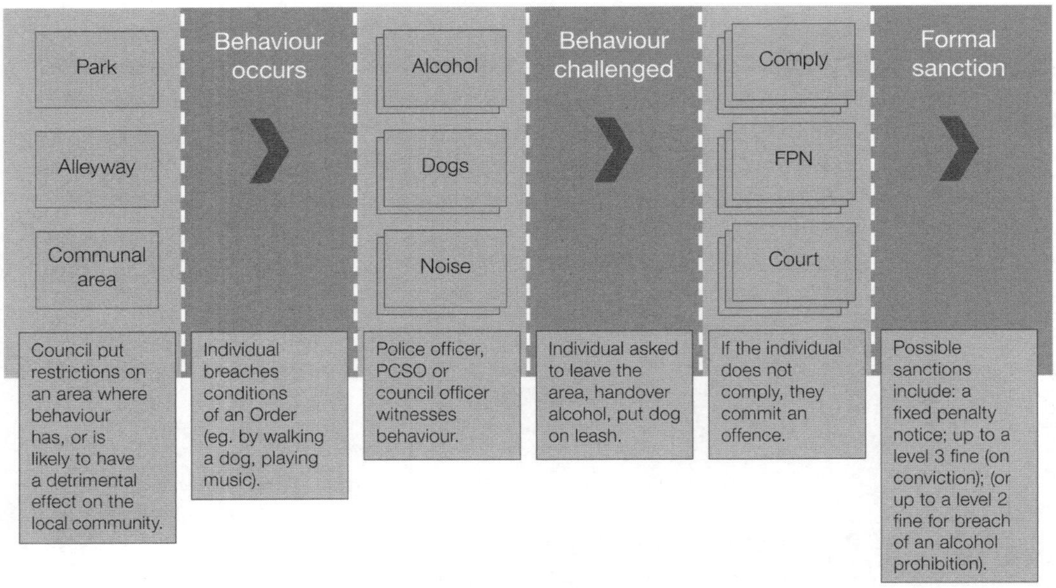

Purpose

Public spaces protection orders (PSPOs) are intended to deal with a particular nuisance or problem in a particular area that is detrimental to the local community's qualify of life, by imposing conditions on the use of that area which apply to everyone. They are designed to ensure the law-abiding majority can use and enjoy public spaces, safe from anti-social behaviour.

Who can make a PSPO?

Councils will be responsible for making the new PSPO although enforcement powers will be much broader. District councils will take the lead in England with county councils undertaking the role only where there is no district council. In London, borough councils will be able to make PSPOs, as will the Common Council of the City of London and the Council of the Isles of Scilly. In Wales, responsibility will fall to county councils or county borough councils. The new power is not available to parish councils and town councils in England, or community councils in Wales. Section 71 ensures that bodies other than local authorities can make PSPOs in certain circumstances by order of the Secretary of State. This will allow the City of London Corporation to continue managing a number of public spaces with the permission of, and on behalf of, local authorities.

Test

The test is designed to be broad and focus on the impact anti-social behaviour is having on victims and communities. A PSPO can be made by the council if they are satisfied on reasonable grounds that the activities carried out, or likely to be carried out, in a public space:

- have had, or are likely to have, a detrimental effect on the quality of life of those in the locality;
- is, or is likely to be, persistent or continuing in nature;
- is, or is likely to be, unreasonable; and
- justifies the restrictions imposed.

Putting victims first: In deciding to place restrictions on a particular public space, councils should consider the knock on effects of that decision. Introducing a blanket ban on a particular activity may simply displace the behaviour and create victims elsewhere.

Details

Where can it apply? The council can make a PSPO on any public space within its own area. The definition of public space is wide and includes any place to which the public or any section of the public has access, on payment or otherwise, as of right or by virtue of express or implied permission, for example a shopping centre.

Working with partners: Before making a PSPO, the council must consult with the local police. This should be done formally through the chief officer of police and the Police and Crime Commissioner, but details could be agreed by working level leads. This is an opportunity for the police and council to share information about the area and the problems being caused as well as discuss the practicalities of enforcement. In addition, the owner or occupier of the land should be consulted. This should include the County Council (if the PSPO application is not being led by them) where they are the Highway Authority.

The council must also consult whatever community representatives they think appropriate. This could relate to a specific group, for instance the residents association, or an individual or group of individuals, for instance, regular users of a park or specific activities such as busking or other types of street entertainment. Before the PSPO is made, the council also has to publish the draft order in accordance with regulations published by the Secretary of State.

Box G: Land requiring special consideration

Before a council makes a PSPO, it should consider whether the land falls into any of the following categories:

- **Registered common land:** There are around 550,000 hectares of registered common land in England and Wales. Common land is mapped as open access land under the Countryside and Rights of Way (CROW) Act 2000 with a right of public access on foot. Some commons, particularly those in urban districts, also have additional access rights and these may include rights for equestrian use.
- **Registered town or village green:** Town and village greens developed under customary law as areas of land where local people indulged in lawful sports and pastimes. These might include organised or ad-hoc games, picnics, fetes and similar activities, such as dog walking.
- **Open access land:** Open access land covers mountain, moor, heath and down and registered common land, and also some voluntarily dedicated land, for example the Forestry Commission's or Natural Resources Wales' freehold estate. Open access land provides a right of open-air recreation on foot although the landowner can voluntarily extend the right to other forms of access, such as for cycling or horse-riding.

This can be done by contacting the Commons registration authority (county council in two-tier areas; unitary authority elsewhere). If the land in question is a registered common, the council will be able to find out what common land rights exist and the access rights of any users. Defra considers the model set out in 'A Common Purpose' to be good practice in consulting directly affected persons (including commoners) and the public about any type of potential change in the management of a common.

If land is a registered green, it receives considerable statutory protection under the 'Victorian Statutes'. In terms of open access land, there are various national limitations on what activities are included within the access rights. It is possible for local restrictions on CROW rights to be put in place to meet wider land use needs, and this system is normally administered by Natural England.

Where an authority is considering an order on one of these types of land, the council should consider discussing this with relevant forums and user groups (e.g. Local Access Forums, Ramblers or the British Horse Society) depending on the type of provision that is contemplated in the order. It could also be appropriate to hold a local public meeting when considering whether to make an order for an area of such land to ensure all affected persons are given the opportunity to raise concerns.

What to include in a PSPO? The PSPO can be drafted from scratch based on the individual issues being faced in a particular public space. A single PSPO can also include multiple restrictions and requirements in one order. It can prohibit certain activities, such as the drinking of alcohol, as well as placing requirements on individuals carrying out certain activities, for instance making sure that people walking their dogs keep them on a lead. However, activities are not limited to those covered by the orders being replaced and so the new PSPO can be used more flexibly to deal with local issues.

When deciding what to include, the council should consider scope. The PSPO is designed to make public spaces more welcoming to the majority of law abiding people and communities and not simply restrict access. Restrictions or requirements can be targeted at specific people, designed to apply only at certain times or apply only in certain circumstances.

Putting victims first: Although it may not be viable in each case, discussing potential restrictions and requirements prior to issuing an order with those living or working nearby may help to ensure that the final PSPO better meets the needs of the local community and is less likely to be challenged.

In establishing which restrictions or requirements should be included, the council should ensure that the measures are necessary to prevent the detrimental effect on those in the locality or reduce the likelihood of the detrimental effect continuing, occurring or recurring.

When the final set of measures is agreed on, the PSPO should be published in accordance with regulations made by the Secretary of State and must:

- identify the activities having the detrimental effect;
- explain the potential sanctions available on breach; and
- specify the period for which the PSPO has effect.

Box H: Controlling the presence of dogs

When deciding whether to make requirements or restrictions on dogs and their owners, local councils will need to consider whether there are suitable alternatives for dogs to be exercised without restrictions.

Under the Animal Welfare Act 2006, owners of dogs are required to provide for the welfare needs of their animals and this includes providing the necessary amount of exercise each day. Councils should be aware of the publicly accessible parks and other public places in their area which dog walkers can use to exercise their dogs without restrictions. Consideration should also be made on how any restrictions affect those who rely on assistance dogs.

In relation to dogs and their owners, a PSPO could, for example:

- exclude dogs from designated areas (e.g. a children's play area in a park);
- require dog faeces to be picked up by owners;
- require dogs to be kept on leads;
- restrict the number of dogs that can be walked by one person at any one time; and
- put in place other restrictions or requirements to tackle or prevent any other activity that is considered to have a detrimental effect on the quality of life of those in the locality, or is likely to have such an effect.

Restricting alcohol: A PSPO can be used to restrict the consumption of alcohol in a public space where the test has been met. However, as with the Designated Public Place Order which it replaces, there are a number of limitations on using the power for this end.

A PSPO cannot be used to restrict the consumption of alcohol where the premises or its curtilage (a beer garden or pavement seating area) is licensed for the supply of alcohol. There are also limitations where either Part 5 of the Licensing Act 2003 or section 115E of the Highways Act 1980 applies. This is because the licensing system already includes safeguards against premises becoming centres for anti-social behaviour. It would create confusion and duplication if PSPOs were introduced here.

Restricting access: In the past, Gating Orders have been used to close access to certain public rights of way where the behaviour of some has been anti-social. The PSPO can also be used to restrict access to a public right of way. However, when deciding on this approach, the council must consider a number of things.

- **Can they restrict access?** A number of rights of way may not be restricted due to their strategic value.
- **What impact will the restriction have?** For instance, is it a primary means of access between two places and is there a reasonably convenient alternative route?
- **Are there any alternatives?** Previously gating was the only option, but it may be possible under a PSPO to restrict the activities causing the anti-social behaviour rather than access in its totality.

There are also further consultation requirements where access is to be restricted to a public right of way. This includes notifying potentially affected persons of the possible restrictions. This could include people who regularly use the right of way in their day to day travel as well as those who live nearby. Interested persons should be informed about how they can view a copy of the proposed order, and be given details of how they can make representations and by when. The council should then consider these representations.

It will be up to the council to decide how best to identify and consult with interested persons. In the past newspapers have been used. However in the digital age, other channels such as websites and social media may be more effective. Where issues are more localised, councils may prefer to deal with individual households. Alternatively, where appropriate, councils may decide to hold public meetings and discuss issues with regional or national bodies (such as the Local Access Forum) to gather views.

Duration of a PSPO: The maximum duration of a PSPO is three years but they can last for shorter periods of time where appropriate. Short-term PSPOs could be used where it is not certain that restrictions will have the desired effect, for instance, when closing a public right of way, councils may wish to make an initial PSPO for 12 months and then review the decision at that point.

At any point before expiry, the council can extend a PSPO by up to three years if they consider that it is necessary to prevent the original behaviour from occurring or recurring. They should also consult with the local police and any other community representatives they think appropriate.

Changing the terms: The new PSPO can cover a number of different restrictions and requirements so there should be little need to have overlapping orders in a particular public space. However, if a new issue arises in an area where a PSPO is in force, the council can vary the terms of the order at any time. This can change the size of the restricted area or the specific requirements or restrictions. For instance, a PSPO may exist to ensure dogs are kept on their leads in a park but, after 12 months, groups start to congregate in the park drinking alcohol which is having a detrimental effect on those living nearby. As a result, the council could vary the PSPO to deal with both issues.

As well as varying the PSPO, a council can also seek to discharge it at any time. For instance when the problem has ceased to exist or the land ceases to be classified as a public space.

Penalty on breach

It is an offence for a person, without reasonable excuse, to:

- do anything that the person is prohibited from doing by a PSPO (other than consume alcohol – see below); or
- fail to comply with a requirement to which the person is subject under a PSPO.

A person does not commit an offence by failing to comply with a prohibition or requirement that the council did not have power to include in the PSPO. A person guilty of an offence is liable on summary conviction to a fine not exceeding level 3 on the standard scale.

It is not an offence to drink alcohol in a controlled drinking zone. However, it is an offence to fail to comply with a request to cease drinking or surrender alcohol in a controlled drinking zone. This is also liable on summary conviction to a fine not exceeding level 2 on the standard scale. If alcohol is confiscated, it can be disposed of by the person who confiscates it.

Depending on the behaviour in question, the enforcing officer could decide that a fixed penalty notice (FPN) would be the most appropriate sanction. The FPN can be issued by a police officer, PCSO, council officer or other person designated by the council. In making the decision to issue a FPN, the officer should consider that if issued, payment of the FPN would discharge any liability to conviction for the offence. However, where the FPN is not paid within the required timescale, court proceedings can be initiated (prosecution for the offence of failing to comply with the PSPO).

Appeals

Any challenge to the PSPO must be made in the High Court by an interested person within six weeks of it being made. An interested person is someone who lives in, regularly works in, or visits the restricted area. This means that only those who are directly affected by the restrictions have the power to challenge. This right to challenge also exists where an order is varied by a council.

Interested persons can challenge the validity of a PSPO on two grounds. They could argue that the council did not have power to make the order, or to include particular prohibitions or requirements. In addition, the interested person could argue that one of the requirements (for instance, consultation) had not been complied with.

When the application is made, the High Court can decide to suspend the operation of the PSPO pending the verdict in part or in totality. The High Court has the ability to uphold the PSPO, quash it, or vary it.

Enforcement

Although PSPOs are made by the council in an area, enforcement should be the responsibility of a wider group. Council officers will be able to enforce the restrictions and requirements, as will other groups that they designate, including officers accredited under the community safety accreditation scheme. In addition, police officers and PCSOs will have the ability to enforce the order.

Transition

Where a designated public place order, gating order or dog control order is currently in force, this will continue to be valid for a period of three years following commencement of the new power. At this point it will be treated as a PSPO. However, councils need not wait for this to happen and could decide to review the need for their current orders ahead of that transition to simplify the enforcement landscape.

2.7 Closure power

Purpose	To allow the police or council to quickly close premises which are being used, or likely to be used, to commit nuisance or disorder.
Applicants	• Local council. • Police.
Test	The following has occurred, or will occur, if the closure power is not used: Closure notice (up to 48 hours): • Nuisance to the public; or • Disorder near those premises. Closure order (up to six months): • Disorderly, offensive or criminal behaviour; • Serious nuisance to the public; or • Disorder near the premises.
Details	• A closure notice is issued out of court in the first instance. Flowing from this the closure order can be applied for through the courts. • Notice: can close a premises for up to 48 hrs out of court but cannot stop owner or those who habitually live there accessing the premises. • Order: can close premises for up to six months and can restrict all access. • Both the notice and the order can cover any land or any other place, whether enclosed or not including residential, business, non-business and licensed premises.
Penalty on breach	Breach is a criminal offence. • Notice: Up to three months in prison; • Order: Up to six months in prison; • Both: Up to an unlimited fine for residential and non-residential premises.
Who can appeal	• Any person who the closure notice was served on; • Any person who had not been served the closure notice but has an interest in the premises; • The council (where closure order was not made and they issued the notice); • The police (where closure order was not made and they issued the notice).
Important changes/ differences	• A single closure power covering a wider range of behaviour. Quick, flexible and can be used for up to 48 hours out of court.

Closure powers

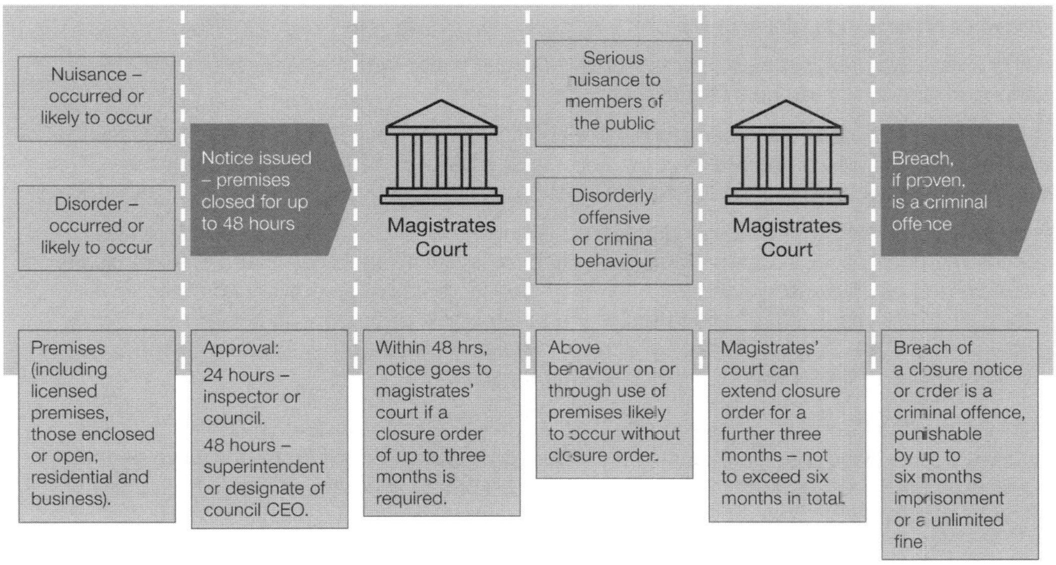

Purpose

The closure power is a fast, flexible power that can be used to protect victims and communities by quickly closing premises that are causing nuisance or disorder.

Applicants

The power comes in two stages: the closure notice and the closure order which are intrinsically linked. The closure notice can be used by the council or the police out of court. Following the issuing of a closure notice, an application must be made to the magistrates' court for a closure order, unless the closure notice has been cancelled.

The test

A closure notice can be issued for 24 hours if the council or police officer (of at least the rank of inspector) is satisfied on reasonable grounds:

- that the use of particular premises has resulted, or (if the notice is not issued) is likely soon to result, in nuisance to members of the public; or
- that there has been, or (if the notice is not issued) is likely soon to be, disorder near those premises associated with the use of those premises, and that the notice is necessary to prevent the nuisance or disorder from continuing, recurring or occurring.

The closure notice can be issued in the first instance for 48 hours or extended from 24 hours up to a maximum of 48 hours by the council's chief executive officer (head of paid service) or designate thereof, or by a police superintendent.

A closure order can subsequently be issued if the court is satisfied:

- that a person has engaged, or (if the order is not made) is likely to engage, in disorderly, offensive or criminal behaviour on the premises; or
- that the use of the premises has resulted, or (if the order is not made) is likely to result, in serious nuisance to members of the public; or
- that there has been, or (if the order is not made) is likely to be, disorder near those premises associated with the use of those premises, and that the order is necessary to prevent the behaviour, nuisance or disorder from continuing, recurring or occurring.

A closure notice cannot prohibit access in respect of anyone who habitually lives on a premises. This means that the notice cannot prohibit those who routinely or regularly live at those premises. It is therefore unlikely to disallow access to, for example, students who live away from the family home for part of the year but routinely return to the family home or those who spend the majority of the week living at the pub in which they work. However, a closure order, granted by the court, can prohibit access to those who routinely live at a premises.

In prohibiting access through a closure notice it will be important to consider who is responsible for the premises and who may need access to secure a premises. This might not always be the owner, for example an individual managing a premises on behalf of an owner who lives abroad may need to secure the premises on their behalf.

Putting victims first: In deciding the effect of the behaviour and courses of action the police and local council should speak to the victim to obtain their view on how the behaviour is affecting them and what outcome they would like to see.

Details

Approvals: The level or role of employee within the council who can issue a notice for up to 24 hours has not been specified due to the different structures locally. In considering who should be authorised as designates of the chief executive officer for the issuing of the 48 hour notice, councils will also want to consider who is delegated to issue the closure notice for 24 hours and consider whether the extension to 48 hours should be authorised by an officer of greater seniority, as is the case for the police. This may take into consideration the need for the power to be used quickly, its flexible nature, and equivalent requirement for a police inspector to issue a closure notice for 24 hours.

Notifications: With every issue of a closure notice, an application must be made to the magistrates' court for a closure order. Where the intention is to cancel the notice prior to the end of the 48 hour period because a closure order or a temporary order is not deemed necessary, this should be communicated to the court on application for a hearing for the closure order.

The police and council will want to consider when the courts will be able to hear the application for the closure order. The courts are required to hear the application within 48 hours of the service of the closure notice. This 48 hour period for the courts excludes Christmas day. To avoid undue pressure on the courts to hear applications for closure orders within 48 hours of serving the closure notice, careful thought should be given as to exactly when to serve the closure notice. Where possible, it is advisable to liaise with the court's listing office before serving the closure notice so that victims can be effectively protected at the earliest opportunity.

Putting victims first: The issuing body should undertake to inform the victim of the anti-social behaviour of the closure notice and to inform them of the details of the closure order hearing where possible and appropriate.

Temporary orders: Courts can consider giving an extension of the closure notice if required. This can be considered as an option by the magistrates' court at the hearing for the closure order. The court can order a closure notice to stay in force for a further 48 hours if satisfied this meets the test required for a closure notice.

A court may also order that a closure notice continue in force for a period of not more than 14 days in circumstances where the hearing is adjourned A hearing can be adjourned for no more that 14 days to enable the occupier or anyone with an interest in the premises to show why a closure order should not be made.

Partnership working: Consultation is required as part of the closure notice. Before issuing a notice the police or council must ensure that they consult with anyone they think appropriate. This should include the victim, but could also include other members of the public that may be affected positively or negatively by the closure, community representatives, other organisations and bodies, the police or local council (where not the issuing organisation) or others that regularly use the premises. There may also be people who use the premises as access to another premises that is not subject to the closure notice but may be impacted on by the closure.

The method of consultation will depend on the situation and urgency. The police or council will want to consider how to keep a record of those consulted in case challenged at a later date (for instance, as part of a court case).

What to include in a closure notice? The closure notice should:

- identify the premises;
- explain the effect of the notice;
- state that failure to comply with the notice is an offence;
- state that an application will be made for a closure order;
- specify when and where the application will be heard;
- explain the effect of the closure order; and
- give information about the names of, and means of contacting, persons and organisations in the area that provide advice about housing and legal matters.

Information should be displayed clearly in simple language, avoiding the use of jargon.

Putting victims first: It is not necessary to include information about those consulted within an order so as to protect those who may have made a complaint from any retribution. However, the officer issuing the closure notice should keep a record of those consulted.

Access: There may be times where the closure of premises through a closure order has a wider impact. An item may have been left in the premises or access has become restricted to another premises. Where an item has been left on premises it is expected that the police and local council will use their discretion in either allowing access temporarily to enable the individual to retrieve their item or retrieving the item on their behalf. Where an individual accesses the premises themselves without communication to the police or council they commit an offence unless they have a reasonable excuse. Therefore it is sensible for the police and council to have clear communication with individuals affected.

Where a closure order restricts access to another premises or part of a premises that is not subject to a closure order the individuals affected will be able to apply to the appropriate court to have the order considered. The court may make any order it thinks appropriate. This may be a variation order to vary the terms of the order or it could cancel the order if considered inappropriate for it to remain in place.

Penalty on breach

An offence is committed when a person, without reasonable excuse, remains on or enters a premises in contravention of a closure notice or a closure order.

Closure notice and temporary order: Breaching a closure notice or temporary order is a criminal offence carrying a penalty of either imprisonment for a period of up to three months or an unlimited fine or both.

Closure order: Breaching a closure order is a criminal offence carrying a penalty of either imprisonment for a period of up to six months or an unlimited fine, or both.

Obstruction: It is a criminal offence to obstruct a police officer or local council employee who is:

- serving a closure notice, cancellation notice or variation notice;
- entering the premises; or
- securing the premises.

This offence carries a penalty of either imprisonment for a period of up to three months or an unlimited fine, or both.

Who can appeal?

A closure notice cannot be appealed. A closure order can be appealed. Appeals are to the Crown Court and must be made within 21 days beginning with the date of the decision to which the appeal relates.

An appeal against the decision to issue the order may be made by:

- a person who was served the closure notice; or
- anyone who has an interest in the premises upon whom the notice was not served.

Where the court decides not to issue a closure order the following may appeal:

- the police may only appeal where they issued the closure notice;
- the local council may only appeal where they issued the closure notice.

On appeal, the Crown Court may make whatever order it thinks appropriate. If the premises is licensed the court must inform the licensing authority. It should also be considered whether it is appropriate and possible to update the victim on the progress of the case.

2.8 New absolute ground for possession

Overview	The Act introduces a new absolute ground for possession of secure and assured tenancies where anti-social behaviour or criminality has already been proven by another court.
Purpose	To expedite the eviction of landlords' most anti-social tenants to bring faster relief to victims.
Applicants / Who can use the new ground	• Social landlords (local authorities and housing associations). • Private rented sector landlords.
Test	The tenant, a member of the tenant's household, or a person visiting the property has met one of the following conditions: • convicted of a serious offence (specified in Schedule 2A to the Housing Act 1985); • found by a court to have breached a civil injunction; • convicted for breaching a criminal behaviour order (CBO); • convicted for breaching a noise abatement notice; or • the tenant's property has been closed for more than 48 hours under a closure order for anti-social behaviour.
Details	• Offence/breach needs to have occurred in the locality of the property or affected a person with a right to live in the locality or affected the landlord or his or her staff/ contractors; • Secure tenants of local housing authorities will have a statutory right to request a review of the landlord's decision to seek possession. Private registered providers are encouraged to adopt a similar practice.
Result of action	• If the above test is met, the court must grant a possession order (subject to any available human rights defence raised by the tenant, including proportionality) where the correct procedure has been followed.
Important changes/ differences	• Unlike the existing discretionary grounds for possession, the landlord will not be required to prove to the court that it is reasonable to grant possession. This means the court will be more likely to determine cases in a single, short hearing; • This will offer better protection and faster relief for victims and witnesses of anti-social behaviour, save landlords costs, and free up court resources and time; • It will provide new flexibility for landlords to obtain possession through this faster route for persistently anti-social tenants; • The court will not be able to postpone possession to a date later than 14 days after the making of the order except in exceptional circumstances, and will not be able to postpone for later than six weeks in any event.

New absolute ground for possession

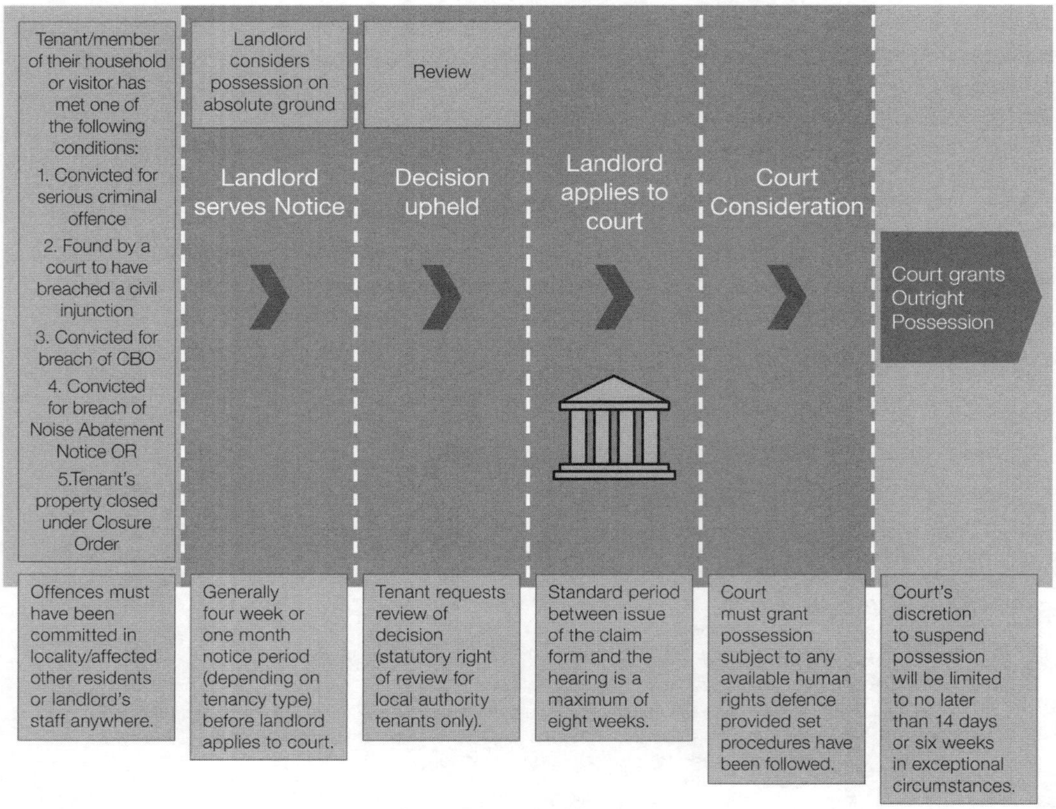

Overview

Prevention and early intervention should be at the heart of all landlords' approaches to dealing with anti-social behaviour. The evidence shows this is the case with over 80% of anti-social behaviour complaints resolved by social landlords through early intervention and informal routes without resorting to formal tools.

It is, however, a source of frustration for landlords and victims that in exceptional cases where anti-social behaviour (or criminality) persists and it becomes necessary to seek possession, the existing process for evicting anti-social tenants is often very lengthy and expensive for landlords and the courts and, most importantly, prolongs the suffering of victims, witnesses and the community.

Purpose

The purpose of the new absolute ground for possession is to speed up the possession process in cases where anti-social behaviour or criminality has been already been proven by another court.

As the landlord will no longer need to prove that it is reasonable to grant possession, the court will be more likely to determine cases in a single, short hearing. This will strike a better balance between the rights of victims and perpetrators, and provide swifter relief for victims, witnesses and the community. **The new absolute ground is intended for the most serious cases of anti-social behaviour and landlords should ensure that the ground is used selectively.**

Informing the tenant: Landlords should ensure that tenants are aware from the commencement of their tenancy that anti-social behaviour or criminality either by the tenant, people living with them, or their visitors could lead to a loss of their home under the new absolute ground.

Applicants

The new absolute ground will be available for secure and assured tenancies, and, therefore, will be able to be used by both social landlords and private rented sector landlords.

In practice, it is likely that private rented sector landlords will generally use the 'no fault' ground for possession, in section 21 of the Housing Act 1988, where this is available. This does not require the tenant to be in breach of any of the terms of their tenancy and, therefore, does not require the landlord to show that it is reasonable to grant possession as long as the relevant notice has been served. However, the 'no fault' ground can only be used at the end of the fixed term of the tenancy, which must be at least six months from the initial inception of the tenancy. This often limits private landlords' ability to seek possession where a tenant commits serious anti-social behaviour or criminality in the early stages of the tenancy. The new absolute ground should assist private rented sector landlords to end tenancies quickly in cases of serious anti-social behaviour or criminality that occur during the fixed term of an assured short-hold tenancy.

Test

The court must grant possession (subject to any available human rights defence raised by the tenant, including proportionality) provided the landlord has followed the correct procedure and at least one of the following five conditions is met:

- the tenant, a member of the tenant's household, or a person visiting the property has been convicted of a serious offence;
- the tenant, a member of the tenant's household, or a person visiting the property has been found by a court to have breached a civil injunction;
- the tenant, a member of the tenant's household, or a person visiting the property has been convicted for breaching a criminal behaviour order (CBO);
- the tenant's property has been closed for more than 48 hours under a closure order for anti-social behaviour; or
- the tenant, a member of the tenant's household, or a person visiting the property has been convicted for breaching a noise abatement notice or order.

The offence or anti-social conduct must have been committed in, or in the locality of, the property, affected a person with a right to live in the locality of the property or affected the landlord or the landlord's staff or contractors.

Serious offences for this purpose include, for example: violent and sexual offences and those relating to offensive weapons, drugs and damage to property. A list of the relevant offences is found in Schedule 2A to the Housing Act 1985.

Details

The new absolute ground is based on the existing process for ending introductory tenancies for local authority tenants set out in sections 127 to 129 of the Housing Act 1996, and existing mandatory grounds for possession for rent arrears for housing association tenants, which generally work well for landlords.

The new ground will be available to landlords in addition to the existing discretionary grounds for possession set out in Schedule 2 to the Housing Act 1985 for secure tenants and Schedule 2 to the Housing Act 1988 for assured tenants. Landlords will be able to choose to use the new ground, in addition to, or instead of the existing discretionary grounds for anti-social behaviour where one or more of the five conditions are met.

Partnership working: Close working relationships with the police, local councils and other local agencies will be important to ensure that the landlord is always aware when one or more of the triggers for the new absolute ground has occurred.

Box I: Secured and Assured Tenancies

Secure tenants are generally tenants of local councils with a very high level of security of tenure. Apart from the new absolute ground, secure tenants can only be evicted from their property on the discretionary grounds for possession in Schedule 2 to the Housing Act 1985.

Tenants of housing associations generally have **non-shorthold assured tenancies** giving them a high level of security of tenure (although not fully equivalent to that of secure tenants). They can already be evicted under mandatory grounds for possession provided for in Schedule 2 to the Housing Act 1988 (for example, for rent arrears) as well as discretionary grounds for possession.

Private rented sector tenants generally have **assured shorthold tenancies** giving them limited security of tenure. They can be evicted under existing grounds for possession in Schedule 2 to the Housing Act 1988 as well as the 'no fault' ground in section 21 of the Housing Act 1988. This simply requires the landlord to give the tenant the proper notice before seeking a court order (usually without a hearing).

Notice requirements: In order to seek possession under the new absolute ground, landlords will need to serve a notice of the proceedings on the tenant, either:

- within 12 months of the relevant conviction or finding of the court being relied on (or if there is an appeal against the finding or conviction within 12 months of the appeal being finally determined, abandoned or withdrawn); or
- within three months where the tenant's property has been closed under a closure order (or if there is an appeal against the making of the closure order, within three months of the appeal being finally determined, abandoned or withdrawn).

The minimum notice period for periodic tenancies is four weeks, or the tenancy period (i.e. the rent period) if longer. In the case of a fixed term tenancy the minimum notice period is one month. The notice is valid for 12 months.

The notice must include the following information:

- the landlord's intention to seek possession under the new absolute ground;
- the reasons why they are seeking possession;
- which of the five conditions for the absolute ground the landlord proposes to rely on;
- the relevant conviction, finding of the court, or closure order the landlord proposes to rely on;
- details of any right that the tenant may have to request a review of the landlord's decision to seek possession, and the time within which the request must be made;
- where and how a tenant may seek advice on the notice; and
- the date after which possession proceedings may be begun.

If the landlord wishes to seek possession on one or more of the existing discretionary grounds as well, he or she must also specify and give details of the relevant discretionary ground/s in the notice.

The court has no power to dispense with service of a notice for possession under the new absolute ground. Therefore where a landlord decides to seek possession for anti-social behaviour on the new absolute ground alongside one or more of the discretionary grounds, the court will not be able to dispense of the notice as they would have been able to if the possession was sought solely on the discretionary ground.

Review procedure:

- Local council tenants will have a statutory right to request a review of the landlord's decision to seek possession under the new absolute ground.
- The request for a review must be made in writing within seven days of the notice to seek possession being served on the tenant.
- The review must be carried out before the end of the notice.
- The landlord must communicate the outcome of the review to the tenant in writing.
- If the decision is to confirm the original decision to seek possession, the landlord must also notify the tenant of the reasons for the decision.
- If the review upholds the original decision, the landlord will proceed by applying to the court for the possession order.
- The statutory review procedure will not apply to housing associations tenants. However, we would expect housing associations to offer a similar non-statutory review procedure (in the same way that they have done so for starter tenancies for example).

Putting victims first: In preparation for the court process, landlords should consider:

- reassuring victims and witnesses by letting them know what they can expect to happen in court;
- using professional witnesses where possible; and
- taking necessary practical steps with court staff to reassure and protect vulnerable victims and witnesses in court (e.g. the provision of separate waiting areas and accompanying them to and from court).

Landlords should also consider providing support/protection for victims and witnesses out of court, at home, and beyond the end of the possession proceedings when necessary.

Court hearing and defences:

- Tenants will be entitled to a court hearing.
- As with other grounds of possession, tenants of public authorities or landlords carrying out a public function will be able to raise any available human rights defence, including proportionality, against the possession proceedings.
- The court will consider whether such a defence meets the high threshold of being 'seriously arguable' established by the Supreme Court.
- Subject to any available human rights defence raised by the tenant, the court must grant an order for possession where the landlord has followed the correct procedure.

Suspension of possession order: The court may not postpone the giving up of possession to a date later than 14 days after the making of the order; unless exceptional hardship would result in which case it may be postponed for up to six weeks.

Important changes/differences

- Unlike with the existing discretionary grounds for possession, landlords will not need to prove to the court that it is reasonable to grant possession. This means that the court will be more likely to determine cases in a single hearing, thereby expediting the process.
- The new ground is an additional tool which will provide more flexibility for landlords but will be applicable only in limited circumstances – where a court has already found a tenant or member of their household guilty of anti-social behaviour or criminality in the locality of the property.
- The court has no power to dispense with service of a notice for possession under the new absolute ground as they can do under the discretionary ground for anti-social behaviour.
- Local council tenants will have a statutory right to request a review of the landlord's decision to seek possession under the absolute ground. We would expect housing associations to make a similar non-statutory review procedure available to their tenants.
- The court will only have the discretion to suspend a possession order made under the new ground to a date no later than 14 days after the making of the order (unless it appears to the court that exceptional hardship would be caused, in which case it may be postponed to a date no later than six weeks after the making of the order.)

ISBN: 978-1-78246-408-2

© Crown Copyright 2014

APPENDIX 6

SENTENCING GUIDELINES COUNCIL: BREACH OF AN ANTI-SOCIAL BEHAVIOUR ORDER

SGC

Sentencing Guidelines Council

Breach of an Anti-Social Behaviour Order

Definitive Guideline

FOREWORD

In accordance with section 170(9) of the Criminal Justice Act (CJA) 2003, the Sentencing Guidelines Council issues this guideline as a definitive guideline. By virtue of section 172 of the CJA 2003, every court must have regard to a relevant guideline. This guideline applies to the sentencing of offenders convicted of breaching an anti-social behaviour order (ASBO) who are sentenced on or after **5 January 2009**.

The Council has previously set out the approach to dealing with breaches of orders in its guidelines on *New Sentences: Criminal Justice Act 2003*[1] and *Breach of Protective Orders*.[2] The main aim of sentencing for breach of a court order is to achieve the purpose of the order; in the case of an ASBO that is to protect the public from behaviour that is likely to cause harassment, alarm or distress.

Any perception that the courts do not treat seriously a failure to comply with a court order can undermine public confidence and is therefore an important additional consideration.

Since the ability of a court to deal appropriately with an order that has been breached depends on how it was made, Annex A to the guideline summarises the key principles and considerations applicable to the making of an ASBO.

This guideline applies to the sentencing of adult and young offenders. It is recognised that a large proportion of orders are imposed on persons under 18 years of age. Although the sentencing framework for youths is very different from that for adults, and a guideline for sentencing young offenders will follow in due course, the Council considered that sentencers would find it helpful to have guiding principles for sentencing young offenders for breach of an ASBO.

The Council has appreciated the work of the Sentencing Advisory Panel in preparing the advice on which this guideline is based and is grateful to those who responded to the consultation of both the Panel and Council. The advice and this guideline are available on www.sentencing-guidelines.gov.uk or can be obtained from the Sentencing Guidelines Secretariat at 4th Floor, 8–10 Great George Street, London SW1P 3AE. A summary of the responses to the Council's consultation also appears on the website.

Chairman of the Council
December 2008

1 *New Sentences: Criminal Justice Act 2003*, published 16 December 2004, www.sentencing-guidelines.gov.uk

2 *Breach of a Protective Order*, published 7 December 2006, www.sentencing-guidelines.gov.uk

BREACH OF AN ANTI-SOCIAL BEHAVIOUR ORDER

A. Statutory provision

1. Section 1 of the Crime and Disorder Act 1998 provides:

   "(10) If without reasonable excuse a person does anything which he is prohibited from doing by an anti-social behaviour order, he shall be liable-

   (a) on summary conviction, to imprisonment for a term not exceeding six months or to a fine not exceeding the statutory maximum or to both; or

   (b) on conviction on indictment, to imprisonment for a term not exceeding five years or to a fine, or to both."

2. Where a person is convicted of an offence of breach of an anti-social behaviour order (ASBO), it is not open to the court to make an order discharging the offender conditionally.[3]

B. Introduction

3. An ASBO is a preventative order that can be made in either civil or criminal proceedings; its aim is to protect the public from behaviour that causes, or is likely to cause, harassment, alarm or distress. An order may be made on application to a magistrates' court, on conviction, or in conjunction with other proceedings in the County Court.

4. Since the ability of a court to deal appropriately with an order that has been breached depends on how it was made, Annex A summarises the key principles and considerations applicable to the making of an ASBO.

5. This guideline relates to the sentencing of both adult and young offenders. As the sentencing framework that applies to offenders aged under 18 is significantly different from that for older offenders, the guidance for young offenders is in the form of principles particularly regarding the circumstances in which a custodial sentence might be justified. The maximum penalty in the case of a young offender is detention for 24 months.

6. Breach of this type of order is different from breach of a community order or failure to surrender to custody because it has the potential to affect a community or the public at large in a way that causes direct harm.

   The main aim of sentencing for breach of a court order is to achieve the purpose of the order. Therefore, the sentence for breach of an ASBO should primarily reflect the harassment, alarm or distress involved; the fact that it constituted breach of a court order is a secondary consideration.

C. Assessing seriousness

7. The sentence for breach of an ASBO must be commensurate with the seriousness of the offence; that is determined by assessing the culpability of the offender and any harm which the offence caused, was intended to cause or might foreseeably have caused.[4]

---

3 Crime and Disorder Act 1998, s.1(11)

4 Criminal Justice Act 2003, s.143(1)

8. A community sentence can be imposed only if a court considers that the offence is serious enough to justify it,[5] and a custodial sentence can be imposed only if a court considers that a community sentence or a fine alone cannot be justified in view of the seriousness of the offence.[6] The Council has published a definitive guideline on seriousness that guides sentencers through the process of determining whether the respective sentencing thresholds have been crossed.[7]

9. A wide range of prohibitions can be attached to an order; consequently the degree of harm resulting from a breach will vary greatly and may be experienced by the wider community as well as by individuals.

10. In order properly to assess the seriousness of a breach of an ASBO, a court needs to be aware of the purpose of the order and the context in which it was made. A breach may b of one or more prohibitions in an order; the approach to sentencing is based on an assessment of the seriousness of the harm arising from the breach (or intended by the offender) rather than the number of prohibitions not complied with.

(i) Culpability and harm

11. When a court is considering the seriousness of breach of an order such as an ASBO, it will need to consider two aspects of culpability:

(a) The degree to which the offender intended to breach the order.

Culpability is variable and an offender may have:

- intended the breach
- been reckless as to whether the order was breached
- been aware of the risk of breach; or
- been unaware of this risk due to an incomplete understanding of the terms of the order.

(b) The degree to which the offender intended to cause the harm that resulted (could have resulted).

Culpability will be higher where the offender foresaw the harm likely to be caused by th breach and will be at its highest where such harm was intended.

12. There are also two dimensions to the harm involved in breach of an ASBO:

(a) the breach may itself cause harassment, alarm or distress, which can reduce the quality of life in a community.

(b) breach of an ASBO contravenes an order of the court, and this can undermine publi confidence in the effective administration of justice.

13. The assessment of the seriousness of an individual offence must take into account not only the harm actually caused by an offence but also any harm that was intended or might foreseeably have been caused.[8]

[5] Criminal Justice Act 2003, s.148(1)
[6] ibid., s.152(2)
[7] *Overarching Principles: Seriousness*, published 16 December 2004, www.sentencing-guidelines.gov.uk
[8] Criminal Justice Act 2003, s.143(1)

14. The test of foreseeability is objective[9] but as the prohibitions imposed must have been considered by a court to be necessary to prevent anti-social behaviour, some degree of harm must always be foreseeable whenever an order is breached. Where a breach causes harm that was not readily foreseeable, the level of culpability should carry more weight than harm when assessing offence seriousness.[10]

(ii) Relevance of the originating conduct

15. The **original conduct** that led to the making of an order is a relevant consideration in so far as it indicates the level of harm caused and whether this was intended.[11]

16. High culpability and/or harm may be indicated if the breach continues a pattern of behaviour against an identifiable victim. Conversely, where there is little connection between the breach and the behaviour that the order was aimed at, this may indicate a less serious offence.

17. The court should examine the prohibitions of the order itself (particularly those in older orders which may have been made without the benefit of the guidance summarised in Annex A), their necessity and reasonableness in all the circumstances.[12]

(iii) Breach of an interim order

18. Breach of an interim order or a final order is equally serious and the same approach to sentencing should be taken.

19. Sentence for a breach of an interim order should be imposed as soon as possible. If the hearing regarding the final order can be brought forward, this should be done so that the two issues can be considered together. However, sentencing for the breach of the interim order should not be delayed for this purpose.

20. Where an interim order is breached the court should consider the extent to which an urgent need for specific interim prohibitions was demonstrated, or if the interim order was sought principally to obtain additional time to prepare a case for the full hearing.[13]

21. Where an interim order has been made without notice to the subject, the order does not take effect until it has been served. If doubts arise about the extent to which the subject has understood the prohibitions but the defence of reasonable excuse is not made out, a lack of understanding of the terms of the order may still mitigate the seriousness of the offence through reducing culpability.

---

9 Harm must have been foreseeable by 'a reasonable person'

10 *Overarching Principles: Seriousness*, published 16 December 2004, www.sentencing-guidelines.gov.uk

11 *Breach of a Protective Order*, published 7 December 2006, www.sentencing-guidelines.gov.uk

12 Where appropriate, an application may be made separately for the order to be varied: Crime and Disorder Act 1998, ss.1(8) or 1CA. See also the Magistrates' Courts (Anti-Social Behaviour Orders) Rules 2002. Where the subject/offender is aged under 18, Practice Direction (Magistrates' Courts: Anti-Social Behaviour Orders: Composition of Benches) [2006] 1 AER 886 provides for the constitution of the court

13 A report commissioned by the YJB concluded that there may be grounds for interim ASBOs only where there is an urgent need for specific prohibitions: Aikta-Reena Solanki, Tim Bateman, Gwyneth Boswell and Emily Hill, Anti-social Behaviour Orders, YJB (2006)

(iv) A breach that also constitutes another criminal offence

22. Whether one offence or two has been charged, the sentence should reflect all relevant aspects of the offence so that, provided the facts are not in issue, the result should be the same.[14]

(a) if the substantive offence only has been charged, the fact that it constitutes breach of an ASBO should be treated as an aggravating factor;

(b) if breach of the order only has been charged, the sentence should reflect the full circumstances of the breach, which will include the conduct that could have been charged as a substantive offence.

23. Where breach of an ASBO also constitutes another offence with a lower maximum penalty than that for breach of the order, this penalty is an element to be considered in the interests of proportionality, although the court is not limited by it when sentencing an adult or youth for breach.

(v) Aggravating and mitigating factors

24. The Council guideline *Overarching Principles: Seriousness* identifies a number of factors that might increase or mitigate the seriousness of an offence. For ease of reference, the factors are set out in Annex B.

(vi) Personal mitigation

25. Offender mitigation is particularly relevant to breach of an ASBO as compliance with the order depends on the ability to understand its terms and make rational decisions in relation to these. Sentence may be mitigated where:

- the offender has a lower level of understanding due to mental health issues or learning difficulties
- the offender was acting under the influence of an older or more experienced offender; or
- there has been compliance with an Individual Support Order or Intervention Order imposed when the ASBO was made.

[14] *Breach of a Protective Order*, published 7 December 2006, www.sentencing-guidelines.gov.uk

D. Sentencing guideline – Adult offenders

Sentencing ranges and starting points

1. This guideline applies to a *"first time offender"* who has been **convicted after a trial**. In common with other proceedings based on breach of a court order,[15] it is likely that an offender in breach of an ASBO will have previous convictions. That has been taken into account in determining the starting points and ranges. Therefore, within this guideline, a "first time offender" is a person who does not have a conviction for breach of an ASBO rather than the usual approach which is based on the existence of any conviction which, by virtue of section 143(2) of the Criminal Justice Act 2003, must be treated as an aggravating factor.

2. As an aid to consistency of approach, the guideline describes a number of types of activity which would fall within the broad definition of the offence. These are set out in a column headed 'Nature of failure & harm'.

3. The expected approach is for a court to identify the description that most nearly matches the particular facts of the offence for which sentence is being imposed. This will identify a **starting point** from which the sentencer can depart to reflect aggravating or mitigating factors affecting the seriousness of the offence (beyond those contained within the column describing the nature of the failure or of the harm) to reach a **provisional sentence**.

4. The **sentencing range** is the bracket into which the provisional sentence will normally fall after having regard to factors which aggravate or mitigate the seriousness of the offence. The particular circumstances may, however, make it appropriate that the provisional sentence falls outside the range.

5. Where the offender has previous convictions which aggravate the seriousness of the current offence, that may take the provisional sentence beyond the range given particularly where there are significant other aggravating factors present.

6. Once the provisional sentence has been identified by reference to those factors affecting the seriousness of the offence, the court will take into account any relevant factors of personal mitigation, which may take the sentence beyond the range given.

7. Where there has been a guilty plea, any reduction attributable to that plea will be applied to the sentence at this stage. Again, this reduction may take the sentence below the range provided.

8. A court must give its reasons for imposing a sentence of a different kind or outside the range provided in the guidelines.[16]

---

[15] for example, failing to surrender to bail

[16] Criminal Justice Act 2003, s.174(2)(a)

The decision making process

The process set out below is intended to show that the sentencing approach for the offence of breach of an anti-social behaviour order is fluid and requires the structured exercise of discretion.

1. Identify the appropriate starting point

Identify the description that most nearly matches the particular facts of the offence for which sentence is being imposed.

2. Consider relevant aggravating factors, both general and those specific to the type of offence

This may result in a sentence level being identified that is higher than the suggested starting point, sometimes substantially so.

3. Consider mitigating factors and personal mitigation

There may be offence or offender mitigation which could result in a sentence that is lower than the suggested starting point (possibly substantially so), or a sentence of a different type.

4. Reduction for guilty plea

The court will then apply any reduction for a guilty plea following the approach set out in the Council Guideline *Reduction in Sentence for a Guilty Plea* (revised July 2007).

5. Consider ancillary orders

The court should consider whether ancillary orders are appropriate or necessary.

6. The totality principle

The court should review the total sentence to ensure that it is proportionate to the offending behaviour and properly balanced.

7. Reasons

When a court imposes a sentence of a different type or outside the range provided, it should explain its reasons for doing so.

Factors to take into consideration

1. The starting points and sentencing ranges are for a *"first time offender"* who pleaded not guilty. In this guideline, a *"first time offender"* is one who does not have a previous conviction for breach of an ASBO.

2. Where a court determines that there are other convictions which it is reasonable to treat as a factor aggravating the seriousness of the breach,[17] that factor will be taken into account at stage 2 of the sentencing process set out on page 7.

3. An ASBO may be breached in a wide range of circumstances and may involve one or more prohibitions not being complied with. The examples given below are intended to illustrate how the scale of the conduct that led to the breach, taken as a whole, might come within the three levels of seriousness:

   - **Serious harm caused or intended** – breach at this level of seriousness will involve the use of violence, significant threats or intimidation or the targeting of individuals or groups of people in a manner that leads to a fear of violence.
   - **Lesser degree of harm intended or likely** – examples may include lesser degrees of threats or intimidation, the use of seriously abusive language, or causing more than minor damage to property.
   - **No harm caused or intended** – in the absence of intimidation or the causing of fear of violence, breaches involving being drunk or begging may be at this level, as may prohibited use of public transport or entry into a prohibited area, where there is no evidence that harassment, alarm or distress was caused or intended.

4. The suggested starting points are based on the assumption that the offender had the highest level of culpability.

5. Aggravating and mitigating factors specifically relevant to sentencing for breach of an ASBO are included in the guideline. Care needs to be taken to ensure that there is no double counting where an element of the breach determines the level of seriousness where it might in other circumstances be an aggravating factor. When assessing the seriousness of an offence, the court must always refer to the full list of aggravating and mitigating factors in the Council guideline on Seriousness (see Annex B).[18]

6. In the most serious cases, involving repeat offending and a breach causing serious harassment together with the presence of several aggravating factors, such as the use of violence, a sentence beyond the highest range will be justified.

7. Once the provisional sentence has been identified by reference to factors affecting the seriousness of the offence, the court will take into account any relevant factors of personal mitigation (see paragraph 25 above), and, in accordance with the Council guideline[19] consider reducing the sentence where a guilty plea was entered.

8. When imposing a community order, the court must ensure that the requirements imposed are proportionate to the seriousness of the breach, compatible with each other,[20] and also with the prohibitions of the ASBO if the latter is to remain in force. Even where the threshold for a custodial sentence is crossed, a custodial sentence is not inevitable.[21]

17 in accordance with Criminal Justice Act 2003, s.143(2)
18 *Overarching Principles: Seriousness*, published 16 December 2004, www.sentencing-guidelines.gov.uk
19 *Reduction in Sentence for a Guilty Plea*, published 20 July 2007, www.sentencing-guidelines.gov.uk
20 *New Sentences: Criminal Justice Act 2003*, published 16 December 2004, www.sentencing-guidelines.gov.uk
21 ibid.

9. An offender may be sentenced for more than one offence of breach, which occurred on different days. While consecutive sentences may be imposed in such cases, the overall sentence should reflect the totality principle.

Breach of an Anti-Social Behaviour Order

Crime and Disorder Act 1998 (section 1(10))

Maximum Penalty: 5 years imprisonment

Note: A conditional discharge is not available as a sentence for this offence

Nature of failure & harm	Starting point	Sentencing range
Serious harassment, alarm or distress has been caused or where such harm was intended	**26 weeks custody**	**Custody threshold – 2 years custody**
Lesser degree of harassment, alarm or distress, where such harm was intended, or where it would have been likely if the offender had not been apprehended	**6 weeks custody**	**Community Order (MEDIUM) – 26 weeks custody**
No harassment, alarm or distress was actually caused by the breach and none was intended by the offender	**Community Order (LOW)**	**Fine Band B – Community Order (MEDIUM)**

Aggravating factors	Mitigating factors
1. Offender has a history of disobedience to court orders. 2. Breach was committed immediately or shortly after the order was made. 3. Breach was committed subsequent to earlier breach proceedings arising from the same order. 4. Targeting of a person the order was made to protect or a witness in the original proceedings.	1. Breach occurred after a long period of compliance. 2. The prohibition(s) breached was not fully understood, especially where an interim order was made without notice.

E. Sentencing principles: Young Offenders

1. The approach to assessing the seriousness of a breach outlined above at paragraphs 7 to 25 applies equally to youths. A court must impose a community or custodial sentence only if such a sentence is warranted by the seriousness of the offence and no lesser sentence can be justified.

2. When sentencing a young offender, the normal approach is for the penalty to reflect both the reduction in culpability (for example, due to a lesser ability to foresee the consequences of actions) and the more onerous effects of punishments on education and personal development in comparison with an adult offender.

3. The sentencing framework that applies to offenders aged under 18 is significantly different from that for adult offenders and key principles are set out in Annex C. The maximum penalty for this offence when committed by a young offender is a 24 month detention and training order (DTO). With the exception of a conditional discharge,[22] the full range of disposals of the youth court is available, and these are also outlined in Annex C.[23]

4. In most cases of breach by a young offender convicted after a trial, the appropriate sentence will be a community sentence.[24] Within the sentence(s) available, a range of requirements can be attached; the court will consider the seriousness of the breach, which requirement(s) will best prevent further offending and the individual circumstances of the offender.

5. The court must ensure that the requirements imposed are compatible both with each other and with the prohibitions of the ASBO if the latter is to remain in force, and that the combination of both is not so onerous as to make further breaches likely.

6. The particular stage of intellectual or emotional maturity of the individual (which may not correspond with actual age) will also influence sentence. A young offender is likely to perceive a particular time period as being longer in comparison with an adult, and this may be of relevance when considering how much time has elapsed between imposition and breach of the order.

[22] Crime and Disorder Act 1998, s.1(11) and s.1C(9)

[23] If the young offender has also been charged with a grave crime under s.91 Powers of Criminal Courts (Sentencing) Act 2000, the case may be committed to the Crown Court. Similarly, where the young offender is committed to the Crown Court for sentence under the dangerous offender provisions

[24] though see paragraph 7 below

7. The principles to be followed when sentencing a youth for breach of an ASBO are as follows:

"First time offender"[25] pleading guilty: the court[26] must make a referral order unless it imposes an absolute discharge, a custodial sentence or a hospital order;

In all other cases:

(i) in some less serious cases, such as where the breach has not involved any harassment, alarm or distress, a fine may be appropriate if it will be paid by the offender, or otherwise a reparation order;

(ii) in most cases, the appropriate sentence will be a community sentence;

(iii) the custody threshold should be set at a significantly higher level than the threshold applicable to adult offenders;

(iv) the custody threshold usually will not be crossed unless the breach involved serious harassment, alarm or distress through either the use of violence, threats or intimidation or the targeting of individuals/groups in a manner that led to a fear of violence;

(v) exceptionally, the custody threshold may also be crossed where a youth is being sentenced for more than one offence of breach (committed on separate occasions within a short period) involving a lesser but substantial degree of harassment, alarm or distress;

(vi) even where the custody threshold is crossed, the court should normally impose a community sentence in preference to a DTO, as custody should be used only as a measure of last resort; and

(vii) where the court considers a custodial sentence to be unavoidable, the starting point for sentencing should be 4 months detention, with a range of up to 12 months. Where a youth is being sentenced for more than one breach involving serious harassment, alarm or distress, sentence may go beyond that range.

[25] For the purpose of this requirement, a "first time offender" is an offender who has never been convicted by or before a court in the United Kingdom of any offence other than the offence and any connected offence, or been bound over in criminal proceedings; Powers of Criminal Court (Sentencing) Act 2000, s.17(1)(b) and (c)

[26] A referral order may be made by a youth court or other magistrates' court; Powers of Criminal Courts (Sentencing) Act 2000, s.16(1)

Aggravating and mitigating factors

8. As with adult offenders, factors that are likely to aggravate an offence of breach of an anti-social behaviour order are:
   - history of disobedience of court orders
   - the breach was committed immediately or shortly after the order was made
   - the breach was committed subsequent to earlier breach proceedings arising from the same order
   - targeting of a person the order was made to protect or of a witness in the original proceedings.

9. Factors that are likely to mitigate the seriousness of the breach are:
   - the breach occurred after a long period of compliance
   - the prohibition(s) breached was not fully understood, especially where an interim order was made without notice.

Personal mitigation

10. Offender mitigation is particularly relevant to breach of an ASBO as compliance with the order depends on the ability to understand its terms and make rational decisions in relation to these. Sentence may be mitigated where:
    - the offender has a lower level of understanding due to mental health issues or learning difficulties
    - the offender was acting under the influence of an older or more experienced offender; or
    - there has been compliance with an Individual Support Order or Intervention Order imposed when the ASBO was made.

11. Other offender mitigating factors that may be particularly relevant to young offenders include peer pressure and a lack of parental support.

Annex B: Aggravating and mitigating factors identified in the Council guideline *Overarching Principles: Seriousness*

The factors below apply to a wide range of offences. Not all will be relevant to the offence of breach of an anti-social behaviour order

Factors indicating higher culpability:

- Offence committed whilst on bail for other offences
- Failure to respond to previous sentences
- Offence was racially or religiously aggravated
- Offence motivated by, or demonstrating, hostility to the victim based on his or her sexual orientation (or presumed sexual orientation)
- Offence motivated by, or demonstrating, hostility based on the victim's disability (or presumed disability)
- Previous conviction(s), particularly where a pattern of repeat offending is disclosed
- Planning of an offence
- An intention to commit more serious harm than actually resulted from the offence
- Offenders operating in groups or gangs
- 'Professional' offending
- Commission of the offence for financial gain (where this is not inherent in the offence itself)
- High level of profit from the offence
- An attempt to conceal or dispose of evidence
- Failure to respond to warnings or concerns expressed by others about the offender's behaviour
- Offence committed whilst on licence
- Offence motivated by hostility towards a minority group, or a member or members of it
- Deliberate targeting of vulnerable victim(s)
- Commission of an offence while under the influence of alcohol or drugs
- Use of a weapon to frighten or injure victim
- Deliberate and gratuitous violence or damage to property, over and above what is needed to carry out the offence
- Abuse of power
- Abuse of a position of trust

Factors indicating a more than usually serious degree of harm:

- Multiple victims
- An especially serious physical or psychological effect on the victim, even if unintended
- A sustained assault or repeated assaults on the same victim

- Victim is particularly vulnerable
- Location of the offence (for example, in an isolated place)
- Offence is committed against those working in the public sector or providing a service to the public
- Presence of others e.g. relatives, especially children or partner of the victim
- Additional degradation of the victim (e.g. taking photographs of a victim as part of a sexual offence)
- In property offences, high value (including sentimental value) of property to the victim, or substantial consequential loss (e.g. where the theft of equipment causes serious disruption to a victim's life or business)

Factors indicating significantly lower culpability:

- A greater degree of provocation than normally expected
- Mental illness or disability
- Youth or age, where it affects the responsibility of the individual defendant
- The fact that the offender played only a minor role in the offence

APPENDIX 7

ACPO GUIDELINES FOR THE PROSECUTION OF BREACHES OF CPNS AND PSPOS

ASSOCIATION OF
CHIEF POLICE OFFICERS

National Policing Guidelines on the Prosecution for Breaches of Community Protection Notices and Public Spaces Protection Order

The Association of Chief Police Officers has agreed to these guidelines being circulated to, and adopted by, Police Forces in England, Wales & Northern Ireland.

It is NOT PROTECTIVELY MARKED under the Government Protective Marking Scheme and any referrals for advice and rationale in relation to Freedom of Information Act disclosure, should be made to the ACPO Central Referral Unit at acpo.request@foi.pnn.police.uk.

© 2014 – ACPO

Document information

Protective marking	**NOT PROTECTIVELY MARKED**
Author	**ACPO**
Force/Organisation	**ACPO**
National Policing Business Area	**Local Policing & Partnerships**
Contact details	**020 7084 8959**
Review date	**December 2016**
Version	**1.0**

These guidelines have been produced and approved by the National Local Policing and Partnerships Business Area on the 22nd December 2014. Guidelines produced by ACPO should be used by chief officers to shape police responses to ensure that the general public experience consistent levels of service. The implementation of all guidance will require operational choices to be made at local level in order to achieve the appropriate police response. These guidelines are intended to provide clarity to relevant agencies in respect of enforcement for breaches of two of the six provisions of the Anti-Social Behaviour, Crime and Policing Act 2014. It will be updated and re-published as necessary.

Any queries relating to this document should be directed to either the author detailed above or the ACPO Programme Support Office on 020 7084 8959/8958.

Contents

1. SECTION 1 – INTRODUCTION

1.1 This document is intended to provide clarity and guidance to relevant agencies in respect of enforcement for breaches of two of the six provisions of the Anti-Social Behaviour, Crime and Policing Act 2014, namely: the **Community Protection Notice** (CPN) and the **Public Spaces Protection Order** (PSPO).

1.2 These guidelines have been issued following consultation with the Home Office, the Crown Prosecution Service (CPS), College of Policing (CoP) and the Local Government Association.

2. SECTION 2 – COMMUNITY PROTECTION NOTICE

2.1 Under Section 43 of the Act, a Constable, a Police Community Support Officer (PCSO) designated by the Chief Constable, a local authority or a person designated by the local authority may issue a notice to a person aged 16 or over or to a body if they are satisfied on reasonable grounds that:

A. The conduct of the individual or body is having a detrimental effect, of a persistent or continuing nature, on the quality of life of those in the locality, and;
B. The conduct is unreasonable.

2.2 The CPN is intended to impose a requirement upon a person or a body to stop doing specific things, or a positive requirement to do specific things, in order to reduce or remove the detrimental effects of their conduct.

2.3 The CPN must only be issued if the person or body has been issued with a written warning and that, having had sufficient warning to address the conduct, it continues to have a detrimental effect.

2.4 A failure to comply with the terms of a CPN is summary criminal offence under Section 48 of the Act.

2.5 A constable or authorised person may issue a Fixed Penalty Notice to any person they have reason to believe has committed the offence.

2.6 The offence can be tried summarily and any person convicted of the offence is liable to a fine not exceeding Level 4 (for an individual) or £20,000 (a body).

2.7 Section 52 (2) of the Act makes it clear that in every case, the Fixed Penalty Notice for a breach of the CPN will be payable to the local authority, irrespective of which agency issued the CPN or which agency issued the Fixed Penalty Notice.

2.8 The agency issuing the CPN will generally be responsible for enforcement of a breach, either by way of a Fixed Penalty Notice or prosecution at a Magistrates' Court or Youth Court (for those aged 16).

2.9 Example of the above:

- A local authority issues a CPN to a company for persistent noise during unsociable hours. Following further complaints from local residents, the local authority gathers evidence that the company has failed to comply with the terms of the CPN. The local authority will therefore issue a Fixed Penalty Notice or, if this is not accepted or appropriate to the circumstances, the local authority will be responsible for bringing any prosecution.

2.10 Similarly, if the police issued the CPN to a person responsible for persistent anti-social behaviour, the police would be responsible for issuing the Fixed Penalty Notice, gathering evidence for prosecution and bringing any charges. In this case, the evidence would be submitted to the Crown Prosecution Service (CPS) as the prosecuting agency.

2.11 It is anticipated there will occasionally be circumstances in which it is more practical for a non-issuing agency to take enforcement for a breach under Section 48.

3. SECTION 3 – BREACH OF CPNs ISSUED BY THE LOCAL AUTHORITY

3.1 The local authority which issued a CPN will be the prosecuting authority for breach of the terms of the CPN. The local authority will also be responsible for the prosecution of breaches of CPNs issued by a person designated with the power to issue the CPN by the local authority under Section 53(1)(c) on its behalf, for example housing providers.

3.2 There will be occasions, however, when the police are involved in the enforcement process, for example:

- A local police officer, aware that an individual has been issued with a CPN by the local authority to address their anti-social behaviour, observes that a person(s) behaving in an anti-social manner and the circumstances necessitate immediate action. The officer can:
    - Issue a Fixed Penalty Notice, payable to the local authority;
    - Report the person for summons;
    - Arrest the person if the "necessity" test (Serious Organised Crime and Police Act 2005) is met.

3.3 The Fixed Penalty Notice would be issued by the officer to the offender, payable to the local authority (Section 52).

3.4 If a Fixed Penalty Notice is refused, or it is not appropriate to issue a Fixed Penalty Notice due to factors such as antecedents, the person may be reported for summons. The police will in those circumstances gather evidence of the offence, which will include interviewing the suspect under caution if appropriate. The police will then provide the evidence to the local authority to consider prosecution.

3.5 "ARREST CASES"

3.5.1 Only the police have a power of arrest for breach of a CPN if the "necessity test" is met. In these circumstances, the person responsible for the breach will be detained for as long as one of the "necessary" conditions under the Serious Organised Crime and Police Act (SOCPA) 2005 exist.

3.5.2 If the necessary conditions for detention cease to exist, the police should inform the person that they will be reported for the offence of failing to comply with the CPN or issued with a Fixed Penalty Notice. Any evidence obtained by the police must be provided to the local authority as the prosecuting authority.

3.6 "IN CUSTODY CASES"

3.6.1 If there is a necessity to detain a person in custody, the police will be responsible for gathering evidence whilst they are in custody, with a view to charging them with an offence of failing to comply with the CPN.

3.6.2 The local authority must be notified of arrest and detention at the earliest opportunity. The local authority will be the prosecuting authority and will be responsible for the provision of a prosecuting lawyer at the person's appearance at magistrates' court or Youth Court (for an offender aged 16). This will include cases in which a person has been remanded in custody to the next available court hearing.

3.6.3 An exception to this general rule will be if police arrest a person for other offences in addition to the breach of the CPN. In these circumstances it would be practicable for all offences to be charged and prosecuted together by the CPS.

4. SECTION 4 – BREACH OF CPNs ISSUED BY THE POLICE

4.1 The CPS will be the prosecuting authority for offences of failing to comply with a CPN issued by the police.

4.2 In cases in which the police issued the CPN and the local authority has obtained or is otherwise in possession of evidence of a breach, that evidence will be provided to the police.

5. SECTION 5 – NON-PAYMENT OF FIXED PENALTY NOTICE

5.1 No proceedings may be taken against a person issued with a Fixed Penalty Notice within 14 days of the date of the notice.

5.2 In the event of the failure to pay the Fixed Penalty Notice, a person will be liable to prosecution under Section 43 for the offence of failing to comply with the terms of the CPN.

5.3 The agency that issued the CPN will be responsible for prosecution. For CPNs issued by the police, the CPS will be the prosecuting authority. In the case of CPNs issued by a person designated by the local authority, the local authority will be the prosecuting agency.

6. SECTION 6 – PUBLIC SPACES PROTECTION ORDERS

6.1 A local authority may make a Public Spaces Protection Order under Section 59 of the Act if it is necessary to prevent persistent or continuing activities which have a detrimental effect on the quality of life in the locality. The duration of an order will be for up to three years unless extended.

6.2 An order may prohibit certain activities which have a detrimental effect on the locality within a specified area. It may also place a positive requirement upon anyone undertaking activities in that area to do something which prevents those activities from having a detrimental.

7. SECTION 7 – BREACH OF A PSPO

7.1 Failure to comply with an order without reasonable excuse is a summary criminal offence which can be enforced by a constable, a designated PCSO or a local authority officer.

7.2 A constable, a PCSO designated by the Chief Constable or a person authorised by the local authority may issue a Fixed Penalty Notice to any person they have reason to believe has committed an offence under Section 63 (consumption of alcohol in a prohibited area) or Section 67 (failing to comply with the terms of the PSPO).

7.3 A person issued with a Fixed Penalty Notice will not be liable for prosecution for the offence of failing to comply with the PSPO if they make payment to the local authority within 14 days.

7.4 In some circumstances in which the police are the enforcing agency, it may be necessary to arrest a person for failure to comply with the PSPO. In those circumstances, the person responsible for the breach will be detained for as long as one of the "necessary" conditions of the SOCAP Act 2005 exists. If the necessary conditions for detention cease to exist, the police should inform the person that they will be reported for the offence of failing to comply with the PSPO or issue them with a Fixed Penalty Notice. Any evidence obtained by the police must be provided to the local authority as the prosecuting authority.

7.5 "IN CUSTODY CASES"

7.5.1 If there is a necessity to detain a person in custody, the police will be responsible for gathering evidence with a view to charging them with an offence of failing to comply with the PSPO.

7.5.2 The local authority must be notified of arrest and detention at the earliest opportunity. The local authority will be the prosecuting authority and will be responsible for the provision of a prosecuting lawyer at the person's appearance at magistrates' court or Youth Court. This will include cases in which a person has been remanded in custody to the next available court hearing.

7.5.3 The CPS will not be responsible for the prosecution of any offence under Sections 63 and 67.

8. SECTION 8 – FAILURE TO PAY A FIXED PENALTY NOTICE

8.1 Failure to make a payment for the Fixed Penalty Notice to the local authority will result in prosecution for the offence of failing to comply with the PSPO.

8.2 The local authority will, in all cases, be the prosecuting authority.

APPENDIX 8

PARENTING CONTRACTS AND ORDERS GUIDANCE (SS 4–8, ANNEXES D–E)

Section 4: Free-standing Parenting orders

The procedure for making free-standing parenting orders is different from that for orders linked to a conviction or order on the child, set out in section 5. The content and operation of the actual order will be the same, as in sections 6-8.

(a) Availability of the order

4.1 In considering whether the necessary conditions for a free-standing parenting order are fulfilled, YOTs should have regard to their statutory duties and to the points set out in section 2 of this guidance.

4.2 A member of the YOT can apply to the Magistrates' Court for a parenting order in respect of a parent or guardian of a child or young person who has been referred to the YOT.

4.3 To make a free-standing parenting order, a Magistrates' Court needs to be satisfied of two conditions:

(a) that the child or young person has engaged in criminal conduct or anti-social behaviour; and

(b) that making the order would be desirable in the interests of preventing further criminal conduct or anti-social behaviour.

4.4 For the first condition to be met, magistrates will need to make a finding about alleged criminal conduct or anti-social behaviour by the child or young person. The legislation does not specify a standard of proof for this, but courts might in practice insist on a criminal standard of proof.[1] The second condition is a judgement, so does not involve a standard of proof. Note sections 6 and 7 of this guidance which will have a bearing on evidence.

(b) Assessing whether order is appropriate

4.5 Free-standing parenting orders require parents to co-operate to tackle early patterns of offending or anti-social behaviour. The intention is to steer the child away from criminal conduct or anti-social behaviour.

4.6 YOTs should form a view about the suitability of a parent for a parenting order following assessment of the child and family circumstances. In deciding whether a parenting order might be appropriate, the YOT must make a judgement about whether parenting is a significant factor in the child or young person's behaviour, whether a parenting programme could remedy this, what other requirements might be useful in an order to address the behaviour and whether the parent can be engaged on a voluntary basis.

4.7 A YOT should normally only apply for a free-standing order after a parent has refused to enter into or failed to comply with a parenting contract or the YOT has failed in attempts to gain parental co-operation on a voluntary basis without attempting a contract, for which evidence has been kept.

---

1 See for instance the case of *McCann* where the House of Lords held that anti-social behaviour orders are civil orders to which the criminal standard of proof applies to the past acts of anti-social behaviour. House of Lords [2002] UKHL 39. *Clingham (formerly C (a minor)) v Royal Borough of Kensington and Chelsea (on Appeal from a Divisional Court of the Queen's Bench Division); Regina v Crown Court at Manchester Ex p McCann (FC) and Others (FC).*

(c) Evidence of criminal conduct or anti- social behaviour

4.8 The YOT will need to prepare evidence in support of the application. A child or young person referred to a YOT will generally have been involved in criminal conduct or anti-social behaviour and may have already received a police reprimand, final warning or penalty notice for disorder. If parents deny such past involvement by their child, YOTs will need to present evidence and ensure any witnesses including staff from other agencies are able to attend. If a YOT is not sure whether there is sufficient evidence it should seek legal advice before applying.

4.9 The supporting evidence could include witness statements of officers who attended incidents or of people affected by the behaviour, evidence of complaints recorded by the police, statements from professional witnesses, video or CCTV evidence, previous convictions, reprimands and final warnings and copies of custody records of previous arrests relevant to the application.

(d) Evidence that making the order would be desirable in the interests of preventing further criminal conduct or anti-social behaviour

4.10 The court has discretion to consider all the circumstances of the case in deciding whether it is desirable to make a parenting order, including the evidence of parents and other witnesses in court. The YOT's assessments of the child or young person and the parents or guardians and details of its ability to provide the parenting programme should be presented in support of the application.

4.11 Hearsay evidence may be admissible in these proceedings because of their civil nature. This may, for example, allow the identity of witnesses, who are too fearful to give evidence, to be protected. If there is an intention to rely upon hearsay evidence, the complainant must act in accordance with the Civil Evidence Act 1995 and the notice procedure set down by the Magistrates Courts (Hearsay Evidence in Civil Proceedings) Rules 1999.

4.12 The YOT should also provide evidence of any experience of trying to engage with the parents through a parenting contract. Magistrates are obliged to take into account any refusal by a parent or guardian to enter into, or failure to comply with, a parenting contract. The YOT needs to be clear what evidence there is of this. If parents or guardians are ready to engage fully with voluntary support, a parenting order would not usually be desirable.

(e) Application form and time limits

4.13 Applications must be made in accordance with the Magistrates' Courts (Parenting Order) Rules [2004] (being revised Autumn 2007) which specify the form of application that should be used. A form is attached at Annex D.

4.14 Under Section 127 of the Magistrates' Court Act 1980 a complaint must be made within six months of the criminal or anti-social behaviour concerned. If that is done, a summons may be issued to the parents later, but not so late as to prejudice them through unreasonable delay.

4.15 The YOT will need to disclose the supporting evidence to the parent, at the latest, once the summons has been issued.

Section 5: Parenting orders linked to conviction or to another order

(a) Availability

5.1 A court can make a parenting order in any proceedings where:

(a) a child safety order is made or the court determines a child has failed to comply with a requirement of a child safety order;

(b) a parental compensation order is made;[2]

(c) an anti-social behaviour order or sexual offences prevention order is made in respect of a child or young person;

(d) a child or young person is convicted of an offence (including where he/she receives a referral order); or

(e) a parent is referred back to court by a Youth Offender Panel after failing to attend panel meetings.

5.2 This means that parenting orders can be made in any of the following courts:

(i) a Family Proceedings Court;

(ii) a Magistrates' Court acting under civil jurisdiction;

(iii) all criminal courts, i.e. a Youth Court, an adult Magistrates' Court or the Crown Court.

5.3 The parenting order is made under the court's own motion (suggested forms for the order are at Annex E). The consent of the parent or guardian is not required.

5.4 There are conditions, one of which must apply before the court can make a parenting order. They are that the court is satisfied that the order would be desirable in the interests of preventing:

(a) a repetition of the kind of behaviour which led to a child safety order, an anti-social behaviour order or a sexual offences prevention order being made; or

(b) the commission of further offences, where the child or young person has been convicted of an offence or issued with a referral order.

5.5 There is an additional condition when a Youth Offender Panel refers a parent back to court. The court may make a parenting order if it is proved to its satisfaction that the parent has failed without reasonable excuse to comply with the order to attend panel meetings and the court is satisfied that the parenting order would be desirable in the interests of preventing the commission of any further offence by the child or young person.

5.6 The court has discretion to consider all the circumstances of the case in deciding whether it is desirable to make a parenting order. The court may wish to consider, for example, how much help, support and encouragement the parent or guardian has offered the child, and whether they are willing to receive assistance and support from the YOT or other provider on a voluntary basis. Where the parent is fully co-operating or willing to co-operate voluntarily a parenting order will not usually be desirable. If the parent has attended a programme without changing his or her behaviour, then an order might be called for.

5.7 Under s 9 of the CDA, where a child or young person under the age of 16 has been convicted of an offence (except where a referral order is made) or made subject to an anti-social behaviour order, the court is required to make a parenting order if it is satisfied that it is desirable to do so in the interests of preventing further offending or anti-social behaviour by the child or young person. If it is not so satisfied, the court must state this in open court and explain why not.

(b) Assessing when parenting order is appropriate

5.8 The suitability of a parent or guardian for a parenting order is normally determined by an assessment process carried out by a practitioner from a YOT. If the assessments provide evidence that parents could be supported to positively influence their child's behaviour and the parents are not willing to engage with support voluntarily it will usually be appropriate to recommend a parenting order to the court. The recommendation should take into consideration the potential needs of both the parents or guardians and the child and the likely effectiveness in terms of changing their behaviour.

5.9 A judgment about the suitability of a parenting intervention and recommendations are usually made in a written report or, in criminal proceedings, in a pre-sentence report ("PSR").

5.10 YOTs are expected to include an assessment of parenting support needs in all youth court PSRs.

---

[2] PCO is available in pilot areas only.

5.11 When preparing PSRs in cases where a parenting order is inappropriate due to, for example, domestic violence, abuse or continuing civil disputes, practitioners will need to take into account the level of information the court needs to make a decision. It may be that detailed sensitive information will not be necessary and that a general phrase such as 'while family tensions or civil matters are to be resolved' will be sufficient for the purpose.

5.12 Before making a parenting order with a referral order the court has to consider a report by an "appropriate officer" because the court needs to have the information necessary to decide whether a parenting order would be desirable. An "appropriate officer" can be an officer of a local probation board,[3] a social worker or a member of a YOT. The report should say which requirements should be included in the order and why they are in the interest of preventing further offending and, where the child or young person is below 16, give information about the person's family circumstances and the likely effect of the order on them.

5.13 If the court is considering serious offences when a referral order could be made and a PSR is required, in appropriate cases, the court may request a parenting assessment at the same time.

5.14 Parenting orders would normally only be made at the same time as referral orders if there is enough already known about the parents and family circumstances to enable a satisfactory report to be written in the time before the hearing. This would usually be where the YOT has already attempted to engage with parents for instance where a young person has received a Final Warning with an intervention. In this case the YOT may be able to provide the court with a report describing the attempts to engage the parents, with an update of the original parenting assessment in the time between notification and court appearance.

5.15 Where the parents are not already known to the YOT in this way, the courts are likely to want to provide the opportunity for the Youth Offender Panel to engage parents and young people in agreeing a contract which could include provision of parenting support on a voluntary basis or through a parenting order. If the parents do not attend the panel their case can be referred back to court, and the YOT would provide an assessment. The court would then consider whether a parenting order is desirable.

Section 6: Procedural points common to all parenting orders

(a) Information about family circumstances

6.1 Before making a parenting order where the child or young person is under the age of 16, the court must obtain and consider information about the child or young person's family circumstances and the likely effect of the order on those circumstances. Where a young person is aged 16 or 17, the court may obtain such information but is not required to do so.

6.2 This recognises that young people aged 16 and 17 are at a transitional stage between childhood and adulthood. Their emotional, social, intellectual and physical development and circumstances will vary greatly. Some may have left school, be living independently of their parents and possibly have family responsibilities of their own. Others may be in full-time education and fully dependent upon their parents.

6.3 The YOT's assessment (see section 2d) and subsequent report, should cover the family circumstances and the likely effect of the order on those circumstances although the court may decide to obtain further information by questioning the YOT officer in court or the parents or guardians if they are in court. The court could therefore rely on an oral report by the YOT in court (e.g. where the family circumstances are known to the YOT), or ask questions of the parent or, if necessary, of the child if present in court. The format in which this information should be presented will be for the court to determine and will depend on the circumstances of the case.

---

[3] An "officer of a local probation board" is to be replaced if the provisions of the Offender Management Bill, currently in Parliament, are enacted.

(b) Parental attendance at court

6.4 The Government believes that parents need to be in court when their children appear so as to support them and help take responsibility for tackling their offending behaviour. Magistrates' Courts, including Youth Courts, and Crown Courts, have powers to enforce parental attendance at court where appropriate. It is usually desirable to ensure both parents attend court and are involved in any parenting intervention. An important exception to this may be where one parent has a history of being violently or sexually abusive towards the child or other parent.

6.5 In discussions and correspondence with parents before coming to court, whenever possible YOTs will wish to encourage them to attend court. However, parents, particularly single parents, will sometimes find it difficult to attend court hearings. YOTs should explain that if a parent cannot attend court, reasons should be communicated to the court and that if valid reasons are not provided, any parent who does not attend will risk being subject to a parenting order. YOTs will also wish to consider whether a non-resident parent should be encouraged to attend. The courts can adjourn to secure attendance and have power to require attendance if thought necessary. But against this they will also weigh up the desirability of completing proceedings.

(i) In a criminal court or a Magistrates' Court acting under civil jurisdiction

6.6 Section 34A of the Children and Young Persons Act 1933 provides that, where a child or young person is charged with an offence or is for any other reason brought before a court, the court may in any case and shall in the case of a child or young person who is under the age of 16 require a person who is a parent or guardian to attend the court during all stages of the proceedings, unless the court is satisfied that it would be unreasonable to do so.

6.7 The court can issue a summons to secure the attendance of the parents or guardians.

6.8 Section 34A applies to Crown Courts and Magistrates' Courts when dealing with either civil or criminal proceedings against the child or where the child's actions are the subject of a parenting order application. Because the provision relates not only to offences but to cases where the child or young person is for any other reason brought before the court, section 34A applies in the case of all proceedings in relation to parenting orders where the child or young person is brought before the court and his or her actions act as the trigger for the parenting order. Parents who fail to attend such hearings will be subject to the existing rules of those courts.

(ii) In a Family Proceedings Court

6.9 These courts hear applications for, and breaches of, Child Safety Orders. The child is not required to attend, but under the Family Proceedings Courts (Children Act 1989) Rules 1991 the court may require a parent or guardian to attend.

(iii) In an adult Magistrates' Court (where an application is made for a free-standing parenting order).

6.10 When a YOT has applied for a free-standing parenting order, the court should then summons the parents to attend the proceedings.

(iv) Where a parent fails to attend

6.11 It is important that courts consider making orders in relation to both parents even if only one attends. Often it is just the mother who attends court whereas engaging both the mother and father will be most effective in tackling their child's misbehaviour. In fact where one or both parents do not attend and there is no reasonable explanation, this may lend weight to an existing recommendation for a parenting order. Where there has been no recommendation for a parenting order, particularly if there were a pattern of non-attendance without valid reasons, then the court may consider whether there is now sufficient evidence for an order. Alternatively, the court may consider whether the YOT should be asked to re-assess the need for an order and return to the court at a later date with a recommendation (if proceedings involving the child have not been completed) or an application for a free standing order (if proceedings have already been completed).

(c) Explaining the order to the parent

6.12 Before making a parenting order the court must as required by s 9(3) of the CD Act 1998, explain to the parent or guardian in ordinary language the effect of the order and of the requirements proposed to be included; the consequences which may follow if he or she fails to comply with any of them; and that the court has the power to review the order on the application of the parent or guardian or of the responsible officer. This requirement can be dealt with if the parent or guardian is present in court using an interpreter where appropriate.

6.13 Experience has shown it is crucial how a parenting order is explained to parents or guardians. It should be stressed that parenting orders are not a punishment and emphasis should be placed on building parents' existing strengths and skills.

6.14 It is highly desirable for parents to be present in court but a parenting order can be made in their absence. Where the parent or guardian is not present, the court will need to find a different way to comply with s 9(3) before it can make a parenting order.[4] One would be to write to the parents or guardians (provided literacy is not a problem), explaining that the court has decided to make a parenting order, when the hearing will be, the effect of the order, the nature of its requirements and the consequences of non-compliance; and to invite the parent or guardian to attend the hearing. The YOT or other agency responsible for the proceedings could deliver the letter. There must be proof that the letter has been served.

6.15 A court may include more than one parent or guardian in an order or issue separate orders to different parents or guardians. Consideration should include whether the parents or guardians are being asked to comply with the same requirements over the same period. All parents or guardians named in an order should be given copies.

Section 7: Requirements of parenting orders

7.1 The requirements of parenting orders or in directions given under them should, as far as practicable, avoid any conflict with the parent's religious beliefs and any interference with the times when the parent normally works or attends educational courses.

(a) Requirement for a parenting programme

7.2 The core requirement of a parenting order is that the parent attends, for a period not exceeding three months, a parenting programme.[5] The court will decide the length of this requirement. All orders must include this requirement unless the parent or guardian has previously received a parenting order.

7.3 The parenting programme can be delivered at any time during the currency of the order "specific requirements" (see 7.18 below). The programme does not have to run from the date the order is made.

7.4 The specific requirements will usually need to be longer than the parenting programme to allow for programme to be delivered, and, if appropriate, an allowance of time to enable parents to catch up with missed sessions. If the only requirement included in the order is attendance at a programme then the court could set the requirement for up to 12 months if it considers it reasonable to do so.

7.5 YOTs should recommend to the court what the length of the requirement should be and explain why. The YOT should therefore make sure the court is aware that the order should allow time for activities including:

---

4 New court rules including this are being considered by the Criminal Procedure Rules Committee.

5 Referred to in legislation as a counselling or guidance programme.

- assessing parents in advance of the programme;
- any work with individual parents needed to prepare for the programme;
- any waiting time before the programme can start;
- the duration of the programme itself;
- a contingency for missed sessions to be provided.

7.6 Details of the programme are specified in directions given by the responsible officer.

7.7 The responsible officer will need to assess what kind of programme is required, in consultation with the provider (if not provided by the responsible officer) and the parent and in light of the planned intervention with the child. This should cover for example who will provide the sessions; whether they should be group, individual or family-based; and whether there are particular cultural and social factors to be considered.

7.8 The responsible officer should set directions in writing and include details of when and where each session will be. A copy should be kept on file.

7.9 During the programme the responsible officer and the programme provider (if different) will need to monitor the parents' progress at suitable intervals.

7.10 The parent might also find it helpful to be involved in some voluntary follow-up work when the order has been completed, such as attending a parent support group.

(b) Residential requirement

7.11 A parenting order can include a residential course but only if two conditions are met:
(a) that the attendance of the parent or guardian at a residential course is likely to be more effective than their attendance at a non-residential course in preventing the child or young person from engaging in a repetition of the behaviour which led to the making of the order; and
(b) that any likely interference with family life is proportionate in all the circumstances.

7.12 These conditions are designed to ensure that residential requirements are made only where proportionate under Article 8 of the European Convention on Human Rights (Right to respect for private and family life).

7.13 A YOT recommending a parenting order with a residential component should provide details of the programme and evidence that these conditions are met. The conditions may be met where the parents' home life is so chaotic that they need a structured setting where sustained counselling and guidance can be undertaken. The YOT will need to take account of all those affected by the residential course and the suitability or unsuitability of the proposed environment for particular children.

7.14 A residential element need not be continuous; a small number of residential weekends structured within a wider non-residential programme may be suitable.

7.15 Normally the child (and any siblings and dependants) should be invited to attend on a voluntary basis as work with a whole family can be beneficial. Where they do not attend, arrangements for their care will be a crucial consideration.

7.16 YOTs will need to meet all statutory requirements for such courses (depending on their content and format) covering health and safety, criminal record checks and registration with the National Care Standards Commission.

7.17 A residential course could be used to bring together work with the parents and child; to reinforce lessons; to allow practitioners to witness the parent/child relationship first hand and to provide intensive family support.

(c) Specific requirements

7.18 The court may also include in a parenting order specific requirements for the parent to comply with for not more than 12 months if it considers them to be desirable in the interests of preventing any repetition of the particular behaviour which led to the order or any further offence by the child or young person.

7.19 The YOT should recommend requirements to the court and how long the parenting order should be imposed for. This will depend on the circumstances of the case but it will be desirable to recommend to the court that the parenting order should last for the full 12 months where this more likely to bring about sustained improvement as a consequence of the support and monitoring delivered through the order.

7.20 Any requirements would need to be tailored to address the problems which led to the parenting order and should, if possible, be linked to the requirements of any order imposed on the child or young person. They could include requiring the parent to ensure that the child:

- attends school or other relevant educational activities, such as mentoring in literacy or numeracy or a homework club;
- attends a programme or course to address relevant problems, such as anger management or drug or alcohol misuse;
- avoids contact with disruptive and, possibly, older children;
- avoids unsupervised visits to certain areas such as shopping centres;
- is at home during certain hours at night and is effectively supervised.

7.21 It may be helpful to include a requirement for the parent to attend all appointments made by the responsible officer. This would ensure the responsible officer can complete any assessment and other preparatory work needed before the parenting programme begins, regularly review progress with the parent and to help with monitoring compliance.

7.22 When formulating specific requirements it is important to recognise that failing without reasonable excuse to comply with requirements of the order or with directions of the responsible officer is a criminal offence. Requirements and directions must therefore be specific and clear enough for a parent or guardian to know when they are breaching them and for the responsible officer to be able to monitor the parent's compliance.

Section 8: Managing parenting orders and further court involvement

(a) Role of the responsible officer

8.1 A parenting order must name an individual person as responsible officer, who will be a member of a YOT or a social worker from a local authority social services department, an officer of a local probation board[6] or a person nominated by the director of children's services or chief education officer such as an education welfare officer. The responsible officer will need to provide or arrange for the provision of the parenting programme, and supervise any other requirements included in the order.

8.2 Where a parenting order is made and the young offender is, or is going to be, supervised by the YOT, it may be appropriate for a member of the team to act as responsible officer under the parenting order, to help ensure a coherent approach to the family situation as a whole. Similarly, where the child is being supervised by a social worker, for instance under a child safety order, it may be appropriate for a social worker from the social services department to act as responsible officer under the parenting order.

8.3 If a member of the YOT is not due to attend court, the relevant social worker or other person who is there will need to consult the YOT before advising the court on who is to be responsible officer. If the RO is not a YOT member, he or she must consult relevant agencies, such as the YOT, as appropriate.

---

6 See footnote 29 regarding "an officer of local probation board".

8.4 Paragraph 8.74 of the YJB National Standards for Youth Justice Services 2004 says: "The first contact between the YOT officer or other responsible officer and the parent must be before the end of the next working day following the court hearing." At the meeting the responsible officer should:

- Provide the parent with a copy of the order;
- Explain the requirements of the order;
- Outline the monitoring arrangements;
- Explain how progress will be reviewed.
- Outline what support the parent can expect;
- Explain what would constitute a reasonable excuse for failing to comply; and
- Explain the potential consequences of failing to comply.

8.5 Under paragraph 8.75, if the counselling or guidance programme under the order is to be provided by someone else, he or she should meet the parent up to two weeks before the programme is due to start.

8.6 It is important for the responsible officer to establish a good relationship with the parent or guardian because this will help ensure the order is successfully completed. Whilst the requirements of the order are in force, the responsible officer should maintain regular contact with the parent or guardian. This should enable the responsible officer to determine the extent to which the parent is complying with the requirements of the order. If the requirements are proving difficult to comply with through no fault of the parent or guardian, the responsible officer may consider the need to apply to the court for the order to be varied.

(b) Variation and discharge

8.7 While a parenting order is in force the court which made the order may vary or discharge it on the application of the responsible officer or the parent or guardian. Under Rule 114 of the Magistrates' Courts Rules 1981, as amended, application is by complaint. These are civil procedures and are governed by sections 51–57 of the Magistrates' Courts Act 1980 and Rules 4 and 98 of the 1981 Rules. These sections and Rules deal with, amongst other things, issuing summonses and parties failing to attend court.

8.8 The order can be varied either by adding or replacing any provision that could originally have been included, or by cancelling any provision.

8.9 Parenting orders may be varied for a number of reasons, for example where the family moves to another area or where the original requirements are not proving effective.

8.10 An order may be discharged for instance if the parent has fully complied with the requirements and the behaviour of the child has improved.

8.11 Where an application to discharge a parenting order has been dismissed, no further application may be made without the court's consent. This is largely to prevent spurious or repeat applications.

(c) Appeals

8.12 Where a parenting order has been made:

- in proceedings relating to the making or breach of a child safety order, an appeal against it can be made to the High Court (the Divisional Court of the Queen's Bench Division);
- in the same proceedings as an anti-social behaviour order, parental compensation order, sexual offences prevention order or proceedings when a parent fails to attend meetings of a youth offender panel, an appeal against it can be made to the Crown Court.

8.13 Appeals against a free-standing order can be made to the Crown Court.

8.14 Where a child or young person has been convicted of an offence, a person subject to a related parenting order has the same right of appeal against it as if he or she had committed the offence leading to the order. For example, if the parenting order were made in a youth court, the appeal would be to the Crown Court and if the parenting order were made in the Crown Court, the appeal would be to the Court of Appeal.

(d) Breach

8.15 A parent is in breach who without reasonable excuse fails to comply with any requirement included in the parenting order, or specified in directions given by the responsible officer.

8.16 The order is primarily designed to help parents to address their child's behaviour so the responsible officer should aim to secure and maintain the parent's co-operation and compliance with the requirements of the order to ensure that it is successfully completed, and will need to make a judgment about what is reasonable in all the circumstances of the case. Where parents have not initially complied with the order, enforcement action short of prosecution such as warning by the responsible officer or police caution may in some cases be sufficient to secure compliance. Formal breach proceedings may however be required in some cases to ensure the order is complied with.

8.17 The process of bringing a breach of a parenting order before a court is different to that for breached community orders – where the responsible officer can apply to court for enforcement action. Breach of a parenting order without reasonable excuse is a summary offence that the CPS may decide to prosecute following a police investigation and referral.

(e) Time limit for breach proceedings

8.18 Section 127 of the Magistrates' Court Act 1980 allows breach proceedings to be brought up to 6 months after the breach occurred. This allows some time for the police and CPS to consider a case. Proceedings can be brought after an order has expired but early action allows more opportunity to secure attendance at a programme and compliance with specific requirements for the remainder of the order.

(f) Monitoring compliance

8.19 Monitoring compliance with a requirement to attend a parenting programme will be straightforward. Any failure by the parent to attend should be immediately reported by the programme provider if different from the responsible officer. Where a parent has failed to fully comply with the requirement to attend the programme as directed by the responsible officer, the responsible officer can direct the parent to attend enough sessions to make up the missed sessions or, if that is impractical, a whole new programme if there is enough time left in the order for the new programme to take place.

8.20 How the responsible officer monitors specific requirements will depend on the circumstances. For example, where attending school is a requirement, the responsible officer should ask the school authorities to inform him or her of any non-attendance. Where the parents are required to ensure their child does not go to a particular area unsupervised, the responsible officer may be informed of a breach after the police receive a complaint about further anti-social or criminal behaviour by the child in that area.

8.21 Under paragraph 8.78 of the National Standards: "If the parent(s) fail(s) to comply with a requirement, including missing an appointment, the responsible officer must make contact with the parent within one working day by visit, telephone or letter. If there is no acceptable reason for the failure, a formal warning must be issued." Any letter should be sent by registered post and a copy placed on file. Any conversation should be recorded on file.

8.22 What constitutes a reasonable excuse will depend on circumstances and the responsible officer will need to make a judgment on each occasion taking into account all the circumstances.

8.23 In some cases it may be reasonable to expect the parents to provide evidence to support their explanation – for instance a doctor's note where illness prevents them from complying.

8.24 Where non-compliance relates to a specific requirement, the responsible officer will need to consider the extent to which the parents have tried to meet the requirement and how far they are able to control their child's behaviour. Where the parents have made all reasonable efforts to control the child, even if he or she commits a further offence, this will not constitute a breach of a specific requirement.

8.25 Other agencies working with the family may be aware of extenuating circumstances and should be consulted before breach procedures are undertaken.

(g) Warnings

8.26 Under the Youth Justice National Standards, as described at paragraph 8.21 above, a formal warning must be issued. The purpose of the warning is to secure the parent's compliance during the remaining period of the order.

(h) Review meeting

8.27 Under paragraph 8.79 of the National Standards, if there is more than one unacceptable failure to comply within three months the responsible officer should meet the parent to review the order and how it can be made to work. It may be appropriate to draw up a new plan with the parents better suited to their needs and circumstances. Variation of the order may be an option. If the responsible officer cannot make contact with the parents or agree a positive way forward the responsible officer should consider whether the failure should be reported to the police for investigation. Whatever is decided, the responsible officer should ensure that a full record is kept.

(i) Referral to the police

8.28 The police are responsible for investigating the alleged breach. Where they consider there is sufficient evidence they may refer the case to the CPS or administer a caution.

8.29 If a parent continues to fail to comply following a review meeting it will usually be appropriate to refer the case to the police.

8.30 If the responsible officer decides to refer the parent to the police, he/she should provide:

- a chronology of events,
- a copy of the parenting order,
- a copy of the directions he or she has set,
- details of the proceedings that surrounded the making of the order,
- details of any compliance as well as failures to comply with the order,
- evidence of any warnings issued to the parent,
- details of any repetition of the kind of behaviour by the child that led to the parenting order,
- a copy of the parenting plan (if there is one), and
- copies of correspondence with the parent.

8.31 The police will then ask the responsible officer to make a statement.

8.32 The police investigation should establish whether the parent failed to comply with a requirement and if so whether they had a reasonable excuse. Normally this will consist of interviews with the parent, the responsible officer, and any other witnesses (such as the programme provider if different from the responsible officer).

8.33 Unless the order has expired or been discharged, the parent will still be required to comply with the order and the responsible officer should continue to monitor compliance. The responsible officer should update the police about any changes in the parent's attitude to the order and any further breaches or compliance.

8.34 Police have power under section 110 of the Serious and Organised Crime and Police Act 2005 to arrest a person they have reasonable grounds for suspecting of committing an offence provided the officer has reasonable grounds to believe the arrest is necessary for one of the reasons specified in s110 (5). The most likely relevant reason would be "to allow the prompt and effective investigation of the offence or of the conduct of the person in question."

This reason might be relevant where a parent has refused to cooperate when the YOT has tried to establish any reasons for non–compliance.

(j) Cautions

8.35 Where a parent admits to breaching a parenting order and there is sufficient evidence to bring a charge the police have discretion to caution the parent if this would be in the public interest.

8.36 Key considerations should include whether the parent has substantially complied with the order, whether the parent is of previous good character and whether there has been any repetition of the kind of behaviour by the child which led to the order being made.

8.37 The decision to proceed by way of a simple caution can be taken by either the police or CPS. There is no requirement for the police to consult CPS before issuing a caution although they may wish to do so.

8.38 If the police do issue a caution they should inform the responsible officer. Where the parenting order has not expired, the responsible officer should continue to try and work with the parent who, following the caution, may be prepared to comply with the remained of the order.

8.39 The responsible officer should immediately report to the police for investigation any further unreasonable failures to comply. If a parent continues to fail to comply with an order after receiving a caution the public interest is more likely to favour a prosecution.

(k) Referral to the Crown Prosecution Service

8.40 If the police decide to refer the case to the CPS the file should include:

- a copy of the parenting order;
- the date on which it was made and details of the proceedings proceeding the order (If the parenting order was made in the family proceedings court, the CPS will only have access to the court papers with the leave of the relevant justices' clerk or the court.)
- information about the order's duration;
- a copy of the responsible officers directions to attend the programme;
- details of any compliance;
- admissible evidence of the alleged breach including a statement by the responsible officer, evidence/copies of any warnings, details of any explanations given by the parent;
- details of any repeat of the behaviour by the child that led to the order; and
- a PNC print of any previous convictions/cautions/reprimands/final warnings for the parent.

8.41 The CPS is responsible for deciding whether there is a realistic prospect of conviction and whether or not the public interest favours a prosecution rather than a caution or taking no further action.

8.42 The Code for Crown Prosecutors will be applied to all cases. Paragraph 6.4(1) of the code lists breach of a court order as a common public interest factor in favour of prosecution, although crown prosecutors must have regard to all the circumstances of the case in reaching a decision.

8.43 Crown prosecutors may decide the public interest favours a simple caution and refer the case back to the police. Where this happens but it proves impossible to caution the parent they should be charged (section 37B (7) PACE).[7]

---

[7] Conditional cautions are a new disposal introduced through the Criminal Justice Act 2003 and are only available in pilot areas. The CPS in those areas may decide the public interest would be best served by a condition caution.

(l) Court hearing

8.44 If a prosecution is brought and the parent pleads not guilty, there will be a summary trial to decide whether the parent has failed without reasonable excuse to comply with a requirement of a parenting order. This will be heard in the adult Magistrates' Court. Where the parent pleads guilty the case will proceed to sentence.

8.45 If the parent is convicted, the court could impose any sentence available for a non-imprisonable offence – that is a fine not exceeding level 3 on the standard scale (up to £1,000), absolute or conditional discharge or community order.[8] The decision on the nature and level of penalty to impose will be a matter for the court following consideration of all the facts of the case, such as the family circumstances and the means of the parents.

8.46 The offence is not a recordable offence for the purposes of PACE.

(m) Further engagement with parents

8.47 It is important for responsible officers to be informed of the outcome of the breach hearing. The court cannot make a new parenting order during breach proceedings but if the order has not expired or been discharged the parent will still have to comply with specific requirements and the responsible officer's directions to attend a parenting programme.

8.48 If the parent has failed to attend a programme in its entirety or particular sessions of a programme, the responsible officer can direct the parent to attend a new programme or a number of sessions to make up for the missed one, provided there is enough time left in the order (i.e. the duration of specific requirements).

8.49 If the order has expired the responsible officer will still need to know the outcome of the hearing in order to make further efforts to engage with the parent and to consider whether another parenting order is appropriate.

Legal advice /assistance

Publicly funded legal advice/ assistance may be available to financially eligible parents. Parents may seek advice as to the availability of public funding from a solicitor with a legal aid contract and can find a solicitor with a contract in their area by telephoning Community Legal Service Direct's help line on 0845 345 4345 or visiting their website at: www.clsdirect.org.uk

Enquiries

For enquiries about this guidance contact the Ministry of Justice, Youth Justice and Children Unit:

Tel: 020 7035 1255 or email: Public_Enquiry.YJCU@justice.gsi.gov.uk

For enquiries about operational matters and the National Standards on Youth Justice contact the Youth Justice Board:

Enquiries line tel: 020 7271 3033 or email: enquiries@yjb.gov.uk

---

[8] Section 177 of the Criminal Justice Act 2003 refers.

Dealing with failure to comply – summary

1 If a parent fails to comply with a requirement of the order, the responsible officer should make contact with the parent within one working day by visit, telephone or letter.

- If there is no acceptable reason for the non-compliance, the responsible officer should give the parent a written warning and if possible a warning in person.
- If the parent has good reason for the failure to comply with the requirements of the parenting order, it may be appropriate for the responsible officer to change the directions for the parenting programme or consider whether to apply to the court for the terms of the order to be varied.

2 If there is more than one unacceptable failure to comply within a period of three months, the responsible officer should meet the parent to review the order and how it can be made to work. A written record is kept. Responsible officer should consider whether the failure to comply should be reported to the police for investigation.

3 Responsible officer should consider whether the failure to comply should be reported to the police for investigation.

4 If reported to the police, police then investigate. Police may issue a caution or provide the results of their investigation to the CPS.

5 CPS will have to be satisfied that there is sufficient evidence to prosecute and decide whether or not it is in the public interest to bring a prosecution.

6 If CPS decides to prosecute, case is heard in the adult magistrates' court. The hearing will determine whether the parent is guilty of failing without reasonable excuse to comply with a requirement of a parenting order or a direction of a responsible officer.

7 Court will determine whether to impose on conviction:

- a fine not exceeding level 3 on the standard scale and/or
- a community penalty
- an absolute or conditional discharge or community order.

8 The YOT will consider whether to pursue monitoring of order or revised directions and further engagement with parent.

Annex D: Suggested form to apply for free-standing parenting orders

Application for Parenting Order (Anti-social Behaviour Act 2003, section 26)

Date: .... Magistrates' Court
Child or young person: (Code)
Child or young person's address:
Child or young person's age and date of birth (or date on which they are believed to have been born):

Parent/ Guardian:
Parent/ Guardian's address:

Parent/ Guardian:
Parent/ Guardian's address:

Applicant: Responsible officer: It is alleged that:

(a) the child or young person has acted on [*insert date(s)*] at [*insert place(s)*] in an anti-social manner, that is to say, in a manner that caused or was likely to cause harassment, alarm or distress to one or more persons not of the same household as himself; or
(b) the child or young person has on [*insert date(s)*] at [*insert place(s)*] engaged in criminal conduct.

Short description of acts:

[Evidence of these acts is attached.]

[The parent(s)/ guardian(s) entered into a parenting contract on [*insert date*].] [It is alleged that the parent(s)/ guardian(s) have failed to comply with the parenting contract, a copy of which is attached to this application form.

Short description of alleged failure to comply with parenting contract: Evidence of this alleged failure to comply is attached.]

[It is alleged that the parent(s)/guardian(s) have refused to enter into a parenting contract.]

[The child or young person is under 16. Information as to the family circumstances of the child or young person is attached.]

It is alleged that making the order would be desirable in the interests of preventing the child or young person from engaging in further criminal conduct or further anti-social behaviour. The court is requested to make such an order in respect of [*insert person's name*] [and] [*insert person's name.*].

[The applicant requests the court to order that the person (s) named above attend for a period of [*insert number*] months a counselling or guidance programme to be specified in directions given by the responsible officer.]

[It is alleged that:

(a) the attendance of the parent(s)/ guardian(s) at a residential course is likely to be more effective than their attendance at a non-residential course in preventing the child or young person from engaging in further criminal conduct or anti-social behaviour; and
(b) any interference with family life which is likely to result from the attendance of the parent(s)/guardian(s) at a residential course is proportionate in all the circumstances.

The court is requested to order that the counselling or guidance programme may [include][consist of] a residential course.

Evidence to support the request for a residential requirement is attached.]

Short description of such residential course to be attended by the parent(s)/guardian(s):

The applicant requests the court to order that the parent(s)/guardian(s) comply for a period of [*insert number*] months with requirements to be specified in the Parenting Order as follows:

Annex E: Suggested forms of parenting orders

(A) Parenting Order (Anti-Social Behaviour Act 2003 section 26)

Date: .... Magistrates' Court
Person(s) named in order: .... (Code)

Age(s) : ....years (if under 18)
....years (if under 18)

Address(es): ....
....

Applicant Youth Offending Team: ....

Responsible officer: ....

[*insert child's/ young person's name*] of [*insert address*], who is believed to have been born on [*insert date of birth*], has [behaved in a manner which is anti-social, that is to say, in a manner that caused or was likely to cause harassment, alarm or distress to one or more persons not of the same household as himself] [engaged in criminal conduct] [*delete as applicable*].

Decision: In exercise of its powers under section 26(3) of the Anti-social Behaviour Act 2003 (the "2003 Act") and having complied with its duties under that section[, and having complied with its duty under section 27(1) of the 2003 Act in considering the failure of the persons named above to [enter into][comply with] a parenting contract], the court has decided to impose a parenting order on the person(s) named above because the court considers that the order would be desirable in the interests of preventing the child or young person from engaging in further [anti-social behaviour] [criminal conduct] [*delete as applicable*].

The requirements of the order are as follows:

[*insert person's name*] shall for a period of [*insert length of requirement*] beginning with the date of the order comply with such requirements as are listed in the Schedule to the order.

[*insert person's name*] shall for a concurrent period of [*insert length of requirement*] not exceeding three months attend a counselling or guidance programme as directed by the responsible officer.

[[*insert person's name*] shall on [*insert dates*] attend a residential course at [*insert address*] as directed by the responsible officer. The court is satisfied that the requirements of section 26(7) and (8) of the 2003 Act have been met.]

[(*In the event that the child/ young person is under 16.*) The court has complied with its duties under section 27(2) of the 2003 Act and has obtained and considered information about the child's/ young person's family circumstances, and the likely effect of the order on those circumstances.]

The court has complied with its duties under section 27(3) of the 2003 Act, and has explained to the person(s) named above the effect of the order and its requirements, what may happen if he/she/they fail(s) to comply with these requirements (as set out in section 9(7) of the Crime and Disorder Act 1998), and that the court has power (under section 9(5) of the Crime and Disorder Act 1998) to review the order on the application of the person(s) named above or the responsible officer.

Justice of the Peace
[or By order of the Court, Clerk of the Court]

SCHEDULE

Any requirement(s) imposed by the court under section 26(4)(a) and (b) of the 2003 Act should be listed here.

(B) Parenting Order (Crime and Disorder Act 1998 section 8)

.... [Family Proceedings][Youth]{Magistrates'] Court

(Code)

Date: ....

Person(s) named in order: ....

Age(s): ....years (if under 18)
....years (if under 18)

Address(es): ....
....
....
Responsible officer: ....

[[*insert child's/ young person's name*] of [*insert address*] who is believed to have born on [*insert date of birth*], has been [made subject to a [child safety order or the court has determined that a child has failed to comply with any requirement included in such an order] [anti-social behaviour order][sexual offences prevention order][referral order]][found guilty of an offence, namely, [brief details of offence and statute]] [or a parental compensation order has been made in relation to the child's behaviour]]. [The above named has been convicted of an offence under [section 443][section 444] of the Education Act 1996] [delete as applicable].

Decision: In exercise of its powers under section 8 of the Crime and Disorder Act 1998 (the "1998 Act") and having complied with its duties under [section 9(1) and (2)] [section 9(2) and (2A) (in the case of a referral order) of the 1998 Act, the court has decided to impose a parenting order on the person(s) named above because the court considers that the order would be desirable in the interests of preventing [a repetition of the kind of behaviour which led to the imposition of a [child safety order][anti-social behaviour order][sexual offences prevention order]][parental compensation order] [the commission of further offences by the child or young person][the commission of further offences under [section 443][section 444] of the Education Act 1996] [delete as applicable].

The requirements of the order are as follows:

[insert person's name] shall for a period of [insert length of requirement] beginning with the date of the order comply with such requirements as are listed in the Schedule to the order.

[insert person's name] shall, for a concurrent period of not exceeding three months attend a counselling or guidance programme as directed by the responsible officer.[[insert person's name] shall, on [insert dates] attend a residential course at [insert address] as directed by the responsible officer. The court is satisfied that the requirements of section 8(7A) of the 1998 Act have been met.]

[(In the event that the child/ young person is under 16.) The court has complied with its duties under section 9(2) of the 1998 Act and has obtained and considered information about the child's/ young person's family circumstances, and the likely effect of the order on those circumstances.]

The court has complied with its duties under section 9(3) to 9(7) of the 1998 Act, and has explained to the person(s) named above the effect of the order and its requirements, what may happen if he/she/they fail(s) to comply with these requirements, and that the court has power to review the order on the application of the person(s) named above or the responsible officer.

Justice of the Peace

[or By order of the Court, Clerk of the Court]

SCHEDULE

Any requirement(s) imposed by the court under section 8(4)(a) and (b) of the 1998 Act should be listed here.

(C) Parenting Order (Powers of Criminal Courts (Sentencing) Act 2000 Schedule 1 paragraph 9D)

Date: .... Magistrates' Court
(Code)

Person(s) named in order: ....
....

Age(s) :
.... years (if under 18)
.... years (if under 18)

Address(es): ....
....

Child or Young person: ....

Applicant Youth Offender Panel: ....

Responsible officer: ....

[*insert parent's name*] of [*insert address*], the parent of [*insert name of child or young person*], has failed without reasonable excuse to comply with the order made under section 20 of the Powers of Criminal Courts (Sentencing) Act 2000 (the "2000 Act") to attend meetings of the youth offender panel dated [insert date(s)], a copy of which is attached to this order.

Decision: Having complied with its duties under paragraph 9D of Schedule 1 to the 2000 Act(a), the court has decided to impose a parenting order on the person(s) named above because the court is satisfied that the order would be desirable in the interests of preventing the commission of any further offence by the child or young person.

The requirements of the order are as follows:

[insert person's name] shall for a period of [insert length of requirement] not exceeding twelve months beginning with the date of the order comply with such requirements as are listed in the Schedule to the order.

[insert person's name] shall, for a concurrent period of [insert length of requirement] not exceeding three months attend a counselling or guidance programme as directed by the responsible officer.[[insert person's name] shall on [insert dates] attend a residential course at [insert address] as directed by the responsible officer. The court is satisfied that the requirements of paragraph 9D(5) of Schedule 1 to the 2000 Act have been met.]

[(In the event that the child/ young person is under 16.) The court has complied with its duties under paragraph 9D(6) of Schedule 1 to the 2000 Act and has obtained and considered information about the child's/ young person's family circumstances, and the likely effect of the order on those circumstances.]

The court has complied with its duties under paragraph 9D(7) of Schedule 1 to the 2000 Act, and has explained to the person(s) named above the effect of the order and its requirements, what may happen if he/she/they fail(s) to comply with these requirements (as set out in section 9(7) of the Crime and Disorder Act 1998), and that the court has power (under section 9(5) of the Crime and Disorder Act 1998) to review the order on the application of the person(s) named above or the responsible officer.

Justice of the Peace
[or By order of the Court,
Clerk of the Court]

SCHEDULE

Any requirement(s) imposed by the court under paragraph 9D(2) of Schedule 1 to the 2000 Act should be listed here.

INDEX

References are to paragraph numbers.